Mathematical Techniques in Finance

Mathematical Techniques in Finance

Tools for Incomplete Markets

Aleš Černý

Princeton University Press

Princeton and Oxford

Published by Princeton University Press,
41 William Street, Princeton, New Jersey 08540

In the United Kingdom: Princeton University Press,
3 Market Place, Woodstock, Oxfordshire OX20 1SY

Library of Congress Cataloguing-in-Publication Data

Černý, Aleš, 1971–
Mathematical techniques in finance: tools for incomplete markets / Aleš Černý.
p.cm.
Includes bibliographical references and index.
ISBN 0-691-08806-3 (alk. paper) — ISBN 0-691-08807-1 (pbk.: alk. paper)
1. Finance—Mathematical models. 2. Pricing—Mathematical models.
3. Risk management—Mathematical models. 4. Derivative securities—Mathematical models. I. Title.

HG106.C47 2004
332′.01′51—dc21   2003053593

British Library Cataloguing-in-Publication Data

A catalogue record for this book is available from the British Library

This book has been composed in Times and
typeset by T&T Productions Ltd, London
Printed on acid-free paper ⊗
www.pupress.princeton.edu

Printed in the United States of America

10 9 8 7 6 5 4 3 2 1

To my parents, with love

Give me but one firm spot on which to stand,
and I will move the earth

Δὸς μοι ποῦ στῶ καί κινῶ τὴν Γῆν

Archimedes

Contents

Preface

Modern finance overlaps with many fields of mathematics, in particular, probability theory, linear algebra, calculus, partial differential equations, stochastic calculus, numerical mathematics, and not least programming. The diversity of mathematical skills makes finance a very challenging subject, putting a lot of strain on its prospective students. *Mathematical Techniques in Finance* offers an introduction to the mathematical tools which are needed to price uncertain income streams such as derivative securities. It is primarily intended as a textbook for Masters in Finance courses with a significant quantitative element, although it has also been popular with Finance PhD students here at Imperial College London, and it has found its way on to the desks of financial analysts.

This book is about the *active and practical use* of mathematics with the main focus on three interrelated financial topics: asset pricing, portfolio allocation, and risk measurement. The book contains a mix of applications and theory working together in a happy union; theory underpins the applications and the applications illustrate the theory. Working out the exercises is more important than trying to memorize the financial and mathematical theory contained in the text.

Study Guide

Before you start reading the book take a look at the book's website

http://pup.princeton.edu/titles/7606.html

to find out what resources are available. Secondly, set up your computer. The computer programs in this book are written in GAUSS, which is a simple language based on vectors and matrices. GAUSS LIGHT is an inexpensive student version that has all the functionality of GAUSS, except it will only handle matrices with no more than 10 000 elements, which is appropriate for most applications in the book. Many economics and finance departments already have a GAUSS license; on the other hand engineering departments seem to prefer MATLAB. This book may provide support to MATLAB and Visual Basic users in the future—watch the website. There is no need to worry about using C++ at this stage; it runs fast but the set-up costs are high. To use an analogy, GAUSS is a car with an automatic gearbox, whereas C++ has a manual one. At this stage we are quite happy just turning the steering wheel and admiring the view without having to worry about the gear shifts. There is always time to learn C++ later if you decide that you really like programming.

Not all the material in this book is suitable for all students. There are essentially two long coherent themes appropriate for Masters programmes, and several digressions intended for short courses aimed at doctoral students. The difficulty is largely conceptual, not mathematical. The book uses linear algebra at the level of Anton (2000), calculus at the level of Binmore and Davies (2001), and probability at the level of Mood et al. (1974); all three are standard undergraduate textbooks. The background to Itô calculus is self-contained and the applications of Itô calculus require little more than partial differentiation and ordinary integration.

Longer Masters Courses

The *discrete-time complete market trail* (Chapters 1, 2, 5 and 6) has a number of exciting computer simulations looking into dynamic asset pricing. Here one can get away with very little mathematics, especially if one is willing to take a few crucial results on trust.

Chapter 1 establishes the basics of the one-period model, shows how securities can be represented by vectors and matrices, and introduces the concept of hedging. It also provides a simple context in which to explore the GAUSS commands. Chapter 2 introduces important financial notions such as returns, arbitrage and state prices, and gives examples of asset pricing both in complete and incomplete markets. Sections 2.1–2.4 are not essential for the complete market modelling and can be skipped.

Chapter 5 introduces the multi-period binomial model for stock prices and computes a dynamic hedging strategy that replicates a given option. We observe how the risk-neutral probabilities arise within the multi-period framework and how the option price can be expressed as a risk-neutral expectation. The calculations are implemented in a spreadsheet.

Chapter 6 takes the binomial modelling one step further by introducing more/ shorter time periods. To achieve consistency across models one must make sure that the mean and variance of annual returns match the empirical data, which brings up the basic properties of mean and variance. At this stage it may be desirable to revise the elementary concepts in Appendix B on probability. Once the model is calibrated we realize that with many periods it is extremely time-consuming to implement it in a spreadsheet. This difficulty is overcome by a simple GAUSS program where we can use some of the matrix algebra of Chapters 1 and 2. Once the model is up and running it is natural to explore the continuous-time limit; on a computer one can consider hedging as frequently as every 10 min.

The discrete-time numerical explorations are a natural springboard to more theoretical calculations on the *continuous-time complete market trail* (Chapters 6, 10, 11). The numerical simulations show that the option price settles down as the rehedging intervals shorten; the real challenge is to work out the limit with pen and paper. This brings up the notions of the central limit theorem and continuous random variables, in particular the normal distribution. The optional (hard) calculations needed to work out the risk-neutral mean and variance of log returns are in Section 6.2.4; it is a good exercise in Taylor expansions and limits. The Black–Scholes integral (Section 6.2.5) is easier and likely to be compulsory in most finance courses. Chapter 6 demonstrates an important point: there are computations one can do with pen and paper that even the fastest computers cannot perform. Here, our productivity tool is standard calculus.

The second half of Chapter 6 deals with the Poisson jump limit of the binomial model. Some courses may wish to discuss the jumps there and then to show that Brownian motion is *not the only* continuous-time limit logically possible. An alternative is to leave jumps as an optional reading and stay on the Brownian motion path moving straight to Chapter 10, where we introduce continuous-time Brownian motion, Itô processes, and most importantly Itô calculus. Itô calculus is another great productivity tool, and it receives plenty of attention in Chapters 10 and 11. In my experience it is hard to *understand* the Itô calculus, but it is possible to *get used to* it and to apply it quickly and consistently; the main focus is therefore on practice. There is a large number of worked examples in Chapter 10, and the end-of-chapter exercises offer yet more opportunities to practise.

With Itô calculus under the belt, Section 11.2 explains the martingale approach to pricing; it represents the condensed wisdom of continuous-time asset pricing. Section 11.2 draws heavily on the martingale properties discussed in Chapter 9; these can be taken for granted if time is at a premium. For a good understanding one will also need the notion of state variable, Markov process and information filtration, which can be found in Chapter 8.

Section 11.3 discusses the Girsanov Theorem (required in Section 11.2) and its use in investment evaluation. Section 11.4 extends 11.2 to several risky assets. Sections 11.3 and 11.4 are more advanced and can be skipped on a first read. Section 11.5 talks about the relationship between martingales and partial differential equations, which is central to most finance applications. Section 11.6 surveys numerical methods used in continuous-time pricing.

The above trails on discrete and continuous-time complete markets are suitable for a core Masters course and can be covered in approximately 40 hours of lectures and 20 hours of tutorials.

Complete market pricing is remarkable by the conspicuous absence of risk, which is mathematically convenient but clearly at odds with reality. Risk is omnipresent in financial markets, as documented by the fate of Long Term Capital Management. Where there is risk one must, first of all, be able to measure it and only then one can come up with a price. Hence the other major theme in this book is *risk measurement and asset pricing in incomplete markets* (Chapters 3 and 4, and the first half of Chapter 12).

Chapter 3 starts by explaining how risky investment opportunities are ranked by the expected utility paradigm. Expected utility is often criticized for being ad hoc, for using meaningless units, for its results being dependent on initial wealth, etc., in short, for being worlds apart from mean–variance analysis. Chapter 3 dispels this *dangerous myth*. When correct measurement units are used all utility functions look exactly the same for small risks, and their investment advice is consistent with mean–variance analysis. When the risks are large and/or asymmetric the mean–variance analysis may lead to investment decisions that are logically inconsistent, whereas increasing utility functions will give consistent advice, albeit one that depends on the investor's attitude to large risks. Formally, this is shown by examining the scaling properties of the HARA class of utility functions. We will see that the risk–return trade-off of utility functions can be measured in terms of generalized Sharpe ratios similar to the standard Sharpe ratio of mean-to-standard deviation.

Naturally, one wishes to achieve the best risk–return trade-off, which leads to the maximization of expected utility. Chapter 4 discusses the numerical techniques that are needed for this task because, sadly, closed-form formulae are not available in incomplete markets. On the other hand the algorithms are quite simple and intuitive.

The use of numerical techniques in Chapter 4 is not an attempt to be innovative at all costs, rather, this chapter follows a trend that is increasingly apparent in financial economics as it relies more and more on numerical analysis to provide answers to pressing practical problems that are beyond the reach of closed-form solutions. As these developments take root financial economics will soon need a large number of professionals who are confident and competent users of numerical techniques. Chapter 4 is an accessible introduction to the economic and mathematical issues of numerical optimization that will prepare the reader for the road ahead.

Chapters 3 and 4 are set in a one-period environment. Chapter 12 transports the reader into a multi-period model where option hedging is risky. In Section 12.1 we describe the optimal hedging strategy and the minimum hedging error, and compute these quantities in a spreadsheet. Section 12.2 discusses the option pricing business in incomplete markets. Section 12.3 then talks about the continuous-time limit, where we will see that continuous hedging is *not* riskless, after all.

Chapter 3, with small digressions to Chapter 4, and the first two sections of Chapter 12 will need at least 15 hours of lectures and tutorials. Ideally, students should be given plenty of space to experiment with the programs and to feed the programs with real market data. This material is suitable for an elective Masters course.

Shorter PhD Courses

The book offers opportunities for short courses targeted at doctoral students.

In the absence of introductory textbooks on dynamic programming one can use Chapter 12, and particularly Section 12.4 to helicopter students into the issues of dynamic programming, its advantages, challenges, principles, and the mathematical language. Chapter 12 is the simplest multi-period optimization problem one will ever encounter (quadratic target function, linear controls) and therefore it is an ideal pedagogical tool. It is the only set-up that does not require iterative numerical optimization. Dynamic programming highlights the importance of the information set, Markov property and state variables covered in Chapter 8.

To complement the dynamic programming one may wish to introduce the martingale duality approach that appears in Section 9.4. This naturally leads to the connection between pricing kernels and the best investment opportunities (Hansen–Jagannathan duality) in Section 9.4.6 and via the extension theorem leads to the equilibrium price kernel restrictions used in the diagnostics of asset-pricing models (Cochrane 2001).

Chapter 7 gives an introduction to the fast Fourier transform (FFT) in finance, and it will appeal mainly to students specializing in derivative pricing. Chapter 7 offers the best of discrete and continuous-time worlds, fast pricing in combination with rich structure (affine models). Motivation for the FFT can be given quickly by referring to the numerical examples in Chapter 6. Complex numbers are introduced with minimum fuss by appealing to their geometric properties. The FFT naturally leads to the continuous-time limit, continuous Fourier transforms and characteristic functions, and it opens a new world of opportunities for numerical and theoretical explorations. The practical usefulness of the FFT can be seen, for example, in Section 12.3.2.

Exercises

The book is about empowering students and helping them to become confident users of the techniques they have seen in the lectures. For this purpose each chapter is accompanied by a tutorial that gives students an opportunity to practise the material just covered. Exercises are an integral part of the book, and solutions are freely available on this book's website (see p. xiii). If the reader can solve the exercises, then he or she can be pretty sure to have understood the theoretical concepts, and vice versa.

Related Reading

Hull (1997) is a classical all-round finance text with accessible mathematics, plenty of institutional details and many different types of financial instruments. There are several *intermediate* texts that concentrate more on the valuation methodology and less on the market practicalities, namely Baxter and Rennie (1996), Neftci (1996), Pliska (1997) and Luenberger (1998); *Mathematical Techniques* belongs to this category. Wilmott (1998) gives a practitioner's prospective of financial engineering mathematics, biased towards partial differential equations, but with plenty of numerical examples and many important topics. Duffie (1996) and Hunt and Kennedy (2000) represent *advanced* textbooks that start almost directly with continuous-time stochastic processes and martingale pricing. Further to this general list of textbooks each chapter provides references to sources and suggested reading.

Acknowledgments

My fascination with applied mathematics goes back a long way and I would like to take this opportunity to thank those who made my journey through the mathematical world both rewarding and enjoyable. First and foremost are my loving parents, who were my first maths and physics teachers. Next comes Bohuš Sivák and the staff at the Pedagogical University in Banská Bystrica who ran a phenomenally entertaining series of summer camps for young mathematicians. Maja Sadloňová and the staff at GVOZA (Maths High School in Žilina) have provided refuge for many generations of budding mathematicians. The introduction to complex numbers in Chapter 7 goes back to Žilina days and Ivo Čáp's afternoon lectures in physics. I would like to thank the staff at the Mathematics Department of the Faculty of Nuclear Sciences and Physical Engineering for the support, enthusiasm and inspiration they provided me with during my undergraduate studies.

My interest in financial economics took longer to develop. I am grateful to the staff at CERGE in Prague for providing an opportunity to study solid theoretical economics. Aydin Hayri is in many ways responsible for the rest of the story; he helped me to enroll as a PhD student at Warwick and, some time later, sent me to a talk by Darrell Duffie. This was a talk that I did not understand, but it nevertheless changed the course of my professional life. It contained heaps of fascinating mathematics, mentioning *martingales* in every other sentence and, best of all, seemed to say something about the real world around us. I have been exploring the fascinating world of continuous-time finance ever since and this book is an opportunity to share parts of that journey with the reader.

In economics and finance no amount of mathematical sophistication can compensate for the ability to identify important problems and then, in spite of complicated analysis needed to generate the solution, communicate the results in simple terms. It has been my privilege to learn the craft from experienced financial economists, Stewart Hodges and David Miles. Stewart is one of the fathers of the incomplete market pricing paradigm and the exposition in Chapter 3 owes much to his pioneering work on the generalized Sharpe ratio. David, my colleague and co-author at Imperial, has taught me the value of numerical analysis in solving real world economic questions. He is the inspiration behind much of the numerical exploration in the book.

This book reflects numerous research discussions I have had with professional colleagues and co-authors. My thanks go to Karim Abadir, David Barr, Simon Benninga, Antonio Bernardo, Tomas Björk, Francis Breedon, Ian Buckley, Lara Cathcart, Martin Cripps, John Cochrane, Keith Cuthbertson, Bernard Dumas, Lina El-Jahel, Bob Flood, Stefano Galluccio, Hélyette Geman, Aydin Hayri, Berthold Herrendorf, Stewart Hodges, Lane Hughston, Tomáš Jandík, Stefan Jaschke, Jan Kallsen, Turalay Kenc, Jo Kennedy, Dima Kramkov, Harold Kushner, David Miles, Marcus Miller, Dirk Nitzsche, Huyên Pham, Nick Schmidt, James Sefton, Euan Sinclair, Jeremy Smith, Andrea Roncoroni, Walter Schachermayer, Martin Schweizer and Martin Weale.

This textbook has taken more than three years to write, and it would have been impossible to complete without the support of people around me. I would like to thank my wife, Barbora, for her care, support and understanding during this campaign. My thanks go to the Business School at Imperial College London, and particularly to Keith Cuthbertson for organizing my teaching and administrative workload efficiently, which freed up the time for the book. I am grateful to Ian Buckley, who provided me with his own lecture notes when I started at Imperial five years ago and who has since contributed many excellent ideas, in particular his trademark multiple choice questions. David Miles has read large parts of the typescript and suggested important clarifications. I have received valuable feedback from four anonymous referees. The book is a testament to the professionalism and perseverance of the PUP team. I am indebted to Jonathan Wainwright for an extremely meticulous editing and typesetting of the manuscript and for the many improvements he has suggested. A big thanks goes to Richard Baggaley, who initiated this project in November 1999 and guided it through the perilous waters of peer reviews, editorial boards and missed deadlines right to the end.

Last, but not least, I have received valuable feedback from five generations of students at Imperial, and I hope that we will join forces in the years to come.

Mathematical Techniques in Finance

1

The Simplest Model of Financial Markets

The main goal of the first chapter is to introduce the one-period finite state model of financial markets with elementary financial concepts such as *basis assets*, *focus assets*, *portfolio*, *Arrow–Debreu securities*, *hedging* and *replication*. Alongside the financial topics we will encounter mathematical tools—linear algebra and matrices—essential for formulating and solving basic investment problems. The chapter explains vector and matrix notation and important concepts such as linear independence.

After reading the first two chapters you should understand the meaning of and be able to solve questions of the following type.

Example 1.1 (replication of securities). Suppose that there is a risky security (call it stock) with tomorrow's value $S = 3$, 2 or 1 depending on the state of the market tomorrow. The first state (first scenario) happens with probability $\frac{1}{2}$, the second with probability $\frac{1}{6}$ and the third with probability $\frac{1}{3}$. There is also a risk-free security (bond) which pays 1 no matter what happens tomorrow. We are interested in replicating two call options written on the stock, one with strike 1.5 and the second with strike 1.

1. Find a portfolio of the stock, bond and the first call option that replicates the second call option (so-called gamma hedging).
2. If the initial stock price is 1 and the risk-free rate of return is 5%, what is the no-arbitrage price of the second option?
3. Find the portfolio of the bond and stock which is the best hedge to the first option in terms of the expected squared replication error (so-called delta hedging).

This chapter is important for two reasons. Firstly, the one-period model of financial markets is the main building block of a dynamic multi-period model which will be discussed later and which represents the main tool of any financial analyst. Secondly, matrices provide an effective way of describing the relationships among several variables, random or deterministic, and as such they are used with great advantage throughout the book.

1.1 One-Period Finite State Model

It is a statement of the obvious that the returns in financial markets are uncertain. The question is how to model this uncertainty. The simplest model assumes that

Table 1.1. Hypothetical scenarios.

Event	Scenario #1 probability $\frac{1}{4}$	Scenario #2 probability $\frac{1}{6}$	Scenario #3 probability $\frac{1}{3}$	Scenario #4 probability $\frac{1}{4}$
Value of FTSE100	5000	4500	4200	4100
LIBOR rate	6.25	6.5	6.75	7.00
Weather	Rain	Rain	Rain	Rain and fog
Chelsea–Wimbledon etc.	5:0	4:0	2:3	0:9

there are only two dates, which we will call today and tomorrow, but which could equally well be called this week and next week, this year and next year, or now and in 10 min. The essential feature of our two-date, one-period model is that no investment decisions are taken between the two dates. One should be thinking of a world which is at a standstill apart from at 12 noon each day when all economic activity (work, consumption, trading, etc.) is carried out in a split second.

It is assumed that we do not know today what the market prices will be tomorrow, in other words the state of tomorrow's world is uncertain. However, we assume that there is only a finite number of scenarios that can take place, each of which is known today down to the smallest detail. One of these scenarios is drawn at random, using a controlled experiment whereby the probability of each scenario being drawn is known today. The result of the draw is made public at noon tomorrow and all events take place as prescribed by the chosen scenario (see Table 1.1 for illustration).

Let us stop for a moment and reflect how realistic the finite state model is. First of all, how many scenarios are necessary? In the above table we have four random variables: the value of the FTSE index, the level of UK base interest rate, UK weather and the result of the Chelsea–Wimbledon football game. Assuming that each of these variables has five different outcomes and that any combination of individual outcomes is possible we would require $5^4 = 625$ different scenarios. Given that in finance one usually works with two or three scenarios, 625 seems more than sufficient. And yet if you realize that this only allows five values for each random variable (only five different results of the football match!), then 625 scenarios do not appear overly exigent.

Next, do we know the probability of each of the 625 scenarios? Well, we might have a *subjective* opinion on how much these probabilities are but since the weather, football match or development in financial markets can hardly be thought of as controlled random experiments we do not know what the *objective* probabilities of those scenarios are. There is even a school of thought stating that objective probabilities do not exist; see the notes at the end of the chapter.

Hence the finite state model departs from reality in two ways: firstly, with a small number of scenarios (states of the world) it provides only a patchy coverage of the actual outcomes, and secondly we do not know the objective probabilities of each scenario, we only have our subjective opinion of how much they might be.

1.2 Securities and Their Pay-Offs

Security is a legal entitlement to receive (or an obligation to pay) an amount of money. A security is characterized by its known price today and its generally uncertain pay-off tomorrow. What constitutes the pay-off depends to some extent on the given security. For example, consider a model with just two scenarios and one security, a share in publicly traded company TRADEWELL Inc. Let us assume that the initial price of the share is 1, and tomorrow it can either increase to 1.2 or drop to 0.9. Assume further that the shareholders will receive a dividend of 0.1 per share tomorrow, no matter what happens to the share price.

> The **security pay-off** is the amount of money one receives after selling the security tomorrow plus any additional payment such as the dividend, coupon or rebate one is entitled to by virtue of holding the security. In our case the pay-off of one TRADEWELL share is 1.3 or 1 depending on the state of the world tomorrow.
>
> Security price plays a dual role. The stock price today is just that—a price. The stock price tomorrow is part of the stock's uncertain pay-off.

Throughout this chapter and for a large part of the next chapter we will ignore today's prices and will only talk about the security pay-offs. We will come back to pricing in Chapter 2, Section 2.5. Throughout this book we assume **frictionless trading**, meaning that one can buy or sell any amount of any security at the market price without transaction costs. This assumption is justified in liquid markets.

Example 1.2. Suppose S is the stock price at maturity. A **call option** with strike K is a derivative security paying

$$S - K \quad \text{if } S > K,$$
$$0 \quad \text{if } S \leqslant K.$$

The pay-offs of options in Example 1.1 are in Table 1.2.

1.3 Securities as Vectors

An n-tuple of real numbers is called an n-dimensional vector. For

$$x = \begin{bmatrix} x_1 \\ x_2 \\ \vdots \\ x_n \end{bmatrix} \quad \text{and} \quad y = \begin{bmatrix} y_1 \\ y_2 \\ \vdots \\ y_n \end{bmatrix}$$

we write $x, y \in \mathbb{R}^n$. Each n-dimensional vector refers to a point in n-dimensional space. The above is a representation of such a point as a *column vector*, which is nothing other than an $n \times 1$ matrix, since it has n rows and 1 column. Of course, the same point can be written as a row vector instead. Whether to use columns or rows is a matter of personal taste, but it is important to be consistent.

Table 1.2.   Call option pay-offs.

Probability	$\frac{1}{2}$	$\frac{1}{6}$	$\frac{1}{3}$
Stock	3	2	1
Call option #1 ($K = 1.5$)	1.5	0.5	0
Call option #2 ($K = 1$)	2	1	0

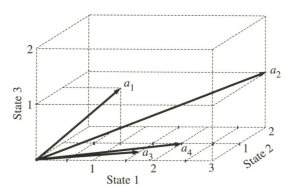

Figure 1.1.   Graphical representation of security pay-offs.

Example 1.3. Consider the four securities from the introductory example. Let us write the pay-offs of each security in the three states (scenarios) as a three-dimensional column vector:

$$a_1 = \begin{bmatrix} 1 \\ 1 \\ 1 \end{bmatrix}, \qquad a_2 = \begin{bmatrix} 3 \\ 2 \\ 1 \end{bmatrix}, \qquad a_3 = \begin{bmatrix} 1.5 \\ 0.5 \\ 0 \end{bmatrix}, \qquad a_4 = \begin{bmatrix} 2 \\ 1 \\ 0 \end{bmatrix}.$$

These securities are depicted graphically in Figure 1.1.

In GAUSS one would write

```
a1 = 1|1|1;
a2 = 3|2|1;
a3 = 1.5|0.5|0;
a4 = 2|1|0;
```

1.4   Operations on Securities

We can multiply vectors by a scalar. For any $\alpha \in \mathbb{R}$ we define

$$\alpha x = \begin{bmatrix} \alpha x_1 \\ \alpha x_2 \\ \vdots \\ \alpha x_n \end{bmatrix}.$$

This operation represents α units of security x.

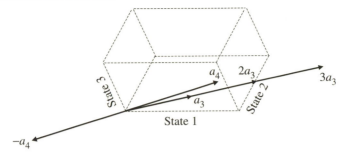

Figure 1.2. Different amounts of the same security have pay-offs that lie along a common direction.

Example 1.4. Two units of the third security will have the pay-off

$$2a_3 = 2 \begin{bmatrix} 1.5 \\ 0.5 \\ 0 \end{bmatrix} = \begin{bmatrix} 3 \\ 1 \\ 0 \end{bmatrix}.$$

If we buy two units of the third security today, tomorrow we will collect 3 pounds (dollars, euros) in the first scenario, 1 in the second scenario and nothing in the third scenario. In GAUSS one would type

$$3*a3;$$

If we issued (wrote, sold) 1 unit of the fourth security, then our pay-off tomorrow would be

$$-a_4 = -1 \begin{bmatrix} 2 \\ 1 \\ 0 \end{bmatrix} = \begin{bmatrix} -2 \\ -1 \\ 0 \end{bmatrix}.$$

In other words, we would have to pay the holder of this security 2 in the first scenario, 1 in the second scenario and nothing in the third scenario. In GAUSS one types

$$-a4;$$

Various amounts of securities a_3 and a_4 are represented graphically in Figure 1.2.

One can also add vectors together:

$$x + y = \begin{bmatrix} x_1 + y_1 \\ x_2 + y_2 \\ \vdots \\ x_n + y_n \end{bmatrix}.$$

With this operation we can calculate portfolio pay-offs. A **portfolio** is a combination of existing securities, which tells us how many units of each security have to be bought or sold to create the portfolio. Naturally, *portfolio pay-off* is what the name suggests: the pay-off of the combination of securities. The word 'portfolio' is sometimes used as an abbreviation of 'portfolio pay-off', creating a degree of ambiguity in the terminology.

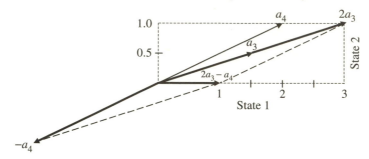

Figure 1.3.   Pay-off of the portfolio containing
two units of security a_3 and minus one unit of security a_4.

Example 1.5. A portfolio in which we hold two units of the first option and issue one unit of the second option will have the pay-off

$$2a_3 - a_4 = \begin{bmatrix} 2 \times 1.5 - 2 \\ 2 \times 0.5 - 1 \\ 2 \times 0 - 0 \end{bmatrix} = \begin{bmatrix} 1 \\ 0 \\ 0 \end{bmatrix}.$$

Graphically, this situation is depicted in Figure 1.3. In GAUSS the portfolio pay-off is

$$2*a3-a4;$$

1.5   The Matrix as a Collection of Securities

Often we need to work with a collection of securities (vectors). It is then convenient to stack the column vectors next to each other to form a matrix.

Example 1.6. The vectors a_1, a_2, a_3, a_4 from Example 1.3 form a 3×4 pay-off matrix, which we denote A,

$$A = \begin{bmatrix} a_1 & a_2 & a_3 & a_4 \end{bmatrix} = \begin{bmatrix} 1 & 3 & 1.5 & 2 \\ 1 & 2 & 0.5 & 1 \\ 1 & 1 & 0 & 0 \end{bmatrix}.$$

The market scenarios (states of the world) are in rows, securities are in columns. In GAUSS

$$A = a1\text{\textasciitilde}a2\text{\textasciitilde}a3\text{\textasciitilde}a4;$$

1.6   Transposition

Sometimes we need a *row vector* rather than a column vector. This is achieved by *transposition* of a column vector:

$$x = \begin{bmatrix} x_1 \\ x_2 \\ \vdots \\ x_n \end{bmatrix}, \qquad x^* = \begin{bmatrix} x_1 & x_2 & \cdots & x_n \end{bmatrix}.$$

Note that x^* (transpose of x) is a $1 \times n$ matrix. Conversely, transposition of a row vector gives a column vector. Should we perform the transposition twice, we will end up with the original vector:

$$(x^*)^* = x.$$

Example 1.7.

$$a_1^* = \begin{bmatrix} 1 & 1 & 1 \end{bmatrix},$$
$$a_2^* = \begin{bmatrix} 3 & 2 & 1 \end{bmatrix},$$
$$a_3^* = \begin{bmatrix} 1.5 & 0.5 & 0 \end{bmatrix},$$
$$a_4^* = \begin{bmatrix} 2 & 1 & 0 \end{bmatrix}.$$

In GAUSS transposition is achieved by attaching a prime to the matrix name. For example, a_1^* would be written as

```
a1';
```

The vectors $a_1^*, a_2^*, a_3^*, a_4^*$ stacked under each other form a 4×3 matrix B

$$B = \begin{bmatrix} a_1^* \\ a_2^* \\ a_3^* \\ a_4^* \end{bmatrix} = \begin{bmatrix} 1 & 1 & 1 \\ 3 & 2 & 1 \\ 1.5 & 0.5 & 0 \\ 2 & 1 & 0 \end{bmatrix}, \tag{1.1}$$

in GAUSS

```
B = a1'|a2'|a3'|a4';
```
(1.2)

Matrix B from equation (1.1) is in fact the *transpose of matrix A*

$$B = A^*,$$

thus instead of (1.2) in GAUSS one would simply write

```
B = A';
```

In general, we can have an $m \times n$ matrix M (denoted $M \in \mathbb{R}^{m \times n}$), where m is the number of rows and n is the number of columns. The element in the ith row and jth column is denoted M_{ij}. The entire jth column is denoted $M_{\bullet j}$ while the entire ith row is denoted $M_{i\bullet}$. According to our needs we can think of the matrix M as if it were composed of m row vectors or n column vectors:

$$M = \begin{bmatrix} M_{11} & M_{12} & \cdots & M_{1n} \\ M_{21} & M_{22} & \cdots & M_{2n} \\ \vdots & \vdots & \ddots & \vdots \\ M_{m1} & M_{m2} & \cdots & M_{mn} \end{bmatrix} = \begin{bmatrix} M_{1\bullet} \\ M_{2\bullet} \\ \vdots \\ M_{m\bullet} \end{bmatrix} = \begin{bmatrix} M_{\bullet 1} & M_{\bullet 2} & \cdots & M_{\bullet n} \end{bmatrix}.$$

The transpose of a matrix is obtained by changing the columns of the original matrix into the rows of the transposed matrix:

$$M^* = \begin{bmatrix} M_{11} & M_{21} & \cdots & M_{m1} \\ M_{12} & M_{22} & \cdots & M_{m2} \\ \vdots & \vdots & \ddots & \vdots \\ M_{1n} & M_{2n} & \cdots & M_{mn} \end{bmatrix} = \begin{bmatrix} (M_{\bullet 1})^* \\ (M_{\bullet 2})^* \\ \vdots \\ (M_{\bullet m})^* \end{bmatrix}$$

$$= \begin{bmatrix} (M_{1\bullet})^* & (M_{2\bullet})^* & \cdots & (M_{n\bullet})^* \end{bmatrix}.$$

Hence, for example, $M^*_{1\bullet} = (M_{\bullet 1})^*$ and $M^*_{\bullet 1} = (M_{1\bullet})^*$, which in words says that the first row of the transposed matrix is the transpose of the first column of the original matrix.

Example 1.8. Suppose a 3×4 pay-off matrix A is given. To extract the pay-off of the third security in all states, in GAUSS one would simply write

```
A[.,3];
```

On the other hand, if one wanted to know the pay-off of all four securities in the first market scenario, one would look at the row

```
A[1,.];
```

1.7 Matrix Multiplication and Portfolios

The basic building block of matrix multiplication is the multiplication of a row vector by a column vector. Let $A \in \mathbb{R}^{1 \times k}$ and $B \in \mathbb{R}^{k \times 1}$:

$$A = \begin{bmatrix} a_1 & a_2 & \cdots & a_k \end{bmatrix}, \qquad B = \begin{bmatrix} b_1 \\ b_2 \\ \vdots \\ b_k \end{bmatrix}.$$

In this simple case the matrix multiplication AB is defined as follows:

$$AB = \begin{bmatrix} a_1 & a_2 & \cdots & a_k \end{bmatrix} \begin{bmatrix} b_1 \\ b_2 \\ \vdots \\ b_k \end{bmatrix} = a_1 b_1 + a_2 b_2 + \cdots + a_k b_k. \qquad (1.3)$$

Note that A is a $1 \times k$ matrix, B is $k \times 1$ matrix and the result is a 1×1 matrix. One often thinks of a 1×1 matrix as a number.

Example 1.9. Suppose that we have a portfolio of the four securities from the introductory example which consists of x_1, x_2, x_3, x_4 units of the first, second, third and fourth security, respectively. In the third state the individual securities pay $1, 1, 0, 0$ in turn. The pay-off of the portfolio in the third state will be

$$x_1 \times 1 + x_2 \times 1 + x_3 \times 0 + x_4 \times 0.$$

If we take

$$A_{3\bullet} = \begin{bmatrix} 1 & 1 & 0 & 0 \end{bmatrix} \quad \text{and} \quad x = \begin{bmatrix} x_1 \\ x_2 \\ x_3 \\ x_4 \end{bmatrix},$$

then the portfolio pay-off can be written in matrix notation as $A_{3\bullet}x$.

In general one can multiply a matrix U ($m \times k$) with a matrix V ($k \times n$), regarding the former as m row vectors in $\mathbb{R}^k$ and the latter as n column vectors in $\mathbb{R}^k$. One multiplies each of the m row vectors in U with each of the n column vectors in V using the simple multiplication rule (1.3):

$$UV = \begin{bmatrix} U_{1\bullet} \\ U_{2\bullet} \\ \vdots \\ U_{m\bullet} \end{bmatrix} \begin{bmatrix} V_{\bullet 1} & V_{\bullet 2} & \cdots & V_{\bullet n} \end{bmatrix} = \begin{bmatrix} U_{1\bullet}V_{\bullet 1} & U_{1\bullet}V_{\bullet 2} & \cdots & U_{1\bullet}V_{\bullet n} \\ U_{2\bullet}V_{\bullet 1} & U_{2\bullet}V_{\bullet 2} & \cdots & U_{2\bullet}V_{\bullet n} \\ \vdots & \vdots & \ddots & \vdots \\ U_{m\bullet}V_{\bullet 1} & U_{m\bullet}V_{\bullet 2} & \cdots & U_{m\bullet}V_{\bullet n} \end{bmatrix}.$$

Facts.

- Matrix multiplication is not, in general, commutative:
$$UV \neq VU.$$

- The result of matrix multiplication does not depend on the order in which the multiplication is carried out (associativity property):
$$(UV)W = U(VW).$$

- Transposition reverses the order of multiplication!
$$(UV)^* = V^*U^*.$$

Example 1.10. Suppose we issue 2 units of call option #1 and 1 unit of call option #2. To balance this position we will buy 2 units of the stock and borrow 1 unit of the bond. What is the total exposure of this portfolio in the three scenarios?

Solution. The portfolio pay-off in the first scenario is

$$\begin{bmatrix} 1 & 3 & 1.5 & 2 \end{bmatrix} \begin{bmatrix} -1 \\ 2 \\ -2 \\ -1 \end{bmatrix} = 1 \times (-1) + 3 \times 2 + 1.5 \times (-2) + 2 \times (-1) = 0.$$

The pay-off in the second state is

$$\begin{bmatrix} 1 & 2 & 0.5 & 1 \end{bmatrix} \begin{bmatrix} -1 \\ 2 \\ -2 \\ -1 \end{bmatrix} = 1 \times (-1) + 2 \times 2 + 0.5 \times (-2) + 1 \times (-1) = 1$$

	A	B	C	D	E	F	G	H
1	pay-off matrix A					portfolio weights x		portfolio pay-off
2	1	3	1.5	2		−1		0
3	1	2	0.5	1		2		1
4	1	1	0	0		−2		1
5						−1		
6								
7						To multiply matrix A with vector x		
8						select the whole area H2:H4,		
9						then type in the formula		
10						=MMULT(A2:D4;F2:F5)		
11						and press CTRL+SHIFT+ENTER		

Figure 1.4. Matrix multiplication in Excel.

and the pay-off in the third state will be

$$\begin{bmatrix} 1 & 1 & 0 & 0 \end{bmatrix} \begin{bmatrix} -1 \\ 2 \\ -2 \\ -1 \end{bmatrix} = 1 \times (-1) + 1 \times 2 + 0 \times (-2) + 0 \times (-1) = 1.$$

The pay-off in *all three states together* is now

$$\begin{bmatrix} 1 & 3 & 1.5 & 2 \\ 1 & 2 & 0.5 & 1 \\ 1 & 1 & 0 & 0 \end{bmatrix} \begin{bmatrix} -1 \\ 2 \\ -2 \\ -1 \end{bmatrix} = \begin{bmatrix} 0 \\ 1 \\ 1 \end{bmatrix}.$$

Thus the portfolio pay-off can be expressed using the pay-off matrix A and the portfolio vector

$$x^* = \begin{bmatrix} -1 & 2 & -2 & -1 \end{bmatrix}$$

as Ax. In GAUSS this reads A*x.

Example 1.11. You can perform the same matrix multiplication in Excel, using the instructions in Figure 1.4.

1.8   Systems of Equations and Hedging

A system of m equations for n unknowns $x_1, \ldots, x_n$,

$$\left.\begin{aligned} A_{11}x_1 + A_{12}x_2 + \cdots + A_{1n}x_n &= b_1, \\ A_{21}x_1 + A_{22}x_2 + \cdots + A_{2n}x_n &= b_2, \\ &\vdots \\ A_{m1}x_1 + A_{m2}x_2 + \cdots + A_{mn}x_n &= b_m, \end{aligned}\right\} \tag{1.4}$$

can be written in matrix form as

$$\begin{bmatrix} A_{11} \\ A_{21} \\ \vdots \\ A_{m1} \end{bmatrix} x_1 + \begin{bmatrix} A_{12} \\ A_{22} \\ \vdots \\ A_{m2} \end{bmatrix} x_2 + \cdots + \begin{bmatrix} A_{1n} \\ A_{2n} \\ \vdots \\ A_{mn} \end{bmatrix} x_n = \begin{bmatrix} b_1 \\ b_2 \\ \vdots \\ b_m \end{bmatrix}$$

or

$$A_{\bullet 1}x_1 + A_{\bullet 2}x_2 + \cdots + A_{\bullet n}x_n = b$$

or

$$Ax = b, \tag{1.5}$$

where

$$x = \begin{bmatrix} x_1 \\ x_2 \\ \vdots \\ x_n \end{bmatrix}, \qquad b = \begin{bmatrix} b_1 \\ b_2 \\ \vdots \\ b_m \end{bmatrix}.$$

One can think of the columns of A as being n securities in m states, x being a portfolio of the n securities and b another security that we want to hedge. In such a situation the securities in A are called **basis assets** and the security b is called a **focus asset**. We know that Ax gives the pay-off of the portfolio x of basis assets. To solve a system of equations $Ax = b$ therefore means finding a portfolio x of basis assets that replicates (perfectly hedges) the focus asset b.

Typically, the basis assets are liquid securities with known prices, whereas the focus asset b is an over-the-counter (OTC) security issued by an investment bank. Such securities are issued between two parties and do not have a liquid secondary market. The question is, what is a fair price of the OTC security?

By issuing the focus asset b the bank commits itself to pay different amounts of money in different states of the world and thus it enters into a risky position. **Hedging** is a simultaneous purchase of another portfolio that reduces this risk, and a **perfect hedge** is a portfolio that eliminates the risk completely. Suppose that portfolio x is a perfect hedge to the focus asset b. The bank will issue asset b (promise to pay b_i in state i tomorrow) and simultaneously purchase the **replicating portfolio** x of basis assets.

How much will the bank charge for issuing the OTC security? To break even, it will charge exactly the cost of the replicating portfolio (plus a fee to cover its overheads). Tomorrow, when the payment of b becomes due it will liquidate the hedging portfolio x. Since x was a perfect hedge, the pay-off of the hedging portfolio Ax will exactly match the liability b in each state of the world. Hence the bank will not have incurred any risk in this operation.

Example 1.12. Let us answer parts (1) and (2) of the introductory Example 1.1. To replicate the fourth security we need to find a portfolio

$$x^* = \begin{bmatrix} x_1 & x_2 & x_3 \end{bmatrix}$$

such that

$$\begin{bmatrix} A_{\bullet 1} & A_{\bullet 2} & A_{\bullet 3} \end{bmatrix} x = A_{\bullet 4}.$$

Thus we are solving

$$
\begin{array}{ccccccc}
1 \times x_1 & + & 3 \times x_2 & + & 1.5 \times x_3 & = & 2, \\
1 \times x_1 & + & 2 \times x_2 & + & 0.5 \times x_3 & = & 1, \\
1 \times x_1 & + & 1 \times x_2 & + & 0 \times x_3 & = & 0.
\end{array}
$$

After a short manipulation we find that $x_1 = -1$, $x_2 = 1$, $x_3 = 0$ is a unique solution. In GAUSS one can obtain the replicating portfolio by typing

```
x=inv(A[.,1:3])*A[.,4];
```

Part (2) assumes that the risk-free security costs $1/1.05$ today, whereas the stock costs 2. The value of the replicating portfolio is therefore

$$\frac{x_1}{1.05} + 2x_2 = \frac{-1}{1.05} + 2 = 1.048.$$

This is how much the bank would charge for the second call option.

1.8.1 Complications

In the preceding example the hedging portfolio x

$$\begin{bmatrix} A_{\bullet 1} & A_{\bullet 2} & A_{\bullet 3} \\ \text{bond} & \text{stock} & \text{option \#1} \end{bmatrix} x = \begin{matrix} A_{\bullet 4} \\ \text{option \#2} \end{matrix} \tag{1.6}$$

is unique and it can be expressed using an inverse matrix

$$x = \begin{bmatrix} A_{\bullet 1} & A_{\bullet 2} & A_{\bullet 3} \end{bmatrix}^{-1} A_{\bullet 4}.$$

However, if we swap the two call options around,

$$\begin{bmatrix} A_{\bullet 1} & A_{\bullet 2} & A_{\bullet 4} \\ \text{bond} & \text{stock} & \text{option \#2} \end{bmatrix} x = \begin{matrix} A_{\bullet 3} \\ \text{option \#1} \end{matrix}, \tag{1.7}$$

we will find that (1.7) suddenly does not have a solution, and, what is more, the matrix

$$\begin{bmatrix} A_{\bullet 1} & A_{\bullet 2} & A_{\bullet 4} \end{bmatrix}$$

is not invertible; this can be seen by typing `inv(A[.,1 2 4]);`.

To add to the confusion, the system

$$\begin{bmatrix} A_{\bullet 1} & A_{\bullet 2} \end{bmatrix} x = A_{\bullet 4} \tag{1.8}$$

has a unique solution ($x_1 = -1$, $x_2 = 1$) even though the inverse of $\begin{bmatrix} A_{\bullet 1} & A_{\bullet 2} \end{bmatrix}$ does not exist; try `inv(A[.,1:2])`. At the same time the system

$$\begin{bmatrix} A_{\bullet 1} & A_{\bullet 2} \end{bmatrix} x = A_{\bullet 3} \tag{1.9}$$

does not have a solution.

It should be stressed that the hedging problems (1.6)–(1.9) arise naturally; these are *not* special cases that you will never see in practice. Clearly, $m = n$ is neither necessary nor sufficient to find a solution and the same holds for the existence or non-existence of the inverse matrix. The next few sections explain how one solves the hedging problem in full generality. Sections 1.9 and 1.10 provide the terminology, Sections 1.11–1.14 discuss the special case when A has an inverse, and Section 2.1 solves the general case.

1.9   Linear Independence and Redundant Securities

Let the column vectors $A_{\bullet 1}, A_{\bullet 2}, \ldots, A_{\bullet n} \in \mathbb{R}^m$ represent n securities in m states of the world, in the sense discussed above.

Definition 1.13. We say that vectors (securities) $A_{\bullet 1}, A_{\bullet 2}, \ldots, A_{\bullet n}$ are **linearly independent** if the only solution to

$$A_{\bullet 1}x_1 + A_{\bullet 2}x_2 + \cdots + A_{\bullet n}x_n = 0$$

is the trivial portfolio

$$x_1 = 0, \quad x_2 = 0, \quad \ldots, \quad x_n = 0.$$

Mathematicians call the sum $A_{\bullet 1}x_1 + A_{\bullet 2}x_2 + \cdots + A_{\bullet n}x_n$ a **linear combination** of vectors $A_{\bullet 1}, A_{\bullet 2}, \ldots, A_{\bullet n}$ and the numbers $x_1, \ldots, x_n$ are coefficients of the linear combination. To us $x_1, \ldots, x_n$ represent numbers of units of each security in a portfolio and the linear combination represents the portfolio pay-off.

The meaning of linear independence is best understood if we look at a situation where $A_{\bullet 1}, A_{\bullet 2}, \ldots, A_{\bullet n}$ are *not* linearly independent. From the definition it means that there is a linear combination where at least one of the coefficients $x_1, \ldots, x_n$ is non-zero and

$$A_{\bullet 1}x_1 + A_{\bullet 2}x_2 + \cdots + A_{\bullet n}x_n = 0. \tag{1.10}$$

Without loss of generality we can assume that $x_1 \neq 0$. One can then solve (1.10) for $A_{\bullet 1}$:

$$A_{\bullet 1} = -\left(A_{\bullet 2}\frac{x_2}{x_1} + \cdots + A_{\bullet n}\frac{x_n}{x_1} \right).$$

The last equality means that $A_{\bullet 1}$ is a linear combination of vectors $A_{\bullet 2}, \ldots, A_{\bullet n}$ with coefficients $-x_2/x_1, \ldots, -x_n/x_1$. In conclusion, if the vectors $A_{\bullet 1}, \ldots, A_{\bullet n}$ are not linearly independent, then at least one of them can be expressed as a linear combination of the remaining $n - 1$ vectors. And vice versa, if vectors $A_{\bullet 1}, \ldots, A_{\bullet n}$ *are* linearly independent, then none of them can be expressed as a linear combination of the remaining $n - 1$ vectors.

Securities that are linear combinations of other securities are called **redundant** and the portfolio which achieves the same pay-off as that of a redundant security is called a *replicating portfolio*. Redundant securities do not add anything new to the market because their pay-off can be synthesized from the pay-off of the remaining securities; instead of trading a redundant security we might equally well trade the replicating portfolio with the same result.

The practical significance of linearly independent securities, on the other hand, is that each additional linearly independent security has a pay-off previously unavailable in the market. The **marketed subspace** is formed by pay-offs of all possible portfolios (linear combinations) of basis assets and is denoted $\text{Span}(A_{\bullet 1}, A_{\bullet 2}, \ldots, A_{\bullet n})$. As was mentioned above each linearly independent security adds something new to the market—it adds one extra dimension to the marketed subspace. Consequently, the maximum number of linearly independent securities in the marketed subspace is called the **dimension** of the marketed subspace. The definition of dimension is made meaningful by the following theorem.

Theorem 1.14 (Dimensionality Theorem). *Suppose $A_{\bullet 1}, A_{\bullet 2}, \ldots, A_{\bullet n}$ are n linearly independent vectors. Suppose*

$$B_{\bullet 1}, B_{\bullet 2}, \ldots, B_{\bullet k} \in \text{Span}(A_{\bullet 1}, A_{\bullet 2}, \ldots, A_{\bullet n})$$

are linearly independent. Then

$$\text{Span}(B_{\bullet 1}, B_{\bullet 2}, \ldots, B_{\bullet k}) = \text{Span}(A_{\bullet 1}, A_{\bullet 2}, \ldots, A_{\bullet n})$$

if and only if $k = n$.

Proof. See website.   □

We say that the **market is complete** if the marketed subspace

$$\text{Span}(A_{\bullet 1}, A_{\bullet 2}, \ldots, A_{\bullet n})$$

includes all possible pay-offs over the m states, that is, if it contains all possible m-dimensional vectors. A complete market means that whatever distribution of wealth in the m market scenarios one may think of, it can always be achieved as a pay-off from a portfolio of marketed securities. Since the dimension of $\mathbb{R}^m$ is m, another way of saying that the market is complete is to claim that there are m linearly independent basis securities or that the dimension of the marketed subspace is m.

1.10   The Structure of the Marketed Subspace

There is a simple procedure for finding out the dimension of the marketed subspace, based on the following two facts, which are a direct consequence of the Dimensionality Theorem.

- Suppose that $A_{\bullet 1}, A_{\bullet 2}, \ldots, A_{\bullet k}$ are linearly independent. For the next security $A_{\bullet k+1}$ there are only two possibilities. Either $A_{\bullet 1}, A_{\bullet 2}, \ldots, A_{\bullet k+1}$ are linearly independent, or $A_{\bullet k+1}$ is *redundant*, that is, there is a replicating portfolio

  $$x^* = \begin{bmatrix} x_1 & x_2 & \cdots & x_k \end{bmatrix}$$

  such that

  $$A_{\bullet k+1} = A_{\bullet 1}x_1 + A_{\bullet 2}x_2 + \cdots + A_{\bullet k}x_k.$$

- With m states there cannot be more than m linearly independent securities.

This allows us to sort basis assets into two groups: in one group we have linearly independent securities that span the whole marketed subspace and in the other group we have redundant securities. There is more than one way of splitting the basis assets into these two groups, and the same security may appear once as linearly independent and another time as redundant—there is no contradiction in this. However, the *number* of linearly independent securities in the first group is always the same, and we know that it is equal to the dimension of the marketed subspace.

Example 1.15. Let us split the four securities from the introductory example into linearly independent and redundant securities.

1. We will start with the first security

$$A_{\bullet 1} = \begin{bmatrix} 1 \\ 1 \\ 1 \end{bmatrix}$$

and place it among the linearly independent securities.

2. For

$$A_{\bullet 2} = \begin{bmatrix} 3 \\ 2 \\ 1 \end{bmatrix}$$

there are now two possibilities: either

(a) it is redundant, which means there is x_1 such that $A_{\bullet 2} = x_1 A_{\bullet 1}$, or

(b) $A_{\bullet 1}, A_{\bullet 2}$ are linearly independent.

Let us examine (a), that is, try to find x_1 so that $A_{\bullet 2} = x_1 A_{\bullet 1}$ holds

$$\begin{bmatrix} 3 \\ 2 \\ 1 \end{bmatrix} = x_1 \begin{bmatrix} 1 \\ 1 \\ 1 \end{bmatrix} = \begin{bmatrix} x_1 \\ x_1 \\ x_1 \end{bmatrix}.$$

This implies that $x_1 = 3$ *and* $x_1 = 2$ *and* $x_1 = 1$, which is impossible. Since (a) is impossible (b) must hold, therefore we add the second security to the basket of linearly independent securities, already containing the first security.

3. Let us examine the third security:

$$A_{\bullet 3} = \begin{bmatrix} 1.5 \\ 0.5 \\ 0 \end{bmatrix}.$$

Either

(a) $A_{\bullet 3}$ is redundant, $A_{\bullet 3} = x_1 A_{\bullet 1} + x_2 A_{\bullet 2}$, or

(b) $A_{\bullet 1}, A_{\bullet 2}, A_{\bullet 3}$ are linearly independent.

Possibility (a) would imply

$$\begin{bmatrix} 1.5 \\ 0.5 \\ 0 \end{bmatrix} = x_1 \begin{bmatrix} 1 \\ 1 \\ 1 \end{bmatrix} + x_2 \begin{bmatrix} 3 \\ 2 \\ 1 \end{bmatrix} = \begin{bmatrix} x_1 + 3x_2 \\ x_1 + 2x_2 \\ x_1 + x_2 \end{bmatrix}.$$

Subtracting the third equation from the second equation we have $0.5 = x_2$, whereas the first equation minus the second equation gives $1 = x_2$ and these two statements are contradictory. Since (a) is not possible the securities $A_{\bullet 1}, A_{\bullet 2}, A_{\bullet 3}$ are linearly independent and therefore $A_{\bullet 3}$ goes into the basket with securities one and two.

4. Finally, we examine the fourth security. We could go through the process outlined above, but there is a faster way. We have three states, hence we know that there cannot be *more* than three linearly independent securities. And we already have three linearly independent securities, namely $A_{\bullet 1}, A_{\bullet 2}$ and $A_{\bullet 3}$. Since $A_{\bullet 4}$ cannot be independent it has to be redundant.

Note. Had we started with $A_{\bullet 4}$ and then continued with $A_{\bullet 3}, A_{\bullet 2}$ and $A_{\bullet 1}$, we would have found that $A_{\bullet 4}, A_{\bullet 3}, A_{\bullet 2}$ are linearly independent and that $A_{\bullet 1}$ is then redundant.

We can conclude that the market containing securities $A_{\bullet 1}$, $A_{\bullet 2}$, $A_{\bullet 3}$ and $A_{\bullet 4}$ is complete, since with three states three linearly independent securities are (necessary and) sufficient to span the whole market.

Recall that we can stack the securities into a matrix $A = \begin{bmatrix} A_{\bullet 1} & A_{\bullet 2} & \cdots & A_{\bullet n} \end{bmatrix}$ and that the portfolio pay-off can be written as $A_{\bullet 1}x_1 + A_{\bullet 2}x_2 + \cdots + A_{\bullet n}x_n = Ax$. Mathematicians call the maximum number of linearly independent columns of a matrix its **rank** and denote it $r(A)$. For us $r(A)$ is nothing other than the dimension of the marketed subspace.

Facts.

- The rank of A^*A is the same as the rank of A.
- $r(AB) \leqslant \min(r(A), r(B))$.
- The ranks of A and A^* are the same—it does not matter whether we look at columns or rows.
- For the $m \times n$ matrix A it is always true that $r(A) \leqslant \min(m, n)$.

Proof. Readers with a particular interest in linear algebra can find the proofs on the website.   □

When $r(A) = \min(m, n)$ we say that A has **full rank**. Square matrices with full rank are called **regular** (**non-singular, invertible**).

1.11   The Identity Matrix and Arrow–Debreu Securities

A square matrix of the form

$$\begin{bmatrix} 1 & 0 & \cdots & 0 \\ 0 & 1 & \ddots & \vdots \\ \vdots & \ddots & \ddots & 0 \\ 0 & \cdots & 0 & 1 \end{bmatrix}$$

is called the identity matrix and is denoted I (or sometimes I_n to denote the dimension). The identity matrix is closely linked to **Arrow–Debreu securities**.

There are as many Arrow–Debreu securities (also called pure securities or elementary state securities) as there are states of the world. The Arrow–Debreu security for state j (denoted e_j) pays 1 in state j and 0 in all other states. Ordering all Arrow–Debreu securities into a matrix $\begin{bmatrix} e_1 & e_2 & \cdots & e_m \end{bmatrix}$ gives

$$\begin{bmatrix} 1 & 0 & \cdots & 0 \\ 0 & 1 & \ddots & \vdots \\ \vdots & \ddots & \ddots & 0 \\ 0 & \cdots & 0 & 1 \end{bmatrix},$$

an $m \times m$ identity matrix.

1.12 Matrix Inverse

Recall that a square matrix with full rank is called invertible (regular, non-singular).

- For every square matrix A with full rank (and only for such matrices!) there is a unique matrix B such that
$$AB = BA = I.$$
The matrix B is called the *inverse* to matrix A and it is more commonly denoted A^{-1}. Thus
$$AA^{-1} = A^{-1}A = I.$$
- When C and D are invertible, then CD is also invertible and $(CD)^{-1} = D^{-1}C^{-1}$.
- Trivially, $(A^{-1})^{-1} = A$.

1.13 Inverse Matrix and Replicating Portfolios

Remember that a matrix A must be square with linearly independent columns to have an inverse. Throughout this book we will assume that an efficient procedure for computation of A^{-1} is available. In GAUSS this procedure is called inv(). In this section we are interested in the *interpretation* of the inverse matrix. Let us begin with the definition:

$$AA^{-1} = I. \tag{1.11}$$

If we divide the matrices A^{-1} and I into n columns, the matrix equality (1.11) is split into n systems of the form

$$AA^{-1}_{\bullet j} = e_j,$$

where $A^{-1}_{\bullet j}$ is the jth column of the inverse matrix and e_j is the jth column of the identity matrix (see also Section 1.11), $j = 1, 2, \ldots, n$.

Thus, for example, the solution x of the system

$$Ax = \begin{bmatrix} 1 \\ 0 \\ \vdots \\ 0 \end{bmatrix}$$

gives us the first column of the inverse matrix.

Again, if we think of A as containing pay-offs of n basis assets in n states, then solving

$$Ax = e_j$$

means finding a portfolio x that replicates the Arrow–Debreu security for state j. Existence of the inverse matrix therefore requires existence of the replicating portfolio for *each* Arrow–Debreu security and this explains why $r(A)$ must equal n for the inverse to exist.

The argument goes as follows. For the inverse to exist each elementary state security must lie in the marketed subspace formed by the basis assets (columns of matrix A). But the elementary state securities are linearly independent and if they all belong to the marketed subspace, that means that the dimension of the marketed subspace is n. We know from Section 1.9 that the dimension of the marketed subspace is equal to $r(A)$. Thus for an inverse to exist we must have $r(A) = n$.

Example 1.16. Find the inverse of

$$A = \begin{bmatrix} 1 & 3 & 1.5 \\ 1 & 2 & 0.5 \\ 1 & 1 & 0 \end{bmatrix}.$$

Solution. In GAUSS we would type

```
inv(A[.,1:3]);
```

which gives

$$A^{-1} = \begin{bmatrix} 1 & -3 & 3 \\ -1 & 3 & -2 \\ 2 & -4 & 2 \end{bmatrix}.$$

To find the inverse by hand one must solve n systems of the type $Ax = I_{\bullet i}$ for $i = 1, 2, \ldots, n$. This is best performed by Gaussian elimination, but there are other possibilities, for example, the Cramer rule applied to $Ax = I_{\bullet i}$ will lead to the computation of the adjoint matrix ($A^{-1} = \operatorname{adj} A / \det A$). This book does not teach how to solve systems of linear equations by hand; the reader should consult the references at the end of the chapter for a detailed exposition of Gaussian elimination, the Cramer rule and related topics.

Just for illustration let us solve $Ax = I_{\bullet 1}$, that is,

$$
\begin{array}{ccccccl}
x_1 & + & 3x_2 & + & 1.5x_3 & = & 1, \qquad\qquad (1a) \\
x_1 & + & 2x_2 & + & 0.5x_3 & = & 0, \qquad\qquad (2a) \\
x_1 & + & x_2 & + & & = & 0, \qquad\qquad (3a)
\end{array}
$$

by Gaussian elimination. In the first instance we subtract Equation (1a) from both Equation (2a) and Equation (3a),

$$
\begin{array}{ccccccl}
x_1 & + & 3x_2 & + & 1.5x_3 & = & 1, \qquad\qquad (1b) \\
 & - & x_2 & - & x_3 & = & -1, \qquad\quad (2b) \\
 & - & 2x_2 & - & 1.5x_3 & = & -1. \qquad\quad (3b)
\end{array}
$$

Now subtract $2 \times$ Equation (2b) from Equation (3b),

$$
\begin{array}{ccccccl}
x_1 & + & 3x_2 & + & 1.5x_3 & = & 1, \qquad\qquad (1c) \\
 & - & x_2 & - & x_3 & = & -1, \qquad\quad (2c) \\
 & & & & 0.5x_3 & = & 1. \qquad\qquad (3c)
\end{array}
$$

Equation (3c) gives $x_3 = 2$, from Equation (2c) we then have $x_2 = -1$ and finally Equation (1c) gives $x_1 = 1$. Note that x represents the first column of A^{-1} as expected.

Excel commands for computing an inverse matrix are described in Figure 1.5.

	A	B	C	D	E	F	G	H	I	J
1	Matrix A				A inverse					
2	1	3	1.5		1	−3	3			
3	1	2	0.5		−1	3	−2			
4	1	1	0		2	−4	2			
5					To calculate the inverse of matrix A					
6					select the whole area E2:G4,					
7					then type in the formula					
8					=MINVERSE(A2:D4)					
9					and press CTRL+SHIFT+ENTER					

Figure 1.5. Computation of A^{-1} in Excel.

1.14 Complete Market Hedging Formula

The inverse of the pay-off matrix can be used to compute replicating portfolios. Recall that the hedging equation reads

$$Ax = b.$$

If A^{-1} exists, we can apply it on both sides to obtain x:

$$A^{-1}Ax = x = A^{-1}b.$$

Complete market without redundant basis assets. Suppose that $A \in \mathbb{R}^{m \times n}$ represents the pay-off of n securities in m states. If A represents a complete market without redundant assets, then $r(A) = m = n$, which means that A is a square matrix with full rank and therefore has an inverse A^{-1}. In this case any focus asset b can be hedged perfectly; there is x such that $Ax = b$. The hedging portfolio x is unique and is given by formula

$$x = A^{-1}b. \tag{1.12}$$

Hedging formula (1.12) has a simple financial interpretation. Recall that the columns of A^{-1} represent portfolio weights that perfectly replicate Arrow–Debreu state securities. The focus asset b is a combination of Arrow–Debreu securities with exactly b_i units of the ith state security. Therefore, the hedging portfolio x is a linear combination of columns in A^{-1}; $x = A^{-1}b$.

Example 1.17. Let us take part (1) of the introductory Example 1.1. We have

$$A = \begin{bmatrix} 1 & 3 & 1.5 \\ 1 & 2 & 0.5 \\ 1 & 1 & 0 \end{bmatrix} \quad \text{and} \quad b = \begin{bmatrix} 2 \\ 1 \\ 0 \end{bmatrix}.$$

We have calculated A^{-1} in Example 1.16:

$$A^{-1} = \begin{bmatrix} 1 & -3 & 3 \\ -1 & 3 & -2 \\ 2 & -4 & 2 \end{bmatrix}.$$

	A	B	C	D	E	F	G	H	I	J
1	Matrix A				b		x			
2	1	3	1.5		2		−1			
3	1	2	0.5		1		1			
4	1	1	0		0		0			
5					To calculate the replicating portfolio					
6					select the whole area G2:G4,					
7					then type in the formula					
8					=MMULT(MINVERSE(A2:C4), E2:E4)					
9					and press CTRL+SHIFT+ENTER					

Figure 1.6.   Solution of the hedging problem using A^{-1}.

The replicating portfolio is therefore

$$x = A^{-1}b = \begin{bmatrix} 1 & -3 & 3 \\ -1 & 3 & -2 \\ 2 & -4 & 2 \end{bmatrix} \begin{bmatrix} 2 \\ 1 \\ 0 \end{bmatrix} = \begin{bmatrix} -1 \\ 1 \\ 0 \end{bmatrix}. \tag{1.13}$$

Excel commands for computing expression (1.13) are given in Figure 1.6.

1.14.1   To Invert or not to Invert?

Note that we have already found the same x in Example 1.12, that time without computing A^{-1}. Which of the two computations would we use in practice?

The main difference between Example 1.12 and Example 1.17 is that the former solves $Ax = b$ for one specific focus asset b; if we changed b, we would have to redo the whole calculation from scratch. In contrast, once we know A^{-1} in Example 1.17 it is easy to recalculate the perfect hedge for *any* focus asset b; we just perform one matrix multiplication $A^{-1}b$. It is also true that solving $Ax = b$ for one fixed value of b (which is what we have done in Example 1.12) is about three times faster than computing the entire inverse matrix A^{-1}. Thus the conclusion is clear. If we are required to solve the hedging problem just once, it is quicker *not* to use the inverse matrix; however, if we have to solve many hedging problems with the same set of basis assets, then it will be far more economical to compute A^{-1} once at the beginning and then recycle it using the formula

$$x = A^{-1}b. \tag{1.14}$$

This will be particularly useful in dynamic option replication of Chapter 4, where the number of one-period hedging problems is large.

1.15   Summary

- The simplest model of financial markets has two periods and a finite number of states. While today's prices of all securities are known, tomorrow's security pay-offs are uncertain. Nevertheless, this uncertainty is rather organized. The security pay-offs must follow one of the finite number of scenarios and the contents of each of these scenarios is known today together with the probability of each scenario.

- If m is the number of scenarios (states of the world), then the pay-off of each security can be represented as an m-dimensional vector.
- The pay-off of n securities is captured in an $m \times n$ pay-off matrix A.
- A portfolio is a combination of existing securities. If we write down the number of units of each security in the portfolio into an n-dimensional portfolio vector x, then the portfolio pay-off can be calculated from the matrix multiplication Ax.
- An asset whose pay-off can be obtained as a combination of pay-offs of other securities is called redundant. The portfolio which has the same pay-off as a redundant asset is called a replicating portfolio.
- Any system of linear equations can be written down as a matrix equality and vice versa; see equations (1.4) and (1.5).
- A hedging problem with m states of the world, n basis assets and a focus asset b can be expressed as a system of m linear equations for n unknowns x, with right-hand side b:
$$Ax = b.$$

The $m \times n$ system matrix A contains pay-offs of the basis assets as its columns. The solution x of the system, if it exists, represents a portfolio of basis assets which replicates the focus asset b.

- A matrix A has an inverse if and only if it is square with full rank. The inverse, if it exists, is denoted A^{-1} and has the property,
$$AA^{-1} = A^{-1}A = I.$$

- If A is a pay-off matrix of basis assets, then the individual columns of A^{-1} represent replicating portfolios to individual Arrow–Debreu securities.
- In a complete market one can hedge perfectly any focus asset b, and when there are no redundant basis assets one can express the perfect hedge as
$$x = A^{-1}b.$$

Here one can interpret x as a linear combination of portfolios that perfectly replicate Arrow–Debreu securities.

1.16 Notes

Anton (2000) and Grossman (1994) are comprehensive guides to matrix calculations and to the underlying theory.

1.17 Exercises

Exercise 1.1. Which of the following is true of matrix multiplication of matrices A and B?

(a) It can be performed only if A and B are square matrices.

(b) Each entry of the result c_{ij} is the product of a_{ij} and b_{ij}.

(c) $AB = BA$.

(d) It can be performed only if the number of columns of A is equal to the number of rows B.

Exercise 1.2. The result of the matrix multiplication $\begin{bmatrix} 1 \\ 1 \end{bmatrix}\begin{bmatrix} 1 & 2 & 3 \end{bmatrix}$ is

(a) not defined;

(b) $\begin{bmatrix} 6 \end{bmatrix}$;

(c) $\begin{bmatrix} 1 & 2 & 3 \\ 1 & 2 & 3 \end{bmatrix}$;

(d) none of the above.

Exercise 1.3. Which of the following is true of matrices A and B if AB is a column vector?

(a) B is a column vector.

(b) A is a row vector.

(c) A and B are square matrices.

(d) The number of rows in A must equal the number of columns in B.

Exercise 1.4. The rank of the $n \times n$ identity matrix is

(a) 0;

(b) 1;

(c) n^2;

(d) none of the above.

Exercise 1.5. The rank of the $m \times n$ matrix is

(a) equal to $\max(m, n)$;

(b) only defined when $m = n$, in which case it is equal to m;

(c) not greater than $\min(m, n)$;

(d) none of the above.

Exercise 1.6. The last column of a transposed matrix is the same as

(a) the first column of the original matrix;

(b) the last row of the original matrix, but transposed;

(c) the first row of the original matrix, but transposed;

(d) none of the above.

Exercise 1.7. Let A be an $m \times n$ matrix representing the pay-off of n securities in m states of the world. The assertion 'market is complete' means that

(a) $m \geqslant n$;

(b) $n \geqslant m$;

(c) $r(A) = m$;

(d) $r(A) = n$.

Exercise 1.8. When there are more securities than states of the world, then

(a) some securities are redundant;

(b) markets are complete;

(c) markets are incomplete;

(d) none of the above.

Exercise 1.9. The number of redundant securities is equal to

(a) $m - \min(m, n)$;

(b) $m - r(A)$;

(c) $n - r(A)$;

(d) none of the above.

Exercise 1.10. If A has full rank, this means that

(a) markets are complete;

(b) there are no redundant securities;

(c) sometimes (a), sometimes (b) and sometimes both;

(d) none of the above.

Exercise 1.11 (terminal wealth). An investor with initial wealth £10 000 chooses between a risk-free rate of return of 2% and a risky security with rate of return $-20\%, -10\%, -5\%, 0\%, 5\%, 10\%, 20\%, 30\%$ with probability 0.05, 0.10, 0.15, 0.20, 0.20, 0.15, 0.10, 0.05, respectively. If α denotes the proportion of initial wealth invested in the risky asset, explain how one can express in matrix notation

(a) terminal wealth;

(b) expected terminal wealth.

Exercise 1.12 (redundant securities). In this question an $m \times n$ matrix A represents the pay-off of n securities in m states. In each of the markets below divide securities into linearly independent and redundant:

(a) $A = \begin{bmatrix} 2 & 1 & 1 \\ 1 & 1 & 0 \\ 0 & 1 & -1 \end{bmatrix}$;

(b) $A = \begin{bmatrix} 2 & 1 & 0 & 3 & 1 \\ 1 & 1 & 1 & 2 & 1 \\ 0 & 1 & 2 & 1 & 0 \end{bmatrix}$;

(c) $A = \begin{bmatrix} 2 & 0 \\ 1 & 1 \\ 0 & 2 \end{bmatrix}$.

Exercise 1.13 (quadratic forms). Define a symmetric 2×2 matrix

$$H = \begin{bmatrix} h_{11} & h_{12} \\ h_{12} & h_{22} \end{bmatrix}$$

and a 2×1 vector

$$x = \begin{bmatrix} x_1 \\ x_2 \end{bmatrix}.$$

(a) Perform the matrix multiplication x^*Hx. The result of the multiplication is a quadratic form in x.

(b) Consider a quadratic form $x_1^2 - 6x_1x_2 + 2x_2^2$. Find a symmetric matrix H such that

$$x_1^2 - 6x_1x_2 + 2x_2^2 = x^*Hx.$$

(c) Write the expression

$$\frac{\partial^2 f}{\partial x^2}(x - x_0)^2 + 2\frac{\partial^2 f}{\partial x \partial y}(x - x_0)(y - y_0) + \frac{\partial^2 f}{\partial y^2}(y - y_0)^2$$

in matrix form.

Exercise 1.14 (probability matrices). A probability matrix is a square matrix having two properties: (i) every component is non-negative and (ii) the sum of elements in each row is 1. The following are probability matrices:

$$P = \begin{bmatrix} \frac{1}{3} & \frac{1}{3} & \frac{1}{3} \\ \frac{1}{4} & \frac{1}{2} & \frac{1}{4} \\ 0 & 0 & 1 \end{bmatrix} \quad \text{and} \quad Q = \begin{bmatrix} \frac{1}{6} & \frac{1}{6} & \frac{2}{3} \\ 0 & 1 & 0 \\ \frac{1}{5} & \frac{1}{5} & \frac{3}{5} \end{bmatrix}.$$

(a) Show that PQ is a probability matrix.

(b) Show that for any pair of probability matrices P and Q the product PQ is a probability matrix.

2

Arbitrage and Pricing in the One-Period Model

2.1 Hedging with Redundant Securities and Incomplete Market

We have seen in the previous chapter that in a complete market without redundant assets any focus asset can be hedged perfectly and the replicating portfolio is given by

$$x = A^{-1}b.$$

In general, the market need not be complete, and at the same time redundant basis assets may be present.

We know that in the general case we can divide the securities into linearly independent and redundant:

$$A = \underbrace{A_1}_{r(A) \text{ columns}} \mid \underbrace{A_2}_{n-r(A) \text{ columns}},$$

$$r(A_1) = r(A).$$

Because the redundant securities do not add anything new to the marketed subspace, *the existence of a solution is entirely determined by the relative position of linearly independent securities A_1 and the focus asset b*. If b is redundant (and this can happen even if the market A_1 is not complete), then we have a solution. Mathematically, this case is described by

$$r(A_1) = r(A_1 \mid b). \tag{2.1}$$

In particular, when market A is complete, then $r(A) = m$ and A_1 is a square $m \times m$ matrix with full rank and then necessarily (2.1) is satisfied for any b, because $r(A_1 \mid b) \leqslant \min(m, m+1) = m$.

In an incomplete market it will often happen that the assets in A_1 and asset b are linearly independent,

$$r(A_1) < r(A_1 \mid b),$$

in which case a perfect hedge does not exist.

While redundant basis assets do not affect the existence or non-existence of a perfect hedge, every redundant basis asset introduces one free parameter into the hedging portfolio. Thus the number of solutions, if at least one solution exists, depends purely on the number of redundant securities $n - r(A)$.

The four combinations (complete, incomplete) × (no redundant basis assets, redundant basis assets) are described below and summarized in Table 2.1.

2.1.1 $r(A) = m = n$
(Complete Market, Basis Assets Are Linearly Independent)

Matrix A is square and has full rank, therefore the inverse exists. Applying A^{-1} from the left,

$$A^{-1}Ax = A^{-1}b,$$
$$x = A^{-1}b.$$

$A^{-1}b$ is the unique solution.

2.1.2 $r(A) = m < n$
(Market Is Complete, but There Are $n - m$ Redundant Basis Assets)

Then A can be partitioned into linearly independent and redundant assets, that is, it can be divided into two matrices A_1, A_2 with m and $n - m$ columns such that $r(A_1) = m$ and there is an $m \times (n - m)$ matrix C of replicating portfolios such that $A_2 = A_1 C$. The vector x too must be partitioned correspondingly,

$$x = \begin{bmatrix} x^{(1)} \\ x^{(2)} \end{bmatrix},$$

where $x^{(1)}$ denotes the portfolio of linearly independent basis assets and $x^{(2)}$ is the portfolio of redundant basis assets. Now the system can be written as

$$A_1 x^{(1)} + A_2 x^{(2)} = b.$$

Since A_2 contains redundant assets, we can express assets in A_2 as portfolios of linearly independent assets in A_1

$$A_1 x^{(1)} + A_1 C x^{(2)} = b,$$

and factor out A_1

$$A_1(x^{(1)} + C x^{(2)}) = b. \tag{2.2}$$

Matrix A_1 is square with full rank, therefore it is invertible. Multiplying both sides of (2.2) by A_1^{-1} we have

$$x^{(1)} + C x^{(2)} = A_1^{-1}b. \tag{2.3}$$

Now we can *choose* the portfolio of redundant basis assets $x^{(2)}$ arbitrarily and calculate the required portfolio of linearly independent basis assets from (2.3):

$$x^{(1)} = A_1^{-1}b - C x^{(2)}.$$

Since we have $n - m$ redundant basis assets, the vector $x^{(2)}$ has $n - m$ entries and therefore the solution has $n - m$ *free parameters*.

Example 2.1. See Example 2.13.

2.1.3 $r(A) = n < m$
(Market Is Incomplete, all Basis Assets Are Linearly Independent)

Multiplying by A^* from the left we have

$$A^*Ax = A^*b. \tag{2.4}$$

Matrix A^*A is square $n \times n$ and it has rank n, therefore it is invertible. Now apply $(A^*A)^{-1}$ from the left in (2.4)

$$\left. \begin{array}{l} (A^*A)^{-1}A^*Ax = (A^*A)^{-1}A^*b, \\ \hat{x} = (A^*A)^{-1}A^*b. \end{array} \right\} \tag{2.5}$$

This is a solution to the modified equation (2.4). To verify whether $\hat{x}$ solves the original equation, substitute $\hat{x}$ back into $Ax = b$; this gives us the following condition:

$$A \underbrace{(A^*A)^{-1}A^*b}_{\hat{x}} = b. \tag{2.6}$$

If (2.6) is satisfied, then b is a redundant security and we have a unique perfect hedge $x = (A^*A)^{-1}A^*b$. Otherwise, there is no solution (b and basis assets are linearly independent).

Example 2.2. Let us see whether we can find a perfect hedge in part (3) of Example 1.1:

$$A = \begin{bmatrix} A_{\bullet 1} & A_{\bullet 2} \end{bmatrix} = \begin{bmatrix} 1 & 3 \\ 1 & 2 \\ 1 & 1 \end{bmatrix}, \qquad x = \begin{bmatrix} x_1 \\ x_2 \end{bmatrix}, \qquad b = A_{\bullet 3} = \begin{bmatrix} 1.5 \\ 0.5 \\ 0 \end{bmatrix}.$$

The two securities in A are linearly independent and hence the unique candidate for the perfect hedging portfolio is given by equation (2.5):

$$\hat{x} = (A^*A)^{-1}A^*b. \tag{2.7}$$

In GAUSS one would type

```
A=(1~3)|(1~2)|(1~1);
b=1.5|0.5|0;
xhat=inv(A'A)*A'b;
```

which gives

$$\hat{x} = \begin{bmatrix} -\frac{2.5}{3} \\ 0.75 \end{bmatrix}.$$

It remains to verify whether this solves the original problem:

$$A\hat{x} = \begin{bmatrix} \frac{4.25}{3} \\ \frac{2}{3} \\ \frac{0.25}{3} \end{bmatrix} \neq \begin{bmatrix} 1.5 \\ 0.5 \\ 0 \end{bmatrix} = b. \tag{2.8}$$

In this case b is a non-redundant security and a perfect hedge does not exist.

When b is changed to

$$b = A_{\bullet 4} = \begin{bmatrix} 2 \\ 1 \\ 0 \end{bmatrix},$$

then the same procedure yields

$$\hat{x} = \begin{bmatrix} -1 \\ 1 \end{bmatrix} \quad \text{and} \quad A\hat{x} = b,$$

which means that this time b can be hedged perfectly, even though the market is not complete.

2.1.4 $r(A) < m, r(A) < n$
(Market Is Incomplete, There Are $n - r(A)$ Redundant Assets)

As in Section 2.1.2 the original problem boils down to

$$A_1(x^{(1)} + Cx^{(2)}) = b. \tag{2.9}$$

Matrix A_1 is not square but it has full rank; we can therefore use the trick from Section 2.1.3, that is, multiply by A_1^* and then by $(A_1^*A_1)^{-1}$:

$$x^{(1)} + Cx^{(2)} = (A_1^*A_1)^{-1}A_1^*b. \tag{2.10}$$

The portfolio of redundant assets $x^{(2)}$ can be chosen arbitrarily.

As in Section 2.1.3 we need to verify that this solution indeed solves the original problem (2.9). On substituting (2.10) into (2.9) we obtain the condition,

$$A_1(A_1^*A_1)^{-1}A_1^*b = b. \tag{2.11}$$

In conclusion, if condition (2.11) is satisfied, then b can be perfectly hedged and the replicating portfolio can be constructed in infinitely many ways according to (2.10) with $x^{(2)}$ arbitrary. Mathematically, there are infinitely many solutions with $n - r(A)$ free parameters. If the condition (2.11) is violated, then there is no solution—the focus asset b is not in the marketed subspace generated by the basis assets in matrix A.

Example 2.3. Consider a hedging problem with

$$A = \begin{bmatrix} 1 & 3 & 2 \\ 1 & 2 & 1 \\ 1 & 1 & 0 \end{bmatrix}, \qquad b = \begin{bmatrix} 1.5 \\ 0.5 \\ 0 \end{bmatrix}.$$

Then the third basis asset is redundant, namely, we have

$$A_1 = \begin{bmatrix} 1 & 3 \\ 1 & 2 \\ 1 & 1 \end{bmatrix}, \qquad A_2 = \begin{bmatrix} 2 \\ 1 \\ 0 \end{bmatrix}, \qquad C = \begin{bmatrix} -1 \\ 1 \end{bmatrix}, \qquad A_2 = A_1C,$$

$$x^{(1)} = \begin{bmatrix} x_1 \\ x_2 \end{bmatrix}, \qquad x^{(2)} = \begin{bmatrix} x_3 \end{bmatrix}.$$

Table 2.1. General solution of the hedging problem with two special cases.

	$r(A) = r(A \mid b)$ b is redundant	$r(A) < r(A \mid b)$ b is non-redundant
$r(A) \leqslant m$ general case	$A_1(A_1^* A_1)^{-1} A_1 b = b$ $x^{(1)} + Cx^{(2)} = (A_1^* A_1)^{-1} A_1 b$ $x^{(2)}$ arbitrary	$A_1(A_1^* A_1)^{-1} A_1 b \neq b$ no solution of $Ax = b$
$r(A) = m = n$ complete market no redundant securities	$x = A^{-1} b$	cannot happen
$r(A) = n < m$ incomplete market no redundant securities	$A(A^* A)^{-1} Ab = b$ $x = (A^* A)^{-1} Ab$	$A(A^* A)^{-1} Ab \neq b$ no solution of $Ax = b$

The solution exists if and only if $A_1 (A_1^* A_1)^{-1} A_1^* b = b$. We have checked this condition in Example 2.2, equation (2.8), and we know that it is not satisfied. Therefore, for

$$b = \begin{bmatrix} 1.5 \\ 0.5 \\ 0 \end{bmatrix}$$

a perfect hedge does not exist.

However, if we change b to

$$b = \begin{bmatrix} 2.5 \\ 1.5 \\ 0.5 \end{bmatrix},$$

a call option with strike 0.5, then we have infinitely many solutions of the form

$$x^{(1)} + Cx^{(2)} = (A_1^* A_1)^{-1} A_1^* b = \begin{bmatrix} -0.5 \\ 1 \end{bmatrix},$$

$$\begin{bmatrix} x_1 \\ x_2 \end{bmatrix} = \begin{bmatrix} -0.5 + x_3 \\ 1 - x_3 \end{bmatrix},$$

where x_3 is a free parameter corresponding to the number of units of the redundant security.

2.2 Finding the Best Approximate Hedge

When the basis assets do not span the whole market (the market is not complete, $r(A) < m$), then some focus assets cannot be hedged perfectly. That is, the solution to

$$Ax = b$$

does not always exist. Nevertheless, we would like to find at least the best *approximate* hedge. The deviation of the basis asset portfolio pay-off from the focus asset is called the **replication error**:

$$\varepsilon = Ax - b.$$

A frequently used criterion is to minimize the sum of squared replication errors (SSREs) over all states:

$$\text{SSRE} = \varepsilon_1^2 + \varepsilon_2^2 + \cdots + \varepsilon_m^2 = (A_{1\bullet}x - b_1)^2 + \cdots + (A_{m\bullet}x - b_m)^2.$$

Fact. Assuming that the securities in A are linearly independent, the portfolio minimizing the squared replication error is given as

$$\hat{x} = (A^*A)^{-1}A^*b. \tag{2.12}$$

Note that this portfolio has already come up as the candidate for the perfect hedge in Section 2.1.3. Now we know that even if it is not the perfect hedge, it is in some sense the best hedge that one can find.

The pay-off of the best hedge is

$$A\hat{x} = A(A^*A)^{-1}A^*b.$$

The procedure of finding x by minimizing the sum of squared errors is known as the **least-squares method**.

2.2.1 Geometric Interpretation of the Best Hedge

We say that two column vectors x and y are at *right angles* (are *orthogonal* or *perpendicular* to each other) if $x^*y = 0$. The quantity

$$\|x\| = \sqrt{x^*x}$$

is called the length (norm) of the vector x.

We can reinterpret the sum of the squared hedging errors as the squared length of the vector ε

$$\text{SSRE} = \|\varepsilon\|^2.$$

Since $\varepsilon = Ax - b$, the best approximate hedge achieves the *shortest distance* between the focus asset b and the marketed subspace Span(A). Using three-dimensional examples it is easy to verify that the shortest distance is achieved when the hedging error ε is *perpendicular* to the marketed subspace Span(A). Thus the optimality condition requires that ε is at right angles to each column in A

$$A^*\hat{\varepsilon} = 0.$$

Substituting for $\hat{\varepsilon}$ we obtain

$$A^*(A\hat{x} - b) = 0,$$
$$A^*A\hat{x} = Ab,$$
$$\hat{x} = (A^*A)^{-1}Ab,$$

which is exactly the equation (2.12).

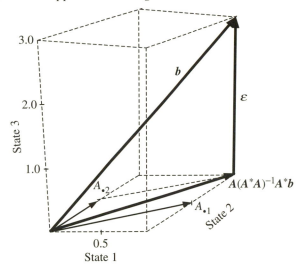

Figure 2.1. Geometric illustration of the best approximate hedge.

Example 2.4. Let us find the best approximate hedge to

$$b^* = \begin{bmatrix} 1 & 2 & 3 \end{bmatrix}$$

using two basis assets

$$A^*_{\bullet 1} = \begin{bmatrix} 1 & 1 & 0 \end{bmatrix} \quad \text{and} \quad A^*_{\bullet 2} = \begin{bmatrix} 0 & 1 & 0 \end{bmatrix}.$$

We set

$$A = \begin{bmatrix} 1 & 0 \\ 1 & 1 \\ 0 & 0 \end{bmatrix}$$

and find

$$\hat{x} = (A^*A)^{-1}A^*b = \begin{bmatrix} 1 \\ 1 \end{bmatrix}.$$

Graphically, when we are looking for the best hedge to the focus asset b in terms of basis assets $A_{\bullet 1}$ and $A_{\bullet 2}$, we are trying to minimize the distance between the focus asset b and the points in the marketed subspace formed by the basis assets $A_{\bullet 1}$ and $A_{\bullet 2}$. The marketed subspace in this case is the horizontal plane formed by the vectors $A_{\bullet 1}$ and $A_{\bullet 2}$. The point of shortest distance is the one where the replication error (the vector ε) is perpendicular to the marketed subspace. If A is the pay-off matrix of the basis assets, then the pay-off of the best hedge is equal to $A(A^*A)^{-1}A^*b$, as indicated in Figure 2.1.

If the columns of A are not linearly independent, then we can partition them into linearly independent and redundant columns, as in Section 2.1.4. Then the best hedge can be constructed in many different ways,

$$\hat{x}^{(1)} + C\hat{x}^{(2)} = (A_1^*A_1)^{-1}A_1^*b,$$

with $\hat{x}_2$ arbitrary. However, the pay-off of the best hedge is unique:

$$A\hat{x} = A_1(\hat{x}^{(1)} + C\hat{x}^{(2)}) = A_1(A_1^*A_1)^{-1}A_1^*b.$$

2.3 Minimizing the Expected Squared Replication Error

The sum of squared replication errors assigns equal weight to each market scenario. However, in reality some states of the world are more likely than others; for example, historically, a weekly rate of return on the FTSE100 Index of between -0.5% and $+0.5\%$ has a probability of 0.35, whereas a return of between -6.5% and -5.5% has a probability of less than 0.01. Consequently, we are less concerned with the sum of the squared errors and more interested in finding a hedging portfolio that minimizes the *expected squared replication error* (ESRE). That is, instead of minimizing the total sum of squared replication errors over all states,

$$\min_{x,\varepsilon=Ax-b} \text{SSRE} = \varepsilon_1^2 + \varepsilon_2^2 + \cdots + \varepsilon_m^2, \tag{2.13}$$

we want to minimize the expected squared error,

$$\min_{x,\varepsilon=Ax-b} \text{ESRE} = p_1\varepsilon_1^2 + p_2\varepsilon_2^2 + \cdots + p_m\varepsilon_m^2, \tag{2.14}$$

where $p_1, p_2, \ldots, p_m > 0$ are the objective probabilities of the individual states of the world. We shall proceed in two steps.

1. Transform the problem (2.14) into minimizing the total sum of squared replication errors by writing

$$\begin{aligned} \text{ESRE} &= p_1\varepsilon_1^2 + p_2\varepsilon_2^2 + \cdots + p_m\varepsilon_m^2 \\ &= \tilde{\varepsilon}_1^2 + \tilde{\varepsilon}_2^2 + \cdots + \tilde{\varepsilon}_m^2, \end{aligned}$$

where

$$\tilde{\varepsilon} = \tilde{A}x - \tilde{b} \tag{2.15}$$

for the as yet unknown matrices $\tilde{A}$ and $\tilde{b}$. If we succeed, then the problem of minimizing $\text{ESRE} = p_1\varepsilon_1^2 + p_2\varepsilon_2^2 + \cdots + p_m\varepsilon_m^2$ has been transformed into minimizing SSRE,

$$\min_{x,\tilde{\varepsilon}=\tilde{A}x-\tilde{b}} \tilde{\varepsilon}_1^2 + \tilde{\varepsilon}_2^2 + \cdots + \tilde{\varepsilon}_m^2,$$

for which the optimal portfolio is known to be

$$\hat{x} = (\tilde{A}^*\tilde{A})^{-1}\tilde{A}^*\tilde{b}.$$

2. Find the matrices $\tilde{A}$ and $\tilde{b}$. First of all we know the relationship between $\tilde{\varepsilon}_i^2$ and $p_i\varepsilon_i^2$,

$$\tilde{\varepsilon}_i^2 = p_i\varepsilon_i^2 = (\sqrt{p_i}\varepsilon_i)^2,$$

which means that we may take

$$\tilde{\varepsilon}_i \triangleq \sqrt{p_i}\varepsilon_i. \tag{2.16}$$

Recall that $\varepsilon = Ax - b$, implying

$$\varepsilon_i = A_{i\bullet}x - b_i.$$

Substitute this into (2.16) to obtain

$$\tilde{\varepsilon}_i = \sqrt{p_i}\varepsilon_i = \sqrt{p_i}A_{i\bullet}x - \sqrt{p_i}b_i. \tag{2.17}$$

Finally, compare (2.17) with (2.15) to realize that we should take

$$\tilde{A}_{i\bullet} \triangleq \sqrt{p_i}A_{i\bullet}, \tag{2.18}$$

$$\tilde{b}_i \triangleq \sqrt{p_i}b_i. \tag{2.19}$$

Consider a hedging problem $Ax = b$ with replication error $\varepsilon = Ax - b$. To minimize the expected squared replication error,

$$\min_{x,\varepsilon=Ax-b} p_1\varepsilon_1^2 + p_2\varepsilon_2^2 + \cdots + p_m\varepsilon_m^2,$$

compute new matrices $\tilde{A}$ and $\tilde{b}$ by multiplying each row of A, b by the square root of the probability for the corresponding state. The optimal hedging portfolio is then given by

$$\hat{x} = (\tilde{A}^*\tilde{A})^{-1}\tilde{A}^*\tilde{b}.$$

Example 2.5. Let us solve part (3) of the introductory example.

Solution. Firstly, we note the pay-off of basis and focus assets and the objective probabilities

$$A = \begin{bmatrix} 1 & 3 \\ 1 & 2 \\ 1 & 1 \end{bmatrix}, \qquad b = \begin{bmatrix} 1.5 \\ 0.5 \\ 0 \end{bmatrix}, \qquad p^{(1)} = \begin{bmatrix} \frac{1}{2} \\ \frac{1}{6} \\ \frac{1}{3} \end{bmatrix}.$$

The transformed matrices are obtained, according to (2.18) and (2.19), by multiplying each row of the matrix A by the square root of the corresponding state probability,

$$\tilde{A} = \begin{bmatrix} \sqrt{\frac{1}{2}} & 3\sqrt{\frac{1}{2}} \\ \sqrt{\frac{1}{6}} & 2\sqrt{\frac{1}{6}} \\ \sqrt{\frac{1}{3}} & \sqrt{\frac{1}{3}} \end{bmatrix}, \qquad \tilde{b} = \begin{bmatrix} 1.5\sqrt{\frac{1}{2}} \\ 0.5\sqrt{\frac{1}{6}} \\ 0 \end{bmatrix}.$$

In GAUSS type

```
Atil   =   A.*sqrt(p)
btil   =   b.*sqrt(p)
```

The '. *' operator signifies element-by-element multiplication, rather than a standard matrix multiplication. To obtain $\hat{x}$ and $\hat{\varepsilon}$ simply type

```
xhat   =   inv(Atil'Atil)*Atil'btil
epshat  =   A*xhat-b
```

If you are calculating $\hat{x}$ by hand, it is probably faster to solve the system,

$$(\tilde{A}^*\tilde{A})\hat{x} = \tilde{A}^*\tilde{b}, \qquad \tilde{A}^*\tilde{A} = \begin{bmatrix} 1 & \frac{13}{6} \\ \frac{13}{6} & \frac{11}{2} \end{bmatrix}, \qquad \tilde{A}^*\tilde{b} = \begin{bmatrix} \frac{5}{6} \\ \frac{29}{12} \end{bmatrix},$$

$$\hat{x}_1 + \tfrac{13}{6}\hat{x}_2 = \tfrac{5}{6},$$

$$\tfrac{13}{6}\hat{x}_1 + \tfrac{11}{2}\hat{x}_2 = \tfrac{29}{12},$$

which gives

$$\hat{x}_1 = -\tfrac{47}{58}, \qquad \hat{x}_2 = \tfrac{22}{29}, \qquad \hat{\varepsilon}^{(1)} = \begin{bmatrix} -\frac{1}{29} \\ \frac{6}{29} \\ -\frac{3}{58} \end{bmatrix} = \begin{bmatrix} -0.0345 \\ 0.2069 \\ -0.0517 \end{bmatrix}.$$

Just out of curiosity let us see what happens with

$$p^{(2)} = \begin{bmatrix} \frac{1}{3} \\ \frac{1}{3} \\ \frac{1}{3} \end{bmatrix}.$$

The same procedure as above gives

$$\hat{x} = \begin{bmatrix} -\frac{5}{6} \\ \frac{3}{4} \end{bmatrix} \quad \text{and} \quad \hat{\varepsilon}^{(2)} = \begin{bmatrix} -\frac{1}{12} \\ \frac{1}{6} \\ -\frac{1}{12} \end{bmatrix} = \begin{bmatrix} -0.0833 \\ 0.1667 \\ -0.0833 \end{bmatrix}.$$

Let us compare the two vectors of residuals side by side, together with the probabilities in the two cases,

$$p^{(1)} = \begin{bmatrix} \frac{1}{2} \\ \frac{1}{6} \\ \frac{1}{3} \end{bmatrix}, \quad p^{(2)} = \begin{bmatrix} \frac{1}{3} \\ \frac{1}{3} \\ \frac{1}{3} \end{bmatrix}, \quad \hat{\varepsilon}^{(1)} = \begin{bmatrix} -0.0345 \\ 0.2069 \\ -0.0517 \end{bmatrix}, \quad \hat{\varepsilon}^{(2)} = \begin{bmatrix} -0.0833 \\ 0.1667 \\ -0.0833 \end{bmatrix}.$$

Moving from $p^{(1)}$ to $p^{(2)}$, the probability of the first state decreases and the first residual becomes larger in absolute value. The probability of the second state increases twofold from $\frac{1}{6}$ to $\frac{1}{3}$, this state is becoming more important (more likely) and therefore the optimal replication error in the second state decreases from 0.207 to 0.167. Intuitively, the portfolio minimizing the expected squared replication error will assign smaller errors (in absolute value) to the states with high probability and higher errors to the states with low probability.

2.4 Numerical Stability of Least Squares

Computer arithmetic operates with a fixed number of decimal places (most commonly 16). This means every arithmetical operation on a computer is subject to round-off errors, which sometimes leads to unexpected results, for example,

$$10^{17} + 1 - 10^{17} = 0$$

but

$$10^{17} - 10^{17} + 1 = 1$$

in computer arithmetic.

Because of the round-off errors, two methods for solving the same system of linear equations may generate very different results when implemented on a computer, even though they would give the same result with pen and paper. Not all linear systems exhibit numerical instability; those that do are called **ill-conditioned**. As an example consider a hedging problem with three basis assets: bond, stock and a call option struck at $1 + \delta$ $(1 > \delta > 0)$, with pay-off matrix

$$A_\delta = \begin{bmatrix} 1 & 4 & 3 - \delta \\ 1 & 3 & 2 - \delta \\ 1 & 2 & 1 - \delta \\ 1 & 1 & 0 \end{bmatrix}.$$

For $1 > \delta > 0$ this matrix has full rank but with $\delta = 0$ the call option is a redundant asset and A_0 does not have a full rank. Assume that the focus asset is a call option struck at 1.5,

$$b = \begin{bmatrix} \frac{5}{2} \\ \frac{3}{2} \\ \frac{1}{2} \\ 0 \end{bmatrix}.$$

2.4.1   Round-Off Errors

For δ close to 0 the system

$$(A_\delta^* A_\delta) x = A_\delta^* b$$

is ill-conditioned. In practice, it is not a good idea to compute the best hedging portfolio directly from the formula,

$$x^{(1)} = (A_\delta^* A_\delta)^{-1} A_\delta^* b, \tag{2.20}$$

when A_δ is close to *not* having a full rank, because then $A_\delta^* A_\delta$ is even closer to not having full rank, very much like for a close to 0 (say $a = 0.001$), a^2 is even closer to 0 ($a^2 = 0.000\,001$).

In equation (2.20) we are using all basis assets *simultaneously* and this creates problems when the basis assets are close to being linearly dependent. A better alternative is to perform the least squares *sequentially*. In GAUSS the sequential least-squares algorithm is called olsqr (ordinary least squares with QR decomposition):

$$x^{(2)} = \text{olsqr}(b, A_\delta). \tag{2.21}$$

The olsqr algorithm is explained in the appendix at the end of this chapter.

Below we compare the numerical values of $x^{(1)}$, $\varepsilon^{(1)}$ and $x^{(2)}$, $\varepsilon^{(2)}$ for $\delta = \frac{1}{2}10^{-4}$, generated by GAUSS program *chapter2sect4a.gss*:

$$x^{(1)} = \begin{bmatrix} 9998.94 \\ -9998.94 \\ 9999.94 \end{bmatrix}, \quad x^{(2)} = \begin{bmatrix} 9999 + 5 \times 10^{-8} \\ -9999 - 5 \times 10^{-8} \\ 10\,000 + 5 \times 10^{-8} \end{bmatrix}, \quad x_{\text{exact}} = \begin{bmatrix} 9999 \\ -9999 \\ 10\,000 \end{bmatrix},$$

$$\varepsilon^{(1)} = \begin{bmatrix} -6.5 \times 10^{-6} \\ -4.6 \times 10^{-6} \\ -2.7 \times 10^{-6} \\ -3.8 \times 10^{-6} \end{bmatrix}, \quad \varepsilon^{(2)} = \begin{bmatrix} 8.3 \times 10^{-12} \\ 4.6 \times 10^{-12} \\ 2.8 \times 10^{-12} \\ 1.8 \times 10^{-12} \end{bmatrix}, \quad \varepsilon_{\text{exact}} = \begin{bmatrix} 0 \\ 0 \\ 0 \\ 0 \end{bmatrix}.$$

It is clear that the `olsqr` algorithm performs much better in terms of numerical precision.

2.4.2   Measurement Errors and Spurious Precision

In the preceding paragraph we were striving for as much precision as possible, which is fine if we know the value of δ with high precision. The situation is very different if δ is subject to measurement errors. Suppose the true value of δ is 0 but we have made a small measurement error and believe that $\delta = 0.005$. In our mistaken belief we would construct a 'perfect' hedge

$$x_{0.005} = \begin{bmatrix} 99 \\ -99 \\ 100 \end{bmatrix}$$

only to discover that the true hedging error is

$$\varepsilon = A_0 x_{0.005} - b = \begin{bmatrix} 0.5 \\ 0.5 \\ 0.5 \\ 0 \end{bmatrix}!$$

The problem is that we are putting too much faith in the value of δ. The `olsqr` algorithm can help to find more reliable hedging coefficients by treating basis assets that are 'almost redundant' as completely redundant. This is done by setting the parameter `_olsqtol` to the size of expected measurement errors. For example,

$$\texttt{\_olsqtol} = 10^\wedge - 2$$

will generate

$$\varepsilon = A_0 \texttt{olsqr}(b, A_{0.005}) - b = \begin{bmatrix} -0.1 \\ 0.05 \\ 0.2 \\ -0.15 \end{bmatrix}$$

and this result is robust with respect to small changes in δ (see the program *chapter2sect4b.gss*).

2.5 Asset Prices, Returns and Portfolio Units

At long last we can talk about asset *prices*. Let S (standing for stock) be the vector of prices for n basis assets. The pay-off of the basis assets is stored in the $m \times n$ matrix A. Practitioners hardly ever talk about pay-offs; they prefer the word *return*. There are two commonly used measures of return: total return and rate of return. **Total return** is the pay-off of the security divided by its price. If a security costs \$4 and pays \$3, its total return is $\frac{3}{4} = 0.75$, or 75%. The **rate of return** is the total return minus one. In the previous example it is $\frac{3}{4} - 1 = -0.25 = -25\%$. If the pay-offs are random, then returns will be random and vice versa. Typically, one of the basis assets is a **risk-free bond** with total return R_f. By 'risk-free' we mean that the pay-off of the bond is the same in all states of the world: we are certain to obtain R_f pounds (euros, dollars) tomorrow for every pound (euro, dollar) we invest in the bond today. *'Risk-free' does not necessarily mean that our pay-off will exceed the initial investment*, that is, one can have situations where $R_f < 1$. By **excess return** we mean the difference between the total return of a given security and a fixed reference return (the reference return is in most cases the risk-free return).

Why did we talk about pay-offs and not use returns from the beginning? The problem with returns is that they are not well defined for securities with zero price. This might not have been a great limitation in the era when only stocks and commodities were traded, but with the advent of derivative securities we have to deal with this problem every day. For example, one cannot talk of the return to a futures contract because the cost of entering a futures contract is (barring technicalities) zero. Thus to make the pricing theory generally applicable one needs to use pay-offs instead of returns. In many cases, however, returns are well defined and in what follows we shall restrict our attention to such situations.

2.5.1 Four Useful Ways of Writing Down the Replication Equation

Suppose we have two states of the world and two assets, one risk-free and one risky, with pay-offs

$$A = \begin{bmatrix} 110 & 60 \\ 110 & 40 \end{bmatrix}$$

and prices

$$S = \begin{bmatrix} 100 \\ 50 \end{bmatrix}.$$

The focus asset pays

$$b = \begin{bmatrix} 450 \\ 410 \end{bmatrix}.$$

1. The solution of $Ax = b$ is

$$x = \begin{bmatrix} 3 \\ 2 \end{bmatrix}.$$

The vector x signifies the *number of basis securities* in the replicating portfolio.

2. Note that $Ax = b$ really means

$$A_{\bullet 1}x_1 + A_{\bullet 2}x_2 = b \tag{2.22}$$

and that this can be rewritten as

$$\frac{A_{\bullet 1}}{S_1}S_1x_1 + \frac{A_{\bullet 2}}{S_2}S_2x_2 = b. \tag{2.23}$$

Define $\hat{A}$ as the *matrix of returns*, whereby each column of A is *divided* by the respective price (that is $\hat{A}_{\bullet i} = A_{\bullet i}/S_i$):

$$\hat{A} = \begin{bmatrix} \frac{110}{100} & \frac{60}{50} \\ \frac{110}{100} & \frac{40}{50} \end{bmatrix}.$$

Then, naturally, the solution of $\hat{A}\hat{x} = b$ is x *multiplied* by the respective price ($\hat{x}_i = x_i S_i$):

$$\hat{x} = \begin{bmatrix} 3 \times 100 \\ 2 \times 50 \end{bmatrix} = \begin{bmatrix} 300 \\ 100 \end{bmatrix}.$$

The vector $\hat{x}$ expresses the *amount of money* invested in each security.

3. Now manipulate (2.23) by adding and subtracting $(A_{\bullet 1}/S_1)S_2x_2$:

$$\frac{A_{\bullet 1}}{S_1}(S_1x_1 + S_2x_2) + \left(\frac{A_{\bullet 2}}{S_2} - \frac{A_{\bullet 1}}{S_1}\right)S_2x_2 = b.$$

Define $\bar{A}$ as the matrix of *excess returns,* whereby we subtract the first column of $\hat{A}$ from all the remaining columns:

$$\bar{A} = \begin{bmatrix} \frac{110}{100} & \frac{60}{50} - \frac{110}{100} \\ \frac{110}{100} & \frac{40}{50} - \frac{110}{100} \end{bmatrix}.$$

The solution of $\bar{A}\bar{x} = b$ has the following interpretation: $\bar{x}_1 = S_1x_1 + S_2x_2$ is the no-arbitrage value of pay-off b; $\bar{x}_2 = S_2x_2$ signifies the money invested in the risky security:

$$\bar{x} = \begin{bmatrix} 400 \\ 100 \end{bmatrix}.$$

4. How should one set up the matrix $\tilde{A}$ so that the solution of $\tilde{A}\tilde{x} = b$ has the following interpretation: $\tilde{x}_1$ is the no-arbitrage value of pay-off b, and $\tilde{x}_2$ is the number of units of the second security in the replicating portfolio?

2.6 Arbitrage

Let x be an arbitrary portfolio of basis assets. Our first concern is with the prices of basis assets being inconsistent, providing possibilities of riskless profit: *arbitrage*. Mathematically, arbitrage can arise in two different ways: type II involves redundant basis assets, whereas type I arbitrage does not.

Type I arbitrage. There is a portfolio that costs nothing to purchase (or one is paid to hold it) and has non-negative pay-off in all states, with a strictly positive pay-off in at least one state:

$$S^*x \leqslant 0 \qquad \text{pay nothing, or receive some money today,} \qquad (2.24)$$

$$Ax \geqslant 0 \qquad \text{receive a non-negative amount tomorrow,} \qquad (2.25)$$

$$Ax \neq 0 \qquad \text{this amount is strictly positive in at least one state.} \qquad (2.26)$$

Example 2.6. Consider a market with the first two securities from Example 1.1 in Chapter 1. Suppose that the prices of these securities were $S_1 = 1$ and $S_2 = 1$. Then we could sell one unit of the first security and buy one unit of the second security, which would cost nothing, and obtain a non-negative pay-off $\begin{bmatrix} 2 & 1 & 0 \end{bmatrix}$:

$$S^*x = \begin{bmatrix} 1 & 1 \end{bmatrix} \begin{bmatrix} -1 \\ 1 \end{bmatrix} = 0,$$

$$Ax = \begin{bmatrix} 1 & 3 \\ 1 & 2 \\ 1 & 1 \end{bmatrix} \begin{bmatrix} -1 \\ 1 \end{bmatrix} = \begin{bmatrix} 2 \\ 1 \\ 0 \end{bmatrix} > 0.$$

This is very much like receiving a lottery ticket for free. With nothing to pay we have the chance of obtaining 2 in the first state or 1 in the second state without the risk of losing anything in the third state.

Another way of looking at the same situation is to realize that the second security pays at least as much as the first security in all states, in mathematical terminology we would say that the pay-off of the first security is **stochastically dominated** by the pay-off of the second security. Therefore, the second security is unambiguously more valuable than the first security, and it must command a higher price than the first security to prevent arbitrage. In our example both securities have the same price—hence the arbitrage opportunity.

Type II arbitrage. The second type of arbitrage is even better. There is a portfolio that has negative price (you are given some money today to hold this portfolio) and pays identically zero in all states tomorrow:

$$S^*x < 0, \qquad (2.27)$$

$$Ax = 0. \qquad (2.28)$$

Note that the second type of arbitrage cannot occur if the basis assets are linearly independent, because linear independence implies that $Ax = 0$ only if $x = 0$, in which case trivially $S^*x = 0$. In plain English the second type of arbitrage implies that there is a **mispriced** redundant basis asset. What is meant is the following. The redundant basis asset has a certain price. The redundant asset can also be perfectly replicated from other basis assets. If this replicating portfolio is cheaper or more expensive than the redundant asset itself, the redundant asset is mispriced and there is an easy arbitrage profit from selling the redundant asset and buying the replicating portfolio or vice versa.

Example 2.7. Consider the four securities from Example 1.1 with prices $S_1 = 1$, $S_2 = 2$, $S_3 = 1$, $S_4 = 2$. Show that the fourth security is mispriced relative to the first three securities.

Solution. From Example 1.12 in Chapter 1 we know that the portfolio consisting of minus 1 unit of the first security, 1 unit of the second security and 0 units of the third security has exactly the same pay-off as the fourth security. However, the price of this replicating portfolio is

$$-1 \times S_1 + 1 \times S_2 = 1,$$

whereas the price of the fourth security is

$$S_4 = 2.$$

To create arbitrage we would therefore sell the fourth security and buy its replicating portfolio. This position implies

$$x = \begin{bmatrix} -1 \\ 1 \\ 0 \\ -1 \end{bmatrix}.$$

We can verify that with this choice of x

$$Ax = \begin{bmatrix} 1 & 3 & 1.5 & 2 \\ 1 & 2 & 0.5 & 1 \\ 1 & 1 & 0 & 0 \end{bmatrix} \begin{bmatrix} -1 \\ 1 \\ 0 \\ -1 \end{bmatrix} = \begin{bmatrix} 0 \\ 0 \\ 0 \end{bmatrix}$$

and

$$S^* x = \begin{bmatrix} 1 & 2 & 1 & 2 \end{bmatrix} \begin{bmatrix} -1 \\ 1 \\ 0 \\ -1 \end{bmatrix} = -1 < 0,$$

consistently with the definition of the second type of arbitrage.

The absence of the second type of arbitrage means that every marketed pay-off has a unique price (the so-called law of one price) and that *prices are linear*: the price of a security with pay-off Ax must be $S^* x$.

2.7   No-Arbitrage Pricing

Having verified that there is no arbitrage among basis assets we can now use the no-arbitrage principle to determine the price of any asset with known pay-off. We will refer to the asset whose price we wish to determine as a *focus asset*. This is known as **relative pricing**, since we are trying to calculate the value of the focus asset by taking the prices and pay-offs of the basis assets as given.

The two types of arbitrage present themselves differently in pricing, too. If the focus asset is redundant, we can find a replicating portfolio and from the absence of *type II* arbitrage we conclude that the value of the focus asset is equal to the value of the replicating portfolio.

Example 2.8. Assume that securities $A_{\bullet 1}, A_{\bullet 2}, A_{\bullet 3}$ are priced as in the previous example, $S_1 = 1, S_2 = 2, S_3 = 1$. Find the implied no-arbitrage price of the elementary security e_1 (the first Arrow–Debreu security).

We know from Example 1.16 that portfolio $\begin{bmatrix} 1 & -1 & 2 \end{bmatrix}$ replicates the first Arrow–Debreu security. By the linearity of pricing, the price of e_1 must be the same as the price of this replicating portfolio, which is

$$1 \times 1 + 2 \times (-1) + 1 \times 2 = 1.$$

Suppose now that the focus asset is not redundant. Does this mean we can say nothing about its price? Not quite. We will not be able to pin down the price uniquely, but the absence of *type I* arbitrage will restrict the price to a range. We can squeeze the pay-off of the focus asset between two basis asset portfolios: so-called **super-replicating portfolios** such that one super-replicating portfolio is unambiguously better than the focus asset, whereas, conversely, the other super-replicating portfolio performs worse than the focus asset in all states (the second portfolio should really be called infer-replicating because its pay-off is in all states inferior to the focus asset pay-off). Consequently, the price of the focus asset will have to lie between the values of the two super-replicating portfolios.

Example 2.9. Suppose we have one basis asset with pay-off

$$A_{\bullet 1} = \begin{bmatrix} 1 \\ 2 \\ 3 \end{bmatrix}$$

and price $S_1 = 2$. Let us find the no-arbitrage price bounds for the asset b with pay-off:

$$b = \begin{bmatrix} 1 \\ 1 \\ 2 \end{bmatrix}.$$

Solution. We notice that one unit of the first security performs 'just' better than the second security,

$$b = \begin{bmatrix} 1 \\ 1 \\ 2 \end{bmatrix} \leqslant \begin{bmatrix} 1 \\ 2 \\ 3 \end{bmatrix} = 1 \times A_{\bullet 1},$$

the word 'just' referring to the pay-off in the first state which is the same for both the focus asset and the super-replicating portfolio. On the other hand, half a unit of the first security performs 'just' worse than the focus asset:

$$0.5 \times A_{\bullet 1} = \begin{bmatrix} 0.5 \\ 1 \\ 1.5 \end{bmatrix} \leqslant \begin{bmatrix} 1 \\ 1 \\ 2 \end{bmatrix} = b.$$

Now the word 'just' refers to the pay-offs in the second state. All in all, the super-replication price bounds for the focus asset are

$$0.5 \times S_1 < S_2 < 1 \times S_1,$$
$$1 < S_2 < 2.$$

2.8 State Prices and the Arbitrage Theorem

The price of an elementary (Arrow–Debreu) security e_j is called a **state price** and is denoted ψ_j. The vector of all state prices is denoted ψ:

$$\psi = \begin{bmatrix} \psi_1 \\ \psi_2 \\ \vdots \\ \psi_s \end{bmatrix}.$$

In Example 2.8 we took the elementary security e_1 as a focus asset and priced it by the perfect replication argument. In a *complete market* all elementary securities can be perfectly replicated and we can therefore find their unique no-arbitrage prices—the state prices—by the perfect replication argument. Note that the elementary securities have non-negative pay-off and, therefore, in the absence of type I arbitrage must command positive price. To sum up, no arbitrage in a complete market implies *positive state prices*.

The converse is also true: positive state prices imply no arbitrage, and this is very easy to establish. First of all, if we only take elementary state securities as basis assets, then there can be no type II arbitrage because elementary state securities are linearly independent. Secondly, the elementary state securities span the whole market—the market is complete—and so we can determine uniquely the no-arbitrage price of any other security with known pay-off. It turns out that the no-arbitrage price of the pay-off b is exactly $\psi^* b$ (see the next example). Now, having $\psi > 0$ and $b \geqslant 0$, $b \neq 0$ implies $\psi^* b > 0$, meaning that with strictly positive state prices any non-negative pay-off will always have positive price. Therefore, with strictly positive state prices type I arbitrage cannot arise. Since we have already excluded type II arbitrage we have demonstrated that strictly positive state prices imply no arbitrage.

Example 2.10. Suppose that there are three states of the world and we know that the state prices are ψ_1, ψ_2, ψ_3. Find the no-arbitrage price of the security with pay-off:

$$b = \begin{bmatrix} b_1 \\ b_2 \\ b_3 \end{bmatrix}.$$

Solution. We need to write b as a portfolio of elementary securities e_1, e_2, e_3. Trivially,

$$b = b_1 \begin{bmatrix} 1 \\ 0 \\ 0 \end{bmatrix} + b_2 \begin{bmatrix} 0 \\ 1 \\ 0 \end{bmatrix} + b_3 \begin{bmatrix} 0 \\ 0 \\ 1 \end{bmatrix}$$

so that the portfolio which combines pay-off b from elementary securities e_1, e_2, e_3 is in fact $x = b$. Thus, by the linearity of no-arbitrage pricing, the price of b is

$$\psi^* x = \psi^* b.$$

Following the previous example, given the state price vector ψ the implied price of securities $A_{\bullet 1}, A_{\bullet 2}, \ldots, A_{\bullet n}$ is

$$S^* = \begin{bmatrix} S_1 & S_2 & \cdots & S_n \end{bmatrix} = \begin{bmatrix} \psi^* A_{\bullet 1} & \psi^* A_{\bullet 2} & \cdots & \psi^* A_{\bullet n} \end{bmatrix} = \psi^* A$$

and after transposition

$$A^* \psi = S. \tag{2.29}$$

2.8.1 State Prices as an Indicator of Arbitrage

The *state prices* can be used with great advantage as an *indicator of arbitrage*.

Theorem 2.11 (Arbitrage Theorem). *A market with n securities, m states of the world, a security pay-off matrix $A \in \mathbb{R}^{m \times n}$ and a security price vector $S \in \mathbb{R}^n$ admits no arbitrage if and only if there is a strictly positive state price vector $\psi \in \mathbb{R}^m$ consistent with the security price vector S, that is,*

$$S = A^* \psi. \tag{2.30}$$

Proof. See website. $\qquad\square$

In a complete market the theorem does not tell us anything new. We have already concluded in Section 2.8 that absence of type II arbitrage implies unique state prices and that absence of type I arbitrage forces these state prices to be strictly positive.

In an incomplete market not all state prices are uniquely determined because not all elementary securities are marketed. Mathematically, the system

$$S = A^* \psi$$

has infinitely many solutions (the situation where there is no solution would imply type II arbitrage). The theorem now has a deeper meaning: it claims that in the absence of arbitrage we can *choose* these undetermined state prices to be strictly positive. It also claims that if we are unable to do so, then there is arbitrage among the marketed assets.

The following two examples discuss separately the complete and incomplete market cases.

Example 2.12. Suppose we have a market with

$$A = \begin{bmatrix} 1 & 3 & 1.5 & 2 \\ 1 & 2 & 0.5 & 1 \\ 1 & 1 & 0 & 0 \end{bmatrix} \quad \text{and} \quad S^* = \begin{bmatrix} 1 & 2 & 0.6 & 1 \end{bmatrix}.$$

Decide whether there are any arbitrage opportunities.

Solution. According to the Arbitrage Theorem there is no arbitrage if and only if there is a vector of strictly positive state prices such that

$$S = A^*\psi, \tag{2.31}$$

$$\begin{bmatrix} 1 \\ 2 \\ 0.6 \\ 1 \end{bmatrix} = \begin{bmatrix} 1 & 1 & 1 \\ 3 & 2 & 1 \\ 1.5 & 0.5 & 0 \\ 2 & 1 & 0 \end{bmatrix} \begin{bmatrix} \psi_1 \\ \psi_2 \\ \psi_3 \end{bmatrix}. \tag{2.32}$$

Since $r(A) = 3$ the unique candidate for a solution is

$$\psi = (AA^*)^{-1}AS = \begin{bmatrix} 0.2 \\ 0.6 \\ 0.2 \end{bmatrix}$$

and it is easy to verify that this value of ψ solves the state price equation (2.31). Since all elements of ψ are positive, there is no arbitrage.

Example 2.13. Decide whether there are arbitrage opportunities in the following market:

$$A = \begin{bmatrix} 1 & 3 \\ 1 & 2 \\ 1 & 1 \end{bmatrix}, \quad S = \begin{bmatrix} 1 \\ 2 \end{bmatrix}.$$

Solution. Here the market is not complete and with two linearly independent assets and three states we should expect one free parameter in the solution for the state prices.

We are solving $S = A^*\psi$:

$$\psi_1 + \psi_2 + \psi_3 = 1, \qquad 3\psi_1 + 2\psi_2 + \psi_3 = 2.$$

Take ψ_3 as a free parameter and solve for ψ_1 and ψ_2

$$\psi_1 = \psi_3 \tag{2.33}$$

and from the first equation

$$\psi_2 = 1 - 2\psi_3. \tag{2.34}$$

Now we have to decide whether there are values of the free parameter ψ_3 such that all state prices are strictly positive. The condition $\psi_2 > 0$ and (2.33) imply $\psi_3 > 0$, while $\psi_1 > 0$ and (2.34) require $\psi_3 < \frac{1}{3}$. Consequently, for $0 < \psi_3 < \frac{1}{3}$ the solution (2.33) and (2.34) of the original state price system is strictly positive, meaning there is *no arbitrage*. *It does not matter that there are also negative solutions.* We would only conclude that there is arbitrage if *none* of the state price solutions were strictly positive (or if there were no solution at all).

2.9 State Prices and Asset Returns

When asset prices are not zero, we can rewrite the state price equation $S = A^*\psi$ in terms of returns. Take the original system:

$$S_1 = A_{11}\psi_1 + A_{21}\psi_2 + \cdots + A_{m1}\psi_m,$$
$$S_2 = A_{12}\psi_1 + A_{22}\psi_2 + \cdots + A_{m2}\psi_m,$$
$$\vdots$$
$$S_n = A_{1n}\psi_1 + A_{2n}\psi_2 + \cdots + A_{mn}\psi_m.$$

Now, divide each equation by its respective price to obtain total returns on the right-hand side. Assuming that the first asset is risk-free, the first equation implies

$$1 = R_f(\psi_1 + \psi_2 + \cdots + \psi_m),$$

whereas for the risky assets we have

$$1 = \frac{A_{12}}{S_2}\psi_1 + \frac{A_{22}}{S_2}\psi_2 + \cdots + \frac{A_{m2}}{S_2}\psi_m,$$
$$\vdots$$
$$1 = \frac{A_{1n}}{S_n}\psi_1 + \frac{A_{2n}}{S_n}\psi_2 + \cdots + \frac{A_{mn}}{S_n}\psi_m.$$

From now on we will treat the risk-free asset separately from the risky ones. Let us denote the matrix of risky returns $\hat{R}$,

$$\hat{R}^* = \begin{bmatrix} \dfrac{A_{12}}{S_2} & \dfrac{A_{22}}{S_2} & \cdots & \dfrac{A_{m2}}{S_2} \\ \vdots & \vdots & \vdots & \vdots \\ \dfrac{A_{1n}}{S_n} & \dfrac{A_{2n}}{S_n} & \cdots & \dfrac{A_{mn}}{S_n} \end{bmatrix}.$$

To sum up, the state price equations can be written as

$$1 = R_f(\psi_1 + \psi_2 + \cdots + \psi_m), \tag{2.35}$$
$$1 = \hat{R}^*\psi. \tag{2.36}$$

From these two identities it is clear that *state prices are determined by the basis asset return*, independently of the basis asset price.

2.10 Risk-Neutral Probabilities

If instead of the state price vector ψ we use a normalized vector q,

$$\begin{bmatrix} q_1 \\ \vdots \\ q_m \end{bmatrix} = \begin{bmatrix} R_f\psi_1 \\ \vdots \\ R_f\psi_m \end{bmatrix}, \tag{2.37}$$

then the bond pricing equation (2.35) reads

$$q_1 + q_2 + \cdots + q_m = 1,$$

that is, we can think of q_i as probabilities. It is interesting to see how the pricing formula for risky assets (2.36) changes in this new light. From (2.37) we have $\psi = q/R_f$ and substituting this into (2.36) we obtain

$$1 = \hat{R}^* \frac{q}{R_f} \tag{2.38}$$

and consequently

$$R_f = \hat{R}^* q. \tag{2.39}$$

What we have on the left-hand side is the risk-free return, whereas on the right-hand side we obtain the *expected return of the risky assets under probabilities q_i*.

Equivalently, to go back to the prices and pay-offs let us multiply each equation in the system (2.38) by its respective price, whereby we obtain

$$S = \frac{1}{R_f} A^* q. \tag{2.40}$$

Taking the risk-free return as the discount rate, we find that the price of each security is the present discounted value of its expected pay-off under probabilities q_i. Note that this identity follows from the definition of q_i, or, rather, it defines q_i from the returns of basis assets. As such (2.40) contains no deep economic intuition but on the basis of it the values q_i are called *risk-neutral probabilities*. Let us try to explain why.

First of all, recall the problems of determining objective state probabilities. Since events in financial markets, unlike rolling a fair die, are not controlled random experiments, every market participant has his/her own assessment of the situation, by means of so-called subjective probabilities. It is difficult to get inside the heads of market participants, so let us simplify matters further by supposing that the market as a whole assigns probabilities to different outcomes.

We know from economic theory that a *risk-neutral agent* with subjective probabilities p would price assets according to the formula,

$$S = \frac{1}{R_f} A^* p. \tag{2.41}$$

Assuming that the *market* as a whole *is risk-neutral,* the comparison of (2.40) with (2.41) reveals that we may then interpret q as the subjective state probabilities seen by the market as a whole; hence the name risk-neutral probabilities. The argument assumes that the market is actually risk-neutral and that it makes sense to think of the market as one uniform entity, but it does not imply one or the other.

2.11 State Prices and No-Arbitrage Pricing

We have seen in Section 2.8.1 that state prices can be used as an indicator of arbitrage among basis assets. Analogously, they can be used to price focus assets.

Theorem 2.14 (Arbitrage Pricing Theorem). *Consider a market with basis assets characterized by pay-off matrix A and price vector S. Suppose we wish to price a focus asset b, assuming that the presence of b does not affect prices of the existing basis assets. The pricing procedure has two steps.*

1. *Find all strictly positive state prices ψ consistent with the price of the basis assets,*

$$A^*\psi = S.$$

If this set is empty, there is arbitrage among basis assets. If it is a singleton (a set containing only one state price vector), the market is complete. In the remaining cases the market is incomplete.

2. *Price the focus asset using all the state prices found above. The set of prices thus obtained is equal to the set of all possible no-arbitrage prices for the focus asset. This set is a singleton if and only if the focus asset is redundant.*

The only material difference from Section 2.8.1 is that now we have to find all strictly positive state prices, whereas to conclude that there was no arbitrage it was enough to find one. It is often more practical to use risk-neutral probabilities instead of state prices; in that case one finds q from (2.39) and prices focus assets using equation (2.40).

Example 2.15. In a market with three basis assets,

$$A = \begin{bmatrix} 1 & 1 & 3 \\ 0 & 1 & 1 \\ 1 & 0 & 2 \end{bmatrix}, \qquad S = \begin{bmatrix} \frac{1}{3} \\ \frac{1}{3} \\ 1 \end{bmatrix},$$

we wish to introduce a new security with pay-off

$$\begin{bmatrix} 1 & 1 & 1 \end{bmatrix}.$$

If the introduction of the new security leaves the prices of basis assets unchanged, find the no-arbitrage price range for the new security.

Solution. In Example 2.13 we have found the set of strictly positive state prices consistent with the basis assets. These were

$$\psi_1 = \tfrac{1}{3} - \psi_3, \tag{2.42}$$
$$\psi_2 = \psi_3, \tag{2.43}$$
$$0 < \psi_3 < \tfrac{1}{3}. \tag{2.44}$$

The no-arbitrage price of the pay-off

$$\begin{bmatrix} 1 & 1 & 1 \end{bmatrix}$$

is

$$S_4 = 1 \times \psi_1 + 1 \times \psi_2 + 1 \times \psi_3.$$

Substituting in the state prices from (2.42) and (2.43) we obtain

$$S_4 = (\tfrac{1}{3} - \psi_3) + \psi_3 + \psi_3 = \tfrac{1}{3} + \psi_3$$

and taking into account the restriction (2.44) we can see that the no-arbitrage price bounds for the focus asset are

$$\tfrac{1}{3} < S_4 < \tfrac{2}{3}.$$

2.12 Summary

- A system of equations may have zero, one or infinitely many solutions. Suppose that we interpret the left-hand side of the system as a pay-off of a portfolio of basis assets and the right-hand side as a pay-off of a focus asset. Whether a solution exists is purely determined by the *position of the focus asset relative to the marketed subspace formed by basis assets*. If the focus asset is redundant, we have a solution, otherwise there is no solution. If basis assets span the whole market (the market is complete), then a solution necessarily always exists.

  On the other hand the uniqueness of a solution (provided that one exists, as discussed above) is purely determined by the number of *redundant basis assets*. With redundant basis assets there will be infinitely many solutions, without redundant basis asset the solution is unique (always assuming that a solution exists in the first place).

- Assuming that the basis assets in the matrix A are linearly independent, the portfolio minimizing the sum of squared replication errors relative to focus asset b is given by

$$\hat{x} = (A^*A)^{-1}A^*b.$$

- When calculating $\hat{x}$ in a computer program, it is advisable to use QR decomposition of A rather than invert A^*A, because A^*A is extremely close to being singular if columns of A are nearly linearly dependent. In terms of GAUSS code

```
xhat=olsqr(b,A)
```

  is preferable to

```
xhat=inv(A'A)*A'b
```

- The best approximating portfolio constitutes a perfect hedge if

$$b = A\hat{x} = A(A^*A)^{-1}A^*b,$$

  in which case b is a redundant security.

- If we wish to minimize the expected squared replication error, it is enough to replace A and b with $\tilde{A}, \tilde{b}$ obtained by multiplying each row of A and b by the square root of the probability of the corresponding scenario.

- There are two types of arbitrage. Type I arbitrage resembles a lottery ticket given away for free, nothing to pay (or receive some money) today and positive gain in some states tomorrow. Type II arbitrage provides sure payment today against zero liabilities tomorrow. It only arises when there is a mispriced redundant basis asset.

- Absence of the second type of arbitrage implies the following relationship between assets prices and state prices:

$$S = A^* \psi.$$

- The state prices implied by basis assets need not be unique (this will happen when the market is not complete), but in the absence of arbitrage they can be chosen strictly positive.

- If there is a marketed risk-free asset with total return R_f, then the *risk-neutral probabilities* are related to the state prices as follows:

$$q = R_f \psi.$$

The risk-neutral probabilities can be calculated from the system,

$$R_f = \hat{R}^* q,$$

which in words says that the risk-neutral expected return on the risky assets must equal the risk-free return.

- The pricing equation with risk-neutral probabilities states that the price of any asset is equal to the present discounted value of the asset's expected pay-off under the risk-neutral probabilities:

$$\text{no-arbitrage value}(b) = \frac{b^* q}{R_f}.$$

When pricing focus assets in an incomplete market we let q go over all strictly positive values consistent with the prices of basis assets:

$$S = \frac{A^* q}{R_f}.$$

2.13 Notes

The definition of type I and type II arbitrage is due to Ingersoll (1987). The Arbitrage Theorem appears in Ross (1978). The term 'risk-neutral probabilities' is due to Arrow (1971). Both the Arbitrage Theorem and the Arbitrage Pricing Theorem are a consequence of the separation theorem for convex sets (see Duffie 1996, Chapter 1).

2.14 Appendix: Least Squares with QR Decomposition

2.14.1 Least Squares with One Explanatory Variable

Suppose we are given two n-dimensional vectors x and y. We can think of y as the dependent variable and of x as the explanatory variable. Our task is to find the least-squares approximation of y using x:

$$\min_\alpha (y - \alpha x)^* (y - \alpha x).$$

The first-order conditions read

$$x^* (y - \alpha x) = 0,$$

which means that the vector of residuals $y - \alpha x$ is at a right angle to the explanatory variable. From here we solve for α:

$$\hat{\alpha} = \frac{x^* y}{x^* x}.$$

We have decomposed y into two components, one that is parallel to x and one that is orthogonal to x:

$$y = \underbrace{\hat{\alpha} x}_{\text{parallel to } x} + \underbrace{y - \hat{\alpha} x}_{\text{orthogonal to } x}.$$

2.14.2 Gramm–Schmidt Orthogonalization

Suppose now we have several explanatory variables $x_1, \ldots, x_m$ each represented by an n-dimensional vector.

1. Take x_1 and normalize it to have unit length

$$\varepsilon_1 = \frac{x_1}{r_{11}}, \tag{2.45}$$

$$r_{11} = \|x_1\|. \tag{2.46}$$

2. Now take x_2 and decompose it into a component parallel to ε_1 and a component orthogonal to ε_1:

$$x_2 = r_{12}\varepsilon_1 + (x_2 - r_{12}\varepsilon_1). \tag{2.47}$$

The coefficient r_{12} turns out to be

$$r_{12} = \varepsilon_1^* x_2. \tag{2.48}$$

Take the residual, normalize it to have length 1 and call it ε_2:

$$\varepsilon_2 = \frac{x_2 - r_{12}\varepsilon_1}{r_{22}}, \tag{2.49}$$

$$r_{22} = \|x_2 - r_{12}\varepsilon_1\|. \tag{2.50}$$

3. Take x_3 and decompose it into a vector parallel to ε_1, a vector parallel to ε_2 (which is itself orthogonal to ε_1) and a residual orthogonal to both ε_1 and ε_2:

$$x_3 = r_{13}\varepsilon_1 + r_{23}\varepsilon_2 + (x_3 - r_{13}\varepsilon_1 + r_{23}\varepsilon_2), \tag{2.51}$$

$$r_{13} = \varepsilon_1^* x_3, \qquad r_{23} = \varepsilon_2^* x_3. \tag{2.52}$$

Normalize the residual to have length 1 and call it ε_3:

$$\varepsilon_3 = \frac{x_3 - r_{13}\varepsilon_1 - r_{23}\varepsilon_2}{r_{33}}, \tag{2.53}$$

$$r_{33} = \|x_3 - r_{13}\varepsilon_1 - r_{23}\varepsilon_2\|, \quad \text{etc.} \tag{2.54}$$

If $x_1, \ldots, x_m$ are linearly independent, then $\varepsilon_1, \ldots, \varepsilon_m$ generated by the Gramm–Schmidt process are orthogonal to each other and

$$\text{Span}(x_1, \ldots, x_m) = \text{Span}(\varepsilon_1, \ldots, \varepsilon_m).$$

2.14.3 QR Decomposition

The QR decomposition is a byproduct of the orthogonalization process. Namely, we can write

$$x_1 = \varepsilon_1 r_{11},$$
$$x_2 = \varepsilon_1 r_{12} + \varepsilon_2 r_{22},$$
$$\vdots$$
$$x_m = \varepsilon_1 r_{1m} + \cdots + \varepsilon_m r_{mm},$$

which in matrix form reads

$$X = QR,$$
$$X = \begin{bmatrix} x_1 & x_2 & \cdots & x_m \end{bmatrix},$$
$$Q = \begin{bmatrix} \varepsilon_1 & \varepsilon_2 & \cdots & \varepsilon_m \end{bmatrix}.$$

The elements of R on and above diagonal equal r_{ij} computed in equations (2.45)–(2.54), the elements below diagonal are 0. Because the vectors ε_i are orthogonal with length 1 by construction, we have

$$Q^*Q = I_m,$$

which means that Q is an **orthogonal matrix.**

Example 2.16. In Section 2.4 we have $A_\delta = QR$ with

$$Q = \begin{bmatrix} \frac{1}{2} & \frac{3}{10}\sqrt{5} & 2\frac{\sqrt{30}}{30} \\ \frac{1}{2} & \frac{1}{10}\sqrt{5} & -\frac{\sqrt{30}}{30} \\ \frac{1}{2} & -\frac{1}{10}\sqrt{5} & -4\frac{\sqrt{30}}{30} \\ \frac{1}{2} & -\frac{3}{10}\sqrt{5} & 3\frac{\sqrt{30}}{30} \end{bmatrix}, \qquad R = \begin{bmatrix} 2 & 5 & 3 - \frac{3}{2}\delta \\ 0 & \sqrt{5} & (1 - \frac{3}{10}\delta)\sqrt{5} \\ 0 & 0 & 3\frac{\sqrt{30}}{30}\delta \end{bmatrix}.$$

2.14.4 Least-Squares and QR Decomposition

We have concluded in Example 2.4 that the optimal hedging error ε,

$$\varepsilon = A\hat{x} - b, \qquad (2.55)$$

must be orthogonal to all basis assets in A and by construction of the QR decomposition ε will therefore be orthogonal to all vectors in Q:

$$Q^*\varepsilon = 0.$$

Now substitute QR for A in (2.55) and multiply both sides by Q^*:

$$\underbrace{Q^*\varepsilon}_{0} = \underbrace{Q^*Q}_{I} R\hat{x} - Q^*b.$$

Then $\hat{x}$ is obtained simply by solving

$$R\hat{x} = Q^*b$$

and because R is upper triangular this step does not require matrix inversion.

In GAUSS, instead of

```
xhat = inv(A'A)*A'b
```

which is numerically unstable, we would write

```
xhat = olsqr(b,A)
```

The columns of matrix A for which $r_{jj} <$ `olsqtol` are considered redundant and their portfolio weight in procedure `olsqr` (ordinary least squares with QR decomposition) is set to zero.

2.15 Exercises

Exercise 2.1. The best hedging portfolio is *unique* when (circle one answer)
   (a) the securities available for hedging are linearly independent;
   (b) $r(A) < m$;
   (c) there are fewer states than securities;
   (d) none of the above.

Exercise 2.2. The pay-off of the best hedging portfolio is always the same, even if the best portfolio itself is not unique:
   (a) TRUE;
   (b) FALSE.

Exercise 2.3 (identifying arbitrage). In each of the following markets decide whether there are any arbitrage opportunities and if so try to identify them by constructing a type I or type II arbitrage portfolio x. If there is no arbitrage, give a vector of strictly positive state prices consistent with the price of basis assets.

(a) $A = \begin{bmatrix} 2 & 1 & 1 \\ 1 & 1 & 0 \\ 0 & 1 & -1 \end{bmatrix}$, $\quad S = \begin{bmatrix} 2 \\ 1 \\ 0.5 \end{bmatrix}$, $\quad x_3 =$

(b) $A = \begin{bmatrix} 2 & 1 & 0 & 3 & 1 \\ 1 & 1 & 1 & 2 & 1 \\ 0 & 1 & 2 & 1 & 0 \end{bmatrix}$, $\quad S = \begin{bmatrix} 1 \\ 1 \\ 1 \\ 2 \\ \frac{1}{3} \end{bmatrix}$, $\quad x_5 =$

(c) $A = \begin{bmatrix} 2 & 0 \\ 1 & 1 \\ 0 & 2 \end{bmatrix}$, $\quad S = \begin{bmatrix} 1 \\ 1001 \end{bmatrix}$, $\quad x_2 =$

Exercise 2.4 (no-arbitrage pricing in incomplete market). Suppose that there are four market scenarios, and there are three basis assets with pay-off matrix and price vector,

$$A = \begin{bmatrix} 1 & 0 & 3 \\ 0 & 1 & 3 \\ 0 & 2 & 3 \\ 1 & 0 & 3 \end{bmatrix}, \qquad S = \begin{bmatrix} \frac{1}{3} \\ \frac{1}{2} \\ 2 \end{bmatrix}.$$

(a) What is the return on the riskless bond?

(b) Find all state prices which are consistent with A and S, and based on this finding decide whether there are any arbitrage opportunities.

(c) Is the market in this model complete?

(d) What are the risk-neutral probabilities?

(e) A focus asset with pay-off $\begin{bmatrix} 1 & 2 & 0 & 1 \end{bmatrix}$ is introduced, without affecting the price of the basis assets. What are the possible no-arbitrage prices of the focus asset? (Hint: price the new security using the state prices calculated in (b) or the risk-neutral probabilities calculated in (d).)

Exercise 2.5 (option pricing with several basis assets). Suppose that R_1 and R_2 are two stock returns, and assume further that these returns are independent and identically distributed (you may need to review the concept of *stochastic independence* in Appendix B),

$$P(R_1 = 1.2) = P(R_2 = 1.2) = \tfrac{1}{2},$$
$$P(R_1 = 1.0) = P(R_2 = 1.0) = \tfrac{1}{2}.$$

Suppose that there is another security with a risk-free return $R = 1.05$.

(a) How many scenarios are needed to describe the joint distribution of R_1 and R_2?

(b) Taking the safe asset and the two risky securities as basis assets find the (range of) risk-neutral probabilities in this model and decide whether there are arbitrage opportunities.

(c) Take the three securities above as basis assets. A new asset, which can be thought of as a digital call option on a stock market index, is introduced. The pay-offs of the digital call are

$$D = 1 \quad \text{for} \quad \frac{R_1 + R_2}{2} > 1.05,$$

$$D = 0 \quad \text{for} \quad \frac{R_1 + R_2}{2} \leqslant 1.05.$$

Find the no-arbitrage price (or a range of prices as the case may be) for the digital call.

Exercise 2.6 (option hedging). Find the portfolio minimizing the expected squared replication error in the case with eight states of the world, two securities available for hedging with pay-offs

$$\begin{bmatrix} 1 & 1 & 1 & 1 & 1 & 1 & 1 & 1 \end{bmatrix}$$

and

$$\begin{bmatrix} 0.80 & 0.90 & 0.95 & 1.00 & 1.05 & 1.10 & 1.20 & 1.30 \end{bmatrix},$$

respectively, when the security to be hedged pays

$$\begin{bmatrix} 0 & 0 & 0 & 0 & 50 & 100 & 200 & 300 \end{bmatrix}$$

in the individual states. The objective state probabilities are

$$\begin{bmatrix} 0.05 & 0.1 & 0.15 & 0.20 & 0.20 & 0.15 & 0.1 & 0.05 \end{bmatrix}.$$

Use Excel or GAUSS to avoid lengthy calculations by hand.

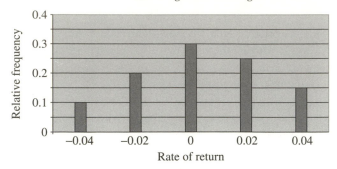

Figure 2.2. Empirical distribution of returns.

Table 2.2. Amount X to be hedged.

PFCo stock return	X
0.04	£2000
0.02	£1000
0	£100
−0.02	£20
−0.04	£0

Exercise 2.7 (valuation of hedging portfolio). The historical distribution of monthly returns on the PFCo shares is shown in Figure 2.2.

An option trader wishes to hedge a random amount X, with X depending on the realized monthly PFCo stock return as shown in Table 2.2. The risk-free rate is 0% and PFCo shares currently trade at £2.

(a) Using the stock and the risk-free bank account, hedge exposure X so as to minimize the expected squared replication error. State the required number of shares and the bank account balance.

(b) What is the cost of the optimal hedge?

Exercise 2.8 (programming). Design an *algorithm* that inputs an $m \times n$ matrix A, returns the rank of A and partitions (splits) the columns of A into two groups (submatrices) A^1 and A^2 such that A^1 contains $r(A)$ linearly independent columns and A^2 contains the remaining $n - r(A)$ columns which can be expressed as linear combinations of the columns in A_1. Store these linear combinations (portfolios) in an $r(A) \times (n - r(A))$ matrix C.

Assume that there is a procedure `Inv(X)` which returns X^{-1} when X is invertible, but when X is not invertible it causes an unrecoverable error. You do not have to use a specific programming language; use a diagram to describe the algorithm if you prefer. (Hint: think of the procedure for splitting securities into linearly independent and redundant described in Section 1.10 of Chapter 1.)

Exercise 2.9 (GAUSS). Program the above algorithm in GAUSS.

3

Risk and Return in the One-Period Model

Striking a balance between risk and return is a daily routine of every finance professional. This chapter will outline standard measurements of attitude to risk and the resulting investment decisions. The main tools needed for this analysis are calculus and probability.

> **Example 3.1 (optimal investment).** An investor with a total wealth of £1 000 000 and risk-free income of £200 000 a year wishes to invest her wealth for one year. She can split her wealth between two assets: a security bearing 2% per annum risk-free, or a risky asset with a return of −10% or 20% with equal probability. Suppose the investor's attitude to risk is characterized by a coefficient of relative risk aversion equal to 5. Find the optimal amount to be invested in the risky asset. How much worse off would the investor be in the absence of the risky asset?

This example may seem theoretical because not many investors walk around with the coefficient of relative risk aversion written on their forehead. On the other hand, if one is able to come up with an investment decision that matches a given attitude to risk (coefficient of relative risk aversion), then in turn the attitude to risk can be inferred from investment decisions. With this observation in mind we now turn our attention to the theoretical foundations. The important concepts to watch out for are the *risk premium*, the *HARA utility*, *baseline risk aversion*, *local risk aversion*, the *certainty equivalent,* the *investment potential* and the *Sharpe ratio*.

3.1 Utility Functions

The evaluation of risky cash flows is based on three premises. The first two are that *investors prefer more to less* and that *positive deviations from average wealth cannot compensate for equally large and equally probable negative deviations* from average wealth. These first two assumptions are summarized in an increasing concave function called the *utility function* (see Figure 3.1).

The third assumption maintains that *risky distribution of wealth is valued by the certainty equivalent of its expected utility*, $E[U(V)]$.

The process of evaluating an uncertain distribution of wealth is described in Figure 3.2. We start with a *distribution of wealth*, depicted in this case by five bars, on the horizontal (wealth) axis. Each bar corresponds to one level of wealth and the height of each bar captures the probability of achieving that value of wealth. The arrows take us to the utility function and then to the vertical axis. The five bars on the

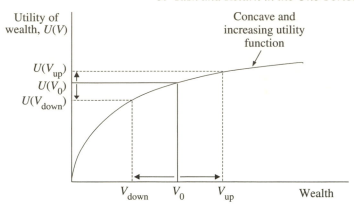

Figure 3.1. With a concave utility function, equally large upside and downside wealth movements from the average wealth level V_0 will cause larger downside movement in utility. This captures an investor's 'risk aversion'.

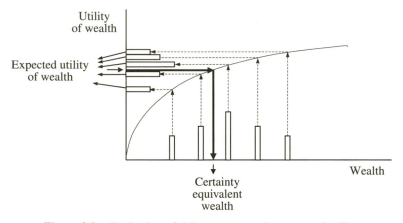

Figure 3.2. Evaluation of risky outcomes using expected utility.

vertical axis depict the *distribution of the utility of wealth.* Note that while the five bars on the horizontal axis are placed symmetrically around the middle value, the corresponding bars on the vertical axis are skewed towards lower values of utility, that is, the investor puts higher emphasis on losses and lower emphasis on gains. We now compute the expected utility of wealth which corresponds to the average position of the five bars on the vertical (utility) axis. The bold arrow is taking us back from expected utility via the utility function to the certainty equivalent wealth. Note that the certainty equivalent falls below the average level of risky wealth. The difference is known as the **risk premium**:

$$\text{risk premium} = \text{average wealth} - \text{certainty equivalent wealth}.$$

This measures the amount of compensation that must be given to a risk-averse investor in order for her to be willing to hold risky assets.

3.1.1   Constant Absolute Risk Aversion (CARA)

Because we are evaluating distributions of wealth relative to an initial level of wealth V_0, we may as well look at the quantity $E[U(V)]/U(V_0)$. Assuming that V_0 is risk free we may write this as $E[U(V)/U(V_0)]$. It is natural to inquire which utility functions look the same relative to the origin V_0, regardless of where that origin lies. To capture this invariance property we write

$$\frac{U(V)}{U(V_0)} = f(V - V_0) \tag{3.1}$$

for all V, V_0 and the as yet undetermined function f. It turns out that the only utility function meeting this condition is exponential (see Exercise 3.10). Of course, not all exponential functions are increasing and concave, but it is easy to verify that

$$U(V) = -e^{-aV} \quad \text{with } a > 0 \tag{3.2}$$

meets our requirements.

The coefficient a is called the *coefficient of absolute risk aversion*, and the negative exponential utility (3.2) is known as the *constant absolute risk-aversion* (CARA) *utility*. Why 'constant absolute' is clear from equation (3.1); the utility reacts to deviations in *absolute* wealth (as opposed to percentage deviations) and the reaction is *constant* with respect to the choice of origin V_0. There is a more technical definition of the coefficient of absolute risk aversion that we will simply state as a fact.

Fact. For a general utility function $U(V)$, the **coefficient of (local) absolute risk aversion** $a(V)$ is defined as

$$a(V) = -\frac{U''(V)}{U'(V)}. \tag{3.3}$$

Consider an investor with risk-free wealth V_{safe} who faces a *small* risk with mean zero and variance $\sigma^2 \approx 0$. To accept the risk the investor requires a risk premium of the size $a(V_{\text{safe}})\sigma^2$.

Proof. See website. $\square$

3.1.2   Constant Relative Risk Aversion (CRRA)

Suppose we wish to find a utility function with constant response to *relative* change in wealth V/V_0, so that

$$\frac{U(V)}{U(V_0)} = f\left(\frac{V}{V_0}\right). \tag{3.4}$$

The utility function satisfying (3.4) is called the *constant relative* risk-aversion (CRRA) utility. It takes the form

$$U_\gamma(V) = \frac{V^{1-\gamma}}{1-\gamma} \quad \text{with } \gamma > 0,\ \gamma \neq 1; \tag{3.5}$$

see Exercise 3.11. The parameter γ is the *coefficient of (local) relative risk aversion*. The expression (3.5) is not well defined for $\gamma = 1$, but it can be shown that

$$\lim_{\gamma \to 1} \frac{V^{1-\gamma} - 1}{1 - \gamma} = \ln V; \tag{3.6}$$

see Exercise 3.9.

For a general utility function $U(V)$ the **coefficient of relative risk aversion** $\tilde{\gamma}(V)$ is defined as

$$\tilde{\gamma}(V) = Va(V), \tag{3.7}$$

where $a(V)$ is the coefficient of absolute risk aversion defined in (3.3). For the CRRA utility in (3.5) we have $\tilde{\gamma}(V) = \gamma$.

Example 3.2. Find the coefficient of relative risk aversion of logarithmic utility. By definition (3.7),

$$\tilde{\gamma} = -\frac{V(\ln V)''}{(\ln V)'}.$$

The first derivative is $(\ln V)' = 1/V$ and the second $(\ln V)'' = (1/V)' = -1/V^2$, consequently

$$\tilde{\gamma} = -\frac{V(-1/V^2)}{1/V} = 1,$$

as might be expected from (3.6). The logarithmic utility is a CRRA utility with a coefficient of relative risk aversion equal to 1.

3.1.3 Hyperbolic Absolute Risk Aversion (HARA)

The most frequently used utility function is a generalization of the CRRA and CARA utility. The best way to think of the HARA utility is to imagine that an investor with a CRRA utility receives extra risk-free wealth $\bar{V}$ so that her utility becomes

$$U_{\gamma,\bar{V}}(V) = \frac{(\bar{V} + V)^{1-\gamma}}{1 - \gamma}. \tag{3.8}$$

The coefficient of local relative risk aversion of the HARA utility is

$$\tilde{\gamma}(V) = \frac{VU''_{\gamma,\bar{V}}(V)}{U'_{\gamma,\bar{V}}(V)} = \gamma \frac{V}{\bar{V} + V} = \gamma \left(\frac{\bar{V}}{V} + 1\right)^{-1}. \tag{3.9}$$

Naturally, the more extra risk-free wealth $\bar{V}$ the investor perceives she has, the lower her coefficient of risk aversion.

We will refer to γ in (3.8) as the **baseline risk aversion**, whereas $\tilde{\gamma}$ in (3.9) evaluated at the risk-free level of wealth V_{safe} will be called **local risk aversion**. Intuitively, local risk aversion describes an investor's attitude to small symmetric risks, whereas baseline risk aversion comes into play when the investor undertakes asymmetric risks with small downside and large upside.

The CRRA utility is a special case of the HARA utility when the baseline and local risk aversion coincide. We jump ahead a little by saying that, in a sense to be made precise in Section 3.8.1, the CARA utility with absolute risk aversion a corresponds to the HARA utility with $\gamma = +\infty$ and $\tilde{\gamma} = a$.

3.2 Expected Utility Maximization

Having established what we mean by constant relative risk aversion, we are now in a position to find the optimal investment for our investor. Denote by R_f the risk-free return, $\hat{R}$ the risky return, $\tilde{\alpha}$ the share of initial wealth invested in the risky asset, y the income, and V_0 the initial wealth.

The end-of-period wealth is

$$V(\tilde{\alpha}) = \underbrace{\tilde{\alpha} V_0}_{\text{money in risky asset}} \hat{R} + \underbrace{(1 - \tilde{\alpha}) V_0}_{\text{money in safe asset}} R_f + y. \tag{3.10}$$

Depending on the realization of the risky return, the wealth will be either

$$V_{\text{up}}(\tilde{\alpha}) = 1\,000\,000[1.2\tilde{\alpha} + 1.02(1 - \tilde{\alpha})] + 200\,000$$
$$= 1\,220\,000 + \tilde{\alpha}\,180\,000$$

if $\hat{R} = R_{\text{up}} = 1.2$, or

$$V_{\text{down}}(\tilde{\alpha}) = 1\,000\,000[0.9\tilde{\alpha} + 1.02(1 - \tilde{\alpha})] + 200\,000$$
$$= 1\,220\,000 - \tilde{\alpha}\,120\,000$$

if $\hat{R} = R_{\text{down}} = 0.9$, each with probability one-half. Thus we are solving

$$\max_{\tilde{\alpha}} \text{E}[U(V(\tilde{\alpha}))] = \max_{\tilde{\alpha}} \text{E}\left[\frac{V(\tilde{\alpha})^{1-\gamma}}{1 - \gamma}\right]$$

$$= \max_{\tilde{\alpha}} \frac{1}{2} \frac{V_{\text{up}}^{1-\gamma}(\tilde{\alpha})}{1 - \gamma} + \frac{1}{2} \frac{V_{\text{down}}^{1-\gamma}(\tilde{\alpha})}{1 - \gamma}$$

$$= \frac{1\,220\,000^{1-\gamma}}{2} \max_{\tilde{\alpha}} \left[\frac{(1 + \frac{18}{122}\tilde{\alpha})^{1-\gamma}}{1 - \gamma} + \frac{(1 - \frac{12}{122}\tilde{\alpha})^{1-\gamma}}{1 - \gamma}\right].$$

To find the maximum we must differentiate the expression above with respect to $\tilde{\alpha}$ and equate it to zero. This gives the so-called *first-order condition*:

$$\frac{18}{122}\left(1 + \frac{18}{122}\tilde{\alpha}_{\text{opt}}\right)^{-\gamma} - \frac{12}{122}\left(1 - \frac{12}{122}\tilde{\alpha}_{\text{opt}}\right)^{-\gamma} = 0. \tag{3.11}$$

Simplify (3.11) by moving the powers of $\tilde{\alpha}_{\text{opt}}$ to opposite sides of the equation and by raising both sides to the power of $-1/\gamma$ to obtain expressions that are linear in $\tilde{\alpha}$:

$$1.5\left(1 + \frac{18}{122}\tilde{\alpha}_{\text{opt}}\right)^{-\gamma} = \left(1 - \frac{12}{122}\tilde{\alpha}_{\text{opt}}\right)^{-\gamma},$$

$$(1.5)^{-1/\gamma}\left(1 + \frac{18}{122}\tilde{\alpha}_{\text{opt}}\right) = 1 - \frac{12}{122}\tilde{\alpha}_{\text{opt}},$$

$$\tilde{\alpha}_{\text{opt}} = \frac{61}{6}\frac{1 - (1.5)^{-1/\gamma}}{1 + (1.5)^{1-1/\gamma}}.$$

With $\gamma = 5$ we obtain

$$\tilde{\alpha}_{\text{opt}} = 0.3323. \tag{3.12}$$

The highest attainable utility is

$$\mathrm{E}[U(V(\tilde{\alpha}_{\text{opt}}))] = \frac{1\,220\,000^{-4}}{-4}\left(\frac{(1 + \frac{18}{122}0.3323)^{-4}}{2} + \frac{(1 - \frac{12}{122}0.3323)^{-4}}{2}\right)$$

$$= -1.1104 \times 10^{-25}.$$

With the optimal investment $\tilde{\alpha}_{\text{opt}} = 0.3323$, the investor's wealth at the end of the period will be either

$$V_{\text{up}}(\tilde{\alpha}_{\text{opt}}) = 1\,220\,000 + 0.3323 \times 180\,000$$

$$= 1\,279\,814$$

if she is lucky and the risky return is high, or

$$V_{\text{down}}(\tilde{\alpha}_{\text{opt}}) = 1\,220\,000 - 0.3323 \times 120\,000$$

$$= 1\,180\,124$$

if the risky return is low.

3.3   Reporting Expected Utility in Terms of Money

Only the level of wealth associated with the utility function, not its value, has a direct economic meaning. Therefore, we do not report the desirability of an investment strategy in terms of expected utility but rather in terms of wealth generating that level of expected utility. To explain this in more detail consider a distribution of wealth V:

$$V = V_{\text{up}} \text{ with probability } \tfrac{1}{2},$$

$$V = V_{\text{down}} \text{ with probability } \tfrac{1}{2}.$$

The expected utility of receiving random wealth V is $\mathrm{E}[U(V)] = \frac{1}{2}U(V_{\text{up}}) + \frac{1}{2}U(V_{\text{down}})$. It is depicted in Figure 3.3 on the vertical axis, between $U(V_{\text{up}})$ and $U(V_{\text{down}})$. To describe this level of utility we will trace it back to the horizontal axis; we can see that it is generated by the wealth level V_{certain}. To sum up, we say that V_{certain} is the **certainty equivalent** of the random distribution of wealth V.

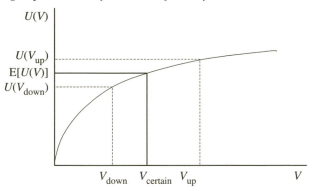

Figure 3.3. Calculation of certainty equivalent wealth.

Let us see how to find V_{certain} computationally. Suppose

$$E[U(V(\tilde{\alpha}_{\text{opt}}))] = -1.110\,397 \times 10^{-25}. \tag{3.13}$$

To find V_{certain} we must solve

$$\left.\begin{aligned}
U(V_{\text{certain}}) &= -1.110\,397 \times 10^{-25}, \\
\frac{V_{\text{certain}}^{-4}}{-4} &= -1.110\,397 \times 10^{-25}, \\
V_{\text{certain}}^{-4} &= 4.441\,588 \times 10^{-25}, \\
V_{\text{certain}} &= (4.441\,588 \times 10^{-25})^{-1/4} = 1\,224\,942.
\end{aligned}\right\} \tag{3.14}$$

We conclude that the investor is better off by £4942 compared with her holding only the risk-free asset.

3.3.1 Inverse of the Utility Function

In computing the value of V_{certain} we have unwittingly used the **inverse function** of the utility function. We have done this by setting $U(V) = u$ and solving for V as a function of u, where u represents expected utility.

Let us see in detail how this is done for the HARA utility:

$$\left.\begin{aligned}
U(V) &= \frac{(\bar{V} + V)^{1-\gamma}}{1 - \gamma} = u, \\
(\bar{V} + V)^{1-\gamma} &= (1 - \gamma)u, \\
\bar{V} + V &= ((1 - \gamma)u)^{1/(1-\gamma)}, \\
V &= ((1 - \gamma)u)^{1/(1-\gamma)} - \bar{V}.
\end{aligned}\right\} \tag{3.15}$$

The inverse of the utility function is denoted U^{-1}; for the HARA utility we have from (3.15)

$$U^{-1}(u) = ((1 - \gamma)u)^{1/(1-\gamma)} - \bar{V}. \tag{3.16}$$

Thus the calculation (3.13) and (3.14) of the previous section can be concisely written as

$$V_{\text{certain}}(\alpha) = U^{-1}(E[U(V(\alpha))]). \tag{3.17}$$

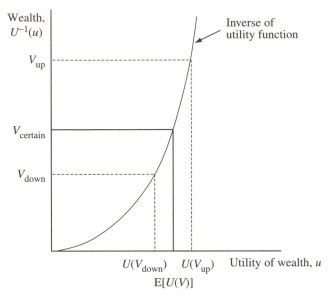

Figure 3.4. Inverse utility function.

Graphically the inverse function is found by rotating Figure 3.3 around the 45° line, as shown in Figure 3.4.

3.4 Scale-Free Formulation of the Optimal Investment Problem with the HARA Utility

Let us see how the level of risk-free wealth affects the investment decision of an investor with the HARA utility. First of all, we will denote the end-of-period risk-free wealth by V_{safe},

$$V_{\text{safe}} \triangleq R_{\text{f}} V_0 + y,$$

and rewrite the investor's terminal wealth (3.10) as

$$V(\tilde{\alpha}) = V_{\text{safe}} + \tilde{\alpha} V_0 (\hat{R} - R_{\text{f}}). \tag{3.18}$$

To simplify the notation denote the excess return by X,

$$X \triangleq \hat{R} - R_{\text{f}}, \tag{3.19}$$

and factor out the risk-free wealth V_{safe} from the investor's total wealth (3.18),

$$V(\tilde{\alpha}) = V_{\text{safe}} \left(1 + \underbrace{\frac{\tilde{\alpha} V_0}{V_{\text{safe}}}}_{\alpha} X \right). \tag{3.20}$$

As the last step we will start measuring risky investment in terms of α, which represents money invested in the risky asset as a fraction of V_{safe},

$$\alpha \triangleq \frac{\tilde{\alpha} V_0}{R_{\text{f}} V_0 + y}, \tag{3.21}$$

whereby (3.20) simplifies to

$$V(\alpha) = V_{\text{safe}}(1 + \alpha X).$$ (3.22)

From (3.8) the HARA utility of terminal wealth reads

$$U_{\gamma,\bar{V}}(V(\alpha)) = \frac{(\bar{V} + V(\alpha))^{1-\gamma}}{1 - \gamma},$$ (3.23)

where γ is the baseline risk aversion. After the substitution of (3.22) into (3.23) we have

$$U_{\gamma,\bar{V}}(V(\alpha)) = \frac{V_{\text{safe}}^{1-\gamma}}{1 - \gamma}\left(1 + \frac{\bar{V}}{V_{\text{safe}}} + \alpha X\right)^{1-\gamma}.$$ (3.24)

3.4.1 Coefficient of Local Risk Aversion

We will now define $\tilde{\gamma}$ as the coefficient of **local** relative **risk aversion** evaluated at the risk-free wealth V_{safe}; from (3.9) we have

$$\tilde{\gamma} \triangleq \gamma\left(1 + \frac{\bar{V}}{V_{\text{safe}}}\right)^{-1}.$$ (3.25)

Since it is preferable to work with $\tilde{\gamma}$ rather than $\bar{V}$, we will substitute (3.25) into (3.24) to obtain

$$U_{\gamma,\tilde{\gamma}}(V(\alpha)) = \frac{V_{\text{safe}}^{1-\gamma}}{1 - \gamma}\left(\frac{\gamma}{\tilde{\gamma}} + \alpha X\right)^{1-\gamma}.$$ (3.26)

Here $U_{\gamma,\tilde{\gamma}}$ stands for the HARA utility with baseline risk aversion γ and local risk aversion $\tilde{\gamma}$.

3.4.2 Expected Utility

Let us now evaluate the expected HARA utility; from (3.26) we obtain

$$E[U_{\gamma,\tilde{\gamma}}(V(\alpha_{\gamma,\tilde{\gamma}}))] = E\left[\frac{V_{\text{safe}}^{1-\gamma}}{1 - \gamma}\left(\frac{\gamma}{\tilde{\gamma}} + \alpha_{\gamma,\tilde{\gamma}}X\right)^{1-\gamma}\right].$$ (3.27)

In (3.27) we have explicitly captured the fact that the choice of α *depends both on the local risk aversion and on the baseline risk aversion.*

Because the expression $V_{\text{safe}}^{1-\gamma}/(1 - \gamma)$ in (3.27) is not random, it can be taken in front of the expectation,

$$E[U_{\gamma,\hat{\gamma}}(V(\alpha_{\gamma,\tilde{\gamma}}))] = \frac{V_{\text{safe}}^{1-\gamma}}{1 - \gamma}E\left[\left(\frac{\gamma}{\tilde{\gamma}} + \alpha_{\gamma,\tilde{\gamma}}X\right)^{1-\gamma}\right].$$ (3.28)

3.4.3 Scaling of Portfolio Choices

If we factor out $1/\tilde{\gamma}$ from the expected utility (3.28),

$$E[U_{\gamma,\tilde{\gamma}}(V(\alpha_{\gamma,\tilde{\gamma}}))] = \frac{((1/\tilde{\gamma})V_{\text{safe}})^{1-\gamma}}{1 - \gamma}E[(\gamma + \tilde{\gamma}\alpha_{\gamma,\tilde{\gamma}}X)^{1-\gamma}],$$ (3.29)

it becomes clear that the choice of $\tilde{\gamma}\alpha_{\gamma,\tilde{\gamma}}$ is independent of $\tilde{\gamma}$ because the square bracket on the right-hand side of (3.29), apart from $\tilde{\gamma}\alpha_{\gamma,\tilde{\gamma}}$, only depends on γ and X. Note that for $\tilde{\gamma} = 1$ we have

$$\tilde{\gamma}\alpha_{\gamma,\tilde{\gamma}} = \alpha_{\gamma,1}; \tag{3.30}$$

hence we can interpret $\alpha_{\gamma,1}$ as the risky portfolio choice per unit of local risk tolerance. From (3.30) we also have

$$\alpha_{\gamma,1} = \gamma\alpha_{\gamma,\gamma},$$

where $\alpha_{\gamma,\gamma}$ is the portfolio choice of a CRRA investor with relative risk aversion γ.

Equation (3.30) means that the portfolio choice of an HARA investor has two components:

$$\alpha_{\gamma,\tilde{\gamma}} = \underbrace{\frac{1}{\tilde{\gamma}}}_{\substack{\text{local risk} \\ \text{tolerance}}} \times \underbrace{\alpha_{\gamma,1}}_{\substack{\text{portfolio choice} \\ \text{per unit of local} \\ \text{risk tolerance}}}. \tag{3.31}$$

The HARA investor looks at the *portfolio choice* of a CRRA investor *per unit of local risk tolerance* and then adjusts her portfolio choice to accommodate her *local risk aversion*. The baseline portfolio is independent of the local risk aversion.

3.4.4   *Scaling of Certainty Equivalents; Investment Potential*

Our starting point is equation (3.29)

$$E[U_{\gamma,\tilde{\gamma}}(V(\alpha_{\gamma,\tilde{\gamma}}))] = \frac{((\gamma/\tilde{\gamma})V_{\text{safe}})^{1-\gamma}}{1-\gamma}E[(\gamma + \tilde{\gamma}\alpha_{\gamma,\tilde{\gamma}}X)^{1-\gamma}].$$

From (3.17) the certainty equivalent wealth corresponding to investment $\alpha_{\gamma,\tilde{\gamma}}$ is

$$V_{\gamma,\tilde{\gamma}\text{ certain}}(\alpha_{\gamma,\tilde{\gamma}}) = U^{-1}(E[U(V(\alpha_{\gamma,\tilde{\gamma}}))]), \tag{3.32}$$

where $U^{-1}(.)$ was given in (3.16). Substituting (3.16) and (3.29) into (3.32) we have

$$V_{\gamma,\tilde{\gamma}\text{ certain}}(\alpha_{\gamma,\tilde{\gamma}}) = \frac{1}{\tilde{\gamma}}V_{\text{safe}}(E[(\gamma + \tilde{\gamma}\alpha_{\gamma,\tilde{\gamma}}X)^{1-\gamma}])^{1/(1-\gamma)} - \bar{V}. \tag{3.33}$$

Divide both sides of (3.33) by the risk-free wealth V_{safe} and substitute for $\bar{V}$ from (3.25):

$$\frac{V_{\gamma,\tilde{\gamma}\text{ certain}}(\alpha_{\gamma,\tilde{\gamma}})}{V_{\text{safe}}} = \frac{1}{\tilde{\gamma}}(E[(\gamma + \tilde{\gamma}\alpha_{\gamma,\tilde{\gamma}}X)^{1-\gamma}])^{1/(1-\gamma)} - \left(\frac{\gamma}{\tilde{\gamma}} - 1\right). \tag{3.34}$$

Now set $\tilde{\gamma} = 1$ in (3.34),

$$\frac{V_{\gamma,1\text{ certain}}(\alpha_{\gamma,1})}{V_{\text{safe}}} - 1 = (E[(\gamma + \alpha_{\gamma,1}X)^{1-\gamma}])^{1/(1-\gamma)} - \gamma \tag{3.35}$$

and substitute (3.35) back into (3.34):

$$\frac{V_{\gamma,\tilde{\gamma}\text{ certain}}(\alpha_{\gamma,\tilde{\gamma}})}{V_{\text{safe}}} - 1 = \frac{1}{\tilde{\gamma}}\left(\frac{V_{\gamma,1\text{ certain}}(\alpha_{\gamma,1})}{V_{\text{safe}}} - 1\right). \tag{3.36}$$

Define the **investment potential** IP_γ as the percentage increase in certainty equivalent per unit of local risk tolerance:

$$IP_\gamma(\alpha_{\gamma,1}, X) = \left(\frac{V_{\gamma,1\ \text{certain}}(\alpha_{\gamma,1})}{V_{\text{safe}}} - 1\right). \tag{3.37}$$

By $IP_\gamma(X)$ denote the **maximum investment potential** associated with the risky asset

$$IP_\gamma(X) \triangleq \max_\alpha IP_\gamma(\alpha, X). \tag{3.38}$$

From (3.36) the percentage increase in certainty equivalent of an HARA investor due to risky investment has two distinct components:

$$\underbrace{\frac{\max_{\alpha_{\gamma,\tilde{\gamma}}} V_{\gamma,\tilde{\gamma}\ \text{certain}}(\alpha_{\gamma,\tilde{\gamma}})}{V_{\text{safe}}} - 1}_{\substack{\text{maximum percentage increase} \\ \text{in certainty equivalent}}} = \underbrace{\frac{1}{\tilde{\gamma}}}_{\substack{\text{local risk} \\ \text{tolerance}}} \times \underbrace{IP_\gamma(X)}_{\substack{\text{baseline} \\ \text{investment} \\ \text{potential}}}. \tag{3.39}$$

One is the maximum baseline investment potential of the risky asset, which only depends on the baseline risk aversion and the distribution of returns. The other is local risk tolerance, which determines to what extent the investor is able to benefit from the investment potential of the risky security; clearly, the higher $\tilde{\gamma}$ the less benefit accrues to the investor in terms of certainty equivalent. We will see in Sections 3.4.6 and 3.5.3 that for symmetrically distributed excess returns offering relatively small risk premiums the maximum investment potential *does not depend* on the baseline risk aversion γ, and that $IP_\gamma(X)$ is closely related to the Sharpe ratio $E[X]/\sqrt{\text{Var}(X)}$ of the risky asset.

3.4.5 Numerical Example: Scaling Properties

How are the scaling properties (3.31) and (3.39) used in practice? Typically, one is given a numerical procedure, called say HARAmax, that maximizes the normalized HARA utility in (3.36), and returns the maximum investment potential IP_γ and the normalized optimal investment $\alpha_{\gamma,1\ \text{opt}}$. The inputs are the coefficient of baseline risk aversion gama (please note that gamma is a reserved word in GAUSS and cannot be used to name a variable), the values of excess return X, and the probability distribution of excess returns Xdistr. For example, to solve Example 3.1 in GAUSS we would set

```
gama  =  5;
   X  =  0.18~-0.12;
Xdistr  =  0.5~0.5;
```

and run the command

```
{IP,alpha1}  =  HARAmax;
```

which produces

$$\left.\begin{aligned} IP = 0.020\,253 &= \frac{V_{\gamma,1\ \text{certain}}(\alpha_{\gamma,1\ \text{opt}})}{V_{\text{safe}}} - 1, \\ \text{alpha1} = 1.362 &= \alpha_{\gamma,1\ \text{opt}}. \end{aligned}\right\} \tag{3.40}$$

Table 3.1. Optimal portfolio choice and the resulting investment potential for different values of baseline risk aversion. Asset returns are taken from Example 3.1.

γ	0.5	1	2	5	10	10^4
$\alpha_{\gamma,1\ \text{opt}}$	1.389	1.389	1.375	1.362	1.357	1.351
IP_γ	0.0208	0.0206	0.0204	0.0203	0.0202	0.0201

If we wish to recover the optimal investment as a proportion of initial wealth, then by virtue of (3.21) and (3.30)

$$\tilde{\alpha}_{\gamma\ \text{opt}} = \frac{\alpha_{\gamma\ \text{opt}}}{V_0} V_{\text{safe}} = \frac{\alpha_{\gamma,1\ \text{opt}}}{\gamma V_0}(R_f V_0 + y) = \frac{1.362}{5}\frac{1\,220\,000}{1\,000\,000} = 0.3323,$$

which is exactly what we had found in (3.12).

The certainty equivalent of the risky investment is easily found from (3.40):

$$V_{\gamma,\gamma\ \text{certain}}(\alpha_{\gamma,\gamma\ \text{opt}}) = \left(1 + \frac{\text{IP}_\gamma(X)}{\gamma}\right)V_{\text{safe}}$$

$$= 1.004\,050\,6 \times 1\,220\,000 = 1\,224\,942.$$

Again, this is exactly what we discovered in (3.14). The use of scaling properties is illustrated in the GAUSS program *chapter3sect4a.gss*.

3.4.6 Numerical Example: Invariance of Investment Potential

We found in Section 3.4.4 that the investment potential only depends on the baseline risk aversion and the distribution of asset returns. It turns out that in many cases the dependence on baseline risk aversion is quite weak. Consider the distribution of returns from Example 3.1. In the previous section we have calculated the investment potential and portfolio decision corresponding to baseline risk aversion $\gamma = 5$. Let us repeat this exercise for a range of baseline risk aversions from 0.5 to 10^4. The results are shown in Table 3.1 and can be generated by running the GAUSS program *chapter3sect4b.gss*.

We can see in Table 3.1 that the optimal portfolio choice for this risky asset is consistently around 1.36 and that the investment potential is between 2 and 2.1% for all values of γ. For symmetric risks with small investment potential it is always the case that the baseline risk aversion plays a small role. Essentially, for small symmetric risks all utility functions behave like a quadratic utility which corresponds to $\gamma = -1$; this link is pursued formally in Section 3.5.3. In addition, Section 3.6 shows that the investment potential measured by the quadratic utility is closely related to a widely used performance measure, the Sharpe ratio. The baseline risk aversion only comes into play when asset returns are highly asymmetric; we illustrate this phenomenon in Section 3.8 with the example of mispriced options.

3.5 Quadratic Utility

Closed-form solutions to optimal investment problems are more of an exception than the rule. The quadratic utility is the only case that can be solved in closed form in full generality when markets are incomplete. The quadratic utility is important for another reason: its certainty equivalent is closely linked to a widely used performance measure, the Sharpe ratio. These rather attractive properties are outweighed by a significant drawback: the quadratic utility is not increasing for all levels of wealth.

Every quadratic utility has a bliss point beyond which utility decreases with increasing wealth (see Figure 3.5). However, one might hope that if one chooses V_{bliss} sufficiently large, then one is unlikely to reach the declining part of the utility function. We will examine this point in more detail in Section 3.6.3.

The quadratic utility may be written as

$$U(V) = -\tfrac{1}{2}(V - V_{\text{bliss}})^2. \tag{3.41}$$

Apart from the change of sign the quadratic utility (3.41) is a special case of the HARA utility (3.8) with $\gamma = -1$ and $\bar{V} = -V_{\text{bliss}}$. We will therefore denote quadratic utility with local risk aversion $\tilde{\gamma}$ by $U_{-1,\tilde{\gamma}}$ and the normalized utility with $\tilde{\gamma} = 1$ simply by U_{-1}.

From (3.25) with $\gamma = -1$ and $\bar{V} = -V_{\text{bliss}}$ we obtain

$$\tilde{\gamma} = -1\left(1 + \frac{\bar{V}}{V_{\text{safe}}}\right) = \left(\frac{V_{\text{bliss}}}{V_{\text{safe}}} - 1\right)^{-1}. \tag{3.42}$$

For example, $\tilde{\gamma} = 1$ when $V_{\text{bliss}} = 2V_{\text{safe}}$, whereas we have $\tilde{\gamma} = 5$ when V_{bliss} is only 20% higher than the risk-free wealth.

3.5.1 Scale-Free Formulation

Using the previously established notation, the terminal wealth can be expressed as

$$V(\alpha) = \underbrace{(V_0 R_{\text{f}} + y)}_{V_{\text{safe}}}(1 + \alpha X), \tag{3.43}$$

where X is the excess return and α is the proportion of risky investment in V_{safe}. We are maximizing the expected quadratic utility

$$-\mathrm{E}[(V_{\text{bliss}} - V_{\text{safe}}(1 + \alpha X))^2]. \tag{3.44}$$

Let us rephrase the expected utility using the local coefficient of risk aversion. Once we factor out the risk-free wealth from (3.44) and substitute in the definition of $\tilde{\gamma}$, we obtain the following expression for the expected quadratic utility

$$\mathrm{E}[U_{-1,\tilde{\gamma}}(V(\alpha_{-1,\tilde{\gamma}}))] = -V_{\text{safe}}^2 \mathrm{E}\left[\left(\frac{V_{\text{bliss}}}{V_{\text{safe}}} - (1 + \alpha_{-1,\tilde{\gamma}}X)\right)^2\right]$$

$$= -V_{\text{safe}}^2 \mathrm{E}[(\tilde{\gamma}^{-1} - \alpha_{-1,\tilde{\gamma}}X)^2]. \tag{3.45}$$

Solving for the certainty equivalent (see Exercise 3.7), we obtain

$$\frac{V_{-1,\tilde{\gamma}\ \text{certain}}(\alpha_{-1,\tilde{\gamma}})}{V_{\text{safe}}} - 1 = \frac{1}{\tilde{\gamma}}(1 - (\mathrm{E}[(1 - \tilde{\gamma}\alpha_{-1,\tilde{\gamma}}X)^2])^{1/2}).$$

Apart from a change of sign, equation (3.45) is exactly the same as (3.34).

The investment potential, as measured by quadratic utility, is

$$\text{IP}_{-1}(\alpha_{-1,1}, X) = \frac{V_{-1,1 \text{ certain}}(\alpha_{-1,1})}{V_{\text{safe}}} - 1 = 1 - (\text{E}[(1 - \alpha_{-1,1} X)^2])^{1/2}. \quad (3.46)$$

The optimal decision $\alpha_{-1,1}$ found by maximizing (3.46) represents the optimal investment per unit of local risk tolerance. For risk tolerance different from 1, the optimal portfolio scales according to (3.30):

$$\alpha_{-1,\tilde{\gamma}} = \frac{1}{\tilde{\gamma}} \alpha_{-1,1}. \quad (3.47)$$

The percentage increase in certainty equivalent due to risky investment is again directly proportional to the investor's local risk tolerance:

$$\frac{V_{-1,\tilde{\gamma} \text{ certain}}(\alpha_{-1,\tilde{\gamma}})}{V_{\text{safe}}} - 1 = \frac{1}{\tilde{\gamma}} \text{IP}_{-1}(\alpha_{-1,1}, X). \quad (3.48)$$

3.5.2 Optimal Investment

To find the optimum investment for an investor with a unit risk aversion, one must maximize the investment potential in (3.46)

$$\max_{\alpha}(1 - (\text{E}[(1 - \alpha X)^2])^{1/2}),$$

which is equivalent to solving

$$\min_{\alpha}(\text{E}[(1 - \alpha X)^2])^{1/2},$$

which in turn is equivalent to maximizing the normalized quadratic utility

$$\min_{\alpha} u(\alpha) = \min_{\alpha} \text{E}[(1 - \alpha X)^2]. \quad (3.49)$$

We could write down the first-order conditions for (3.49) straight away, but it is useful to get α outside of the expectation E[.] before we attempt any optimization. First, we will expand the round bracket inside the expectation:

$$u(\alpha) = \text{E}[1 - 2\alpha X + \alpha^2 X^2]. \quad (3.50)$$

Expression (3.50) can be simplified further by using elementary properties of expectation:

$$u(\alpha) = 1 - 2\alpha \text{E}[X] + \alpha^2 \text{E}[X^2]. \quad (3.51)$$

Now is the right time to write down the first-order conditions of $\min_\alpha u(\alpha)$:

$$0 = u'(\alpha) = 2\alpha \text{E}[X^2] - 2\text{E}[X]. \quad (3.52)$$

Solving for α in (3.52) we obtain

$$\alpha_{-1,1 \text{ opt}} = \frac{\text{E}[X]}{\text{E}[X^2]}. \quad (3.53)$$

Now substitute the optimal portfolio decision (3.53) into the expression for the maximum investment potential, (3.46):

$$\text{IP}_{-1}(X) = 1 - \left(1 - \frac{(\text{E}[X])^2}{\text{E}[X^2]}\right)^{1/2}. \quad (3.54)$$

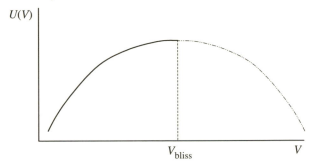

Figure 3.5. Every quadratic utility has a bliss point, here V_{bliss}, beyond which the utility decreases with increasing wealth. The decreasing part contradicts our assumption that investors prefer more wealth to less.

Let us summarize the main findings so far.

The quadratic utility optimization admits a general closed-form solution. The maximum investment potential is

$$\text{IP}_{-1}(X) = 1 - \left(1 - \frac{(\text{E}[X])^2}{\text{E}[X^2]}\right)^{1/2} \tag{3.55}$$

and the optimal portfolio per unit of local risk tolerance is

$$\alpha_{-1,1\,\text{opt}} = \frac{\text{E}[X]}{\text{E}[X^2]}. \tag{3.56}$$

For local risk aversion different from 1, we have the standard scaling properties of the HARA utility:

$$\underbrace{\frac{\max_{\alpha_{-1,\bar{\gamma}}} V_{-1,\bar{\gamma}\,\text{certain}}(\alpha_{\gamma,\bar{\gamma}})}{V_{\text{safe}}} - 1}_{\substack{\text{maximum percentage increase in certainty}\\ \text{equivalent due to risky investment}}} = \underbrace{\frac{1}{\bar{\gamma}}}_{\substack{\text{local risk}\\ \text{tolerance}}} \times \underbrace{\text{IP}_{-1}(X)}_{\substack{\text{baseline}\\ \text{investment}\\ \text{potential}}}. \tag{3.57}$$

The corresponding optimal investment strategy is

$$\alpha_{-1,\bar{\gamma}\,\text{opt}} = \frac{1}{\bar{\gamma}}\alpha_{-1,1\,\text{opt}}. \tag{3.58}$$

3.5.3 *Quadratic Utility as an Approximation to the CRRA Utility*

If the risky investment is relatively small, the resulting wealth will not depart dramatically from the risk-free wealth V_{safe}. In such circumstances one can approximate the CRRA utility by a quadratic utility around the risk-free wealth V_{safe} by writing down a second-order Taylor expansion at V_{safe}. The required algebra is in Exercise 3.8. However, formal computations are not really necessary. The original utility and its quadratic approximation share the value of the first two derivatives at V_{safe}; therefore, they also share the value of local risk aversion at V_{safe}. This tells us that we should expect the portfolio decisions per unit of local risk tolerance to be similar.

The same goes for the percentage increase in certainty equivalent per unit of risk tolerance, in other words, we expect the investment potentials IP_γ and IP_{-1} to be similar.

An HARA utility with local risk aversion $\tilde{\gamma}$ can be approximated by a quadratic utility with local risk aversion $\tilde{\gamma}$. As a consequence

$$\alpha_{\gamma,1 \text{ opt}} \approx \alpha_{-1,1 \text{ opt}}, \qquad IP_\gamma \approx IP_{-1},$$

as long as $\alpha_{\gamma,1 \text{ opt}}$ is small.

Returning to the numerical example of Section 3.4.6, the optimal investment dictated by a quadratic utility is

$$\alpha_{-1,1 \text{ opt}} = \frac{E[X]}{E[X^2]} = \frac{0.5(0.18 - 0.12)}{0.5(0.18^2 + 0.12^2)} = 1.282$$

compared with $\alpha_{\gamma,1}$ of around 1.37 in Table 3.1. The investment potential generated by a quadratic utility is

$$IP_{-1} = 1 - \sqrt{1 - \frac{(E[X])^2}{E[X^2]}} = 1 - \sqrt{1 - \frac{0.5^2(0.18 - 0.12)^2}{0.5(0.18^2 + 0.12^2)}} = 0.0194,$$

compared with an IP_γ in Table 3.1 of around 0.02.

3.6   Reporting Investment Potential in Terms of Sharpe Ratios

3.6.1   The Sharpe Ratio

Equation (3.57) shows that assets with the same value of

$$1 - \frac{(E[X])^2}{E[X^2]} \tag{3.59}$$

will lead to the same improvement in expected quadratic utility. Practitioners like to work with the expected excess return $\mu_X = E[X]$ and the variance of the excess return $\sigma_X^2 = E[X^2] - (E[X])^2$; let us therefore express (3.59) in terms of these two quantities:

$$1 - \frac{(E[X])^2}{E[X^2]} = \frac{E[X^2] - (E[X])^2}{E[X^2] - (E[X])^2 + (E[X])^2}$$

$$= \frac{\sigma_X^2}{\sigma_X^2 + \mu_X^2} = \frac{1}{1 + (\mu_X/\sigma_X)^2}. \tag{3.60}$$

We can now see that the certainty equivalent wealth depends on the risky return through μ_X/σ_X; this quantity is known as the **Sharpe ratio** of the risky return and is denoted $SR(X)$.

Table 3.2.   Asset A stochastically dominated by asset B.

Probability	$\frac{1}{6}$	$\frac{1}{2}$	$\frac{1}{3}$
Excess return of asset A	-1%	1%	2%
Excess return of asset B	-1%	1%	11%

The Sharpe ratio is closely related to quadratic utility; there is a one-to-one relationship between the maximum quadratic utility attainable in a market and the market Sharpe ratio:

$$\frac{\max_{\alpha_{-1,\tilde{\gamma}}} V_{-1,\tilde{\gamma}\text{ certain}}(\alpha_{-1,\tilde{\gamma}})}{V_{\text{safe}}} - 1 = \frac{1}{\tilde{\gamma}}(1 - (1 + \mathrm{SR}^2(X))^{-1/2}). \qquad (3.61)$$

Even though the investment potential is a very useful measure of investment opportunities, most practitioners prefer to use the Sharpe ratio. From (3.60) and (3.55) we can find a simple conversion formula,

$$\mathrm{IP}_{-1} = 1 - (1 + \mathrm{SR}^2)^{-1/2},$$

which simplifies further when SR is small,

$$\mathrm{IP}_{-1} = \tfrac{1}{2}\mathrm{SR}^2 + o(\mathrm{SR}^2). \qquad (3.62)$$

Conversely,

$$\mathrm{SR} = ((1 - \mathrm{IP}_{-1})^{-2} - 1)^{1/2} = \sqrt{2\mathrm{IP}_{-1}} + o(\sqrt{\mathrm{IP}_{-1}}).$$

By substituting (3.60) into (3.49), we obtain the computational definition of the Sharpe ratio:

$$\min_{\alpha_{-1,1}} \mathrm{E}[(1 - \alpha_{-1,1}X)^2] = \frac{1}{1 + \mathrm{SR}^2(X)}. \qquad (3.63)$$

The optimal $\alpha_{-1,1}$ in (3.63) maximizes the Sharpe ratio and gives the optimal portfolio decision per unit of risk tolerance for an investor with quadratic utility. We will see in Section 4.6 that with multiple assets, too, the quadratic utility identifies the highest Sharpe ratio available in the market.

3.6.2   Problems with the Standard Sharpe Ratio

Consider two assets A and B with excess returns as given in Table 3.2. Asset B performs no worse than asset A in all states; one would therefore expect the Sharpe ratio of B to outperform the Sharpe ratio of A, because any investor is better off using asset B rather than asset A.

Let us now calculate the two Sharpe ratios. For asset A we have

$$\mathrm{E}[X_A] = -1 \times \tfrac{1}{6} + 1 \times \tfrac{1}{2} + 2 \times \tfrac{1}{3} = 1,$$
$$\mathrm{E}[X_A^2] = (-1)^2 \times \tfrac{1}{6} + 1^2 \times \tfrac{1}{2} + 2^2 \times \tfrac{1}{3} = 2,$$
$$\sigma_{X_A}^2 = \mathrm{E}[X_A^2] - (\mathrm{E}[X_A])^2 = 1,$$

$$\text{SR}(X_A) = \frac{\text{E}[X_A]}{\sigma_{X_A}} = \frac{1}{1} = 1,$$

and for asset B we obtain

$$\text{E}[X_B] = -1 \times \tfrac{1}{6} + 1 \times \tfrac{1}{2} + 11 \times \tfrac{1}{3} = 4,$$

$$\text{E}[X_B^2] = (-1)^2 \times \tfrac{1}{6} + 1^2 \times \tfrac{1}{2} + 11^2 \times \tfrac{1}{3} = 41,$$

$$\sigma_{X_B}^2 = \text{E}[X_B^2] - (\text{E}[X_B])^2 = 41 - 4^2 = 25,$$

$$\text{SR}(X_B) = \frac{\text{E}[X_B]}{\sigma_{X_B}} = \tfrac{4}{5} = 0.8.$$

Surprisingly, as measured by the Sharpe ratio, *asset B appears less attractive than asset A*: $\text{SR}(X_B) < \text{SR}(X_A)$!

3.6.3   The Bliss Point Condition

The previous example illustrates that the Sharpe ratio is *not* a good reward-for-risk measure; its relationship with the quadratic utility explains why this is the case. A quadratic utility has a bliss point: one is penalized for achieving wealth beyond this point. The penalty will not be incurred as long as

$$V(\alpha_{-1,\tilde{\gamma}\text{ opt}}) \leqslant V_{\text{bliss}}. \tag{3.64}$$

Now substitute from (3.43) and (3.58) into (3.64) to express the optimal wealth in terms of the excess return:

$$V_{\text{safe}}\left(1 + \tilde{\gamma}^{-1}\frac{\text{E}[X]}{\text{E}[X^2]}X\right) \leqslant V_{\text{bliss}}. \tag{3.65}$$

Divide (3.65) by $V_{\text{safe}} > 0$, subtract 1 from both sides and use (3.42) to obtain

$$\tilde{\gamma}^{-1}\frac{\text{E}[X]}{\text{E}[X^2]}X \leqslant \tilde{\gamma}^{-1}. \tag{3.66}$$

The whole analysis only makes sense if $\tilde{\gamma}$ is positive, in which case (3.66) simplifies to

$$\text{E}[X]X \leqslant \text{E}[X^2]. \tag{3.67}$$

Finally, let us denote by x_{max} the highest possible value of the excess return and by x_{min} the lowest possible value of the excess return and restate the bliss point condition (3.67) in terms of x_{max} and x_{min}:

$$\text{E}[X]x_{\text{max}} \leqslant \text{E}[X^2] \quad \text{if } \text{E}[X] > 0, \tag{3.68}$$

$$\text{E}[X]x_{\text{min}} \geqslant \text{E}[X^2] \quad \text{if } \text{E}[X] < 0. \tag{3.69}$$

Most of the time one deals with risky assets that have positive risk premiums, $\text{E}[X] > 0$; therefore, the bliss point condition usually takes the form (3.68).

Let us examine assets A and B in the light of the bliss point condition (3.68). For asset A the bliss point condition is satisfied,

$$\underbrace{\text{E}[X_A]}_{1}\underbrace{x_{A\,\text{max}}}_{2} \leqslant \underbrace{\text{E}[X_A^2]}_{2},$$

whereas for asset B it is violated,

$$\underbrace{E[X_B]}_{4}\,\underbrace{x_{B\,max}}_{11} \not\leq \underbrace{E[X_B^2]}_{41}.$$

The optimal wealth in market A does not extend beyond the bliss point, whereas in market B it does. This is why asset A achieves a higher Sharpe ratio than the unambiguously more attractive asset B.

To conclude, as long as $V(\alpha_{-1,\tilde{\gamma}\,\text{opt}}) < V_{\text{bliss}}$, the Sharpe ratio is a meaningful reward-for-risk measure. For excess returns that do not meet conditions (3.68) and (3.69), the optimal wealth will go beyond the bliss point and the expected quadratic utility will therefore understate the true value of the investment to an individual who prefers more to less. By virtue of (3.61), the Sharpe ratio, as an equivalent expression of expected utility, will understate the true investment potential associated with the risky asset.

3.6.4 A Better Alternative: the Arbitrage-Adjusted Sharpe Ratio

We concluded in the previous section that the expected quadratic utility is made *worse* by all states in which the excess return X exceeds $E[X^2]/E[X]$. One can alleviate this problem by performing the following thought experiment.

The investor will increase her expected utility by setting aside part of her wealth when returns are high (when her wealth exceeds the bliss point). Suppose the investor sets aside that part of the excess return which exceeds the value of x_{cap}. Effectively, we now have a new distribution of the excess return X_{cap} such that $\max(X_{\text{cap}}) = x_{\text{cap}}$. Let us perform the optimal investment analysis with X_{cap} instead of X. The Sharpe ratio determining the maximum expected quadratic utility is given by

$$\frac{(E[X_{\text{cap}}])}{\sqrt{E[X_{\text{cap}}^2] - (E[X_{\text{cap}}])^2}} \tag{3.70}$$

and the bliss point condition becomes

$$x_{\text{cap}}E[X_{\text{cap}}] \leqslant E[X_{\text{cap}}^2]. \tag{3.71}$$

At the beginning the investor will set x_{cap} at x_{max}. If the bliss point condition (3.71) is satisfied, the standard Sharpe ratio is an appropriate reward-for-risk measure. If, however, (3.71) is violated, then setting x_{cap} a little lower will improve the Sharpe ratio in (3.70), because we will only dispose of wealth above the bliss point. Intuitively, the investor should stop lowering the truncation point x_{cap} as soon as

$$x_{\text{cap}}E[X_{\text{cap}}] = E[X_{\text{cap}}^2]. \tag{3.72}$$

At this point one has decomposed the original excess return X into two parts,

$$X = X_{\text{cap}} + (X - X_{\text{cap}}),$$

where $X - X_{\text{cap}}$ is the non-negative amount of money one is setting aside and X_{cap} achieves the highest possible Sharpe ratio without requiring extra resources. We

Table 3.3.   Distribution of an excess return X.

x	-25%	-15%	-5%	5%	15%	25%	35%
$P(X = x)$	0.01	0.04	0.25	0.40	0.25	0.04	0.01

Table 3.4.   Decomposition of excess return into the arbitrage component and the maximum Sharpe ratio component.

X_{cap}	-25%	-15%	-5%	5%	15%	24.04%	24.04%
$X - X_{\text{cap}}$	0%	0%	0%	0%	0%	0.96%	10.96%
x	-25%	-15%	-5%	5%	15%	25%	35%
$P(X = x)$	0.01	0.04	0.25	0.40	0.25	0.04	0.01

can think of X_{cap} as the pure Sharpe ratio component and of $(X - X_{\text{cap}})$ as the pure arbitrage component of X,

$$X = \underbrace{X_{\text{cap}}}_{\text{pure Sharpe ratio part}} + \underbrace{(X - X_{\text{cap}})}_{\text{pure arbitrage part}},$$

$$\text{SR}_{\text{A}}(X) \triangleq \text{SR}(X_{\text{cap}}),$$

and we define the **arbitrage-adjusted Sharpe ratio** $\text{SR}_{\text{A}}(X)$ as the maximum Sharpe ratio when part of the return can be set aside into an arbitrage fund.

Example 3.3. Consider a risky security with the distribution of the excess return as given in Table 3.3. Find the Sharpe ratio and the arbitrage-adjusted Sharpe ratio of this security and decompose its excess return into the pure Sharpe ratio and the pure arbitrage part.

Solution.

$$\begin{aligned} \text{E}[X] &= -25 \times 0.01 - 15 \times 0.04 - 5 \times 0.25 + 5 \times 0.4 \\ &\quad + 15 \times 0.25 + 25 \times 0.04 + 35 \times 0.01 \\ &= 5.0, \\ \text{E}[X^2] &= 25^2 \times 0.01 + 15^2 \times 0.04 + 5^2 \times 0.25 + 5^2 \times 0.4 \\ &\quad + 15^2 \times 0.25 + 25^2 \times 0.04 + 35^2 \times 0.01 \\ &= 125.0. \end{aligned}$$

The standard Sharpe ratio is

$$\text{SR}(X) = \frac{5}{\sqrt{125 - 5^2}} = 0.5.$$

Now let us examine the bliss point condition (3.68),

$$\underbrace{x_{\max}}_{35} \underbrace{\text{E}[X]}_{5} \not\lessgtr \underbrace{\text{E}[X^2]}_{125}.$$

In the present case the optimal wealth exceeds the bliss point. We will guess that the optimal truncation point x_{cap} occurs below 25% and find x_{cap} from the condition (3.72). First we must evaluate $E[X_{cap}]$,

$$E[X_{cap}] = -25 \times 0.01 - 15 \times 0.04 - 5 \times 0.25 + 5 \times 0.4 + 15 \times 0.25$$
$$+ x_{cap} \times 0.04 + x_{cap} \times 0.01$$
$$= 3.65 + 0.05x_{cap}, \tag{3.73}$$

then evaluate $E[X_{cap}^2]$,

$$E[X_{cap}^2] = 25^2 \times 0.01 + 15^2 \times 0.04 + 5^2 \times 0.25 + 5^2 \times 0.4$$
$$+ 15^2 \times 0.25 + x_{cap}^2 \times 0.04 + x_{cap}^2 \times 0.01$$
$$= 87.75 + 0.05x_{cap}^2,$$

and finally solve for x_{cap} from (3.72),

$$x_{cap}E[X_{cap}] = E[X_{cap}^2],$$
$$x_{cap}(3.65 + 0.05x_{cap}) = 87.75 + 0.05x_{cap}^2,$$
$$x_{cap} = \frac{87.75}{3.65} = 24.041.$$

This means that all the returns in excess of 24.04% should be set aside into an arbitrage fund. The decomposition into the pure Sharpe ratio and the pure arbitrage part is given in Table 3.4.

The arbitrage-adjusted Sharpe ratio is

$$SR_A(X) = SR(X_{cap}) = \frac{E[X_{cap}]}{\sqrt{E[X_{cap}^2] - (E[X_{cap}])^2}}.$$

This can be simplified by substituting for X_{cap}^2 from (3.72) and dividing both the numerator and denominator by $E[X_{cap}]$

$$SR_A(X) = \frac{1}{\sqrt{(x_{cap}/E[X_{cap}]) - 1}}. \tag{3.74}$$

It remains to evaluate $E[X_{cap}]$ from (3.73)

$$E[X_{cap}] = 3.65 + 0.05 \times 24.041 = 4.852$$

and substitute this value into (3.74) to find the arbitrage-adjusted Sharpe ratio,

$$SR_A(X) = \frac{1}{\sqrt{(24.041/4.852) - 1}} = 0.503.$$

3.6.5 Arbitrage-Adjusted Sharpe Ratio and the Truncated Quadratic Utility

To formalize the intuition behind the arbitrage-adjusted Sharpe ratio, let us consider a quadratic utility truncated after the bliss point (see Figure 3.6).

The truncation in the utility function means that the investor is neither penalized nor rewarded for having wealth above V_{bliss}; therefore, the truncation acts *as if the*

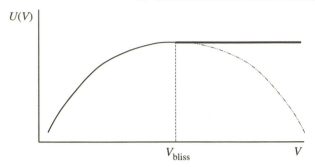

Figure 3.6.   Truncated quadratic utility.

investor is setting aside all the wealth above V_{bliss}. How much money is set aside is determined by the arbitrage-adjusted risky share $\alpha_{-1A,\tilde{\gamma}}$. Namely, a specific value of $\alpha_{-1A,\tilde{\gamma}}$ corresponds to the truncation of excess return at the point x_{cap} as follows:

$$V_{\text{safe}}(1 + \alpha_{-1A,\tilde{\gamma}} x_{\text{cap}}) = V_{\text{bliss}}.$$

Solving for x_{cap} and using definition (3.7) we obtain

$$x_{\text{cap}} = \frac{1}{\tilde{\gamma}\alpha_{-1A,\tilde{\gamma}}} = \frac{1}{\alpha_{-1A,1}}, \tag{3.75}$$

where $\alpha_{-1A,1}$ is interpreted as the arbitrage-adjusted portfolio weight per unit of local risk tolerance.

Recall from (3.63) that the standard Sharpe ratio $\text{SR}(X)$ is related to the quadratic utility maximization as follows,

$$\min_{\alpha_{-1,1}} \text{E}[(1 - \alpha_{-1,1}X)^2] = \frac{1}{1 + \text{SR}^2(X)};$$

analogously for the arbitrage-adjusted Sharpe ratio $\text{SR}_A(X)$, we will have

$$\min_{\alpha_{-1A,1}} \text{E}[(\max(0, 1 - \alpha_{-1A,1}X))^2] = \frac{1}{1 + \text{SR}_A^2(X)}. \tag{3.76}$$

Having computed $\alpha_{-1A,1 \text{ opt}}$ in (3.76) we can recover x_{cap} from (3.75):

$$x_{\text{cap}} = \frac{1}{\alpha_{-1A,1 \text{ opt}}}. \tag{3.77}$$

It can be shown that x_{cap} from (3.77) is the same as x_{cap} implied by (3.72); in fact, (3.72) is the first-order condition for the maximization of the expected truncated quadratic utility in (3.76). While (3.72) is very intuitive, it only applies in situations with one risky asset. With multiple risky assets the first-order conditions become too complicated to provide useful intuition and we have to rely on the equivalent formulation (3.76). Truncation of the utility unfortunately means that *closed-form solutions are no longer available* and that one has to use numerical techniques (see Chapter 4).

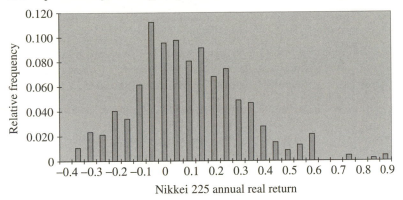

Figure 3.7. Histogram of annual real returns 1960–2000, year on year, monthly data.

3.7 The Importance of Arbitrage Adjustment

How much does it matter whether one uses the Sharpe ratio or the arbitrage-adjusted Sharpe ratio? Example 3.3 has shown that for investment in equities the difference is negligible, both in terms of investment decisions ($\alpha_{-1,1\,\mathrm{opt}} = 1/0.25$, $\alpha_{-1A,1\,\mathrm{opt}} = 1/0.2404$) and in terms of certainty equivalents ($\mathrm{SR}(X) = 0.5$, $\mathrm{SR}_A(X) = 0.503$).

The situation is very different when dealing with mispriced options. Suppose an investor buys an at-the-money call option on the Nikkei 225 Index, maturing in one year. The pay-off of the option is $\max(R - 1, 0)$, where R is the annual return on the Nikkei 225. Suppose the investor believes that the distribution of the Nikkei 225 annual returns is identical to the historical distribution depicted in Figure 3.7. When the option price is very low the option return will be strongly skewed towards high values and the bliss point condition is likely to be violated.

To examine this effect we will consider a range of prices for the option, the highest being the Black–Scholes value and the lowest being $-1/10$ of the Black–Scholes price. The lower the option price the higher the skew in option returns and the more divergence between the standard and arbitrage-adjusted Sharpe ratio. The resulting investment decisions and their value in terms of Sharpe ratios are reported in Table 3.5. The necessary computations are implemented in the GAUSS program *chapter3sect7.gss* (detailed discussion of the computational techniques can be found in Chapter 4).

One should think of the Black–Scholes value as the 'fair' value of the option. We observe that when the option is valued fairly (see the last column of Table 3.5) there is very little difference between the standard Sharpe ratio and the arbitrage-adjusted Sharpe ratio and the corresponding portfolio decisions are virtually the same. In contrast, in the second column the option is severely underpriced, and here the Sharpe ratio is a very poor guide to the true investment potential of the option.

There are two ways in which the standard Sharpe ratio understates the investment potential of the option. Firstly, it chooses the wrong α, we invest less money in the option than we should because we are selecting α using the wrong criterion (the Sharpe ratio instead of the arbitrage-adjusted Sharpe ratio). This results in a lower

Table 3.5. The standard Sharpe ratio understates the true investment potential of underpriced options. α_{-1}-portfolio choice without arbitrage adjustment, α_{-1A}-portfolio choice with arbitrage adjustment.

Option price	Arbitrage −0.0048	0.0048	0.0241	0.0361	0.0433	BS value 0.0481
$\alpha_{-1,1}$	−0.0158	0.0150	0.0632	0.0800	0.0838	0.0832
$\alpha_{-1A,1}$	−0.9804	0.0458	0.0895	0.0933	0.0900	0.0872
$SR(\alpha_{-1,1})$	0.645	0.574	0.432	0.344	0.291	0.256
$SR_A(\alpha_{-1,1})$	0.698	0.612	0.447	0.350	0.293	0.257
$SR_A(\alpha_{-1A,1})$	$+\infty$	0.716	0.462	0.352	0.294	0.257

arbitrage-adjusted Sharpe ratio, $SR_A(\alpha_{-1,1}) < SR_A(\alpha_{-1A,1})$. For example, in the second column of Table 3.5 the investment-maximizing Sharpe ratio is $\alpha_{-1} = 0.015$, whereas the risky investment maximizing the arbitrage-adjusted Sharpe ratio is three times as high, $\alpha_{-1A,1} = 0.0458$. The suboptimal investment represents a drop in arbitrage-adjusted Sharpe ratio from 0.716 to 0.612.

Secondly, the standard Sharpe ratio makes any choice of α look worse than it actually is because the standard Sharpe ratio quite unreasonably penalizes high returns, $SR(\alpha_{-1,1}) < SR_A(\alpha_{-1,1})$. For example, in the second column of Table 3.5 we have a standard Sharpe ratio of $SR(\alpha_{-1,1}) = 0.574$; however, if we decomposed the wealth generated by the investment $\alpha_{-1,1} = 0.015$ into the pure Sharpe ratio part and the pure arbitrage part, we would realize that its pure Sharpe ratio part has a value of $SR_A(\alpha_{-1,1}) = 0.612$. This could mean that a project with positively skewed returns may be rejected in favour of a less profitable project that does not exhibit skewed returns.

Matters come to a head when the option price is negative, say $-1/10$ of the Black–Scholes price (see the first column of Table 3.5). The investor is now paid to hold the option. The Sharpe ratio does not notice the arbitrage opportunity, it collects only 1.58% of the risk-free wealth from the option premium and achieves a lowly value of $SR(\alpha_{-1,1}) = 0.645$. The arbitrage-adjusted Sharpe ratio, however, adopts a much more reasonable strategy: it collects option premiums worth 98.04% of risk-free wealth and achieves the princely level of $SR_A(\alpha_{-1A,1}) = +\infty$, that is, it correctly reports that the pure Sharpe ratio part of this investment strategy is non-negative and risk-free.

3.8 Portfolio Choice with Near-Arbitrage Opportunities

The arbitrage-adjusted quadratic utility is an improvement on the standard quadratic utility, because it does not penalize high values of wealth, but it still exhibits too much risk aversion when near-arbitrage opportunities are available. In this section we will examine portfolio choices generated by the HARA class of utility functions with different values of baseline risk aversion. We will see that to generate reasonable portfolio choice when returns are highly skewed, one needs a baseline risk aversion close to 1.

Table 3.6. CRRA investment potential of a fairly priced option.

γ	(Option price)/(Black–Scholes value) $= 1$						
	$-1A$	1	2	5	15	10^4	10^8
$\alpha_{\gamma,1 \text{ opt}}$	0.145	0.242	0.223	0.209	0.202	0.198	0.198
$IP_\gamma (\alpha_{-1A,1 \text{ opt}})$	0.041	0.052	0.050	0.049	0.049	0.048	0.048
IP_γ	0.041	0.061	0.057	0.054	0.052	0.052	0.052

In Table 3.6 the option is valued at the Black–Scholes price and its return exhibits a relatively weak skew. The truncated quadratic utility reports the smallest investment potential of 4.1%, whereas the log utility reports the highest figure of 6.1%. These differences are very small if we note that the arbitrage-adjusted Sharpe ratio investment delivers an investment potential of 5.2% to a log utility investor and that these figures correspond to unit local risk aversion. A typical investor has a local risk aversion of 5 so that the resulting increase in certainty equivalent of a log investor who uses a suboptimal quadratic portfolio is $5.2\%/5 = 1.04\%$, whereas the optimal portfolio delivers $6.1\%/5 = 1.22\%$.

The situation is more dramatic when we price the option at half of its fair value (see Table 3.7). Now the portfolio maximizing arbitrage-adjusted quadratic utility is 0.15, while the optimal log utility portfolio at 0.44 is almost three times as high. Because the option is now much more attractive, the risky investment in Table 3.7 exceeds the risky investment in Table 3.6.

Suppose the option is sold at 10% of its fair value, which means the option is almost an arbitrage opportunity and its return is skewed severely towards high values. The portfolio choices are depicted in Table 3.8. An interesting phenomenon occurs. For all utility functions, apart from the log utility, the proportion of money invested in the option drops, even though the option is five times cheaper than it was in Table 3.7. To appreciate what is happening one must look at the distribution of terminal wealth corresponding to Table 3.8. This can be done by running the GAUSS program *chapter3sect8.gss*. The log investor is giving up 11.5% of her safe wealth with probability 40% to have a 60% chance of increasing her wealth by 50% or more, whereas an investor with baseline risk aversion $\gamma = 2$ only gives up 7% of her wealth with probability 40% to have a 60% chance of increasing her wealth by 30% or more.

The different level of aggressiveness can be seen more graphically when the option price drops further to almost zero, as shown in Table 3.9. The portfolio weights generated by all the utility functions, apart from the log utility, now seem inadequately small. However, the situation looks different when one examines the resulting wealth distributions. Essentially, a log investor keeps the downside exposure constant (in our case she stands to lose 12% of her safe wealth with probability 40%) and makes her upside earning potential very high (at least a 68-fold increase in wealth with probability 60%). On the other hand, an investor with baseline risk aversion $\gamma = 2$ will increase the upside potential by a smaller amount and at the same time lower the downside exposure, giving up only 1.2% of her wealth with probability 40% in compensation for a 60% chance to increase her wealth 7.6 times or more.

Table 3.7.   CRRA investment potential of an underpriced option.

	(Option price)/(Black–Scholes value) = 0.5						
γ	$-1A$	1	2	5	15	10^4	10^8
$\alpha_{\gamma,1\text{ opt}}$	0.154	0.436	0.368	0.314	0.289	0.278	0.278
$\text{IP}_\gamma(\alpha_{-1A\text{ opt}})$	0.142	0.227	0.214	0.204	0.199	0.197	0.197
IP_γ	0.142	0.362	0.295	0.255	0.239	0.231	0.231

An HARA investor with baseline risk aversion $\gamma = 1$ is much more aggressive than investors with $\gamma > 1$ when asset returns are strongly skewed towards high values. The biggest change in portfolio decisions is seen around $\gamma = 1$, while for $\gamma > 15$ all portfolio decisions are virtually identical.

3.8.1   The CARA Utility as a Limit of the HARA Utility

We noticed in the previous section that the risky investment per unit of risk tolerance $\alpha_{\gamma,1}$ does not change very much when γ is large. Similarly, the investment potential IP_γ seems to achieve a steady level as $\gamma \to +\infty$. We will now explore this phenomenon in more detail.

Suppose we have a market with finitely many states. Denote the limiting value of the optimal risky investment per unit of local risk tolerance for large values of baseline risk aversion by $\alpha_{+\infty,1\text{ opt}}$,

$$\alpha_{+\infty,1\text{ opt}} = \lim_{\gamma \to +\infty} \alpha_{\gamma,1\text{ opt}}. \tag{3.78}$$

We claim that in the absence of arbitrage the limit in (3.78) $\alpha_{+\infty,1\text{ opt}}$ exists and is finite and that it is obtained from the maximization of the negative exponential utility with the coefficient of absolute risk aversion equal to unity:

$$\alpha_{+\infty,1\text{ opt}} = \arg\min_{\alpha} \text{E}[e^{-\alpha X}]. \tag{3.79}$$

Similarly, denote the limiting value of the investment potential by IP_∞

$$\text{IP}_\infty = \lim_{\gamma \to +\infty} \text{IP}_\gamma,$$

then

$$\text{IP}_\infty = -\ln \text{E}[e^{-\alpha_{+\infty,1\text{ opt}} X}]. \tag{3.80}$$

Thus the optimal portfolio of an investor with negative exponential utility and absolute risk aversion a is identical to the portfolio of an investor with the HARA utility $\alpha_{\gamma,\tilde{\gamma}}$, $\tilde{\gamma} = a$ and γ very large.

The quantity $\sqrt{2\text{IP}_\infty}$ is known as the **Hodges ratio** HR and it has the notable property of being equal to the standard Sharpe ratio when excess returns X are normally distributed. Furthermore, the Hodges ratio has a very simple relationship with investment potential which copies the asymptotic behaviour of Sharpe ratio in (3.62),

$$\text{IP}_\infty = \tfrac{1}{2}\text{HR}^2.$$

Table 3.8. CRRA investment potential of a severely underpriced option.

| γ | (Option price)/(Black–Scholes value) $= 0.1$ | | | | | | |
	-1A	1	2	5	15	10^4	10^8
$\alpha_{\gamma,1\text{ opt}}$	0.079	0.563	0.343	0.226	0.190	0.174	0.174
$\text{IP}_\gamma\,(\alpha_{-1\text{A opt}})$	0.289	0.759	0.663	0.588	0.551	0.532	0.532
IP_γ	0.289	2.189	1.128	0.771	0.663	0.617	0.617

Table 3.9. CRRA investment potential of a near-arbitrage opportunity.

| γ | (Option price)/(Black–Scholes value) $= 0.001$ | | | | | | |
	-1A	1	2	5	15	10^4	10^8
$\alpha_{\gamma,1\text{ opt}}$	0.002	0.590	0.058	0.016	0.010	0.009	0.009
$\text{IP}_\gamma\,(\alpha_{-1\text{A opt}})$	0.368	1.570	1.211	0.955	0.845	0.793	0.793
IP_γ	0.368	48.669	2.726	1.268	1.006	0.911	0.911

The results (3.79), (3.80) are not difficult to show if we accept as given that there is a finite number $\tilde{\alpha}$ such that $\lim_{\gamma\to+\infty}\alpha_{\gamma,1}=\tilde{\alpha}$. Then we can write

$$\lim_{\gamma\to+\infty}\text{E}\left[\left(1+\frac{\alpha_{\gamma,1\text{ opt}}}{\gamma}X\right)^{1-\gamma}\right]=\lim_{\gamma\to+\infty}\text{E}\left[\left(1+\left(\frac{\tilde{\alpha}}{\gamma}+o\left(\frac{1}{\gamma}\right)\right)X\right)^{1-\gamma}\right].$$

With finitely many states we can take the limit inside the expectation,

$$=\text{E}\left[\underbrace{\lim_{\gamma\to+\infty}\left(1+\left(\frac{\tilde{\alpha}}{\gamma}+o\left(\frac{1}{\gamma}\right)\right)X\right)^{1-\gamma}}_{I}\right].$$

Now compute the Taylor expansion of

$$\frac{\ln I}{1-\gamma}=\ln\left(1+\left(\frac{\tilde{\alpha}}{\gamma}+o\left(\frac{1}{\gamma}\right)\right)X\right)$$

with respect to $1/\gamma$ for $1/\gamma$ very small,

$$\frac{\ln I}{1-\gamma}=\frac{\tilde{\alpha}}{\gamma}X+o\left(\frac{1}{\gamma}\right),$$

which implies

$$\lim_{\gamma\to+\infty}\ln I=-\tilde{\alpha}X.$$

Because exponential is a continuous function we have

$$\lim_{\gamma\to+\infty}I=\lim_{\gamma\to+\infty}e^{\ln I}=e^{\lim_{\gamma\to+\infty}\ln I}=e^{-\tilde{\alpha}X},$$

$$\lim_{\gamma\to+\infty}\text{E}\left[\left(1+\frac{\alpha_{\gamma,1\text{ opt}}}{\gamma}X\right)^{1-\gamma}\right]=\text{E}[e^{-\tilde{\alpha}X}],$$

which proves the main part of our claim. It remains to show that $\tilde{\alpha}$ maximizes the expression $\text{E}[e^{-\tilde{\alpha}X}]$, but that is easy because if $\tilde{\alpha}$ did not maximize $\text{E}[e^{-\tilde{\alpha}X}]$, then

$$\alpha_\gamma=(\tilde{\alpha}/\gamma)+o(1/\gamma)$$

could not be the optimal portfolio for $E[(1 + \alpha_\gamma X)^{1-\gamma}]$ when γ is large. The proof of (3.80) is in Exercise 3.12.

3.9   Generalization of the Sharpe Ratio

It turns out that the definition of the Sharpe ratio can be meaningfully extended to the entire family of HARA utility functions by suitably redefining (3.63),

$$1 + \text{SR}^2 = (1 - \text{IP}_{-1})^{-2}, \tag{3.81}$$

for all values of γ. We will denote by SR_γ the **generalized Sharpe ratio** of an investor with baseline relative risk aversion γ, and define

$$1 + \text{SR}_\gamma^2 \triangleq \left(1 + \frac{\text{IP}_\gamma}{\gamma}\right)^{2\gamma}, \tag{3.82}$$

whereby the standard Sharpe ratio becomes a special case of SR_γ with $\gamma = -1$. In the limit $\gamma \to \infty$,

$$1 + \text{SR}_\infty^2 = e^{2\text{IP}_\infty},$$

with IP_∞ given in (3.80).

The generalized Sharpe ratio (3.82) has four important properties:

(1) SR_{-1} is the standard Sharpe ratio;

(2) $\text{SR}_\gamma \approx \text{SR}_{-1}$ for SR_γ small;

(3) for all values of γ, SR_γ has the same time-scaling property: if the highest Sharpe ratio over time dt is $\text{SR}_\gamma \sqrt{dt}$, then the highest Sharpe ratio over time T is $\sqrt{\exp(\text{SR}_\gamma^2 T) - 1}$;

(4) in the continuous-time Black–Scholes model, the SR_γ of the optimal dynamic trading strategy coincides for all γ (see Exercise 11.11).

3.9.1   *Summary of Computational Definitions*

Below we summarize the definitions of HARA investment potential for arbitrary γ. For $\gamma < 0$ we give two versions, one with and one without arbitrage adjustment:

$$\text{IP}_\gamma = \gamma\left(\left(\min_\alpha E[(1 + \alpha X)^{1-\gamma}]\right)^{1/(1-\gamma)} - 1\right) \quad \text{for } \gamma > 1, \tag{3.83}$$

$$\text{IP}_\gamma = \gamma\left(\left(\max_\alpha E[(1 + \alpha X)^{1-\gamma}]\right)^{1/(1-\gamma)} - 1\right) \quad \text{for } 0 < \gamma < 1, \tag{3.84}$$

$$\text{IP}_\gamma = \exp\left(\max_\alpha E[\ln(1 + \alpha X)]\right) \quad \text{for } \gamma = 1, \tag{3.85}$$

$$\text{IP}_\gamma = \gamma\left(\left(\min_\alpha E[|1 + \alpha X|^{1-\gamma}]\right)^{1/(1-\gamma)} - 1\right) \quad \text{for } \gamma < 0, \tag{3.86}$$

$$\text{IP}_{\gamma A} = \gamma\left(\left(\min_\alpha E[(\max(1 + \alpha X, 0))^{1-\gamma}]\right)^{1/(1-\gamma)} - 1\right) \quad \text{for } \gamma < 0. \tag{3.87}$$

The optimal α from (3.83)–(3.87) divided by γ represents the optimal investment per unit of local risk aversion.

3.10 Summary

- When large sums are at stake investors appear to be risk averse, putting more weight on downside deviations from average wealth than on equally likely upside deviations. This attitude to risk can be captured using a concave and increasing function, called a utility function. Particularly useful is the HARA utility

$$U(\text{risky wealth}) = \frac{\text{safe wealth}^{1-\gamma}}{1-\gamma}\left(\frac{\gamma}{\tilde{\gamma}} + \frac{\text{risky wealth}}{\text{safe wealth}} - 1\right)^{1-\gamma},$$

  characterized by two coefficients of relative risk aversion γ and $\tilde{\gamma}$. The local risk aversion $\tilde{\gamma}$, which ranges from about 3 for aggressive investors to about 10 for conservative investors, governs attitude to small symmetric risks. The baseline risk aversion γ only comes into play when the distribution of returns is highly skewed; its value is likely to be close to 1. Important special cases are the quadratic utility, $\gamma = -1$, and the exponential utility, $\gamma = \pm\infty$.

- One evaluates a risky distribution of wealth by looking at its expected utility, or rather the certainty equivalent of it. Certainty equivalent is the non-random level of wealth that gives a utility equal to the expected utility. The certainty equivalent of an HARA investor is indirectly proportional to her local risk aversion,

$$\frac{\text{maximum certainty equivalent}_{\gamma,\tilde{\gamma}}}{\text{safe wealth}} - 1$$
$$= \frac{1}{\tilde{\gamma}}\left(\frac{\text{maximum certainty equivalent}_{\gamma,1}}{\text{safe wealth}} - 1\right),$$

  as is the optimal portfolio choice,

$$\text{optimal portfolio}_{\gamma,\tilde{\gamma}} = \frac{1}{\tilde{\gamma}}\text{optimal portfolio}_{\gamma,1}.$$

- The percentage increase in certainty equivalent per unit of local risk tolerance is called the investment potential,

$$\text{investment potential}_{\gamma} = \left(\frac{\text{maximum certainty equivalent}_{\gamma,1}}{\text{safe wealth}} - 1\right).$$

  For relatively unattractive investment opportunities the investment potential (almost) does not depend on γ.

- The quadratic utility formally looks like the HARA utility with $\gamma = -1$. For all practical purposes it represents the only case that can be solved in closed form when markets are incomplete:

$$\text{optimal portfolio}_{-1,1} = \frac{E[\text{excess return}]}{E[(\text{excess return})^2]},$$

$$\text{investment potential}_{-1} = 1 - \sqrt{1 - \frac{(E[\text{excess return}])^2}{E[(\text{excess return})^2]}}.$$

- The Sharpe ratio is a popular reward-for-risk measure. It is computed as the ratio of the mean excess return of a risky security to the standard deviation of that return. The Sharpe ratio is closely related to the certainty equivalent wealth of the quadratic utility investor,

$$\text{investment potential}_{-1} = 1 - (1 + (\text{Sharpe ratio})^2)^{-1/2},$$

  and via the quadratic approximation it can be related to the certainty equivalent gain of other utility functions. In particular, for the HARA utility we have that

$$\text{investment potential}_\gamma \approx \tfrac{1}{2}(\text{Sharpe ratio})^2$$

  when the investment potential is small.
- The Sharpe ratio is not a good reward-for-risk measure when returns are asymmetric or exhibit fat tails. In this case the Sharpe ratio can actually get worse as the distribution of the returns improves. To remedy this problem one can decompose the excess return into a pure Sharpe ratio part and a pure arbitrage part. Computationally, this procedure is carried out by maximizing the truncated quadratic utility. The pure Sharpe ratio then replaces the standard Sharpe ratio as a consistent reward-for-risk measure.
- The portfolio choices generated by the truncated quadratic utility are too conservative when near-arbitrage opportunities are available. A better alternative seems to be an HARA utility with γ close to 1. To be able to report investment potential in commonly accepted units one can extend the definition of the Sharpe ratio to $\gamma \neq -1$ by postulating that

$$1 + (\text{Sharpe ratio}_\gamma)^2 = \left(1 + \frac{\text{investment potential}_\gamma}{\gamma}\right)^{2\gamma}.$$

  For small symmetric risks one will always have

$$\text{Sharpe ratio}_\gamma \approx \text{Sharpe ratio}_{-1}.$$

- For γ large the HARA utility transforms into a negative exponential utility with absolute risk aversion $\tilde{\gamma}$.

3.11 Notes

Von Neumann and Morgenstern (1944) proposed ranking of risky investment opportunities by expected utility. Markowitz (1952) is a first practical application of quadratic utility in portfolio selection. A number of authors have examined and confirmed the robustness of portfolio choice implied by different utility functions (see Grinold 1999; Kallberg and Ziemba 1983; Kroll et al. 1984; Pulley 1981). The bliss-point condition for quadratic utility was first examined in Wippern (1971). The HARA class of utility functions appears in Ingersoll (1987), who also shows that the exponential utility is obtained in the limit $\gamma \to \infty$. The use of the Sharpe ratio as a performance evaluation measure was suggested in Sharpe (1966). The undesirable properties of Sharpe ratio and its generalization in the sense of changing the utility function from quadratic to another (exponential) appear in Hodges (1998). The arbitrage-adjusted Sharpe ratio and the HARA class Sharpe ratios appear in Černý (2003). Cochrane and Saá-Requejo (2000) find option price bounds based on the absence of high arbitrage-adjusted Sharpe ratios.

Dowd (1999) uses the term generalized Sharpe ratio for the quadratic utility with multiple assets, in the following sense. Suppose one already holds asset X and in addition one has to decide between buying asset Y or Z. Then Y is more attractive than Z if $SR(X, Y) > SR(X, Z)$. The quantity $SR(X, Y)$ is, in Dowd's terminology, the generalized Sharpe ratio of Y.

3.12 Exercises

Exercise 3.1 (calibrating risk aversion). Suppose we do not know the relative risk aversion of our investor. We know, however, that her financial situation is the same as in Example 3.1 and that the available assets display the same characteristics. Furthermore, we have just learned that our investor has decided to invest £300 000 in the risky asset for one year. Assuming that her preferences are described by CRRA utility, find her coefficient of relative risk aversion.

Exercise 3.2 (rational investor and lottery). Another investor in an identical financial situation buys a lottery ticket for £1 with a one-in-two-million chance of winning £1 000 000. Assuming power utility, compute her coefficient of risk aversion. How much better off is this investor with the lottery ticket? How much worse off would she be if her preferences were described by a power utility with $\gamma = 5$?

Exercise 3.3 (impact of the risk-free rate on borrowing). Consider an investor with an initial wealth of $V_0 = $ £500, an annual income of $y = $ £30 000 and a CRRA utility with $\gamma = 5$. Assets are the same as in Example 3.1. Describe the optimal investment. How does the optimal investment change if the rate for risk-free borrowing goes up from 2 to 4% per annum?

Exercise 3.4 (utility or certainty equivalent?). We have searched for the optimal investment by maximizing the expected utility of the corresponding wealth distribution. Yet we prefer to measure the performance of an investment using the money equivalent of the expected utility. Surely, to be consistent, we should be maximizing the money equivalent rather than the expected utility itself! Is there a contradiction in our approach?

Exercise 3.5 (the quadratic utility as an approximation of the power utility). Use the histogram of the Nikkei 225 Real Annual Returns to find an optimal investment strategy for an investor with an initial wealth of ¥100 000 000 and an annual income of ¥10 000 000. Assume a risk-free rate of 2% and a power utility with $\gamma = 5$. Compute the same investment decision when the power utility is approximated by the quadratic utility. (Hint: modify the program *chapter3sect4a.gss* by copying and pasting the distribution of Nikkei returns from the program *chapter3sect7.gss*.)

Exercise 3.6 (arbitrage-adjusted Sharpe ratio). Consider a risky security with the distribution of excess return as given in Table 3.10. Using just pen and paper find the arbitrage-adjusted Sharpe ratio of the security and decompose its excess return into a pure Sharpe ratio part and a pure arbitrage part.

Table 3.10.   Distribution of excess returns.

x	-1%	2%	11%
$P(X = x)$	$\frac{1}{3}$	$\frac{1}{3}$	$\frac{1}{3}$

Exercise 3.7 (certainty equivalent wealth of expected quadratic utility). Solve the equation

$$-(V_{\text{bliss}} - V_{-1,\tilde{\gamma} \text{ certain}})^2 = -V_{\text{safe}}^2 \mathrm{E}[(\tilde{\gamma}^{-1} - \alpha_{-1,\tilde{\gamma}} X)^2]$$

for $V_{-1,\tilde{\gamma} \text{ certain}}/V_{\text{safe}}$.

Exercise 3.8 (approximation of the CRRA utility by the quadratic utility). Use a quadratic utility to approximate the CRRA utility around the risk-free wealth V_{safe}. What is the value of the local risk aversion of the approximating utility?

Exercise 3.9 (the logarithmic utility as a limit of the power utility). Find the value of $(a^X - 1)/x$ as x approaches 0. Do this by expressing the numerator as a first-order Taylor expansion around $x = 0$. Based on your result, what is the value of

$$\frac{w^{1-\gamma} - 1}{1 - \gamma}$$

as γ approaches 1?

Exercise 3.10 (the CARA utility). Find $U(w)$ such that

$$\frac{U(w)}{U(w_0)} = f(w - w_0)$$

for all w and w_0 with f unspecified.

Exercise 3.11 (the CRRA utility). Find $U(w)$ such that

$$\frac{U(w)}{U(w_0)} = f\left(\frac{w}{w_0}\right)$$

for all w and w_0 with f unspecified.

Exercise 3.12 (investment potential with large baseline risk aversion). Suppose that

$$\lim_{\gamma \to \infty} a(\gamma) = a$$

is finite. Show that

$$\lim_{\gamma \to \infty} \gamma (a(\gamma)^{1/(1-\gamma)} - 1) = -\ln a.$$

Numerical Techniques for Optimal Portfolio Selection in Incomplete Markets

One would not need special numerical techniques if all investment decisions could be performed using the quadratic utility. The previous chapter highlighted that the quadratic utility is a very flexible tool that works well in many commonly encountered market situations, particularly with equities. However, we also saw that the quadratic utility will lead to underinvestment when security returns are skewed, which is particularly true with mispriced options.

This chapter provides an introduction to the numerical algorithms necessary for the analysis of optimal investment decisions with a non-quadratic utility in an incomplete market. We used these algorithms to generate numerical examples in the previous chapter; now we will study them in their own right.

Sections 4.1–4.3 discuss optimal portfolio selection for a CRRA agent and one risky asset; the resulting numerical algorithm is adapted to the HARA utility in Section 4.4. In Section 4.5 we allow for several risky assets, and finally in Section 4.6 we examine closed-form solutions to optimal portfolio selection with multiple assets and a quadratic utility.

4.1 Sensitivity Analysis of Portfolio Decisions with the CRRA Utility

Whenever one solves optimization problems, it is very important to gauge the impact of a small change in the choice variable (risky portfolio share α) on the target function (certainty equivalent of expected utility relative to risk-free wealth). The purpose of such an exercise is twofold. Firstly, it quantifies the magnitude of the rounding errors. If we know that a 1% change in α causes a 0.001% change in certainty equivalent and if 0.001% precision in certainty equivalent is deemed sufficient, then we only need to report α with precision 1%, that is, instead of $\alpha_{\text{opt}} = 0.332\,291\ldots$ we will write $\alpha_{\text{opt}} = 0.332$. Secondly, suppose we are unable to compute α_{opt} quickly with arbitrary precision (such a situation is common in practice). Sensitivity analysis provides a tool for identifying optimal α with sufficient precision (there is more on this topic in Section 4.2).

4.1.1 Target Function and Optimality Condition

The investor wishes to maximize her certainty equivalent wealth. To simplify the notation let us denote the target function $F(\alpha)$,

$$F(\alpha) = \frac{V_{\gamma,\gamma\text{ certain}}(\alpha)}{V_{\text{safe}}} = (\mathrm{E}[(1 + \alpha X)^{1-\gamma}])^{1/(1-\gamma)} \quad \text{for } \gamma > 0, \ \gamma \neq 1, \quad (4.1)$$

where $\alpha = \alpha_{\gamma,\gamma}$ represents a portfolio choice of a CRRA investor with relative risk aversion γ. Before we write down the first-order conditions it is convenient to introduce notation for the expected utility $u(\alpha)$,

$$u(\alpha) \triangleq \mathrm{E}[(1 + \alpha X)^{1-\gamma}], \tag{4.2}$$

which means we can write the target function as

$$F(\alpha) = (u(\alpha))^{1/(1-\gamma)}. \tag{4.3}$$

The optimal portfolio α_{opt} is found from the first-order condition,

$$F'(\alpha_{\mathrm{opt}}) = 0. \tag{4.4}$$

Applying a chain rule for differentiation in (4.3) we obtain

$$F'(\alpha_{\mathrm{opt}}) = \underbrace{\frac{1}{1 - \gamma}(u(\alpha_{\mathrm{opt}}))^{\gamma/(1-\gamma)}}_{\neq 0}\, u'(\alpha_{\mathrm{opt}}) = 0,$$

and consequently the optimality condition simplifies to

$$u'(\alpha_{\mathrm{opt}}) = 0. \tag{4.5}$$

The optimization of certainty equivalent amounts to the optimization of expected utility.

4.1.2 *Approximately Optimal Solution*

In general it is unlikely that we will manage to solve the first-order condition (4.5) exactly; therefore, we should try to understand the magnitude of the error if we stop with α_ε such that

$$u'(\alpha_\varepsilon) = \varepsilon$$

with ε small.

Let us first of all estimate how far α_ε is from α_{opt}. If ε is small, we would expect α_ε and α_{opt} to be close to each other, close enough to use a Taylor expansion of u' around α_ε with high precision. This gives

$$u'(\alpha_{\mathrm{opt}}) = u'(\alpha_\varepsilon) + u''(\alpha_\varepsilon)(\alpha_{\mathrm{opt}} - \alpha_\varepsilon) + \tfrac{1}{2}u'''(\xi)(\alpha_{\mathrm{opt}} - \alpha_\varepsilon)^2$$

where ξ is a number between α_ε and α_{opt}. Assuming that the quadratic term is negligible, and realizing that $u'(\alpha_{\mathrm{opt}}) = 0$, we obtain

$$0 = u'(\alpha_\varepsilon) + u''(\alpha_\varepsilon)(\alpha_{\mathrm{opt}} - \alpha_\varepsilon), \qquad \alpha_{\mathrm{opt}} - \alpha_\varepsilon = \frac{-u'(\alpha_\varepsilon)}{u''(\alpha_\varepsilon)}. \tag{4.6}$$

This solves half of our problem. Namely, we now know that to compute α_{opt} with a precision of 10^{-2}, we can stop our search as soon as

$$\left|\frac{-u'(\alpha_\varepsilon)}{u''(\alpha_\varepsilon)}\right| < 10^{-2}.$$

4.1.3 Required Precision

But what precision is really necessary? It could be the case that even a minute change in α makes a large impact on the certainty equivalent. We will not know unless we can estimate the impact of the change in α on our target function. To this end we write down the second-order Taylor expansion of u:

$$u(\alpha_{\text{opt}}) = u(\alpha_\varepsilon) + u'(\alpha_\varepsilon)(\alpha_{\text{opt}} - \alpha_\varepsilon) + \tfrac{1}{2}u''(\alpha_\varepsilon)(\alpha_{\text{opt}} - \alpha_\varepsilon)^2 + \tfrac{1}{6}u'''(\xi)(\alpha_{\text{opt}} - \alpha_\varepsilon)^3. \tag{4.7}$$

Substituting from equation (4.6) we have

$$u(\alpha_{\text{opt}}) = u(\alpha_\varepsilon) - \frac{1}{2}\frac{(u'(\alpha_\varepsilon))^2}{u''(\alpha_\varepsilon)}, \tag{4.8}$$

assuming again that the last term on the right-hand side of (4.7) can be neglected.

To find the percentage difference between the optimal and the approximately optimal certainty equivalent, divide both sides of equation (4.8) by $u(\alpha_\varepsilon)$ and raise both sides to $1/(1-\gamma)$ power:

$$\underbrace{\left(\frac{u(\alpha_{\text{opt}})}{u(\alpha_\varepsilon)}\right)^{1/(1-\gamma)}}_{F(\alpha_{\text{opt}})/F(\alpha_\varepsilon)} = \left(1 - \frac{1}{2}\frac{(u'(\alpha_\varepsilon))^2}{u(\alpha_\varepsilon)u''(\alpha_\varepsilon)}\right)^{1/(1-\gamma)}.$$

One last touch, we can approximate the right-hand side using the first-order expansion of $(1+x)^{1/(1-\gamma)}$ around $x = 0$ (see Exercise 4.1):

$$\frac{F(\alpha_{\text{opt}})}{F(\alpha_\varepsilon)} - 1 = \frac{V_{\gamma,\gamma \text{ certain}}(\alpha_{\text{opt}})}{V_{\gamma,\gamma \text{ certain}}(\alpha_\varepsilon)} - 1 = -\frac{1}{2(1-\gamma)}\frac{(u'(\alpha_\varepsilon))^2}{u(\alpha_\varepsilon)u''(\alpha_\varepsilon)}. \tag{4.9}$$

Consider a CRRA investor with relative risk aversion γ and an approximately optimal portfolio α_ε such that

$$u'(\alpha_\varepsilon) = \varepsilon \approx 0.$$

The estimated distance of the approximately optimal portfolio from the optimal portfolio is

$$\alpha_{\text{opt}} - \alpha_\varepsilon = -\frac{u'(\alpha_\varepsilon)}{u''(\alpha_\varepsilon)} \tag{4.10}$$

and the estimated percentage difference in certainty equivalents is

$$\frac{V_{\gamma,\gamma \text{ certain}}(\alpha_{\text{opt}})}{V_{\gamma,\gamma \text{ certain}}(\alpha_\varepsilon)} - 1 = -\frac{1}{2(1-\gamma)}\frac{(u'(\alpha_\varepsilon))^2}{u(\alpha_\varepsilon)u''(\alpha_\varepsilon)}. \tag{4.11}$$

4.1.4 Numerical Example

Let us revisit Example 3.1 of the previous chapter to see how useful the two approximations (4.10) and (4.11) are. We have $\gamma = 5$, and the excess return X takes two values, $+18\%$ or -12%, with equal probability 0.5. The normalized expected utility is therefore

$$u(\alpha) = \text{E}[(1 + \alpha X)^{1-\gamma}] = 0.5(1 + 0.18\alpha)^{-4} + 0.5(1 - 0.12\alpha)^{-4}. \tag{4.12}$$

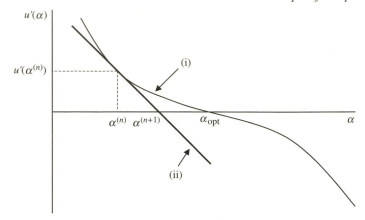

Figure 4.1. Illustration of root finding using Newton's method. (i) The exact value of $u'(\alpha)$. (ii) $u'(\alpha) = u'(\alpha^{(n)}) + u''(\alpha^{(n)})(\alpha - \alpha^{(n)})$. The line represents the first-order Taylor expansion of $u'(\alpha)$ around the point $\alpha^{(n)}$.

We will find $u'(\alpha)$ and $u''(\alpha)$ by direct evaluation:

$$u'(\alpha) = -2(0.18(1 + 0.18\alpha)^{-5} - 0.12(1 - 0.12\alpha)^{-5}), \qquad (4.13)$$

$$u''(\alpha) = 10(0.18^2(1 + 0.18\alpha)^{-6} + 0.12^2(1 - 0.12\alpha)^{-6}). \qquad (4.14)$$

The normalized optimal investment can be found directly by solving the optimality condition $u'(\alpha_{opt}) = 0$. Alternatively, one can simply scale the solution (3.12) by the ratio of initial wealth to risk-free wealth along the lines of (3.21):

$$\alpha_{opt} = \frac{\tilde{\alpha}_{opt}}{1.22} = \frac{0.332\,291}{1.22} = 0.272\,370. \qquad (4.15)$$

With α_{opt} given in (4.15), let us take an approximately optimal portfolio decision,

$$\alpha_\varepsilon = 0.273, \qquad (4.16)$$

$$\alpha_\varepsilon - \alpha_{opt} = 0.000\,63. \qquad (4.17)$$

Numerically,

$$F(\alpha_{opt}) = (u(0.272\,370))^{-1/4} = 0.844\,302\,514, \qquad (4.18)$$

$$F(\alpha_\varepsilon) = (u(0.273))^{-1/4} = 0.844\,302\,496, \qquad (4.19)$$

$$u'(\alpha_\varepsilon) = u'(0.273) = 2.641 \times 10^{-4},$$

$$u''(\alpha_\varepsilon) = u''(0.273) = 0.4188.$$

We have predicted in (4.10) that

$$\alpha_{opt} - \alpha_\varepsilon = \frac{-u'(\alpha_\varepsilon)}{u''(\alpha_\varepsilon)} = -6.306 \times 10^{-4},$$

while from (4.17) the true deviation is -6.3×10^{-4}, a very nice match.

For the target function we have predicted in (4.11)

$$\frac{F(\alpha_{opt})}{F(\alpha_\varepsilon)} - 1 = \frac{1}{8} \frac{(u'(\alpha_\varepsilon))^2}{u(\alpha_\varepsilon)u''(\alpha_\varepsilon)} = 2.115 \times 10^{-8},$$

whereas in reality substituting from (4.18) and (4.19)

$$\frac{F(\alpha_{\text{opt}})}{F(\alpha_\varepsilon)} - 1 = \frac{0.844\,302\,514}{0.844\,302\,496} - 1 = 2.13 \times 10^{-8}, \tag{4.20}$$

again spot on!

Equation (4.20) means the investor knows her certainty equivalent wealth to the last penny even though (4.17) implies that she knows the amount invested in the risky asset with a tolerance of roughly £700. It is difficult to believe that individuals optimize their certainty equivalent with a precision of 10^{-8}; one would more realistically expect a precision in the region of 10^{-3} to 10^{-5} of total financial wealth, which in turn means that the required precision in α is about 10^{-2}.

Then it must be the case that individuals cannot really make up their mind about the optimal level of α if the differences in α fall below 10^{-2}. This has important consequences for the calibration of risk aversion. Suppose the investor in our example knows her V_{certain} with precision 10^{-5}. If, in an experiment, she claims that her optimal level of α is 0.273, this level can correspond to $\gamma = 5.5$ or $\gamma = 4.5$ or any value in between because for all these values $\alpha = 0.273$ approximates the certainty equivalent of the optimal decision with tolerance 10^{-5}.

4.2 Newton's Algorithm for Optimal Investment with CRRA Utility

Let us stay with the introductory Example 3.1, characterized by equations (4.12)–(4.14):

$$u(\alpha) = 0.5(1 + 0.18\alpha)^{-4} + 0.5(1 - 0.12\alpha)^{-4},$$

$$u'(\alpha) = -2(0.18(1 + 0.18\alpha)^{-5} - 0.12(1 - 0.12\alpha)^{-5}),$$

$$u''(\alpha) = 10(0.18^2(1 + 0.18\alpha)^{-6} + 0.12^2(1 - 0.12\alpha)^{-6}).$$

In contrast to the preceding section, however, let us pretend that we do *not* know how to solve $u'(\alpha) = 0$ in closed form. How can one get a computer to solve it?

We will concentrate on a numerical root-finding algorithm called **Newton's method**. Suppose that after n steps of the numerical procedure we have an approximate solution $\alpha^{(n)}$. The idea is to approximate $u'(\alpha^{(n)})$ around $\alpha^{(n)}$ using a first-order Taylor expansion and then find the root of the approximating line instead of finding the root of $u'(\alpha)$ itself (see Figure 4.1).

Mathematically, $\alpha^{(n+1)}$ is described as the point on the Taylor expansion line that crosses the horizontal axis

$$u'(\alpha^{(n)}) + u''(\alpha^{(n)})(\alpha^{(n+1)} - \alpha^{(n)}) = 0, \tag{4.21}$$

$$\alpha^{(n+1)} = \alpha^{(n)} - \frac{u'(\alpha^{(n)})}{u''(\alpha^{(n)})}. \tag{4.22}$$

Note that the relationship between $\alpha^{(n+1)}$ and $\alpha^{(n)}$ is the same as the relationship between α_{opt} and α_ε captured in equation (4.6); in particular, we can reuse (4.11) to estimate the optimality of the approximate solution $\alpha^{(n)}$:

$$\frac{V_{\text{certain}}(\alpha_{\text{opt}})}{V_{\text{certain}}(\alpha^{(n)})} - 1 = -\frac{1}{2(1-\gamma)} \frac{(u'(\alpha^{(n)}))^2}{u(\alpha^{(n)})u''(\alpha^{(n)})}. \tag{4.23}$$

We will stop the iteration as soon as the improvement in $u(\alpha)$, or more precisely in the certainty equivalent of $u(\alpha)$, is negligible. Suppose we want to know the certainty equivalent with precision 10^{-5}, then we should stop as soon as

$$\left| \frac{V_{\text{certain}}(\alpha_{\text{opt}})}{V_{\text{certain}}(\alpha^{(n)})} - 1 \right| = |\text{error}_V(\alpha^{(n)})| < 10^{-5}. \tag{4.24}$$

Exercise 4.2 discusses why (4.24) is a sensible stopping rule.

Let us see the whole procedure in practice. A natural starting point is

$$\alpha^{(0)} = 0. \tag{4.25}$$

The zero iteration gives

$$u(0) = 1.0,$$
$$u'(0) = -0.12,$$
$$u''(0) = 0.468.$$

The error in the certainty equivalent is

$$\text{error}_V(\alpha^{(0)}) = \frac{1}{8} \frac{(-0.12)^2}{1.0 \times 0.468} = 3.8 \times 10^{-3},$$

and because it does not satisfy condition (4.24) we have to carry on. In the first iteration one obtains

$$\alpha^{(1)} = \alpha^{(0)} - \frac{u'(\alpha^{(0)})}{u''(\alpha^{(0)})} = 0 - \frac{-0.12}{0.468} = 0.2564,$$
$$u(0.2564) = 0.984\,01,$$
$$u'(0.2564) = -6.705 \times 10^{-3},$$
$$u''(0.2564) = 0.4209,$$
$$\text{error}_V(\alpha^{(1)}) = \frac{1}{8} \frac{(-6.705 \times 10^{-3})^2}{0.9840 \times 0.4209} = 1.4 \times 10^{-5}.$$

Since the error is larger than the tolerance we have set in (4.24), we need to compute another iteration:

$$\alpha^{(2)} = \alpha^{(1)} - \frac{u'(\alpha^{(1)})}{u''(\alpha^{(1)})} = 0.2564 - \frac{-6.705 \times 10^{-3}}{0.4209} = 0.2723,$$
$$u(0.2723) = 0.983\,96,$$
$$u'(0.2723) = -2.557 \times 10^{-5},$$
$$u''(0.2723) = 0.2814,$$
$$\text{error}_V(\alpha^{(2)}) = \frac{1}{8} \frac{(-2.557 \times 10^{-5})^2}{0.983\,96 \times 0.2814} = -3.0 \times 10^{-10}.$$

```
@*******************@
@   initialization  @
@*******************@

CertaintyEqTolerance = 10^(-5);
alpha = 0;
iteration=0;
CertaintyEqPrecision=2*CertaintyEqTolerance;
du = 0;
ddu = 1;


@*******************@
@   the main loop   @
@*******************@

do until abs(CertaintyEqPrecision) < CertaintyEqTolerance;

    alpha = alpha - du/ddu;
    u= 0.5*(1+0.18*alpha)^-4+0.5*(1-0.12*alpha)^-4;
    du=-2*(0.18*(1+0.18*alpha)^-5-0.12*(1-0.12*alpha)^-5);
    ddu=10*(0.18^2*(1+0.18*alpha)^-6+0.12^2*(1-0.12*alpha)^-6);

    @ precision of current alpha @
    aPrecision = -du/ddu;
    @ precision in certainty equivalent wealth @
    CertaintyEqPrecision = 1/8*du^2/ddu/u;

print "iteration                           " iteration;
print "certainty equivalent                " u^(-1/4);
print "estimated precision in c.e.         " CertaintyEqPrecision;
print "alpha                               " alpha;
print "estimated precision in alpha        " aPrecision;
print "u(alpha)                            " u;
print "u'(alpha)                           " du;
print "u''(alpha)                          " ddu;
iteration=iteration+1;
endo;
end;
```

right-hand side of eqn (4.24)
eqn (4.25)

eqn (4.24)

eqn (4.22)
eqn (4.12)
eqn (4.13)
eqn (4.14)

eqn (4.10)

eqn (4.23)

Figure 4.2. Implementation of Newton's method in GAUSS; program *chapter4sect2.gss*.

Here the iteration ends since (4.24) is now satisfied. According to equation (4.6) the corresponding error in α is

$$\text{error}_\alpha(\alpha^{(2)}) = -\frac{u'(\alpha^{(1)})}{u''(\alpha^{(1)})} = \frac{2.557 \times 10^{-5}}{0.2814} = 9.1 \times 10^{-5}.$$

4.2.1 GAUSS Implementation

Figure 4.2 shows that Newton's method can easily be programmed in GAUSS. The numerical results of the previous section can be reproduced by running the program, *chapter4sect2.gss*.

4.3 Optimal CRRA Investment Using Empirical Return Distribution

The implementation of Newton's algorithm provides a very powerful tool because we can now tackle investment problems that do not permit a closed-form solution of the optimality condition $u'(\alpha) = 0$. Most incomplete market investment problems fall into this category. Consider as an example an investor in the Japanese equity

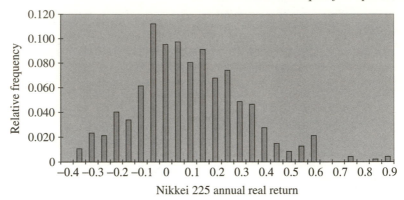

Figure 4.3. Histogram of annual real returns on the Nikkei, 1960–2000, year on year, monthly data.

market who wishes to pursue a buy-and-hold strategy for a year. The empirical distribution of the relevant returns is depicted in Figure 4.3.

4.3.1 Automatic Generation of the Target Function and Its Derivatives

One weakness of the portfolio optimizing program in Figure 4.2 is that one must type in the expected utility and all its derivatives by hand. It would be much nicer to simply provide the values of excess return and the corresponding probabilities and let the program take care of everything else.

To achieve this goal we will write the target function in a more schematic way:

$$u(\alpha) = \mathrm{E}[(1 + \alpha X)^{1-\gamma}].$$

The vector of excess returns

$$X = \underbrace{\begin{bmatrix} -0.37 & -0.32 & \cdots & 0.83 & 0.87 \end{bmatrix}}_{\text{26 entries}},$$

and the vector of probabilities corresponding to the 26 levels of risky return

$$\mathrm{XDistr} = \underbrace{\begin{bmatrix} 0.011 & 0.023 & \cdots & 0.002 & 0.004 \end{bmatrix}}_{\text{26 entries}}$$

are given. The investor also knows her γ: $\gamma = 5$.

To compute the expectation $\mathrm{E}[(1 + \alpha X)^{1-\gamma}]$, say for $\alpha = 0.1$, one will first evaluate the normalized wealth $1 + \alpha X$,

$$V = 1 + 0.1X$$
$$= \begin{bmatrix} 1 - 0.037 & 1 - 0.032 & \cdots & 1 + 0.083 & 1 + 0.087 \end{bmatrix}$$
$$= \begin{bmatrix} 0.963 & 0.968 & \cdots & 1.083 & 1.087 \end{bmatrix},$$

then generate the vector of utility levels $(1 + \alpha X)^{1-\gamma}$

$$V^{-4} = \begin{bmatrix} 0.963^{-4} & 0.968^{-4} & \cdots & 1.083^{-4} & 1.087^{-4} \end{bmatrix}$$
$$= \begin{bmatrix} 1.163 & 1.139 & \cdots & 0.727 & 0.716 \end{bmatrix},$$

and finally compute the expected utility (the weighted average of utility levels) as a matrix product between the row vector of utilities V^{-4} and the column vector of probabilities XDistr* (XDistr transposed):

$$E[(1 + \alpha X)^{1-\gamma}] = (1 + \alpha X)^{1-\gamma} \text{XDistr}^*$$

$$= \begin{bmatrix} 1.163 & 1.139 & \cdots & 0.727 & 0.716 \end{bmatrix} \begin{bmatrix} 0.011 \\ 0.023 \\ \vdots \\ 0.002 \\ 0.004 \end{bmatrix} = 0.973.$$

(4.26)

In GAUSS

```
wealth = 1 + alpha*X;
u = (wealth^(1-gama))*XDistr';
```

We now have to obtain the values of $u'(\alpha)$ and $u''(\alpha)$. Recall from (4.26) that the target function is effectively a weighted average of utility levels, with weights equal to the probabilities of obtaining different values of excess return. Note that the weights (probabilities) *do not* depend on the choice variable α, only the utility levels do. Because the weights remain constant, it is easy to realize that the change in the weighted average of utility levels is the same as the weighted average of changes in utility levels in individual states, in other words

$$u'(\alpha) = \frac{d}{d\alpha} E[(1 + \alpha X)^{1-\gamma}] = E\left[\frac{d}{d\alpha}(1 + \alpha X)^{1-\gamma}\right]. \qquad (4.27)$$

Applying this fact twice consecutively we obtain

$$u''(\alpha) = \frac{d^2}{d\alpha^2} E[(1 + \alpha X)^{1-\gamma}] = E\left[\frac{d^2}{d\alpha^2}(1 + \alpha X)^{1-\gamma}\right]. \qquad (4.28)$$

Evaluation of derivatives on the right-hand side of (4.27) and (4.28) tells us how to express $u'(\alpha)$ and $u''(\alpha)$ in terms of expectations,

$$u'(\alpha) = (1 - \gamma)E[X(1 + \alpha X)^{-\gamma}], \qquad (4.29)$$

$$u''(\alpha) = \gamma(\gamma - 1)E[X^2(1 + \alpha X)^{-\gamma-1}]. \qquad (4.30)$$

The computation of $u'(\alpha)$ and $u''(\alpha)$ in GAUSS proceeds similarly to the evaluation of $u(\alpha)$ described above. To find the random variable $X(1 + \alpha X)^{-\gamma}$ we first form a row vector $(1 + \alpha X)^{-\gamma}$

$$-(1 + 0.1X)^{-5} = V^{-5}$$

$$= \begin{bmatrix} 0.963^{-5} & 0.968^{-5} & \cdots & 1.083^{-5} & 1.087^{-5} \end{bmatrix}$$

$$= \begin{bmatrix} 1.207 & 1.177 & \cdots & 0.671 & 0.659 \end{bmatrix}$$

and **multiply** it **element by element** with the row vector X,

$$X(1 + 0.1X)^{-5}$$
$$= \begin{bmatrix} -0.37 & -0.32 & \cdots & 0.83 & 0.87 \end{bmatrix}$$
$$\times \begin{bmatrix} 1.207 & 1.177 & \cdots & 0.671 & 0.659 \end{bmatrix}$$
$$= \begin{bmatrix} -0.37 \times 1.207 & -0.32 \times 1.177 & \cdots & 0.83 \times 0.671 & 0.87 \times 0.659 \end{bmatrix}$$
$$= \begin{bmatrix} -0.447 & -0.377 & \cdots & 0.558 & 0.573 \end{bmatrix}.$$

Finally, we compute the expectation by multiplying the row vector $X(1+0.1X)^{-5}$ with the column vector XDistr*:

$$E[X(1 + \alpha X)^{-\gamma}] = (X(1 + \alpha X)^{-\gamma})\text{XDistr}^*$$

$$= \begin{bmatrix} -0.447 & -0.377 & \cdots & 0.558 & 0.573 \end{bmatrix} \begin{bmatrix} 0.011 \\ 0.023 \\ \vdots \\ 0.002 \\ 0.004 \end{bmatrix}$$

$$= -0.218.$$

In GAUSS

```
du  =  (1-gama)*(X.*wealth^(-gama))*XDistr';
ddu =  gama*(gama-1)*(X^2.*wealth^(-gama-1))*Xdistr';
```

Note the special operator . * for the element-by-element multiplication. Analogously . / represents element-by-element division.

4.3.2 CRRA Portfolio Optimizer Wrapped Up as a Procedure

In practice, the portfolio optimizer will be used inside a larger program whose task it is to process data, deliver the data as an input to the optimizer, take the output from the optimizer and present it graphically or otherwise to the user. If we simply leave the optimizer in the main body of the large program, there is a danger that a variable used in the optimizer, say `alpha`, is also used elsewhere in the larger program for a completely different purpose. To prevent the optimizer interfering with the rest of the program it is a very good idea to encase the optimizer in a **procedure**, which acts like a protective shield.

Firstly, one must have a name for the procedure: we shall call it `CRRAmax`. Secondly, one must determine how many outputs the procedure will have, in our case we are after the maximum certainty equivalent and the optimal portfolio decision. To say in GAUSS that the procedure `CRRAmax` has two outputs one writes

$$\text{proc(2)} = \text{CRRAmax};$$

Next one must determine which variables inside the procedure are **local**, meaning they are never allowed to interfere with variables of the same name outside the procedure. To make `alpha`, `CEq`, u, du, ddu local we would use a command

$$\text{local alpha,CEq,u,du,ddu};$$

```
proc(2) = CRRAmax;
@*******************@
@ initialization @
@*******************@
local alpha,iteration,CEqPrecision,wealth,u,du,ddu,CEq;
alpha = 0;
iteration=0; du=0; ddu=1;
CEqPrecision=2*CertaintyEqTolerance;
format /ro 12,4; @ output rounded to 4 decimal places @
@*******************@
@ the main loop @
@*******************@

do until abs(CEqPrecision) < CertaintyEqTolerance;          eqn (4.24)
    wealth = 1 + X*alpha;
    u = (wealth^(1-gama))*XDistr';                          eqn (4.26)
    du = (1-gama)*(X.*(wealth^(-gama)))*XDistr';            eqn (4.29)
    ddu = gama*(gama-1)*((X^2).*(wealth^(-gama-1)))*XDistr';  eqn (4.30)
    CEq=u^(1/(1-gama));
    CEqPrecision = 1/2/(1-gama)*du^2/ddu/u;                 eqn (4.23)

if_output>0;
  print "iteration                           " iteration;
  print "Certainty equivalent/Safe wealth    " CEq;
  print "estimated precision in CEq          " CEqPrecision;
  print "alpha                               " alpha;
  print "estimated precision in alpha        " -du/ddu;
endif;
iteration=iteration+1;
endo;
retp(CEq,alpha);
endp;
```

Figure 4.4. CRRA portfolio optimizer as a procedure, program *chapter4sect3.gss*.

In contrast to local variables all variables initialized outside of procedures are called **global**. Global variables can be used inside and outside procedures, but it is *not* advisable to change them inside procedures because it makes error tracking next to impossible; they are best used in procedures as an input. The entire procedure CRRAmax is shown in Figure 4.4.

Having computed the outputs the procedure will return them via a special command retp. To return the certainty equivalent CEq and the optimal portfolio alpha one writes

retp(CEq,alpha);

The procedure ends with the statement

endp;

The required inputs X, XDistr, gama and _output are passed to the procedure as *global* variables. The parameter _output controls the printouts from the optimizer, setting

_output = 0

switches off all printed output from the procedure.

4.3.3 First Iteration of CRRA Optimizer and Quadratic Utility

With the portfolio optimization neatly tucked away in the procedure CRRAmax, the main body of the program only contains a few lines defining X, XDistr and gama,

Table 4.1. Iterations of Newton's method applied to optimal investment in the Japanese stock market.

Iteration	α	$u^{1/(1-\gamma)}(\alpha)$	%error$_V$
0	0.0000	1.000	1.2×10^{-2}
1	0.2974	1.0138	6.0×10^{-4}
2	0.3749	1.0144	8.4×10^{-8}

receiving outputs from the optimizer

$$\{\texttt{CEq,alpha}\}=\texttt{CRRAmax}$$

and reporting the results on the screen. The program also compares the optimal portfolio choice $\alpha_{\gamma,\gamma}$ with the optimal portfolio of quadratic utility investor with the same local risk aversion $\alpha_{-1,\gamma}$. The main body of the code is given in Figure 4.5.

The program *chapter4sect3.gss* converges after two iterations and the results are summarized in Table 4.1.

For the quadratic investor with local risk aversion $\tilde{\gamma}=5$ we obtain

$$\alpha_{-1,5}=\tfrac{1}{5}\alpha_{-1,1}=\frac{1}{5}\frac{E[X]}{E[X^2]}=0.2974,$$

which is the same as the α from the first iteration in Table 4.1. This is not a coincidence; in general,

$$\alpha^{(1)}=\underbrace{\alpha^{(0)}}_{0}-\frac{u'(\alpha^{(0)})}{u''(\alpha^{(0)})}=-\frac{u'(0)}{u''(0)},$$

and from (4.29) and (4.30)

$$u'(0)=(1-\gamma)E[X],$$
$$u''(0)=\gamma(\gamma-1)E[X^2],$$

so that

$$\alpha^{(1)}=-\frac{(1-\gamma)E[X]}{\gamma(\gamma-1)E[X^2]}=\frac{1}{\gamma}\frac{E[X]}{E[X^2]}.$$

> For a CRRA investor with risk aversion γ the first iteration of the CRRA portfolio optimizer is identical to the optimal portfolio choice of a quadratic utility investor with local risk aversion $\tilde{\gamma}=\gamma$.

To find out how much the CRRA investor would lose by pursuing the suboptimal quadratic utility investment $\alpha_{-1,\gamma}$, we simply note that this investment strategy is in the second row of Table 4.1 and that the corresponding error in certainty equivalent is 6×10^{-4}; thus the investor loses 6×10^{-4} part of her risk-free wealth. Suppose the risk-free wealth is $1\,220\,000$, then the investor foregoes £732 in certainty equivalent wealth if she pursues an investment strategy dictated by quadratic utility instead of the optimal strategy.

```
@*******************@
@    parameters     @
@*******************@
@ row vector of rates of return from -35% to 90% in 5% increments @
Risky1 = seqa(-0.35,0.05,26);
RiskFreeRate = 0.02;
@*****************************************@
@     global parameters for utility      @
@        maximizing procedure CRRAmax     @
@*****************************************@
_output=1;
gama=5;
CertaintyEqTolerance=10^-5;
@relative frequency of annual real returns on NIKKEI 225@
XDistr = 0.011~ 0.023~ 0.021~ 0.041~ 0.034~ 0.061~ 0.112~ 0.095~ 0.097~
0.081~ 0.091~ 0.068~ 0.074~ 0.049~ 0.047~ 0.028~ 0.015~ 0.008~ 0.013~
0.021~ 0.000~ 0.000~ 0.004~ 0.000~ 0.002~ 0.004;
X = Risky1-RiskFreeRate;

@***********************************************@
@ Computations for quadratic utility investor @
@***********************************************@
EX = X*XDistr';@ E[X] @
EX2 = X^2*XDistr';@ E[X^2] @

@***************************@
@ main body of the programme @
@***************************@
{CEq,alpha}=CRRAmax;
print "Certainty equivalent wealth/Safe wealth   " CEq;
print "CRRA alpha                                " alpha;
print "quadratic utility alpha                   " EX/EX2/gama;
end;
```

Figure 4.5. Optimal portfolio choice of a Japanese equity investor with CRRA utility. Main body of GAUSS program *chapter4sect3.gss*.

4.4 HARA Portfolio Optimizer

So far we have dealt with the optimization of the CRRA utility, which forces local and baseline risk aversion to be the same. With the HARA investor we wish to decouple the local and baseline risk aversion; hence we are interested in the percentage increase in certainty equivalent wealth per unit of local risk tolerance (equals the investment potential IP) and portfolio decision per unit of local risk tolerance alpha1. If CEq and alpha are outputs from the procedure CRRAmax, it is a simple matter to recompute IP and alpha1 from the scaling properties (3.31) and (3.39):

$$IP = gama*(CEq-1); \qquad (4.31)$$

$$alpha1 = gama*alpha; \qquad (4.32)$$

There is a catch, however. With γ large the CRRA investor is so risk averse that the optimal $\alpha_{\gamma,\gamma}$ is identically zero, and the optimal certainty equivalent over safe wealth is 1. If we simply design the procedure HARAmax as the CRRAmax procedure with transformations (4.31), (4.32), the output for γ large will be zero risky investment. This can be seen by running the program *chapter4sect4a.gss*.

In these circumstances we have to make sure the certainty equivalent of an investor with *unit* local risk aversion is computed with sufficient precision. Thus, instead of requiring

$$\left| \frac{V_{\gamma,\gamma \text{ certain}}(\alpha_{\text{opt}})}{V_{\gamma,\gamma \text{ certain}}(\alpha^{(n)})} - 1 \right| < \text{tolerance},$$

we should go for

$$\left| \frac{V_{\gamma,1 \text{ certain}}(\alpha_{\text{opt}})}{V_{\gamma,1 \text{ certain}}(\alpha^{(n)})} - 1 \right| < \text{tolerance},$$

bearing in mind that there are very few investors with local risk aversion less than one.

Our problem now is that, although we know the value of

$$\frac{V_{\gamma,\gamma \text{ certain}}(\alpha_{\text{opt}})}{V_{\gamma,\gamma \text{ certain}}(\alpha^{(n)})} - 1$$

in terms of $u(\alpha^{(n)})$, we have no such expression for

$$\frac{V_{\gamma,1 \text{ certain}}(\alpha_{\text{opt}})}{V_{\gamma,1 \text{ certain}}(\alpha^{(n)})} - 1.$$

Exercise 4.3 shows that

$$\frac{V_{\gamma,1 \text{ certain}}(\alpha_{\text{opt}})}{V_{\gamma,1 \text{ certain}}(\alpha^{(n)})} - 1$$

$$= \frac{\gamma \left(V_{\gamma,\gamma \text{ certain}}(\alpha^{(n)})/V_{\text{safe}} \right)}{1 + \gamma \left((V_{\gamma,\gamma \text{ certain}}(\alpha^{(n)})/V_{\text{safe}}) - 1 \right)} \left(\frac{V_{\gamma,\gamma \text{ certain}}(\alpha_{\text{opt}})}{V_{\gamma,\gamma \text{ certain}}(\alpha^{(n)})} - 1 \right),$$

which can be rephrased in terms of $u(\alpha^{(n)})$ as follows:

$$\frac{V_{\gamma,1 \text{ certain}}(\alpha_{\text{opt}})}{V_{\gamma,1 \text{ certain}}(\alpha^{(n)})} - 1 = -\frac{\gamma (u(\alpha^{(n)}))^{1/(1-\gamma)}}{1 + \gamma ((u(\alpha^{(n)}))^{1/(1-\gamma)} - 1)} \frac{1}{2(1-\gamma)} \frac{(u'(\alpha^{(n)}))^2}{u(\alpha^{(n)}) u''(\alpha^{(n)})}.$$

$$(4.33)$$

Most of the time $(u(\alpha^{(n)}))^{1/(1-\gamma)}$ is close to 1 and the error estimate is therefore close to

$$\frac{\gamma}{2(1-\gamma)} \frac{(u'(\alpha^{(n)}))^2}{u(\alpha^{(n)}) u''(\alpha^{(n)})}$$

so that γ in the numerator compensates for $1 - \gamma$ in the denominator when γ is large.

With the error estimate (4.33) in hand, one only needs to change a few lines in Figure 4.4 to obtain the procedure HARAmax (see Figure 4.6).

4.5   HARA Portfolio Optimization with Several Risky Assets

Let us consider a case with two risky assets with returns X_1 and X_2 given in Table 4.2. Assuming that the two returns are independent, the joint distribution takes the form given in Table 4.3.

This model has four states of the world and two choice variables α_1 and α_2; our aim is to maximize

$$u(\alpha_1, \alpha_2) = \text{E}[(1 + \alpha_1 X_1 + \alpha_2 X_2)^{1-\gamma}].$$

```
proc(2) = HARAmax;
@*******************@
@   initialization   @
@*******************@
local alpha,iteration,CertaintyEqPrecision,wealth,u,du,ddu,CEq;
alpha = 0;
CertaintyEqPrecision=2*CertaintyEqTolerance;
du=0; ddu=1;
@*******************@
@    the main loop   @
@*******************@
do until abs(CertaintyEqPrecision) < CertaintyEqTolerance;
alpha = alpha - du/ddu;
wealth = 1 + X*alpha;
u = (wealth^(1-gama))*XDistr';
du = (1-gama)*(X.*(wealth^(-gama)))*XDistr';
ddu = gama*(gama-1)*((X^2).*(wealth^(-gama-1)))*XDistr';
CEq = u^(1/(1-gama));
CertaintyEqPrecision = -1/2/(1-gama)*du'inv(ddu)*du/u*
                       gama*CEq/(1+gama*(CEq-1));          eqn (4.33)
endo;
retp(gama*(CEq-1),gama*alpha);
endp;
```

Figure 4.6. HARA portfolio optimizer, *chapter4sect 4b.gss*.

Recall that with one risky asset the portfolio optimizer dictates

$$\alpha^{(n+1)} = \alpha^{(n)} - (u''(\alpha^{(n)}))^{-1}u'(\alpha^{(n)}). \tag{4.34}$$

With several risky assets (4.34) remains the same, except α is now a vector, u' is a vector (the so-called **gradient**) and u'' is a matrix (called **Hessian**):

$$G(\alpha) = \begin{bmatrix} \dfrac{\partial u(\alpha_1, \alpha_2)}{\partial \alpha_1} \\[2mm] \dfrac{\partial u(\alpha_1, \alpha_2)}{\partial \alpha_2} \end{bmatrix}, \tag{4.35}$$

$$H(\alpha) = \begin{bmatrix} \dfrac{\partial^2 u(\alpha_1, \alpha_2)}{\partial \alpha_1^2} & \dfrac{\partial^2 u(\alpha_1, \alpha_2)}{\partial \alpha_1 \partial \alpha_2} \\[2mm] \dfrac{\partial^2 u(\alpha_1, \alpha_2)}{\partial \alpha_1 \partial \alpha_2} & \dfrac{\partial^2 u(\alpha_1, \alpha_2)}{\partial \alpha_2^2} \end{bmatrix}, \tag{4.36}$$

$$\underbrace{\alpha^{(n+1)}}_{2\times 1 \text{ vector}} = \underbrace{\alpha^{(n)}}_{2\times 1 \text{ vector}} - \underbrace{H^{-1}(\alpha^{(n)})}_{\text{inverse of } 2\times 2 \text{ matrix}} \underbrace{G(\alpha^{(n)})}_{2\times 1 \text{ vector}}. \tag{4.37}$$

The gradient and Hessian are evaluated the same way as the derivatives u' and u'' in (4.29) and (4.30); for example, the first entry in the gradient is

$$\frac{\partial}{\partial \alpha_1} \mathrm{E}[(1 + \alpha_1 X_1 + \alpha_2 X_2)^{1-\gamma}] = \mathrm{E}\left[\frac{\partial}{\partial \alpha_1}(1 + \alpha_1 X_1 + \alpha_2 X_2)^{1-\gamma}\right]$$

$$= (1 - \gamma)\mathrm{E}[X_1(1 + \alpha_1 X_1 + \alpha_2 X_2)^{-\gamma}].$$

Having performed the necessary algebra in (4.35) and (4.36) we obtain

$$G(\alpha) = (1 - \gamma)\begin{bmatrix} \mathrm{E}[X_1(1 + \alpha^* X)^{-\gamma}] \\ \mathrm{E}[X_2(1 + \alpha^* X)^{-\gamma}] \end{bmatrix}, \tag{4.38}$$

Table 4.2.   Marginal distribution of two excess returns.

value of X_1	-0.22	0.18	value of X_2	-0.12	0.18
probability	$\frac{1}{4}$	$\frac{3}{4}$	probability	$\frac{1}{2}$	$\frac{1}{2}$

Table 4.3.   Joint distribution of two excess returns.

value of (X_1, X_2)	$(-0.22, -0.12)$	$(0.18, 0.18)$	$(0.18, -0.12)$	$(0.18, 0.18)$
probability	$\frac{1}{4} \times \frac{1}{2}$	$\frac{1}{4} \times \frac{1}{2}$	$\frac{3}{4} \times \frac{1}{2}$	$\frac{3}{4} \times \frac{1}{2}$

$$H(\alpha) = \gamma(\gamma - 1)\begin{bmatrix} \mathrm{E}[X_1^2(1+\alpha^*X)^{-\gamma-1}] & \mathrm{E}[X_1 X_2(1+\alpha^*X)^{-\gamma-1}] \\ \mathrm{E}[X_1 X_2(1+\alpha^*X)^{-\gamma-1}] & \mathrm{E}[X_2^2(1+\alpha^*X)^{-\gamma-1}] \end{bmatrix},$$

$$(4.39)$$

using matrix notation α^*X for $\alpha_1 X_1 + \alpha_2 X_2$.

With several risky assets Newton's method of equation (4.22) generalizes to

$$\alpha^{(n+1)} = \alpha^{(n)} - H^{-1}(\alpha^{(n)})G(\alpha^{(n)}),$$

where

$$G(\alpha) = (1 - \gamma)\mathrm{E}[X^*(1+\alpha^*X)^{-\gamma}],$$
$$H(\alpha) = \gamma(\gamma - 1)\mathrm{E}[XX^*(1+\alpha^*X)^{-\gamma}].$$

In analogy with (4.6)

$$\mathrm{error}_\alpha(\alpha^{(n)}) = -H^{-1}(\alpha^{(n)})G(\alpha^{(n)})$$

signifies the distance of $\alpha^{(n)}$ from optimal α and the quadratic form,

$$\mathrm{error}_V(\alpha^{(n)}) = -\frac{1}{2(1-\gamma)}\frac{G^*(\alpha^{(n)})[H(\alpha^{(n)})]^{-1}G(\alpha^{(n)})}{u(\alpha^{(n)})},$$

is the precision of certainty equivalent wealth, in analogy with (4.20).

4.5.1   *Automatic Generation of the Target Function and Its Derivatives*

Our aim is to calculate the first and second derivatives $G(\alpha)$ and $H(\alpha)$ in a manner general enough to allow for any number of risky securities, not just two. To this end we will represent the two securities X_1, X_2 and probabilities XDistr in matrix form, with columns corresponding to the four states in the order given in Table 4.3,

$$X = \begin{bmatrix} X_1 \\ X_2 \end{bmatrix} = \begin{bmatrix} -0.22 & -0.22 & 0.18 & 0.18 \\ -0.12 & 0.18 & -0.12 & 0.18 \end{bmatrix},$$

$$\mathrm{XDistr} = \begin{bmatrix} \frac{1}{8} & \frac{1}{8} & \frac{3}{8} & \frac{3}{8} \end{bmatrix}.$$

Suppose we have

$$\alpha = \begin{bmatrix} \alpha_1 \\ \alpha_2 \end{bmatrix} = \begin{bmatrix} 0.1 \\ 0.2 \end{bmatrix}.$$

To evaluate the target function $u(\alpha) = \mathrm{E}[(1 + \alpha^* X)^{1-\gamma}]$ we first compute the normalized wealth,

$$V = 1 + \alpha^* X,$$

in GAUSS

```
wealth = 1+alpha'X;
```

yielding

$$V = 1 + \begin{bmatrix} 0.1 & 0.2 \end{bmatrix} \begin{bmatrix} -0.22 & -0.22 & 0.18 & 0.18 \\ -0.12 & 0.18 & -0.12 & 0.18 \end{bmatrix}$$

$$= 1 + \begin{bmatrix} -0.046 & 0.014 & -0.006 & 0.054 \end{bmatrix}$$

$$= \begin{bmatrix} 0.954 & 1.014 & 0.994 & 1.054 \end{bmatrix}.$$

Next we evaluate the utility levels $V^{1-\gamma}$ and compute their expected value by multiplying $V^{1-\gamma}$ with the column vector of probabilities XDistr*

$$u(\alpha) = V^{1-\gamma}\text{XDistr}^*$$

$$= \begin{bmatrix} 0.954^{-4} & 1.014^{-4} & 0.994^{-4} & 1.054^{-4} \end{bmatrix} \begin{bmatrix} \frac{1}{8} \\ \frac{1}{8} \\ \frac{1}{8} \\ \frac{3}{8} \\ \frac{3}{8} \end{bmatrix} = 0.957,$$

in GAUSS

```
u = (wealth^(1-gama))*XDistr'
```

The evaluation of the gradient is only slightly more complicated. To get the dimensions right we will multiply the marginal utility $V^{-\gamma}$ with individual probabilities element by element,

$$V^{-\gamma}\text{XDistr} = \begin{bmatrix} 0.954^{-5} & 1.014^{-5} & 0.994^{-5} & 1.054^{-5} \end{bmatrix} \begin{bmatrix} \frac{1}{8} & \frac{1}{8} & \frac{3}{8} & \frac{3}{8} \end{bmatrix}$$

$$= \begin{bmatrix} 0.158 & 0.117 & 0.386 & 0.288 \end{bmatrix}$$

and use this adjusted vector of 'probabilities' to compute the expectation,

$$G = (1 - \gamma)\mathrm{E}[XV^{-\gamma}]$$

$$= -4X(V^{-\gamma}\text{XDistr})^* = -4 \begin{bmatrix} -0.22 & -0.22 & 0.18 & 0.18 \\ -0.12 & 0.18 & -0.12 & 0.18 \end{bmatrix} \begin{bmatrix} 0.158 \\ 0.117 \\ 0.386 \\ 0.288 \end{bmatrix}$$

$$= \begin{bmatrix} -0.243 \\ -0.0305 \end{bmatrix}.$$

In GAUSS

```
du = (1-gama)*X*((wealth^(-gama)).*XDistr)';
```

Using the same logic the expression for the Hessian is

```
ddu = gama*(gama-1)*X*(X.*(wealth^(-gama-1)).*XDistr)';
```

To allow for multiple assets one simply replaces the main body of procedure HARAmax with the following code.

```
do until abs(IPPrecision) < IPPrecisionTolerance;
alpha = alpha - inv(ddu)*du;
wealth = 1 + alpha'X;
u = (wealth^(1-gama))*XDistr';
du = (1-gama)*X*(XDistr.*(wealth^(-gama)))';
ddu = gama*(gama-1)*X*(X.*XDistr.*(wealth^(-gama)))';
CE=u^(1/(1-gama));
IPPrecision = -1/2/(1-gama)*du'inv(ddu)*du/u*gama*CE/(1+gama*(CE-1));
endo;
retp(gama*(CE-1),gama*alpha);
endp;
```

4.6 Quadratic Utility Maximization with Multiple Assets

The main advantage of using the quadratic utility is the availability of closed-form solutions with multiple assets. We will use the set-up of Section 4.5 assuming that we have two risky assets with a distribution of excess returns as given in Table 4.3.

The expected utility takes the form

$$u(\alpha) = E[(1 - \alpha_1 X_1 - \alpha_2 X_2)^2].$$

The expression

$$I(\alpha) = (1 - \alpha_1 X_1 - \alpha_2 X_2)^2$$

inside the expectation is a quadratic form. In order to separate the random and non-random parts in I it is useful to write it in matrix notation:

$$I(\alpha) = \underbrace{\begin{bmatrix} 1 & -\alpha_1 & -\alpha_2 \end{bmatrix}}_{\text{non-random}} \underbrace{\begin{bmatrix} 1 & X_1 & X_2 \\ X_1 & X_1^2 & X_1 X_2 \\ X_2 & X_1 X_2 & X_2^2 \end{bmatrix}}_{\text{random}} \underbrace{\begin{bmatrix} 1 \\ -\alpha_1 \\ -\alpha_2 \end{bmatrix}}_{\text{non-random}}.$$

All the random elements now appear inside the matrix.

We are now ready to compute the expected utility. Because the coefficients in the vector $\begin{bmatrix} 1 & \alpha_1 & \alpha_2 \end{bmatrix}$ are non-random, the expectation will only affect the terms inside the matrix:

$$u(\alpha) = E[I(\alpha)]$$

$$= \begin{bmatrix} 1 & -\alpha_1 & -\alpha_2 \end{bmatrix} \begin{bmatrix} 1 & E[X_1] & E[X_2] \\ E[X_1] & E[X_1^2] & E[X_1 X_2] \\ E[X_2] & E[X_1 X_2] & E[X_2^2] \end{bmatrix} \begin{bmatrix} 1 \\ -\alpha_1 \\ -\alpha_2 \end{bmatrix}$$

$$= 1 - 2 \begin{bmatrix} \alpha_1 & \alpha_2 \end{bmatrix} \underbrace{\begin{bmatrix} E[X_1] \\ E[X_2] \end{bmatrix}}_{\mu_X} + \begin{bmatrix} \alpha_1 & \alpha_2 \end{bmatrix} \underbrace{\begin{bmatrix} E[X_1^2] & E[X_1 X_2] \\ E[X_1 X_2] & E[X_2^2] \end{bmatrix}}_{\Omega_X} \begin{bmatrix} \alpha_1 \\ \alpha_2 \end{bmatrix}.$$

Let us now differentiate the expected utility with respect to α_1 and α_2 to obtain two first-order conditions

$$-2\underbrace{\begin{bmatrix} E[X_1] \\ E[X_2] \end{bmatrix}}_{\mu_X} +2\underbrace{\begin{bmatrix} E[X_1^2] & E[X_1 X_2] \\ E[X_1 X_2] & E[X_2^2] \end{bmatrix}}_{\Omega_X} \underbrace{\begin{bmatrix} \alpha_1 \\ \alpha_2 \end{bmatrix}}_{\alpha_{-1\,\mathrm{opt}}} = 0,$$

$$\alpha_{-1\,\mathrm{opt}} = \Omega_X^{-1}\mu_X.$$

Substituting this value into $u(\alpha)$ we obtain

$$u(\alpha_{-1\,\mathrm{opt}}) = 1 - 2\alpha_{-1\,\mathrm{opt}}^*\mu_X + \alpha_{-1\,\mathrm{opt}}^*\Omega_X\alpha_{-1\,\mathrm{opt}}$$

$$= 1 - \mu_X^*\Omega_X^{-1}\mu_X. \tag{4.40}$$

4.6.1 Variance–Covariance Matrix

The matrix Ω_X represents the second non-central moments of the distribution of excess returns. However, professional investors prefer to work with central moments, that is variances and covariances. The **variance–covariance matrix** Σ_X is defined as

$$\Sigma_X = \begin{bmatrix} E[(X_1 - E[X_1])^2] & E[(X_1 - E[X_1])(X_2 - E[X_2])] \\ E[(X_1 - E[X_1])(X_2 - E[X_2])] & E[(X_2 - E[X_2])^2] \end{bmatrix}.$$

Just as in the univariate case we have $\sigma_X^2 = E[X^2] - \mu_X^2$, in the multivariate case Σ_X and Ω_X are closely related

$$\Sigma_X = \Omega_X - \mu_X\mu_X^*.$$

Similarly, in the univariate case we can write

$$\alpha_{-1\,\mathrm{opt}} = \frac{\mu_X}{E[X^2]} = \frac{\mu_X/\sigma_X^2}{1 + \mu_X^2/\sigma_X^2};$$

it is left as an exercise to show that in the multivariate case $\alpha_{-1\,\mathrm{opt}}$ can be expressed analogously as

$$\alpha_{-1\,\mathrm{opt}} = \Omega_X^{-1}\mu_X = \frac{\Sigma_X^{-1}\mu_X}{1 + \mu_X^*\Sigma_X^{-1}\mu_X}. \tag{4.41}$$

Substituting (4.41) into the expected utility (4.40) we obtain

$$u(\alpha_{-1\,\mathrm{opt}}) = 1 - \frac{\mu^*\Sigma_X^{-1}\mu_X}{1 + \mu_X^*\Sigma_X^{-1}\mu_X} = \frac{1}{1 + \mu_X^*\Sigma_X^{-1}\mu_X}. \tag{4.42}$$

Another exercise shows that, in direct analogy with (3.60), $\mu_X^*\Sigma_X^{-1}\mu_X$ is the square of the highest Sharpe ratio attainable from investing in the two risky assets:

$$\mathrm{SR}^2(X) \triangleq \mu_X^*\Sigma_X^{-1}\mu_X. \tag{4.43}$$

The highest Sharpe ratio available with several risky assets is sometimes called the *market Sharpe ratio* (it is implicitly understood that the 'market' is restricted to the risky securities being analysed). The relationship (4.43) together with (4.42) gives an exact analogy of the relationship between the Sharpe ratio and the expected quadratic utility for one risky asset.

Coming back to our risky assets,

$$E[X] = X\,\text{XDistr}^* = \begin{bmatrix} -0.22 & -0.22 & 0.18 & 0.18 \\ -0.12 & 0.18 & -0.12 & 0.18 \end{bmatrix} \begin{bmatrix} 0.125 \\ 0.125 \\ 0.375 \\ 0.375 \end{bmatrix} = \begin{bmatrix} 0.08 \\ 0.03 \end{bmatrix}.$$

The computation of the variance–covariance matrix is best done in two stages, using the identity

$$\Sigma_X = E[XX^*] - E[X]E[X^*].$$

Since we already know $E[X]$, it is easy to calculate $E[X]E[X^*]$:

$$E[X]E[X^*] = \begin{bmatrix} 0.08 \\ 0.03 \end{bmatrix} \begin{bmatrix} 0.08 & 0.03 \end{bmatrix} = 10^{-2} \begin{bmatrix} 0.64 & 0.24 \\ 0.24 & 0.09 \end{bmatrix}.$$

What remains to be computed is $E[XX^*]$. There are many ways of doing this, one particularly attractive way being

$$E[XX^*] = X(X\,\text{XDistr})^*$$

$$= \begin{bmatrix} -0.22 & -0.22 & 0.18 & 0.18 \\ -0.12 & 0.18 & -0.12 & 0.18 \end{bmatrix} \begin{bmatrix} -0.22 \times 0.125 & -0.12 \times 0.125 \\ -0.22 \times 0.125 & 0.18 \times 0.125 \\ 0.18 \times 0.375 & -0.12 \times 0.375 \\ 0.18 \times 0.375 & 0.18 \times 0.375 \end{bmatrix}$$

$$= 10^{-2} \begin{bmatrix} 3.64 & 0.24 \\ 0.24 & 2.34 \end{bmatrix}.$$

The variance–covariance matrix is, therefore,

$$\Sigma_X = 10^{-2} \begin{bmatrix} 3.64 & 0.24 \\ 0.24 & 2.34 \end{bmatrix} - 10^{-2} \begin{bmatrix} 0.64 & 0.24 \\ 0.24 & 0.09 \end{bmatrix} = 10^{-2} \begin{bmatrix} 3 & 0 \\ 0 & 2.25 \end{bmatrix}.$$

It is not a coincidence that the covariance between X_1 and X_2 is zero. When X_1 and X_2 are independent, as it is the case here; it is always true that they are also uncorrelated. You can find out more about the very important concept of independence and its consequences in Appendix B.

4.7 Summary

- Optimal investment problems admit closed-form solution only when the market is complete. The only exception is the quadratic utility, which admits closed-form solutions with both multiple risky assets and incomplete markets.

- One can approximate any utility function by the corresponding second-order Taylor expansion and solve the investment problem for the approximating quadratic utility instead. The result is the same as the first iteration of Newton's algorithm described in Section 4.2. Typically, one requires more than one iteration to reach a reasonable degree of optimality, therefore the quadratic approximation does not often suffice.

4.8 Notes

Newton's root-finding algorithm is standard and can be found in most textbooks on numerical mathematics, such as Cheney and Kincaid (1999). Economists use whole chains of optimizations to find optimal portfolio allocations and optimal consumption of individuals over their lifetime. An introduction to these types of models can be found in Heer and Maußner (2004).

4.9 Exercises

Exercise 4.1 (Taylor expansion). Find the first-order Taylor expansion of

$$(1 + x)^{1/(1-\gamma)}$$

around $x = 0$. This expansion was used to derive the percentage error of certainty equivalent wealth in (4.20).

Exercise 4.2 (stopping rule). Newton's algorithm of Section 4.2 stops when

$$\text{stopping rule A:} \quad \left| \frac{V_{\text{certain}}(\alpha_{\text{opt}})}{V_{\text{certain}}(\alpha^{(n)})} - 1 \right| < \texttt{tolerance}$$

is small. But perhaps we should stop when

$$\text{stopping rule B:} \quad \left| \frac{(V_{\text{certain}}(\alpha_{\text{opt}})/V_{\text{safe}}) - 1}{(V_{\text{certain}}(\alpha^{(n)})/V_{\text{safe}}) - 1} \right| < \texttt{tolerance}$$

is small? Argue which stopping rule is more appropriate.

Exercise 4.3 (stopping rule for HARA investor with unit local risk aversion). Using the scaling property (3.36) show that

$$\frac{V_{\gamma,1\,\text{certain}}(\alpha_{\text{opt}})}{V_{\gamma,1\,\text{certain}}(\alpha^{(n)})} - 1$$

$$= \frac{\gamma(V_{\gamma,\gamma\,\text{certain}}(\alpha^{(n)})/V_{\text{safe}})}{1 + \gamma((V_{\gamma,\gamma\,\text{certain}}(\alpha^{(n)})/V_{\text{safe}}) - 1)} \left(\frac{V_{\gamma,\gamma\,\text{certain}}(\alpha_{\text{opt}})}{V_{\gamma,\gamma\,\text{certain}}(\alpha^{(n)})} - 1 \right).$$

Exercise 4.4 (arbitrage-adjusted Sharpe ratio). Assume that the risk-free return is 2% per annum. Decompose the NIKKEI 225 return into a pure Sharpe ratio part and a pure arbitrage part. Compute the standard and the arbitrage-adjusted Sharpe ratios. Do this by adapting procedure HARAmax in program *chapter4sect4b.gss*.

Exercise 4.5 (quadratic approximation with multiple risky assets). Use the set-up of Section 4.5 to compute the optimal investment for $\gamma = 5$ using the second-order Taylor approximation of the power utility. Compare the outcome with the exact results obtained in Section 4.5. Reduce the Sharpe ratio of the risky assets to 0.1 and recompute the exact portfolio weights together with the quadratic approximation weights. Note that the approximation improves dramatically.

Exercise 4.6 (mean–variance efficient portfolio). Let X be a vector of risky excess returns. Denote the vector of expected excess returns μ and define the square matrix Ω of second non-central moments,

$$\Omega = \text{E}[XX^*].$$

By definition the variance–covariance matrix Σ of excess returns X is given as

$$\Sigma = E[XX^*] - E[X]E[X^*] = \Omega - \mu\mu^*.$$

The vectors $\Omega^{-1}\mu$ and $\Sigma^{-1}\mu$ differ only by a scalar multiple and both represent the so-called **mean–variance efficient portfolio**. Express $\Omega^{-1}\mu$ in terms of $\Sigma^{-1}\mu$. (Hint: define $b = \Omega^{-1}\mu$ and express Ωb using Σb.)

Exercise 4.7 (maximum Sharpe ratio). Given a vector of risky excess returns X find the market Sharpe ratio, that is, maximize

$$SR^2(X) = \max_\alpha \frac{(E[\alpha^* X])^2}{E[(\alpha^* X)^2] - (E[\alpha^* X])^2}. \tag{4.44}$$

Exercise 4.8 (perfectly correlated assets). Let X_1 and X_2 be two random excess returns. Describe the circumstances under which the matrix Ω

$$\Omega = \begin{bmatrix} E[X_1^2] & E[X_1 X_2] \\ E[X_1 X_2] & E[X_2^2] \end{bmatrix}$$

is not invertible. Repeat the same exercise with

$$\Sigma = \begin{bmatrix} E[X_1^2] - (E[X_1])^2 & E[X_1 X_2] - E[X_1]E[X_2] \\ E[X_1 X_2] - E[X_1]E[X_2] & E[X_2^2] - (E[X_2])^2 \end{bmatrix}.$$

5

Pricing in Dynamically Complete Markets

The one-period model is often too simple for practical purposes. An individual investor has approximately 50 years of adult life when she is making choices over savings, investment and consumption. If important investment decisions are taken every five years, we need at least a 10-period model. Professional investors trade even more frequently. A trader on a stock exchange may adjust his or her portfolio several times a day resulting in more than 500 investment decisions a month.

This chapter explains the essentials of dynamic decision-making in frictionless complete markets where every source of financial risk is priced in the market. Even though real financial markets are never complete, the complete market approximation is an extremely useful one, firstly because it facilitates the mathematical analysis and secondly because it gives a reasonably good approximation of what is going on in reality. The latter point will be examined in greater detail in Chapter 12, which looks at dynamic decision-making in incomplete markets.

The aim of this chapter is to introduce reader to the techniques which are instrumental in tackling asset pricing in a dynamic framework. We use a simple set-up with the European call option as a focus asset in a discrete-time model to illustrate the backward recursive pricing procedure and to recover the option price as an unconditional expectation under risk-neutral probabilities. Further important concepts related to dynamic portfolio selection are introduced in Chapter 8 on information management and in Chapter 9 on the change of measure.

5.1 Options and Portfolio Insurance

Consider the following hypothetical situation. Due to an exceptionally high number of new employees, pension fund 'A' will receive £10 million in pension contributions one year from now. The fund will want to invest this amount in the FTSE 100 Index, but is worried that the price of shares may become over-inflated over the next year before it does so. Consequently, the fund decides to buy a 5% out-of-the-money European call option expiring in one year's time. It means that the fund is buying the right (but not the obligation) to buy shares in the FTSE 100 Index in one year's time at a price 5% higher than the current price. Consequently, the fund is protected against price increases in excess of 5%.

Consider pension fund 'B'. Currently, the fund has £20 million invested in the FTSE 100 Index, but due to an exceptional number of retiring employees fund 'B' will have to pay £10 million in one year's time. The fund is concerned about a potential short-term slump; therefore, it buys a 10% out-of-the-money European put option expiring in one year. This gives the fund the right (but not the obligation) to sell FTSE 100 shares at a price 10% lower than the current price one year from today, and protects it against price decreases larger than 10%.

To summarize, buying a call option is equivalent to securing the potential upside gains beforehand, while buying a put option provides a beforehand protection from downside losses. Conversely, the seller (issuer) of a call option is giving up the potential upside gains for a fixed up-front payment, while the seller (issuer) of a put option is providing insurance against potential downside losses for a fixed premium up front. The price specified in the option contract (that is, the price at which the holder of the option has the right to buy or sell the underlying stock) is called the **strike price**.

What is a fair price for a call option? Intuitively, if the underlying stock price is very likely to go up, we would expect the call to be more expensive than if the price is almost certainly expected to fall. Quite surprisingly, in many situations this intuition turns out to be a poor guide. Our intuition is based on the fact that the option pay-off is not a linear function of the stock return and, therefore, the option is not a redundant security relative to the stock and the risk-free bond. This, of course, is only true if one takes into account 'static' replicating portfolios where the proportion of stock holding is fixed over time. But as soon as one considers time-dependent replicating strategies the intuition becomes less clear. It turns out that dynamic replicating portfolios consisting of time-varying proportions of the underlying stock and a risk-free bond can match the pay-off of options quite well, and in some idealized instances perfectly.

5.2 Option Pricing

5.2.1 *Representation of Stock Prices*

Our aim is to determine the option price relative to the current stock price. First of all we have to choose a basis time interval at which we will trade the stock. Our aim is to price equity options, a specific example we have in mind is European call options on the FTSE 100 Index. To keep the example as simple as possible, we will make several simplifying assumptions. Firstly, for a realistic analysis one would have to consider trading at least once a week, but that would result in more trading periods than one can comfortably fit on a page. Hence we will consider trading once a month, with the initial time to expiry three months. The second simplification is to ignore transaction costs, which in reality can contribute significantly to the cost of a replicating strategy. Thirdly, the risk-free rate is assumed to be the same both for borrowing and lending. Last, but not least, we will exclude other options from the replicating portfolio.

The simplest model of stock prices assumes that the monthly returns are independent and identically distributed, in short IID. More specifically, we will assume that the monthly return can only take two values, high and low, R_u and R_d. It is not a terribly realistic model, but anything more sophisticated would take us into

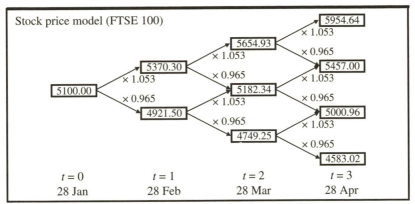

Figure 5.1. Binomial model for the FTSE 100 Index.

the world of incomplete markets, which is somewhat more complex and will be discussed later in Chapter 12.

The next step is to **calibrate** the model to monthly returns. Calibration is a process of matching at least some aspects of real data by selecting suitable values of parameters in the model. The average monthly return on the FTSE 100 between 1984 and 2001 was about 0.9%, but in five-year subsamples this figure varies from 0.15% to 1.3%. The standard deviation between 1984 and 2001 was about 4.4%, in five-year subsamples it varies between 3.7% and 6.2%. The variation of the average return and of its standard deviation contradicts our assumption of identically distributed returns, but we shall ignore this contradiction for the time being. To match the monthly expected return and its standard deviation our task is to find numbers R_u, R_d and p such that

$$p R_u + (1 - p) R_d = 1.009,$$
$$p R_u^2 + (1 - p) R_d^2 = 0.044^2 + 1.009^2.$$

Since we have two equations and three unknowns there is a certain degree of arbitrariness in the choice of p; we will simply choose $p = \frac{1}{2}$. Solving for R_u and R_d yields

$$R_u = 1.053 \quad \text{with } p_u = \tfrac{1}{2}, \tag{5.1}$$
$$R_d = 0.965 \quad \text{with } p_d = \tfrac{1}{2}. \tag{5.2}$$

The probabilities p_u and p_d are called **objective probabilities**; they are our best assessment of the frequency with which R_u and R_d will occur in reality.

The entire model for stock prices is described in Figure 5.1. Our model has three periods, each corresponding to one month, and four dates

$$t = 0, 1, 2, 3.$$

If $t = 0$ corresponds to 28 January, then $t = 3$ corresponds to the expiry date three months from the starting date, 28 April of the same year. For the purpose of this example we assume the value of the FTSE 100 Index on 28 January is 5100.00 points.

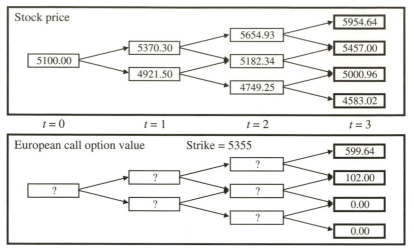

Figure 5.2.   Intrinsic value of a European call option struck at $K = 5355$.

The last ingredient is the risk-free interest rate. Assuming a constant rate equivalent to 4% per annum, the monthly risk-free return is

$$R_f = 1.04^{1/12} = 1.0033.$$

5.2.2   Intrinsic Option Value

Consider now a 5% out-of-the-money call option that expires in three months. Such an option gives its owner the right to buy FTSE 100 shares at the strike price $K = £5100 \times 1.05 = £5355$ in three months. Clearly, this right is worthless if the FTSE 100 is below 5355 points in three months' time; in such a case we say that the option has expired out of the money. In the top two nodes at time $t = 3$, however, the option is in the money, and exercising it will lead to an immediate gain of $5954.64 - 5355 = £599.64$ and $5457 - 5355 = £102$, respectively. The pay-off from exercising the option is known as the **intrinsic value** of the option. The stock price and the option value at expiry are depicted in Figure 5.2.

5.2.3   Static Replicating Strategy

How much should we pay for the option at $t = 0$? Suppose we have x_1 pounds (dollars, euros, yen) in the bank account and we buy x_2 FTSE 100 shares. After three periods the money in the bank account becomes $R_f^3 x_1 = 1.0099 x_1$, while the value of the shares will depend on the FTSE value at $t = 3$, the value of the shares is either $5954.64 x_2$ or $5467 x_2$ or $5000.96 x_2$ or $4583.02 x_2$. Perfect replication of the option pay-off therefore requires

$$
\underbrace{\begin{bmatrix} 1.0099 \\ 1.0099 \\ 1.0099 \\ 1.0099 \end{bmatrix}}_{\text{safe return}} x_1 +
\underbrace{\begin{bmatrix} 5954.64 \\ 5467.00 \\ 5000.96 \\ 4583.02 \end{bmatrix}}_{\text{stock price}} x_2 =
\underbrace{\begin{bmatrix} 599.64 \\ 102.00 \\ 0.00 \\ 0.00 \end{bmatrix}}_{\text{option pay-off}}.
\tag{5.3}
$$

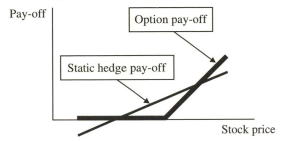

Figure 5.3. Static replicating portfolio and option value.

Using the techniques of Chapter 2 one can easily verify that (5.3) does not have a solution. Intuitively, this is quite clear; the left-hand side is linear in the stock price, whereas the right-hand side, being equal to $\max(0, \text{stock price} - 5355)$, is not linear in the stock price. This situation is depicted in Figure 5.3.

5.3 Dynamic Replicating Trading Strategy

One of the greatest insights of modern finance is that dynamic hedging can significantly reduce, and sometimes completely eliminate, the hedging error of a static hedge. It is important to realize that if one looks only one period ahead, then each node in our decision tree represents the familiar one-period model with two states (high stock return, low stock return) and two securities (stock and bond). This allows the hedge to be chosen separately in each node of the decision tree. Since we know the option pay-off at $t = 3$ it is quite natural to find the replicating strategy working backwards from time $t = 2$ to time $t = 0$.

5.3.1 One-Period Hedge

We begin in the highest node at time $t = 2$ (see Figure 5.4). We want to replicate the option pay-off in the next period, which is known to be

$$b = \begin{bmatrix} 599.64 \\ 102.00 \end{bmatrix} = \begin{bmatrix} C_u \\ C_d \end{bmatrix}.$$

There are two basis assets available for hedging, a risk-free bond (bank account) with initial value 1 and terminal pay-off 1.0033, and the stock with initial value $S_{\text{now}} = 5654.93$ and terminal pay-off either $S_u = 5954.64$ or $S_d = 5457.00$. In the established notation the pay-off matrix of basis assets is

$$A = \begin{bmatrix} 1.0033 & 5954.64 \\ 1.0033 & 5457.00 \end{bmatrix} = \begin{bmatrix} R_f & S_u \\ R_f & S_d \end{bmatrix},$$

with basis asset prices equal to

$$S = \begin{bmatrix} 1 \\ 5654.93 \end{bmatrix} = \begin{bmatrix} 1 \\ S_{\text{now}} \end{bmatrix}.$$

We are looking for the replicating portfolio x such that

$$Ax = b.$$

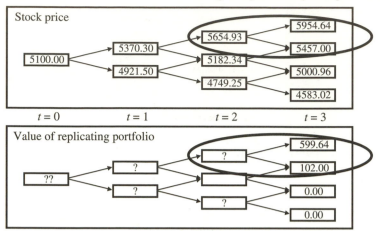

Figure 5.4.   One-period model determining the value of option replicating portfolio in the contingency with the highest stock price at $t = 2$.

The solution is

$$\begin{bmatrix} x_1 \\ x_2 \end{bmatrix} = \begin{bmatrix} 1.0033 & 5954.64 \\ 1.0033 & 5457.00 \end{bmatrix}^{-1} \begin{bmatrix} 599.64 \\ 102.00 \end{bmatrix} = \begin{bmatrix} -5337.39 \\ 1 \end{bmatrix}.$$

The value of x_1 represents the amount of money in the bank account and x_2 is the number of shares. This means we must hold one unit of the stock and borrow £5337.39 from the bank to generate the same pay-off as that of the option. Intuitively, this is quite clear: because the option ends in the money, its pay-off is a linear combination of the stock price minus strike price; therefore, one must hold one unit of the stock and have to borrow enough to repay K, the strike price. Recall that $K = 5355$ and consequently the amount to borrow is $5355/1.0033 = 5337.39$. The total cost of the replicating portfolio is equal to the cost of buying one unit of the stock, £5655, minus the amount borrowed at the risk-free rate, in total $5654.93 - 5337.39 = 317.54$.

5.3.2   Option Hedging Terminology: Option Delta

Practitioners call the number of shares in the hedging portfolio **delta**. It would be natural to denote 'option delta' by Δ, but unfortunately this symbol is used quite frequently to denote change in a variable, for example Δt stands for a small time interval. To avoid confusion we will denote the number of shares θ and we will use this symbol consistently throughout the book. Consequently, option delta will be denoted by θ wherever mathematical notation is required.

5.3.3   General Solution to the One-Period Hedging Problem

It is clear that dynamic hedging will require solution of many one-period hedging problems. It is therefore useful to make a brief digression to find a general solution of the replication problem $Ax = b$ with two states and two securities. Because the

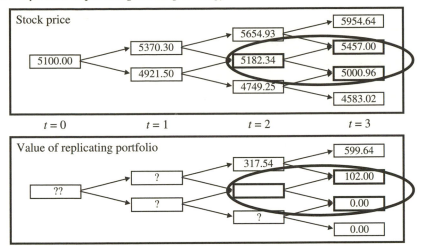

Figure 5.5. One-period model determining the value of option replicating portfolio when $S_2 = 5182.34$.

financial interpretation of x is

$$x = \begin{bmatrix} x_1 \\ x_2 \end{bmatrix} = \begin{bmatrix} \text{bank account} \\ \text{delta} \end{bmatrix}$$

$Ax = b$ becomes

$$\text{bank}\, R_f + \text{delta}\, S_u = C_u, \tag{5.4}$$

$$\text{bank}\, R_f + \text{delta}\, S_d = C_d. \tag{5.5}$$

Subtracting (5.5) from (5.4) we find the option delta

$$\text{delta} = \frac{C_u - C_d}{S_u - S_d},$$

and plugging delta into (5.4) we find the bank account balance

$$\text{bank} = \frac{C_d S_u - C_u S_d}{(S_u - S_d) R_f}.$$

The bank account balance can be expressed in terms of stock returns if we divide both numerator and denominator by the current stock price

$$\text{bank} = \frac{C_d(S_u/S_{now}) - C_u(S_d/S_{now})}{(S_u/S_{now} - S_d/S_{now}) R_f} = \frac{C_d R_u - C_u R_d}{(R_u - R_d) R_f}.$$

The total cost of the replicating portfolio is equal to

$$\text{bank} + \text{delta}\, S_{now} = \frac{C_d R_u - C_u R_d}{(R_u - R_d) R_f} + S_{now} \frac{C_u - C_d}{S_u - S_d} \tag{5.6}$$

$$= \frac{C_d R_u - C_u R_d}{(R_u - R_d) R_f} + \frac{C_u - C_d}{R_u - R_d} \tag{5.7}$$

$$= C_d \frac{R_u - R_f}{(R_u - R_d) R_f} + C_u \frac{R_f - R_d}{(R_u - R_d) R_f}. \tag{5.8}$$

Consider a one-period model with two states and two securities, a safe bank account with interest rate $R_f - 1$ and a risky security with return R_u or R_d corresponding to end-of-period prices S_u and S_d. The perfect replicating portfolio of a pay-off C with values C_u, C_d has the following characteristics:

$$\text{delta} = \frac{C_u - C_d}{S_u - S_d}, \tag{5.9}$$

$$\text{bank} = \frac{C_d R_u - C_u R_d}{(R_u - R_d) R_f}, \tag{5.10}$$

$$\text{no-arbitrage value}(C) = C_d \underbrace{\frac{R_u - R_f}{(R_u - R_d) R_f}}_{\text{state price}_d} + C_u \underbrace{\frac{R_f - R_d}{(R_u - R_d) R_f}}_{\text{state price}_u}. \tag{5.11}$$

Numerically,

$$\text{bank} = 11.927 C_d - 10.930 C_u, \tag{5.12}$$

$$\text{value}(C) = 0.4338 C_u + 0.5629 C_d. \tag{5.13}$$

5.3.4 Dynamic Hedging at $t = 2$, Continued

The situation in the middle node at $t = 2$ is depicted in Figure 5.5. We have

$$\begin{bmatrix} C_u \\ C_d \end{bmatrix} = \begin{bmatrix} 102.00 \\ 0.00 \end{bmatrix}, \qquad \begin{bmatrix} S_u \\ S_d \end{bmatrix} = \begin{bmatrix} 5457.00 \\ 5000.96 \end{bmatrix},$$

and the one-period risky returns are by assumption always the same $R_u = 1.053$, $R_d = 0.965$. From (5.9), (5.10)

$$\text{delta} = \frac{102 - 0}{5457 - 5000.96} = 0.224,$$

$$\text{bank} = \frac{-102.003 \times 0.965}{(1.053 - 0.965) 1.0033} = -1115,$$

$$\text{value}(C) = 0.4338 \times 102 = 44.25.$$

In the lowest node at $t = 2$ (see Figure 5.6), there is nothing to hedge because the option will finish out of the money. Consequently, the replicating portfolio is characterized by

$$\text{delta} = 0, \qquad \text{bank} = 0, \qquad \text{value} = 0.$$

5.3.5 Dynamic Hedging at $t = 1$

The conclusion of the previous section is that at time $t = 2$ we need £317.54 in the highest node, £44.25 in the middle node and £0 in the lowest node to replicate the option pay-off at $t = 3$. Our task has now shifted forward by one period. At $t = 1$ we no longer attempt to replicate the pay-off of the option at $t = 3$; instead we try to replicate the amount of money at $t = 2$ needed to replicate the option pay-off at $t = 3$.

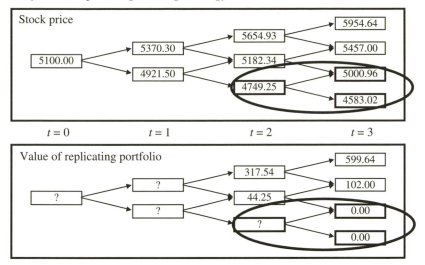

Figure 5.6. One-period model determining the value of
option replicating portfolio when $S_2 = 4749.25$.

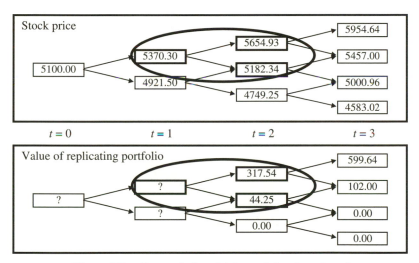

Figure 5.7. One-period model determining the value of
option replicating portfolio at $t = 1$ when $S_1 = 5370.30$.

More specifically, in the upper node at time $t = 1$ (see Figure 5.7) the value to be
replicated is

$$\begin{bmatrix} C_u \\ C_d \end{bmatrix} = \begin{bmatrix} 317.54 \\ 44.25 \end{bmatrix},$$

with the corresponding stock prices

$$\begin{bmatrix} S_u \\ S_d \end{bmatrix} = \begin{bmatrix} 5654.93 \\ 5182.34 \end{bmatrix}.$$

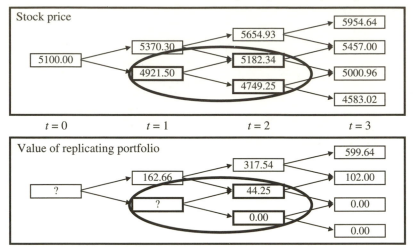

Figure 5.8. One-period model determining the value of option replicating portfolio at $t = 1$ when $S_1 = 4921.50$.

From (5.9)–(5.11)

$$\text{delta} = \frac{317.54 - 44.25}{5654.93 - 5182.34} = 0.578,$$

$$\text{bank} = \frac{44.25 \times 1.053 - 317.54 \times 0.965}{(1.053 - 0.965)1.0033} = -2943,$$

$$\text{value} = 0.4338 \times 317.54 + 0.5629 \times 44.25 = 162.66.$$

The situation at the lower node at $t = 1$ is depicted in Figure 5.8:

$$\text{delta} = \frac{44.25 - 0}{5182.34 - 4749.25} = 0.102,$$

$$\text{bank} = \frac{-44.24 \times 0.965}{(1.053 - 0.965)1.0033} = -484,$$

$$\text{value} = 0.4338 \times 44.25 = 19.19.$$

5.3.6   Hedging at $t = 0$

Finally, at $t = 0$ we are replicating the cost at $t = 1$ needed to replicate the cost at $t = 2$ needed to replicate the option pay-off at $t = 3$. This may sound very complicated, but it is no more difficult than any of the previous steps.

Referring to Figure 5.9 we have

$$\text{delta} = \frac{162.66 - 19.19}{5370.30 - 4921.50} = 0.320,$$

$$\text{bank} = \frac{19.19 \times 1.053 - 162.66 \times 0.965}{(1.053 - 0.965)1.0033} = -1544,$$

$$\text{value} = 0.4338 \times 162.66 + 0.5629 \times 19.19 = 81.36,$$

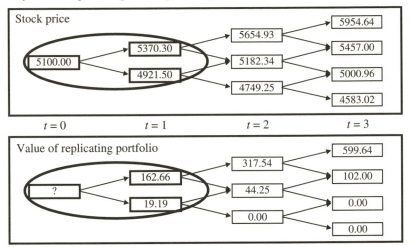

Figure 5.9. One-period model determining the value of
option replicating portfolio at $t = 0$.

$$\begin{bmatrix} C_u \\ C_d \end{bmatrix} = \begin{bmatrix} 162.66 \\ 19.19 \end{bmatrix}, \qquad \begin{bmatrix} S_u \\ S_d \end{bmatrix} = \begin{bmatrix} 5370.30 \\ 4921.50 \end{bmatrix}.$$

5.3.7 Self-Financing Trading Strategy and Option Pricing

To conclude, we have devised a **self-financing trading strategy** which costs
£81.36 and without adding extra resources along the way it generates, after three
months, the same pay-off as the call option. In other words, we have found a
perfect hedge for the option which costs £81.36, consequently £81.36 is the no-
arbitrage price of the call option at $t = 0$. If the option were more expensive we
would sell (or borrow) the option and buy the self-financing portfolio, and vice
versa.

Note that the term 'self-financing' relates only to the interim dates $t = 1, 2$;
at $t = 0$ one has to put in £81.36, at $t = 3$ one will collect a random amount
depending on the terminal stock price.

The entire replicating strategy is summarized in Figure 5.10. The values in Figure 5.10 are precise to the last decimal place, while the values that we have calculated
above differ slightly due to rounding errors.

5.3.8 Numerical Implementation

The binomial option pricing model of this section is implemented as a GAUSS
program *chapter5sect3.gss* and as an Excel spreadsheet *chapter5sect3.xls*. The
GAUSS program stores stock and option prices in a square matrix, where the column
index tt corresponds to the time period $+1$ and the row index ii is equal to the
number of low returns $+1$ (see Figure 5.11).

S0	K	R_u	R_d	r
5100	5355	1.053	0.965	0.0033

Stock prices			
			5954.64
		5654.93	
	5370.30		5457.00
5100.00		5182.34	
	4921.50		5000.96
		4749.25	
			4583.02
$t = 0$	$t = 1$	$t = 2$	$t = 3$

Value of replicating portfolio			
			599.64
		317.54	
	162.66		102.00
81.36		44.25	
	19.19		0.00
		0.00	
			0.00
$t = 0$	$t = 1$	$t = 2$	$t = 3$

Bank account			
			599.64
		−5337.39	
	−2942.92		102.00
−1548.87		−1114.88	
	−483.63		0.00
		0.00	
			0.00

Number of shares			
			0.000
		1.000	
	0.578		0.000
0.320		0.224	
	0.102		0.000
		0.000	
			0.000

Figure 5.10. Dynamic self-financing trading strategy that replicates the cash flows generated by one European call option written on the FTSE 100.

ii \ tt	1	2	3	4
1	5100.00	5370.30	5654.93	5954.64
2		4921.50	5182.34	5457.00
3			4749.25	5000.96
4				4583.02

Figure 5.11. Indexation of stock and option prices in a binomial model. Illustration to the GAUSS program *chapter5sect3.gss*.

```
@************************@
@        market          @
@************************@
S0=5100;                                    @ initial stock price  @
strike=5355;
Rsafe=1.0033;                               @ monthly safe return  @
R=1.053~0.965;                              @ monthly stock return @


@************************@
@     Risk-neutral       @
@     probabilities      @
@************************@
QDistr=((Rsafe-R[2])~(R[1]-Rsafe))/(R[1]-R[2]);


@************************@
@   grid indexation      @
@************************@
Tidx=4;                         @ number of trading dates        @
dlnS=ln(R[1])-ln(R[2]);         @ increment on log price grid     @
highlnR=ln(R[1]);               @ the highest return over one period @
```

```
@ there are tt live cells at time tt, highest stock price at the top    @
@ log price at cell   1 at time tt is ln(S0)+(tt-1)*highlnR             @
@ log price at cell ii at time tt is ln(S0)+(tt-1)*highlnR-(ii-1)*dlnS @

C = zeros(Tidx,Tidx);            @ initialize the grid for call option price @
stock = zeros(Tidx,Tidx);        @ initialize the grid for stock price       @
delta = zeros(Tidx,Tidx);        @ initialize the grid for option delta      @

@************************@
@      option payoff     @
@************************@
S_T=seqa(ln(S0)+(Tidx-1)*highlnR,-dlnS,Tidx); @ log of stock return at T  @
S_T=exp(S_T);                              @ stock price at maturity       @
C_T=maxc((S_T-strike)'|zeros(1,rows(S_T))); @ option payoff at maturity @
stock[.,Tidx]=S_T;                         @ stock price grid at maturity  @
C[.,Tidx]=C_T;                             @ option price =option payoff at T @

@************************@
@       main loop        @
@************************@
for tt (Tidx-1,1,-1);
    for ii (1,tt,1);
        stock[ii,tt]=S0*exp((tt-1)*highlnR-(ii-1)*dlnS);
        C[ii,tt]=(QDistr*C[ii:ii+1,tt+1])/Rsafe;  @ risk-neutral pricing @
        delta[ii,tt]=(C[ii,tt+1]-C[ii+1,tt+1])
                        /(R[1]-R[2])/stock[ii,tt];
    endfor;
endfor;
```

5.4   Risk-Neutral Probabilities in a Multi-Period Model

In the preceding section we have computed an entire self-financing strategy which generates the option value at expiry, and we have concluded that the initial outlay of this strategy must be equal to the initial option price. It is remarkable that the option value can be computed *without knowing the option delta*; indeed, looking at equation (5.13), one only needs to know option values in the next period to work out the current value of the option.

This result is not accidental. Each one-period submodel we have dealt with in the previous section is complete. Chapter 2 tells us that every complete market has a unique set of state prices which moreover only depend on the basis asset returns (see (2.36)). In our particular case asset returns are IID, which means they are the same in all one-period submodels, which implies one has the same pricing equation, namely (5.13), in all of them.

Chapter 2 also tells us that we can rephrase state prices in terms of risk-neutral probabilities; specifically, the no-arbitrage price of pay-off

$$\begin{bmatrix} C_u \\ C_d \end{bmatrix}$$

is given as the risk-neutral expectation of the discounted pay-off

$$\text{no-arbitrage value}(C) = \frac{q_u C_u + q_d C_d}{R_f}, \tag{5.14}$$

where the risk-neutral probabilities q_u and q_d are chosen such that the risk-neutral expectation of return on all basis assets is equal to the risk-free return,

$$q_u + q_d = 1,$$
$$q_u R_u + q_d R_d = R_f.$$

This gives conditional risk-neutral probabilities,

$$q_u = \frac{R_f - R_d}{R_u - R_d} = \frac{1.0033 - 0.965}{1.053 - 0.965} = 0.435\,23, \tag{5.15}$$

$$q_d = \frac{R_u - R_f}{R_u - R_d} = \frac{1.053 - 1.0033}{1.053 - 0.965} = 0.564\,77, \tag{5.16}$$

and the valuation formula

$$\text{no-arbitrage value}(C) = \frac{0.435\,23 C_u + 0.564\,77 C_d}{1.0033}. \tag{5.17}$$

Note that (5.17) is identical to (5.13), that is, risk-neutral probabilities are a clever mathematical shortcut for writing down the no-arbitrage value of a replicating portfolio.

5.4.1   *Valuation Formula as a Conditional Expectation*

Denoting C_t the option price at time t we can write the option pricing formula (5.17) more elegantly as a conditional expectation:

$$C_2 = \mathrm{E}_2^Q\left[\frac{C_3}{R_f}\right]. \tag{5.18}$$

The letter Q in E_2^Q denotes risk-neutral probability, the subscript '2' in E_2^Q signifies the expectation *conditional on the information at time $t = 2$*. In words the option value at time $t = 2$ is the risk-neutral expectation, *conditional on the information at time $t = 2$*, of the option price at time $t = 3$ discounted at the risk-free rate. The nice thing about equation (5.18) is that it holds for *all nodes* at time $t = 2$ simultaneously, namely, the statement

$$C_2 = \mathrm{E}_2^Q\left[\frac{C_3}{R_f}\right]$$

is, in our model, equivalent to three separate identities (see Figure 5.12):

$$317.54 = \frac{599.64 q_u + 102.00 q_d}{1.0033},$$

$$44.25 = \frac{102.00 q_u + 0.00 q_d}{1.0033},$$

$$0.00 = \frac{0.00 q_u + 0.00 q_d}{1.0033}.$$

Similarly, the option price *in all nodes* at time $t = 1$ can be expressed in terms of C_2 as

$$C_1 = \mathrm{E}_1^Q\left[\frac{C_2}{R_f}\right]. \tag{5.19}$$

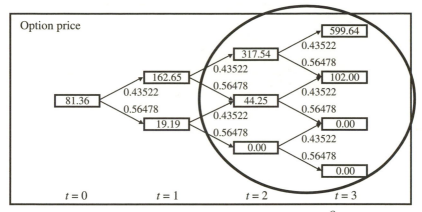

Figure 5.12. Illustration to conditional expectation $E_2^Q[C_3]$.

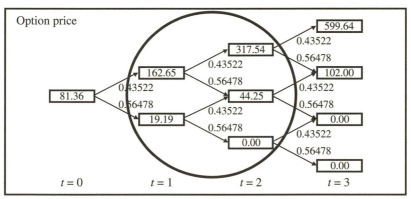

Figure 5.13. Illustration to conditional expectation $E_1^Q[C_2]/R_f$.

This expression stands for two equalities

$$162.65 = \frac{317.54 q_u + 44.25 q_d}{1.0033},$$

$$19.19 = \frac{44.25 q_u + 0.00 q_d}{1.0033},$$

graphically depicted in Figure 5.13.

Finally,

$$C_0 = E_0^Q\left[\frac{C_1}{R_f}\right] \tag{5.20}$$

means

$$81.36 = \frac{162.65 q_u + 19.19 q_d}{1.0033}. \tag{5.21}$$

Because the information at $t = 0$ is very simple (there is only one node in the decision tree at $t = 0$) $E_0[.]$ is often called the **unconditional expectation** and the subscript '0' is sometimes dropped.

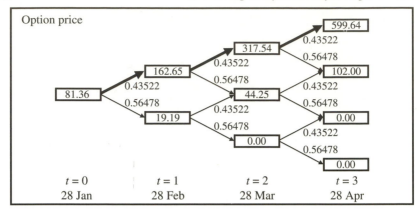

Figure 5.14. Unconditional risk-neutral probability of reaching $C_3 = 599.64$.

To summarize, by substituting (5.18) into (5.19) and the resulting expression into (5.20) we have shown that

$$C_0 = \mathrm{E}_0^{Q}\left[\frac{1}{R_f}\mathrm{E}_1^{Q}\left[\frac{1}{R_f}\mathrm{E}_2^{Q}\left[\frac{C_3}{R_f}\right]\right]\right],$$

which can be simplified to

$$C_0 = \frac{1}{R_f^3}\mathrm{E}_0^{Q}[\mathrm{E}_1^{Q}[\mathrm{E}_2^{Q}[C_3]]] \tag{5.22}$$

due to the fact that R_f is constant.

The **law of iterated expectations** (sometimes called **Bayes law**) states that in a chain of conditional expectations the one with the lowest time index prevails, and consequently we obtain the dynamic no-arbitrage pricing formula:

$$C_0 = \frac{1}{R_f^3}\mathrm{E}_0^{Q}[C_3].$$

5.5 The Law of Iterated Expectations

The law of iterated expectations is a natural consequence of the properties of conditional probabilities. To convince the reader that the law uses only very elementary operations, we will demonstrate that it works in our specific option example. This involves showing that

$$\frac{1}{R_f^3}\mathrm{E}_0^{Q}[\mathrm{E}_1^{Q}[\mathrm{E}_2^{Q}[C_3]]] = \frac{1}{R_f^3}\mathrm{E}_0^{Q}[C_3]. \tag{5.23}$$

Recall from (5.21) that the left-hand side is equal to 81.36. Before we can evaluate the right-hand side, we need to find the distribution of C_3 as seen at time $t = 0$.

There is only one path starting at $t = 0$ that reaches $C_3 = 599.64$ (see Figure 5.14), and the risk-neutral probability of following this path is simply the product of one-step conditional probabilities on this path (this is a consequence of the chain rule

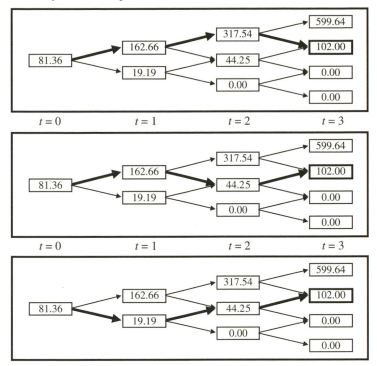

Figure 5.15. Paths reaching $C_3 = 102.00$.

for conditional probabilities discussed in Appendix B). Mathematically,

$$Q(C_3 = 599.64 \mid S_0 = 5100) = q_u^3 = 0.08244.$$

There are three ways to reach $C_3 = 102.00$, which are depicted in Figure 5.15. The probability of each of these paths is $q_u^2 q_d$ because in each case we go up twice and down once. As a result

$$Q(C_3 = 102.00 \mid S_0 = 5100) = 3q_u^2 q_d = 3 * 0.43522^2 * 0.56478 = 0.32094.$$

In the remaining cases $C_3 = 0.00$ and hence

$$Q(C_3 = 0.00 \mid S_0 = 5100) = 1 - 0.08244 - 0.33094 = 0.58662.$$

With the distribution of C_3 (as of $t = 0$) in hand it is straightforward to evaluate the right-hand side of (5.23),

$$\frac{1}{R_f^3} E_0^Q[C_3] = \frac{0.08244 \times 599.64 + 0.32094 \times 102.00 + 0.586626 \times 0.00}{1.0033^3}$$

$$= 81.36;$$

thus we have

$$\frac{1}{R_f^3} E_0^Q[E_1^Q[E_2^Q[C_3]]] = \frac{1}{R_f^3} E_0^Q[C_3].$$

5.6 Summary

- A multi-period model of financial markets is complete as long as all one-period models corresponding to individual nodes in the decision tree are complete.

- The complete market model with stock and risk-free short-term borrowing makes many simplifying assumptions. The most crucial are absence of transaction costs and limited short-term variability in stock prices—we can allow for only two values of stock return over any one period. The risk-free rate can vary over time as long as its variation depends only on the history of stock prices.

- In a complete market with stock and risk-free borrowing any cash flow that depends only on the stock price history has a unique no-arbitrage price. The no-arbitrage price is equal to the cost of a self-financing portfolio that exactly replicates the cash flow. We have used the example of a European call option which has a particularly simple cash flow with pay-off only at expiry date. Security with pay-offs at multiple dates can be thought of as a portfolio of simpler securities, each with pay-off at only one date. In conclusion, the no-arbitrage price of any security is equal to the risk-neutral expectation of the present discounted value of the cash flow it generates. In the European call option example

$$C_0 = \mathrm{E}_0^Q \left[\frac{\max(S_T - K, 0)}{R_{f0} R_{f1} \cdots R_{fT-1}} \right].$$

5.7 Notes

The binomial lattice model of stock prices is due to Sharpe (1978). The risk-neutral valuation approach is due to Ross (1978); more explicit discussion of binomial model appears in Cox et al. (1979).

In this chapter objective and risk-neutral probabilities appear side by side for the first time. Roughly speaking, risk-neutral probabilities reflect the price of wealth in individual states of the market (state prices), whereas objective probabilities tell us how likely those states are to occur. It is important to bear in mind that objective probabilities are in fact our *subjective* guess of how likely the different states are; in reality, we cannot hope that someone behind the scenes is flipping a coin or rolling dice to generate states according to a particular (random) formula. The classic statement of this is by de Finetti (1974a): '[objective] probability does not exist'. One can use probabilistic models with great advantage but every user has to supply his or her own 'objective' probabilities and each user is solely responsible for the actions he or she takes based on such models.

5.8 Exercises

Exercise 5.1 (calibration of a binomial tree and option pricing). From the data we know the following parameters: the monthly risk-free rate is 0.5%, expected monthly rate of stock return is 1%, monthly volatility σ (standard deviation) of the stock return is 3%. Price a European call option (an option to buy the stock at

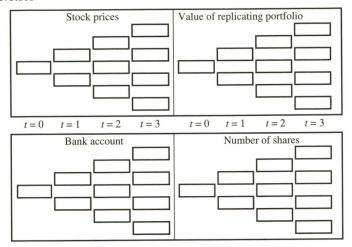

Figure 5.16. Replicating portfolio.

maturity at the strike price) with three months to expiry and strike price $K = £10.1$. Assume that current stock price is $S_0 = £10$ (the option is initially 1% out of the money). Proceed in the following steps.

(a) Calibrate a binomial tree to the stock expected return and volatility, assuming that the one-step conditional probabilities are $p_u = p_d = \frac{1}{2}$ at each node. Take one step to be equal to one month.

$$R_u =$$
$$R_d =$$

(b) Find the self-financing portfolio that replicates the pay-off of the call option. In Figure 5.16 write down how much money you have to keep in the bank and how many units of stock you want to hold.

(c) How is the option price related to the value of the self-financing portfolio in (b)? **Circle one answer.**

   (i) The option price is always greater than the value of the self-financing replicating portfolio.

   (ii) The two are always the same.

   (iii) The option price is always smaller.

   (iv) The relationship changes from node to node.

Exercise 5.2 (path-dependent risk-neutral probabilities and asset pricing). Consider the stock price model in Figure 5.17.

(a) Compute risk-neutral probabilities in each one-period submodel.

   (i) At $t = 0$:

$$q_u =$$
$$q_d =$$

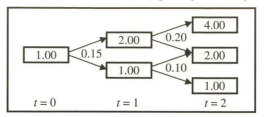

Figure 5.17. Binomial stock price model, no dividends,
stock prices at the nodes, risk-free rate of return between branches.

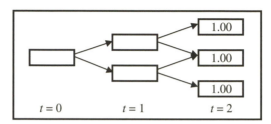

Figure 5.18. No-arbitrage value of pure discount bond with maturity at $t = 2$.

(ii) At $t = 1$ in the upper node:

$$q_u =$$
$$q_d =$$

(iii) At $t = 1$ in the lower node:

$$q_u =$$
$$q_d =$$

(b) How would the answer in part (a) change if the stock also paid a dividend equal to 10% of its price?

(c) Suppose we want to price a security with pay-off 1 at $t = 2$ (the so-called pure discount bond). Find the no-arbitrage price of the pure discount bond at $t = 0, 1$ and write it into the tree in Figure 5.18. Use the risk-neutral probabilities calculated in part (a).

(d) Price a European put option on the stock with strike $K = 3$. Write the no-arbitrage value of the option into the tree in Figure 5.19. Use the risk-neutral probabilities calculated in part (a).

Exercise 5.3 (consumption budget). Figure 5.20 depicts stock price scenarios over three dates $t = 0, 1, 2$ and the associated consumption levels of an investor. For example, when the stock market is doing well at $t = 1$, the investor will consume £700 a month, whereas if the stock market is performing poorly at $t = 1$ she will only consume £500.

(a) Calculate how much wealth is needed to finance this consumption strategy if the one-period risk-free rate is 5% and the investor can freely trade in stocks and use the safe bank account.

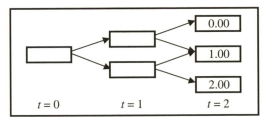

Figure 5.19. No-arbitrage value of a European put option with strike $K = 3$.

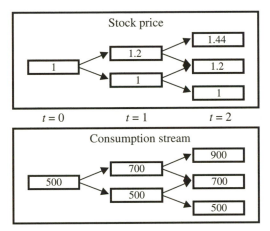

Figure 5.20. Stock prices and corresponding consumption levels.

(b) Consider a general consumption stream c_0, c_1, c_2. Use expectation under risk-neutral probability to express the fact that the consumption stream c_0, c_1, c_2 can be financed by initial wealth V_0.

Exercise 5.4 (calibration in trinomial lattice). Suppose the return on a stock can take three values: u, 1 and $1/u$ with probabilities p_1, p_2 and p_3. Find the values of p_1, p_2 and p_3 that will give an expected rate of return of 6% and a standard deviation of the rate of return equal to 10%.

(a) For $u = 1.10$:

$$p_1 =$$
$$p_2 =$$
$$p_3 =$$

(b) For $u = 1.13$:

$$p_1 =$$
$$p_2 =$$
$$p_3 =$$

6

Towards Continuous Time

In the previous chapter we considered a trading interval of one month. In this chapter we will use the same option pricing model, but we will reduce the trading interval to one week, one day, one hour, one minute, etc., to obtain the continuous-time no-arbitrage value of the option in the limit. However, we will see that there are two ways of reaching the limit. In the first case the logarithm of the stock price is subject to random but continuous movements up or down in what is known as *Brownian motion*; in the second case the stock price moves deterministically in one direction most of the time but once in a while it jumps in the opposite direction by a predetermined amount. The second type of limit is called the *Poisson jump process*. Looking ahead the Brownian motion limit is closely related to the *Itô process*, whereas the Poisson jump limit is a special case of the Lévy process.

6.1 IID Returns, and the Term Structure of Volatility

Assume trading takes place every 5 min; this is frequent enough for most traders. The simplest model assumes that the 5 min returns are independent and identically distributed (IID). Our goal is to examine the distribution of returns on lower frequencies, say hourly, daily or weekly. Let us denote by $R_1(5 \text{ min})$ the return over the first 5 min, by $R_2(5 \text{ min})$ the return over the second 5 min, and so on. The return over the first hour will be

$$R_{\text{hour}} = R_1(5 \text{ min}) R_2(5 \text{ min}) \cdots R_{12}(5 \text{ min}).$$

It is much easier to work with sums than to work with products; a useful trick is to apply logarithms to both sides, yielding

$$\ln R_{\text{hour}} = \ln R_1(5 \text{ min}) + \ln R_2(5 \text{ min}) + \cdots + \ln R_{12}(5 \text{ min}).$$

To continue with the argument we will require several elementary properties of random variables, which are summarized in the box overleaf. Because the 5 min returns are independent and identically distributed, so are the log returns. If log returns are independent, they are necessarily uncorrelated; therefore, it is easy to compute the mean and the variance of $\ln R_{\text{hour}}$ using rules (6.1) and (6.2),

$$E[\ln R_{\text{hour}}] = 12 E[\ln R(5 \text{ min})],$$
$$\text{Var}(\ln R_{\text{hour}}) = 12 \, \text{Var}(\ln R(5 \text{ min})).$$

```
@***************************@
@           trading time              @
@             parameters              @
@***************************@
Minute = 1;
Hour = 60;
HoursInDay  =   8;
DaysInWeek = 5;
DaysInMonth = 21;
Day  = HoursInDay*Hour;
Week = DaysInWeek*Day;
Month = DaysInMonth*Day;
Year = 12*Month;
```

Figure 6.1. Trading time parameters in GAUSS.

The mean and variance of hourly log returns are, in an IID model, 12 times higher than the mean and variance of 5 min log returns. Mean and variance of log returns grow linearly with the time horizon.

Facts.

- For *any* collection of random variables $X_1, X_2, \ldots, X_n$

$$E[X_1 + X_2 + \cdots + X_n] = E[X_1] + E[X_2] + \cdots + E[X_n], \qquad (6.1)$$

  expectation of a sum = sum of expectations.

- If $X_1, X_2, \ldots, X_n$ are *independent* random variables, then for *any* functions $f_1, f_2, \ldots, f_n$ the random variables $f_1(X_1), f_2(X_2), \ldots, f_n(X_n)$ are again *independent*.

- Independent random variables are uncorrelated (however, uncorrelated random variables need not be independent).

- For *uncorrelated* random variables $X_1, X_2, \ldots, X_n$ we have

$$\mathrm{Var}(X_1 + X_2 + \cdots + X_n) = \mathrm{Var}(X_1) + \mathrm{Var}(X_2) + \cdots + \mathrm{Var}(X_n), \qquad (6.2)$$

  variance of a sum = sum of variances.

6.1.1 Trading Time

Consider the daily log returns. It is important to realize that a particular stock exchange is *not* open 24 hours a day, 7 days a week but that it typically runs during normal working hours, 9.00 a.m. to 5.00 p.m. Monday to Friday. Outside this time stocks are not traded and therefore there is no movement in their price; it is as if time stops. Thus, a calendar day has 24 hours, a trading day only 8. A calendar week has 7 days, a trading week 5, etc. (see Figure 6.1).

Because there are only 480 min in a trading day we should expect

$$\mathrm{Var}(\ln R_{\mathrm{day}}) = \frac{480}{5} \, \mathrm{Var}(\ln R_i(5 \text{ min})) = 96 \, \mathrm{Var}(\ln R_i(5 \text{ min})).$$

If we judged the situation mechanically and simply used calendar time, the variance of daily return in the model would come out three times higher!

- In a model with IID returns the mean and variance of log returns grow linearly with the time horizon. This is known as the **linear law for mean and variance**. The linear law gives a good match with the observed data when the time horizon is measured in trading time.
- The returns on a daily horizon are so small that we can write a first-order Taylor expansion $\ln R_{\text{day}} = R_{\text{day}} - 1$ with very high precision and then

$$E[\ln R_{\text{day}}] = E[R_{\text{day}} - 1] = E[R_{\text{day}}] - 1,$$

$$\text{Var}(\ln R_{\text{day}}) = \text{Var}(R_{\text{day}} - 1) = \text{Var}(R_{\text{day}}).$$

Thus for time horizons up to one day we can remove the word 'log' in the previous bullet point.

- If the variance of returns grows linearly with time, then the standard deviation, also called the **volatility**, must grow as a square root of time. The **square root law for volatility of returns** was observed as early as 1863 on the Paris Bourse.

6.2 Towards Brownian Motion

6.2.1 Model of Daily Returns

Recall that in Chapter 5 we calibrated monthly stock returns as follows:

$$R_{\text{u}}(\text{month}) = 1.053 \quad \text{with } p_{\text{u}} = \tfrac{1}{2}, \tag{6.3}$$

$$R_{\text{d}}(\text{month}) = 0.965 \quad \text{with } p_{\text{d}} = \tfrac{1}{2}, \tag{6.4}$$

$$R_{\text{f}}(\text{month}) = 1.0033. \tag{6.5}$$

We now wish to construct a model with daily log returns that would be consistent with the expected monthly log return and its volatility. The simplest way of achieving that is to construct the monthly log return first and then scale it according to the linear law for the mean and variance discussed above. The following properties of mean and variance will be useful.

- Let X be a random variable, and a, b constants. Then

$$E[a + bX] = a + bE[X], \tag{6.6}$$

$$\text{Var}(a + bX) = \text{Var}(bX) = b^2 \, \text{Var}(X). \tag{6.7}$$

- Recall that $\text{Vol}(X) = \sqrt{\text{Var}(X)}$. Consequently, for the volatility we have

$$\text{Vol}(a + bX) = \text{Vol}(bX) = |b| \, \text{Vol}(X). \tag{6.8}$$

Since the mean grows linearly with time, whereas volatility obeys the square root law, the right thing to do is to decompose the monthly log return into two parts, one non-random and one random with mean zero,

$$\ln R_{\text{month}} = \underbrace{E[\ln R_{\text{month}}]}_{\substack{\text{non-random} \\ \text{part}}} + \underbrace{(\ln R_{\text{month}} - E[\ln R_{\text{month}}])}_{\substack{\text{random part} \\ \text{with mean zero}}},$$

and then scale the first part by $\frac{1}{21}$ and the second part by $\sqrt{\frac{1}{21}}$ (remember, a month has 21 trading days),

$$\ln R_{\text{day}} = \tfrac{1}{21} E[\ln R_{\text{month}}] + \sqrt{\tfrac{1}{21}} (\ln R_{\text{month}} - E[\ln R_{\text{month}}]). \qquad (6.9)$$

One can verify using rules (6.6) and (6.7) that in this way we will obtain

$$E[\ln R_{\text{day}}] = \tfrac{1}{21} E[\ln R_{\text{month}}],$$

$$\text{Var}(\ln R_{\text{day}}) = \tfrac{1}{21} \text{Var}(\ln R_{\text{month}}),$$

as required by the linear law for mean and variance.

The safe return, too, obeys the rule (6.9):

$$\ln R_{\text{f}}(\text{day}) = \tfrac{1}{21} \ln R_{\text{f}}(\text{month}). \qquad (6.10)$$

Numerically,

$$E[\ln R_{\text{month}}] = p_{\text{u}} \ln R_{\text{u}}(\text{month}) + p_{\text{d}} \ln R_{\text{d}}(\text{month})$$

$$= \frac{0.0516}{2} - \frac{0.0356}{2} = 0.008,$$

$$\ln R_{\text{u}}(\text{day}) = \frac{0.008}{21} + \sqrt{\frac{1}{21}} (0.0516 - 0.008) = 0.009\,90,$$

$$\ln R_{\text{d}}(\text{day}) = \frac{0.008}{21} + \sqrt{\frac{1}{21}} (-0.0356 - 0.008) = -0.009\,13,$$

$$\ln R_{\text{f}}(\text{day}) = \tfrac{1}{21} \ln(1.0033) = 1.6 \times 10^{-4}.$$

6.2.2 Numerical Implementation

Now we can run through the standard pricing routine of Chapter 5:

$$R_{\text{u}}(\text{day}) = e^{\ln R_{\text{u}}(\text{day})} = e^{0.009\,90} = 1.009\,95,$$

$$R_{\text{d}}(\text{day}) = e^{\ln R_{\text{d}}(\text{day})} = e^{-0.009\,13} = 0.990\,91,$$

$$R_{\text{f}}(\text{day}) = R_{\text{f}}(\text{month})^{1/21} = 1.0033^{1/21} = 1.000\,16,$$

$$q_{\text{u}}(\text{day}) = \frac{R_{\text{f}}(\text{day}) - R_{\text{d}}(\text{day})}{R_{\text{u}}(\text{day}) - R_{\text{d}}(\text{day})} = \frac{1.000\,16 - 0.990\,91}{1.009\,95 - 0.990\,91} = 0.486,$$

$$q_{\text{d}}(\text{day}) = 0.514.$$

The option expires in three months, each month now has 21 trading days, which gives in total 63 trading periods. One could fit this into an Excel spreadsheet, but with a growing number of trading periods this solution becomes less and less practical; for example, a model with hourly rebalancing has as many as $8 \times 63 = 504$ periods.

It is more productive to adapt the option pricing code of Chapter 5 to the new circumstances. With the trading time parameters defined in Figure 6.1 we can program the scaling properties (6.9) and (6.10) very easily (see Figure 6.2).

The main body of the program remains the same, except with a high number of trading dates we cannot afford to store the option prices for all the values of stock price and all intermediate dates; it requires too much memory and slows down the program. Fortunately, it is enough to know the option prices in the next period to

```
@***************************@
@      Hedging Parameters      @
@***************************@
T=3*month;                                          @ Time to maturity    @
RehedgeInterval=1*day;                              @ Trading period       @
S0=5100;                                            @ Initial stock price @
strike=5355;
@***************************@
@      Transformation of       @
@        log returns           @
@***************************@
UnitTime=month;
R1safe=1.0033;                                      @ monthly safe return         @
R1=1.053~0.965;                                     @ monthly return              @
PDistr=0.5~0.5;                                     @ prob. density of monthly   returns @
lnR1=ln(R1);                                        @ monthly log return          @
mu1=lnR1*PDistr';                                   @ expected monthly log return @
sig1=sqrt(((lnR1-mu1)^2)*PDistr');                  @ volatility of monthly log return @

dt = RehedgeInterval/UnitTime;
lnRdt=mu1*dt+(lnR1-mu1)*sqrt(dt);                   @ log return over rehedging interval @
Rdt=exp(lnRdt);
Rdtsafe=R1safe^dt;

@***********************@
@       Risk-neutral      @
@       probabilities     @
@***********************@
QDistr=((Rdtsafe-Rdt[2])~(Rdt[1]-Rdtsafe))/(Rdt[1]-Rdt[2]);
```

Figure 6.2. Brownian scaling of returns.

Table 6.1. No-arbitrage option price for different rebalancing intervals.

Trading interval	1 month	1 day	1 hour	30 min
Option price	81.3643	76.0859	75.9822	75.9414
Option delta	0.31965	0.31703	0.31678	0.31671

find the option price in the current period, so at any time in the program one only needs to remember the last column of option prices. The modified pricing algorithm is shown in Figure 6.3.

The entire program is in the file *chapter6sect2a.gss*; the reader should try different rebalancing frequencies by changing the parameter RehedgeInterval. The output is summarized in Table 6.1.

6.2.3 Distribution of Log Returns in the Limit

The prices in Table 6.1 are different for each length of the trading interval, although they do not change very much as we shorten the trading interval from 1 day to 1 hour to 30 min. Why are the prices different? First of all the conditional risk-neutral probabilities are different in each model. Secondly, the risk-neutral distribution of the unconditional three-month return will be different in each model. Consider the model with monthly rebalancing; this model has three periods and the log return after three months will be either $3 \ln R_u$ or $2 \ln R_u + \ln R_d$ or $\ln R_u + 2 \ln R_d$ or $3 \ln R_d$ with probabilities q_u^3, $3q_u^2 q_d$, $3q_u q_d^2$ and q_d^3, respectively. These probabilities (divided by $\ln R_u - \ln R_d$) are plotted in Figure 6.4.

```
@*************************@
@   grid indexation       @
@*************************@
Tidx=ceil(T/RehedgeInterval)+1;        @ Number of trading dates        @
dlnS=lnRdt[1]-lnRdt[2];                @ increment on log price grid    @
highlnRdt=lnRdt[1];                    @ the highest return over one period @

@ there are tt live cells at time tt, highest stock price at the top      @
@ log price at cell  1 at time tt is ln(S0)+(tt-1)*highlnRdt              @
@ log price at cell ii at time tt is ln(S0)+(tt-1)*highlnRdt-(ii-1)*dlnS  @

@*************************@
@       option payoff     @
@*************************@
S_T=seqa(ln(S0)+(Tidx-1)*highlnRdt,-dlnS,Tidx);  @ log price at maturity   @
S_T=exp(S_T);                                    @ stock price at maturity @
C=maxc((S_T-strike)'|zeros(1,rows(S_T)));        @ option payoff at maturity@

@*************************@
@       main loop         @
@*************************@
starttime = hsec;                       @ start of computation         @
for tt (Tidx-1,1,-1);
Cnext=C;                                @ option value in next period @
for ii (1,tt,1);
C[ii]=(QDistr*Cnext[ii:ii+1])/Rdtsafe;  @ risk-neutral pricing        @
endfor;
endfor;
```

Figure 6.3. Modification of binomial pricing algorithm that
only remembers the latest set of option prices.

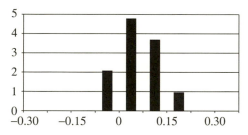

Figure 6.4. Unconditional risk-neutral distribution of
log stock return. Trading interval one month.

Now take the model with daily rehedging. It has 63 periods and the three-month
log return can now range from $63 \ln R_u$ to $63 \ln R_d$. Specifically, the risk-neutral
probability of achieving a log return of size $n \ln R_u + (63 - n) \ln R_d$ is

$$\frac{63!}{n!(63 - n)!} q_u^n q_d^{63-n}.$$

The risk-neutral probabilities (again divided by $\ln R_u - \ln R_d$) are plotted in Figure 6.5.

Finally, we will perform the same exercise in a model with hourly rehedging
(504 periods; see Figure 6.6). Comparing Figure 6.5 with Figure 6.6 one can guess
that the shape of the risk-neutral distribution of the three-month log return does not
change very much as the trading interval goes to zero, and this is why the option
price settles down.

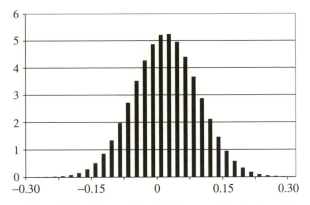

Figure 6.5. Unconditional risk-neutral distribution of log stock returns. Trading interval one day.

Facts.

- The limiting shape of the risk-neutral distribution of the three-month log return is *normal distribution*.
- The normal distribution has two parameters, the mean m and variance s^2. If X is a normal random variable with mean m and variance s^2, we will write
$$X \sim N(m, s^2).$$
The distribution $N(0, 1)$ is called *standard normal*.
- Suppose that $X \sim N(m, s^2)$. Then the probability of X lying in a small interval around value x, divided by the size of that interval, is
$$f(x) = \frac{1}{\sqrt{2\pi}\sigma} \exp\left(-\frac{1}{2}\frac{(x-m)^2}{s^2}\right).$$
Mathematically,
$$\lim_{\Delta x \to 0} \frac{\Pr(x \leqslant X < x + \Delta x)}{\Delta x} = \frac{1}{\sqrt{2\pi}\sigma} \exp\left(-\frac{1}{2}\frac{(x-m)^2}{s^2}\right).$$
In other words, with the correct choice of m and s the curve $f(x)$ will be the limit of the bell-shaped patterns in Figures 6.4–6.6.

6.2.4 Mean and Variance of the Risk-Neutral Distribution of Log Returns

The aim of this section is to find the mean and variance of the limiting distribution in Figure 6.6. Denote by $Q_{\Delta t}$ the risk-neutral probability measure generated by a binomial model with rehedging interval Δt. We wish to find

$$\lim_{\Delta t \to 0} \mathrm{E}^{Q_{\Delta t}}[\ln R(T)], \tag{6.11}$$

$$\lim_{\Delta t \to 0} \mathrm{Var}^{Q_{\Delta t}}(\ln R(T)). \tag{6.12}$$

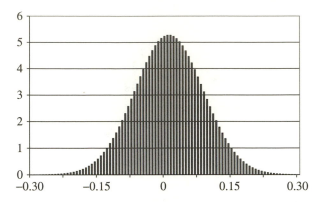

Figure 6.6. Unconditional risk-neutral distribution of
log stock returns. Trading interval one hour.

We shall take as given that the one-period returns are independent under $Q_{\Delta t}$ (this
is in fact obvious, but we lack the necessary terminology at this stage; it will be
introduced in Chapter 8 and Appendix B). Then we can apply rules (6.1) and (6.2)
under $Q_{\Delta t}$, yielding

$$E^{Q_{\Delta t}}[\ln R(T)] = \frac{T}{\Delta t} E^{Q_{\Delta t}}[\ln R(\Delta t)], \qquad (6.13)$$

$$\text{Var}^{Q_{\Delta t}}(\ln R(T)) = \frac{T}{\Delta t} \text{Var}^{Q_{\Delta t}}(\ln R(\Delta t)). \qquad (6.14)$$

Since the rehedging interval is very short, by necessity both

$$E^{Q_{\Delta t}}[\ln R(\Delta t)] \quad \text{and} \quad \text{Var}^{Q_{\Delta t}}(\ln R(\Delta t))$$

are small. Suppose we can show that

$$E^{Q_{\Delta t}}[\ln R(\Delta t)] = \mu_Q \Delta t + o(\Delta t), \qquad (6.15)$$

$$\text{Var}^{Q_{\Delta t}}(\ln R(\Delta t)) = \sigma_Q^2 \Delta t + o(\Delta t), \qquad (6.16)$$

for some constants μ_Q, σ_Q. The combination of (6.13) and (6.14) with (6.15) and
(6.16) then implies

$$\lim_{\Delta t \to 0} E^{Q_{\Delta t}}[\ln R(T)] = \mu_Q T, \qquad (6.17)$$

$$\lim_{\Delta t \to 0} \text{Var}^{Q_{\Delta t}}(\ln R(T)) = \sigma_Q^2 T. \qquad (6.18)$$

Our task has simplified to finding μ_Q and σ_Q^2. To find μ_Q we must evaluate
the left-hand side of (6.15) and in order to do this we need to approximate the
risk-neutral probabilities $q_u(\Delta t), q_u(\Delta t)$. Exercise 6.1 shows that

$$q_u(\Delta t) = p_u + \xi \sqrt{\Delta t} + o(\Delta t), \qquad (6.19)$$

$$q_d(\Delta t) = p_d - \xi \sqrt{\Delta t} + o(\Delta t), \qquad (6.20)$$

with

$$\xi = \frac{r - \mu}{\ln R_u(1) - \ln R_d(1)} - \tfrac{1}{2}\sigma^2, \qquad (6.21)$$

where μ is the expected monthly log return, σ^2 is the variance of the monthly log return (see Exercise 6.2), and r is the risk-free monthly log return,

$$\mu \triangleq E^P[\ln R(1)], \tag{6.22}$$

$$\sigma^2 \triangleq \text{Var}^P(\ln R(1)), \tag{6.23}$$

$$r \triangleq \ln R_f(1). \tag{6.24}$$

In analogy with equations (6.9) and (6.10), the return over period Δt is given by

$$\ln R(\Delta t) \triangleq \mu \Delta t + \sqrt{\Delta t}(\ln R(1) - \mu), \tag{6.25}$$

$$\ln R_f(\Delta t) \triangleq r \Delta t. \tag{6.26}$$

Exercise 6.3 shows that (6.25) together with (6.19) and (6.20) imply

$$E^{Q_{\Delta t}}[\ln R(\Delta t)] = \underbrace{(\mu + \xi(\ln R_u(1) - \ln R_d(1)))}_{r - \sigma^2/2}\Delta t + o(\Delta t), \tag{6.27}$$

$$\text{Var}^{Q_{\Delta t}}(\ln R(\Delta t)) = \sigma^2 \Delta t + o(\Delta t), \tag{6.28}$$

which, after comparison with (6.15) and (6.16), finally gives

$$\mu_Q = r - \tfrac{1}{2}\sigma^2,$$

$$\sigma_Q^2 = \sigma^2.$$

Equations (6.17) and (6.18) then yield the desired result,

$$\lim_{\Delta t \to 0} E^{Q_{\Delta t}}[\ln R(T)] = (r - \tfrac{1}{2}\sigma^2)T,$$

$$\lim_{\Delta t \to 0} \text{Var}^{Q_{\Delta t}}(\ln R(T)) = \sigma^2 T.$$

> In the Brownian motion limit as Δt goes to zero the risk-neutral distribution of $\ln R(T)$ tends to normal distribution with mean $(r - \tfrac{1}{2}\sigma^2)T$ and variance $\sigma^2 T$.

6.2.5 Black–Scholes Option Pricing Formula

1. Recall that the option price is the risk-neutral expectation of the option pay-off discounted by the risk-free rate,

$$C_0 = e^{-rT}E_0^Q[C_T]. \tag{6.29}$$

2. The option pay-off is a (piecewise linear) function of the terminal stock price,

$$C_T = \begin{cases} S_T - K & \text{if } S_T > K, \\ 0 & \text{if } S_T \leqslant K. \end{cases}$$

3. The log return is normally distributed under probability measure Q,

$$\ln R(T) \overset{Q}{\sim} N((r - \tfrac{1}{2}\sigma^2)T, \sigma^2 T).$$

4. The terminal stock price is a product of the initial stock price and the three-month return,

$$S_T = S_0 R(T),$$
$$\ln S_T = \ln S_0 + \ln R(T).$$

Consequently, the risk-neutral distribution of $\ln S_T$ is

$$\ln S_T \overset{Q}{\sim} N(\ln S_0 + (r - \tfrac{1}{2}\sigma^2)T, \sigma^2 T). \tag{6.30}$$

We can now rewrite the option pricing formula (6.29) as follows,

$$C_0 = e^{-rT} E^Q[(e^{\ln S_T} - e^{\ln K}) 1_{\ln S_T > \ln K}], \tag{6.31}$$

where $1_{\ln S_T > \ln K}$ is a step function

$$1_{X > a} \overset{\triangle}{=} \begin{cases} 1 & \text{for } X > a, \\ 0 & \text{for } X \leqslant a. \end{cases}$$

In Appendix A we derive that for $X \sim N(\tilde{\mu}, \tilde{\sigma}^2)$ one has

$$E[(e^X - e^a) 1_{X > a}] = e^{\tilde{\mu} + \tilde{\sigma}^2/2} \Phi\left(\frac{\tilde{\mu} + \tilde{\sigma}^2 - a}{\tilde{\sigma}}\right) - e^a \Phi\left(\frac{\tilde{\mu} - a}{\tilde{\sigma}}\right). \tag{6.32}$$

We can now apply this result to (6.31) $X = \ln S_T$ and $a = \ln K$. From (6.30) we must take

$$\tilde{\mu} = \ln S_0 + (r - \tfrac{1}{2}\sigma^2)T,$$
$$\tilde{\sigma}^2 = \sigma^2 T,$$

and this gives the celebrated Black–Scholes formula:

$$C_0 = S_0 \Phi\left(\frac{\ln(S_0/K) + (r + \sigma^2/2)T}{\sigma\sqrt{T}}\right) - Ke^{-rT} \Phi\left(\frac{\ln(S_0/K) + (r - \sigma^2/2)T}{\sigma\sqrt{T}}\right).$$

Numerically,

$$S_0 = 5100, \qquad K = 5355, \qquad T = 3,$$
$$R_u(1) = 1.053, \qquad R_d(1) = 0.965,$$
$$\mu = \tfrac{1}{2}(\ln 1.053 + \ln 0.965) = 0.008, \tag{6.33}$$
$$\sigma^2 = \tfrac{1}{4}(\ln 1.053 - \ln 0.965)^2 = 0.0019, \tag{6.34}$$
$$r = \ln 1.0033,$$

which yields

$$C_0 = 75.9329.$$

It is interesting to compare this value with the binomial model prices in Table 6.1. Note that in our example the evaluation of Black–Scholes formula is roughly a million times faster than the pricing in a binomial model with a 30 min trading interval. The differences between the limiting value and the binomial approximation can be explored by running the GAUSS program *chapter6sect2b.gss*.

It is worth summarizing what the Black–Scholes formula means (see box overleaf).

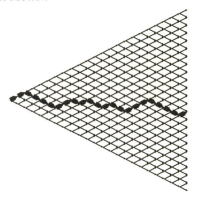

Figure 6.7. Movement in a binomial lattice with Brownian motion limit.

- Fix a trading interval of unit time length (say one month) with risk-free rate $r(1)$ and risky return $R(1)$, where the risky return has two values over a single trading period (binomial tree). Denote by μ and σ^2 the mean and variance of $\ln R(1)$ under objective probabilities, and define the continuously compounded interest rate $r = \ln(1 + r(1))$.
- For any shorter trading interval Δt define a new model with one-period risk-free rate $r(\Delta t)$ and risky return $R(\Delta t)$ as follows:

$$1 + r(\Delta t) \triangleq e^{r \Delta t},$$

$$\ln R(\Delta t) \triangleq \mu \Delta t + \sqrt{\Delta t}(\ln R(1) - \mu).$$

  In this way we can guarantee that the mean and variance of the log return over unit time length are always μ and σ^2, respectively.
- Let us denote the no-arbitrage option price in a model with trading interval Δt by $C_0(\Delta t)$. As Δt goes to zero, the number of trading periods increases to infinity and the option price converges to the Black–Scholes value:

$$\lim_{\Delta t \to 0} C_0(\Delta t) = S_0 \left(\frac{\ln(S_0/K) + (r + \sigma^2/2)T}{\sigma \sqrt{T}} \right)$$
$$- K e^{-rT} \Phi \left(\frac{\ln(S_0/K) + (r - \sigma^2/2)T}{\sigma \sqrt{T}} \right). \quad (6.35)$$

  This happens because as Δt goes to zero the risk-neutral distribution of the log stock price tends to normal with mean $\ln S_0 + (r - \frac{1}{2}\sigma^2)T$ and variance $\sigma^2 T$.

6.2.6 *Black–Scholes Delta*

Recall from Chapter 5 that the number of shares in the option replicating portfolio is

$$\text{delta} = \frac{C_u - C_d}{S_u - S_d}.$$

In the Brownian motion limit the difference between C_u and C_d goes to zero as Δt becomes very small, and so does the difference between S_u and S_d. In the limit the expression for delta looks like the derivative of C with respect to S. It turns out that this intuition is correct,

$$\lim_{\Delta t \to 0} \frac{C_u(\Delta t) - C_d(\Delta t)}{S_u(\Delta t) - S_d(\Delta t)} = C'(S),$$

where $C(S)$ is the Black–Scholes price as a function of initial stock price. Consequently, $C'(S)$ is known as the **Black–Scholes delta**; its value is computed in Exercise A.7:

$$\text{Black–Scholes delta} = \Phi\left(\frac{\ln(S/K) + (r + \sigma^2/2)T}{\sigma\sqrt{T}}\right).$$

Numerically,

$$\text{Black–Scholes delta} = 0.316\,68;$$

compare this value with its binomial counterparts in Table 6.1.

6.3   Towards a Poisson Jump Process

The idea behind the Brownian motion limit was to keep the objective probability of the high and low log return constant ($= \frac{1}{2}$) and let the difference between high and low log return go to zero as the trading interval goes to zero. The Poisson limit does exactly the opposite: we will keep the difference between the two log returns constant and let the probability vary as the trading interval goes to zero. The probability of a high return will approach 1 and the probability of a low return will approach zero as the trading interval goes to zero. This means that most of the time the stock price will be moving smoothly upwards, but once in a while it will jump down by a prespecified amount J.

Mathematically,

$$\ln R_u(\Delta t) \triangleq \tilde{\mu}\Delta t, \tag{6.36}$$
$$\ln R_d(\Delta t) = \tilde{\mu}\Delta t - J,$$
$$p_u = 1 - \lambda_P \Delta t,$$
$$p_d = \lambda_P \Delta t.$$

6.3.1   *Calibration*

As before denote by μ and σ^2 the mean and variance of the log return over a time period of length 1. Exercise 6.4 shows

$$E^P[\ln R(\Delta t)] = (\tilde{\mu} - \lambda_P J)\Delta t, \tag{6.37}$$
$$\text{Var}^P(\ln R(\Delta t)) = J^2 \lambda_P \Delta t - (J\lambda_P \Delta t)^2. \tag{6.38}$$

We know that the log return over a period of length 1 is the sum of $1/\Delta t$ log returns over periods of length Δt. In addition the expectation of a sum equals the sum of expectations, therefore

$$\frac{1}{\Delta t}E^P[\ln R(\Delta t)] = E^P[\ln R(1)] = \mu. \tag{6.39}$$

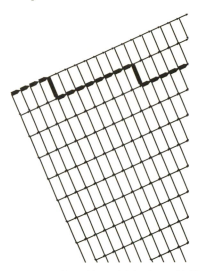

Figure 6.8. Stock price movement in a binomial lattice with Poisson process limit. Up movement is proportional to trading interval size, down movement is fixed. There is a much higher number of up movements (smooth increase in price) than down movements (sudden price decrease).

By assumption the log returns over disjoint time periods are independent and therefore uncorrelated; hence we can use the fact that the variance of a sum equals the sum of variances,

$$\frac{1}{\Delta t} \operatorname{Var}^P (\ln R(\Delta t)) = \operatorname{Var}^P (\ln R(1)) = \sigma^2. \tag{6.40}$$

Substitute (6.39) into equation (6.37) and substitute (6.40) into (6.38) to relate the unknown parameters $J, \lambda_P, \tilde{\mu}$ to the observed parameters μ, σ^2,

$$\tilde{\mu} - \lambda_P J = \mu,$$
$$J^2(\lambda_P - \lambda_P^2 \Delta t) = \sigma^2.$$

Solving for the jump size J and the drift rate $\tilde{\mu}$ we find

$$\tilde{\mu}(\Delta t) = \mu + \frac{\sqrt{\lambda_P}\sigma}{\sqrt{1 - \lambda_P \Delta t}}, \tag{6.41}$$

$$J(\Delta t) = \frac{\sigma}{\sqrt{\lambda_P}\sqrt{1 - \lambda_P \Delta t}}. \tag{6.42}$$

When the rehedging interval is very short, $\Delta t \approx 0$, Δt has a very small impact on the value of $\tilde{\mu}$ and J; it is then all right to use the limiting values for $\tilde{\mu}$ and J with $\Delta t = 0$:

$$\tilde{\mu} = \tilde{\mu}(0) = \mu + \sqrt{\lambda_P}\sigma, \tag{6.43}$$

$$J = J(0) = \frac{\sigma}{\sqrt{\lambda_P}}. \tag{6.44}$$

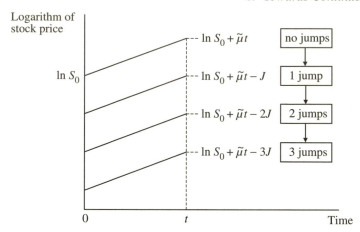

Figure 6.9.   Possible values of the log stock price in the Poisson jump model.

Recall from (6.33) and (6.34) that the observed monthly mean and standard deviation of log returns are

$$\mu = 0.0080, \qquad \sigma = 0.0436.$$

We will see later that λ_P can be interpreted as the average number of jumps per unit of time when Δt is small. With $\lambda_P = 1$ and a short rehedging interval $\Delta t \to 0$ we have, from (6.43) and (6.44),

$$\tilde{\mu} = \mu + \sigma = 5.16\%, \tag{6.45}$$

$$J = \sigma = 4.36\%. \tag{6.46}$$

With one jump a month on average the jump size is equal to 4.36%, and the stock price grows at a rate 5.16% per month during periods when no jumps are present.

6.3.2   Stock Price Dynamics

In the Brownian motion limit the log return $\ln(S_t/S_0)$ can take any value between $-\infty$ and $+\infty$. In the Poisson jump model the situation is very different; the log return $\ln(S_t/S_0)$ can only take a discrete set of values *corresponding to the number of jumps* between time 0 and time t. Specifically, if the stock price does not jump at all, then by assumption (6.36) the log return increases linearly with time at rate $\tilde{\mu}$:

$$\text{no jumps in } [0, t]: \qquad \ln(S_t/S_0) = \tilde{\mu}t.$$

If exactly one jump occurs somewhere between 0 and t, then the log return at the end of the time interval will be lower by the size of the jump:

$$1 \text{ jump in } [0, t]: \qquad \ln(S_t/S_0) = \tilde{\mu}t - J.$$

If two jumps occur in the time interval $[0, t]$, we have

$$2 \text{ jumps in } [0, t]: \qquad \ln(S_t/S_0) = \tilde{\mu}t - 2J, \text{ etc.}$$

See also Figure 6.9.

Denote by N_t the number of jumps that occur between 0 and t; then in general

$$\ln(S_t/S_0) = \tilde{\mu}t - N_t J, \tag{6.47}$$

$$S_t = S_0 e^{\tilde{\mu}t - N_t J}.$$

We observe that the terminal stock price S_t is a function of calendar time and the number of jumps,

$$S_t = S(t, N_t).$$

In the calibrated model (6.45) and (6.46), the numerical values of the FTSE 100 Index after three months are

$$S(3, \underbrace{0}_{\text{no jumps}}) = 5100 e^{0.0516 \times 3} = 5953.86, \tag{6.48}$$

$$S(3, \underbrace{1}_{\text{1 jump}}) = 5100 e^{0.0516 \times 3 - 0.0436 \times 1} = 5699.85, \tag{6.49}$$

$$S(3, \underbrace{2}_{\text{2 jumps}}) = 5100 e^{0.0516 \times 3 - 0.0436 \times 2} = 5456.68, \tag{6.50}$$

$$S(3, \underbrace{3}_{\text{3 jumps}}) = 5100 e^{0.0516 \times 3 - 0.0436 \times 3} = 5223.88, \text{ etc.,} \tag{6.51}$$

by virtue of (6.47).

6.3.3 Distribution of Jumps and Jump Times

The total number of jumps in a given time interval is a random variable. By assumption the numbers of jumps in *disjoint* time intervals are *independent*. Mathematically, $N_{\Delta t}, N_{2\Delta t} - N_{\Delta t}, N_{3\Delta t} - N_{2\Delta t}, N_{4\Delta t} - N_{3\Delta t}, \ldots$ are stochastically independent random variables. Now we would like to find out the probability that exactly 0, 1, 2, 3 jumps happen in time interval $[0, t]$.

If the trading period is Δt, then in the interval $[0, t]$ we have $t/\Delta t$ trading dates. The probability of seeing exactly *zero* low returns over time period $[0, t]$ is

$P(\text{no jumps in } [0, t])$

$$= P(\underbrace{\text{no jumps in } [0, \Delta t] \text{ and no jumps in } [\Delta t, 2\Delta t] \text{ and } \cdots}_{t/\Delta t \text{ independent events each with probability } p_u})$$

$$= p_u^{t/\Delta t} = (1 - \lambda_P \Delta t)^{T/\Delta t}.$$

This probability does not vary much with Δt when Δt is small; Exercise 6.5 shows that

$$\lim_{\Delta t \to 0} P(\text{no jumps in } [0, t]) = e^{-\lambda_P t}. \tag{6.52}$$

Facts (see Mood et al. 1974). For Δt small the probability of having exactly n low returns is

$$\lim_{\Delta t \to 0} P(N_t = n) = \frac{(\lambda_P t)^n}{n!} e^{-\lambda_P t}. \tag{6.53}$$

We say that (in the limit when Δt is very small) the number of jumps N_t has **Poisson distribution** with **arrival intensity** λ_P. The mean and variance of N_t are

$$E^P[N_t] = \lambda_P t, \tag{6.54}$$

$$\text{Var}^P(N_t) = \lambda_P t.$$

Equation (6.54) implies that the arrival intensity λ_P *represents the average number of jumps per unit of time.* Equation (6.52) reveals that the probability of the first jump arriving in $[t, t + dt]$ is

$$P(\text{first jump happens in } [t, t + dt]) = \underbrace{e^{-\lambda_P t}}_{\text{no jumps in } [0,t]} \quad \underbrace{\lambda_P \, dt}_{\text{1 jump in } [t,t+dt]} \quad .$$

We say that the time of the first arrival has an **exponential distribution** with parameter λ_P.

6.3.4 Risk-Neutral Probabilities

What really matters, as we already know, is the distribution of stock returns under the *risk-neutral* probability measure. To this end Exercise 6.6 shows

$$q_u(\Delta t) = 1 + \underbrace{\frac{r - \tilde{\mu}}{1 - e^{-J}}}_{\lambda_Q} \Delta t + o(\Delta t),$$

which means that under the risk-neutral probability, jumps arrive with intensity λ_Q,

$$\lambda_Q = \frac{\tilde{\mu} - r}{1 - e^{-J}}.$$

Numerically,

$$\lambda_Q = \frac{0.0516 - \ln(1.0033)}{1 - e^{-0.0436}} = 1.132,$$

that is, under the risk-neutral measure the jumps will arrive more frequently than under the objective probability measure. The risk-neutral probability of a specific number of jumps in a given time period can be calculated from (6.53) when λ_P is replaced by λ_Q,

$$\lim_{\Delta t \to 0} Q(N_t = n) = \frac{(\lambda_Q t)^n}{n!} e^{-\lambda_Q t}.$$

Specifically, for the three-month period until expiry of the option we have

$$\lim_{\Delta t \to 0} Q(N_3 = 0) = e^{-1.132 \times 3} = 0.0335, \tag{6.55}$$

$$\lim_{\Delta t \to 0} Q(N_3 = 1) = 1.132 \times 3e^{-1.132 \times 3} = 0.1138, \tag{6.56}$$

$$\lim_{\Delta t \to 0} Q(N_3 = 2) = \tfrac{1}{2}(1.132 \times 3)^2 e^{-1.132 \times 3} = 0.1932, \tag{6.57}$$

$$\lim_{\Delta t \to 0} Q(N_3 = 3) = \tfrac{1}{6}(1.132 \times 3)^3 e^{-1.132 \times 3} = 0.2187, \text{ etc.} \tag{6.58}$$

6.3.5 *Poisson Option Pricing Formula*

Let us denote by $C(t, N_t)$ the option price at time t if the stock price has jumped N_t times between 0 and t. Recall that the higher the N_t the further out of the money the option gets. The option pricing formula simply reads

$$C(0, N_0) = e^{-rT} E_0^Q[C(T, N_T)],$$

where at expiry

$$C(T, N_T) = \max(S_T - K; 0) = \max(S_0 e^{\tilde{\mu}T - N_T J} - K; 0).$$

We know from (6.48)–(6.51) that the terminal stock price takes discrete values

$$S_T = \left[\underbrace{5953.86}_{\text{no jumps}} \quad \underbrace{5699.85}_{\text{1 jump}} \quad \underbrace{5456.68}_{\text{2 jumps}} \quad \underbrace{5223.88}_{\text{3 jumps}} \quad \cdots \right],$$

which means the option pay-offs are

$$\max(S_T - K; 0) = \left[\underbrace{598.86}_{\text{no jumps}} \quad \underbrace{344.85}_{\text{1 jump}} \quad \underbrace{101.68}_{\text{2 jumps}} \quad \underbrace{0.00}_{\text{3 jumps}} \quad \cdots \right]; \tag{6.59}$$

from (6.55)–(6.58) the corresponding risk-neutral probabilities are

$$\left[\underbrace{0.0335}_{\text{no jumps}} \quad \underbrace{0.1138}_{\text{1 jump}} \quad \underbrace{0.1932}_{\text{2 jumps}} \quad \underbrace{0.2187}_{\text{3 jumps}} \quad \cdots \right]. \tag{6.60}$$

Putting (6.59) and (6.60) together we find the no-arbitrage price of the option

$$C(0, 0) = \frac{598.86 \times 0.0335 + 344.85 \times 0.1138 + 101.68 \times 0.1932}{1.0033^3} = 78.17.$$

More generally,

$$C(t, N_t) = e^{-r(T-t)} E_t^Q[C(T, N_T)]$$

$$= e^{-(\lambda_Q + r)(T-t)} \sum_{n=0}^{+\infty} \max(S_0 e^{\tilde{\mu}T - (n + N_t)J} - K; 0) \frac{(\lambda_Q(T-t))^n}{n!}.$$

6.3.6 *Poisson Delta*

We know from Chapter 5 that the number of shares in the replicating portfolio is given by

$$\theta = \frac{C_u - C_d}{S_u - S_d}.$$

In the jump model S_d is far from S_u even when the rehedging interval Δt is very small,

$$S_u = S_0 e^{\tilde{\mu}\Delta t} = S_0 + O(\Delta t),$$

$$S_d = S_0 e^{\tilde{\mu}\Delta t - J(\Delta t)} = S_0 e^{-J} + O(\Delta t).$$

Similarly, the gap between C_u and C_d does not vanish as Δt goes to zero,

$$C_u = C(\Delta t, 0) = C(0, 0) + O(\Delta t),$$
$$C_d = C(\Delta t, 1) = C(0, 1) + O(\Delta t),$$

hence in the limit

$$\theta(0, 0) = \lim_{\Delta t \to 0} \frac{C_u - C_d}{S_u - S_d} = \frac{C(0, 0) - C(0, 1)}{S_0(1 - e^{-J})}.$$

We have all the ingredients apart from $C(0, 1)$, which represents the option value when the initial stock price already includes one jump at time 0. From (6.59) the option pay-off in such a case is

$$\max(S_T - K; 0) = \left[\underbrace{344.85}_{\text{1 jump}} \quad \underbrace{101.68}_{\text{2 jumps}} \quad \underbrace{0.00}_{\text{3 jumps}} \quad \underbrace{0.00}_{\text{4 jumps}} \quad \cdots \right]. \qquad (6.61)$$

Because 1 jump has already happened, the corresponding probabilities are again those given in (6.60); 'no jumps' is now interpreted as 'no *extra* jumps'. Numerically,

$$C(0, 1) = \frac{344.85 \times 0.0335 + 101.68 \times 0.1138}{1.0033^3} = 22.90,$$
$$\theta(0, 0) = \frac{C(0, 0) - C(0, 1)}{S_0(1 - e^{-J})} = \frac{78.17 - 22.90}{5100(1 - e^{-0.0436})} = 0.254.$$

6.4   Central Limit Theorem and Infinitely Divisible Distributions

It is remarkable is that in an IID model the *shape* of the distribution of daily returns does not depend, well, almost does not depend, on the shape of the distribution of 5 min returns. This result is illustrated in Figure 6.10. The dotted line depicts (an arbitrarily chosen) distribution of the 5 min return, normalized to have mean zero and variance one:

$$X_{\text{dot}} = \frac{\ln R_1 - \mu}{\sigma}.$$

The dashed line depicts a 20 min log return normalized to have mean zero and variance one,

$$X_{\text{dash}} = \frac{\ln R_1 + \ln R_2 + \ln R_3 + \ln R_4 - 4\mu}{2\sigma},$$

the dot-dash line represents the normalized hourly return, and finally the thin line gives the distribution of a normalized daily log return,

$$X_{\text{thin}} = \frac{\sum_{i=1}^{96} \ln R_i - 96\mu}{\sqrt{96}\sigma}.$$

The thick line gives the limiting standard normal distribution of log returns on longer time horizons,

$$\frac{\sum_{i=1}^{n} \ln R_i - n\mu}{\sqrt{n}\sigma} \longrightarrow N(0, 1), \qquad (6.62)$$

as n goes to infinity. This result is known as the **central limit theorem**, and it is valid for any distribution of $\ln R_i$ with finite variance.

In conclusion, IID returns on short time horizons imply that log returns on long time horizons are distributed normally. When log returns are distributed normally we say that returns have **lognormal distribution**.

The central limit theorem applies in situations when the smallest trading interval is fixed and the number of trading intervals goes to infinity. If we were to fix the time horizon T and let the trading interval go to zero, $\Delta t \to 0$, so that the number of trading intervals $n = T/\Delta t$ again goes to infinity, the limit need not be normal, but in general it will be a so-called **infinitely divisible distribution**. One can show that every infinitely divisible distribution is a sum of a normal variable with independent Poisson variables of different jump sizes and arrival intensities.intensities. If the limit of IID log returns is normal, we say that log returns follow a **Brownian motion process** in the limit. If the limiting distribution also contains jumps, we say that the log return follows a **Lévy process**, of which the Poisson jump process is the simplest example.,

---

Facts. There are two important limit laws in finance. For every fixed Δt let $\{\ln R_i(\Delta t)\}_{i=1,2,\dots}$ be a collection of independent random variables with mean $\mu \Delta t$ and variance $\sigma^2 \Delta t$.

- Central limit theorem (fixed trading interval, number of trades going to infinity):

$$\lim_{\substack{T \to \infty, \\ \Delta t \text{ fixed}, \\ n=T/\Delta t}} \frac{\sum_{i=1}^n \ln R_i(\Delta t) - n\mu \Delta t}{\sqrt{n}\sigma\sqrt{\Delta t}}$$

$$= \lim_{\substack{T \to \infty, \\ \Delta t \text{ fixed}, \\ n=T/\Delta t}} \frac{\sum_{i=1}^n \ln R_i(\Delta t) - \mu T}{\sigma\sqrt{T}} = N(0,1).$$

- Continuous trading limit:

$$\lim_{\substack{T \text{ fixed}, \\ \Delta t \to 0, \\ n=T/\Delta t}} \frac{\sum_{i=1}^n \ln R_i(\Delta t) - n\mu \Delta t}{\sqrt{n}\sigma\sqrt{\Delta t}}$$

$$= \lim_{\substack{T \text{ fixed}, \\ \Delta t \to 0, \\ n=T/\Delta t}} \frac{\sum_{i=1}^n \ln R_i(\Delta t) - \mu T}{\sigma\sqrt{T}}$$

$$= \text{infinitely divisible distribution}(0,1).$$

Every infinitely divisible distribution is a sum of mutually independent normal and (possibly infinitely many) Poisson variables with different jump sizes and arrival intensities.

6.5 Summary

- This chapter examined two continuous-time limits of the binomial stock price lattice: the Brownian motion limit and the Poisson jump limit.

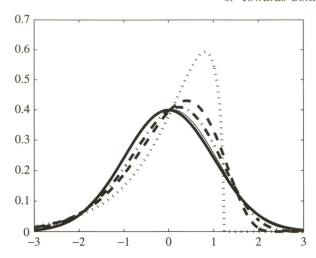

Figure 6.10. The scaled distribution of 5 min, 20 min, hourly and daily returns (dot, dash, dot-dash and thin line, respectively). Thick line corresponds to the standard normal distribution.

- In both cases we have assumed that log returns are IID and we have required the mean and variance of the log return on a fixed time horizon (say one month) to be the same *regardless* of the length of the rehedging interval.

- In a model with IID log returns both the mean and the variance of log returns increase linearly with the time horizon.

- The easiest way to implement the Brownian motion limit is to keep the conditional objective probabilities constant and simply scale down the values of log returns to satisfy the linear law for mean and variance. With the notation $\mu = E^P[\ln R_1]$, $\sigma^2 = \text{Var}^P(\ln R_1)$, the Brownian scaling reads

$$\ln R_{\Delta t} = \mu \Delta t + (\ln R_1 - \mu)\sqrt{\Delta t}.$$

- A simple application of the central limit theorem shows that as $\Delta t \to 0$ the distribution of log returns on a fixed time horizon becomes normal (see Exercise 6.8):

$$\ln R_T \stackrel{P}{\sim} N(\mu T, \sigma^2 T).$$

- In the Brownian motion limit the change of measure does not affect the variance of log returns, only the mean, and the shape of the distribution remains normal (the last assertion is taken for granted, the proof is in Section 7.5.2). Denoting the risk-free yield by $r = \ln R_{f1}$ we have

$$\ln R_T \stackrel{Q}{\sim} N((r - \tfrac{1}{2}\sigma^2)T, \sigma^2 T). \tag{6.63}$$

This is one of the most remarkable results in finance—the risk-neutral distribution of log returns is completely independent of μ.

- With (6.63) in hand it is relatively straightforward to price the European call option by evaluating the risk-neutral expectation,

$$C_0 = E_0^Q \left[\frac{C_T}{e^{rT}} \right] = e^{-rT} E_0^Q [\max(\underbrace{S_0 e^{\ln R_T}}_{S_T} - K, 0)].$$

The result is the famous Black–Scholes formula (6.35).

- In the Brownian motion limit the distance between high and low log return $\ln R_u(\Delta t) - \ln R_d(\Delta t)$ goes to 0 as $\Delta t \to 0$. This means that stock prices move continuously in the limit.

- The Poisson limit works by keeping $\ln R_u(\Delta t) - \ln R_d(\Delta t) = J$ constant and instead changing the probabilities, $p_u = 1 - \lambda_P \Delta t$ and $p_d = \lambda_P \Delta t$. In the limit the log price grows at a constant rate most of the time, but once in a while it jumps by the amount J; we say that the jumps arrive with intensity λ_P.

- Under the risk-neutral measure the rate of growth and the size of jumps remains the same, only the arrival intensity of jumps changes.

- In the Poisson jump limit the call option price

$$C_0 = E_0^Q \left[\frac{C_T}{e^{rT}} \right] = e^{-rT} E_0^Q [\max(\underbrace{S_0 e^{\ln R_T}}_{S_T} - K, 0)]$$

can be expressed as a sum (of possibly infinitely many terms if jumps are upwards rather than downwards).

6.6 Notes

The square root law for the standard deviation of returns was observed as early as 1863 (see Taqqu 2002). The derivation of the Black–Scholes formula via a binomial lattice is due to Cox et al. (1979). The Poisson limit of the binomial lattice appears in Page Jr and Sanders (1986). See notes in Chapter 7 for references to Lévy processes representing IID log returns in continuous time.

6.7 Exercises

Exercise 6.1 (risk-neutral probabilities in Brownian motion limit). Show that

$$q_u(\Delta t) \triangleq \frac{R_f(\Delta t) - R_d(\Delta t)}{R_u(\Delta t) - R_d(\Delta t)}, \tag{6.64}$$

with $R_f(\Delta t), R_f(\Delta t)$ given by (6.25), (6.26) can be approximated as

$$q_u(\Delta t) = p_u + \xi \sqrt{\Delta t} + o(\sqrt{\Delta t}),$$

with

$$\xi = \frac{r - \mu}{\ln R_u(1) - \ln R_d(1)} - \frac{\sigma^2}{2}$$

and r, μ, σ defined in (6.22)–(6.24).

Exercise 6.2 (variance of monthly log return). Consider a random variable Z taking two values Z_u and Z_d with probability p_u and p_d respectively. Show that

$$\text{Var}(Z) = p_u p_d (Z_u - Z_d)^2.$$

Exercise 6.3 (risk-neutral mean and variance of log returns on short horizons). Suppose risk-neutral probabilities satisfy

$$q_u(t) = p_u + \xi\sqrt{t} + o(\sqrt{t}),$$
$$q_d(t) = p_d + \xi\sqrt{t} + o(\sqrt{t}),$$

and that log returns are given by

$$\ln R_t = \mu t + \sqrt{t}(\ln R_1 - \mu).$$

Find the risk-neutral mean and variance of $\ln R_t$ with precision $o(t)$.

Exercise 6.4 (mean and variance of log return in a jump model). In a model with $p_u = 1 - \lambda\Delta t$, $X_u = \tilde{\mu}\Delta t$, $X_d = \tilde{\mu}\Delta t - J$ show that

$$\text{E}^P[X] = (\tilde{\mu} - \lambda J)\Delta t,$$
$$\text{Var}^P(X) = J^2\lambda\Delta t - (J\lambda\Delta t)^2.$$

Exercise 6.5 (probability of no jumps). In a binomial model with $p_u = 1 - \lambda\Delta t$ the probability of no jumps over period $[0, t]$ is

$$p_0(\Delta t) = (1 - \lambda\Delta t)^{t/\Delta t}.$$

Find the limit $p_0 = \lim_{\Delta t \to 0} p_0(\Delta t)$.

Exercise 6.6 (risk-neutral distribution of jumps). Consider a binomial model with

$$\ln R_u(\Delta t) = \tilde{\mu}(\Delta t)\Delta t,$$
$$\ln R_d(\Delta t) = \tilde{\mu}(\Delta t)\Delta t - J(\Delta t),$$
$$\ln R_f(\Delta t) = r\Delta t,$$

where $\tilde{\mu}(\Delta t)$ and $J(\Delta t)$ are given by the calibration (6.41) and (6.42). Show that the one-period risk-neutral probability in this model satisfies

$$q_u(\Delta t) = 1 + \frac{r - \tilde{\mu}}{1 - e^{-J}}\Delta t + o(\Delta t),$$

where $\tilde{\mu}$ and J are given by (6.43) and (6.44).

Exercise 6.7 (option pricing in the Poisson jump model). Compute the no-arbitrage call option price in the model of Section 6.3 with $\lambda = 9$. This model will have nine jumps per month on average with a standard deviation of three jumps per month. This is roughly one jump every other trading day.

Exercise 6.8 (central limit theorem). Use the central limit theorem to find the P-distribution of $\ln(S_t/S_0)$ in the Brownian motion limit of the binomial lattice.

7

Fast Fourier Transform

This chapter explains how one can accelerate the computations in the binomial lattice of Chapter 6 and get closer to the continuous-time limit *numerically* using a fast Fourier transform (FFT). As a by-product we will see that Fourier transform can be used to characterize the continuous-time limit *theoretically* and this will allow us to *prove* what we have assumed in Chapter 6, namely that the risk-neutral distribution of log returns is normal in the Brownian motion limit. We will appreciate the speed of the FFT in Chapter 12 when dealing with the continuous-time limit of an incomplete market model.

7.1 Introduction to Complex Numbers and the Fourier Transform

The Fourier transform is very much about *evenly spaced points on a circle*, and if you have seen a bicycle wheel, you are perfectly qualified to study this topic. From a mathematical point of view, evenly distributed points on a circle are most easily described by complex numbers. This section reviews the geometry of these numbers, which in turn determine the properties of the Fourier transform.

7.1.1 Complex Numbers

Complex numbers are a convenient way of capturing vectors in a two-dimensional space. For example, Figure 7.1 depicts a vector,

$$2 + i.$$

This is a point in the plane two units along the *real* (horizontal) *axis* and one unit along the *imaginary* (vertical) *axis*. This terminology is unfortunate; the imaginary axis is no less real than the real axis. It would be fairer to call the imaginary axis the *north–south axis* and the real axis the *east–west axis*.

The rules for addition of complex numbers are the same as with vectors, for example,

$$\begin{bmatrix} 2 \\ 1 \end{bmatrix} + \begin{bmatrix} 3 \\ -4 \end{bmatrix} = \begin{bmatrix} 5 \\ -3 \end{bmatrix}$$

translated into complex notation would read

$$(2 + i) + (3 - 4i) = 5 - 3i.$$

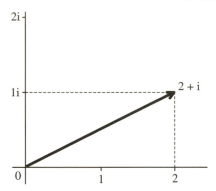

Figure 7.1.   A complex number as a two-dimensional vector.

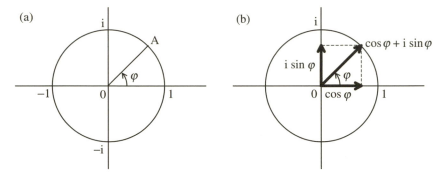

Figure 7.2.   A point on the unit circle expressed as a complex number.

Likewise, multiplication by a scalar (a real number) works as for vectors:

$$-3\begin{bmatrix}2\\1\end{bmatrix}=\begin{bmatrix}-6\\-3\end{bmatrix}$$

translates into complex numbers as

$$-3(2+i)=-6-3i.$$

7.1.2   Complex Multiplication

Complex numbers are very good at describing the movement around a unit circle. As shown in Figure 7.2a, the unit circle intersects the real axis at points -1, 1, and the imaginary axis at points $-i$ and i.

A point A on the unit circle is uniquely characterized by its *argument* φ, the angle between the real axis and the line OA. More specifically, Figure 7.2b shows that the point A can be expressed as $\cos\varphi + i\sin\varphi$.

On most computers the functions sin and cos are implemented in such a way that the angle φ must be given in *radians*. Radians measure the distance travelled on the perimeter of the unit circle. The entire perimeter of the unit circle has length 2π, which corresponds to $360°$. The angle corresponding to i is $90°$ or $\pi/2$, the angle corresponding to -1 is $180°$ or π, and so on, as shown in Table 7.1.

Table 7.1. Conversion table between degrees and radians.

Angle in degrees	0	30	60	90	180	270	360
Angle in radians	0	$\pi/6$	$\pi/3$	$\pi/2$	π	$3\pi/2$	2π

Facts.

- *Multiplying complex numbers* on a unit circle *means adding angles*. The angle of i is $90°$, the angle of $\text{i} \times \text{i}$ will be $90° + 90° = 180°$, which corresponds to -1 (see Figure 7.3a). In standard notation this gives the famous formula,

$$\text{i} \times \text{i} = \text{i}^2 = -1. \tag{7.1}$$

  With (7.1) in hand the general definition of complex multiplication follows naturally:

$$(a_1 + \text{i}b_1) \times (a_2 + \text{i}b_2) = a_1 a_2 + \text{i}(b_1 a_2 + a_1 b_2) + b_1 b_2 \text{i}^2$$
$$= a_1 a_2 - b_1 b_2 + \text{i}(b_1 a_2 + a_1 b_2). \tag{7.2}$$

- It also follows that the 'multiplication is adding angles' rule works quite generally on the unit circle:

$$(\cos \varphi_1 + \text{i} \sin \varphi_1) \times (\cos \varphi_2 + \text{i} \sin \varphi_2)$$
$$= \cos(\varphi_1 + \varphi_2) + \text{i} \sin(\varphi_1 + \varphi_2). \tag{7.3}$$

- One can express points on the unit circle more elegantly using the **Euler formula**,

$$\cos \varphi + \text{i} \sin \varphi = e^{\text{i}\varphi}, \tag{7.4}$$

  whereby (7.3) becomes

$$e^{\text{i}\varphi_1} \times e^{\text{i}\varphi_2} = e^{\text{i}(\varphi_1 + \varphi_2)} \tag{7.5}$$

  (see Figure 7.3b).

7.1.3 Geometry of Spoked Wheels

It is very easy to construct a wheel with evenly placed spokes using complex numbers. Suppose we want to place five points on the unit circle, evenly spaced. One fifth of the full circle is characterized by the angle $2\pi/5$, hence the first spoke will be placed at $e^{\text{i}2\pi/5}$. Let us denote this number by z_5:

$$z_5 \triangleq e^{\text{i}2\pi/5}.$$

Since the multiplication by z_5 causes anticlockwise rotation by one-fifth of the full circle, the second spoke will be $(z_5)^2$, the third spoke at $(z_5)^3$, and so on (see Figure 7.4a).

This provides a natural numbering of the spokes, according to how many elementary rotations are needed to reach the particular spoke (see Figure 7.4b). Note that since we are moving in a circle we will come back to the starting point after five

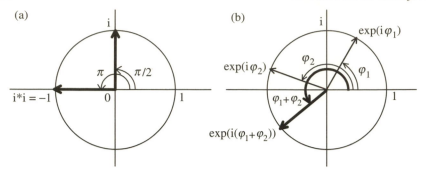

Figure 7.3. Complex multiplication on a unit circle means adding angles.

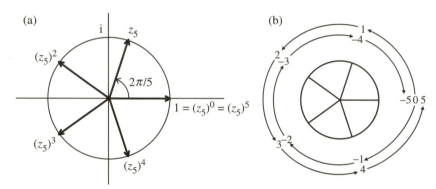

Figure 7.4. Spoke numbering.

rotations anticlockwise,

$$(z_5)^0 = (z_5)^5 = (z_5)^{10} = (z_5)^{15} = \cdots,$$
$$(z_5)^1 = (z_5)^6 = (z_5)^{11} = (z_5)^{16} = \cdots,$$
$$\vdots$$
$$(z_5)^4 = (z_5)^9 = (z_5)^{14} = (z_5)^{19} = \cdots,$$

and also after five rotations clockwise,

$$(z_5)^0 = (z_5)^{-5} = (z_5)^{-10} = (z_5)^{-15} = \cdots,$$
$$(z_5)^1 = (z_5)^{-4} = (z_5)^{-9} = (z_5)^{-14} = \cdots,$$
$$\vdots$$
$$(z_5)^4 = (z_5)^{-1} = (z_5)^{-6} = (z_5)^{-11} = \cdots.$$

Thus the numbering of spokes is not unique; for example, the indices $0, \pm 5, \pm 10$ refer to the same spoke (see Figure 7.4b).

The following box summarizes the most important properties of evenly spaced points on the unit circle. These properties are essential for the understanding of how and why the discrete Fourier transform works.

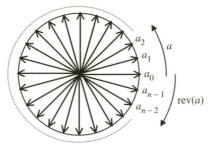

Figure 7.5. Reverse order on a circle.

- Let z_n be a rotation by one-nth of a full circle:

$$z_n \triangleq e^{i2\pi/n}.$$

Then

$$(z_n)^0 + (z_n)^1 + \cdots + (z_n)^{n-1} = 0 \qquad (7.6)$$

for any n. This is because the points $(z_n)^0, (z_n)^1, \ldots, (z_n)^{n-1}$ are evenly distributed on a unit circle and thus the result of summation must not change if we rotate the set of points by one-nth of a full circle. The only vector that remains unchanged after such a rotation is the zero vector.

- One can generalize this result further. Let k be an integer between 1 and $n-1$. Then

$$(z_n^k)^0 + (z_n^k)^1 + \cdots + (z_n^k)^{n-1} = 0 \qquad (7.7)$$

for any n. The reason for this result is again the rotational symmetry of points $(z_n^k)^0, (z_n^k)^1, \ldots, (z_n^k)^{n-1}$. The difference from the above case is that in the sequence $(z_n)^0, (z_n)^1, \ldots, (z_n)^{n-1}$ each spoke occurs *exactly once*, whereas in $(z_n^k)^0, (z_n^k)^1, \ldots, (z_n^k)^{n-1}$ the same spoke can occur several times (try $n = 4, k = 2$).

- The case with $k = 0$ requires special attention. Since $(z_n^0)^j = 1$ for all j we have

$$(z_n^k)^0 + (z_n^k)^1 + \cdots + (z_n^k)^{n-1} = n.$$

To summarize,

$$(z_n^k)^0 + (z_n^k)^1 + \cdots + (z_n^k)^{n-1} = n \quad \text{for } k = 0, \pm n, \pm 2n, \ldots, \quad (7.8)$$

$$(z_n^k)^0 + (z_n^k)^1 + \cdots + (z_n^k)^{n-1} = 0 \quad \text{for } k \neq 0, \pm n, \pm 2n, \ldots. \quad (7.9)$$

7.1.4 Reverse Order on a Circle

Given a sequence of n numbers $a = [a_0, a_1, \ldots, a_{n-1}]$ we can say that

$$\mathrm{rev}(a) \triangleq [a_0, a_{n-1}, \ldots, a_1]$$

is a in *reverse order*. If a is written around a circle in an *anticlockwise* direction, then $\mathrm{rev}(a)$ is found by reading from a_0 in a clockwise direction (see Figure 7.5). Note that $\mathrm{rev}(a)$ *is not* equal to $[a_{n-1}, \ldots, a_1, a_0]$.

- For any k the sequence

$$(z_n^k)^0, (z_n^k)^1, \ldots, (z_n^k)^{n-1}$$

is the same as the sequence

$$(z_n^{-k})^0, (z_n^{-k})^1, \ldots, (z_n^{-k})^{n-1}$$

taken in the reverse order:

$$\mathrm{rev}((z_n^{-k})^0, (z_n^{-k})^1, \ldots, (z_n^{-k})^{n-1}) = (z_n^k)^0, (z_n^k)^1, \ldots, (z_n^k)^{n-1}. \quad (7.10)$$

This is because $(z_n^{-k})^{n-j} = z_n^{-kn+kj} = z_n^{kj} = (z_n^k)^j$ for any j.

7.2 Discrete Fourier Transform (DFT)

As in the previous section take $z_n \triangleq e^{i2\pi/n}$ (this number is called the nth root of unity). Let $a_0, a_1, \ldots, a_{n-1}$ be a sequence of n (in general complex) numbers. The **discrete Fourier transform** of $a_0, a_1, \ldots, a_{n-1}$ is the sequence $b_0, b_1, \ldots, b_{n-1}$ such that

$$b_k = \frac{a_0(z_n^k)^0 + a_1(z_n^k)^1 + \cdots + a_{n-1}(z_n^k)^{n-1}}{\sqrt{n}} \quad (7.11)$$

$$= \frac{1}{\sqrt{n}} \sum_{j=0}^{n-1} a_j z_n^{jk} = \frac{1}{\sqrt{n}} \sum_{j=0}^{n-1} a_j e^{i(2\pi/n)jk}.$$

We write

$$\mathcal{F}(a) = b.$$

Equation (7.11) represents the **forward transform**. The **inverse transform** is

$$\tilde{a}_l = \frac{\tilde{b}_0(z_n^{-l})^0 + \tilde{b}_1(z_n^{-l})^1 + \cdots + \tilde{b}_{n-1}(z_n^{-l})^{n-1}}{\sqrt{n}} \quad (7.12)$$

$$= \frac{1}{\sqrt{n}} \sum_{k=0}^{n-1} \tilde{b}_k z_n^{-kl} = \frac{1}{\sqrt{n}} \sum_{k=0}^{n-1} \tilde{b}_k e^{-i(2\pi/n)kl}$$

and we write

$$\tilde{a} = \mathcal{F}^{-1}(\tilde{b}).$$

- The inverse discrete Fourier transform of the sequence $\tilde{b}_0, \tilde{b}_1, \ldots, \tilde{b}_{n-1}$ is the same as the forward transform of the same sequence in reversed order:

$$\mathcal{F}^{-1}(\tilde{b}) = \mathcal{F}(\mathrm{rev}(\tilde{b})). \quad (7.13)$$

This is a direct consequence of (7.10).

- Appendix 7.7.1 shows that $\mathcal{F}^{-1}$ is indeed an inverse transformation to $\mathcal{F}$, that is,

$$\mathcal{F}^{-1}(\mathcal{F}(a)) = \mathcal{F}(\mathcal{F}^{-1}(a)) = a. \quad (7.14)$$

This result relies on (7.8) and (7.9).

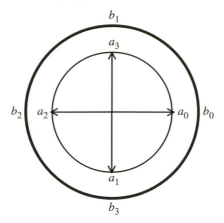

Figure 7.6. Computing the first element of the circular convolution $a \circledast b$.

7.3 Fourier Transforms in Finance

7.3.1 *Option Pricing via Circular Convolution*

For any two n-dimensional vectors $a = [a_0, a_1, \ldots, a_{n-1}], b = [b_0, b_1, \ldots, b_{n-1}]$ we define the *circular convolution* of a and b to be a new vector c

$$c = a \circledast b$$

such that

$$c_j = \sum_{k=0}^{n-1} a_{j-k} b_k. \tag{7.15}$$

One will immediately note that the index $j - k$ can be less than 0. If this occurs, we will simply add n to get the result between 0 and $n - 1$; this practice is consistent with the spoke numbering introduced in Section 7.1.3.

Graphically, one can evaluate the convolution as follows.

1. Set up two concentric circles divided into n equal segments. Write a around the *inner circle clockwise* and b around the *outer circle anticlockwise.* Figure 7.6 shows this for $n = 4$.

2. Perform a scalar multiplication between the two circles. In Figure 7.6 this would give

$$a_0 b_0 + a_3 b_1 + a_2 b_2 + a_1 b_3.$$

The result is c_0.

3. *Turn the inner circle anticlockwise* by $(1/n)$th of a full circle. Repeat the scalar multiplication between the circles. The result is c_1. In Figure 7.7,

$$c_1 = a_1 b_0 + a_0 b_1 + a_3 b_2 + a_2 b_3.$$

4. Repeat this procedure to compute $c_2, \ldots, c_{n-1}$, each time giving the inner circle a $(1/n)$th turn anticlockwise.

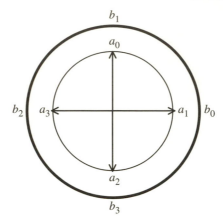

Figure 7.7. Computing the second element of the circular convolution $a \circledast b$.

How can one use convolution for option pricing? Let us go back to the binomial option pricing model of Chapter 5. At time $T = 3$ the option can have four different values:

$$C(3) = \begin{bmatrix} 599.64 \\ 102.00 \\ 0.00 \\ 0.00 \end{bmatrix}.$$

The conditional one-period risk-neutral probabilities are $q_u = 0.435\,23$, $q_d = 0.564\,77$ and the risk-free return is $R_f = 1.0033$. Let us construct two vectors a and b. Vector a will be $C(3)$ in reverse order:

$$a = \text{rev}(C(3)) = \begin{bmatrix} 599.64 \\ 0.00 \\ 0.00 \\ 102.00 \end{bmatrix}.$$

Vector b will contain state prices which we know are equal to the risk-neutral probabilities discounted by the risk-free rate. This quantity is sometimes called the *pricing kernel* or the *stochastic discount factor*. Since we only have two states over one period there are just two state prices; the remaining entries will be padded by zeros:

$$b = \begin{bmatrix} \dfrac{q_u}{R_f} \\ \dfrac{q_d}{R_f} \\ 0.00 \\ 0.00 \end{bmatrix} = \begin{bmatrix} 0.4338 \\ 0.5629 \\ 0.00 \\ 0.00 \end{bmatrix}.$$

Now let us compute $c = a \circledast b$ using the graphical method described above (see Figure 7.8).

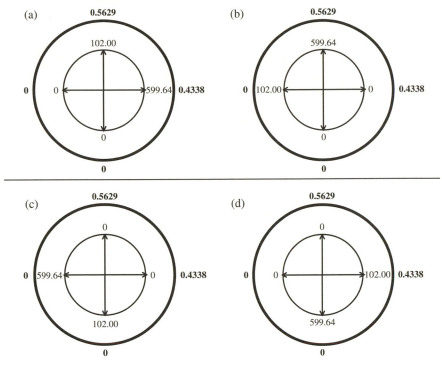

Figure 7.8. Option pricing via circular convolution. (a) $c_0 = 599.64 \times 0.4338 + 102.00 \times 0.5629$; (b) $c_1 = 599.64 \times 0.5629$; (c) $c_2 = 0$; (d) $c_3 = 102.00 \times 0.4338$.

Numerically,

$$c_0 = 317.54, \qquad c_1 = 337.54, \qquad c_2 = 0, \qquad c_3 = 44.25.$$

We will write the result c in reverse order

$$\mathrm{rev}(c) = \begin{bmatrix} 317.54 \\ 44.25 \\ 0 \\ 337.54 \end{bmatrix}$$

and compare it with the no-arbitrage price of the option at $t = 2$:

$$C(2) = \begin{bmatrix} 317.54 \\ 44.25 \\ 0 \end{bmatrix}.$$

We can see that $\mathrm{rev}(c)$ corresponds to $C(2)$ except that the last entry in $\mathrm{rev}(c)$ is meaningless; it is the no-arbitrage price of the pay-off

$$\begin{bmatrix} 0 \\ 599.64 \end{bmatrix}.$$

We have just shown that

$$\mathrm{rev}(C(2)) = \mathrm{rev}(C(3)) \circledast b.$$

Similarly,

$$\text{rev}(C(1)) = \text{rev}(C(2)) \circledast b,$$
$$\text{rev}(C(0)) = \text{rev}(C(1)) \circledast b.$$

By backward substitution,

$$\text{rev}(C(2)) = \text{rev}(C(3)) \circledast b,$$
$$\text{rev}(C(1)) = \text{rev}(C(3)) \circledast b \circledast b,$$
$$\text{rev}(C(0)) = \text{rev}(C(3)) \circledast b \circledast b \circledast b,$$

where b is the vector containing the pricing kernel $q/(1+r)$ padded by zeros to have the same dimension as $C(3)$. The vectors $C(0)$, $C(1)$, $C(2)$ computed in this manner have more entries than needed; the useful entries are at the top end of each vector. Numerically, we have

Number of low returns	$C(0)$	$C(1)$	$C(2)$	$C(3)$
0	**81.36**	**162.66**	**317.54**	**599.64**
1	115.28	**19.19**	**44.25**	**102.00**
2	265.47	190.01	**0.00**	**0.00**
3	232.62	325.17	337.54	**0.00**

The relevant entries are highlighted. Compare this result with Figure 5.10 in Chapter 5.

7.3.2   Option Pricing via Discrete Fourier Transform

The discrete Fourier transform has one very useful property: it turns convolutions into products,

$$\mathcal{F}(a \circledast b) = \sqrt{n}\mathcal{F}(a)\mathcal{F}(b) \tag{7.16}$$

(see Appendix 7.7.2). This can be used to a great advantage in pricing. Recall from the preceding section that

$$\text{rev}(C_0) = \text{rev}(C_T) \circledast \overbrace{b \circledast b \circledast \cdots \circledast b}^{T \text{ times}}.$$

Now apply the forward transform $\mathcal{F}$ to both sides, using property (7.16) on the right-hand side:

$$\mathcal{F}(\text{rev}(C_0)) = \mathcal{F}(\text{rev}(C_T)) \times (\sqrt{n}\mathcal{F}(b))^T. \tag{7.17}$$

Recall from (7.13) that $\mathcal{F}(\text{rev}(C_0)) = \mathcal{F}^{-1}(C_0)$ and substitute this into (7.17)

$$\mathcal{F}^{-1}(C_0) = \mathcal{F}^{-1}(C_T) \times (\sqrt{n}\mathcal{F}(b))^T.$$

Finally, apply the forward transform to both sides again and use (7.14) on the left-hand side:

$$C_0 = \mathcal{F}(\mathcal{F}^{-1}(C_T) \times (\sqrt{n}\mathcal{F}(b))^T).$$

Table 7.2. Comparison of DFT pricing algorithm with standard binomial recursion. Execution times for Pentium III 750 MHz, 128 Mb RAM.

Trading interval in minutes	Number of periods	Execution time in seconds	
		DFT	recursion
60	504	0.15	0.4
30	1008	0.6	1.6
15	2016	2.3	6.4
5	6048	20.8	61.6

Option pricing via discrete Fourier transform. Consider a model with IID stock returns and a constant interest rate, represented by a recombining binomial tree with T periods and $T + 1$ trading dates. Let the $(T + 1)$-dimensional vector C_T be the pay-off of the option at expiry. Let b contain the one-step state prices as the first two entries, with the remaining $T - 1$ entries being zeros. Then the first element of the $(T + 1)$-dimensional vector C_0,

$$C_0 = \mathcal{F}(\mathcal{F}^{-1}(C_T) \times (\sqrt{T + 1}\mathcal{F}(b))^T), \qquad (7.18)$$

is the no-arbitrage price of the option at time 0.

Every textbook, and indeed every computer language, defines the forward and inverse transforms slightly differently. In GAUSS the two transforms are called dfft and dffti, respectively, and they are related to $\mathcal{F}$ and $\mathcal{F}^{-1}$ as follows:

$$\text{dfft}(a) \triangleq \frac{\mathcal{F}(a)}{\sqrt{n}},$$

$$\text{dffti}(a) \triangleq \sqrt{n}\mathcal{F}^{-1}(a),$$

with n being the dimension of vector a. Equation (7.18) translated into GAUSS becomes

$$C_0 = \text{dfft}(\text{dffti}(C_T) \times ((T + 1)\text{dfft}(b))^T). \qquad (7.19)$$

Suppose the vectors C_T and b have already been defined in GAUSS. To compute the option price at $t = 0$ we would write

```
C_0 = dfft( dffti(C_T). * ((T+1) * dfft(b))^T );
print "no-arbitrage price at t=0 is" C_0[1,1];
```

The program *chapter7sect3.gss* illustrates this point in full. It is instructive to compare the speed of the DFT algorithm with the speed of the standard recursive pricing procedure *chapter6sect2b*. The DFT algorithm is approximately three times faster; the computational time for both algorithms grows quadratically with the number of periods (see Table 7.2).

7.4 Fast Pricing via the Fast Fourier Transform (FFT)

There is a fast version of the discrete Fourier transform that considerably saves on computational time. It comes almost for free—only one adjustment is needed: the length of the input vector must be of the form $2^p 3^q 5^r$. The next two subsections describe the FFT algorithm in more detail; those interested in applications can jump straight to Section 7.4.4.

7.4.1 Description of Basic FFT Algorithm

The number of complex multiplications required to compute the discrete Fourier transform from its definition (7.11) is proportional to n^2. The fast Fourier transform is an algorithm that will compute the same transform with only $n \log_2 n$ complex multiplications. With $n = 1024$ this represents only $10\,240$ as opposed to $n^2 = 1\,048\,576$ operations—a 100-fold improvement in speed.

Here is the basic idea of FFT.

1. Take n to be a power of 2:

$$n \triangleq 2^p.$$

   If the original dimension is not a power of 2, add zeros at the end of the original vector.

2. Calculate the Fourier transform, summing over the even and odd spokes separately:

$$
\begin{aligned}
b_k &= \frac{1}{\sqrt{n}} \sum_{j=0}^{n-1} a_j (z_n^k)^j \\
&= \frac{1}{\sqrt{n}} \underbrace{\sum_{j=0}^{(n/2)-1} a_{2j} (z_n^k)^{2j}}_{\text{even indices}} + \frac{1}{\sqrt{n}} \underbrace{\sum_{j=0}^{(n/2)-1} a_{2j+1} (z_n^k)^{2j+1}}_{\text{odd indices}} \\
&= \frac{1}{\sqrt{n}} \sum_{j=0}^{(n/2)-1} a_{2j} ((z_n^2)^k)^j + \frac{1}{\sqrt{n}} z_n^k \sum_{j=0}^{(n/2)-1} a_{2j+1} ((z_n^2)^k)^j.
\end{aligned}
$$

The two sums represent transforms of length $n/2$, the number z_n^k in front of the second sum is known as the *twiddle factor*. Crucially, we can reuse the same half transforms to compute $b_{k+n/2}$ (recall that $z_n^n = 1$ is a rotation by a full circle, while $z_n^{n/2} = -1$ is a rotation by half a circle):

$$
\begin{aligned}
b_{k+n/2} &= \frac{1}{\sqrt{n}} z_n^n \sum_{j=0}^{(n/2)-1} a_{2j} ((z_n^2)^k)^j + \frac{1}{\sqrt{n}} z_n^{k+n/2} \sum_{j=0}^{(n/2)-1} a_{2j+1} ((z_n^2)^k)^j \\
&= \frac{1}{\sqrt{n}} \sum_{j=0}^{(n/2)-1} a_{2j} ((z_n^2)^k)^j - \frac{1}{\sqrt{n}} z_n^k \sum_{j=0}^{(n/2)-1} a_{2j+1} ((z_n^2)^k)^j.
\end{aligned}
$$

3. To summarize, the sums

$$\sum_{j=0}^{(n/2)-1} a_{2j}((z_n^2)^k)^j \quad \text{and} \quad \sum_{j=0}^{(n/2)-1} a_{2j+1}((z_n^2)^k)^j$$

only need to be computed for $k = 0, 1, \ldots, (n/2) - 1$, their value for $k = n/2$ is the same as with $k = 0$, the value for $(n/2) + 1$ is the same as with $k = 1$, etc. These two sums for different k represent two Fourier transforms of length $n/2$. To obtain b_k for $k = 0, 1, \ldots, n - 1$ the only extra computation required is n complex multiplications by the '*twiddle factors*' z_n^k. To compute one transform of length n we need 2 transforms of length $n/2$ plus n complex multiplications, which we can think of as $n/2$ transforms of length 2. This is called the *divide-and-conquer approach* and it can be generalized to any composite length $n = n_1 n_2$, which can be broken down to n_1 transforms of length n_2 and n_2 transforms of length n_1.

4. The process of splitting indices into even and odd is called *decimation in time*. A similar algorithm that divides indices into the top and bottom half (on the unit circle) is known as *decimation in frequency*. The difference between these two approaches lies in the ordering of input and output; the former has naturally ordered input, whereas the latter yields naturally ordered output.

Let $\text{Op}(n)$ denote the number of complex multiplications required for a transform of size n. For simplicity let us agree that $\text{Op}(1) = 1$. We would like to evaluate $\text{Op}(n)$. Above we have shown that

$$\text{Op}(n) = 2\,\text{Op}(n/2) + n.$$

Apply the same reduction to the transform of size $n/2$,

$$\text{Op}(n/2) = 2\,\text{Op}(n/4) + n/2,$$

then to the transform of size $n/4$,

$$\text{Op}(n/4) = 2\,\text{Op}(n/8) + n/4,$$

and so on,

$$\text{Op}(n) = 2\,\text{Op}(n/2) + n = 2(2\,\text{Op}(n/4) + n/2) + n = 4\,\text{Op}(n/4) + n + n$$

$$= \cdots \overset{\text{after } p \text{ steps}}{=} 2^p\,\text{Op}(n/2^p) + \underbrace{n + \cdots + n}_{p \text{ times}}.$$

Recall that $n = 2^p$ and $\text{Op}(1) = 1$, hence

$$\text{Op}(n) = pn + n = n\log_2 n + n.$$

7.4.2 FFT of Lengths Different from 2^p

The FFT algorithm for $n = 2^p$ is referred to as a radix-2 algorithm. When $n \neq 2^p$ one has to use more complex algorithms.

(1) For low prime numbers $n = 2, 3, 5, 7$ use the definition of the discrete Fourier transform.

(2) If $n > 7$ is a prime number (it has no divisors other than 1 and n), use the so-called *Rader algorithm* that reduces to a Fourier transform of size $n - 1$, using convolution. Note that $n - 1$ will not be a prime.

(3) If n is not a prime $n = n_1 n_2$, and n_1, n_2 have no common divisors, then use the *prime factor algorithm*. Like the standard divide-and-conquer approach it requires n_1 transforms of length n_2 and n_2 transforms of size n_1 but it saves on twiddle factor multiplications by cleverly reordering the indices.

(4) Finally, if $n = n_1^p$ with n_1 prime use the *radix-n_1 algorithm*, analogous to the radix-2 algorithm. There is one exception: transforms of length 2^p should use the radix-4 algorithm as much as possible.

Generally, the higher the n the slower the radix-n algorithm per output length. There is one notable exception: radix-4 is faster than radix-2 by about 25%. In practice, one uses transforms of size $n = 2^p 3^q 5^r$, which are evaluated by sequential applications of rules (1), (3), (4), and if the original vector size is not of this form, then a sufficient number of zeros is added. The advantage of using mixed-radix algorithms is twofold: firstly, more transform lengths are available, which means one need not pad the input with too many zeros; and, secondly, one can use the operation-saving prime factor algorithm. For example, with vector size $2^{10} + 1 = 1025$ the next available size for the radix-2 algorithm is $n = 2048 = 2^{11}$, but with a mixed 2,3,5-radix algorithm one could use the length $n = 1080 = 2^3 3^3 5$, which is nearly twice as small and consequently the Fourier transform evaluation is twice as fast when compared with the radix-2 algorithm.

7.4.3   Computational Considerations

One can refine the basic FFT algorithms in many ways. For example, not all twiddle factors z_n^k are complex and one can therefore reduce the number of complex operations in short length transforms. One can save complex multiplications by shifting data in the memory; for small n this will help a little. However, for large n shifting numbers in the memory can be as time-consuming as complex multiplication, partly because the processor speed is generally higher than the memory speed. A good algorithm will strike a balance between the two operations. It is also possible, instead of moving numbers in the memory, to change the way numbers are indexed in the memory. One example of this procedure is 'bit reversal', which swaps odd and even indices in a vector.

Because of different processor speeds and memory access, FFT algorithms will score differently in speed ranking on different computers. For small n (100–1000) the gain in speed by choosing different algorithms can be as much as 400%, for large n (1 000 000) it is around 25%. See the notes at the end of chapter for specialized references. In practice, if the 2,3,5-radix FFT algorithm is not fast enough for your application, then it is probably more productive to rethink the application rather than try to optimize the FFT code further.

7.4.4   GAUSS Implementation of FFT

In GAUSS the padding by zeros is done automatically; therefore, extra caution is needed. The fast Fourier forward and inverse transforms are performed by the

Table 7.3. Comparison of DFT and FFT pricing speeds.
Execution times for Pentium III 750 MHz, 128 Mb RAM.

Trading interval in minutes	Number of periods	Execution time in seconds	
		DFT	FFT
30	1 008	0.6	0.003
15	2 016	2.3	0.006
5	6 048	20.8	0.022
1	30 240	510	0.27

Table 7.4. Option value in a binomial model as a function of
rebalancing frequency Δt. Output from program *chapter7sect4*.

Δt (seconds)	60	10	1	Black–Scholes
Option price	75.933 99	75.932 93	75.932 90	75.932 88
Option delta	0.316 685 36	0.316 683 47	0.316 683 34	0.316 683 31

functions `fftn` and `ffti`, respectively. These functions use a mixed 2,3,5,7-radix algorithm. If n is the input dimension, the output dimension from `fftn` and `ffti` will be `nextn(n)`. The option pricing GAUSS formula (7.19) will therefore change to

$$C_0 = \texttt{fftn}(\texttt{ffti}(C_T) \times (\texttt{nextn}(T+1) \times \texttt{fftn}(b))^T).$$

In GAUSS code

```
C_0 = fftn( ffti(C_T).*(nextn(T+1)*fftn(b))^T );

print "no-arbitrage price at t=0 is" C_0[1];
```

The program *chapter7sect4.gss* gives a working example of pricing with the fast Fourier transform. The FFT algorithm has a blistering speed compared with the DFT (see Table 7.3).

Because it is so fast one can explore higher trading frequencies and see that the Black–Scholes formula really does describe the limiting value. Note that the Black–Scholes formula is still about 10 000 times faster than the FFT algorithm (see Table 7.4).

7.5 Further Applications of FFTs in Finance

7.5.1 Characteristic Functions, the Lévy Theorem and Convergence in Distribution

What the FFT is to practical applications, the **continuous Fourier transform** is to theoretical work. Let X be a random variable with probability density $f_X(x)$. The continuous Fourier transform of f is defined as

$$\phi_X(\lambda) = \mathrm{E}[e^{i\lambda X}] \quad \text{for } \lambda \in \mathbb{R}. \tag{7.20}$$

Thus, when X is a discrete variable with n equally spaced values $x_0, x_1, \ldots, x_{n-1}$, then

$$\mathrm{E}[e^{i\lambda X}] = \sum_{k=0}^{n-1} f(x_k)e^{i\lambda x_k}$$

very much resembles the discrete Fourier transform of the vector of probabilities $f(x_k)$.

In probability theory ϕ_X is known as the **characteristic function** of the random variable X. Let Y be a sum of IID random variables X_k,

$$Y = X_1 + X_2 + \cdots + X_n,$$

then for the characteristic function of Y we have

$$\phi_Y(\lambda) = \mathrm{E}[e^{i\lambda Y}] = \mathrm{E}[e^{i\lambda(X_1+X_2+\cdots+X_n)}]$$
$$= \mathrm{E}[e^{i\lambda X_1}e^{i\lambda X_2}\cdots e^{i\lambda X_n}].$$

If X_k are independent, then $e^{i\lambda X_k}$ are also independent; we know that for independent variables the expectation of a product is a product of expectations:

$$\phi_Y(\lambda) = \mathrm{E}[e^{i\lambda X_1}]\mathrm{E}[e^{i\lambda X_2}]\cdots \mathrm{E}[e^{i\lambda X_n}] \qquad (7.21)$$
$$= (\mathrm{E}[e^{i\lambda X}])^n = (\phi_X(\lambda))^n.$$

In probability theory the density of a sum of IID random variables equals the convolution of individual densities. Hence equation (7.21) is analogous to the convolution theorem (7.16).

In the option pricing model Y represents the logarithm of the stock return to maturity and $X = X_{\Delta t}$ is the logarithm of the one-period return, where one period has length Δt. Expectations are taken under the risk-neutral measure $Q_{\Delta t}$; this measure is different for different values of time step,

$$\phi_{\Delta t, \ln R_T}(\lambda) = \mathrm{E}^{Q_{\Delta t}}[e^{i\lambda \ln R_T}]$$
$$= (\mathrm{E}^{Q_{\Delta t}}[e^{i\lambda \ln R_{\Delta t}}])^{T/\Delta t} = (\phi_{\Delta t, \ln R_{\Delta t}}(\lambda))^{T/\Delta t}. \qquad (7.22)$$

The fact that the risk-neutral distribution of log returns in Figure 6.6 has a limit as $\Delta t \to 0$ is now mathematically captured by saying that $\phi_{\Delta t, \ln R_T}(\lambda)$ converges pointwise (for each λ separately) to a fixed characteristic function $\phi_{\ln R_T}(\lambda)$ as $\Delta t \to 0$. **Lévy's continuity theorem** states that pointwise convergence of characteristic functions implies that for *any* bounded continuous function $g(\ln R_T)$ we have

$$\mathrm{E}^{Q_{\Delta t}}[g(\ln R_T)] \to \mathrm{E}^Q[g(\ln R_T)], \qquad (7.23)$$

where Q is the probability measure corresponding to $\phi_{\ln R_T}(\lambda)$. The relationship (7.23) is known as the **convergence in distribution** (more technically, the weak convergence in measure).

7.5.2 *The Distribution of Log Returns in the Brownian Limit*

Explicitly, in the binomial model the characteristic function of log returns reads

$$\phi_{\Delta t, \ln R_{\Delta t}}(\lambda) = \mathrm{E}^{Q_{\Delta t}}[e^{i\lambda \ln R_{\Delta t}}] = q_\mathrm{u}(\Delta t)e^{i\lambda \ln R_\mathrm{u}(\Delta t)} + q_\mathrm{d}(\Delta t)e^{i\lambda \ln R_\mathrm{d}(\Delta t)}.$$

Since $\ln R(\Delta t)$ is small we can approximate the exponentials by a second-order Taylor expansion,

$$E^{Q_{\Delta t}}[e^{i\lambda \ln R_{\Delta t}}] = E^{Q_{\Delta t}}[1 + i\lambda \ln R_{\Delta t} - \lambda^2 \tfrac{1}{2}(\ln R_{\Delta t})^2 + o(\Delta t)].$$

The hard-earned results of Section 6.2.4 tell us that

$$E^{Q_{\Delta t}}[\ln R_{\Delta t}] = (r - \tfrac{1}{2}\sigma^2)\Delta t + o(\Delta t),$$

$$E^{Q_{\Delta t}}[(\ln R_{\Delta t})^2] = \sigma^2 \Delta t + o(\Delta t),$$

and consequently

$$\phi_{\Delta t, \ln R_{\Delta t}}(\lambda) = 1 + (i\lambda(r - \tfrac{1}{2}\sigma^2) - \lambda^2 \tfrac{1}{2}\sigma^2)\Delta t + o(\Delta t). \tag{7.24}$$

Plug (7.24) into (7.22) to obtain

$$\phi_{\Delta t, \ln R_T}(\lambda) = (1 + (i\lambda(r - \tfrac{1}{2}\sigma^2) - \lambda^2 \tfrac{1}{2}\sigma^2)\Delta t + o(\Delta t))^{T/\Delta t}.$$

Exercise 6.5 has shown that for x real $\lim_{\Delta t \to 0}(1 + x\Delta t + o(\Delta t))^{T/\Delta t} = e^{xT}$; the same result works for x complex so that in the limit,

$$\lim_{\Delta t \to 0} \phi_{\Delta t, \ln R_T}(\lambda) = \exp(i\lambda(r - \tfrac{1}{2}\sigma^2)T - \tfrac{1}{2}\lambda^2 \sigma^2 T).$$

The right-hand side is the characteristic function of a normal distribution with mean $(r - \tfrac{1}{2}\sigma^2)T$ and variance $\sigma^2 T$. We have now *proved* that log returns are distributed normally in the limit under risk-neutral measure.

7.5.3   *Working Out Probabilities from the Characteristic Function via FFT*

Theorists are often able to furnish us with the characteristic function of the log return distribution, but in the more complicated cases it is difficult to work out the corresponding probability density. One can, however, discretize the log return and find the density of the discretized variable using FFT. Here is how this procedure works.

We are given the theoretical value of $\phi(\lambda)$, say $\phi(\lambda) = e^{-\lambda^2/2}$. We know that

$$\phi(\lambda) = E^Q[e^{i\lambda X}] = \int_{-\infty}^{+\infty} e^{i\lambda x} f(x)\, dx,$$

where X is the log return and $f(x)$ is its risk-neutral density. Since f must go to zero at $\pm\infty$ we can approximate the integral on the right-hand side by an integral over a finite interval $[x_{\min}, x_{\max}]$

$$\phi(\lambda) \approx \int_{x_{\min}}^{x_{\max}} e^{i\lambda x} f(x)\, dx,$$

which in turn can be approximated by a sum if we subdivide the interval $[x_{\min}, x_{\max}]$ into n equally sized segments with length $\Delta x = (x_{\max} - x_{\min})/n$,

$$\phi(\lambda) \approx \sum_{j=0}^{n} e^{i\lambda(x_{\min} + (j+1/2)\Delta x)} \underbrace{f(x_{\min} + (j + 1/2)\Delta x)\Delta x}_{q_j},$$

where q_j are the risk-neutral probabilities of the discretized return. Divide both sides by $e^{i\lambda x_{\min}}$ and by $\sqrt{n}$:

$$\frac{\phi(\lambda)e^{-i\lambda(x_{\min}+\Delta x/2)}}{\sqrt{n}} \approx \frac{\sum_{j=0}^{n-1} e^{i\lambda j\Delta x}q_j}{\sqrt{n}}. \tag{7.25}$$

The sum on the right-hand side would look exactly like the discrete Fourier transform (7.11) of the risk-neutral probabilities q if $\lambda j\Delta x$ were equal to $(2\pi/n)jk$:

$$\lambda j\Delta x = (2\pi/n)jk. \tag{7.26}$$

But we know $\phi(\lambda)$ for *all* values of λ, so nothing stops us from selecting n specific values of λ satisfying (7.26),

$$\lambda_k = \frac{2\pi k}{n\Delta x} \quad \text{for } k = -\frac{n}{2}, -\frac{n}{2}+1, \ldots, \frac{n}{2}-1.$$

It is important that k takes both negative and positive signs because $\phi(\lambda)$ comes from a continuous transform and it is *not* periodic in λ.

For these specific values of λ denote the left-hand side of (7.25) by b_k,

$$b_k = \frac{\phi(\lambda_k)e^{-i\lambda_k(x_{\min}+\Delta x/2)}}{\sqrt{n}},$$

then (7.25) can be rephrased in terms of the discrete Fourier transform as

$$b = \mathcal{F}(q).$$

Conversely, we can recover q from b by using the inverse transform,

$$q = \mathcal{F}^{-1}(b).$$

Take the specific example with $\phi(\lambda) = e^{-\lambda^2/2}$. Let us approximate the density in the range $[-3, 3]$ using 600 points. We have $\Delta x = 0.01$ and

$$\lambda_k = \frac{2\pi k}{6} \quad \text{for } k = 0, 1, \ldots, 599,$$

$$b_k = \frac{e^{-(\lambda_k^2/2)+i3\lambda_k}}{\sqrt{600}}.$$

The GAUSS code for the computation of q is given in Exercise 7.3. The numerically obtained density $q/\Delta x$ is indistinguishable from the theoretical values of the standard normal density which corresponds to the characteristic function $\phi(\lambda) = e^{-\lambda^2/2}$.

7.5.4 Affine Processes

Affine processes appear to be the most promising tool in modern financial analysis. They feature prominently in option pricing, interest rate and credit derivative modelling, and are also increasingly used to study optimal portfolio allocation. It would be futile trying to summarize the vast number of existing applications of affine processes in finance; the notes at the end of the chapter only serve as a starting point. This section cannot give an exhaustive treatment; it is here to alert readers to the existence of affine processes and the whole new world of opportunities they offer.

The geometric Brownian motion model of stock prices is the simplest example of an affine structure. In short a process $\ln S$ is affine if the characteristic function of $\ln S_T$, $E_t^Q[e^{i\lambda \ln S_T}]$ is of the exponential affine form $e^{a(t,T,\lambda)+b(t,T,\lambda)\ln S_t}$, where a and b are complex functions of λ. In the Black–Scholes model, for example,

$$E_t^Q[e^{i\lambda \ln S_T}] = e^{i(r-\sigma^2/2)(T-t)\lambda - (\sigma^2 T/2)\lambda^2 + i\lambda \ln S_t}.$$

Affine models offer both flexibility and tractability. They permit asset returns to be serially correlated, allow for correlations across assets and also permit the presence of jumps, which is particularly important for the modelling of fat tails in asset returns. At the same time, the affine structure of the characteristic function often allows coefficients a, b to be evaluated in closed form which then permits, using the technique of Section 7.5.3, simple recovery of the risk-neutral distribution and consequently fast pricing.

Consider as an example the celebrated **Heston model** of stochastic volatility used in option pricing. The Black–Scholes model assumes that the return volatility is constant over time. In practice, price predictions from the constant volatility model do not fit the market data well across different strikes; this phenomenon is known as volatility smile or smirk. Heston's model resolves this problem by allowing volatility to be stochastic,

$$d\sigma_t^2 = (\alpha - \sigma_t^2)\,dt + \tilde{\sigma}\sigma_t\,dB_1^Q,$$
$$d\ln S = (r - \tfrac{1}{2}\sigma_t^2)\,dt + \sigma_t\,dB_2^Q,$$

where the volatility shocks dB_1^Q can be correlated with the stock return shocks dB_2^Q. The characteristic function of $\ln S_T$ has the affine exponential form,

$$E_t^Q[e^{i\lambda \ln S_T}] = e^{a(T-t,\lambda)+b(T-t,\lambda)\sigma_t^2 + i\lambda \ln S_t},$$

where a and b are known in closed form. Once the characteristic function is known fast option pricing is available via the techniques of Section 7.5.3.

7.6 Notes

The fast Fourier transform does not appear in undergraduate textbooks on numerical mathematics and the most useful references on the introductory level are web based (see http://www.fftw.org/links.html and in particular the online manual by Hey (1999)). A fast implementation of the FFT, taking into account computer architecture, is suggested in Frigo and Johnson (1998); it is implemented in Matlab. Duhamel and Vetterli (1990) is an excellent survey of FFT algorithms. The classic account of radix-n FFT is in Cooley and Tukey (1965). The improvement of the radix-4 over the radix-2 algorithm is documented in Yavne (1968) and more accessibly in Duhamel and Holman (1984). The prime factor algorithm is due to Kolba and Parks (1977). The prime length algorithm appears in Rader (1968). Number theoretical transforms (NTTs) are closely related to FFTs and can be used to calculate circular convolutions (see McClellan and Rader 1979; Pollard 1971). Efficient implementation of mixed 2,3,5-radix algorithm is due to Temperton (1992); it is used in GAUSS.

Affine processes find a large number of applications in finance. For an exhaustive characterization of affine processes see Duffie et al. (2003). Heston (1993) is the example given in the main text of this chapter. Exponential Lévy processes represent a special class of affine processes used to model IID stock returns with fat-tailed distribution (see Eberlein and Keller 1995; Madan and Seneta 1990). The use of FFTs in option pricing in conjunction with continuous Fourier transforms was pioneered in Carr and Madan (1999). Convergence in distribution and Lévy's continuity theorem can be found in Ash and Doléans-Dade (1999).

7.7 Appendix

7.7.1 Inverse Discrete Fourier Transform

To show $\mathcal{F}^{-1}(\mathcal{F}(a)) = a$ we need to prove that for $b = \mathcal{F}(a)$ defined in (7.11) we have $\mathcal{F}^{-1}(b) = a$. Denote $\tilde{a} = \mathcal{F}^{-1}(b)$ and express $\tilde{a}$ from definition (7.12):

$$\tilde{a}_l = \frac{1}{\sqrt{n}} \sum_{k=0}^{n-1} b_k z_n^{-kl}.$$

Now substitute for b_k from (7.11)

$$= \frac{1}{n} \sum_{k=0}^{n-1} \left(\sum_{j=0}^{n-1} a_j z_n^{jk} \right) z_n^{-kl},$$

move z_n^{-kl} inside the inner summation

$$= \frac{1}{n} \sum_{k=0}^{n-1} \left(\sum_{j=0}^{n-1} a_j z_n^{k(j-l)} \right),$$

change the order of summation

$$= \frac{1}{n} \sum_{j=0}^{n-1} \left(\sum_{k=0}^{n-1} a_j z_n^{k(j-l)} \right),$$

and take a_j in front of the inner sum (it does not depend on k)

$$= \frac{1}{n} \sum_{j=0}^{n-1} a_j \left(\sum_{k=0}^{n-1} (z_n^{j-l})^k \right).$$

By virtue of (7.8) and (7.9) the inner sum $\sum_{k=0}^{n-1} (z_n^{j-l})^k$ equals 0 for $j \neq l$ and for $j = l$ it equals n. Consequently,

$$\tilde{a}_l = \frac{1}{n} \sum_{j=0}^{n-1} a_j \left(\sum_{k=0}^{n-1} (z_n^{j-l})^k \right) = a_l$$

for all l, which proves that $\mathcal{F}^{-1}(\mathcal{F}(a)) = a$.

7.7.2 Fourier Transform of Convolutions

We wish to show $\mathcal{F}(a \circledast b) = \mathcal{F}(a)\mathcal{F}(b)$. Let us begin by computing $c = a \circledast b$. From the definition (7.15),

$$c_j = \sum_{k=0}^{n-1} a_{j-k} b_k. \tag{7.27}$$

Set $d = \mathcal{F}(c)$, and use the definition (7.11) to evaluate d_l

$$d_l = \frac{1}{\sqrt{n}} \sum_{j=0}^{n-1} c_j z_n^{jl}.$$

Now substitute for c_j from (7.27)

$$= \frac{1}{\sqrt{n}} \sum_{j=0}^{n-1} \left(\sum_{k=0}^{n-1} a_{j-k} b_k \right) z_n^{jl},$$

move z^{jl} inside the inner bracket, writing it as a product $z^{jl} = z^{(j-k)l} z^{kl}$,

$$= \frac{1}{\sqrt{n}} \sum_{j=0}^{n-1} \sum_{k=0}^{n-1} a_{j-k} z^{(j-k)l} b_k z^{kl},$$

change the order of summation

$$= \frac{1}{\sqrt{n}} \sum_{k=0}^{n-1} \sum_{j=0}^{n-1} a_{j-k} z^{(j-k)l} b_k z^{kl},$$

and take $b_k z^{kl}$ in front of the inner summation (it does not depend on j)

$$= \frac{1}{\sqrt{n}} \sum_{k=0}^{n-1} b_k z^{kl} \left(\sum_{j=0}^{n-1} a_{j-k} z^{(j-k)l} \right). \tag{7.28}$$

It is easy to realize that the inner sum does not depend on k, because it always adds the same n elements, only the order in which they are added depends on k (we are completing one full turn around the circle, starting at the kth spoke). Hence we have

$$\sum_{j=0}^{n-1} a_{j-k} z^{(j-k)l} = \sum_{j=0}^{n-1} a_j z^{jl} \quad \text{for all } k,$$

and substituting this into (7.28) we finally obtain

$$d_l = \sqrt{n} \underbrace{\left(\frac{1}{\sqrt{n}} \sum_{k=0}^{n-1} b_k z^{kl} \right)}_{\tilde{b}_l} \underbrace{\left(\frac{1}{\sqrt{n}} \sum_{j=0}^{n-1} a_j z^{jl} \right)}_{\tilde{a}_l},$$

where, from the definition of the forward transform (7.11),

$$\tilde{a} = \mathcal{F}(a),$$
$$\tilde{b} = \mathcal{F}(b),$$

which completes the proof.

7.8   Exercises

Exercise 7.1 (unconditional distribution of returns and FFT). Consider a 3-period binomial model with conditional risk-neutral probabilities $q_u = q_d = 0.5$. It is easy to verify that the unconditional probability of reaching the four nodes at $T = 3$ is $\begin{bmatrix} 0.125 & 0.375 & 0.375 & 0.125 \end{bmatrix}$. The same result can be obtained from DFT as follows. Take $n = T + 1$, $b = \begin{bmatrix} q_u & q_d & 0 & 0 \end{bmatrix}$ and evaluate $\mathcal{F}^{-1}((\sqrt{n}\mathcal{F}(b))^T)$. Your task is to use the same principle to generate data for Figures 6.4–6.6.

Exercise 7.2 (real FFT). Suppose that sequence a contains only real numbers. In such a case the image $b = \mathcal{F}(a)$ will have a degree of symmetry and we only need to compute the first $(n/2) + 1$ entries of the sequence b. Conversely, the inverse transform takes the complex half sequence and transforms it to the full-size real original. The advantage of the real FFT is that it saves half of the mathematical operations and therefore runs twice as fast as the ordinary FFT.

In GAUSS the forward and inverse real FFTs are named `rfftp` and `rfftip`. Rewrite the option pricing algorithm *chapter7sect4.gss* in terms of the real FFT. Set the rehedging interval to one month and compare the results with the original program.

Exercise 7.3 (recovering risk-neutral distributions from the characteristic function). Implement Section 7.5.3 in GAUSS using fast Fourier transforms.

8

Information Management

In Chapter 5 we were deliberately vague about the meaning of 'information available at time t'. It turns out that the amount of information needed to price a security or to solve a dynamic optimal investment problem varies from case to case, and that the information plays a crucial role in implementing the solution in reality. This chapter introduces the necessary terminology to describe the different amounts of information that are used in theory and practice, discussing notions of *path dependency*, *state variables*, *Markov property of stochastic processes*, *information filtration*, *adaptedness* and *measurability*. The required background reading for this chapter is Section 5.4.

8.1 Information: Too Much of a Good Thing?

A specific feature of the option pricing example in Chapter 5 is that *one does not need all the information* available at time t to value the option. By 'all the information' we mean the whole history of stock prices until the present day. In our model, whether the stock price goes up and then down or down and then up, the option price at $t = 2$ is still the same £44.25 (see Figure 8.1).

In such a case we say that the option price is independent of the path of stock prices, in short it is *path-independent*. It is definitely a good thing that we *do not have to* use all the information hidden in the history of stock prices, because one can very quickly accumulate too much information. Just consider how many paths there are in our decision tree. For this purpose each path is depicted separately in Figure 8.2.

After 30 periods we accumulate $2^{30} = 10^9$ paths, which proves too much even for modern computers. And 30 periods is nothing if one considers trading once a day for a few months! Consider, on the other hand, the recombining tree in Figure 8.1—it would only have 30 nodes at the end of 30 periods! Path independence significantly reduces the amount of memory storage required to compute the option price; it is therefore essential to understand where the path independence is coming from, which is the topic of the next section.

8.1.1 State Variables: the Information that Matters

Stock prices in our model have the following remarkable feature: the risk-neutral probability of achieving a particular level of stock price in the future does not depend

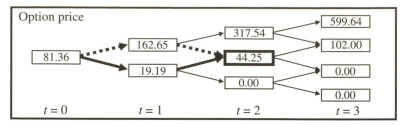

Figure 8.1. Option price exhibiting path independence.

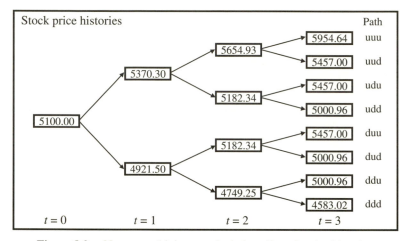

Figure 8.2. Non-recombining tree depicting all stock price histories.

on the history of past prices, only on the last known price. For example,

$$Q(S_3 = 5457.00 \mid S_2 = 5182.34, S_1 = 5370.30, S_0 = 5100.00)$$

is the same as

$$Q(S_3 = 5457.00 \mid S_2 = 5182.34, S_1 = 4921.50, S_0 = 5100.00),$$

namely 0.435 22. The values of S_1 and S_0 do not matter for the conditional distribution of S_3 viewed from $t = 2$, all that matters is the value of S_2.

More generally, if the last known price is S_t, then the distribution of stock price k steps ahead, S_{t+k}, conditional on the price history up to and including time t, $S_0, \ldots, S_t$, only depends on S_t for all t and all k. A process S with this property is called a **Markov process**.

Since our stock price is Markov under the risk-neutral probability, we can take nodes in Figure 8.3 with identical stock prices and put them on top of each other and the corresponding conditional probabilities will perfectly overlap too. We say that the nodes in the tree, and the corresponding probabilities on the branches, **recombine**; the resulting recombining tree is shown in Figure 8.4.

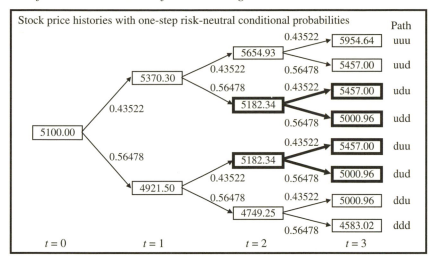

Figure 8.3. Information tree nodes with identical stock price.

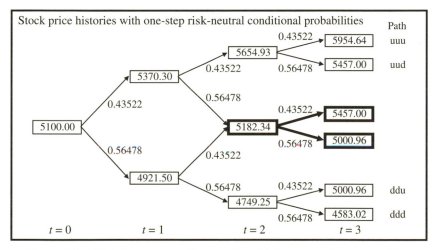

Figure 8.4. A Markov process allows nodes with the same value to recombine, together with the conditional probabilities on the branches.

8.1.2 *Path (In)dependence of Option Prices*

We are now ready to explain the path independence of option prices. Recall that the option price at the terminal date $T = 3$ is equal to the intrinsic value of the option,

$$C_T = \max(S_T - K, 0).$$

For a given option contract the strike K is fixed, therefore C_T only depends on S_T. Recall now that

$$C_{T-1} = \frac{1}{R_{\mathrm{f}}} \mathrm{E}^{Q}_{T-1}[C_T].$$

Table 8.1.   Trading instruction, 'Buy X shares'.

Path	uuu	uud	udu	udd	duu	dud	ddu	ddd
X	1	1	1	1	2	2	2	2

Furthermore, C_T only depends on S_T, and the conditional risk-neutral probabilities of S_T depend only on S_{T-1}. Consequently, $\mathrm{E}^Q_{T-1}[C_T]$ only depends on S_{T-1} and as a result C_{T-1} only depends on S_{T-1}. Now

$$C_{T-2} = \frac{1}{R_\mathrm{f}} \mathrm{E}^Q_{T-2}[C_{T-1}],$$

C_{T-1} depends on S_{T-1}, the conditional distribution of S_{T-1} only depends on S_{T-2} and consequently C_{T-2} depends only on S_{T-2}, etc.

Two factors combine to generate path-independent option prices. Firstly, the *option pay-off at expiry is path-independent*—C_T only depends on S_T and not on the entire history of stock prices. Secondly, *stock price is a Markov process under the risk-neutral probabilities*, which then implies that C_{T-1} depends on S_{T-1}, etc. The stock price acts as a **state variable**; all quantities of interest—the option price and the hedging portfolio—can be written as a function of this state variable. The second state variable is *time*—the option price not only depends on the stock price, it also depends on the time to expiry.

Very few problems in finance exhibit as little path dependency as European call option pricing. For example, the pay-off of an exotic option called the 'lookback option' depends not only on the stock price at expiry but also on the lowest stock price in the period between the day of issue and the expiry date. If the stock price is a Markov process under risk-neutral probabilities, then the no-arbitrage price of a lookback option will depend on three state variables: the current stock price, the lowest stock price to date and the time to expiry.

8.1.3   All Available Information and Insider Trading

The previous section highlighted the importance of state variables in managing the amount of information contained in the history of stock prices. In short, state variables contain *all the relevant information*. But while it is true that one never wants to use more information than necessary in practice, in theoretical work it is often handy to be able to fall back on the notion of *all available information*. First of all, it is often difficult to tell what constitutes the *relevant information* in a given problem beforehand. For example, in optimal investment new state variables are generated in the process of finding the best investment strategy. Secondly, keeping track of all available information at a given point in time is useful for ruling out trading strategies with 'insider' knowledge.

We have already mentioned above that all available information can be represented by the non-recombining stock price tree (see Figure 8.2). Suppose at time $t = 0$ a trader receives the instruction, 'Buy X shares', where X is as given in Table 8.1. Interestingly, the trader does not have to wait until $t = 3$ to execute this order. If the stock price moves up at the beginning, it is clear that the order says, 'Buy 1 share'.

Table 8.2. Two dynamic trading strategies,
represented by the stochastic processes X and Y.

Path	X_0	X_1	X_2	X_3	Y_0	Y_1	Y_2	Y_3
uuu	1	1	1	1	1	1	1	0
uud	1	1	1	0	1	1	0	0
udu	1	1	0	1	1	0	1	0
udd	1	1	0	0	1	0	0	0
duu	1	0	1	1	0	1	1	0
dud	1	0	1	0	0	1	0	0
ddu	1	0	0	1	0	0	1	0
ddd	1	0	0	0	0	0	0	0

If, on the other hand, the stock price goes down at the beginning, then it is clear that the order instructs to 'Buy 2 shares'. We can see that the information available at $t = 1$ is sufficient to pin down the value of X exactly. In such a case mathematicians say that the random variable X is $\mathcal{F}_1$-**measurable**[1], where $\mathcal{F}_t$ is the set of all events identifiable at time t. Naturally, if X is known at $t = 1$, then it is also known at $t = 2, 3$ but not necessarily at $t = 0$, as is the case here.

Now, with the same X, consider the order, 'Buy X shares now!' at $t = 0$. Clearly, this cannot be done unless we know at $t = 0$ what the stock price will do at $t = 1$. People possessing such privileged information are called **insiders** and they face heavy penalties should they use their inside information for trading on their own behalf. This observation gives us a restriction on permissible trading strategies. Namely, if X_t is an instruction to buy X_t shares at time t, then in the absence of insider trading X_t has to be $\mathcal{F}_t$-measurable, that is, X_t must be an instruction that depends only on past and present prices. When this is the case for all $t = 0, 1, 2, 3$ we say that the **stochastic process** $\{X_t\}_{t=0,1,2,3}$ is **adapted to the information filtration** $\{\mathcal{F}_t\}_{t=0,1,2,3}$ generated by the stock prices.

There is an easy way to check whether a process X is adapted to the stock price information. If X can be written into the non-recombining information tree in Figure 8.2 using one number per node, then X is adapted to the filtration generated by stock prices. If more than one number appears at any given node, then X looks into the future and executing it is tantamount to insider trading. As an example consider two trading strategies, X and Y, given in Table 8.2.

Figure 8.5 shows that strategy X is adapted, because it uses only past and current information. In words the strategy says, 'Buy 1 share after the price *has gone up*, otherwise do not trade'. On the other hand, Y is not adapted, quite naturally because the strategy means, 'Buy 1 share if the price *will go up*, otherwise do not trade'.

8.2 Model-Independent Properties of Conditional Expectation

It is essential to be able to evaluate various conditional expectations directly on the tree, as we have done when computing option prices in Chapter 5. But, in prac-

---

[1] For a more detailed explanation refer to Section 8.5.

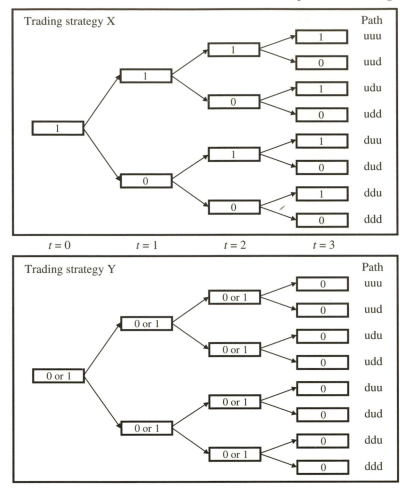

Figure 8.5. Adapted and non-adapted trading strategies depicted in the information tree.

tice, building a physical model costs time and in complex situations can even be counterproductive—just try and put a three-dimensional tree into an Excel spreadsheet! It is therefore equally important to be able to evaluate with just pen and paper conditional expectations without a physical model. In this section we will highlight a few useful manipulations involving conditional expectations that are model independent.

8.2.1   *Conditional Expectation as a Random Variable*

The expectation of X conditional on the information at time t, $E_t[X]$, can have as many values as there are nodes in the information tree at time t. As an example let us calculate $E_1^Q[S_2]$. In the upper node at time $t = 1$ we have

$$E_1^Q[S_2] = 0.435\,22 \times 5654.93 + 0.564\,78 \times 5182.34 = 5388.02$$

Table 8.3. Conditional expectation as a random variable.

Path	uuu	uud	udu	udd	duu	dud	ddu	ddd
$E_1[S_2]$	5388.02	5388.02	5388.02	5388.02	4937.74	4937.74	4937.74	4937.74

and in the lower node

$$E_1^Q[S_2] = 0.435\,22 \times 5182.34 + 0.564\,78 \times 4749.25 = 4937.74.$$

Since the conditional expectation $E_1[S_2]$ can change from node to node we have to treat it as a random variable, as indicated in Table 8.3.

The randomness, however, is always such that $E_1[S_2]$ is known at time 1.

> Regardless of specific model, $E_t[X]$ is always known at time t.

8.2.2 Two Important Rules

Conventional wisdom tells us that $E[aX] = aE[X]$ if a is a non-random entity. Now consider a similar expression,

$$E_1[S_1 S_2],$$

where as before S_1 is known at time $t = 1$, whereas S_2 is only known at time $t = 2$. Since S_1 is known at $t = 1$, it acts as a constant for expectation at $t = 1$ and consequently

$$E_1[S_1 S_2] = S_1 E_1[S_2],$$

and conversely

$$S_1 E_1[S_2] = E_1[S_1 S_2].$$

> This is known as the **law of conditional constant**:
> $$E_t[XY] = X E_t[Y] \quad \text{if } X \text{ is known at time } t.$$
>
> In addition, we have the **law of iterated expectations**, discovered in Section 5.5:
> $$E_t[E_s[X]] = E_s[E_t[X]] = E_t[X] \quad \text{for } t \leqslant s.$$

8.2.3 Examples

Example 8.1. Calculate

$$E_0^P[S_3]$$

if the objective conditional distribution of returns is given by (5.1) and (5.2).

Solution. We can write the terminal stock price in terms of one-step returns

$$S_3 = S_0 \frac{S_1}{S_0} \frac{S_2}{S_1} \frac{S_3}{S_2},$$

obtaining

$$E_0^P[S_3] = E_0^P\left[S_0 \frac{S_1}{S_0} \frac{S_2}{S_1} \frac{S_3}{S_2} \right].$$

Now S_0 is known at $t = 0$; therefore, we can take it in front of the expectation,

$$E_0^P[S_3] = S_0 E_0^P\left[\frac{S_1}{S_0}\frac{S_2}{S_1}\frac{S_3}{S_2}\right].$$

By the law of iterated expectations,

$$E_0^P\left[\frac{S_1}{S_0}\frac{S_2}{S_1}\frac{S_3}{S_2}\right] = E_0^P\left[E_1^P\left[E_2^P\left[\frac{S_1}{S_0}\frac{S_2}{S_1}\frac{S_3}{S_2}\right]\right]\right].$$

Consider the innermost expectation. Because S_2, S_1 and S_0 are known at $t = 2$ we can take $(S_1/S_0)(S_2/S_1)$ in front of $E_2^P[.]$:

$$E_0^P\left[E_1^P\left[E_2^P\left[\frac{S_1}{S_0}\frac{S_2}{S_1}\frac{S_3}{S_2}\right]\right]\right] = E_0^P\left[E_1^P\left[\frac{S_1}{S_0}\frac{S_2}{S_1}E_2^P\left[\frac{S_3}{S_2}\right]\right]\right].$$

Similarly, we can take S_1/S_0 in front of $E_1^P[.]$ to obtain

$$E_0^P\left[\frac{S_1}{S_0}\frac{S_2}{S_1}\frac{S_3}{S_2}\right] = E_0^P\left[\frac{S_1}{S_0}E_1^P\left[\frac{S_2}{S_1}E_2^P\left[\frac{S_3}{S_2}\right]\right]\right].$$

It is easy to compute

$$E_t^P\left[\frac{S_{t+1}}{S_t}\right],$$

from (5.1) and (5.2),

$$E_t^P\left[\frac{S_{t+1}}{S_t}\right] = \tfrac{1}{2}R_u + \tfrac{1}{2}R_d = 1.009.$$

Consequently,

$$E_0^P\left[\frac{S_1}{S_0}E_1^P\left[\frac{S_2}{S_1}E_2^P\left[\frac{S_3}{S_2}\right]\right]\right] = E_0^P\left[\frac{S_1}{S_0}E_1^P\left[\frac{S_2}{S_1}1.009\right]\right]$$

$$= E_0^P\left[\frac{S_1}{S_0}1.009^2\right] = 1.009^3,$$

and as a result

$$E_0^P[S_3] = S_0 1.009^3. \tag{8.1}$$

Note that our calculation does not require returns to be independent, only that the conditional one-step expected return is constant over time.

Example 8.2. Find the conditional variance of S_3 as seen at time $t = 1$ under the objective probability.

Solution. The conditional variance is naturally defined in the same way as the normal variance except one uses the conditional instead of the unconditional expectation, that is,

$$\text{Var}(S_3) \triangleq E_1^P[(S_3 - E_1[S_3])^2] = E_1^P[S_3^2] - (E_1^P[S_3])^2.$$

From the previous exercise we can deduce that $E_1^P[S_3] = 1.009^2 S_1$, so it remains to calculate $E_1^P[S_3^2]$. Using a similar procedure as in the previous exercise we obtain

$$E_1[S_3^2] = S_1^2 E_1\left[\frac{S_2^2}{S_1^2}E_2^P\left[\frac{S_3^2}{S_2^2}\right]\right].$$

Again

$$E_t^P\left[\frac{S_{t+1}^2}{S_t^2}\right]$$

is easy to evaluate

$$E_t^P\left[\frac{S_{t+1}^2}{S_t^2}\right] = \tfrac{1}{2}R_u^2 + \tfrac{1}{2}R_d^2 = 1.009^2 + 0.044^2$$

and therefore

$$E_1^P[S_3^2] = S_1^2(1.009^2 + 0.044^2)^2.$$

To conclude

$$\text{Var}(S_3) = S_1^2((1.009^2 + 0.044^2)^2 - 1.009^4) = 0.003\,95 S_1^2.$$

8.3 Summary

- How much information is needed to determine the security price depends on two factors, firstly how complex is the security's cash flow and secondly how complex is the conditional risk-neutral distribution of the variables determining the cash flow. Regarding the latter aspect, we say that the stock price process is Markov under a given probability measure if the future distribution of stock prices under that measure depends only on the last known price and not on the entire stock price history. Graphically, a *process is Markov* if the nodes with identical value also carry identical one-step conditional probabilities on the branches, that is, when the *nodes* with identical values *recombine*.

- If the stock price is a Markov process under objective probability P, it does not automatically follow that it must be a Markov process under the risk-neutral probability Q, and vice versa. When one talks about the Markov property it is important to specify what probability measure one has in mind. Q is the relevant measure for pricing.

- If the cash flow depends only on the stock price and the stock price is a Markov process under risk-neutral probability, then the stock price and time to expiry is all one needs to determine the no-arbitrage value of the cash flow. We say that the stock price and time act as state variables. In general, *state variables summarize all the necessary information* in a given problem. The use of state variables significantly reduces the amount of information required to express the solution, bearing in mind that information increases exponentially with time.

- In our simple market with one risky asset all available information is represented by the stock price history. The information available at a given time can be depicted using a *non-recombining* tree for stock prices. Mathematically, information filtration is a collection of growing σ-algebras $\{\mathcal{F}_t\}_{t=0,1,\dots,T}$, where $\mathcal{F}_t$ contains all the events that can be verified as true or false at time t.

- To rule out trading strategies that use privileged information about future prices (insider trading), we require that any instruction X_t for trading at time t

depends only on the publicly available information at time t. Mathematically, we require X_t to be a $\mathcal{F}_t$-measurable random variable. When this is the case for all t we say that the trading strategy $\{X_t\}_{t=0,1,\dots,T}$ is a process *adapted* to the stock price filtration. Graphically, process X is adapted if it can be written into the non-recombining stock price tree using one value per node.

- It is often desirable to manipulate conditional expectations without a physical model. Three useful model-independent rules are

    (1) the law of iterated expectations,

    $$E_t[E_s[X]] = E_s[E_t[X]] = E_t[X]$$

    for $t \leqslant s$ and any random variable X;

    (2) the law of conditional constant,

    $$E_t[XY] = XE_t[Y]$$

    if X is known at time t, that is if X is $\mathcal{F}_t$-measurable;

    (3) $E_t[X]$ is always known at time t.

8.4 Notes

The exposition in this chapter follows Pliska (1997). A more detailed and more advanced introduction to probability spaces can be found in Shreve (2004) and Williams (1991); see also references therein.

8.5 Appendix: Probability Space

This appendix is intended for those who are interested in the theoretical foundation of probability. Here the reader will find more detailed definitions of events, σ-algebras, stochastic processes, information filtration, adaptedness, etc. Do not worry if you find this appendix too difficult to grasp—the intuition developed in the main body of the chapter is sufficient for most practical purposes. At the same time this introduction barely scratches the surface of the mathematical complexities needed to develop the theory of stochastic processes in full. The first reference in this direction is Williams (1991).

To set the scene for random variables one needs three essential ingredients: the set of elementary outcomes Ω, the set of all events $\mathcal{F}$ and, if one wishes to talk about expectations, a probability measure, here denoted P. As an example take the non-recombining tree of stock price histories in Figure 8.6.

In this case the set of elementary outcomes is the set of all paths,

$$\Omega = \{\text{uuu, uud, udu, udd, duu, dud, ddu, ddd}\},$$

and the set of all events $\mathcal{F}$ is the set of all subsets of Ω (sometimes called the potential set of Ω and denoted by 2^{Ω}),

$$\mathcal{F} = 2^{\Omega}.$$

The probability P assigns a real number between 0 and 1 to each event in $\mathcal{F}$,

$$P : \mathcal{F} \rightarrow [0, 1].$$

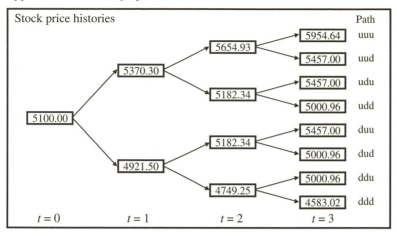

Figure 8.6. Stock price histories.

In addition P must satisfy these two natural conditions:

(1) $P(\Omega) = 1$ 'probability of the certain event is 1';

(2) if $A_1, A_2, \ldots$ is a sequence of mutually exclusive events in $\mathcal{F}$, then

$$P\left[\bigcup_{i=1}^{\infty} A_i\right] = \sum_{i=1}^{\infty} P(A_i) \tag{8.2}$$

'the probability of a countable union of mutually exclusive events is equal to the sum of probabilities of the individual events'.

In the example above there are no more than eight mutually exclusive events, namely {uuu}, {uud}, ..., {ddd}. In this case it suffices to specify the probability for each of these elementary events. The same construction will work with countably many mutually exclusive events.

8.5.1 Too Many Events: σ-Algebra to the Rescue

To motivate what comes next we need to digress a little. As soon as one considers a sample space Ω with uncountably many outcomes, one runs into difficulties with having *too many events*. Let us take Ω to be an interval $[-0.3, 0.3]$ representing elementary outcomes of the random variable 'annual rate of return'. In this case one cannot define the set of events $\mathcal{F}$ as the set of all subsets of Ω, simply because inside this collection there will always be events that cannot be assigned probability without creating contradiction. Namely, any interval Ω can be decomposed into a countable number of mutually exclusive and equally probable events A_i such that $\bigcup_{i=1}^{\infty} A_i = \Omega$. By (8.2) this would imply

$$1 = \sum_{i=1}^{\infty} P(A_i)$$

but since all $P(A_i)$ are the same, it can only be the case that the right-hand side is either 0 or $+\infty$ (for construction of A_i refer to Williams (1991)).

In this instance the right way to define the probability measure P is to determine the probability of events $(-\infty, x]$, making sure that the probability is growing with x. Using property (8.2) one can then compute the probabilities of finite unions and intersections and ultimately the probability of countable unions and intersections of intervals. The ultimate set of events for which probabilities can be computed in this way is called the *Borel σ-algebra* in $\mathbb{R}$ and it contains all the events that can be safely considered within probability theory. The concept of σ-algebra can be extended to very complicated sets of elementary outcomes Ω, which arise if one wants to consider continuous-time stochastic processes, but that is already beyond the scope of this introduction.

8.5.2 Information

Information filtration is a collection of growing σ-algebras indexed by time $\{\mathcal{F}_t\}_{t=0,1,...,T}$. The most important is the set of events attached to the terminal date $\mathcal{F}_T$. Being the largest one it sets the limits and defines our probability space as $\{\Omega, \mathcal{F} = \mathcal{F}_T, P\}$. In Figure 8.6 above the collection of all elementary events corresponds to the nodes at $t = 3$,

$$\mathcal{P}_3 = \{\{uuu\}, \{uud\}, \{udu\}, \{udd\}, \{duu\}, \{dud\}, \{ddu\}, \{ddd\}\}.$$

These 'elementary' events can be combined to generate the set of all events which are identifiable at time $t = 3$, the σ-algebra $\mathcal{F}_3$:

$$\mathcal{F}_3 = \{\{uuu\}, \{uud\}, \{udu\}, \{udd\}, \{duu\}, \{dud\}, \{ddu\}, \{ddd\},$$

$$\{uuu, uud\}, \ldots, \{ddu, ddd\}$$

(all combinations of two events in $\mathcal{P}_3$)

$$\{uuu, uud, udu\}, \ldots, \{dud, ddu, ddd\}$$

(all combinations of three events in $\mathcal{P}_3$)

$$\{uuu, uud, udu, udd\}, \ldots$$

(all combinations of four events in $\mathcal{P}_3$)

(all combinations of five events in $\mathcal{P}_3$)

(all combinations of six events in $\mathcal{P}_3$)

(all combinations of seven events in $\mathcal{P}_3$)

$$\{uuu, uud, udu, udd, duu, dud, ddu, ddd\} \text{ (certain event)} ,$$

$$\emptyset \text{ (impossible event)}\}.$$

The reader should bear in mind that in spite of all the mathematical notation the events in $\mathcal{F}_3$ have real meaning, for example, combination $\{duu, dud, ddu\}$ corresponds to the event 'stock price at $t = 1$ is lower than 5000 and stock price at $t = 3$ is greater than 5000'.

At time $t = 2$ one can distinguish four elementary events, corresponding to the four nodes at time $t = 2$ in Figure 8.6,

$$\mathcal{P}_2 = \{\{uuu, uud\}, \{udu, udd\}, \{duu, dud\}, \{ddu, ddd\}\}.$$

Combinations of these four nodes generate all events discernible at $t = 2$:

$$\mathcal{F}_2 = \{\{\text{uuu, uud}\}, \{\text{udu, udd}\}, \{\text{duu, dud}\}, \{\text{ddu, ddd}\},$$
$$\{\text{uuu, uud, udu, udd}\}, \ldots$$
(all combinations of two events in $\mathcal{P}_2$)
$$\{\text{uuu, uud, udu, udd, duu, dud}\}, \ldots$$
(all combinations of three events in $\mathcal{P}_2$)
$$\Omega \text{ (certain event)},$$
$$\emptyset \text{ (impossible event)}\}.$$

At time $t = 1$ one can distinguish two elementary events, corresponding to the two nodes at time $t = 2$ in Figure 8.6:

$$\mathcal{P}_1 = \{\{\text{uuu, uud, udu, udd}\}, \{\text{duu, dud, ddu, ddd}\}\}.$$

Combinations of these two nodes generate all events identifiable at $t = 1$:

$$\mathcal{F}_1 = \{\{\text{uuu, uud, udu, udd}\}, \{\text{duu, dud, ddu, ddd}\},$$
$$\Omega \text{ (certain event)},$$
$$\emptyset \text{ (impossible event) }\}.$$

Finally, at $t = 0$ we have a trivial algebra of events:

$$\mathcal{P}_0 = \{\Omega\},$$
$$\mathcal{F}_0 = \{\Omega \text{ (certain event)}, \emptyset \text{ (impossible event) }\}.$$

8.5.3 Random Variables

On a probability space $\{\Omega, \mathcal{F}_T, P\}$ a **random variable** is any function X assigning real numbers to elementary outcomes

$$X : \Omega \to \mathbb{R}$$

such that the values of X can be identified using events in $\mathcal{F}_T$, that is,

X is such that for all real numbers u the event $(X \leqslant u)$ belongs to $\mathcal{F}_t$.

In short X is a random variable on $\{\Omega, \mathcal{F}_T, P\}$ if it is $\mathcal{F}_T$-measurable, if it is known at time T. A collection of random variables $\{X_t\}_{t=0,1,\ldots,T}$ indexed by time is called a **stochastic process**. A stochastic process is **adapted to filtration** $\{\mathcal{F}_t\}_{t=0,1,\ldots,T}$ if in addition X_t is $\mathcal{F}_t$-measurable for $t = 0, 1, \ldots, T$.

8.5.4 Conditional Expectation

Let X be a random variable on a filtered probability space $\{\Omega, \{\mathcal{F}_t\}_{t=0,1,\ldots,T}, P\}$. The conditional expectation $E_t[X] = E[X \mid \mathcal{F}_t]$ is formally defined as the $\mathcal{F}_t$-measurable random variable Y minimizing the expectation,

$$E_0[(X - Y)^2].$$

With a countable number of elementary outcomes this boils down to evaluating expectations node by node.

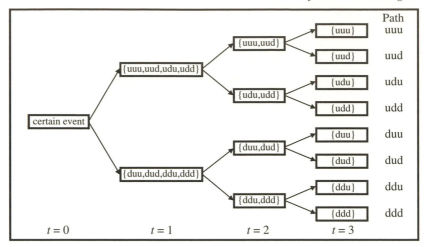

Figure 8.7. Information filtration.

8.6 Exercises

Exercise 8.1 (information filtration). Figure 8.7 represents the resolution of uncertainty over three discrete-time intervals. To describe the information filtration, we identify the smallest events that can be recognized at a given time point. In Figure 8.7 at $t = 3$ these events are {uuu}, {uud}, ..., {ddd}; at time $t = 2$ they are {uuu, uud}, {udu,udd}, {duu, dud}, {ddu, ddd} and so on. We write this down in the following form:

$$\mathcal{P}_3 = \{\{uuu\}, \{uud\}, \{udu\}, \{udd\}, \{duu\}, \{dud\}, \{ddu\}, \{ddd\}\},$$
$$\mathcal{P}_2 = \{\{uuu, uud\}, \{udu, udd\}, \{duu, dud\}, \{ddu, ddd\}\},$$
$$\mathcal{P}_1 = \{\{uuu, uud, udu, udd\}, \{duu, dud, ddu, ddd\}\},$$
$$\mathcal{P}_0 = \{\{uuu, uud, udu, udd, duu, dud, ddu, ddd\}\}.$$

Effectively, the set $\mathcal{P}_t$ describes the nodes at time t in Figure 8.7. The events in the set $\mathcal{P}_t$ generate an algebra of events $\mathcal{F}_t$. In the above case we have $\mathcal{F}_0 \subset \mathcal{F}_1 \subset \mathcal{F}_2 \subset \mathcal{F}_3$, that is, $\{\mathcal{F}_t\}_{t=0}^3$ is indeed an information filtration.

Consider now a recombining tree with the same paths (see Figure 8.8). For example, the meaning of the middle node at time $t = 2$ is 'stock price goes up then down, or first down and then up', which in terms of paths gives an event {udu, udd, duu, dud}.

(a) Describe the nodes of the recombining tree in Figure 8.8.

$$\mathcal{P}_3 =$$
$$\mathcal{P}_2 =$$
$$\mathcal{P}_1 =$$
$$\mathcal{P}_0 =$$

(b) Decide whether the sequence of algebras generated by $\mathcal{P}_0, \ldots, \mathcal{P}_3$ is a filtration.

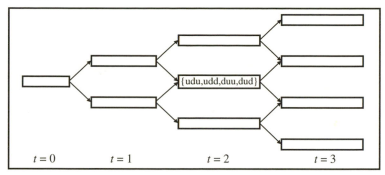

Figure 8.8. Nodes in the recombining tree.

Exercise 8.2. Figure 8.9 represents an information filtration with four distinct time paths uu, ud, du, dd. Tables 8.4 and 8.5 describe five stochastic processes V, W, X, Y, Z.

(a) Which of the processes V, W, X, Y, Z are adapted to the filtration F? Tick the corresponding box in Table 8.6.

(b) Amongst those that are adapted, classify the processes into the following categories by ticking the appropriate box in Table 8.7:

    (1) **deterministic** (U_0, U_1, U_2 all known at time 0, that is, they are all $\mathcal{F}_0$-measurable); these are further divided into

        (i) **constant** (i.e. deterministic and time independent, $U_0 = U_1 = U_2 = $ const.);

        (ii) **time-dependent** (U_0, U_1, U_2 not all equal, but all known at time 0);

    (2) **genuinely stochastic** (that is, NOT deterministic).

(c) When is the value of V_2 (W_2, X_2, Y_2, Z_2) known for the first time with certainty? (Mathematically, what is the smallest t such that V_2 is $\mathcal{F}_t$-measurable?) Tick the appropriate box in Table 8.8.

Exercise 8.3. Table 8.9 gives the unconditional probabilities and a value of the random variable X for each path in a three-step non-recombining binomial tree. Find the following conditional expectations and write them in Table 8.9: $E_2[X]$, $E_1[X]$, $E_2[E_1[X]]$, $E_1[E_2[X]]$, $E_0[X]$.

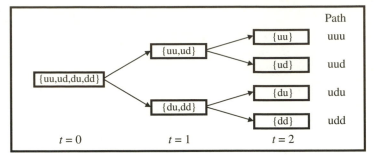

Figure 8.9.   Information filtration.

Table 8.4.   Processes V, W, X.

Path	V_0	V_1	V_2	W_0	W_1	W_2	X_0	X_1	X_2
uu	3	3	3	1	6	6	1	1	1
ud	2	2	2	1	6	6	1	1	1
du	−1	−1	−1	1	4	−3	1	1	1
dd	1	1	1	1	4	−3	1	1	1

Table 8.5.   Processes Y, Z.

Path	Y_0	Y_1	Y_2	Z_0	Z_1	Z_2
uu	1	6	1	1	6	−2
ud	1	6	2	1	6	−2
du	1	2	3	1	6	−2
dd	1	2	−88	1	6	−2

Table 8.6.

Process	V	W	X	Y	Z
Adapted					

Table 8.7. Classification of stochastic processes.

| Process | Deterministic | | Stochastic | Not adapted |
	Constant	Time dependent		
V				
W				
X				
Y				
Z				

Table 8.8. Timing of information disclosure.

| Random variable | First revealed at $t = $? | | |
	$t = 0$	$t = 1$	$t = 2$
V_2			
W_2			
X_2			
Y_2			
Z_2			

Table 8.9. Conditional expectations.

Outcome ω	$P(\{\omega\})$	X	$E_2[X]$	$E_1[X]$	$E_2[E_1[X]]$	$E_1[E_2[X]]$	$E_0[X]$
uuu	$\frac{1}{18}$	8					
uud	$\frac{1}{18}$	7					
udu	$\frac{1}{9}$	6					
udd	$\frac{1}{9}$	5					
duu	$\frac{1}{6}$	4					
dud	$\frac{1}{6}$	3					
ddu	$\frac{1}{6}$	2					
ddd	$\frac{1}{6}$	1					

9

Martingales and Change of Measure in Finance

This chapter has the thankless task of doing the groundwork for continuous-time finance, and some of the concepts studied here, particularly martingales, will not come into play until Chapter 11, when we rederive the Black–Scholes formula in continuous time. The change of measure has a more immediate use in dynamic portfolio selection discussed in Section 9.4. Applications of the law of iterated expectations and the law of conditional constant of Chapter 8 are a recurring theme in this chapter.

9.1 Discounted Asset Prices Are Martingales

9.1.1 Risk-Neutral Pricing Revisited

The plan of this section is to rederive the risk-neutral pricing formula of Section 5.5 allowing for a fully general information structure and stochastic interest rates. We saw in the previous chapter that a multi-period model is a collection of simple one-period models, namely there are as many one-period models as there are nodes in the information tree, excluding the last-period nodes. For example, with three periods and two possible stock returns in each period we have to consider $1+2+4=7$ one-period models (see Figure 9.1). In the presence of a Markov structure some of these submodels may be identical, which helps to reduce the number of computations, but in general each submodel will be different.

In the absence of arbitrage every one-period model has a (perhaps not unique) risk-neutral probability such that

$$R_{\mathrm{f}} = \mathrm{E}^Q[R_i] \quad \text{for all } i, \tag{9.1}$$

where R_i is the return of asset i.

For the purposes of this chapter it is sufficient to examine the individual risky assets in isolation; let us therefore consider one generic asset with return R_t and price S_t.

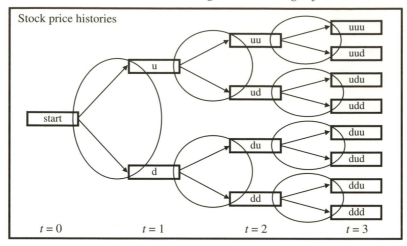

Figure 9.1. Every multi-period model is composed of several one-period models.

- For simplicity we will assume that assets bear no dividends; therefore the risky return between t and $t+1$ is simply

$$R_{t+1} = \frac{S_{t+1}}{S_t}.$$

- Within the multi-period set-up we can capture the one-period pricing equation (9.1) by using the conditional expectation,

$$R_{f\,t} = \mathrm{E}_t^Q\left[\frac{S_{t+1}}{S_t}\right], \qquad (9.2)$$

which in fact takes care of all one-period models in period t.

- The generic asset that we consider from now on can have different financial interpretations; it can be a stock, an option on the stock, a long-dated zero coupon bond, etc.

Recall from Chapter 8 the two important rules for manipulation of conditional expectations.

Law of conditional constant (LawCC):

$$\mathrm{E}_t[XY] = X\mathrm{E}_t[Y], \quad \text{if } X \text{ is known at time } t. \qquad (9.3)$$

Law of iterated expectations (LawIE):

$$\mathrm{E}_s[\mathrm{E}_t[X]] = \mathrm{E}_s[X] \quad \text{for } s \leqslant t. \qquad (9.4)$$

By virtue of LawCC we can rephrase (9.2) as

$$S_t = \mathrm{E}_t^Q\left[\frac{S_{t+1}}{R_{f\,t}}\right]. \qquad (9.5)$$

Starting from the final period (9.5) gives

$$S_{T-1} = E_{T-1}^Q \left[\frac{S_T}{R_{f\,T-1}} \right], \tag{9.6}$$

$$S_{T-2} = E_{T-2}^Q \left[\frac{S_{T-1}}{R_{f\,T-2}} \right], \tag{9.7}$$

$$\vdots$$

$$S_0 = E_0^Q \left[\frac{S_1}{R_{f\,0}} \right]. \tag{9.8}$$

Substituting (9.7) into (9.6) we have

$$S_{T-2} = E_{T-2}^Q \left[\frac{1}{R_{f\,T-2}} E_{T-1}^Q \left[\frac{S_T}{R_{f\,T-1}} \right] \right]$$

$$= E_{T-2}^Q \left[E_{T-1}^Q \left[\frac{S_T}{R_{f\,T-1} R_{f\,T-2}} \right] \right]$$

using the fact that $R_{f\,T-2}$ is known at time $T-2$ and therefore also at $T-1$, and therefore by virtue of LawCC (9.3) it can be moved inside the inner expectation. An application of LawIE (9.4) yields

$$S_{T-2} = E_{T-2}^Q \left[\frac{S_T}{R_{f\,T-1} R_{f\,T-2}} \right].$$

Performing the backward substitution procedure several times, we arrive at

$$S_t = E_t^Q \left[\frac{S_T}{R_{f\,T-1} \cdots R_{f\,t}} \right] \quad \text{for } t = 0, 1, \ldots, T-1. \tag{9.9}$$

Denote by β_t the **compounded return** on bank account deposits from time 0 to time t,

$$\beta_t = R_{f\,0} \cdots R_{f\,t-1},$$

$$\beta_0 = 1,$$

then the risk-neutral valuation formula (9.9) can be written more compactly as

$$\frac{S_t}{\beta_t} = E_t^Q \left[\frac{S_T}{\beta_T} \right].$$

9.1.2 Discounted Asset Price Is a Martingale under Q

The stochastic process $\{X_t\}_{t=0,\ldots,T}$ is a **martingale under measure** P if for all $s \leqslant t \leqslant T$

$$X_s = E_s^P[X_t] \tag{9.10}$$

and $E_0^P[|X_t|]$ is finite for all t.

We have just shown that

$$\frac{S_t}{\beta_t} = \mathrm{E}_t^Q\!\left[\frac{S_T}{\beta_T}\right] \tag{9.11}$$

for all t. But this already implies that the process $\{S_t/\beta_t\}_{t=0,\dots,T}$ is a martingale under Q! Namely, it follows from (9.11) and LawIE that

$$\mathrm{E}_s^Q\!\left[\frac{S_t}{\beta_t}\right] = \mathrm{E}_s^Q\!\left[\mathrm{E}_t^Q\!\left[\frac{S_T}{\beta_T}\right]\right] = \mathrm{E}_s^Q\!\left[\frac{S_T}{\beta_T}\right] = \frac{S_s}{\beta_s}$$

for all $s \leqslant t$.

> For all traded assets *without intermediate dividends the discounted price process is a martingale under the risk-neutral measure.*

At the moment one can think of this result as a mathematical curiosity; it will become important later in continuous-time models.

9.1.3 Two Martingale Propositions

In the last two sections we have unwittingly discovered and proved two important principles that will be exploited time and time again.

Proposition 9.1 (first martingale proposition). *Let* $\{X_t\}_{t=0,1,\dots,T}$ *be a stochastic process with the property,*

$$X_t = \mathrm{E}_t^P[X_{t+1}] \quad \text{for } t = 0, 1, \dots, T-1. \tag{9.12}$$

Then the process $\{X_t\}_{t=0,1,\dots,T}$ *is a martingale under measure* P.

Proof. Use (9.12) iteratively and at the end apply the law of iterated expectations:

$$X_s = \mathrm{E}_s^P[X_{s+1}] = \mathrm{E}_s^P[\mathrm{E}_{s+1}^P[X_{s+2}]] = \cdots$$
$$= \mathrm{E}_s^P[\mathrm{E}_{s+1}^P[\cdots \mathrm{E}_{t-1}^P[X_t]]] = \mathrm{E}_s^P[X_t].$$

$\square$

Proposition 9.2 (second martingale proposition). *Let* Y *be a fixed random variable which is known at time* T. *Define a stochastic process* $\{X_t\}_{t=0,1,\dots,T}$ *by setting*

$$X_t = \mathrm{E}_t^P[Y].$$

Then the process $\{X_t\}_{t=0,1,\dots,T}$ *is a martingale under measure* P, *and* $X_T = Y$.

Proof. By the law of iterated expectations,

$$\mathrm{E}_s^P[X_t] = \mathrm{E}_s^P[\mathrm{E}_t^P[Y]] = \mathrm{E}_s^P[Y] = X_s.$$

$\square$

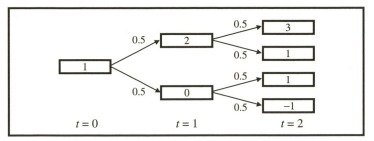

Figure 9.2. Example of a martingale. The process depicted in this figure is a martingale under the probability measure generated by the conditional probabilities on the branches.

9.1.4 What Is a Martingale?

The martingale definition (9.10) does not provide much help and certainly it does not tell us how a martingale is constructed. The best information one can get comes from the first martingale proposition. We can rewrite (9.12) as

$$0 = E_t^P[X_{t+1} - X_t],$$

which means that the *martingale is created by adding shocks with zero conditional mean*:

$$X_t = X_0 + \underbrace{(X_1 - X_0)}_{\text{1st shock}} + \underbrace{(X_2 - X_1)}_{\text{2nd shock}} + \cdots + \underbrace{(X_t - X_{t-1})}_{t\text{th shock}}. \tag{9.13}$$

As an example suppose that the shock values are ± 1 with conditional probability $\frac{1}{2}$ and that $X_0 = 1$. The process X generated by (9.13) is depicted in Figure 9.2.

9.1.5 Wealth of a Self-Financing Trading Strategy Is a Martingale under Q

Now consider a self-financing strategy with cash value V_t and risky investment (number of shares) θ_t,

$$V_{t+1} = R_{ft} V_t + \theta_t S_t \underbrace{\left(\frac{S_{t+1}}{S_t} - R_{ft}\right)}_{\text{excess return}}, \tag{9.14}$$

and apply $E_t^Q[.]$ on both sides using LawCC,

$$E_t^Q[V_{t+1}] = R_{ft} V_t + \theta_t S_t \underbrace{E_t^Q\left[\frac{S_{t+1}}{S_t} - R_{ft}\right]}_{0}. \tag{9.15}$$

From the definition of Q we have $E_t^Q[S_{t+1}/S_t - R_{ft}] = 0$ and after dividing both sides of (9.15) by R_{ft} we obtain

$$V_t = E_t^Q\left[\frac{V_{t+1}}{R_{ft}}\right]. \tag{9.16}$$

Now divide both sides of (9.16) by β_t using LawCC on the right-hand side to obtain

$$\frac{V_t}{\beta_t} = E_t^Q\left[\frac{V_{t+1}}{\beta_{t+1}}\right]. \tag{9.17}$$

Since (9.17) holds for all t, by virtue of the first martingale proposition *the discounted wealth of any self-financing strategy is a martingale under Q*; in particular, we have

$$\frac{V_t}{\beta_t} = E_t^Q\left[\frac{V_T}{\beta_T}\right] \quad \text{for all } t. \tag{9.18}$$

Intuitively, the value of a self-financing strategy is very much like the value of an asset without dividends because one is not allowed to add or withdraw any cash in the intermediate periods. That is why equation (9.18) is identical in form to equation (9.11). Property (9.18) will be instrumental in proving the dynamic arbitrage theorem.

9.2 Dynamic Arbitrage Theorem

Definition 9.3. We say that there is **type I dynamic arbitrage** if one can find a self-financing strategy with initial value $V_0 \leqslant 0$ and terminal value $V_T \geqslant 0$, such that $V_T > 0$ with positive probability. **Type II dynamic arbitrage** is a self-financing trading strategy with $V_0 < 0$ and $V_T = 0$.

Theorem 9.4. *Assume that securities pay no dividends and that $R_{ft} > 0$ in all states for all t. In a model with a finite number of states there is no dynamic arbitrage if and only if there is a strictly positive probability measure Q such that the discounted price process of all securities is a martingale under Q. Equivalently, a multi-period model is arbitrage-free if and only if each constituent one-period model is arbitrage-free.*

Proof. First the easy part. If there is no dynamic arbitrage, then there cannot be a one-period arbitrage in the model, because such one-period opportunity could be exploited dynamically by waiting until the one-period arbitrage comes up (this will happen with positive probability) and then executing the one-period arbitrage trade and investing the proceeds in the risk-free account. This is equivalent to saying that without dynamic arbitrage all the one-step conditional probabilities must be strictly positive. But if all-conditional risk-neutral probabilities are strictly positive, then the unconditional measure Q, being a product of conditional probabilities, is strictly positive and by the construction described in Sections 9.1.1 and 9.1.2, discounted stock prices are martingales under Q.

The proof in the opposite direction is harder. Suppose we are given a strictly positive measure Q under which $\{S_t/\beta_t\}_{t=0,\dots,T}$ is a martingale. Suppose there is type I dynamic arbitrage, a self-financing strategy with $V_0 \leqslant 0$ and $V_T > 0$, then we also have $V_T/\beta_T > 0$ with positive probability. Since Q is strictly positive we must have $E_0^Q[V_T/\beta_T] > 0 \geqslant V_0$. However, the last inequality contradicts the martingale condition (9.18). Suppose there is type II arbitrage, then $E_0^Q[V_T/\beta_T] = 0 > V_0$, which again contradicts the martingale condition (9.18). Equivalently, the absence of one-period arbitrage opportunities implies the existence of strictly positive conditional risk-neutral probabilities under which $R_{ft} = E_t^Q[S_{t+1}/S_t]$ for all t. However, this already implies that Q is strictly positive and that $\{S_t/\beta_t\}_{t=0,\dots,T}$ is a Q-martingale; and we have just shown that these two facts guarantee no dynamic arbitrage. $\square$

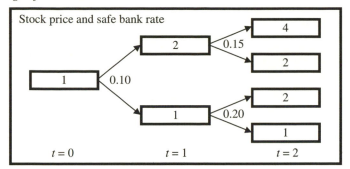

Figure 9.3. Two-period model for stock prices and risk-free investment. Stock prices are at the nodes, the risk-free rate is between the branches.

The measure Q is called the **equivalent martingale measure**. In the present context 'equivalent' means that Q assigns positive probability to all states with positive P probability and vice versa. There are situations of practical importance when a particular measure Q may not be equivalent to P (see Section 12.2.4).

9.3 Change of Measure

In finance one works with two sets of probability measures, objective P and risk-neutral Q. The objective probabilities determine how likely a particular state of the market is *ex ante*, whereas the risk-neutral probabilities, being related to state prices, tell us how expensive it is to buy wealth *ex ante* for that particular state. The ratio of the two probability measures

$$\frac{\text{risk-neutral probability}}{\text{objective probability}}$$

is called the **change of measure**.

If the change of measure is high in a particular scenario, then either the wealth in this scenario is very expensive or this scenario is highly unlikely to occur; in both cases it means one will not want to buy too much wealth for that scenario. Since one is buying the wealth *ex ante*, before the state of the market is revealed, the wealth acts as an insurance against poverty in that state. We can therefore think of states with a *high change of measure* as **uninsurable**. Conversely, states with a low change of measure are relatively cheap to insure against. This trade-off is discussed in Section 9.4 on dynamic optimal portfolio selection in complete markets.

9.3.1 One-Step Conditional Change of Measure

To visualize the definition of the change of measure let us consider a two-period model with IID stock returns,

$$R_u = 2 \text{ with probability } 0.5,$$
$$R_d = 1 \text{ with probability } 0.5.$$

The risk-free rate is initially $r_0 = 10\%$, if the stock price goes up it increases to $r_1(u) = 15\%$ and if the stock price goes down it increases to $r_1(d) = 20\%$. The stock price and the risk-free rate are captured in Figure 9.3.

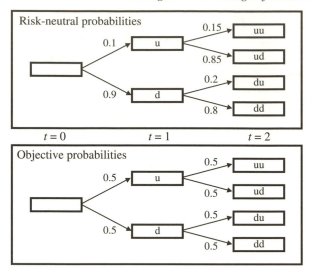

Figure 9.4. Conditional objective and risk-neutral
probabilities of movement in the information tree.

Recall that in this simple model the risk-neutral probabilities are given by

$$q_u = \frac{R_f - R_d}{R_u - R_d} = R_f - 1 = r,$$

and note that r is changing from node to node. The conditional risk-neutral and
objective probabilities are depicted in Figure 9.4

Let us denote the conditional one-step risk-neutral density at time t by

$$q_{t+1|t}$$

and the conditional one-step objective density at time t by

$$p_{t+1|t}.$$

Then we define the **one-step conditional change of measure** as the ratio of risk-
neutral and objective probabilities,

$$m_{t+1|t} \triangleq \frac{q_{t+1|t}}{p_{t+1|t}}.$$

Example 9.5. In the two-period tree of Figure 9.4:

$$q_{2|1}(uu) = 0.15, \qquad p_{2|1}(uu) = 0.5,$$
$$q_{2|1}(ud) = 0.85, \qquad p_{2|1}(ud) = 0.5,$$
$$q_{2|1}(du) = 0.2, \qquad p_{2|1}(du) = 0.5,$$
$$q_{2|1}(dd) = 0.8, \qquad p_{2|1}(dd) = 0.5,$$

$$m_{2|1}(uu) = \frac{0.15}{0.5} = 0.3, \tag{9.19}$$

$$m_{2|1}(ud) = \frac{0.85}{0.5} = 1.7, \tag{9.20}$$

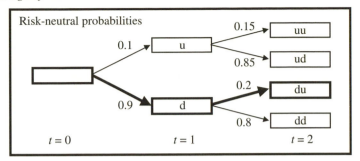

Risk-neutral probabilities

Figure 9.5. Illustration of the multiplication rule for conditional probabilities.

$$m_{2|1}(\mathrm{du}) = \frac{0.2}{0.5} = 0.4, \tag{9.21}$$

$$m_{2|1}(\mathrm{dd}) = \frac{0.8}{0.5} = 1.6, \tag{9.22}$$

$$q_{1|0}(\mathrm{u}) = 0.1, \qquad p_{1|0}(\mathrm{u}) = 0.5,$$

$$q_{1|0}(\mathrm{d}) = 0.9, \qquad p_{1|0}(\mathrm{d}) = 0.5,$$

$$m_{1|0}(\mathrm{u}) = \frac{0.1}{0.5} = 0.2, \tag{9.23}$$

$$m_{1|0}(\mathrm{d}) = \frac{0.9}{0.5} = 1.8. \tag{9.24}$$

- For any random variable X known at $t+1$ we have identically

$$\mathrm{E}_t^Q[X] = \mathrm{E}_t^P\left[\frac{q_{t+1|t}}{p_{t+1|t}} X\right] = \mathrm{E}_t^P[m_{t+1|t} X]. \tag{9.25}$$

- In particular,

$$\mathrm{E}_t^P[m_{t+1|t}] = 1 \quad \text{for all } t \tag{9.26}$$

by applying (9.25) with $X = 1$ and realizing that $\mathrm{E}_t^Q[1] = 1$.

9.3.2 *Unconditional Change of Measure*

Multiplication rule for conditional probabilities. The *ex ante* probability of following a particular path in the decision tree equals the product of conditional probabilities on the branches belonging to that path. This is a simple consequence of the definition of conditional probability discussed in Appendix B.

Example 9.6. The risk-neutral probability at $t = 0$ of following the path down–up is $0.9 \times 0.2 = 0.18$ (see Figure 9.5).

As a consequence of the multiplication rule for conditional probabilities the unconditional densities $p_{T|0}, q_{T|0}$ (that is, densities that define the probability measures

P and Q) satisfy

$$p_{T|0} = p_{1|0} \cdots p_{T-1|T-2} p_{T|T-1},$$

$$q_{T|0} = q_{1|0} \cdots q_{T-1|T-2} q_{T|T-1}.$$

The **unconditional change of measure** is naturally defined as $q_{T|0}/p_{T|0}$:

$$m_T = \frac{q_{T|0}}{p_{T|0}} = \frac{q_{T|T-1} q_{T-1|T-2} \cdots q_{1|0}}{p_{T|T-1} p_{T-1|T-2} \cdots p_{1|0}} = m_{T|T-1} m_{T-1|T-2} \cdots m_{1|0}. \quad (9.27)$$

Symbolically, we write

$$m_T = \frac{\mathrm{d}Q}{\mathrm{d}P};$$

mathematicians call $\mathrm{d}Q/\mathrm{d}P$ the **Radon–Nikodým derivative** of the measure Q with respect to the measure P. In a discrete model with a finite number of states, the change of measure $\mathrm{d}Q/\mathrm{d}P$ is always well defined because we only consider states with positive P probability, which means that the denominator in (9.27) is always different from 0.

Example 9.7. We will find the unconditional change of measure for the information tree in Figure 9.4. First, we first need to evaluate the unconditional path probabilities from the multiplication rule

$$p_{2|0}(uu) = p_{1|0}(u) p_{2|1}(uu) = 0.5 \times 0.5 = 0.25,$$

$$p_{2|0}(ud) = p_{1|0}(u) p_{2|1}(ud) = 0.5 \times 0.5 = 0.25,$$

$$p_{2|0}(du) = p_{1|0}(d) p_{2|1}(du) = 0.5 \times 0.5 = 0.25,$$

$$p_{2|0}(dd) = p_{1|0}(d) p_{2|1}(dd) = 0.5 \times 0.5 = 0.25,$$

$$q_{2|0}(uu) = q_{1|0}(u) q_{2|1}(uu) = 0.1 \times 0.15 = 0.015,$$

$$q_{2|0}(ud) = q_{1|0}(u) q_{2|1}(ud) = 0.1 \times 0.85 = 0.085,$$

$$q_{2|0}(du) = q_{1|0}(d) q_{2|1}(du) = 0.9 \times 0.2 = 0.18,$$

$$q_{2|0}(dd) = q_{1|0}(d) q_{2|1}(dd) = 0.9 \times 0.8 = 0.72,$$

which then yields

$$m_2(uu) = \frac{q_{2|0}(uu)}{p_{2|0}(uu)} = \frac{0.015}{0.25} = 0.06,$$

$$m_2(ud) = \frac{q_{2|0}(ud)}{p_{2|0}(ud)} = \frac{0.085}{0.25} = 0.34,$$

$$m_2(du) = \frac{q_{2|0}(du)}{p_{2|0}(du)} = \frac{0.18}{0.25} = 0.72,$$

$$m_2(dd) = \frac{q_{2|0}(dd)}{p_{2|0}(dd)} = \frac{0.72}{0.25} = 2.88.$$

Alternatively, we can perform the calculation using the precomputed one-period changes of measure in (9.19)–(9.24):

$$m_2(uu) = m_{1|0}(u) m_{2|1}(uu) = 0.2 \times 0.3 = 0.06,$$

$$m_2(ud) = m_{1|0}(u) m_{2|1}(ud) = 0.2 \times 1.7 = 0.34,$$

$$m_2(\text{du}) = m_{1|0}(\text{d})m_{2|1}(\text{du}) = 1.8 \times 0.4 = 0.72,$$
$$m_2(\text{dd}) = m_{1|0}(\text{d})m_{2|1}(\text{dd}) = 1.8 \times 1.6 = 2.88.$$

9.3.3 Density Process of the Change of Measure and Conditional Expectations

Often we are interested in paths running between two intermediate times $s < t$, and not the entire length from 0 to T. For this purpose we will define the so-called **density process** of the change of measure to give us the change of measure from time 0 to time t:

$$m_t \triangleq m_{1|0} \cdots m_{t|t-1}. \tag{9.28}$$

Now if we wish to evaluate the change of measure between times $s < t$, we can take m_t and deselect the probabilities belonging to time interval $[0, s]$ by dividing through m_s,

$$m_{t|s} = m_{s+1|s} \cdots m_{t|t-1} = \frac{m_t}{m_s}. \tag{9.29}$$

The first equality always works, but the second equality in (9.29) only makes sense if $m_s \neq 0$. The case $m_s = 0$ can only occur on paths on which at least one branch has zero conditional Q probability, which then means that measure Q is *not* equivalent to P. It is in this context that equivalence of measures becomes important.

At this point we can generalize the change-of-measure formulae (9.25) and (9.26) to any time interval and obtain two important results that will play a crucial role in the continuous-time models of Chapter 11.

- For $s < t$ and any random variable Y known at time t we have identically

$$E_s^Q[Y] = E_s^P\left[\frac{q_{t|s}}{p_{t|s}}X\right] = E_s^P[m_{t|s}Y]. \tag{9.30}$$

- In particular, (9.30) with $X = 1$ yields

$$E_s^P[m_{t|s}] = 1 \quad \text{for all } s < t. \tag{9.31}$$

Proposition 9.8 (third martingale proposition). *Let $\{X_t\}_{t=0,1,\dots,T}$ be a process adapted to the given information filtration and suppose m_t defined in (9.28) is strictly positive for all t. Then $\{X_t\}_{t=0,1,\dots,T}$ is a martingale under measure Q if and only if $\{m_t X_t\}_{t=0,1,\dots,T}$ is a martingale under measure P.*

Proof. Since the process X is adapted the random variable X_t must be known at time t. Substitute (9.29) into (9.30) with $Y = X_t$ to obtain $E_s^Q[X_t] = E_s^P[m_t X_t / m_s]$. By construction m_s is known at time s; we can therefore take m_s in front of the conditional expectation. Multiplying both sides by m_s we finally obtain

$$m_s E_s^Q[X_t] = E_s^P[m_t X_t] \quad \text{for all } s < t. \tag{9.32}$$

If X is a martingale under Q, then $E_s^Q[X_t] = X_s$ and formula (9.32) implies $m_s X_s = E_s^P[m_t X_t]$ for all $s < t$, which means mX is a martingale under P. Conversely, if mX is a martingale under P, then $E_s^P[m_t X_t] = m_s X_s$ and formula (9.32) implies

$m_s E_s^Q[X_t] = m_s X_s$ and since $m_s > 0$ we have $E_s^Q[X_t] = X_s$ for all $s < t$, meaning X is a martingale under Q.   □

Proposition 9.9 (fourth martingale proposition). *Suppose that m_t defined in (9.28) is strictly positive for all t. Then the density process $\{m_t\}_{t=0,1,\dots,T}$ is a martingale under measure P.*

Proof. Let us take $X_t = 1$ for all t. Then X_t is a martingale under any probability measure, and specifically under Q. By virtue of the third martingale proposition, m_t must be a martingale under P.   □

9.4 Dynamic Optimal Portfolio Selection in a Complete Market

This section shows that the change of measure plays an important role in optimal portfolio allocation problems.

9.4.1 Problem Formulation

An investor with initial wealth $V_0 = £10$ wishes to invest her wealth for two periods without adding or withdrawing money along the way. The investor's trade-off between the risk and return is captured by a CRRA utility with the coefficient of relative risk aversion $\gamma = 5$. Suppose that the only assets available are stock and a risk-free bank account depicted in Figure 9.3.

Let us visualize the evolution of an investor's wealth. If the investor buys θ_0 stocks at $t = 0$, then from the self-financing condition (9.14) her wealth at $t = 1$ will be either

$$V_1(u) = 10 \times 1.1 + \theta_0 S_0(2 - 1.1) \tag{9.33}$$

or

$$V_1(d) = 10 \times 1.1 + \theta_0 S_0(1 - 1.1). \tag{9.34}$$

If the investor receives a high return in the first period, then in the second period she will have either

$$V_2(uu) = V_1(u) \times 1.15 + \theta_1(u) S_1(u)(2 - 1.15) \tag{9.35}$$

or

$$V_2(ud) = V_1(u) \times 1.15 + \theta_1(u) S_1(u)(1 - 1.15), \tag{9.36}$$

but if the first period return is low, then the second period wealth will be either

$$V_2(du) = V_1(d) \times 1.2 + \theta_1(d) S_1(d)(2 - 1.2) \tag{9.37}$$

or

$$V_2(dd) = V_1(u) \times 1.2 + \theta_1(d) S_1(d)(1 - 1.2). \tag{9.38}$$

After substitution of (9.33) and (9.34) into (9.35)–(9.38) we obtain the terminal wealth as a function of the trading strategy θ_0, θ_1:

$$V_2(uu) = 12.65 + 1.035\theta_0 + 1.7\theta_1(u),$$

$$V_2(\text{ud}) = 12.65 + 1.035\theta_0 - 0.3\theta_1(\text{u}),$$
$$V_2(\text{du}) = 13.2 - 0.12\theta_0 + 0.8\theta_1(\text{d}),$$
$$V_2(\text{dd}) = 13.2 - 0.125\theta_0 - 0.2\theta_1(\text{d}).$$

The investor's task is to find numbers $\theta_0, \theta_1(\text{u})$ and $\theta_1(\text{d})$ which maximize the expected utility of the terminal wealth:

$$\mathrm{E}_0^P\left[\frac{V_2^{1-\gamma}}{1-\gamma}\right].$$

Mathematically, we write this problem down as follows:

$$\max_{\theta_0,\theta_1} \mathrm{E}_0^P\left[\frac{V_2^{1-\gamma}}{1-\gamma}\right]; \tag{9.39}$$

it is understood in (9.39) that θ_t is chosen separately for each stock price history at time t, that is, in our particular model θ_1 represents two numbers, $\theta_1(\text{u})$ and $\theta_1(\text{d})$.

9.4.2 Change of Control Variables and Budget Constraint

In practice, (9.39) is the most useful formulation and one can work out the optimal values of θ_1, θ_0 recursively by a procedure known as *dynamic programming*. But since the principle of dynamic programming takes a while to explain, we will defer its discussion to Section 12.4.3. Here we will instead concentrate on the much simpler **martingale duality method**, which sidesteps the need to compute θ_0, θ_1 by finding directly the optimal values of $V_2(\text{uu}), V_2(\text{ud}), V_2(\text{du})$ and $V_2(\text{dd})$.

Instead of looking for the number of shares θ_t in each period, it makes things much simpler to realize that in a complete market any distribution of wealth can be generated if one has enough cash at $t = 0$. How much cash is needed to finance a given distribution of wealth? We know that each cash flow has a unique no-arbitrage price, the no-arbitrage price of V_T is simply $\mathrm{E}_0^Q[V_T/\beta_T]$. We can choose V_T freely in each state but the distribution of wealth must satisfy the **budget constraint**,

$$\underbrace{V_0}_{\text{initial wealth}} = \underbrace{\mathrm{E}_0^Q\left[\frac{V_T}{\beta_T}\right]}_{\substack{\text{no-arbitrage value} \\ \text{of terminal wealth}}}. \tag{9.40}$$

In our model, (9.40) translates into

$$10 = \frac{0.1 \times 0.15 \times V_2(\text{uu}) + 0.1 \times 0.85 \times V_2(\text{ud})}{1.1 \times 1.5}$$
$$+ \frac{0.9 \times 0.2 \times V_2(\text{du}) + 0.9 \times 0.8 \times V_2(\text{dd})}{1.1 \times 1.2}.$$

Thus the optimal utility problem (9.39) can be rephrased equivalently as

$$\max_{V_2} \mathrm{E}_0^P\left[\frac{V_2^{1-\gamma}}{1-\gamma}\right] \tag{9.41}$$

subject to

$$V_0 = E_0^Q\left[\frac{V_2}{R_{f1}R_{f2}}\right]. \tag{9.42}$$

All this crucially relies on the fact that the market is dynamically complete and therefore every cash flow that only depends on stock price history (in our case the cash flow is V_2) can be perfectly replicated using a dynamic self-financing strategy.

9.4.3 Constrained Maximization and Lagrange Multiplier

In this paragraph we will solve the utility maximization (9.41) and (9.42). Let us write (9.41) and (9.42) down explicitly:

$$\max_{V_2(\mathrm{uu}),V_2(\mathrm{ud}),V_2(\mathrm{du}),V_2(\mathrm{dd})} \underbrace{\frac{1}{4}\left(\frac{V_2^{1-\gamma}(\mathrm{uu})}{1-\gamma}+\frac{V_2^{1-\gamma}(\mathrm{ud})}{1-\gamma}+\frac{V_2^{1-\gamma}(\mathrm{du})}{1-\gamma}+\frac{V_2^{1-\gamma}(\mathrm{dd})}{1-\gamma}\right)}_{\text{objective function}}$$

$$\tag{9.43}$$

subject to

$$\underbrace{\frac{0.015V_2(\mathrm{uu})+0.085V_2(\mathrm{ud})}{1.1\times1.2}+\frac{0.18V_2(\mathrm{du})+0.72V_2(\mathrm{dd})}{1.1\times1.15}-10=0}_{\text{constraint}}. \tag{9.44}$$

We will take for granted that the constrained maximization (9.43) and (9.44) is solved by forming the so-called **Lagrangian** function,

$$\text{Lagrangian} = \text{objective function} - \text{Lagrange multiplier} \times \text{constraint},$$

in our case

$$L = \frac{1}{4}\left(\frac{V_2^{1-\gamma}(\mathrm{uu})}{1-\gamma}+\frac{V_2^{1-\gamma}(\mathrm{ud})}{1-\gamma}+\frac{V_2^{1-\gamma}(\mathrm{du})}{1-\gamma}+\frac{V_2^{1-\gamma}(\mathrm{dd})}{1-\gamma}\right)$$
$$-\lambda\left(\frac{0.02V_2(\mathrm{uu})+0.08V_2(\mathrm{ud})}{1.1\times1.2}+\frac{0.135V_2(\mathrm{du})+0.765V_2(\mathrm{dd})}{1.1\times1.15}-10\right),$$

and solving the unconstrained optimization

$$\max_{V_2(\mathrm{uu}),V_2(\mathrm{ud}),V_2(\mathrm{du}),V_2(\mathrm{dd})} L. \tag{9.45}$$

The value of the **Lagrange multiplier** λ must be such that the budget constraint (9.44) holds. Why the Lagrangian works for constrained optimization is explained in Appendix A.

The first-order conditions of the maximization in (9.45) read

$$0 = \frac{\partial L}{\partial V_2(\mathrm{uu})} = 0.25V_2^{-\gamma}(\mathrm{uu}) - \lambda\frac{0.015}{1.1\times1.15},$$

$$0 = \frac{\partial L}{\partial V_2(\mathrm{ud})} = 0.25V_2^{-\gamma}(\mathrm{ud}) - \lambda\frac{0.085}{1.1\times1.15},$$

$$0 = \frac{\partial L}{\partial V_2(ud)} = 0.25V_2^{-\gamma}(du) - \lambda \frac{0.18}{1.1 \times 1.2},$$

$$0 = \frac{\partial L}{\partial V_2(ud)} = 0.25V_2^{-\gamma}(dd) - \lambda \frac{0.72}{1.1 \times 1.2}.$$

Solving for $V_2^{-\gamma}$ we find

$$V_2^{-\gamma}(uu) = \lambda \frac{0.06}{1.1 \times 1.15}, \tag{9.46}$$

$$V_2^{-\gamma}(ud) = \lambda \frac{0.34}{1.1 \times 1.15}, \tag{9.47}$$

$$V_2^{-\gamma}(du) = \lambda \frac{0.72}{1.1 \times 1.2}, \tag{9.48}$$

$$V_2^{-\gamma}(dd) = \lambda \frac{2.88}{1.1 \times 1.2}. \tag{9.49}$$

- On the left-hand side of (9.46)–(9.49) we have the **marginal utility**, whereas on the right-hand side we have the **unconditional change of measure** discounted at the risk-free rate and multiplied by λ.
- This result is not specific to our model, but it is valid generally in the sense that the optimal value of V_T in

$$\max_{V_T} E_0^P[U(V_T)] \quad \text{s.t.} \ V_0 = E_0^Q\left[\frac{V_T}{\beta_T}\right]$$

satisfies

$$U'(V_T) = \lambda \frac{m_T}{\beta_T},$$

where m_T is the ratio of the unconditional risk-neutral probability to the unconditional objective probability on each path in the information tree.
- The ratio m_T/β_T is called the **stochastic discount factor**, the **pricing kernel** or the **state-price density**.

The next step is to solve (9.46)–(9.49) for V_2 with $\gamma = 5$:

$$V_2(uu) = \lambda^{-1/5}\left(\frac{0.06}{1.1 \times 1.15}\right)^{-1/5} = 1.8399\lambda^{-1/5}, \tag{9.50}$$

$$V_2(ud) = \lambda^{-1/5}\left(\frac{0.34}{1.1 \times 1.15}\right)^{-1/5} = 1.3005\lambda^{-1/5}, \tag{9.51}$$

$$V_2(du) = \lambda^{-1/5}\left(\frac{0.72}{1.1 \times 1.2}\right)^{-1/5} = 1.1289\lambda^{-1/5}, \tag{9.52}$$

$$V_2(dd) = \lambda^{-1/5}\left(\frac{2.88}{1.1 \times 1.2}\right)^{-1/5} = 0.8555\lambda^{-1/5}. \tag{9.53}$$

We can see that the investor wishes to hold most wealth in the state with the lowest change of measure; this makes sense since $m/\beta = (q/p)/\beta$ will be small in the states which are likely to occur (p relatively large) and where wealth is cheap to buy (the state price q/β relatively small).

In the final step we will recover the appropriate value of $\lambda^{-1/5}$ by plugging (9.50)–(9.53) into the budget constraint (9.44),

$$10 = \lambda^{-1/5}\left(\frac{0.015 \times 1.8399 + 0.085 \times 1.3005}{1.1 \times 1.15}\right.$$
$$\left. + \frac{0.18 \times 1.1289 + 0.72 \times 0.8555}{1.1 \times 1.2}\right),$$

which yields

$$\lambda^{-1/5} = 13.7028. \tag{9.54}$$

Now substitute $\lambda^{-1/5}$ into (9.50)–(9.53) and obtain values of the optimal terminal wealth:

$$V_2(\text{uu}) = 25.21, \tag{9.55}$$
$$V_2(\text{ud}) = 17.82, \tag{9.56}$$
$$V_2(\text{du}) = 15.47, \tag{9.57}$$
$$V_2(\text{dd}) = 11.72. \tag{9.58}$$

9.4.4   Optimal Trading Strategy and State Variables

Once we know the optimal terminal wealth it is very easy to work out the trading strategy that generates it using formulae (5.9)–(5.11). For example, in the high node at time $t = 1$ we have

$$\theta_1(u) = \frac{V_2(\text{uu}) - V_2(\text{ud})}{S_2(\text{uu}) - S_2(\text{ud})} = \frac{25.21 - 17.82}{4 - 2} = 3.695, \tag{9.59}$$

$$V_1(u) = \frac{q_{2|1}(\text{uu})V_2(\text{uu}) + q_{2|1}(\text{ud})V_2(\text{ud})}{R_{f\,1}(u)}$$

$$= \frac{0.15 \times 25.21 + 0.85 \times 17.82}{1.15} = 16.46, \tag{9.60}$$

$$\text{bank}_1(u) = V_1(u) - \theta_1(u)S_1(u) = 16.46 - 2 \times 3.695 = 9.07. \tag{9.61}$$

The entire optimal investment strategy is captured in Figure 9.6. If our calculations are correct, we must get $V_0 = 10$ in the end.

The procedure (9.59)–(9.61) is very similar to option pricing of Chapter 5 but there is one important difference here in terms of state variables. While European call option prices in the model of Figure 9.3 would only depend on the stock price at any given time, we can see that the optimal wealth in the same model is path dependent, that is, $V_2(\text{ud}) \neq V_2(\text{du})$! This is a typical situation in optimal investment problems; the optimal solution requires an additional state variable, which is the wealth itself. As long as the stock price is a Markov process under P, and the safe interest rate depends only on the current stock price and time, we will find that the optimal trading strategy θ_t is a function of S_t and V_t; fortunately, no more information is required.

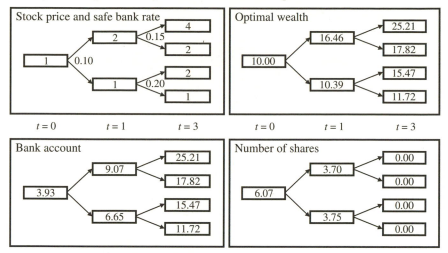

Figure 9.6. Optimal dynamic investment strategy.

9.4.5 Martingale Duality Method on Few Lines

Once the reader is comfortable with the natural calculations (9.43)–(9.61), he or she may be interested in solving the utility maximization symbolically. The symbolic solution is much faster since the numerical values can be entered at the very end and do not have to be carried through the whole calculation.

We start from

$$\max_{V_T(\omega),\omega\in\Omega} \mathrm{E}_0^P\left[\frac{V_T^{1-\gamma}}{1-\gamma}\right] \tag{9.62}$$

$$\text{s.t. } \mathrm{E}_0^P\left[m_T\frac{V_T}{\beta_T}\right] = V_0, \tag{9.63}$$

where we have for convenience put $\mathrm{E}_0^Q[V_T/\beta_T] = \mathrm{E}_0^P[m_T V_T/\beta_T]$ by virtue of (9.30). Since there is just one linear constraint, one solves (9.62) and (9.63) using unconstrained maximization over all states $\omega \in \Omega$ with a Lagrange multiplier:

$$L = \mathrm{E}_0^P\left[\frac{V_T^{1-\gamma}}{1-\gamma}\right] - \lambda\left(\mathrm{E}_0^P\left[m_T\frac{V_T}{\beta_T}\right] - V_0\right)$$

$$= \sum_{\omega} p_{T|0}(\omega)\left(\frac{V_T^{1-\gamma}(\omega)}{1-\gamma} - \lambda m_T(\omega)\frac{V_T(\omega)}{\beta_T(\omega)}\right) + \lambda V_0.$$

The first-order conditions read

$$\frac{\partial L}{\partial V_T(\omega)} = p_{T|0}(\omega)\left(V_T^{-\gamma}(\omega) - \lambda\frac{m_T(\omega)}{\beta_T(\omega)}\right) = 0,$$

$$V_T = \lambda^{-1/\gamma}\left(\frac{m_T}{\beta_T}\right)^{-1/\gamma}. \tag{9.64}$$

The self-financing condition (9.63) implies

$$V_0 = E_0^P\left[\frac{m_T}{\beta_T}V_T\right] = E_0^P\left[\frac{m_T}{\beta_T}\left(\lambda\frac{m_T}{\beta_T}\right)^{-1/\gamma}\right]$$

$$= \lambda^{-1/\gamma}E_0^P\left[\left(\frac{m_T}{\beta_T}\right)^{1-1/\gamma}\right],$$

whereby we obtain

$$\lambda^{-1/\gamma} = \frac{V_0}{E_0^P[(m_T/\beta_T)^{1-1/\gamma}]}. \tag{9.65}$$

Plugging this value back into the optimal wealth equation (9.64) we have

$$V_T = \frac{V_0}{E_0^P[(m_T/\beta_T)^{1-1/\gamma}]}\left(\frac{m_T}{\beta_T}\right)^{-1/\gamma}. \tag{9.66}$$

Example 9.10. Find the optimal wealth level for a CRRA investor with $\gamma = 5$, $V_0 = 10$ with the stock price and short rate from Figure 9.3.

Recall from Example 9.7 on p. 202 that the change of measure is

$$m_2(uu) = 0.06,$$
$$m_2(ud) = 0.34,$$
$$m_2(du) = 0.72,$$
$$m_2(dd) = 2.88.$$

For the cumulative discount we have $\beta_2 = (1+r_0)(1+r_1)$:

$$\beta_2(uu) = \beta_2(ud) = 1.1 \times 1.15 = 1.265,$$
$$\beta_2(du) = \beta_2(dd) = 1.1 \times 1.2 = 1.32.$$

Recall that the unconditional objective probabilities are the same for all paths and are equal to 0.25. Therefore, from (9.65) we have

$$\lambda^{1/\gamma}V_0 = E_0^P\left[\left(\frac{m_T}{\beta_T}\right)^{1-1/\gamma}\right] = E_0^P\left[\left(\frac{m_T}{\beta_T}\right)^{0.8}\right]$$

$$= 0.25\left(\left(\frac{0.06}{1.265}\right)^{0.8} + \left(\frac{0.34}{1.265}\right)^{0.8} + \left(\frac{0.72}{1.32}\right)^{0.8} + \left(\frac{2.88}{1.32}\right)^{0.8}\right)$$

$$= 0.730$$

and from (9.66) we obtain optimal wealth in the final period:

$$V_T(uu) = \frac{10}{0.730}\left(\frac{0.06}{1.265}\right)^{-0.2} = 25.20,$$

$$V_T(ud) = \frac{10}{0.730}\left(\frac{0.34}{1.265}\right)^{-0.2} = 17.82,$$

$$V_T(du) = \frac{10}{0.730}\left(\frac{0.72}{1.32}\right)^{-0.2} = 15.46,$$

$$V_T(\text{dd}) = \frac{10}{0.730}\left(\frac{2.88}{1.32}\right)^{-0.2} = 11.72.$$

This solution is implemented in an Excel spreadsheet *chapter9sect4.xls*.

9.4.6 Measuring Investment Potential in a Dynamically Complete Market

With the expression for optimal wealth (9.66) it is easy to work out the investment potential of dynamic trading. First we will calculate the certainty equivalent, using the notation of Chapter 3:

$$V_{\gamma,\gamma \text{ certain}} = (\text{E}_0^P[V_T^{1-\gamma}])^{1/(1-\gamma)}$$

$$= \frac{V_0}{\text{E}_0^P[(m_T/\beta_T)^{1-1/\gamma}]}\left(\text{E}_0^P\left[\left(\frac{m_T}{\beta_T}\right)^{-(1-\gamma)/\gamma}\right]\right)^{1/(1-\gamma)}$$

$$= V_0\left(\text{E}_0^P\left[\left(\frac{m_T}{\beta_T}\right)^{1-1/\gamma}\right]\right)^{\gamma/(1-\gamma)}. \tag{9.67}$$

The safe wealth depends on how much it costs at time 0 to buy one unit of wealth in each state at time T. From the arbitrage pricing formula the cost is

$$\text{E}_0^Q\left[\frac{1}{\beta_T}\right] = \text{E}_0^P\left[\frac{m_T}{\beta_T}\right]. \tag{9.68}$$

In financial terminology (9.68) represents the price of a zero coupon discount bond. Hence if we invest V_0 into the discount bond with maturity T, we will have in the terminal period

$$V_{\text{safe}} = \frac{V_0}{\text{E}_0^P[m_T/\beta_T]}. \tag{9.69}$$

Combining (9.67) and (9.69) with the definition of investment potential (3.37) we have

$$\text{IP}_\gamma = \gamma\left(\frac{V_{\gamma,\gamma \text{ certain}}}{V_{\text{safe}}} - 1\right) = \gamma\left(\text{E}_0^P\left[\frac{m_T}{\beta_T}\right]\left(\text{E}_0^P\left[\left(\frac{m_T}{\beta_T}\right)^{1-1/\gamma}\right]\right)^{\gamma/(1-\gamma)} - 1\right). \tag{9.70}$$

This formula looks simpler when rephrased in terms of the generalized Sharpe ratio (3.82):

$$1+\text{SR}_\gamma^2 = \left(1+\frac{\text{IP}_\gamma}{\gamma}\right)^{2\gamma} = \left(\text{E}_0^P\left[\frac{m_T}{\beta_T}\right]\right)^{2\gamma}\left(\text{E}_0^P\left[\left(\frac{m_T}{\beta_T}\right)^{1-1/\gamma}\right]\right)^{2\gamma^2/(1-\gamma)}. \tag{9.71}$$

For the standard Sharpe ratio, $\gamma = -1$, we obtain the well-known **Hansen–Jagannathan duality formula**, which links the maximum market Sharpe ratio to the Sharpe ratio of the pricing kernel:

$$\text{SR}_{-1}^2 = \left(\frac{(\text{E}_0^P[m_T/\beta_T])^2}{\text{Var}_0^P(m_T/\beta_T)}\right)^{-1}, \tag{9.72}$$

$$\text{SR}(\text{market}) = \frac{1}{\text{SR}(\text{pricing kernel})}.$$

The duality between market investment opportunities and state prices is important for econometric testing of asset-pricing models where m is typically linked to observed financial behaviour of households via an optimizing model; see the references at the end of the chapter.

9.5 Summary

- We have defined a cumulative return on the bank account deposits β_t:

$$\beta_t = R_{f\,0} \times R_{f\,1} \times \cdots \times R_{f\,t-1},$$
$$\beta_0 = 1.$$

- A process $\{X_t\}_{t\in[0,T]}$ is a martingale if (i) $E_s[X_t] = X_s$ for all $s < t$ and (ii) $E_0[|X_t|]$ is finite for all t. When we talk about martingales in this book we look for property (i) and assume that (ii) is satisfied automatically. In contrast, a mathematical treatment of martingales would place a strong emphasis on the verification of condition (ii), which happens to be a much harder task. Fortunately for us, (ii) is indeed satisfied in frequently encountered models of financial markets which *ex post* justifies us in not giving it much attention in this text.

- Intuitively, a martingale is a process created by adding shocks with zero conditional mean. Mathematically, this statement is captured by the first martingale proposition.

- When an asset bears no dividends the one-period pricing formula reads

$$S_t = E_t^Q\left[\frac{S_{t+1}}{R_{f\,t}}\right].$$

Dividing both sides by β_t we have

$$\frac{S_t}{\beta_t} = E_t^Q\left[\frac{S_{t+1}}{\beta_{t+1}}\right] \quad \text{for all } t$$

and the first martingale proposition then implies that the discounted price process $\{S_t/\beta_t\}$ is a martingale under the risk-neutral measure:

$$\frac{S_s}{\beta_s} = E_s^Q\left[\frac{S_t}{\beta_t}\right] \quad \text{for any } s < t.$$

By taking $t = T$ and $s = 0$ we obtain the risk-neutral pricing formula used in option pricing.

- The wealth of a self-financing strategy behaves exactly like an asset without dividends, since one is not allowed to add or withdraw money at intermediate dates:

$$\frac{V_s}{\beta_s} = E_s^Q\left[\frac{V_t}{\beta_t}\right] \quad \text{for any } s < t.$$

This property is instrumental in proving the multi-period version of the arbitrage theorem: there is no dynamic arbitrage if and only if there is a strictly positive probability measure Q under which the discounted prices of all traded assets are martingales (assuming that assets pay no dividend).

- In finance one uses two sets of probability measures, objective P and risk-neutral Q. Objective probabilities measure the likelihood of individual market scenarios; the risk-neutral probabilities discounted at the safe rate tell us how expensive it is to buy a contract which delivers one unit of wealth at the terminal date when a particular market scenario occurs.

- The ratio of risk-neutral to objective probabilities is called the change of measure. Scenarios with a low change of measure are easy to ensure against, whereas the scenarios with a very high change of measure are uninsurable.

- The change of measure on paths starting at time s and ending at time t is denoted by $m_{t|s}$, with the exception of $m_{t|0}$, which is denoted simply by m_t. For any random variable X known at t we have by definition

$$E_s^Q[X] = E_s^P[m_{t|s}X] \qquad (9.73)$$

and in particular

$$1 = E_s^P[m_{t|s}]. \qquad (9.74)$$

- From the multiplication rule for conditional probabilities the unconditional change of measure is the product of one-step changes of measure,

$$m_{t|s} = m_{s+1|s} \times m_{s+2|s+1} \times \cdots \times m_{t|t-1}.$$

To capture $m_{t|s}$ it is convenient to define *density process* $\{m_t\}_{t=0,1,\dots,T}$:

$$m_t = m_{1|0} \times \cdots \times m_{t-1|t-2} \times m_{t|t-1},$$
$$m_0 = 1.$$

By direct comparison

$$m_{t|s} = \frac{m_t}{m_s}. \qquad (9.75)$$

- Property (9.74) together with (9.75) implies that the process $\{m_t\}_{t=0,1,\dots,T}$ is a martingale under P.

- Property (9.73) together with (9.75) implies that the process $\{X_t\}_{t=0,1,\dots,T}$ is a martingale under Q if and only if $\{m_t X_t\}_{t=0,1,\dots,T}$ is a martingale under P. This characterization becomes useful in the continuous-time limit when dealing with Itô processes.

- Let V_t be the wealth of a self-financing trading strategy with a number of shares θ_t. The dynamic optimal investment problem

$$\max_{\theta_t, t=0,1,\dots,T-1} E_0^P[U(V_T)]$$

with θ_t known at time t can be rephrased equivalently as a constrained optimization over terminal wealth with one linear constraint,

$$\max_{V_T(\omega), \omega \in \Omega} E_0^P[U(V_T)] \qquad (9.76)$$

$$\text{s.t. } E_0^Q\left[\frac{V_T}{\beta_T}\right] = V_0. \qquad (9.77)$$

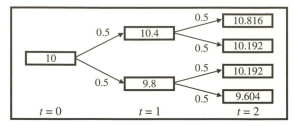

Figure 9.7. Stock price histories and conditional objective probabilities.

The marginal utility at optimum is proportional to the unconditional *state price density* m_T/β_T,

$$U'(V_T) = \lambda \frac{m_T}{\beta_T}.$$

Other commonly used expressions for m_T/β_T are the *pricing kernel* and the *stochastic discount factor*.

- The optimal investment problem typically requires one more state variable, wealth, compared with the corresponding option pricing problem. Thus even though the stock price tree may recombine to form a lattice, it is typically not possible to write the optimal wealth into this lattice.

9.6 Notes

Sections 9.1–9.3 are an elaboration of Chapter 2G in Duffie (1996). The same material is explained very well in Chapter 2 of Baxter and Rennie (1996). The martingale duality approach to dynamic optimal investment and consumption problems was pioneered by Pliska (1986) and developed by Cox and Huang (1989) and Karatzas et al. (1991). The relationship between the variance of the pricing kernel and the market Sharpe ratio appears in Hansen and Jagannathan (1991); for extensions thereof see Černý (2003). For a comprehensive survey of asset pricing that uses pricing kernels as the main tool, see Cochrane (2001). This book ignores the questions of integrability which are central to the proper mathematical use of martingales. Interested reader can learn the technical background from Williams (1991). Lack of uniform integrability is resolved by introducing the notion of local martingale; see Hunt and Kennedy (2000).

9.7 Exercises

Exercise 9.1 (martingale properties). Decide whether each of the following four statements is *true* or *false*.

The process $\{X_t\}_{t=0,1,\dots,T}$ is a martingale if

(a) for all $0 \leqslant s \leqslant t \leqslant T$, $E_s[X_t] = X_s$,

(b) for all $0 \leqslant t \leqslant T$, $E_t[X_T] = X_t$,

(c) for all $0 \leqslant t \leqslant T-1$, $E_t[X_{t+1}] = X_t$,

(d) for all $0 \leqslant t \leqslant T$, $E_0[X_t] = X_0$.

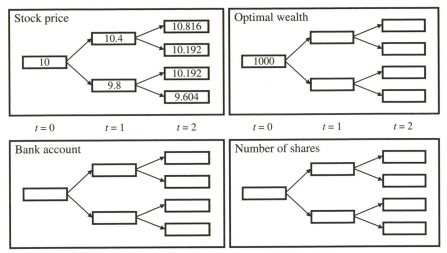

Figure 9.8. Description of the optimal investment strategy.

Exercise 9.2 (dynamic investment with logarithmic utility). Consider the model of Exercise 5.1: the monthly risk-free rate is 0.5%, the monthly stock return can take two values, $R_u = 1.04$, $R_d = 0.98$, with equal probability and monthly stock returns are independent. Assume that the initial stock price is $S_0 = £10$. The stock price model is depicted in Figure 9.7.

Suppose that an investor starts with £1000 and wishes to invest this sum for two months. Her criterion is to maximize the expected log-utility of her wealth in two months' time.

(a) The coefficient of relative risk aversion is defined as

$$-\frac{V U''(V)}{U'(V)}.$$

Is an investor with $U(V) = \ln V$ more or less risk averse than an investor with $U(V) = \sqrt{V}$? Circle one answer.

   (i) Log investor more risk averse than square root investor.

  (ii) Log investor less risk averse than square root investor.

 (iii) Both equally risk averse.

(b) Find the unconditional change of measure in this model.

$$m_{uu} =$$

$$m_{ud} =$$

$$m_{du} =$$

$$m_{dd} =$$

(c) Using the change of measure write down the budget constraint that our investor faces.

$$£10 =$$

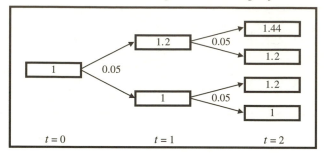

Figure 9.9.   Information tree containing stock price histories and risk-free interest rate.

(d) Rewrite the constrained maximization as an unconstrained problem with a Lagrange multiplier.

$$\max_{V_{\text{uu}}, V_{\text{ud}}, V_{\text{du}}, V_{\text{dd}}}$$

(e) Solve the unconstrained problem with a Lagrange multiplier λ.

$$V_{\text{uu}} =$$
$$V_{\text{ud}} =$$
$$V_{\text{du}} =$$
$$V_{\text{dd}} =$$

(f) Find the correct value of λ from the budget constraint.

$$\lambda =$$

(g) Evaluate the optimal wealth in two months' time for each path.

$$V_{\text{uu}} =$$
$$V_{\text{ud}} =$$
$$V_{\text{du}} =$$
$$V_{\text{dd}} =$$

(h) Find the self-financing portfolio that leads to the optimal wealth distribution. In Figure 9.8 write down investor's total wealth, the number of shares and the cash in bank.

(i) If we take stock price and calendar time as the state variables, are these variables sufficient to describe the optimal wealth of our investor?

Exercise 9.3 (dynamic investment with square root utility). Repeat the above with $U(V) = \sqrt{V}$, and compare the optimal value of V_2 with the result in Exercise 9.2. Is your finding consistent with the ranking of risk aversion found in part (a) of Exercise 9.2?

Exercise 9.4 (dynamic investment with exponential utility). Repeat the above with $U(V) = -e^{-V}$.

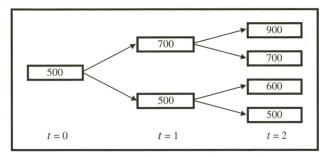

Figure 9.10. Specific consumption stream.

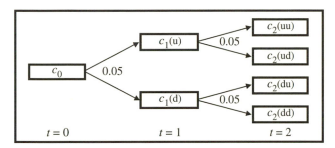

Figure 9.11. General consumption stream.

Exercise 9.5 (dynamic investment with CRRA utility). For the two-period model above, design an Excel spreadsheet that computes the optimal trading strategy for a CRRA investor with arbitrary baseline risk aversion γ. Report also the investment potential and the corresponding Sharpe ratio of the optimal investment strategy.

Exercise 9.6 (optimal intertemporal consumption). Consider a two-period model with two assets: stock and a risk-free bank account. The one-period stock returns are independent and identically distributed, and each can take two values, $R_u = 1.2$ or $R_d = 1.0$ with equal objective probability $p_u = p_d = \frac{1}{2}$. The risk-free rate is constant, $r = 0.05$. The information tree with stock price and risk-free rate is depicted in Figure 9.9.

  (a) Write down the information tree with conditional risk-neutral probabilities clearly depicted on the branches.

  (b) Suppose a consumer chooses her consumption according to Figure 9.10. For example, if the stock price goes up and then down the consumption is $c_0 = 500$, $c_1 = 700$, $c_2 = 700$. Use the risk-neutral probabilities to work out how much wealth the consumer needs at time 0 to finance this stream of consumption.

  (c) Suppose now that the consumption stream is unknown, as shown in Figure 9.11. Write down the budget constraint that the consumption stream must satisfy so that it can be financed with initial wealth $V_0 = 1000$.

  (d) The consumer has an initial wealth 1000 and wishes to maximize the expected utility of consumption,

$$\max_{c_0,c_1,c_2} E_0^P [\ln c_0 + \ln c_1 + \ln c_2],$$

subject to the budget constraint derived in (c). Formulate the problem as an unconstrained optimization with a Lagrange multiplier λ and write down the first-order conditions.

(e) Solve for the consumption as a function of λ, deduce λ from the budget constraint, and enter the optimal value of consumption into the information tree.

10

Brownian Motion and Itô Formulae

In this chapter we will abandon the world with a finite number of states and discrete-time periods to uncover the beauty of continuous-time finance. We briefly review the construction of *Brownian motion*, which was the main topic of Chapter 6. The construction naturally leads to the logarithm of the stock price being expressed as a *stochastic integral*, which implies that the log stock price is an *Itô process*. We will show how to transform one Itô process (logarithm of stock price) into another (level of stock price) by means of the all-important *Itô formula*. We will generalize the formula to the function of several Itô processes depending on several independent Brownian motions. We will use these formulae to find the equation for the discounted price process and to verify the solution for the Ornstein–Uhlenbeck mean-reverting process. At the end of the chapter we will see under what conditions an Itô process becomes a martingale. The tools developed in this chapter will allow us to rederive the Black–Scholes formula in the next chapter using only continuous-time mathematics.

10.1 Continuous-Time Brownian Motion

10.1.1 Discrete Brownian Motion

We will start with a collection of random variables $\varepsilon_1, \varepsilon_2, \ldots, \varepsilon_T$ interpreting ε_t as a *shock* which is revealed at time t but not before. Furthermore, we require the conditional mean of each shock to be zero and the conditional variance to be 1:

$$\mathrm{E}_t[\varepsilon_{t+1}] = 0, \tag{10.1}$$

$$\mathrm{Var}_t(\varepsilon_{t+1}) = \mathrm{E}_t[\varepsilon_{t+1}^2] = 1. \tag{10.2}$$

Exercise 10.1 shows three important properties of the shocks ε_t.

- The mean of ε_t is 0 as of *any* earlier date $s < t$,

$$\mathrm{E}_s[\varepsilon_t] = 0. \tag{10.3}$$

- The variance of ε_t is 1 as of any earlier date $s < t$,

$$\mathrm{Var}_s(\varepsilon_t) = 1. \tag{10.4}$$

- The shocks $\varepsilon_t, \varepsilon_u$ are automatically uncorrelated as of any earlier date $s < t < u$,

$$\mathrm{Cov}_s(\varepsilon_t, \varepsilon_u) = 0. \tag{10.5}$$

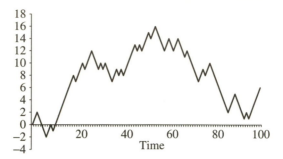

Figure 10.1.   Realization of the process $B_{1,t}$ with $T = 100$.
The shocks ε_t are independent and take values ± 1 with probability 50%.

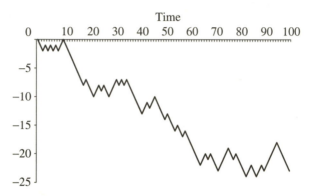

Figure 10.2.   Another realization of the process $B_{1,t}$.

The easiest (but not the only) way to construct shocks ε with properties (10.1) and (10.2) is to assume that $\{\varepsilon_t\}$ are IID (independent identically distributed).

Now consider a new process $B_{1,t}$ that adds up all the shocks up until the time t,

$$B_{1,0} = 0,$$
$$B_{1,1} = \varepsilon_1,$$
$$B_{1,2} = \varepsilon_1 + \varepsilon_2,$$
$$B_{1,T} = \varepsilon_1 + \varepsilon_2 + \cdots + \varepsilon_T.$$

The process $B_{1,t}$ is called a discrete-time **Brownian motion with time step 1** or sometimes also a **random walk**. Figures 10.1 and 10.2 show two realizations of the Brownian motion where the shock values have been taken from a quasi-random number generator in Excel (see Exercise 10.2).

We will notice the following facts about the process $B_{1,t}$. By virtue of (10.1) and of the first martingale proposition the *process B_t is a martingale*. Furthermore, since by virtue of (10.5) the shocks $\{\varepsilon_t\}$ are uncorrelated, the unconditional variance of $B_{1,t}$ equals the sum of unconditional variances of individual shocks, which by virtue of (10.4) are all equal to 1,

$$\mathrm{Var}_0(B_{1,t}) = \mathrm{Var}_0(\varepsilon_1 + \cdots + \varepsilon_t) = \mathrm{Var}_0(\varepsilon_1) + \cdots + \mathrm{Var}_0(\varepsilon_t) = t. \qquad (10.6)$$

For the conditional variance at time s similarly

$$\text{Var}_s(B_{1,t}) = \text{Var}_s(\underbrace{\varepsilon_1 + \cdots + \varepsilon_s}_{\text{known at time } s} + \varepsilon_{s+1} + \cdots + \varepsilon_t)$$

$$= \text{Var}_s(\varepsilon_{s+1} + \cdots + \varepsilon_t) \qquad (10.7)$$

$$= \text{Var}_s(\varepsilon_{s+1}) + \cdots + \text{Var}_s(\varepsilon_t) = t - s. \qquad (10.8)$$

We notice that the *variance* of the process $B_{1,t}$ *increases linearly with time*. This is the same **linear law for variance** that has already appeared in Chapter 6. Also note that the shocks ε *do not* have to be independent or identically distributed for (10.6) and (10.8) to hold.

10.1.2 Refining the Time Step

We can repeat the same construction as above using an arbitrary time step Δt, denoting the resulting Brownian motion $B_{\Delta t, t}$,

$$B_{\Delta t, 0} = 0,$$

$$B_{\Delta t, \Delta t} = \varepsilon_{\Delta t},$$

$$B_{\Delta t, 2\Delta t} = \varepsilon_{\Delta t} + \varepsilon_{2\Delta t},$$

$$B_{\Delta t, T} = \varepsilon_{\Delta t} + \varepsilon_{2\Delta t} + \cdots + \varepsilon_{T-\Delta t} + \varepsilon_T.$$

In order to make sure that $\text{Var}_0(B_{\Delta t, t}) = t$ as before, the variance of the individual shocks must be proportional to Δt,

$$\text{Var}_t(\varepsilon_{t+\Delta t}) = \Delta t, \qquad (10.9)$$

$$\text{E}_t[\varepsilon_{t+\Delta t}] = 0. \qquad (10.10)$$

Example 10.1. With a time step $\Delta t = 1$ we have used shocks of size $\varepsilon_1 = \pm 1$. If we now take a time step of $\Delta t = \frac{1}{16} = 0.0625$, the shock size must drop by the factor $\sqrt{\Delta t} = \frac{1}{4}$. Namely, taking

$$\varepsilon_{\Delta t} = \sqrt{\Delta t}\varepsilon_1$$

and applying standard properties of mean and variance gives

$$\text{E}[\varepsilon_{\Delta t}] = \text{E}[\sqrt{\Delta t}\varepsilon_1] = \sqrt{\Delta t}\text{E}[\varepsilon_1] = 0,$$

$$\text{Var}(\varepsilon_{\Delta t}) = \text{Var}(\sqrt{\Delta t}\varepsilon_1) = \Delta t\,\text{Var}(\varepsilon_1) = \Delta t,$$

as required in (10.9) and (10.10). Therefore, with a time step of $\Delta t = \frac{1}{16}$ we would use shocks of size ± 0.25. One realization of the Brownian motion $B_{1/16, t}$ is shown in Figure 10.3.

As the time step gets smaller we are adding shocks more and more frequently but the variance of the shocks gets smaller proportionally with their number. In the limit $\Delta t \to 0$ *as the size of the shocks goes to zero* the process B_t is defined for all values of $t \in [0; T]$ and we obtain **continuous-time Brownian motion**. A sufficient but not necessary condition to obtain continuous Brownian motion is independence of the ε shocks.

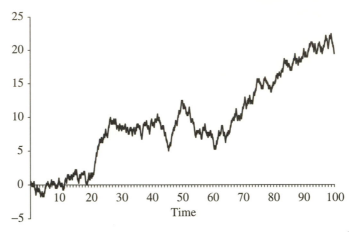

Figure 10.3. Realization of discrete Brownian motion with time step $\frac{1}{16}$.

10.1.3 Continuous-Time Limit, Lévy Processes and Markov Chain Approximations

We are about to leave the comforting world of discrete mathematics to discover the exciting but rather abstract world of continuous stochastic processes. Before we do so it may be useful to elucidate how these two worlds fit together.

- It is important to bear in mind that $B_{\Delta t,T}$ converges to the continuous-time value B_T in terms of its distribution,

$$\lim_{\Delta t \to 0} \mathrm{E}_0[(B_T - B_{\Delta t,T})^2] = 0,$$

but not pathwise. For example, the discrete Brownian motion starting at 0 can cross zero on the interval $[0, T]$ no more than $T/\Delta t$ times, whereas the continuous-time Brownian motion starting at zero crosses zero infinitely many times in an arbitrarily short time interval after the start. Fortunately, what matters in finance are mostly the distributional properties, which we review in the next section.

- To obtain the Brownian motion limit it is absolutely crucial that the size of ε shocks tends to zero (in an appropriate sense) as the time interval Δt shrinks. If the size of shocks *did not* go to zero, then the limit would be a **Poisson jump process**, or more generally a combination of independent Poisson processes—a **Lévy process**. The two different types of limits, Brownian and Poisson, were examined in detail in Chapter 6.

- The mathematical theory describing the limits of discrete-time processes is known under the name of **Markov chain approximation method**; see the references at the end of the chapter. This theory essentially tells us that it is OK to switch between the discrete and continuous-time versions of the same problem, whether it concerns pricing, optimal investment, or indeed a range of other problems in physics, operations research, etc. In practice, one can pick the version that is more practical to solve in the given circumstances.

The discrete version can always be solved by brute force on a computer; on the other hand if a continuous-time solution exists, then it typically evaluates much faster than the discretized model (think of the Black–Scholes formula compared with the speed of the binomial option pricing model). As a rule, the more realistic the model the smaller the chance that it will have a simple closed-form continuous-time solution. The numerical solutions of discrete-time models therefore offer a considerable degree of flexibility. In addition computers are getting faster and models that were numerically impractical 20 years ago today have a new lease of life.

- So far, with the exception of Chapters 8 and 9, the book has been skewed towards numerical methods. It is now time to redress the balance and provide tools for dealing with continuous-time models. To make our task easier we will restrict our attention to Brownian motion; see the notes at the end of the chapter for references dealing with Poisson jump processes. By its very nature the continuous-time Brownian motion is a theoretical abstraction and its manipulation therefore calls for theoretical tools. These tools, namely the Itô integral and Itô calculus, are the main topic of the remainder of the chapter.

10.1.4 Properties of Continuous-Time Brownian Motion

Quite naturally, most of the properties of the continuous-time Brownian motion follow from the properties of its discrete-time counterpart. The only thing that changes is the shape of the distribution, in the limit Brownian increments have jointly **normal** distribution. *It is as if all the shocks ε were distributed identically, independently and normally from the start.*

1. For any $t_1 \leqslant t_2 \leqslant t_3$ the distribution of $B_{t_3} - B_{t_2}$ conditional on the information at time t_1 is normal with mean 0 and variance $t_3 - t_2$. Mathematically, we write

$$B_{t_3} - B_{t_2} \mid \mathcal{F}_{t_1} \sim N(0, t_3 - t_2). \tag{10.11}$$

2. For $t_1 < t_2 \leqslant t_3 < t_4$ the increments $B_{t_2} - B_{t_1}$ and $B_{t_4} - B_{t_3}$ are jointly normal and uncorrelated, and therefore also independent.

3. The *sample paths* of Brownian motion are *continuous*, that is,

$$\lim_{s \to t} B_s - B_t = 0$$

for almost all realizations of the process $\{B_t\}$ and all times t.

4. The sample paths are *not differentiable*, that is,

$$\lim_{s \to t} \frac{B_t - B_s}{t - s}$$

does not exist at any time t for almost all realizations of the process $\{B_t\}$.

The sample path properties rarely find application in finance, and they do not feature elsewhere in this book. On the other hand, property (10.11) is used extensively, not least in the proof of the Itô formula.

Brownian increments in continuous time. Consider a small time step dt and denote the shock $B_{t+dt} - B_t$ by dB_t. Then

$$dB_t \sim N(0, dt),$$
$$\text{Cov}(dB_t, dB_s) = 0 \quad \text{for } t \neq s,$$
$$\text{Cov}(dB_t, dB_t) = \text{Var}(dB_t) = dt.$$

The Brownian shock dB_t is distributed normally with a mean of 0 and variance dt. Brownian shocks over distinct time intervals are uncorrelated.

10.2   Stochastic Integration and Itô Processes

Recall the scaling rule (6.25) for log returns in the discrete-time Brownian motion set-up:
$$\ln R(\Delta t) \triangleq \mu \Delta t + \sqrt{\Delta t}(\ln R(1) - \mu). \tag{10.12}$$
Denoting the variance of $\ln R(1)$ by σ we can rephrase (10.12) as
$$\ln R(\Delta t) = \mu \Delta t + \sigma \underbrace{\frac{\sqrt{\Delta t}(\ln R(1) - \mu)}{\sigma}}_{\varepsilon}, \tag{10.13}$$

where the shock ε has conditional mean zero and variance Δt as required by conditions (10.9) and (10.10). We can reinterpret $\ln R(\Delta t)$ as $\ln S_{t_{i+1}}/S_{t_i}$, whereby (10.13) becomes
$$\ln S_{t_{i+1}} - \ln S_{t_i} = \mu \Delta t + \sigma \varepsilon_{t_{i+1}}. \tag{10.14}$$
This is a recipe for generating values of $\ln S$ always one step ahead. We could make μ and σ time dependent, or even random as of time 0, as long as μ_{t_i}, σ_{t_i} are known at time t_i.

Applying the formula (10.14) n times ($n = T/\Delta t$) we obtain the final-period value $\ln S_{\Delta t, T}$:

$$\ln S_{\Delta t, T} = \ln S_0 + \sum_{i=0}^{n-1} \mu_{t_i} \Delta t + \sum_{i=0}^{n-1} \sigma_{t_i} \varepsilon_{t_{i+1}}. \tag{10.15}$$

Refining the time step $\Delta t \to 0$ in (10.15) $\ln S_{\Delta t, T}$ converges to a continuous-time random variable $\ln S_T$, which is known as the **Itô integral**, symbolically denoted

$$\ln S_T = \ln S_0 + \int_0^T \mu_t \, dt + \int_0^T \sigma_t \, dB_t. \tag{10.16}$$

The collection of the limiting random variables $\{\ln S_t\}$ indexed by the time subscript 't' is called an **Itô process**. Equation (10.16) is often written in differential form,

$$d \ln S_t = \mu_t \, dt + \sigma_t \, dB_t. \tag{10.17}$$

Equation (10.17) is called the **stochastic differential equation**, or SDE for short.

The limiting value of the Itô integral does not depend on the shape of the distribution of the ε shocks as long as conditions (10.9) and (10.10) are satisfied and the shock sizes tend to zero. It is often convenient to think of ε as normally distributed in the limit.

10.2.1 Convergence of Sums to Integrals

As with Brownian motion, the standard construction of the Itô integral assumes mean square convergence, that is, the limit $\ln S_T$ satisfies

$$\lim_{\Delta t \to 0} E_0[(\ln S_T - \ln S_{\Delta t, T})^2] = 0. \tag{10.18}$$

A more modern approach, the Markov chain approximation method, uses convergence in distribution discussed in Section 7.5.1 of Chapter 7. In general, mean square convergence implies convergence in distribution, but not vice versa.

In order for the limit of (10.15) to exist, μ_t and σ_t *must* be identifiable from the history of the shocks ε up to time t. Mathematically, we say that μ_t and σ_t must be adapted to the information filtration generated by the shocks ε. There are good economic reasons for this requirement that are related to insider trading; for more discussion of information issues refer to Chapter 8. Moreover, the cumulative drift and the cumulative volatility must not be too high, otherwise the mean or variance of $\ln S_T$ will be infinite and the limit not well defined. The following restrictions make sure that the limit always exists:

$$E_0\left[\int_0^T |\mu_t|\, dt\right] < \infty, \qquad E_0\left[\int_0^T \sigma_t^2\, dt\right] < \infty.$$

10.2.2 Complete or Incomplete? The Martingale Representation Theorem

What is more important to us, the convergence result (10.18) works in the opposite direction too. Let us take an arbitrary function g and form a new random variable $g(\ln S_{\Delta t, T})$, which we can think of as a '*derivative security pay-off*'. We can now devise a '*dynamic hedging strategy*' θ_t (adapted to the filtration generated by the ε shocks, which are now interpreted as excess returns) that minimizes the expected squared error,

$$E_0\left[\left(g(\ln S_{\Delta t, T}) - E_0[g(\ln S_{\Delta t, T})] - \sum_{i=0}^{n-1} \theta_{t_i} \varepsilon_{t_{i+1}}\right)^2\right]. \tag{10.19}$$

The computation of the optimal θ is done in Chapter 12, but let us leave that aside for the moment. Crucially, we will find that the 'expected squared hedging error' (10.19) goes to zero in the Brownian motion limit as $\Delta t \to 0$, *regardless of how many values ε takes*. For example, we could take a trinomial model for stock prices in which the option cannot be hedged perfectly, yet we are guaranteed that if we rescale the trinomial returns in a Brownian fashion the expected squared hedging error will eventually vanish as $\Delta t \to 0$. This important result is known as the **martingale representation theorem**. It explains the mystery of the continuous-time Black–Scholes model where the market is incomplete if hedging takes place at discrete-time intervals but where the market becomes complete when continuous rebalancing is permitted.

The martingale representation theorem is usually written down in continuous time, which makes it slightly more abstract but nevertheless still useful. We note it here for future reference.

Proposition 10.2 (martingale representation theorem). *Let* $\{B_t\}_{t\in[0,T]}$ *be a Brownian motion and let* $\{\mathcal{F}_t\}_{t\in[0,T]}$ *be the information filtration generated by this Brownian motion. Suppose that the random variable X is known at time T in this information filtration and that* $\mathrm{E}_0[X^2] < \infty$. *Then there is a 'hedging process'* $\{\theta_t\}_{t\in[0,T]}$ *adapted to the filtration* $\{\mathcal{F}_t\}_{t\in[0,T]}$ *such that*

$$X = \mathrm{E}_0[X] + \int_0^T \theta_t \, \mathrm{d}B_t.$$

10.3 Important Itô Processes

10.3.1 Brownian Motion with Drift

Consider a stochastic differential equation along the lines of (10.17). When μ and σ are constant over time, the process $X = \ln S$ becomes a **Brownian motion with drift**:

$$\mathrm{d}X_s = \mu \, \mathrm{d}s + \sigma \, \mathrm{d}B_s,$$

$$X_t - X_0 = \int_0^t \mathrm{d}X_s = \int_0^t \mu \, \mathrm{d}s + \int_0^t \sigma \, \mathrm{d}B_s,$$

$$X_t = X_0 + \mu t + \sigma \underbrace{(B_t - B_0)}_{N(0,t)}. \tag{10.20}$$

The word 'drift' signifies that the expected change in X increases with time:

$$\mathrm{E}_0[X_t - X_0] = \mu t + \underbrace{\mathrm{E}_0[\sigma (B_t - B_0)]}_{0} = \mu t.$$

Since the distribution of $B_t - B_0$ is normal it is easy to see from (10.20) that

$$X_t - X_0 \sim N(\mu t, \sigma^2 t).$$

Replacing 0 with an arbitrary time s, $s < t$, we conclude that, conditional on the information at time s, the random variable $X_t - X_s$ is distributed normally $N(\mu(t - s), \sigma^2(t - s))$. In particular, this means X is a *Markov process*.

10.3.2 Brownian Motion with Non-Stochastic Time-Dependent Drift and Volatility

When μ and σ depend only on calendar time (their time t value is known at time 0), the situation is very similar. In discretized form,

$$X_{\Delta t, T} = X_0 + \sum_{i=0}^{n-1} \mu_{t_i} \Delta t + \sum_{i=0}^{n-1} \sigma_{t_i} \varepsilon_{t_{i+1}}. \tag{10.21}$$

Properties of normal variables.

- If Z is normally distributed and a, b are constants, then $a + bZ$ again has a normal distribution.
- The sum of jointly normal variables is again distributed normally.

By assumption the values μ_{t_i} and σ_{t_i} are known at time 0 and therefore the expression on the right-hand side of (10.21) is a linear combination of normally distributed variables $\sigma_{t_i}\varepsilon_{t_{i+1}}$ plus a constant, hence X_T itself has normal distribution. By virtue of (6.1) its mean is

$$E_0[X_T] = X(0) + \sum_{i=0}^{n-1} \mu_{t_i}\Delta t \tag{10.22}$$

and by virtue of (6.2) its variance is

$$\text{Var}_0(X_T) = \sum_{i=0}^{n-1} \sigma_{t_i}^2 \text{Var}(\varepsilon_{t_i}) = \sum_{i=0}^{n-1} \sigma_{t_i}^2 \Delta t \tag{10.23}$$

because the shocks ε_{t_i} are by construction uncorrelated. Consequently,

$$(X_T - X_0) \mid \mathcal{F}_0 \sim N\left(X(0) + \sum_{i=0}^{n-1} \mu_{t_i}\Delta t, \sum_{i=0}^{n-1} \sigma_{t_i}^2 \Delta t \right).$$

As $\Delta t \to 0$ the sums (10.22) and (10.23) turn into integrals:

$$\sum_{i=0}^{n-1} \mu(t_i)\Delta t \to \int_0^T \mu(t)\,dt,$$

$$\sum_{i=0}^{n-1} \sigma^2(t_i)\Delta t \to \int_0^T \sigma^2(t)\,dt.$$

Let X be an Itô process with non-stochastic drift μ_t and non-stochastic volatility σ_t,

$$dX_t = \mu_t\,dt + \sigma_t\,dB_t.$$

Then for any T the increment $X_T - X_0$ is distributed normally as of time 0,

$$(X_T - X_0) \mid \mathcal{F}_0 \sim N\left(\int_0^T \mu_t\,dt, \int_0^T \sigma_t^2\,dt \right). \tag{10.24}$$

Since we can replace 0 with any starting time $s < T$, (10.24) demonstrates that X is a Markov process.

Example 10.3. Find the distribution of X_T if

$$dX_t = 2t\,dt - \sqrt{t}\,dB_t.$$

Solution. Since both the volatility and drift of dX_t are non-stochastic we can apply the result (10.24) to

$$\mu_t = 2t,$$

$$\sigma_t = \sqrt{t},$$

whereby we obtain

$$\int_0^T \mu_t \, dt = \int_0^T 2t \, dt = [t^2]_0^T = T^2,$$

$$\int_0^T \sigma_t^2 \, dt = \int_0^T (\sqrt{t})^2 \, dt = \int_0^T t \, dt = \tfrac{1}{2}T^2.$$

Hence

$$X_T \mid \mathcal{F}_0 \sim N(X_0 + T^2, \tfrac{1}{2}T^2).$$

10.3.3 Stochastic Drift and Volatility

In this most general case μ_t and σ_t are *not* known at time 0, although they *have to be known at time* t. A frequently encountered example is the **Ornstein–Uhlenbeck process** (also known as the mean-reverting process),

$$dX_t = -\mu X_t \, dt + \sigma \, dB_t,$$

which is known in a discrete-time version from econometrics as an AR(1) process with autocorrelation ρ,

$$X_{t+1} = \rho X_t + \sigma \varepsilon_{t+1}.$$

Another example of a process with stochastic drift and volatility is the **geometric Brownian motion**,

$$\frac{dX_t}{X_t} = \mu \, dt + \sigma \, dB_t,$$

which is used to model stock prices.

10.4 Function of a Stochastic Process: the Itô Formula

Let f be a differentiable function of time, then

$$f(t) = f(0) + \int_0^t f'(s) \, ds.$$

A curious property of Itô processes is that the above identity does not hold any more when t is replaced by an Itô process X_t:

$$f(X_t) \neq f(X_0) + \int_0^t f'(X_s) \, dX_s.$$

Instead, if $dX_t = \mu_t \, dt + \sigma_t \, dB_t$, an extra correction term is needed:

$$f(X_t) = f(X_0) + \int_0^t f'(X_s) \, dX_s + \frac{1}{2} \underbrace{\int_0^t f''(X_s)\sigma_s^2 \, ds}_{\text{Itô correction}}. \tag{10.25}$$

Equation (10.25) is known as the **the Itô formula** and it is often written in differential form,

$$dX_t = \mu_t \, dt + \sigma_t \, dB_t, \tag{10.26}$$

$$df(X_t) = f'(X_t) \, dX_t + \tfrac{1}{2} f''(X_t)\sigma_t^2 \, dt. \tag{10.27}$$

The standard calculus

$$df(X_t) = f'(X_t) \, dX_t$$

can be used either when f is linear in X or when the process X is **locally non-stochastic**, $\sigma_t = 0$.

For the proof of the Itô formula see Section 10.8.

10.5 Applications of the Itô Formula

- The Itô formula is often written and used in the form,

$$dX_t = \mu_t \, dt + \sigma_t \, dB_t, \tag{10.28}$$

$$df(X_t) = \left(f'(X_t)\mu_t + \tfrac{1}{2} f''(X_t)\sigma_t^2 \right) dt + f'(X_t)\sigma_t \, dB_t. \tag{10.29}$$

From experience, it is *not* a good idea to use it in this way. It is hard to remember with one Itô process and it becomes impossible to remember with several Itô processes. It is also difficult to apply, because one has to identify correctly what σ_t is equal to.

- A good way to remember and apply the Itô formula is to think of a second-order Taylor expansion,

$$df(X_t) = f'(X_t) \, dX_t + \tfrac{1}{2} f''(X_t)(dX_t)^2,$$

where $(dX_t)^2$ is replaced by the conditional variance of dX_t:

$$df(X_t) = f'(X_t) \, dX_t + \tfrac{1}{2} f''(X_t) \, \mathrm{Var}_t(dX_t). \tag{10.30}$$

This way one gets the right economic intuition *and* one does not have to remember what dX_t is equal to. This formula changes very little when more state variables are added.

10.5.1 Geometric Brownian Motion

Example 10.4. Suppose that the stock price S_t follows a geometric Brownian motion,

$$\frac{dS_t}{S_t} = \mu \, dt + \sigma \, dB_t; \tag{10.31}$$

let us find the SDE for $\ln S_t$.

Solution. We have $f(S_t) = \ln S_t$. The first and second derivatives with respect to S_t are

$$f'(S_t) = 1/S_t, \tag{10.32}$$

$$f''(S_t) = -1/S_t^2, \tag{10.33}$$

hence the Itô formula (10.30) reads

$$\mathrm{d}\ln S_t = \frac{\mathrm{d}S_t}{S_t} - \frac{1}{2}\frac{\mathrm{Var}_t(\mathrm{d}S_t)}{S_t^2}. \tag{10.34}$$

As the second step we need to evaluate the conditional variance $\mathrm{Var}_t(\mathrm{d}S_t)$. For this purpose we will isolate $\mathrm{d}S_t$ on the left-hand side of the SDE (10.31):

$$\mathrm{d}S_t = \mu S_t \, \mathrm{d}t + \sigma S_t \, \mathrm{d}B_t. \tag{10.35}$$

The conditional variance is evaluated using standard rules for variance (see equation (6.7)). Substituting from (10.35)

$$\mathrm{Var}_t(\mathrm{d}S_t) = \mathrm{Var}_t(\mu S_t \, \mathrm{d}t + \sigma S_t \, \mathrm{d}B_t).$$

By assumption S_t is known at time t so $\mu S_t \, \mathrm{d}t$ acts as a constant and does not affect the variance:

$$\mathrm{Var}_t(\mathrm{d}S_t) = \mathrm{Var}_t(\sigma S_t \, \mathrm{d}B_t).$$

By the same token, σS_t is known at time t and can be taken in front of the variance:

$$\mathrm{Var}_t(\mathrm{d}S_t) = (\sigma S_t)^2 \underbrace{\mathrm{Var}_t(\mathrm{d}B_t)}_{\mathrm{d}t}.$$

Finally, the scaling properties of Brownian motion tell us that $\mathrm{Var}_t(\mathrm{d}B_t) = \mathrm{d}t$ and hence

$$\mathrm{Var}_t(\mathrm{d}S_t) = (\sigma S_t)^2 \, \mathrm{d}t. \tag{10.36}$$

With a little bit of practice one can go straight from (10.35) to (10.36) skipping the intermediate steps.

Substituting (10.35) and (10.36) into the Itô formula (10.34) we obtain

$$\mathrm{d}\ln S_t = (\mu - \tfrac{1}{2}\sigma^2) \, \mathrm{d}t + \sigma \, \mathrm{d}B_t.$$

In conclusion, if the stock price levels follow a geometric Brownian motion, then the logarithm of stock prices follows a Brownian motion with drift and vice versa. Specifically, the conditional distribution of log returns is normal,

$$\ln S_t - \ln S_0 \sim N((\mu - \tfrac{1}{2}\sigma^2)t, \sigma^2 t),$$

which means that returns are distributed lognormally.

10.5.2 Compounded Stochastic Interest Rate

Example 10.5. In continuous time the compounded return on bank deposits is given by

$$\beta_t = \exp\left(\int_0^t r_s \, \mathrm{d}s\right).$$

Find the SDE for β_t assuming that r_t is itself an Itô process.

Solution. We notice that β_t is a function of the Itô process X_t,

$$X_t = \int_0^t r_s \, \mathrm{d}s,$$

for which the SDE reads

$$dX_t = r_t \, dt. \tag{10.37}$$

The cumulative interest rate process X_t is *locally non-stochastic* because the dB_t part is missing in (10.37).

We can now re-express β_t as a function of X_t

$$\beta_t = e^{X_t}$$

and apply the Itô formula to $f(X_t) = e^{X_t}$. Since X_t is locally non-stochastic, the Itô calculus turns into standard calculus,

$$d\beta(t) = \underbrace{f'(X_t)}_{\beta_t} dX(t) + \tfrac{1}{2} f''(X_t) \underbrace{\mathrm{Var}_t(dX_t)}_{0}$$

$$= \beta_t r_t \, dt.$$

This result is frequently written in the form

$$\frac{d\beta_t}{\beta_t} = r_t \, dt,$$

where the left-hand side represents the rate of return on a locally safe bank account deposit.

10.6 Multivariate Itô Formula

The Itô formula changes marginally when we allow f to be a function of m Itô processes $X_{1t}, X_{2t}, \ldots, X_{mt}$ generated by m, possibly correlated, Brownian motions:

$$dX_{1t} = \mu_{1t} \, dt + \sigma_{1t} \, dB_{1t},$$
$$dX_{2t} = \mu_{2t} \, dt + \sigma_{2t} \, dB_{2t},$$
$$dX_{mt} = \mu_{mt} \, dt + \sigma_{mt} \, dB_{mt}.$$

The Itô formula then becomes

$$df(X_t) = \sum_{i=1}^{m} \frac{\partial f}{\partial X_{it}} \, dX_{it} + \frac{1}{2} \sum_{i=1,\, j=1}^{m} \frac{\partial^2 f}{\partial X_{it} \partial X_{jt}} \, \mathrm{Cov}_t(dX_{it}, dX_{jt}), \tag{10.38}$$

where

$$\mathrm{Cov}_t(dX_i, dX_j) = \sigma_{it} \sigma_{jt} \rho_{ijt} \, dt$$

with ρ_{ijt} being the assumed correlation between dB_{it} and dB_{jt}.

Often time appears as one of the state variables determining the value of f. If we set $X_{0t} = t$, then (10.38) becomes

$$df(t, X_t) = \frac{\partial f}{\partial t} \, dt + \sum_{i=1}^{m} \frac{\partial f}{\partial X_{it}} \, dX_{it} + \frac{1}{2} \sum_{i=1,\, j=1}^{m} \frac{\partial^2 f}{\partial X_{it} \partial X_{jt}} \, \mathrm{Cov}_t(dX_{it}, dX_{jt}),$$

$$\tag{10.39}$$

since $\mathrm{Cov}_t(dt, dX_{it}) = 0$. The following elementary properties of covariance are extremely useful in the application of the multivariate Itô formula.

Let X, Y be random variables and a_i, b_i constants:
- $\operatorname{Cov}(X, X) = \operatorname{Var}(X)$;
- $\operatorname{Cov}(X, Y) = \operatorname{Cov}(Y, X)$;
- $\operatorname{Cov}(a_1, Y) = 0$;
- $\operatorname{Cov}(a_1 + b_1 X, a_2 + b_2 Y) = b_1 b_2 \operatorname{Cov}(X, Y)$.

Specifically, in the context of the Itô formula let a_{it}, b_{it} be known at time t, then
- $\operatorname{Cov}_t(a_{1t}\, dt + b_{1t}\, dB_t, a_{2t}\, dt + b_{2t}\, dB_t) = b_{1t} b_{2t}\, dt$.

Two applications of the multivariate Itô formula are given below. Further applications appear in Sections 11.3 and 11.5.

10.6.1   Ornstein–Uhlenbeck Process

Example 10.6. Consider the Ornstein–Uhlenbeck process:

$$dX_t = (\alpha - \beta X_t)\, dt + \sigma\, dB_t. \tag{10.40}$$

Using the Itô formula show that the process X_t,

$$X_t = \frac{\alpha}{\beta} + \left(X_0 - \frac{\alpha}{\beta}\right) e^{-\beta t} + \sigma e^{-\beta t} \int_0^t e^{\beta s}\, dB_s, \tag{10.41}$$

satisfies the Ornstein–Uhlenbeck SDE (10.40).

Solution. Define a new Itô process Z_t,

$$Z_t = \int_0^t e^{\beta s}\, dB_s, \tag{10.42}$$

so that we have

$$X_t = \frac{\alpha}{\beta} + \left(X_0 - \frac{\alpha}{\beta}\right) e^{-\beta t} + \sigma e^{-\beta t} Z_t \tag{10.43}$$

and from (10.42)

$$dZ_t = e^{\beta t}\, dB_t. \tag{10.44}$$

To find the SDE for X apply the Itô formula to the right-hand side of (10.43) treating t and Z_t as state variables. Since the expression (10.43) is linear in Z_t and Z_t is the only random component in it, we will effectively be using standard calculus.

The required partial derivatives are

$$\frac{\partial f(t, Z_t)}{\partial t} = -\beta \left(X(0) - \frac{\alpha}{\beta}\right) e^{-\beta t} - \beta \sigma e^{-\beta t} Z_t$$

$$= \alpha - \beta X_t \text{ by virtue of (10.43)},$$

$$\frac{\partial f(t, Z_t)}{\partial Z_t} = \sigma e^{-\beta t}, \qquad \frac{\partial^2 f(t, Z_t)}{\partial Z_t^2} = 0,$$

and the Itô formula (10.39) gives

$$dX_t = (\alpha - \beta X_t)\, dt + \sigma e^{-\beta t}\, dZ_t$$

$$= (\alpha - \beta X_t)\, dt + \sigma\, dB_t,$$

which is what we wanted to demonstrate.

- The Ornstein–Uhlenbeck process is a Markov process.
- By virtue of (10.41) its increments are normally distributed.
- The discretely sampled Ornstein–Uhlenbeck process is equivalent to the discrete-time autoregressive process (see Exercise 10.9).
- The Ornstein–Uhlenbeck process is the simplest example of an affine process (see Chapter 7, p. 167) with non-IID increments.
- Among many applications it is used to model short rate in the Vašíček model of term structure of interest rates.

10.6.2 Discounted Price Process

Example 10.7. Find the SDE for the discounted stock price,

$$f(\beta_t, S_t) = S_t/\beta_t.$$

Solution. We have seen in Example 10.5 that the compounded bank account return β_t evolves according to

$$d\beta_t = r_t \beta_t \, dt,$$

which means that β is locally non-stochastic. This, and the fact that S_t/β_t is linear in S_t, means that we are effectively using standard calculus. Namely, if we write down the Itô formula for $f(\beta_t, S_t)$ symbolically,

$$df(\beta_t, S_t) = \frac{\partial f(\beta_t, S_t)}{\partial \beta_t} d\beta_t + \frac{\partial f(\beta_t, S_t)}{\partial S_t} dS_t$$

$$+ \frac{1}{2}\left(\frac{\partial^2 f(\beta_t, S_t)}{\partial \beta_t^2} \underbrace{\text{Var}_t(d\beta_t)}_{0} + 2 \frac{\partial^2 f(\beta_t, S_t)}{\partial \beta_t \partial S_t} \underbrace{\text{Cov}_t(d\beta_t, dS_t)}_{0} \right.$$

$$\left. + \frac{\partial^2 f(\beta_t, S_t)}{\partial S_t^2} \underbrace{\text{Var}_t(dS_t)}_{0} \right),$$

it is clear that all quadratic terms vanish. For the first-order terms the requisite partial derivatives are

$$\frac{\partial(S_t/\beta_t)}{\partial \beta_t} = -\frac{S_t}{\beta_t^2}, \qquad \frac{\partial(S_t/\beta_t)}{\partial S_t} = \frac{1}{\beta_t}.$$

The result is therefore

$$d\left(\frac{S_t}{\beta_t}\right) = -\frac{S_t}{\beta_t^2} r_t \beta_t \, dt + \frac{dS_t}{\beta_t},$$

$$\frac{d(S(t)/\beta(t))}{S(t)/\beta(t)} = \frac{dS_t}{S_t} - r_t \, dt. \tag{10.45}$$

The right-hand side of (10.45) is the continuous-time equivalent of one-period excess return. It is worth noting that to arrive at (10.45) one does not need to know the specific form of the SDE for S or r; the derivation works for *any* pair of Itô processes S and r. This is another reason to favour (10.30) over (10.28) and (10.29).

10.7 Itô Processes as Martingales

Much of continuous-time finance revolves around martingales; therefore, we need a simple criterion that can tell us whether a given Itô process is a martingale. The argument given here is heuristic[1]—a proper mathematical treatment would be too technical.

The first martingale proposition tells us that a discrete-time process is a martingale if and only if

$$0 = E_t[X_{t+1} - X_t] \quad \text{for all } t.$$

In continuous time this condition becomes

$$0 = E_t[X_{t+dt} - X_t] = E_t[dX_t]. \tag{10.46}$$

On the other hand, for an Itô process X and dt very small we have

$$dX_t = \mu_t \, dt + \sigma_t \, dB_t. \tag{10.47}$$

Combination of (10.47) with (10.46) gives

$$0 = E_t[dX_t] = \mu_t \, dt + \sigma_t E_t[dB_t] = \mu_t \, dt, \tag{10.48}$$

which means that X is a martingale if and only if $\mu_t = 0$ for all t.

The Itô process X is a martingale if and only if $E_t[dX_t] = 0$ for all t. If $dX_t = \mu_t \, dt + \sigma_t \, dB_t$, then X is a martingale if and only if $\mu_t = 0$ for all t (and σ_t meets certain technical conditions to make $E_0[|X_t|]$ finite).

Example 10.8. Find out whether the process $B_t^2 - t$ is a martingale.

Solution. Apply the Itô formula to $B_t^2 - t$:

$$d(B_t^2 - t) = \underbrace{2B_t \, dB_t - dt}_{\text{standard calculus}} + \underbrace{\tfrac{1}{2} 2 \, \text{Var}_t(dB_t)}_{\text{Itô correction}}$$

$$= 2B_t \, dB_t - dt + dt = 0 \, dt + 2B_t \, dB_t.$$

Since the drift is 0 we have shown that $B_t^2 - t$ is a martingale.

10.7.1 Characterization of Brownian Motion

Lévy gives the following simple characterization of Brownian motion. *An Itô process X_t is a Brownian motion if and only if both processes,*

$$X_t,$$

$$X_t^2 - t,$$

are martingales. This characterization is useful in the proof of the Girsanov theorem, which underpins continuous-time asset pricing.

---

[1] The main reason why the whole argument is heuristic is that the exact value of the increment dX_t is

$$dX_t = \int_t^{t+dt} \mu_s \, ds + \sigma_s \, dB_s$$

and we are taking for granted that (10.47) approximates it well in some sense.

10.8 Appendix: Proof of the Itô Formula

Suppose that we are given an Itô process X_t:

$$dX_t = \mu_t\, dt + \sigma_t\, dB_t. \tag{10.49}$$

The SDE for a new process $f(X_t)$ is given by the Itô formula:

$$df(X_t) = f'(X_t)\, dX_t + \tfrac{1}{2} f''(X_t)\sigma_t^2\, dt.$$

Proof. Here we will sketch the reasoning that leads to the Itô formula. These ideas require no more than a univariate Taylor expansion and the rules for calculating mean and variance. First let us use the Taylor expansion of the function $f(X)$ around a fixed point X up to second order:

$$df(X_t) = f'(X_t)\, dX_t + \tfrac{1}{2} f''(X_t)(dX_t)^2. \tag{10.50}$$

Let us now examine the quadratic term of the Taylor expansion (10.50). Recall that X_t, μ_t and σ_t are known at time t and that $dB_t \sim N(0, dt)$, implying

$$\left.\begin{aligned}
E_t[dB_t] = 0, \qquad & E_t[(dB_t)^2] = dt, \\
E_t[(dB_t)^3] = 0, \qquad & E_t[(dB_t)^4] = 3(dt)^2.
\end{aligned}\right\} \tag{10.51}$$

Let us examine the mean and the variance of the term $(dX_t)^2$. Substituting for dX_t from (10.49) and using standard properties of expectation we have

$$dX_t = \mu_t\, dt + \sigma_t\, dB_t,$$
$$E_t[(dX_t)^2] = \sigma_t^2\, dt + (\mu\, dt)^2,$$
$$\begin{aligned}
\mathrm{Var}_t((dX_t)^2) &= E_t[(dX_t)^4] - (E_t[(dX_t)^2])^2 \\
&= (\mu dt)^4 + 6(\mu\sigma)^2(dt)^3 + 3\sigma^4(dt)^2 - (\sigma_t^2\, dt + (\mu\, dt)^2)^2.
\end{aligned}$$

The only term of order dt is $\sigma_t^2\, dt$. Consequently, in the mean square limit we can write

$$(dX_t)^2 = \sigma_t^2\, dt = \mathrm{Var}_t(dX_t)$$

with precision $(dt)^2$. Substituting this result into the Taylor expansion (10.50) we obtain

$$\begin{aligned}
df(X_t) &= f'(X_t)\, dX_t + \tfrac{1}{2} f''(X_t)\sigma_t^2\, dt \\
&= f'(X_t)\, dX_t + \tfrac{1}{2} f''(X_t)\, \mathrm{Var}_t(dX_t),
\end{aligned}$$

which is the Itô formula. $\qquad\square$

10.9 Summary

- The material in this chapter is difficult to summarize because it is already quite condensed and pretty much everything is important. In these circumstances it is probably most productive to concentrate on the basics.
- Rule 1: Brownian increments over disjoint time intervals are uncorrelated, for example, $B_4 - B_0$ is uncorrelated with $B_{10} - B_4$.
- Rule 2: Brownian increments have mean zero.

- Rule 3: Brownian increments have a jointly normal distribution.
- Rule 4: The variance of a Brownian increment equals the length of the corresponding time interval, for example, $\text{Var}_0(B_{10} - B_4) = 10 - 4$.
- Rule 5: The scalar multiple of normal variable is again normal.
- Rule 6: Scaling of variances $\text{Var}(\mu + \sigma X) = \sigma^2 \text{Var}(X)$.
- Rule 7: The expectation of a sum equals the sum of expectations, always.
- Rule 8: The variance of a sum equals the sum of variances, if summands are uncorrelated.
- Rule 9: The sum of jointly normally distributed variables is again normally distributed.
- Rules 1–9 are key to simple stochastic integration, which is all one needs at this level. For example, to work out the distribution of $\int_0^T e^{\beta s}\, dB_s$ we realize that the shocks dB_s are normally distributed with mean 0 and variance ds (Rules 2 and 4). Then $e^{\beta s}\, dB_s \sim N(0, e^{2\beta s}\, ds)$ by Rules 5 and 6. Finally,

$$\int_0^T e^{\beta s}\, dB_s \sim N\left(0, \int_0^T e^{2\beta s}\, ds\right)$$

  by Rules 1, 7, 8 and 9.
- The multivariate Itô formula: think of a second-order Taylor expansion where all second-order terms containing dt are omitted and $dX_1\, dX_2$ is replaced with the conditional covariance,

$$df(t, X_{1t}, X_{2t}) = \frac{\partial f}{\partial t}\, dt + \frac{\partial f}{\partial X_{1t}}\, dX_{1t} + \frac{\partial f}{\partial X_{2t}}\, dX_{2t}$$

$$+ \frac{1}{2} \sum_{i=1,\, j=1}^{2} \frac{\partial^2 f}{\partial X_{it}\, \partial X_{jt}}\, \text{Cov}_t(dX_{it}, dX_{jt}).$$

  The rules for manipulating covariances are derived in Appendix B and appear in Section 10.6.
- The continuous-time analogy of the first martingale proposition goes as follows. Let B^P be a Brownian motion under measure P. The Itô process X with SDE

$$dX_t = \mu_t\, dt + \sigma_t\, dB_t^P$$

  is a martingale under measure P if and only if $\mu_t = 0$ for all t (and $E_0[|X_t|]$ is finite).

10.10   Notes

The technicalities behind Itô integrals and stochastic calculus can be offputting. Øksendahl (1998) is a rigorous yet accessible introduction to the mathematical aspects of Itô processes and Brownian motion. Shreve (2004) is particularly friendly to students. Another good reference with finance applications is Hunt and Kennedy (2000). The Markov chain approximation method is explained very carefully in Kushner and Dupuis (2001). Neftci (1996) gives a version of the Itô formula with Poisson jumps. de Finetti (1974b) has an accessible introduction to Lévy processes.

10.11   Exercises

Exercise 10.1. Prove (10.3)–(10.5) by using the law of iterated expectations and the law of conditional constant.

Exercise 10.2. Generate 100 steps of the random walk with time step 1 in a spreadsheet.

In the following questions B is a standard Brownian motion.

Exercise 10.3. Calculate $E_s[X_t]$ for $s < t$ and decide whether the process X is a *martingale*:

(a) $X_t = t B_t$,
(b) $X_t = -B_t$,
(c) $X_t = B_t^2 - t$,
(d) $X_t = B_t^3 - t B_t$.

Exercise 10.4 (stochastic integration). Find the conditional distribution of X_t given the information at time s. In each case decide whether the process X is *Markov*:

(a) $dX_t = 3\,dt + 7\,dB_t$,
(b) $dX_t = 2t\,dt - t\,dB_t$,
(c) $dX_t = 0.15X_t\,dt + 0.2X_t\,dB_t$.
    (Hint: use the Itô formula to find the SDE for $\ln X_t$ first.)

Exercise 10.5 (Itô formula). Fill in the right-hand side:

(a) $d(B_t^2 - t) =$

(b) $d(B_t^3 - t B_t) =$

(c) $de^{B_t} =$

Exercise 10.6 (investment evaluation). The prices of two stocks follow a geometric Brownian motion,

$$dS_1(t) = 0.1S_1(t)\,dt + 0.2S_1(t)\,dB_1(t),$$
$$dS_2(t) = 0.15S_2(t)\,dt + 0.4S_2(t)\,dB_2(t),$$
$$S_1(0) = S_2(0) = 1,$$

where $B_1(t)$ and $B_2(t)$ are correlated Brownian motions with $\rho(dB_1(t), dB_2(t)) = 0.6$.

(a) Using the Itô formula find the SDEs for the increments $d\ln S_1(t)$, $d\ln S_2(t)$.
(b) Using your result in part (a), write $\ln S_1(8)$ and $\ln S_2(10)$ as Itô integrals.
(c) Find the mean and variance of $\ln S_1(8)$ as seen at time $t = 0$.
(d) Describe the distribution of $\ln S_1(8) - \ln S_2(10) = \ln S_1(8)/S_2(10)$ as seen at time $t = 0$.
(e) Find the *a priori* probability (as seen at time $t = 0$) for the event that the price of the first stock at time 8 is *at least* twice as large as the price of the second stock at time 10.

(f) Thinking of the second stock as a benchmark, find the level of relative performance $R_{1\%}$ such that $S_1(8)/S_1(0)$ underperforms $R_{1\%}S_2(10)/S_2(0)$ in only 1% of cases.

Exercise 10.7 (solution to the Ornstein–Uhlenbeck SDE). For the Ornstein–Uhlenbeck process X with SDE,

$$dX_t = (\alpha - \beta X_t)\, dt + \sigma\, dB_t, \tag{10.52}$$

find

$$d(e^{\beta t} X_t) =$$

Integrate both sides from 0 to T to find an explicit expression for X_T.

Exercise 10.8 (conditional distribution of the Ornstein–Uhlenbeck process). The risk-free interest rate r_t in the Vašíček model follows the Ornstein–Uhlenbeck process. It is known that r_t can be expressed as a stochastic integral,

$$r_t = 0.03 + (r_0 - 0.03)e^{-0.8t} + 0.002e^{-0.8t} \int_0^t e^{0.8s}\, dB_s,$$

where B is a Brownian motion. Find the distribution of r_t as of time 0. Justify your answer.

Exercise 10.9 (discrete sampling of mean reverting process). Suppose we observe the Ornstein–Uhlenbeck process in equation (10.52) at annual frequency. If we write

$$X_{t+1} = \mu + \rho X_t + \tilde{\sigma}\varepsilon_{t+1}, \tag{10.53}$$

where $\varepsilon_1, \varepsilon_2, \varepsilon_3, \ldots$ are independent standard normal variables such that ε_t is known at time t but not before, what values of μ, ρ, $\tilde{\sigma}$ correspond to α, β, ρ in equation (10.52)? To find out, you will need to compute the conditional distribution of X_{t+1} given X_t implied by (10.52) and compare it with the conditional distribution of X_{t+1} given X_t implied by (10.53):

$$\mu =$$
$$\rho =$$
$$\tilde{\sigma} =$$

Exercise 10.10 (evaluating mean reversion). Evaluate the expectation of the future value of an Ornstein–Uhlenbeck process $E_0[X_t]$ with X_t given in (10.41), using the arguments of Section 10.7.

11

Continuous-Time Finance

In the first part of this chapter we will apply the idea of risk-neutral pricing to the continuous-time model of security prices and rederive the Black–Scholes formula. The second part constructs the change of measure in continuous time and uses it to evaluate dynamic optimal investment in the Black–Scholes model. The third part discusses risk-neutral pricing with several risky securities. The fourth shows how to construct the no-arbitrage partial differential equation from the martingale properties of discounted asset prices. The final part reviews the numerical methods used in asset pricing.

11.1 Summary of Useful Results

11.1.1 The Itô Process as a Martingale

Suppose B^P is a Brownian motion under measure P and that X_t is an Itô process,

$$dX_t = \mu_t \, dt + \sigma_t \, dB_t^P, \qquad (11.1)$$

where the drift μ_t and volatility σ_t are known at time t (they are adapted processes). The same fact is equivalently expressed in integral form as

$$X_t = X_0 + \int_0^t \mu_s \, ds + \int_0^t \sigma_s \, dB_s^P.$$

The process $\{X_t\}_{t \in [0,T]}$ is a **martingale** under measure P if and only if

$$E_t^P[dX_t] = 0$$

for all t; in particular, in conjunction with (11.1) its drift μ_t is zero for all $t \in [0, T]$.

11.1.2 Itô Formula Results

1. If X_t is a geometric Brownian motion with deterministic coefficients μ_t and σ_t,

$$\frac{dX_t}{X_t} = \mu_t \, dt + \sigma_t \, dB_t, \qquad (11.2)$$

then $\ln X_t$ is a Brownian motion with deterministic drift and volatility,

$$d \ln X_t = (\mu_t - \tfrac{1}{2}\sigma_t^2) \, dt + \sigma_t \, dB_t. \qquad (11.3)$$

2. If X_t is as above and

$$\beta_t = \exp\left(\int_0^t r_s \, ds\right), \qquad (11.4)$$

then

$$d\left(\frac{X_t}{\beta_t}\right) = (\mu_t - r_t)\frac{X_t}{\beta_t}\,dt + \sigma_t\frac{X_t}{\beta_t}\,dB_t. \tag{11.5}$$

11.1.3   Expectation of Truncated Lognormal Variable

We derive in Section B.10.2 that for a normally distributed random variable X,

$$X \sim N(m, s^2), \tag{11.6}$$

we have

$$\mathrm{E}[\max(e^X - K, 0)] = \exp(m + \tfrac{1}{2}s^2)\Phi\left(\frac{m + s^2 - \ln K}{s}\right) - K\Phi\left(\frac{m - \ln K}{s}\right), \tag{11.7}$$

where Φ is the cumulative standard normal distribution.

11.2   Risk-Neutral Pricing

In this section we will rederive the Black–Scholes option price formula using the newly acquired Itô calculus. The whole exercise shows how much easier the calculations are in continuous time (once we know what we are doing) compared with the calculation of the normal limit in Chapter 6. The main features of risk-neutral pricing are reiterated in another example, where we price a log contract instead of an option.

11.2.1   The Black–Scholes Formula Revisited

Consider a model with independent and identically distributed log returns,

$$d\ln S_t = \tilde{\mu}\,dt + \sigma\,dB_t^P, \tag{11.8}$$

where B^P is a Brownian motion under the objective probability. Assume that the risk-free rate r is constant. We will now describe how the calculations of Chapter 6 can be captured using Itô calculus.

1. To obtain price levels from (11.8) apply the Itô formula to $e^{\ln S_t}$, or simply use the result (11.2) and (11.3) in reverse:

$$\frac{dS_t}{S_t} = \underbrace{(\tilde{\mu} + \tfrac{1}{2}\sigma^2)}_{\text{denote by }\mu}\,dt + \sigma\,dB_t^P. \tag{11.9}$$

2. From the risk-neutral pricing we know that

$$\mathrm{E}_t^Q\left[\frac{dS_t}{S_t}\right] = r\,dt, \tag{11.10}$$

we will therefore decompose the stock return (11.9) as follows:

$$\frac{dS_t}{S_t} = r\,dt + \sigma\underbrace{\left(\frac{\mu - r}{\sigma}\,dt + dB_t^P\right)}_{dB_t^Q}. \tag{11.11}$$

3. Define a new Itô process B^Q:

$$dB_t^Q = \frac{\mu - r}{\sigma} dt + dB_t^P. \tag{11.12}$$

By virtue of (11.10) and (11.11) the new process is a martingale under measure Q.

4. It turns out that B^Q is not only a martingale under Q but in fact it is a Brownian motion under Q, that is, $\text{Var}_t^Q(dB_t^Q) = dt$. This is one of the consequences of the **Girsanov theorem**, which is discussed in more detail in Section 11.3.

5. To sum up, in $dS_t/S_t = \mu\, dt + \sigma\, dB_t^P$ one can mechanically replace μ with r and dB^P with dB^Q:

$$\frac{dS_t}{S_t} = \mu\, dt + \sigma\, dB_t^P = r\, dt + \sigma\, dB_t^Q. \tag{11.13}$$

Crucially, B^Q is a Brownian motion under the risk-neutral measure. In short, when asset prices are Itô processes, changing measure only affects the conditional mean of asset returns but not their conditional variance. We have realized this already in equations (6.27) and (6.28).

6. Find the distribution of $\ln S_T$ under measure Q. To this end we will apply the Itô formula result (11.2) and (11.3) to equation (11.13) and integrate

$$d \ln S_t = (r - \tfrac{1}{2}\sigma^2)\, dt + \sigma\, dB_t^Q, \tag{11.14}$$

$$\ln S_T = \ln S_t + \int_t^T (r - \tfrac{1}{2}\sigma^2)\, ds + \int_t^T \sigma\, dB_s^Q,$$

$$\ln S_T \mid \mathcal{F}_t \overset{Q}{\sim} N(\ln S_t + (r - \tfrac{1}{2}\sigma^2)(T - t), \sigma^2(T - t)). \tag{11.15}$$

Again, we have seen this result in equation (6.30).

7. The discounted price process of *all* traded assets without dividends is a martingale under Q, specifically for the option we have

$$\frac{C_t}{\beta_t} = E_t^Q\left[\frac{C_T}{\beta_T}\right]. \tag{11.16}$$

Bearing in mind that the terminal option pay-off is $C_T = \max(S_T - K, 0)$ we can use the martingale condition (11.16) to express the current option price as a risk-neutral expectation:

$$C_t = \beta_t E_t^Q\left[\frac{\max(S_T - K, 0)}{\beta_T}\right].$$

In our case the safe rate is deterministic and we can take the discount factor in front of the expectation:

$$C_t = e^{-r(T-t)} E_t^Q[\max(S_T - K, 0)]. \tag{11.17}$$

Apply the formulae (11.6) and (11.7) to (11.15) and (11.17) with $X = \ln S_T$,

$$m = \ln S_t + (r - \tfrac{1}{2}\sigma^2)(T - t),$$
$$s^2 = \sigma^2(T - t).$$

The result is the famous Black–Scholes formula:

$$C_t = S_t \Phi \left(\frac{\ln(S_t/K) + (r + \frac{1}{2}\sigma^2)(T - t)}{\sigma\sqrt{T - t}} \right)$$
$$- K e^{-r(T-t)} \left(\frac{\ln(S_0/K) + (r - \frac{1}{2}\sigma^2)(T - t)}{\sigma\sqrt{T - t}} \right). \tag{11.18}$$

8. The same procedure works with the deterministic time-dependent safe rate and stock return volatility. If we denote by r_{AV}, σ_{AV}^2 the *average* risk-free return and *average* variance of log returns over period $[t, T]$,

$$r_{AV} = \frac{1}{T - t} \int_t^T r_s \, ds,$$

$$\sigma_{AV}^2 = \frac{1}{T - t} \int_t^T \sigma_s^2 \, ds,$$

then it is enough to simply replace r and σ in (11.18) with r_{AV} and σ_{AV}.

11.2.2 Another Example: Log Contract Pricing

Example 11.1. Suppose we have a stock with no dividends and IID log returns:

$$\frac{dS_t}{S_t} = \mu \, dt + \sigma \, dB_t^P.$$

Find the no-arbitrage price of a log contract, which is a security that pays $\ln S_T$ at maturity T.

Solution. We can start straight from step 5. From the Girsanov theorem,

$$\frac{dS_t}{S_t} = r \, dt + \sigma \, dB_t^Q,$$

where B^Q is a Brownian motion under risk-neutral measure. By the Itô formula (11.2) and (11.3), $\ln S$ is a Brownian motion with drift

$$d \ln S_t = (r - \tfrac{1}{2}\sigma^2) \, dt + \sigma \, dB_t^Q$$

and after integration

$$\ln S_T \mid \mathcal{F}_t \overset{Q}{\sim} N(\ln S_t + (r - \tfrac{1}{2}\sigma^2)(T - t), \sigma^2(T - t)). \tag{11.19}$$

Denote by L_t the log contract price, then from the risk-neutral pricing formula,

$$L_t = e^{-r(T-t)} E_t^Q[\ln S_T].$$

By virtue of (11.19),

$$E_t^Q[\ln S_T] = \ln S_t + (r - \tfrac{1}{2}\sigma^2)(T - t)$$

and consequently

$$L_t = e^{-r(T-t)}(\ln S_t + (r - \tfrac{1}{2}\sigma^2)(T - t)).$$

11.2.3 Another Example: Pricing in the Presence of Dividends

Example 11.2. Assume as before that the increments in log stock price are IID,

$$\frac{dS_t}{S_t} = \mu \, dt + \sigma \, dB_t^P,$$

but suppose in addition that the stock pays a dividend $\delta S_t \, dt$. Price a call option in this model.

Solution. The underlying principle of risk-neutral pricing is

$$E_t^Q[\text{risky rate of return}] = \text{risk-free rate of return}.$$

Without dividends the risky rate of return over time dt is exactly

$$\frac{S_{t+dt}}{S_t} - 1 = \frac{dS_t}{S_t}.$$

With dividends being paid at a rate δ the risky rate of return is

$$\underbrace{\frac{\overbrace{S_{t+dt} + \delta S_t \, dt}^{\text{pay-off tomorrow}}}{\underbrace{S_t}_{\text{price today}}} - 1 = \frac{dS_t}{S_t} + \delta \, dt.}$$

The Girsanov theorem tells us that the change of measure does not affect the volatility of risky returns,

$$\text{Var}_t^Q\left(\frac{dS_t}{S_t} + \delta \, dt\right) = \text{Var}_t^P\left(\frac{dS_t}{S_t} + \underbrace{\delta \, dt}_{\text{const.}}\right) = \text{Var}_t^P\left(\frac{dS_t}{S_t}\right) = \sigma^2 \, dt,$$

and therefore the risk-neutral SDE must read

$$\underbrace{\frac{dS_t}{S_t} + \delta \, dt}_{\substack{\text{risky rate} \\ \text{of return}}} = \underbrace{r \, dt}_{\substack{\text{risk-free rate} \\ \text{of return}}} + \underbrace{\sigma \, dB_t^Q}_{\substack{\text{random part} \\ \text{mean 0, variance } \sigma^2 \, dt}},$$

where B^Q is a Brownian motion under the risk-neutral measure.

From here it is easy to figure out the risk-neutral distribution of log returns (the derivation is the same as in points 5 and 6 of the Black–Scholes example):

$$\ln S_T \mid \mathcal{F}_t \overset{Q}{\sim} N(\ln S_t + (r - \delta - \tfrac{1}{2}\sigma^2)(T - t), \sigma^2(T - t)).$$

One then repeats point 7 of the Black–Scholes derivation with the modified distribution of log returns.

11.3 The Girsanov Theorem

In step 3 of the risk-neutral pricing we defined a new Itô process B^Q,

$$dB_t^Q = \frac{\mu - r}{\sigma} \, dt + dB_t^P, \tag{11.20}$$

which we know is a martingale under Q. The **Girsanov theorem** claims the following.

1. The unique change of measure $m_T = dQ/dP$ that turns B^Q into a martingale is given by

$$\ln m_T = \int_0^T -\frac{1}{2}\left(\frac{\mu - r}{\sigma}\right)^2 dt - \int_0^T \left(\frac{\mu - r}{\sigma}\right) dB_t^P. \qquad (11.21)$$

2. $f(t, B_t^Q) = (B_t^Q)^2 - t$ is a martingale under Q, which implies that B^Q is a Brownian motion under Q. More intuitively, one can write

$$\text{Var}_t^P(dB_t^Q) = \text{Var}_t^Q(dB_t^Q) = dt;$$

change of measure does not affect volatility.

Proof of 1. We will construct the required change of measure m_T, taking for granted that m_T can be written as an Itô integral with respect to B^P (this is in fact a consequence of the martingale representation theorem on p. 226):

$$m_T = \underbrace{\text{E}_0^P[m_T]}_{1} + \int_0^T \lambda_s \, dB_s^P.$$

For the next two sentences we need knowledge from Chapter 9. Let $m_t = \text{E}_t^P[m_T]$ be the density process of the change of measure. Since $\text{E}_s^P[dB_s] = 0$ by LawIE and LawCC we have

$$m_t = \text{E}_t^P[m_T] = 1 + \int_0^t \lambda_s \, dB_s^P. \qquad (11.22)$$

Equation (11.22) in differential form reads

$$dm_t = \lambda_t \, dB_t^P. \qquad (11.23)$$

By the third martingale proposition (p. 203), B_t^Q is a martingale under Q if and only if $\{m_t B_t^Q\}$ is a martingale under measure P. This condition will in turn help us to identify the density process m_t.

We will find out whether the process $m B^Q$ is a martingale by looking at its drift. Applying the multivariate Itô formula to $f(m_t, B_t^Q) = m_t B_t^Q$ we obtain

$$d(m_t B_t^Q) = m_t \, dB_t^Q + B_t^Q \, dm_t$$

$$+ \frac{1}{2}\left(\underbrace{\frac{\partial^2 f}{\partial m_t^2} \text{Var}_t^P(dm_t)}_{0} + 2 \underbrace{\frac{\partial^2 f}{\partial m_t \partial B_t^Q} \text{Cov}_t^P(dm_t, dB_t^Q)}_{1}\right.$$

$$\left. + \underbrace{\frac{\partial^2 f}{\partial(B_t^Q)^2} \text{Var}_t^P(dB_t^Q)}_{0}\right). \qquad (11.24)$$

Substituting from (11.20) and (11.23) we have

$$\text{Cov}_t^P(dm_t, dB_t^Q) = \text{Cov}_t^P\left(\lambda_t \, dB_t^P, \frac{\mu - r}{\sigma} \, dt + dB_t^P\right)$$

$$= \lambda_t \, \text{Cov}_t^P(dB_t^P, dB_t^P) = \lambda_t \, dt,$$

and plugging this result back into (11.24) we find

$$d(m_t B_t^Q) = \left(m_t \frac{\mu - r}{\sigma} + \lambda_t\right) dt + (m_t + B_t^Q \lambda_t) \, dB_t^P,$$

$$E_t^P[d(m_t B_t^Q)] = \left(m_t \frac{\mu - r}{\sigma} + \lambda_t\right) dt.$$

By the first martingale proposition, the process $m_t B_t^Q$ is a martingale under P if and only if $E_t^P[d(m_t B_t^Q)] = 0$, which requires

$$m_t \frac{\mu - r}{\sigma} + \lambda_t = 0,$$

$$\lambda_t = -\frac{\mu - r}{\sigma} m_t. \tag{11.25}$$

Now substitute λ_t from (11.25) into the SDE for the density process (11.23),

$$dm_t = -\frac{\mu - r}{\sigma} m_t \, dB_t^P. \tag{11.26}$$

We can see from (11.26) that in the Black–Scholes model the density process is a geometric Brownian motion and that it is unique. It is now easy to find the SDE for $\ln m_t$ from (11.2) and (11.3)

$$d \ln m_t = -\frac{1}{2}\left(\frac{\mu - r}{\sigma}\right)^2 dt - \frac{\mu - r}{\sigma} \, dB_t^P,$$

and after integration

$$\ln m_T = \underbrace{\ln m_0}_{0} - \frac{1}{2}\left(\frac{\mu - r}{\sigma}\right)^2 T - \frac{\mu - r}{\sigma}(B_T - B_0). \tag{11.27}$$

□

Proof of 2. From the Itô formula we have

$$df(t, B_t^Q) = 2B_t^Q \, dB_t^Q - dt + \frac{1}{2} 2 \underbrace{\text{Var}_t^P(dB_t^Q)}_{dt}$$

$$= 2B_t^Q \, dB_t^Q.$$

Since B_t^Q is a martingale under Q we have

$$E_t^Q[df(t, B_t^Q)] = 2B_t^Q E_t^Q[dB_t^Q] = 0,$$

which together with the first martingale proposition implies that

$$f(t, B_t^Q) = (B_t^Q)^2 - t$$

is itself a martingale under Q. Hence both processes B_t^Q and $(B_t^Q)^2 - t$ are martingales under Q, which, by virtue of Section 10.7.1, implies that B^Q is a Brownian motion under Q. □

11.3.1 Application of Girsanov Theorem: Dynamic Optimal Investment

In this section we will demonstrate how the change of measure (11.27) can be used to evaluate the investment potential of dynamic trading. Recall that the investment potential is the percentage increase in certainty equivalent resulting from investing in the risky asset for an agent with unit local risk aversion. When the local risk aversion is more than 1 the percentage gain is proportionally lower.

From (9.70) the expression for the investment potential is

$$\text{IP}_\gamma = \gamma \left(\text{E}_0^P \left[\frac{m_T}{\beta_T} \right] \left(\text{E}_0^P \left[\left(\frac{m_T}{\beta_T} \right)^{1-1/\gamma} \right] \right)^{\gamma/(1-\gamma)} - 1 \right). \qquad (11.28)$$

This expression can be simplified since in the Black–Scholes model β_T is nonrandom. Bearing in mind that $\text{E}_0^P[m_T] = 1$, (11.28) becomes

$$\text{IP}_\gamma = \gamma ((\text{E}_0^P[m_T^{1-1/\gamma}])^{\gamma/(1-\gamma)} - 1). \qquad (11.29)$$

It now remains to evaluate the expectation $\text{E}_0^P[m_T^{1-1/\gamma}]$ inside the round bracket.

Facts. Let $X \sim N(\tilde{\mu}, \tilde{\sigma}^2)$. Then

$$g(\lambda) = \text{E}[e^{\lambda X}] = e^{\lambda \tilde{\mu} + \lambda^2 \tilde{\sigma}^2/2}. \qquad (11.30)$$

As an aside, the function $g(\lambda)$ is called the **moment-generating function** of the random variable X.

We will use (11.30) with $\lambda = 1 - 1/\gamma$ and $X = \ln m_T$ under measure P. From (11.27) we have

$$\tilde{\mu} = \text{E}_0[\ln m_T] = -\frac{1}{2} \left(\frac{\mu - r}{\sigma} \right)^2 T,$$

$$\tilde{\sigma}^2 = \text{Var}_0[\ln m_T] = \left(\frac{\mu - r}{\sigma} \right)^2 T.$$

Formula (11.30) implies

$$\text{E}_0^P[m_T^{1-1/\gamma}] = \text{E}_0^P[e^{(1-1/\gamma)\ln m_T}]$$

$$= \exp\left(\frac{1}{2} \left(1 - \frac{1}{\gamma} \right) \left(\frac{\mu - r}{\sigma} \right)^2 T \left(1 - \frac{1}{\gamma} - 1 \right) \right)$$

$$= \exp\left(-\frac{1}{2\gamma} \left(1 - \frac{1}{\gamma} \right) \left(\frac{\mu - r}{\sigma} \right)^2 T \right). \qquad (11.31)$$

Finally, substitute (11.31) back into the expression for the investment potential

Table 11.1. Investment potential of dynamic trading strategies.

γ	-1	1	3	$+\infty$
IP_γ	11.8%	13.3%	12.8%	12.5%

(11.29) and simplify:

$$
\begin{aligned}
\mathrm{IP}_\gamma &= \gamma \left(\left(\exp\left(-\frac{1}{2\gamma}\left(1 - \frac{1}{\gamma}\right)\left(\frac{\mu - r}{\sigma}\right)^2 T \right) \right)^{\gamma/(1-\gamma)} - 1 \right) \\
&= \gamma \left(\exp\left(\frac{1}{2\gamma}\left(\frac{\mu - r}{\sigma}\right)^2 T \right) - 1 \right).
\end{aligned}
\tag{11.32}
$$

Assuming an annual Sharpe ratio of excess log return of 0.5 and a time horizon of one year, which implies $((\mu - r)/\sigma)^2 T = 0.25$, we have the numerical values given in Table 11.1. In particular, Exercise 11.10 shows that

$$
\mathrm{IP}_{+\infty} = \frac{1}{2}\left(\frac{\mu - r}{\sigma}\right)^2 T.
$$

11.4 Risk-Neutral Pricing and Absence of Arbitrage

The analysis in Section 11.2.1 shows that the crucial step of risk-neutral pricing is not the change of measure (step 3), which is in fact guaranteed by the Girsanov theorem, but the ability to write

$$
\mu_t \, dt + \sigma_t \, dB_t^P
$$

as

$$
r_t \, dt + \sigma_t \left(\frac{\mu_t - r_t}{\sigma_t} \, dt + dB_t^P \right),
$$

that is, step 2 is critical for the functioning of the whole risk-neutral method described above.

Can the second step fail? The answer is, only when there is arbitrage. Note that the **market price of risk** η_t,

$$
\eta_t = \frac{\mu_t - r_t}{\sigma_t},
\tag{11.33}
$$

is not defined when $\sigma_t = 0$. But if $\sigma_t = 0$, then the stock return is riskless at time t and so the return on holding the stock from t to $t + dt$ has to be equal to the risk-free rate $r_t \, dt$, otherwise arbitrage opportunities arise. Thus at any moment when $\sigma_t = 0$ one must have $\mu_t = r_t$ and η_t can then be arbitrary, otherwise we set

$$
\eta_t = \frac{\mu_t - r_t}{\sigma_t}
$$

and the relationship

$$
\frac{dS_t}{S_t} = r_t \, dt + \sigma_t (\eta_t \, dt + dB_t)
$$

will still hold if there is no arbitrage.

The situation is very similar when we have several correlated stocks. Suppose the covariance matrix of three stock returns over time dt is

$$\Sigma \, dt = \begin{bmatrix} 0.09 & 0.03 & 0.072 \\ 0.03 & 0.0676 & 0.0408 \\ 0.072 & 0.0408 & 0.0625 \end{bmatrix} dt$$

and the mean rates of return are

$$E\left[\frac{dS_1}{S_1}\right] = 0.1 \, dt, \qquad E\left[\frac{dS_2}{S_2}\right] = 0.08 \, dt, \qquad E\left[\frac{dS_3}{S_3}\right] = 0.12 \, dt$$

with the safe rate of return $r = 0.02$.

Before we get to the heart of the argument, it is necessary to decompose the stock returns into linearly independent components. By far the best way to achieve this is to make the components uncorrelated. The decomposition process is not complicated, but it requires more than one step and it has interesting ramifications; we shall therefore relegate it to Section 11.9. Mathematically, we are performing a **Cholesky factorization** of the covariance matrix Σ.

Having decomposed the stock returns we obtain

$$\frac{dS_1}{S_1} = 0.11 \, dt + 0.3 \, dB_1, \tag{11.34}$$

$$\frac{dS_2}{S_2} = 0.08 \, dt + 0.1 \, dB_1 + 0.24 \, dB_2, \tag{11.35}$$

$$\frac{dS_3}{S_3} = 0.12 \, dt + 0.07 \, dB_1 + 0.24 \, dB_2, \tag{11.36}$$

where the Brownian increments dB_1 and dB_2 are uncorrelated. *The number of Brownian motions on the right-hand side of (11.34)–(11.36) signifies the number of linearly independent stock returns.*

In matrix notation the stock returns read

$$\frac{dS}{S} = \mu \, dt + \sigma \, dB, \tag{11.37}$$

with

$$\mu = \begin{bmatrix} 0.14 \\ 0.09 \\ 0.12 \end{bmatrix}, \qquad \sigma = \begin{bmatrix} 0.3 & 0 \\ 0.1 & 0.24 \\ 0.24 & 0.07 \end{bmatrix}.$$

In analogy with (11.33) we will try to solve the system $\mu - r = \sigma \eta$,

$$\begin{bmatrix} 0.14 - 0.02 \\ 0.09 - 0.02 \\ 0.12 - 0.02 \end{bmatrix} = \begin{bmatrix} 0.3 & 0 \\ 0.24 & 0.1 \\ 0.24 & 0.07 \end{bmatrix} \begin{bmatrix} \eta_1 \\ \eta_2 \end{bmatrix}.$$

The first equation gives

$$\eta_1 = 0.4,$$

and the second equation then implies

$$\eta_2 = -0.26.$$

It is easy to verify that the third equation is not satisfied because

$$0.1 \neq 0.24 \times 0.4 - 0.07 \times 0.26 = 0.0778.$$

Clearly, $\mu - r = \sigma\eta$ cannot be solved. We claim that this happens because there is *arbitrage* among the three stock returns. Let us now construct the arbitrage trading strategy. The third asset is redundant relative to the first two and to replicate the random part of the third return we will create a portfolio of the first two assets that has the same factor loadings as the third asset. In other words we are looking for portfolio weights α_1, α_2 such that

$$\underbrace{\begin{bmatrix} 0.3\,dB_1 \\ 0\,dB_2 \end{bmatrix}}_{\text{1st asset}} \underbrace{\begin{bmatrix} 0.24\,dB_1 \\ 0.1\,dB_2 \end{bmatrix}}_{\text{2nd asset}} \begin{bmatrix} \alpha_1 \\ \alpha_2 \end{bmatrix} = \underbrace{\begin{bmatrix} 0.24\,dB_1 \\ 0.07\,dB_2 \end{bmatrix}}_{\text{3rd asset}},$$

which gives

$$\alpha_1 = 0.24, \qquad \alpha_2 = 0.7.$$

The randomness of the portfolio which invests 24 pence in the first stock and 70 pence in the second stock is the same as the randomness of the portfolio that invests 100 pence in the third stock. *A fortiori* the portfolio

$$\alpha_1 = -0.24, \qquad \alpha_2 = -0.7, \qquad \alpha_3 = 1 \tag{11.38}$$

is completely riskless. This portfolio costs $-0.24 - 0.7 + 1 = 0.06$; borrowing 6 pence from the bank would cost us $0.06 \times 0.02\,dt$ in interest payments. On the other hand, the capital gain on the portfolio (11.38) is

$$dG = \alpha_1 \frac{dS_1}{S_1} + \alpha_2 \frac{dS_2}{S_2} + \alpha_3 \frac{dS_3}{S_3}$$
$$= -0.24 \times 0.14\,dt - 0.7 \times 0.09\,dt + 1 \times 0.12\,dt = 0.0234\,dt.$$

Consequently, the portfolio (11.38) turns in a risk-free profit of

$$(0.0234 - 0.0012)\,dt = 0.0222\,dt,$$

equivalent to 2.22 pence per unit of time.

Conversely, if the market price of risk equation

$$\mu - r = \sigma\eta \tag{11.39}$$

has a solution (which is unique by construction of σ), then there cannot be arbitrage among the stock returns. To show this let us consider a portfolio α and its capital gain $\alpha^* \, dS/S$. Substituting from (11.37) we have

$$dG = \alpha^* \frac{dS}{S} = \alpha^* \mu \, dt + \alpha^* \sigma \, dB.$$

Can it happen that the capital gain dG is riskless? Yes, but only when

$$\alpha^* \sigma = 0. \tag{11.40}$$

If $\alpha^* \sigma = 0$ and there is no arbitrage, it must be true that the risk-free capital gain $\alpha^* \mu \, dt$ is the same as if we invested the same amount of money into the risk-free bank account:

$$(\alpha_1 \mu_1 + \cdots + \alpha_m \mu_m)\,dt = (\alpha_1 + \cdots + \alpha_m) r \, dt. \tag{11.41}$$

However, equation (11.39) multiplied by α^* from the left tells us that

$$\alpha^*(\mu - r) = \alpha^* \sigma \eta,$$

and if $\alpha^* \sigma = 0$, then we obtain $\alpha^*(\mu - r) = 0$ as required by the no-arbitrage condition (11.41).

Risk-neutral pricing with several risky assets

- Decompose m asset returns using the smallest necessary number of uncorrelated components $dB_1^P, \ldots, dB_n^P$,

$$\frac{dS_t}{S_t} = \mu \, dt + \sigma \, dB_t^P.$$

In the absence of arbitrage there is a unique market price of risk vector η corresponding to shocks $dB_1, \ldots, dB_n$, satisfying

$$\mu - r = \sigma \eta.$$

- Now we can rewrite the asset returns in terms of n risk-neutral Brownian motions dB^Q,

$$\frac{dS_t}{S_t} = \mu \, dt + \sigma \, dB_t^P = r \, dt + \underbrace{(\mu - r)}_{\sigma\eta} \, dt + \sigma \, dB_t^P \qquad (11.42)$$

$$= r \, dt + \sigma \, \underbrace{(\eta \, dt + dB_t^P)}_{dB_t^Q}$$

and apply the Girsanov theorem to

$$dB_t^Q = \eta \, dt + dB_t^P.$$

- The multidimensional Girsanov theorem reads

$$\frac{dQ}{dP} = m_T = \exp\left(-\frac{1}{2}\int_0^T \eta^* \eta \, dt - \int_0^T \eta^* \, dB_t^P\right).$$

If Brownian motions B^P are uncorrelated under P, then the Brownian motions B^Q are uncorrelated under Q and vice versa.

11.4.1   Example: Risk-Neutral Pricing with Two Stocks

Example 11.3. Find the risk-neutral SDEs for the stock prices if the stock returns satisfy

$$\frac{dS_{1t}}{S_{1t}} = 0.08 \, dt + 0.2 \, dB_{1t}^P, \qquad (11.43)$$

$$\frac{dS_{2t}}{S_{2t}} = 0.12 \, dt - 0.15 \, dB_{1t}^P + 0.2 \, dB_{2t}^P, \qquad (11.44)$$

with dB_{1t}^P and dB_{2t}^P uncorrelated. Assume that the risk-free rate is constant:

$$r = 0.02.$$

Solution. In this case the two assets are clearly not perfectly correlated, hence arbitrage is ruled out. Mathematically, σ is a 2×2 full rank matrix and therefore the solution for η exists. Since there is no arbitrage, equation (11.42) tells us that we can mechanically copy down (11.43) and (11.44), replacing P with Q and replacing the drift terms with the risk-free rate:

$$\frac{dS_{1t}}{S_{1t}} = 0.02\,dt + 0.2\,dB_{1t}^{Q},$$

$$\frac{dS_{2t}}{S_{2t}} = 0.02\,dt - 0.15\,dB_{1t}^{Q} + 0.2\,dB_{2t}^{Q}.$$

11.4.2 Example: the Black–Scholes PDE

The no-arbitrage argument works for any collection of assets, not just stocks; in this section we will apply it to stocks and options. Historically, the Black–Scholes formula was derived using an arbitrage argument along the lines of (11.40) and (11.41). Let us examine this argument in more detail.

The starting point of the derivation is to guess that the option price only depends on the stock price and calendar time (in 1973 that was not at all obvious):

$$C_t = C(t, S_t).$$

The capital gains from holding one unit of the option from t to $t + dt$ are equal to dC_t; from the Itô formula,

$$dC_t = \frac{\partial C}{\partial t}\,dt + \frac{\partial C}{\partial S_t}\,dS_t + \frac{1}{2}\frac{\partial^2 C}{\partial S_t^2}\,\mathrm{Var}_t(dS_t)$$

$$= \left(\frac{\partial C}{\partial t} + \frac{\sigma^2 S_t^2}{2}\frac{\partial^2 C}{\partial S_t^2}\right)dt + \frac{\partial C}{\partial S_t}\,dS_t. \tag{11.45}$$

Let us construct a portfolio long one option and short θ stocks. The capital gains on this portfolio are

$$dC_t - \theta\,dS_t. \tag{11.46}$$

Can we find θ such that the capital gains (11.46) are riskless? Substituting from (11.45) we have

$$dC_t - \theta\,dS_t = \left(\frac{\partial C}{\partial t} + \frac{\sigma^2 S_t^2}{2}\frac{\partial^2 C}{\partial S_t^2}\right)dt + \left(\frac{\partial C}{\partial S_t} - \theta\right)dS_t. \tag{11.47}$$

Since the only random part (as of time t) in (11.47) is dS_t, to eliminate randomness we must choose

$$\theta = \frac{\partial C}{\partial S_t}, \tag{11.48}$$

whereby the capital gains of our portfolio become

$$\left(\frac{\partial C}{\partial t} + \frac{\sigma^2 S_t^2}{2}\frac{\partial^2 C}{\partial S_t^2}\right)dt.$$

Because the capital gains are risk-free, in the absence of arbitrage they must equal the interest earned on the value of our portfolio $C_t - \theta S_t$ in the risk-free bank account:

$$\left(\frac{\partial C}{\partial t} + \frac{\sigma^2 S_t^2}{2} \frac{\partial^2 C}{\partial S_t^2}\right) dt = (C_t - \theta S_t) r \, dt. \tag{11.49}$$

Substitution from (11.48) into (11.49) then yields the **Black–Scholes partial differential equation**,

$$\frac{\partial C}{\partial t} + r S_t \frac{\partial C}{\partial S_t} + \frac{\sigma^2 S_t^2}{2} \frac{\partial^2 C}{\partial S_t^2} - r C = 0, \tag{11.50}$$

from which the Black–Scholes formula was originally derived.

11.5 Automatic Generation of PDEs and the Feynman–Kac Formula

We have seen in Section 11.2.1 that pricing of contingent claims which have pay-off $g(S_T)$ at maturity is straightforward when the risk-free rate and stock volatilities are non-stochastic. In that case the expectation determining the price of the contingent claim C_t,

$$C_t = \exp\left(-\int_t^T r_s \, ds\right) E_t^Q[g(S_T)],$$

is easy to calculate because we can work out the risk-neutral distribution of the stock prices, which happens to be lognormal. However, this is no longer true when either the stock volatility or the risk-free rate are stochastic under the risk-neutral measure. In such a case we may not know how to evaluate the expectation,

$$C_t = E_t^Q\left[\exp\left(-\int_t^T r_s \, ds\right) g(S_T)\right], \tag{11.51}$$

directly and at this point we may wish to construct a **no-arbitrage partial differential equation** *à la* Black–Scholes PDE and compute the solution this way.

Specifically, suppose that the risk-neutral SDEs for stock price and risk-free rate are

$$dr_t = \mu_r(r_t, S_t) \, dt + \sigma_r(r_t, S_t) \, dB_t^Q, \tag{11.52}$$

$$dS_t = \mu(r_t, S_t) \, dt + \sigma(r_t, S_t) \, dB_t^Q. \tag{11.53}$$

Then the processes r_t, S_t are jointly Markov under Q and therefore C_t is a function of only r_t, S_t and time t. One could construct the no-arbitrage PDE for $C(t, r_t, S_t)$ by following the no-arbitrage reasoning outlined in Section 11.4.2, but this is hardly the most efficient method because the derivation is long. Instead, there is a much faster way which uses the martingale properties of the option price. This procedure is more direct and therefore more transparent, and any errors in the derivation can be easily spotted.

We know that C_t/β_t is a martingale under Q; we will therefore require

$$E_t^Q\left[d\left(\frac{C_t}{\beta_t}\right)\right] = 0. \tag{11.54}$$

From the Itô formula (10.45),

$$d\left(\frac{C_t}{\beta_t}\right) = \frac{1}{\beta_t}(dC_t - r C_t \, dt). \tag{11.55}$$

Now use the Itô formula again to find $dC(t, r_t, S_t)$ given (11.52) and (11.53),

$$dC = \left(\frac{\partial C}{\partial t} + \frac{\partial C}{\partial r_t}\mu_r + \frac{\partial C}{\partial S_t}\mu + \frac{1}{2}\left(\frac{\partial^2 C}{\partial r_t^2}\sigma_r^2 + 2\frac{\partial^2 C}{\partial r_t \partial S_t}\sigma_r \sigma + \frac{\partial^2 C}{\partial S_t^2}\sigma^2\right)\right) dt$$
$$+ \left(\frac{\partial C}{\partial r_t}\sigma_r + \frac{\partial C}{\partial S_t}\sigma\right) dB_t^Q,$$

which, together with the martingale condition (11.54) and the Itô formula (11.55), yields the no-arbitrage PDE,

$$\frac{\partial C}{\partial t} + \frac{\partial C}{\partial r_t}\mu_r + \frac{\partial C}{\partial S_t}\mu + \frac{1}{2}\left(\frac{\partial^2 C}{\partial r_t^2}\sigma_r^2 + 2\frac{\partial^2 C}{\partial r_t \partial S_t}\sigma_r \sigma + \frac{\partial^2 C}{\partial S_t^2}\sigma^2\right) - rC = 0, \quad (11.56)$$

with a boundary condition

$$C(T, r, S) = g(S). \tag{11.57}$$

- The correspondence among the expectation (11.51), the SDEs for stock price and interest rate (11.52) and (11.53), and the PDE (11.56) with boundary condition (11.57) is called the **Feynman–Kac formula**.
- As an aside, with $r_t = 0$ the interest rate ceases to be a state variable and (11.56) simplifies to **Kolmogorov's backward equation**:

$$\frac{\partial C}{\partial t} + \frac{\partial C}{\partial S_t}\mu + \frac{1}{2}\frac{\partial^2 C}{\partial S_t^2}\sigma^2 = 0. \tag{11.58}$$

- Both PDEs (11.56) and (11.58) reflect the fact that a certain process (C_t/β_t and C_t, respectively) is a martingale under measure Q.

The two ways of pricing derivative securities captured in (11.51)–(11.53) and (11.56) and (11.57) are equivalent, yet they behave quite differently when used in calculations. The next two sections highlight those differences. Suppose we are in the Black–Scholes model,

$$d \ln S_t = (r - \tfrac{1}{2}\sigma^2)\, dt + \sigma\, dB_t^Q, \tag{11.59}$$

and that we wish to price a (slightly silly) derivative security called the *squared log contract*, which pays $(\ln S_T)^2$ at maturity. Our problem leads to the calculation of

$$E_0^Q[(\ln S_T)^2].$$

11.5.1 Example: Pricing with PDEs

A PDE expert, let us call him Mr Wilmott, would proceed as follows.

1. He would define the process X

$$X_t \triangleq E_t^Q[(\ln S_T)^2],$$

and conclude by looking at (11.59) that $\ln S_t$ is a Markov process under Q and therefore X_t depends on time and the current value of the stock S_t,

$$X_t = X(t, \ln S_t).$$

X_0 is what Mr Wilmott wishes to calculate.

2. By virtue of the first martingale proposition the process X is a martingale under Q. Mr Wilmott applies the Itô formula to find the drift of X_t and sets it equal to 0 to obtain Kolmogorov's backward equation:

$$\frac{\partial X}{\partial t} + \frac{\partial X}{\partial \ln S} \underbrace{(r - \tfrac{1}{2}\sigma^2)}_{\text{denote by } \mu} + \frac{1}{2} \frac{\partial^2 X}{\partial (\ln S)^2}\sigma^2 = 0, \qquad (11.60)$$

$$X(T, \ln S) = (\ln S)^2. \qquad (11.61)$$

3. Mr Wilmott now needs to solve the PDE (11.60) with the boundary condition (11.61). Being an experienced mathematician he guesses the solution is a polynomial in $\ln S$:

$$X(t, \ln S) = a(t)(\ln S)^2 + b(t)\ln S + c(t).$$

From the boundary conditions (11.61) he finds

$$a(T) = 1, \qquad (11.62)$$

$$b(T) = c(T) = 0. \qquad (11.63)$$

Substituting this into Kolmogorov's backward equation (11.60) he obtains

$$a'(t)(\ln S)^2 + (2a(t)\mu + b'(t))\ln S + b(t)\mu + a(t)\sigma^2 + c'(t) = 0,$$

which must hold for any S and any t. This is only possible if the time-dependent coefficients standing by the different powers of $\ln S$ are all identically equal to 0,

$$a'(t) = 0, \qquad (11.64)$$

$$2a(t)\mu + b'(t) = 0, \qquad (11.65)$$

$$b(t)\mu + a(t)\sigma^2 + c'(t) = 0. \qquad (11.66)$$

Equation (11.64) means $a(t) = \text{const.}$, and from the boundary condition (11.62) that constant has to be 1:

$$a(t) = 1.$$

Next, from (11.65) and (11.63) one must have

$$b'(t) = -2\mu,$$

$$b(t) = \int_t^T 2\mu \, dt = 2\mu(T - t),$$

and finally (11.66) and (11.63) imply

$$c(t) = \mu^2(T - t)^2 + \sigma^2(T - t).$$

Thus Mr Wilmott's complete solution is

$$X(t, \ln S_t) = (\ln S_t)^2 + 2\mu(T - t)\ln S_t + \mu^2(T - t)^2 + \sigma^2(T - t), \qquad (11.67)$$

$$\mu = r - \tfrac{1}{2}\sigma^2. \qquad (11.68)$$

11.5.2 Example: Pricing with SDEs

Now let us meet Mr Filipović, who is an SDE expert. To find $E_t^Q[(\ln S_T)^2]$ Mr Filipović begins by integrating the SDE (11.59),

$$\ln S_T = \ln S_t + (r - \tfrac{1}{2}\sigma^2)(T - t) + \sigma(B_T^Q - B_t^Q),$$

whereby he realizes that conditional on the information at time t the distribution of $\ln S_T$ is normal

$$\ln S_T \mid \mathcal{F}_t \sim N(\ln S_t + (r - \tfrac{1}{2}\sigma^2)(T - t), \sigma^2(T - t)).$$

Mr Filipović knows the formula $E[X^2] = \mathrm{Var}(X) + (E[X])^2$ and applies it with $X = \ln S_T$,

$$
\begin{aligned}
E_t[(\ln S_T)^2] &= \mathrm{Var}_t(\ln S_T) + (E_t[\ln S_T])^2 \\
&= \sigma^2(T - t) + (S_t + (r - \tfrac{1}{2}\sigma^2)(T - t))^2,
\end{aligned}
$$

which gives him the PDE result (11.67) with much less effort.

11.5.3 The Power of Stochastic Integration: an Example from the Vašíček Model

Inspired by the success of Mr Filipović let us try the stochastic integration method on a harder problem from the theory of fixed-income securities. We wish to price a pure discount bond with maturity T, which is a security that pays 1 at time T. Its price at time 0 is therefore

$$\mathrm{bond}_0 = E_0^Q\left[\frac{1}{\beta_T}\right] = E_0^Q[e^{-\ln\beta_T}].$$

The short rate in the Vašíček model follows the Ornstein–Uhlenbeck process:

$$dr_t = a(b - r_t)\,dt + \sigma\,dB_t^Q. \tag{11.69}$$

From Section 10.6.1 we know that (11.69) has a solution of the form

$$r_T = b + (r_0 - b)e^{-aT} + \sigma e^{-aT}\int_0^T e^{as}\,dB_s^Q. \tag{11.70}$$

For bond pricing it is important to know the distribution of the cumulative interest:

$$\ln\beta_T = \int_0^T r_t\,dt.$$

Substituting for r_t from (11.70) we obtain

$$
\begin{aligned}
\ln\beta_T &= \int_0^T\left(b + (r_0 - b)e^{-at} + \sigma e^{-at}\int_0^t e^{as}\,dB_s^Q\right)dt \\
&= \int_0^T (b + (r_0 - b)e^{-at})\,dt + \sigma\int_0^T\left(\int_0^t e^{a(s-t)}\,dB_s^Q\right)dt \\
&= bT + (r_0 - b)\frac{1 - e^{-aT}}{a} + \sigma\iint_{\substack{0\leqslant t\leqslant T \\ 0\leqslant s\leqslant t}} e^{a(s-t)}\,dB_s^Q\,dt.
\end{aligned}
$$

To simplify the double integral, we will hold s constant and integrate over t first. Formally, this is done by changing the order of integration (see Appendix A.6.5). The double integral above can be written in two equivalent ways:

$$\iint_{\substack{0 \leqslant t \leqslant T \\ 0 \leqslant s \leqslant t}} = \iint_{\substack{0 \leqslant s \leqslant T \\ s \leqslant t \leqslant T}}.$$

Continuing with the latter we obtain

$$\iint_{\substack{0 \leqslant s \leqslant T \\ s \leqslant t \leqslant T}} e^{a(s-t)} \, dB_s^Q \, dt = \int_0^T \left(\int_s^T e^{a(s-t)} \, dt \right) dB_s^Q$$

$$= \int_0^T \frac{1 - e^{a(s-T)}}{a} \, dB_s^Q.$$

In other words we have found a stochastic integral for the yield $\ln \beta_T$:

$$\ln \beta_T = bT + (r_0 - b)\frac{1 - e^{-aT}}{a} + \sigma \int_0^T g_t \, dB_t^Q,$$

$$g_t = \frac{1 - e^{a(t-T)}}{a},$$

$$\int_0^T g_t^2 \, dt = \frac{(e^{aT} - 2)^2 + 2aT - 1}{2a^3}.$$

By virtue of (10.24) $\ln \beta_T$ is distributed normally

$$\ln \beta_T \mid \mathcal{F}_0 \stackrel{Q}{\sim} N\left(bT + (r_0 - b)\frac{1 - e^{-aT}}{a}, \sigma^2 \frac{(e^{aT} - 2)^2 + 2aT - 1}{2a^3} \right).$$

The bond price $E^Q[e^{-\ln \beta_T}]$ can now be calculated from the moment-generating function (11.30) with $X = \ln \beta_T$ and $\lambda = -1$ to obtain the Vašíček result. One can imagine that it is much more demanding to infer the same result from the Feynman–Kac PDE.

11.6 Overview of Numerical Methods

There are essentially three ways of evaluating the expectation (11.51) numerically.

1. If the interest rate or the stock price is strongly path dependent, that is, if more and more state variables are needed to generate S_{t+dt} or r_{t+dt} as t increases, then it is best to evaluate (11.51) by a **Monte Carlo** experiment. In a Monte Carlo experiment one uses a random number generator to simulate a large number of paths, say a million, of a discrete-time version of the risk-neutral Brownian motion B^Q on the time interval $[0, T]$. On each path one evaluates the discretized value of the discounted pay-off $\exp(-\int_0^T r_s \, ds)g(S_T)$ and then one computes the average of the discounted pay-offs over all paths.

2. If, on the other hand, the interest rate and stock price are (jointly) Markov under Q, then it is more advantageous to construct a **no-arbitrage partial differential equation** *à la* Black–Scholes PDE (11.50), because one only has (apart from time) two state variables to contend with and the PDE can be

solved efficiently in the two-dimensional state space grid. PDEs are typically solved by the **finite-difference method**, which appears in two versions: **explicit** and **implicit** (see the references at the end of the chapter). It is worth noting that finite-difference methods are a special case of the **Markov chain approximation method**.

3. In some cases one obtains a closed-form expression for the characteristic function of log returns. Option prices can then be recovered numerically from an integral akin to an inverse Fourier transform of the option pay-off.

4. In the best case we are able to calculate the joint distribution of S_T and β_T in closed form and the expectation can be computed either explicitly or by numerical integration over the joint density.

In terms of speed, with a low number of state variables (3) and (4) are the fastest and (1) is the slowest. In terms of implementation (3) and (4) are the most sophisticated and (1) the simplest.

11.7 Summary

- Asset pricing in the Brownian motion limit is based on two principles. The first is general: the risk-neutral expectation of risky return must equal the risk-free return. The second is specific to Itô processes: the change of measure does not affect the conditional volatility of returns. In the Black–Scholes model this means we can rephrase

$$\frac{\mathrm{d}S_t}{S_t} = \mu\,\mathrm{d}t + \sigma\,\mathrm{d}B_t^P$$

as

$$\frac{\mathrm{d}S_t}{S_t} = \underbrace{r\,\mathrm{d}t}_{\substack{\text{risk-free rate} \\ \text{of return}}} + \underbrace{\sigma\,\mathrm{d}B_t^Q}_{\substack{\text{volatility} \\ \text{unchanged}}}.$$

$$\underbrace{\phantom{\frac{\mathrm{d}S_t}{S_t}}}_{\substack{\text{risky rate} \\ \text{of return}}}$$

- The two equations above imply

$$\mathrm{d}B^Q = \frac{\mu - r}{\sigma}\,\mathrm{d}t + \mathrm{d}B^P.$$

The Girsanov theorem claims that (i) the only measure under which B^Q is a martingale is given by $m_T = \mathrm{d}Q/\mathrm{d}P$ with

$$m_T = \exp\left(-\int_0^T \frac{1}{2}\left(\frac{\mu - r}{\sigma}\right)^2 \mathrm{d}t - \int_0^T \frac{\mu - r}{\sigma}\,\mathrm{d}B_t^P\right),$$

and (ii) B^Q is a Brownian motion under Q, that is, $\mathrm{Var}_t^Q(\mathrm{d}B_t^Q) = \mathrm{d}t$.

- The same procedure works with multiple risky assets, provided that there are no mispriced redundant assets. There can be no mispriced assets if the conditional covariance matrix $\Sigma\,\mathrm{d}t$ of risky returns has full rank. Otherwise, one has to perform Cholesky decomposition of the covariance matrix $\Sigma =$

$\sigma\sigma^*$ to see whether the linearly dependent securities are priced consistently (see Section 11.9). In the absence of arbitrage the system of equations

$$\mu - r = \sigma\eta$$

has a (unique) solution, the risk-neutral Brownian motions become

$$dB^Q = \eta\,dt + dB^P$$

and the change of measure generalizes to

$$m_T = \exp\left(-\int_0^T \tfrac{1}{2}\eta^*\eta\,dt - \int_0^T \eta^*\,dB_t^P\right).$$

- Once we have characterized the risk-neutral SDE of the stock price the option pricing is transformed into calculating expectations of the form

$$C_0 = E_0^Q\left[\exp\left(-\int_0^T r_s\,ds\right)g(S_T)\right].$$

There are effectively three ways of evaluating this expectation: (i) the Monte Carlo simulation of risk-neutral shocks dB^Q, (ii) solving the no-arbitrage Feynman–Kac partial differential equation (numerically, this looks very much like the binomial option pricing model), (iii) trying to work out the joint distribution of S_T and β_T by stochastic integration (we have seen examples in the derivation of the Black–Scholes and Vašíček models).

11.8   Notes

The martingale pricing method follows Duffie (1996); a concise and clear presentation without digressions is in Baxter and Rennie (1996). Finite-difference methods are well explained in Wilmott et al. (1995), and the theory of Markov chain approximations is in Kushner and Dupuis (2001). Numerical inversion of the characteristic function is applied, for example, in Heston (1993) and Carr and Madan (1999). Hull (1997) is an easy introduction to Monte Carlo methods; see also Judd (1998) for a detailed exposition of quasi-random sequences. Cholesky decomposition can be found in Judd (1998). Björk (1998) is a good introduction to fixed-income models and it contains a PDE derivation of bond prices in the Vašíček model.

11.9   Appendix: Decomposition of Asset Returns into Uncorrelated Components

Let Y_1, Y_2, Y_3 be three correlated asset returns with covariance matrix

$$\Sigma_Y = \begin{pmatrix} 0.04 & 0.02 & 0.02 \\ 0.02 & 0.0676 & 0.0244 \\ 0.02 & 0.0244 & 0.0361 \end{pmatrix}.$$

We are looking for uncorrelated random variables ε_1, ε_2, ε_3 with unit variance, and coefficients

$$\begin{pmatrix} \sigma_{11} & 0 & 0 \\ \sigma_{21} & \sigma_{22} & 0 \\ \sigma_{31} & \sigma_{32} & \sigma_{33} \end{pmatrix}$$

such that

$$Y_1 = \sigma_{11}\varepsilon_1, \tag{11.71}$$

$$Y_2 = \sigma_{21}\varepsilon_1 + \sigma_{22}\varepsilon_2, \tag{11.72}$$

$$Y_3 = \sigma_{31}\varepsilon_1 + \sigma_{32}\varepsilon_2 + \sigma_{33}\varepsilon_3. \tag{11.73}$$

The procedure for finding σ_{ij} resembles the Gramm–Schmidt orthogonalization for vectors (see Section 2.14.2). In fact, it *is* the same procedure but instead of vectors we have random variables and the *right angle* between two random variables Y_1, Y_2 is given by the condition $\mathrm{Cov}(Y_1, Y_2) = 0$.

1. (a) The first component ε_1 is simply Y_1 normalized to have unit variance,

$$\sqrt{\mathrm{Var}(Y_1)}\varepsilon_1 = Y_1,$$

which implies

$$\sigma_{11} = \sqrt{\mathrm{Var}(Y_1)} = 0.2. \tag{11.74}$$

(b) Once we know σ_{11} we can immediately work out σ_{21} and σ_{31} from the fact that

$$\sigma_{ij} = \mathrm{Cov}(Y_i, \varepsilon_j). \tag{11.75}$$

Equation (11.75) can be established by calculating the covariance with ε_j on both sides of equations (11.71)–(11.73). Application of (11.75) with $j = 1$ yields

$$\sigma_{21} = \mathrm{Cov}(Y_2, \varepsilon_1) = \frac{\mathrm{Cov}(Y_2, Y_1)}{\sigma_{11}} = \frac{0.02}{0.2} = 0.1, \tag{11.76}$$

$$\sigma_{31} = \mathrm{Cov}(Y_3, \varepsilon_1) = \frac{\mathrm{Cov}(Y_3, Y_1)}{\sigma_{11}} = \frac{0.02}{0.2} = 0.1. \tag{11.77}$$

2. (a) The second component ε_2 is whatever is left over from Y_2 once we take away the part of Y_2 which is perfectly correlated with ε_1. In other words, $Y_2 - \sigma_{21}\varepsilon_1$ normalized by its standard deviation σ_{22} becomes ε_2. We know that $Y_2 = \sigma_{21}\varepsilon_1 + \sigma_{22}\varepsilon_2$ and therefore

$$\mathrm{Var}(Y_2) = \sigma_{21}^2 + \sigma_{22}^2.$$

From here we can find σ_{22}:

$$\sigma_{22} = \sqrt{\mathrm{Var}(Y_2) - \sigma_{21}^2} = \sqrt{0.0676 - 0.1^2} = 0.24. \tag{11.78}$$

(b) Having found σ_{22} it is now possible to work out σ_{32} from the condition (11.75),

$$\sigma_{32} = \mathrm{Cov}(Y_3, \varepsilon_2) = \mathrm{Cov}\left(Y_3, \frac{Y_2 - \sigma_{21}\varepsilon_1}{\sigma_{22}}\right) \tag{11.79}$$

$$= \frac{\mathrm{Cov}(Y_3, Y_2) - \sigma_{21}\,\mathrm{Cov}(Y_3, \varepsilon_1)}{\sigma_{22}}, \tag{11.80}$$

since we have already computed σ_{21} and $\mathrm{Cov}(Y_3, \varepsilon_1) = \sigma_{31}$ in the previous step. Numerically,

$$\sigma_{32} = \frac{0.0244 - 0.1^2}{0.24} = 0.06. \tag{11.81}$$

3. Finally, we evaluate σ_{33} from the condition,

$$\text{Var}(Y_3) = \sigma_{31}^2 + \sigma_{32}^2 + \sigma_{33}^2,$$

which yields

$$\sigma_{33} = \sqrt{\text{Var}(Y_3) - \sigma_{31}^2 - \sigma_{32}^2} = \sqrt{0.0361 - 0.1^2 - 0.06^2} = 0.15.$$

11.9.1 Cholesky Decomposition

There is a simple relationship between the matrices σ and Σ_Y. By definition we have

$$Y = \sigma\varepsilon, \tag{11.82}$$

and by virtue of the portfolio rule for covariances (11.82) implies

$$\Sigma_Y = \sigma\Sigma_\varepsilon\sigma^*. \tag{11.83}$$

Since by assumption the ε shocks have unit variance and are uncorrelated, the covariance matrix Σ_ε is an identity matrix and (11.83) simplifies to

$$\Sigma_Y = \sigma\sigma^*. \tag{11.84}$$

When, as in our case, σ is a lower triangular matrix, (11.84) is known as the **Cholesky decomposition** of the matrix Σ_Y. The reader can verify that

$$\sigma = \begin{pmatrix} 0.2 & 0 & 0 \\ 0.1 & 0.24 & 0 \\ 0.1 & 0.06 & 0.15 \end{pmatrix}$$

calculated in equations (11.74)–(11.81) satisfies equation (11.84).

All respectable numerical software packages have a routine that performs Cholesky decomposition. In GAUSS

```
chol(sigY)
```

will return the upper triangular matrix σ^* (see the GAUSS program *chapter11sect9a. gss*).

11.9.2 Redundant Assets

The Cholesky algorithm will break down when one of the assets Y_1, Y_2, Y_3 is redundant. For example, if Y_2 is perfectly correlated with Y_1, then in step (2b) we will find $\sigma_{22} = 0$ and then we cannot compute σ_{32}. The good news is that we do not need to. Since ε_2 is zero we can simply ignore it and proceed with calculating ε_3 (and once ε_3 is computed rename it ε_2). The bad news is there are not many numerical packages that perform the simple alteration in Cholesky decomposition to enable it to handle perfectly correlated variables. If the reader wishes to locate such a procedure, it is useful to know that a covariance matrix of linearly independent variables is *positive definite*, whereas the covariance matrix of potentially linearly dependent variables is *positive semidefinite*. We are after *Cholesky decomposition for positive semidefinite matrices*; a functioning version can be found in the file *chapter11sect9b.gss*.

Redundant assets are an issue of great practical importance. An equity analyst will work with large numbers of assets and there is every chance that not all of them will be linearly independent. One way of dealing with this situation has been suggested in the previous paragraph. Another possibility is to avoid the Cholesky decomposition altogether. In practice, covariance matrices do not fall from the sky like they sometimes do in textbooks. Instead, a covariance matrix would be estimated from historical data. Suppose we have an $N \times 3$ matrix Y_{data} containing N observations of asset returns for three assets Y_1, Y_2, Y_3. For simplicity suppose that we have already preprocessed the data so that Y_{data} represents the deviations of returns from their respective sample mean. Then the sample covariance matrix is obtained simply as the matrix product

$$\Sigma_Y = Y_{\text{data}}^* Y_{\text{data}}.$$

It is natural to perform the orthogonal decomposition directly on the columns of the data matrix Y_{data} (see Section 2.14 for details). This will give

$$Y_{\text{data}} = QR$$

and

$$\Sigma_Y = R^* \underbrace{Q^* Q}_{I} R = R^* R.$$

If the QR decomposition is performed without permuting columns of the data matrix, we will find that $R^* = \sigma$ is the lower triangular matrix from the Cholesky decomposition of the covariance matrix Σ_Y. For an example see *chapter11sect9c.gss*.

11.10 Exercises

Exercise 11.1 (return and yield). If the stock price is given by the following SDE,

$$\frac{dS_t}{S_t} = \mu \, dt + \sigma \, dB_t,$$

and there are no dividends, then the parameter μ can be calculated as (circle one answer)

(a) the yield calculated from expected return;

(b) the expected yield;

(c) none of the above.

Exercise 11.2 (Feynman–Kac formula). The stock price is given by the following SDE,

$$\frac{dS_t}{S_t} = \mu \, dt + \sigma \, dB_t^P,$$

where B_t^P is a Brownian motion under measure P and the short rate is constant at r, with $\beta_t = e^{rt}$. Suppose we define

$$\frac{X_t}{\beta_t} = E_t^P \left[\frac{S_T}{\beta_T} \right].$$

Then (circle one answer)

(a) $X_t = X(t, S_t)$, where

$$\tfrac{1}{2}\sigma^2 S^2 \frac{\partial^2 X}{\partial S^2} + \mu S \frac{\partial X}{\partial S} + \frac{\partial X}{\partial t} = 0.$$

(b) $X_t = X(t, S_t)$, where

$$\tfrac{1}{2}\sigma^2 S^2 \frac{\partial^2 X}{\partial S^2} + (\mu - r) S \frac{\partial X}{\partial S} + \frac{\partial X}{\partial t} = 0.$$

(c) $X_t = X(t, S_t)$, where

$$\tfrac{1}{2}\sigma^2 \frac{\partial^2 X}{\partial S^2} + (r - \tfrac{1}{2}\sigma^2) \frac{\partial X}{\partial S} + \frac{\partial X}{\partial t} = 0.$$

(d) None of the above.

Exercise 11.3 (the multivariate Itô formula and the Girsanov theorem). You are given an Itô process X_t,

$$dX_t = \eta_t \, dt + dB_t^P,$$
$$X_0 = 0,$$

where B_t^P is a Brownian motion under measure P and η_t is a process adapted to the filtration generated by B^P. There is also another Itô process m_t,

$$dm_t = -\eta_t m_t \, dB_t^P, \qquad (11.85)$$
$$m_0 = 1. \qquad (11.86)$$

(a) Which of the three processes X_t, m_t, B_t^P are martingales under P?

(b) Consider a new process $Y_t = X_t^2 - t$. Using the Itô formula find the SDE for the process Y_t:

$$dY_t =$$

(c) Use the multivariate Itô formula to find the SDE of the process $m_t Y_t$. Is the process $m_t Y_t$ a martingale under P?

$$d(m_t Y_t) =$$

(d) Discuss the significance of your finding in part (c).

Exercise 11.4 (digital option pricing). Suppose you want to value a digital option on the S&P500 Index. From the historical data you have estimated that the average monthly return on the S&P500 is 1% and the standard deviation of this return is 4%. You decide to model the S&P500 as a geometric Brownian motion with constant parameters:

$$\frac{dX_t}{X_t} = \mu \, dt + \sigma \, dB_t.$$

Your expert on interest rates tells you that the rates will go up at a constant rate from the current 5% to 7% over one year and then will stay at 7% indefinitely.

(a) Find the correct value of μ and σ.

$$\mu =$$

$$\sigma =$$

(b) Plot the evolution of the short rate.

(c) Calculate the cumulative discount $\beta_t = e^{\int_0^t r_s \, ds}$.

$$\beta_t =$$

(d) Write down the SDE for the index X_t using the risk-neutral Brownian motion:

$$dX_t = \qquad dt + \qquad dB_t^Q.$$

(e) From (d) find the SDE for $\ln X_t$:

$$d \ln X_t = \qquad dt + \qquad dB_t^Q.$$

(f) Find the risk-neutral distribution of $\ln X_t$, i.e. find the distribution of $\ln X_t$ under measure Q.

$$(\ln X_t | \mathcal{F}_0) \stackrel{Q}{\sim}$$

(g) Price a digital option on the index with expiry date T and strike $K = 1400$. Such an option pays £1 when $X_T > 1400$ and 0 otherwise. Assume that the current value of the index is $X_0 = 1400$ and that the option matures in 12 months. (Hint: write the option price as an expectation. Realize that this expectation is equal to a probability of an event. To find this probability transform the event as we did when we looked for quantiles in Section B.11.)

$$D_t =$$

NB. You are pricing the option as if there were no dividends on the S&P500. This is not the case, in practice, the earned dividends *are* calculated into the monthly returns and the pricing then has to be adjusted accordingly.

Exercise 11.5 (quadratic call option in the Black–Scholes model). The commercial bank Exotiq wants to sell a new derivative security, the quadratic call option. If S_T is the stock price at expiry, the quadratic call option with strike K will pay $\max(S_T^2 - K^2, 0)$. Suppose that stock returns follow a geometric Brownian motion with an average rate of return equal to 8% per year and an annual volatility of log return of 20% a year. The risk-free rate is 2% per annum, the contract expires in one year and the initial stock price is 10. You have been hired as an analyst to price the quadratic call option with strike 10. Proceed in steps.

(a) Write down the SDE for stock price using B^P, which is a Brownian motion under the objective probability.

(b) Rephrase the same equation using B^Q, which is a Brownian motion under the risk-neutral probability.

(c) Find the risk-neutral distribution of $\ln S_T$ as of time 0.

(d) Express the price of a quadratic call option as a risk-neutral expectation.

(e) Evaluate this expectation using formulae (11.6) and (11.7). (Hint: write $S_T^2 = \exp(2 \ln S_T)$ and find the distribution of $2 \ln S_T$.)

Exercise 11.6 (calculating expectations with PDEs and SDEs). Find

$$E_0^Q[S_T^2]$$

if

$$\frac{dS_t}{S_t} = \mu \, dt + \sigma \, dB_t^Q.$$

Use

(a) the PDE martingale approach by setting $X_t = E_t^Q[S_T^2]$ and guessing that

$$X_t = X(t, S_t) = S_t^2 e^{a(t)},$$

where $a(t)$ is a function of the calendar time only.
PDE for X:

$$a(t) =$$

(b) the SDE approach (by passing to $\ln S_t$):

$$\ln S_T \mid \mathcal{F}_0 \overset{Q}{\sim}$$
$$E_0^Q[S_T^2] = E_0^Q[e^{2 \ln S_T}] =$$

Exercise 11.7 (pricing bonds with PDEs in a Gaussian model of term structure).
Consider a term-structure model with stochastic interest rates:

$$dr_t = 0.01 \, dt + 0.1 \, dB_t^Q, \tag{11.87}$$
$$r_0 = 0.1,$$
$$\beta_t = \exp\left(\int_0^t r_u \, du\right).$$

Suppose we want to price a zero coupon bond in this model. Such a bond pays 1 at maturity; if the interest rate were deterministic, the price of the bond would be 1 discounted back at the risk-free rate, $X_0 = 1/\beta_T$, and intermediate prices would be

$$X_t = \frac{1}{\exp(\int_t^T r_u \, du)} = \frac{\beta_t}{\beta_T}. \tag{11.88}$$

However, since r is stochastic the deterministic formula (11.88) changes to

$$X_t = E_t^Q\left[\frac{\beta_t}{\beta_T}\right] = E_t^Q\left[\exp\left(\int_t^T r_u \, du\right)\right]. \tag{11.89}$$

The task is to find the PDE that the bond price must satisfy, proceeding in steps.

(a) Denote the bond price process by X. Looking at the equation (11.89) and using the Markov properties of process r, decide which variables X_t depend upon (apart from the calendar time):

$$X_t = X(t, \qquad\qquad).$$

(b) Using (a) and the Itô formula write down the SDE for the discounted bond price X_t/β_t:

$$d\left(\frac{X_t}{\beta_t}\right) =$$

(c) Assuming that B^Q is a Brownian motion under the risk-neutral measure, write down the PDE which captures the fact that X_t/β_t is a martingale under the risk-neutral measure:

PDE for X:

(d) Write down the boundary condition for the function X (stating that $X_T = 1$):

$$X(\quad , \quad) =$$

Exercise 11.8 (Gaussian model of term structure and bond pricing using SDEs). Take the same model as above

$$dr_t = 0.01 \, dt + 0.1 \, dB_t^Q,$$
$$r(0) = 0.1,$$

where r is the overnight interest rate on bank deposits. Denote by $y(t, T)$ the cumulative interest on bank account deposits from time t to time T,

$$y(t, T) = \int_t^T r_u \, du. \tag{11.90}$$

Our aim is to find the price of a zero coupon discount bond in this model

$$X_0 = E_0^Q\left[\frac{1}{\beta_T}\right] = E_0^Q[e^{-y(0,T)}].$$

(a) Express r_u as an Itô integral from time 0:

$$r_u = r_0 +$$

(b) Substitute r_u into the formula for the compounded interest rate with (11.90) and change the order of integration to obtain an Itô integral for the cumulative interest $y(0, T)$.

(c) Describe the risk-neutral distribution of $y(0, T)$ as perceived at time 0.

$$y(0, T)|\mathcal{F}_0 \overset{Q}{\sim}$$

(d) Using the result in (c) calculate $X_0 = E_0^Q[e^{-y(0,T)}]$.

Exercise 11.9 (relationship between PDEs and SDEs). Proceed as in Exercise 11.8 above.

(a) Describe the distribution of $y(t, T)$ as seen at an intermediate time t.

(b) Find the no-arbitrage price X_t of a pure discount bond maturing T years from now at any intermediate time t, $0 < t < T$.

(c) Note that X_t is a function of t and r_t only (taking T as given). Plug this function $X(t, r_t)$ into the PDE derived in Exercise 11.7. What do you observe?

Exercise 11.10 (limiting value of investment potential). Write down a first-order Taylor expansion of $e^{ax} - 1$ around $x = 0$ and use it to prove that

$$\lim_{x \to 0} \frac{e^{ax} - 1}{x} = a.$$

Consequently, show that for IP_γ given in (11.32) we have

$$\lim_{\gamma \to +\infty} \mathrm{IP}_\gamma = \frac{1}{2} \frac{(\mu - r)^2}{\sigma^2}.$$

Exercise 11.11 (generalized Sharpe ratio in the Black–Scholes model). Rephrase the investment potential (11.32) in terms of the generalized Sharpe ratios (3.82). How do the GSRs depend on the baseline risk aversion γ?

Exercise 11.12 (stock return correlation). For the two stock returns in Section 11.4.1 evaluate the instantaneous correlation between stock returns under both P and Q.

12

Dynamic Option Hedging and Pricing in Incomplete Markets

The models of Chapters 5, 6 and 11 imply that option hedging is a riskless business. In practice, this is far from true. In this chapter we will describe the simplest way of measuring and computing the risk of dynamic option hedging strategies. The chapter has four sections.

Section 12.1 starts out by constructing a reasonably realistic distribution of stock returns, allowing for larger-than-normal price movements on short to medium time horizons. We then define the hedging risk as the expected squared replication error to maturity. We will describe the dynamically optimal strategy (the so-called *variance-optimal hedge*) and the locally optimal strategy that turns out to be virtually identical to the continuous-time Black–Scholes hedge. We will evaluate the expected replication error of these two strategies. We will show how the unconditional replication error is related to the option's *gamma* and to the kurtosis of stock returns. The first part concludes by examining the properties of *variance-optimal martingale measure* and the way it can be used to describe the convergence of variance-optimal hedge to the Black–Scholes strategy.

The first section tacitly assumes that the average hedging error is zero, but, in practice, options are sold at a premium. It makes better sense to view the option and the associated hedging strategy as an investment. Section 12.2 shows how to evaluate the expected utility of option hedging strategies and calculates their dynamic Sharpe ratio.

Section 12.3 explores the continuous-time limit. We will observe that the hedging error disappears in the Brownian motion limit, but that in reality returns are far from normal and hedging errors remain high even with very short rebalancing intervals.

Section 12.4 describes the mathematical technology needed to derive the optimal hedging strategy. It motivates *Bellman's principle of optimality* and carefully describes the principle of *dynamic programming*. We derive and interpret the optimal hedging strategy and show how all quantities of interest can be obtained from a simple least-squares regression.

12.1 The Risk in Option Hedging Strategies

12.1.1 A More Realistic Stock Price Model

In Chapter 5, to keep the model complete, we could only allow two values of stock return in any one period. In this chapter we will allow for seven values of weekly

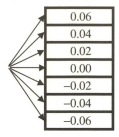

Figure 12.1.   Model of weekly log return.

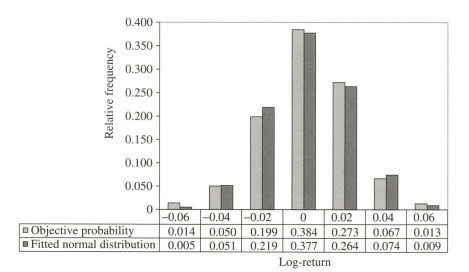

	−0.06	−0.04	−0.02	0	0.02	0.04	0.06
▨ Objective probability	0.014	0.050	0.199	0.384	0.273	0.067	0.013
▪ Fitted normal distribution	0.005	0.051	0.219	0.377	0.264	0.074	0.009

Log-return

Figure 12.2.   Histogram of weekly log returns.

returns, but having more is not a problem. What is important is to space the log returns out regularly, so that our tree recombines.[1] In this particular example we will use a gap of 2% (see Figure 12.1).

Next we have to get the empirical distribution of weekly stock returns. For the purpose of this chapter we will consider weekly returns on FTSE 100 Index, assuming that the weekly returns are distributed independently. To produce an appropriate histogram we will divide the log returns into seven categories (bins), the first bin containing all the log returns below −5%, the second bin containing all the returns between −5% and −3%, and so on, with the last bin ranging from 5% upwards. The resulting histogram of weekly returns[2] in the period 1984–2001 is depicted in Figure 12.2.

---

[1]This gives the simplest implementation of the model. Numerically, it is often more efficient to set up a stock price grid but then to allow stock returns to fall between grid points. Such an arrangement requires interpolation between grid points, but it gives greater flexibility in modelling conditional returns, which is particularly advantageous at short time horizons, where returns can have a range of 20 standard deviations.

[2]For simplicity this example assumes that the risk-free rate has been constant between 1984 and 2001.

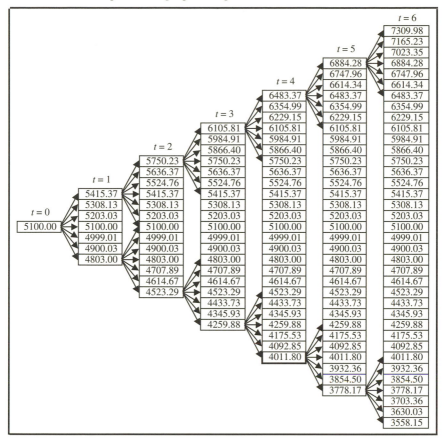

Figure 12.3. Lattice of stock prices.

Our aim is to price a European call option with six weeks to expiry, rehedging once a week. We will assume that the initial value of the index is $S_0 = 5100$. The resulting stock price lattice is depicted in Figure 12.3 (see also Exercise 12.1). The conditional probabilities of movement within the lattice are taken from the histogram in Figure 12.2 (see Figure 12.4). The option is struck at $K = 5355$, that is, initially 5% out of the money.

12.1.2 Mean–Variance Hedging

We will now describe the goal of dynamic hedging. With seven possible values of return and only two assets to hedge with, our market is incomplete; we therefore expect any option hedging strategy to entail some hedging error, which of course means risk. Chapter 3 taught us that economists weigh up risks and returns using utility functions. In particular, we know that for small risks all utility functions are virtually equivalent and that the simplest utility function to use is quadratic. Since our situation is complicated by having to deal with many periods, we will happily settle for a quadratic utility; it is a good starting point that can inform future

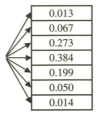

Figure 12.4.   Conditional objective probabilities of stock price movement.

extensions to exponential or logarithmic utility. Besides, if one hedges frequently, it is likely that the risks involved are small.

Mathematically, we will formulate the problem as follows. The goal is to *minimize the time 0 expected squared replication error at maturity*. This is achieved by choosing the adapted self-financing trading strategy $\{\theta_t\}_{t=0,1,\dots,T}$ to solve

$$\min_{\{\theta_t\}_{t=0,1,\dots,T}} E_0^P[(V_T - H_T)^2] \tag{12.1}$$

$$\text{s.t. } V_T = R_f^T V_0 + \sum_{t=0}^{T-1} R_f^{T-t} \theta_t S_t (R_{t+1} - R_f), \tag{12.2}$$

where H_T is the pay-off of the option at expiry, V_T denotes the terminal value of the hedging portfolio generated by holding θ_t units of the stock at time t (thus θ_t represents what is commonly known as the option delta) with the remaining money deposited safely in (or borrowed from) the risk-free bank account with safe return R_f. $\{R_t\}_{t=1,\dots,T}$ are IID stock returns with conditional objective probability density given in Figure 12.4.

12.1.3   Guide to Mean–Variance Hedging Strategies

We will describe two hedging strategies. The *dynamically optimal hedge* that solves (12.1) and (12.2) is denoted θ_t^D and called the **variance-optimal hedge**. It depends on the stock price, the calendar time *and* the current value of the hedging portfolio V_t^D. We will also encounter a closely related suboptimal strategy θ_t^L, which only depends on the stock price and the calendar time. We will call this strategy the **locally optimal hedge**. The solution is characterized by the processes H and $(\varepsilon^D)^2$ and $(\varepsilon^L)^2$; all three are functions of stock price and calendar time only.

The process H is called the **mean value process** because the replicating portfolio with value H_t has zero expected hedging risk. In a complete market the hedging risk is identically zero and H is the no-arbitrage price of the option.

The ε^2 processes capture the minimum expected squared replication error (the minimum attainable hedging risk); they are always non-negative and in a complete market they are identically equal to zero. In addition, with IID returns we always have $(\varepsilon_t^D)^2 \leqslant (\varepsilon_t^L)^2$.

We now describe the construction of H, θ^L, θ^D and ε^L, ε^D in turn. The results are simplified to the special case with IID returns and constant interest rate. The solution method and the general solution are described in Section 12.4.

12.1.4 Mean Value Process

This process is constructed with the help of special risk-neutral probabilities called *variance-optimal probabilities*. The variance-optimal probabilities in turn are computed from the distribution of excess returns. The variance-optimal measure will be denoted Q to distinguish it from the objective probability measure P. The corresponding change of measure is given by the formula,

$$\frac{dQ}{dP} = m_{1|0}m_{2|1}\cdots m_{T|T-1}, \tag{12.3}$$

$$m_{t+1|t} \triangleq \frac{q_{t+1|t}}{p_{t+1|t}} = \frac{1 - aX_{t+1}}{b}; \tag{12.4}$$

for a detailed discussion of the change of measure and its role in finance, refer to Chapter 9. The all-important parameters, a and b, are closely linked to quadratic utility maximization (see Chapter 3); a represents the optimal investment in the basis asset (stock) per unit of risk tolerance, b represents the maximum utility, which in turn is related to the Sharpe ratio of the basis asset:

$$X_{t+1} \triangleq R_{t+1} - R_f, \tag{12.5}$$

$$a = \frac{E_t^P[X_{t+1}]}{E_t^P[X_{t+1}^2]}, \tag{12.6}$$

$$b = 1 - \frac{(E_t^P[X_{t+1}])^2}{E_t^P[X_{t+1}^2]} = \frac{1}{1 + SR^2(X)}. \tag{12.7}$$

We will assume that the risk-free interest rate is 4% per annum, equivalent to a risk-free return of $R_f = 1.04^{1/52}$ per week. Numerically,

$$R_{t+1} = \begin{bmatrix} e^{0.06} & e^{0.04} & e^{0.02} & e^{0.00} & e^{-0.02} & e^{-0.04} & e^{-0.06} \end{bmatrix},$$

$$R_f = 1.00075,$$

$$X_{t+1} = \begin{bmatrix} 6.108 & 4.006 & 1.945 & -0.075 & -2.056 & -3.997 & -5.899 \end{bmatrix} \times 10^{-2},$$

$$E_t^P[X_{t+1}] = 1.58 \times 10^{-3},$$

$$E_t^P[X_{t+1}^2] = 4.72 \times 10^{-4},$$

$$a = \frac{1.58 \times 10^{-3}}{4.72 \times 10^{-4}} = 3.35,$$

$$b = 1 - \frac{1.58^2 \times 10^{-6}}{4.72 \times 10^{-4}} = 0.9947,$$

$$m_{t+1|t} = \begin{bmatrix} 0.7995 & 0.8704 & 0.9398 & 1.0079 & 1.0746 & 1.1400 & 1.2041 \end{bmatrix},$$

$$q_{t+1|t} = m_{t+1|t}\,p_{t+1|t}$$
$$= \begin{bmatrix} 0.010 & 0.058 & 0.257 & 0.387 & 0.214 & 0.057 & 0.017 \end{bmatrix}.$$

The risk-neutral probabilities q and the option pay-off H_T define the mean value

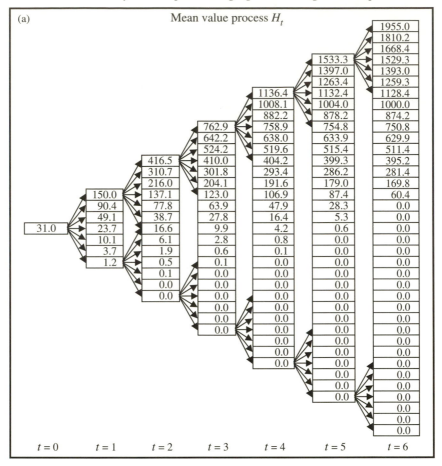

Figure 12.5. Comparison of (a) the mean value process H with (b) the corresponding continuous-time Black–Scholes prices.

process $\{H_t\}_{t=0,1,\dots,T}$ as follows:

$$H_t = E_t^Q\left[\frac{H_T}{R_f^{T-t}}\right].$$

In our special case with IID returns and a deterministic interest rate the conditional variance-optimal probabilities $q_{t+1|t}$ coincide with the risk-neutral probabilities of the one-period **Markowitz Capital Asset Pricing Model (CAPM)**. Thus H_{T-1} is the CAPM price of the option at time $T-1$, H_{T-2} is the CAPM price of H_{T-1} at time $T-2$ and so on.

The value of H_t is computed recursively using the risk-neutral probabilities and starting from the last period as in the complete market case:

$$H_t = E_t^Q\left[\frac{H_{t+1}}{R_f}\right], \quad t = T-1,\dots,0. \tag{12.8}$$

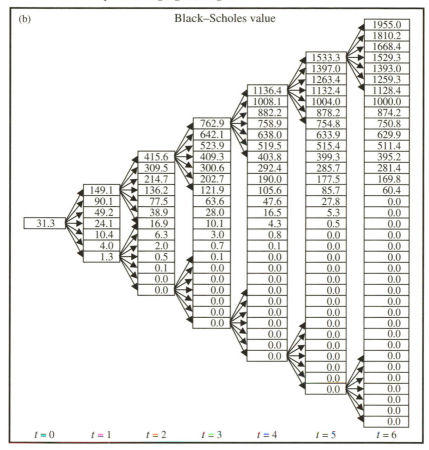

Figure 12.5. See opposite for description.

However, formula (12.8) differs from its complete market counterpart in one important respect. While in a complete market there is a self-financing portfolio with value H_t that perfectly replicates H_{t+1}, in an incomplete market such a portfolio generally does not exist. Exercise 12.2 implements the mean value process in a spreadsheet.

The mean value process H_t is depicted in Figure 12.5, together with the corresponding Black–Scholes value for comparison. It turns out that the mean value H_t is very close to the Black–Scholes value, even though many of the assumptions of the Black–Scholes model are violated here. Consider, for example, the middle node at $t = 1$. The BS formula dictates that

$$C(S, K, r, \sigma, \tau) = S\Phi\left(\frac{\ln(S/K) + (r + \frac{1}{2}\sigma^2)\tau}{\sigma\sqrt{\tau}}\right)$$
$$- e^{-r\tau}K\Phi\left(\frac{\ln(S/K) + (r - \frac{1}{2}\sigma^2)\tau}{\sigma\sqrt{\tau}}\right)$$

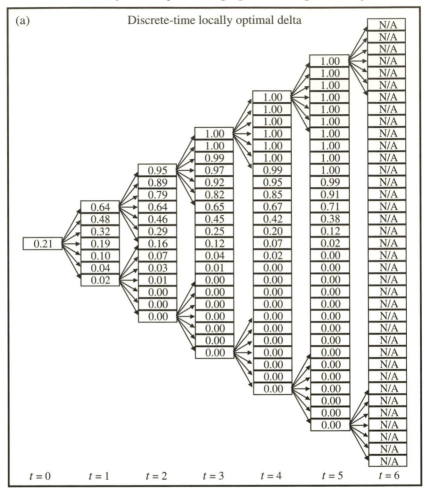

Figure 12.6. Comparison between (a) the discrete-time and (b) continuous-time Black–Scholes delta.

with

$$S = 5100.00, \qquad K = 5355,$$

$$r = \ln(1.04^{1/52}), \qquad \tau = 6 - 1 = 5,$$

$$\sigma = \sqrt{4.72 \times 10^{-4} - 1.58^2 \times 10^{-6}} = 2.16 \times 10^{-2},$$

resulting in $C = 24.1$, as compared with $H = 23.7$ in the same node. Black–Scholes requires continuous trading and lognormally distributed returns, while the trading in our model is far from continuous and the lognormality of stock returns is questionable too. This shows that the BS formula is extremely robust, and no doubt this is the main reason for its popularity. Where the robustness is coming from is discussed in Section 12.3.4.

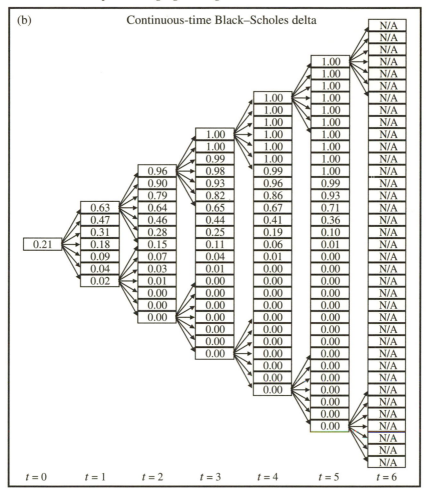

Figure 12.6. See opposite for description.

12.1.5 *Black–Scholes Delta and Optimal Hedging Strategy*

It turns out that the dynamically optimal hedging strategy θ_t^D is obtained from the minimization of the one-step-ahead hedging error $E_t[(V_{t+1} - H_{t+1})^2]$. Using the self-financing condition $V_{t+1} = R_f V_t + \theta_t S_t(R_{t+1} - R_f)$ the squared error can be written as

$$E_t^P[(R_f V_t + \theta_t S_t X_{t+1} - H_{t+1})^2] \tag{12.9}$$

and it is clear that the optimal value of θ_t depends not only on H_{t+1} but also on V_t.

The nature of the self-financing portfolio is such that once we arrive at time t we cannot choose V_t; it is given by our past trading strategy and realizations of stock prices. But it makes sense to inquire what value of V_t we *would* prefer *if* we had the choice. It turns out that the optimal pair V_t, θ_t minimizing (12.9) is $V_t = H_t$,

Table 12.1. One random draw for stock returns.

$\ln(S_1/S_0)$	$\ln(S_2/S_1)$	$\ln(S_3/S_2)$	$\ln(S_4/S_3)$	$\ln(S_5/S_4)$	$\ln(S_6/S_5)$
-0.04	0.02	0.00	-0.02	0.02	0.00

$\theta_t = \theta_t^{\mathrm{L}}$,

$$\theta_t^{\mathrm{L}} = \frac{\mathrm{E}_t^P[(H_{t+1} - R_f H_t)X_{t+1}]}{S_t \mathrm{E}_t^P[X_{t+1}^2]}, \tag{12.10}$$

where θ_t^{L} is the locally optimal delta. Effectively, the locally optimal hedging strategy assumes that the value of the hedging portfolio is always at its optimum H_t. In an incomplete market this is obviously not always the case; therefore, the dynamically optimal strategy makes an adjustment for the difference between V_t and H_t:

$$\theta_t^{\mathrm{D}} = \theta_t^{\mathrm{L}} + R_f a \frac{H_t - V_t^{\mathrm{D}}}{S_t}. \tag{12.11}$$

The coefficient a is computed from (12.6), numerically $a = 3.35$. In a *bull market*, $a > 0$, the delta is adjusted downward when the self-financing portfolio is above the target value H_t and vice versa. In a *bear market* the adjustments are exactly the opposite.

The locally optimal delta is easily computed from formula (12.10), because we already know the values of H_{t+1} in all nodes (see Exercise 12.3). Figure 12.6 compares θ_t^{L} with its Black–Scholes counterpart. We note that the difference never exceeds two percentage points. In practice, the continuous-time Black–Scholes delta is a very good approximation to the locally optimal delta because the expected squared hedging error of the two strategies is virtually identical. But the question remains how inefficient is the Black–Scholes strategy compared with the dynamically optimal strategy, and that will be the focus of the next two sections.

12.1.6 Monte Carlo Simulation of Hedging Errors

Let us visualize the outcome of the two competing hedging strategies θ_t^{L} and θ_t^{D}. Consider a randomly chosen sequence of returns written down in Table 12.1 and depicted in Figure 12.7.

Our aim is to simulate the resulting value of the locally and dynamically optimal hedging portfolios. From the self-financing condition we have

$$V_{t+1}^{\mathrm{L}} = R_f V_t^{\mathrm{L}} + \theta_t^{\mathrm{L}}(S_{t+1} - S_t R_f), \tag{12.12}$$

$$V_{t+1}^{\mathrm{D}} = R_f V_t^{\mathrm{D}} + \theta_t^{\mathrm{D}}(S_{t+1} - S_t R_f), \tag{12.13}$$

and the dynamically optimal delta is obtained from (12.11):

$$\theta_t^{\mathrm{D}} = \theta_t^{\mathrm{L}} + R_f a \frac{H_t - V_t^{\mathrm{D}}}{S_t}.$$

The initial value of the hedging portfolio is the same for both strategies $V_0^{\mathrm{D}} = V_0^{\mathrm{L}} = H_0$ and consequently also $\theta_0^{\mathrm{D}} = \theta_0^{\mathrm{L}}$. From Figure 12.6a we find $\theta_0^{\mathrm{L}} = 0.21$.

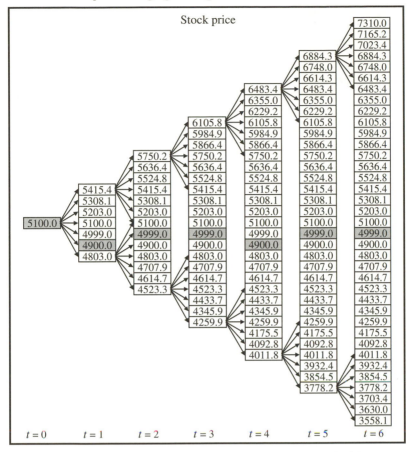

Figure 12.7. Illustration of a Monte Carlo experiment generating hedging errors.

From the self-financing condition (12.12) we have

$$
\begin{aligned}
V_1^L &= R_f V_0^L + \theta_0^L (S_1 - S_0 R_f) \\
&= 1.000\,75 \times 30.95 + 0.2145 \times (4900.03 - 5100 \times 1.000\,75) \\
&= -12.74.
\end{aligned}
$$

An identical calculation applies to V_1^D; therefore, at $t = 1$ we have $V_1^D = V_1^L = -12.74$. Both portfolios are short of the target value $H_1 = 3.75$.

From Figure 12.6a we find the locally optimal delta at $t = 1$ to be $\theta_1^L = 0.0428$. Unlike the locally optimal hedge, the dynamically optimal delta takes into account that the value of the hedging portfolio has fallen short of the target,

$$
\begin{aligned}
\theta_1^D &= \theta_1^L + R_f a \frac{H_1 - V_1^D}{S_1} \\
&= 0.0427 + 1.000\,75 \times 3.35 \times \frac{3.75 + 12.74}{4900.0} = 0.0540,
\end{aligned}
$$

Table 12.2. Comparison of Black–Scholes and variance-optimal hedging
strategies in one Monte Carlo experiment.

t	0	1	2	3	4	5	6
S_t	5100.00	4900.03	4999.01	4999.01	4900.03	4999.01	4999.01
H_t	30.95	3.75	6.05	2.83	0.09	0.00	0.00
θ_t^{L}	0.2145	0.0427	0.0697	0.0419	0.0025	0.0000	N/A
θ_t^{D}	0.2145	0.0540	0.0788	0.0491	0.0114	0.0080	N/A
V_t^{L}	30.95	-12.74	-8.69	-8.96	-13.27	-13.05	-13.06
V_t^{D}	30.95	-12.74	-7.61	-7.92	-12.97	-11.89	-11.93

Table 12.3. Monte Carlo simulation of hedging errors.

	Average hedging error		Average squared hedging error	
Number of runs	L	D	L	D
10 000	0.143	0.167	1069.83	1055.92
100 000	-0.0657	-0.0622	1063.40	1052.12
1 000 000	-0.0767	-0.0746	1072.11	1061.72

with the adjustment equal roughly to one percentage point. The value of the two
hedging portfolios at $t = 2$ is again obtained from the self-financing conditions
(12.12) and (12.13):

$$V_2^{L} = R_f V_1^{L} + \theta_1^{L}(S_2 - S_1 R_f)$$
$$= 1.000\,75 \times (-12.74) + 0.0427 \times (4999.01 - 4900.03 \times 1.000\,75)$$
$$= -8.68, \tag{12.14}$$

$$V_2^{D} = R_f V_1^{D} + \theta_1^{D}(S_2 - S_1 R_f)$$
$$= 1.000\,75 \times (-12.74) + 0.054 \times (4999.01 - 4900.03 \times 1.000\,75)$$
$$= -7.60, \quad \text{etc.} \tag{12.15}$$

Table 12.2 details the remaining calculations (results in equations (12.14) and
(12.15) contain small rounding errors). First of all we note that the value of both
hedging portfolios is at the end quite far from the option pay-off, $V_6^{L} = -13.06$ and
$V_6^{D} = -11.93$, whereas the option expires out of the money $H_6 = 0.00$. Secondly,
we note that the locally optimal delta is very close to the dynamically optimal delta,
the difference always less than 1.5 percentage points and consequently the values
of the two portfolios remain close together.

These observations are only valid for the sequence of stock returns given in
Table 12.1. To see what happens in general one has to perform a *Monte Carlo
simulation*. This requires generating Table 12.1 randomly many times, and for each
sequence of returns in Table 12.1 producing the corresponding Table 12.2, storing
the resulting hedging shortfalls, $H_6 - V_6^{L}$ and $H_6 - V_6^{D}$.

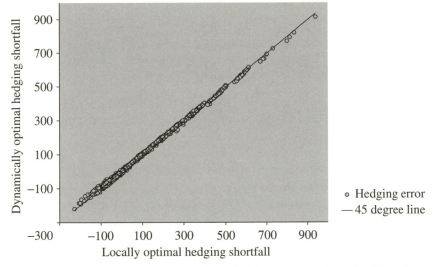

Figure 12.8. Scatter plot of Black–Scholes hedging errors (horizontal axis) against variance-optimal errors (vertical axis).

Figure 12.8 plots the resulting values of $H_6 - V_6^L$ against $H_6 - V_6^D$ for 10 000 randomly chosen stock price histories. The hedging errors can be quite large—their magnitude varies from -230 to 900—compared with the Black–Scholes price of 30. It is also apparent that the errors move together along the 45° line signifying there is little difference between the locally optimal and the dynamically optimal hedging strategy. The numerical values of the average squared hedging error from the Monte Carlo simulations are reported in Table 12.3 (see the GAUSS program *chapter12sect1.gss*).

In conclusion,

- discrete-time hedging errors are non-trivial;
- little is gained from following a dynamically optimal hedging strategy instead of the Black–Scholes hedge.

Monte Carlo may be a natural way of comparing and evaluating the performance of alternative hedging strategies, but this method does have its own shortcomings. First of all, it is difficult to generate truly random numbers. Secondly, the number of simulations required to generate a representative sample of stock price histories is very high. Thirdly, the result of a Monte Carlo study is itself random. Therefore, one may have to run several million simulations before one is convinced that the results obtained are representative. All this is, of course, time-consuming. In the next section we will show how the performance of the two competing hedging strategies can be evaluated by a simple recursive procedure in a tree.

12.1.7 Squared Error Process ε_t^2

The mean value process H_t represents the target value the hedging portfolio V_t is trying to achieve. It can be shown that $V_t = H_t$ minimizes the expected squared replication error as seen at time t, $E_t^P[(V_T - H_T)^2]$. The size of the error in the ideal case $V_t = H_t$ is measured by the **squared error process** ε_t^2:

$$E_t^P[(V_T - H_T)^2] = k_t(V_t - H_t)^2 + \varepsilon_t^2.$$

Specifically, ε_t^2 only depends on the stock price and the calendar time and it is computed recursively from

$$\varepsilon_t^2 = E_t^P[\varepsilon_{t+1}^2] + k_{t+1}\text{ESRE}_t^P(H_{t+1}), \tag{12.16}$$

$$\varepsilon_T = 0. \tag{12.17}$$

The term $\text{ESRE}_t^P(H_{t+1})$ is the *one-period* expected squared replication error from hedging the pay-off H_{t+1}, and it is the *same* for the locally and dynamically optimal hedging strategies:

$$\text{ESRE}_t^P(H_{t+1}) = E_t^P[(R_f H_t + \theta_t^L S_t X_{t+1} - H_{t+1})^2]. \tag{12.18}$$

Theorem 12.1 (IID hedging theorem). *The only difference between the two strategies (L, D) in terms of the hedging error is the proportion k_{t+1} of the one-period error that is carried over to the previous period:*

$$k_t^L = R_f^{2(T-t)} = 1.0015^{T-t}, \tag{12.19}$$

$$k_t^D = R_f^{2(T-t)}b^{T-t} = 0.9962^{T-t}. \tag{12.20}$$

Proof. See Section 12.4.7.   □

This proportion is smaller for the dynamically optimal strategy by the factor of b^{T-t}. Recall from (12.7) that $b = 1 - (E_t^P[X_{t+1}])^2/E_t^P[X_{t+1}^2]$. An econometrician would interpret $(E_t^P[X_{t+1}])^2/E_t^P[X_{t+1}^2]$ as the non-central R^2 from the regression of the risk-free rate onto the excess return. Naturally, the excess return performs very poorly in explaining the variation in the risk-free rate; consequently, the R^2 will be small and b will be very close to 1, which is one reason why the expected squared error of the dynamically optimal hedge is only marginally smaller than the expected squared error of the locally optimal hedge.

12.1.8 One-Period Hedging Errors

Since the one-period hedging errors are a crucial ingredient of the total hedging error, we will now briefly review how one computes $\text{ESRE}_t^P(H_{t+1})$. The reader may wish to revisit the material in Section 2.3

Consider the middle node in the penultimate period, $S_5 = 5100$. The basis assets are the stock and the bank account deposit/overdraft, the focus asset is the option. The pay-off of basis assets is in matrix A, the amount to be hedged is in vector b, and objective probabilities are given by p:

$$A = \begin{bmatrix} 1.00075 & 5415.37 \\ 1.00075 & 5308.13 \\ 1.00075 & 5203.03 \\ 1.00075 & 5100.00 \\ 1.00075 & 4999.01 \\ 1.00075 & 4900.03 \\ 1.00075 & 4803.00 \end{bmatrix}, \quad b = \begin{bmatrix} 60.37 \\ 0.00 \\ 0.00 \\ 0.00 \\ 0.00 \\ 0.00 \\ 0.00 \end{bmatrix}, \quad p = \begin{bmatrix} 0.013 \\ 0.067 \\ 0.273 \\ 0.384 \\ 0.199 \\ 0.051 \\ 0.014 \end{bmatrix}.$$

Because we are after the *expected* squared replication error, we will generate $\tilde{A}, \tilde{b}$ by multiplying each row of A and b with the square root of the probability for the corresponding state. The optimal hedge then takes the form of least-squares coefficients:

$$x = (\tilde{A}^* \tilde{A})^{-1} \tilde{A}^* \tilde{b}. \tag{12.21}$$

Numerically,

$$x = \begin{bmatrix} -98.5 \\ 1.94 \times 10^{-2} \end{bmatrix},$$

and the expected squared error is $\tilde{\varepsilon}^* \tilde{\varepsilon}$, where $\tilde{\varepsilon} = \tilde{A}x - \tilde{b}$. In our case,

$$\tilde{\varepsilon}^* = \begin{bmatrix} -6.14 & 1.14 & 1.23 & 0.22 & -0.71 & -0.79 & -0.64 \end{bmatrix},$$

$$\tilde{\varepsilon}^* \tilde{\varepsilon} = 42.11. \tag{12.22}$$

As a result of the way we have set up the matrix A, the coefficient x_1 is interpreted as the amount of money deposited in the bank account and x_2 is the number of shares (option delta). For a spreadsheet implementation of $\mathrm{ESRE}_t^P (H_{t+1})$, see Exercise 12.5.

Figure 12.9a depicts the one-period expected squared hedging errors, with the result (12.22) highlighted. The largest replication errors are concentrated at the money, whereas far in and out of the money the replication error is virtually zero. This makes sense, since far in and out of the money the option pay-off is linear in stock price and the option therefore becomes a redundant asset. The non-linearity of option pay-off at the money is traditionally captured by the option **gamma**, which is the second derivative of Black–Scholes price with respect to stock price. We discuss the gamma and its relationship to $\mathrm{ESRE}_t^P (H_{t+1})$ in the next section.

12.1.9 Black–Scholes Gamma

We saw in Section 12.1.4 that H_t is very close to the Black–Scholes price of the option. Thus we may believe that the hedging error $\mathrm{ESRE}_t^P (H_{t+1})$ will be well approximated by the hedging error implied by the Black–Scholes formula, which is examined in Appendix 12.7. We find that the one-period squared hedging error is proportional to the kurtosis of asset returns and to gamma squared:

$$\mathrm{ESRE}_t (H_{t+1}) \approx (\tfrac{1}{2} \gamma_t S_t^2 \, \mathrm{Var}_t^P (R_{t+1}))^2 (\mathrm{kurt}_t^P (R_{t+1}) - 1). \tag{12.23}$$

The explicit value of γ is computed in the exercises of Appendix A:

$$\gamma_t = \frac{1}{\sigma\sqrt{T-t}\,S_t}\,\exp\left(-\frac{1}{2}\left(\frac{\ln(S_t/K)+(r+\frac{1}{2}\sigma^2)(T-t)}{\sigma\sqrt{T-t}}\right)^2\right). \qquad (12.24)$$

In the Black–Scholes setting, returns are virtually normally distributed and the kurtosis of returns is therefore equal to 3. This generates the standard result for the variance of one-step errors in a discretely rehedged Black–Scholes model:

$$\mathrm{ESRE}_t(H_{t+dt}) = \tfrac{1}{2}\sigma^4\gamma^2 S_t^4(\mathrm{d}t)^2.$$

In our model the kurtosis is 3.28 and therefore the standard formula becomes

$$\mathrm{ESRE}_t(H_{t+dt}) = \frac{2.28}{4}\sigma^4\gamma^2 S_t^4(\mathrm{d}t)^2. \qquad (12.25)$$

The Black–Scholes approximation of $\mathrm{ESRE}_t(H_t + dt)$ is depicted in Figure 12.9b.

12.1.10   Unconditional Hedging Errors and Toft's Formula

Having computed the one-period errors, the next task is to combine them to evaluate the total expected squared hedging error. Using equation (12.16) recursively we obtain

$$\varepsilon_0^2 = \mathrm{E}_0^P\left[\sum_{t=0}^{T-1} k_{t+1}\mathrm{ESRE}_t^P(H_{t+1})\right], \qquad (12.26)$$

that is the total squared hedging error is equal to the expectation of the sum of one-period squared hedging errors. Because in our case the process k is deterministic we can simplify (12.26) further by taking k in front of the expectation

$$\varepsilon_0^2 = \sum_{t=0}^{T-1} k_{t+1}\mathrm{E}_0^P[\mathrm{ESRE}_t^P(H_{t+1})]. \qquad (12.27)$$

Table 12.4 gives numerical values of $\mathrm{E}_0^P[\mathrm{ESRE}_t^P(H_{t+1})]$ for individual periods t, together with weights k for the two hedging strategies.

The total expected squared error of the locally optimal strategy is

$$\begin{aligned}(\varepsilon_0^L)^2 &= 1.0076 \times 101.4 + 1.0061 \times 119.0 + 1.0045 \times 139.5 \\ &\quad + 1.0030 \times 167.1 + 1.0015 \times 212.8 + 1.0000 \times 328.9 \\ &= 1071.6,\end{aligned} \qquad (12.28)$$

whereas for the dynamically optimal strategy we have

$$\begin{aligned}(\varepsilon_0^D)^2 &= 0.9811 \times 101.4 + 0.9849 \times 119.0 + 0.9886 \times 139.5 \\ &\quad + 0.9924 \times 167.1 + 0.9962 \times 212.8 + 1.0000 \times 328.9 \\ &= 1061.3.\end{aligned} \qquad (12.29)$$

These exact figures should be compared with the Monte Carlo estimates in Table 12.3.

Table 12.4. Composition of the total error for
the dynamically optimal and locally optimal strategy.

t	0	1	2	3	4	5
$E_0^P[\text{ESRE}_t^P(H_{t+1})]$	101.4	119.0	139.5	167.1	212.8	328.9
Locally optimal k	1.0076	1.0061	1.0045	1.0030	1.0015	1.0000
Dynamically optimal k	0.9811	0.9849	0.9886	0.9924	0.9962	1.0000

- Table 12.4 indicates why the locally optimal strategy performs nearly as well as the dynamically optimal hedge. It shows that the errors close to maturity contribute three times as much to the total error than the errors in the first hedging period. Yet the gain from following the dynamically optimal strategy is the largest in the early hedging periods and it vanishes as one gets closer to maturity.

- One can approximate the total hedging error by means of **Toft's formula**, which replaces $\text{ESRE}_t^P(H_{t+1})$ in (12.27) with the gamma approximation (12.23) (see also Exercise 12.9). Toft's formula adjusted for excess kurtosis seems to work very well on historical equity data; however, it is only an approximation and has to be used cautiously. One can easily construct *artificial* return distributions for which the kurtosis-adjusted Toft formula will hugely overestimate the true hedging errors.

Formula (12.27) is useful for a comparison between the errors of the dynamically and locally optimal strategies, but it is not a very practical recipe for computing ε_t^2. Just think how many computations are required to evaluate $E_0^P[\text{ESRE}_5^P[H_6]]$, then $E_0^P[\text{ESRE}_4^P[H_5]]$, and so on, even when all ESREs are already known. A better strategy is to take advantage of the recursive relationship (12.16):

$$\varepsilon_t^2 = E_t^P[\varepsilon_{t+1}^2] + k_{t+1}\text{ESRE}_t^P(H_{t+1})$$

(see Exercise 12.6).

The values of ε_t^2 are shown in Figure 12.10, where we can see that the total expected squared hedging error of the dynamically optimal strategy is 1061.4 and the locally optimal error is 1071.7, confirming the results in equations (12.28) and (12.29).

12.2 Incomplete Market Option Price Bounds

12.2.1 Sharpe Ratio of Option Hedging Strategies

So far we have tacitly assumed that options are bought and sold at the mean value H_0. But suppose now that we are able to sell a call option at a premium $\pi > 0$, receiving $H_0 + \pi$. If we simply plough this amount of money into the hedging strategy by taking $V_0 = H_0 + \pi$, then the expected squared replication error actually increases

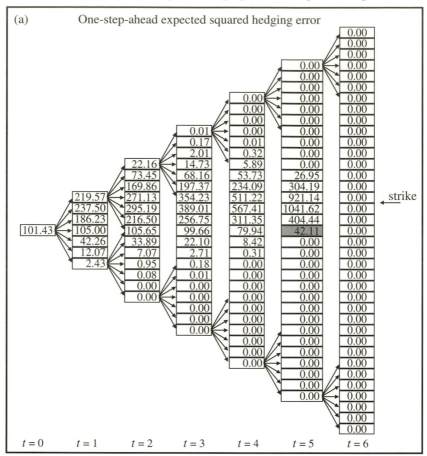

Figure 12.9. Comparison of (a) one-step-ahead expected squared hedging error based on the discrete model and (b) on discrete application of the continuous Black–Scholes formula.

for both the D and L hedge, because for both strategies

$$E_0[(V_T - H_T)^2] = k_0(V_0 - H_0)^2 + \varepsilon_0^2$$

and this value is the smallest for $V_0 = H_0$. If $V_0 \neq H_0$, then the squared replication error alone does not tell us how good a given option deal is. In this section we will examine option hedging strategies in the context of optimal investment, discussed in Section 3.5. The result will not only tell us how many units of the option to sell at a given price and what is the optimal hedge to maturity, but most importantly we will be able to evaluate the investment potential of the whole package.

Let us establish the following notation. Let C_0 be the initial (ask) price of the option; suppose our total financial wealth before trading is V_{safe}/R_f^T, the utility function bliss point is V_{bliss} and we are considering selling η units of the option with pay-off H_T. Then the optimal investment problem with quadratic utility has

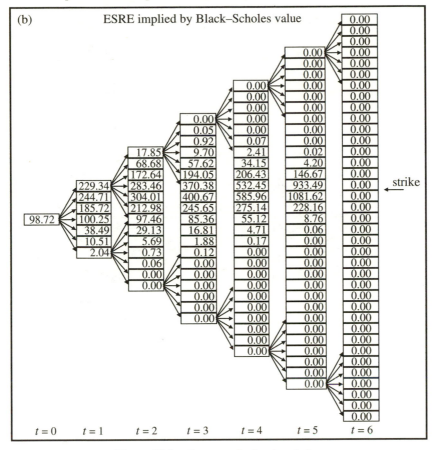

Figure 12.9. See opposite for description.

the form,

$$\max_{\theta_0,\theta_1,\dots,\theta_{T-1}} -E_0[(V_{\text{bliss}} - (V_T - \eta H_T))^2], \tag{12.30}$$

$$V_0 = \eta C_0 + \frac{V_{\text{safe}}}{R_{\text{f}}^T}. \tag{12.31}$$

Equation (12.30) very much resembles the optimal hedging problem (12.1). By comparing (12.30) with (12.1) we can see that for a fixed η the maximum is achieved by the dynamically optimal strategy whereby we start with wealth V_0 and optimally hedge the amount $\tilde{H}_T = V_{\text{bliss}} + \eta H_T$. Therefore,

$$u(\eta) = \max_{\theta_0,\theta_1,\dots,\theta_{T-1}} -E_0[(V_{\text{bliss}} - (V_T - \eta H_T))^2]$$

$$= k_0 \underbrace{\left(V_0 - \frac{V_{\text{bliss}}}{R_{\text{f}}^T} - \eta H_0\right)^2}_{V_0 - \tilde{H}_0} + \varepsilon_0^2(V_{\text{bliss}} + \eta H_T), \tag{12.32}$$

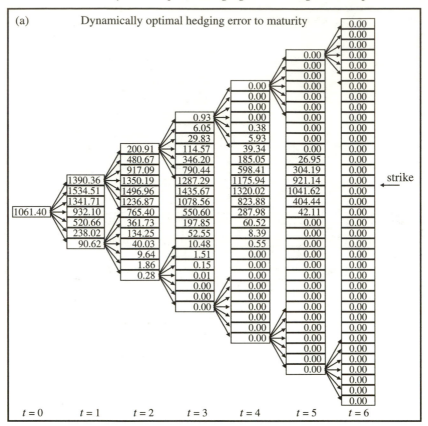

Figure 12.10. Comparison of squared error processes of the variance-optimal and the discrete Black–Scholes strategies.

where $\varepsilon_0^2(V_{\mathrm{bliss}} + \eta H_T)$ is the squared error process from hedging the amount $V_{\mathrm{bliss}} + \eta H_T$. It is intuitively clear that

$$\varepsilon_0^2(V_{\mathrm{bliss}} + \eta H_T) = \varepsilon_0^2(\eta H_T) \tag{12.33}$$

because the risk-free amount V_{bliss} can be hedged perfectly. Similarly, the error has a linear scaling property:

$$\varepsilon_0^2(\eta H_T) = \eta^2 \varepsilon_0^2(H_T). \tag{12.34}$$

Putting (12.31)–(12.34) together we have

$$u(\eta) = \max_{\theta_0, \theta_1, \dots, \theta_{T-1}} -E_0[(V_{\mathrm{bliss}} - (V_T - \eta H_T))^2]$$

$$= k_0 \left(\frac{V_{\mathrm{safe}} - V_{\mathrm{bliss}}}{R_{\mathrm{f}}^T} + \eta(C_0 - H_0) \right)^2 + \eta^2 \varepsilon_0^2(H_T). \tag{12.35}$$

This is a good opportunity to deal with the scaling properties of our investment problem. We can set the local risk aversion equal to 1 by letting $V_{\mathrm{bliss}} = 2V_{\mathrm{safe}}$

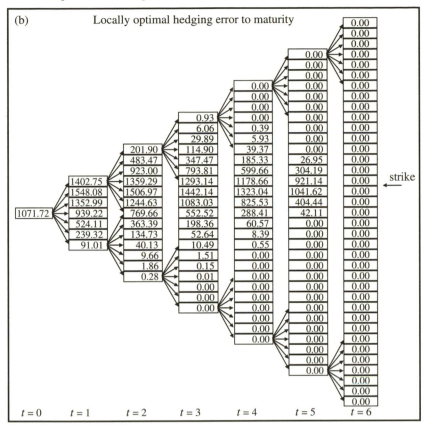

Figure 12.10. See opposite for description.

and introduce $\alpha_{-1,1} = \eta C_0 R_{\mathrm{f}}^T / V_{\mathrm{safe}}$ as the proportion of the option sales in the safe wealth per unit of risk tolerance. In this fashion (12.35) is rephrased as

$$-\frac{u(\alpha_{-1,1})}{(V_{\mathrm{safe}}/C_0 R_{\mathrm{f}}^T)^2} = k_0(\alpha_{-1,1}(C_0 - H_0) - C_0)^2 + \alpha_{-1,1}^2 \varepsilon_0^2(H_T). \qquad (12.36)$$

The last step requires finding the optimal number of options to sell, that is, maximizing the right-hand side of (12.36) with respect to α. The first-order conditions give

$$2k_0(\alpha_{-1,1}(C_0 - H_0) - C_0)(C_0 - H_0) + 2\alpha_{-1,1}\varepsilon_0^2(H_T) = 0,$$

$$\alpha_{-1,1\,\mathrm{opt}} = \frac{k_0 C_0(C_0 - H_0)}{\varepsilon_0^2(H_T) + k_0(C_0 - H_0)^2}, \qquad (12.37)$$

and the optimized utility becomes

$$\max_{\alpha} -\frac{u(\alpha_{-1,1})}{(V_{\mathrm{safe}}/C_0 R_{\mathrm{f}}^T)^2} = \frac{k_0 C_0^2 \varepsilon_0^2(H_T)}{\varepsilon_0^2(H_T) + k_0(C_0 - H_0)^2}. \qquad (12.38)$$

We know from Section 3.5 that the quadratic utility is related to the Sharpe ratio of the investment strategy as follows:

$$\max_{\alpha} -\frac{u(\alpha_{-1,1})}{V_{\text{safe}}^2} = \frac{1}{1 + \text{SR}^2}. \tag{12.39}$$

Comparing (12.39) with (12.38) we find

$$\frac{1}{1 + \text{SR}^2} = \frac{(k_0/R_{\text{f}}^{2T})\varepsilon_0^2(H_T)}{\varepsilon_0^2(H_T) + k_0(C_0 - H_0)^2},$$

$$1 + \text{SR}^2 = \frac{R_{\text{f}}^{2T}}{k_0} + \frac{R_{\text{f}}^{2T}(C_0 - H_0)^2}{\varepsilon_0^2(H_T)}. \tag{12.40}$$

The same procedure applies to both the dynamically and the locally optimal strategies; in fact, (12.37) and (12.40) hold generally for any hedging strategy that depends at most linearly on V if k and H are computed in the right way.

Let C_0 be the option price, H_0 the mean value of the option and $\varepsilon_0^2(H_T)$ the expected squared replication error.

- For an investor with local risk aversion $\tilde{\gamma}$ and no initial risky assets, the maximum investment potential is achieved by investing proportion α of the initial risk-free wealth into the option deal where

$$\alpha^{\text{D}} = \frac{1}{\tilde{\gamma}} \frac{b^T(1 - H_0/C_0)}{(\varepsilon_0^{\text{D}}(H_T)/R_{\text{f}}^T C_0)^2 + b^T(1 - H_0/C_0)^2},$$

$$\alpha^{\text{L}} = \frac{1}{\tilde{\gamma}} \frac{(1 - H_0/C_0)}{(\varepsilon_0^{\text{L}}(H_T)/R_{\text{f}}^T C_0)^2 + (1 - H_0/C_0)^2},$$

for the dynamically optimal investment and for the locally optimal investment, respectively.

- The corresponding maximum Sharpe ratios are

$$\text{SR}^{\text{D}} = \sqrt{\underbrace{\frac{1 - b^T}{b^T}}_{\text{basis SR}} + \underbrace{\left(\frac{(C_0 - H_0)R_{\text{f}}^T}{\varepsilon_0^{\text{D}}(H_T)}\right)^2}_{\text{option SR}}},$$

$$\text{SR}^{\text{L}} = \frac{(C_0 - H_0)R_{\text{f}}^T}{\varepsilon_0^{\text{L}}(H_T)}.$$

12.2.2 Numerical Examples

Consider the stock market model of the first section and the option mentioned there. We have calculated the mean value of the option to be $H_0 = 31.0$. Recall that 31.3 is the Black–Scholes price of the option at which the implied volatility coincides with the objective volatility of the stock. Suppose that the option can be sold at $C_0 = 39.4$; this corresponds to an implied volatility of 10% above the objective volatility. The optimal α^{D} is

$$\alpha^{D}_{-1,1} = \frac{0.9947^{6}(1 - 31.0/39.4)}{(\sqrt{1061.4}/(1.04^{6/52}39.4))^{2} + 0.9947^{6}(1 - 31.0/39.4)^{2}} = 0.286.$$

Hence the option sales revenue of an investor with risk aversion $\tilde{\gamma} = 3$ would be equal to $0.286/3 = 9.5\%$ of her risk-free wealth, provided that the investor uses weekly rehedging and the dynamically optimal strategy. The Sharpe ratio of this strategy is 0.315. It is a combination of the basis Sharpe ratio

$$SR_{basis} = \sqrt{\frac{1 - 0.9947^{6}}{0.9947^{6}}} = 0.180$$

obtained by investing in the risk-free bank account and the stock only, and the Sharpe ratio of the dynamically optimal option hedge,

$$SR^{D}_{option} = \frac{(39.4 - 31.0)1.04^{6/52}}{\sqrt{1061.4}} = 0.259,$$

$$SR^{D} = \sqrt{0.180^{2} + 0.259^{2}} = 0.315.$$

In contrast, the Black–Scholes hedge gives

$$\alpha^{L}_{-1,1} = \frac{(1 - 31.0/39.4)}{(\sqrt{1061.4}/(1.04^{6/52}39.4))^{2} + (1 - 31.0/39.4)^{2}} = 0.295,$$

$$SR^{L} = \frac{(39.4 - 31.0)1.04^{6/52}}{\sqrt{1071.7}} = 0.257.$$

Compared with the dynamically optimal investment we are losing out by not investing a little more in the stock.

12.2.3 Option Price Bounds

So far we have looked at the investment potential of a hedging strategy with option price given. One can revert this procedure to find a 'sensible' range of prices for the option. The basic idea is that one should not observe option prices in the market that lead to highly attractive hedging strategies, so-called **good deals** or **near-arbitrage opportunities**. Suppose we can agree that a Sharpe ratio of 1 represents an extremely attractive investment. In such a case the option price should obey

$$\frac{|C_{0} - H_{0}|R_{f}^{T}}{\varepsilon_{0}^{D}(H_{0})} < 1. \tag{12.41}$$

Obviously, the better the hedge we can come up with the smaller the hedging error ε and the narrower the price bounds. The interpretation of the bounds is simple: if the price drops below the lower bound, then buy the option; if it increases beyond the upper bound then sell. The complete market world now becomes a special case with $\varepsilon = 0$, where the investor makes a move as soon as the price deviates from H_{0}.

The idea sounds deceptively simple, so where is the catch? We are using a quadratic utility which is extremely conservative when dealing with skewed risks.

Consider the price bounds given by equation (12.41). Numerically, we have

$$C_{\text{low}} = H_0 - \frac{\varepsilon_0^D(H_0)}{R_f^T} = 31.0 - \frac{\sqrt{1061.4}}{1.04^{6/52}} = -1.4,$$

$$C_{\text{high}} = H_0 + \frac{\varepsilon_0^D(H_0)}{R_f^T} = 31.0 + \frac{\sqrt{1061.4}}{1.04^{6/52}} = 63.4.$$

The lower price bound is negative. This is a familiar story from Chapter 3; the quadratic utility is not very good at recognizing arbitrage opportunities. When the option price is low we would like to buy the option, which means we have a limited downside risk and a large upside potential. The quadratic utility, however, penalizes the upside and hence the Sharpe ratio of this wonderful investment opportunity is low. This problem is not as dramatic when we are selling the option, but even there it is theoretically possible to find a selling price that gives us an arbitrage opportunity and only a finite level of Sharpe ratio.

To conclude, Sharpe ratio price bounds are ultra cautious. If we want a more sensitive criterion, we need to be able to solve the hedging problem with a non-decreasing utility. The exponential utility is the easiest to work with, but that is already beyond the scope of this book. If the reader is comfortable with the material in Chapters 3 and 4 and with the last part of this chapter, then it is a very interesting and feasible project to try to extend the analysis of this chapter to the exponential utility.

12.2.4 Is H_0 a No-Arbitrage Price of the Option?
Properties of Variance-Optimal Measure

The peculiar behaviour of the quadratic utility raises one interesting question: could it happen that the mean value price H_0 permits arbitrage? To *guarantee* that H_0 admits no arbitrage it is enough to show that (i) the variance-optimal measure Q is a martingale measure *and* (ii) the variance-optimal probabilities are strictly positive. The rest then follows from the dynamic arbitrage theorem. To demonstrate (i) one must show that this measure prices the stock returns correctly at all times and in all contingencies,

$$E_t^Q[R_{t+1}] = R_f,$$

or equivalently

$$E_t^Q[X_{t+1}] = E_t^Q[R_{t+1} - R_f] = 0. \qquad (12.42)$$

Because R_{t+1} is known at time $t+1$ we can rewrite (12.42) using the one-step-ahead conditional change of measure $m_{t+1|t}$:

$$E_t^Q[X_{t+1}] = E_t^P[X_{t+1}m_{t+1|t}] \qquad (12.43)$$

(refer also to equation (9.25)). Recall the definition of the variance-optimal measure from (12.4)

$$m_{t+1|t} \triangleq \frac{1 - aX_{t+1}}{b}$$

and substitute it into (12.43)

$$E_t^Q[X_{t+1}] = \frac{E_t^P[X_{t+1}] - aE_t^P[X_{t+1}^2]}{b}.$$

Now recall from (12.6) that $a = E_t^P[X_{t+1}]/E_t^P[X_{t+1}^2]$, which immediately implies that the right-hand side of the above equation is zero.

We should perhaps verify at this point that $m_{t+1|t}$ is a conditional change of measure. To this end we have

$$E_t^P[m_{t+1|t}] = E_t^P\left[\frac{1 - aX_{t+1}}{b}\right] = \frac{1 - aE_t^P[X_{t+1}]}{b}$$
$$= \frac{1 - (E_t^P[X_{t+1}])^2/E_t^P[X_{t+1}^2]}{b} = 1,$$

by virtue of (12.6) and (12.7), as required by condition (9.26).

Finally, and most importantly, we need $m_{t+1|t} > 0$ so that all risk-neutral probabilities are non-negative. From the definition of $m_{t+1|t}$ this implies

$$\frac{1 - aX_{t+1}}{b} > 0.$$

Now, b is always positive, therefore we have

$$1 > aX_{t+1}, \tag{12.44}$$

which is the familiar bliss point condition (3.67) from Chapter 3. Thus as long as (12.44) holds the variance-optimal measure Q is an *equivalent* martingale measure and therefore H_t is guaranteed to be a no-arbitrage price of H_T. If the bliss point condition (12.44) is violated, then H_t *may or may not* be a no-arbitrage price of H_T. The less frequent the rehedging the more of a problem this could pose. In practice, however, unless the hedge is completely static, one is unlikely to encounter a situation where H_0 gives rise to arbitrage. To give a numerical example, on a monthly horizon the FTSE 100 returns between 1984 and 2001 averaged 0.9% with a standard deviation of 4.8%, which corresponds to a bliss point of

$$\frac{4.8^2 + 0.9^2}{0.9} = 26.5\%,$$

whereas the maximum monthly return in that period was 21% (between 5 October 1998 and 4 November 1998).

When m takes both positive and negative values, we say that Q is a **signed** (rather than equivalent) **measure**.

12.3 Towards Continuous Time

12.3.1 Brownian Motion Limit

What happens to the option price and the hedging error as the rehedging interval goes to zero? We can find out by extending the binomial model programmed in *chapter6sect2.gss* to accommodate the multinomial model of this chapter. First of all, we need to adjust the inputs.

```
@****************************@
@    Transformation of       @
@        log returns         @
@****************************@
UnitTime=week;
R1safe=1.04^(1/52);                          @ weekly safe return                  @
lnR1   =0.060~0.040~0.02~0.000~-0.02~
        -0.04~-0.06;                         @ weekly return                       @
PDistr=0.013~0.067~0.273~0.384~0.199~
        0.050~0.014;                         @ prob. density of weekly  returns    @
mu1=lnR1*PDistr';                            @ expected weekly log return          @
sig1=sqrt(((lnR1-mu1)^2)*PDistr');           @ volatility of weekly log return     @

dt = RehedgeInterval/UnitTime;
lnRdt=mu1*dt+(lnR1-mu1)*sqrt(dt);            @ log return over rehedging interval  @
Rdt=exp(lnRdt);
Rdtsafe=R1safe^dt;
```

Note that the scaling remains exactly the same as in Chapter 6, that is, we keep the probabilities constant and only vary the size of log returns to keep the unconditional mean and variance constant. Next we must calculate the risk-neutral probabilities.

```
@**************************@
@      Risk-neutral        @
@      probabilities       @
@**************************@
X = Rdt - Rdtsafe;                           @ excess return             @
EX= X*PDistr';                               @ E[X]                      @
EX2=(X^2)*PDistr';                           @ E[X^2]                    @
sigX=sqrt(EX2-(EX)^2);                       @ st. dev. of returns       @
kurt=((X-EX)^4)*PDistr'/(sigX^4);            @ kurtosis of returns       @
a=EX/EX2;                                    eq. (12.6)
b=1-EX^2/EX2;                                eq. (12.7)
QDistr=PDistr.*((1-a*X)/b);                  eq. (12.4)
```

Finally, we will adjust the main loop so that it evaluates the squared error to maturity.

```
@**************************@
@   grid indexation        @
@**************************@
Tidx=ceil(T/RehedgeInterval)+1;             @ Number of trading dates            @
dlnR=lnRdt[1]-lnRdt[2];                      @ increment on log price grid        @
highlnRdt=lnRdt[1];                          @ the highest return over one period @
n=cols(lnRdt);                               @ number of branches over one period @

@ there are 1+(n-1)*(tt-1) live cells at time tt,
                                             highest stock price at the top @
@ log price at cell  1 at time tt is ln(S0)+(tt-1)*highlnRdt          @
@ log price at cell ii at time tt is ln(S0)+(tt-1)*highlnRdt-(ii-1)*dlnR  @


@**************************@
@     option payoff        @
@**************************@
MaxDim=1+(n-1)*(Tidx-1);                          @ no. of cells at time T   @
S_T=seqa(ln(S0)+(Tidx-1)*highlnRdt,
                        -dlnR,MaxDim);           @ log price at maturity    @
S_T=exp(S_T);                                    @ stock price at maturity  @
H=maxc((S_T-strike)'|zeros(1,MaxDim));           @ option payoff at maturity @
eps2_D=zeros(rows(S_T),1);                        eq. (12.17)
k_D=rev(seqm(1,b*Rdtsafe^2,Tidx));               eq. (12.20)
```

Table 12.5. Towards continuous time. Hedging errors in the Brownian motion limit.

Frequency	H_0	ε_0^2	Kurtosis	Computation time (s)
5 min	31.238	**2.7**	3.30	312
15 min	31.229	**8.1**	3.30	34
30 min	31.221	**16.1**	3.30	8.2
1 hour	31.205	**31.9**	3.29	2.1
1 day	31.022	**243.5**	3.29	0.00

```
@***********************@
@      main loop        @
@***********************@
for tt (Tidx-1,1,-1);
    Hnext=H;                             @ mean value in next period    @
    epsnext=eps2_D;                      @ squared error in next period @
    for ii (1,1+(n-1)*(tt-1),1);
        focus=Hnext[ii:ii+n-1]';
        H[ii]=(QDistr*focus')/Rdtsafe;                    eq. (12.8)
        hedge=(PDistr.*X)*(focus-Rdtsafe*H[ii])'/EX2;     eq. (12.10)
        HedgeError=focus-hedge*X-Rdtsafe*H[ii];           @ hedging error @
        ESRE=(HedgeError.*PDistr)*HedgeError';            @ ESRE          @
        eps2_D[ii]=PDistr*epsnext[ii:ii+n-1]              eq. (12.16)
                   +k_D[tt+1]*ESRE;
    endfor;
endfor;
```

The entire program is in the file *chapter12sect3.gss*. The reader can now experiment with changing the `RehedgeInterval`. The results are summarized in Table 12.5. It is apparent that the hedging error tends to zero as we make the rehedging interval shorter. This is very interesting, since each of the models we are looking at is incomplete and the degree of incompleteness (in terms of the number of branches in one period) does not change. Here we have a numerical 'proof' that continuous rehedging in the Black–Scholes model is indeed riskless. Mathematically, we are observing a very special case of the martingale representation theorem under the variance-optimal measure.

12.3.2 Numerical Implementation at High Rehedging Frequencies

Returns on short time horizons in real financial markets do not follow the Brownian limit, and modelling them brings new challenges. For example, while a weekly return takes values within ± 3 standard deviations, a 5 min return is spread over ± 20 standard deviations, which is reflected in the increasing size of kurtosis at shorter time intervals seen in Table 12.6. The wider spread of return values requires a higher number of branches in the stock price lattice. To model 5 min returns accurately one may have to use as many as $n = 100$ values of the return in any one period. With more branches *and* more time periods one is facing very long computational times if one uses the straightforward multinomial tree and backward recursion.

The problem can be alleviated by using the fast Fourier transform method described in Chapter 7. Recall the Fourier transform pricing formula (7.18),

$$H_0 = \mathcal{F}(\mathcal{F}^{-1}(H_T) \times (\sqrt{n}\,\mathcal{F}(\text{price kernel}))^T),$$

Table 12.6.   Descriptive statistics of FTSE 100 returns in the period 1990–2000.
Reprinted from Oomen (2002).

Frequency	Skewness	Kurtosis
1 min	1.6	3305
5 min	−0.4	508
10 min	−1.9	345
30 min	−1.1	115
1 hour	−0.3	84
1 day	0.05	5.4

which allows us to 'hop' from H_T straight to H_0. In our case the price kernel vector will contain the variance-optimal probabilities divided by the risk-free return at the top with the remaining entries being padded by zeros. It is important to bear in mind that the Fourier pricing formula will only work with equidistantly spaced log returns because the discrete Fourier transform itself is based on evenly spaced numbers on a circle. The program *chapter12sect3a.gss* demonstrates the working of Fourier pricing in the septanomial model of Section 12.1.

If FFT makes the calculation of H_0 relatively straightforward, computing the squared error process is an entirely different matter. To be able to evaluate ε_0^2 one must know the mean value process H in *every* node of the stock price lattice, not just at the beginning. Computing *all* the values of H is bound to be time-consuming no matter how one does it. To make the computation feasible at high rehedging frequencies we have to be selective about the values of H that we want to consider. Section 12.1.10 tells us that one-period errors close to maturity contribute relatively more to the total error. Furthermore, the values of $E_0^P[\mathrm{ESRE}_t^P(H_{t+1})]$ for t small do not seem to change very much. Hence a good strategy might be to create a time grid that has more time points at maturity and progressively fewer points away from maturity, then compute H_{t+1} at these selected time points using the Fourier formula, then evaluate $\mathrm{ESRE}_t^P(H_{t+1})$ using standard regression node by node, and then compute $E_0^P[\mathrm{ESRE}_t^P(H_{t+1})]$ again using the Fourier formula (this time with objective probabilities and without discounting). The GAUSS program *chapter12sect3b.gss* applies the accelerated algorithm to a model calibrated on FTSE 100 Index data with 5 min rehedging interval. For comparison (if you have a spare afternoon), the same computation using backward recursion in the multinomial lattice is in the file *chapter12sect3c.gss*.

We are most interested in the results. We are pricing a European call option on the FTSE 100 Equity Index. The current value (on 26 February 2003) of the index is $S_0 = 3576$, the option is struck at 3625 and expires on 17 April 2003, currently with 33 trading days to maturity. We will hedge once in 5 min and consider two distributions for the returns. The *market model* will use the historical distribution of 5 min returns over the period January 2002 to January 2003, the Black–Scholes model will use the lognormal distribution with the same mean and variance. For both models we calculate the mean value, the hedging error and the optimal delta and give a price range corresponding to a hedging strategy with Sharpe ratio equal to 0.5. The results are summarized in Table 12.7.

Table 12.7. Comparison of hedging errors between a model with observed market returns and a model with lognormal returns.

	Market model	Black–Scholes model
H_0	110.08	110.13
ε_0^2	87±1	3.8
kurtosis	50	3
Toft's estimate of ε_0^2	92	3.8
delta	0.4793	0.4786
SR = 0.5 price range	105.4–114.7	109.2–111.1

Conversely, one could ask what is the risk compensation required by traders who sell the option. The option in question had an ask price of 139, this implies

$$\text{SR} = \frac{139 - 110}{\sqrt{87}} = 3.1,$$

which seems rather high. We have not incorporated any transaction costs, however, which would make the option less attractive to hedge and the risk premium would then drop.

12.3.3 Continuous Hedging Is not Riskless after All

The analysis of the preceding section applied at 1 min intervals turns up $\varepsilon_0^2 = 65$ for the market model compared with $\varepsilon_0^2 = 0.8$ for the Black–Scholes model. By all accounts frequent hedging in reality is not riskless, even though it would have been in the Black–Scholes model. This idea is pursued theoretically in Exercises 12.16–12.18.

12.3.4 Limiting Properties of the Mean Value Process H

It is somewhat surprising that even in the presence of jumps the mean value process is close to the Black–Scholes values. This section outlines the mathematical forces that push H towards the Black–Scholes price. The basic idea is that the distribution of the log return $X_{N,\Delta t} \triangleq \ln R_{1,\Delta t} + \cdots + \ln R_{N,\Delta t}$ converges to normal under some circumstances when $\ln R_{i,\Delta t}$ are IID. One limit of interest takes $N \to \infty$ for Δt fixed and can be viewed as facing longer and longer time to maturity with fixed rebalancing frequency. In this case the limiting distribution is *always normal*: $(X_{N,\Delta t} - \mathrm{E}[X_{N,\Delta t}])/\sqrt{\mathrm{Var}(X_{N,\Delta t})} \to N(0, 1)$. Depending on how far the one-period log return is from normality we will need smaller or larger N to achieve normality in the limit. In the extreme case when the one-period log return is normal we have normality for all N. The second limiting case is more complicated, it takes $N \to \infty$ and $\Delta t \to 0$ such that $N \Delta t = T$ remains fixed. This limit corresponds to continuous trading with a fixed maturity. The result is a *not necessarily normal distribution*; this crucially depends on how non-normal the returns become as $\Delta t \to 0$. In general we are only guaranteed that the limit (if it exists) is an *infinitely divisible distribution*.

Example 12.2. Take

$$\ln R_{\Delta t} = (\mu - \sigma^2/p)\Delta t - \Gamma(\sigma^2 \Delta t/p^2, p),$$

where $\Gamma(\sigma^2 \Delta t/p^2, p)$ represents a random variable Z with density

$$f(z) = \frac{z^{\sigma^2 \Delta t/p^2 - 1} e^{-z/p}}{\Gamma(\sigma^2 \Delta t/p^2) p^{\sigma^2 \Delta t/p^2}}.$$

If $\ln R_{i,\Delta t}$ are IID with distribution Z, then one can show that

$$\ln R_{1,\Delta t} + \cdots + \ln R_{N,\Delta t} = \left(\mu - \frac{\sigma^2}{p}\right)N\Delta t - \Gamma\left(\frac{\sigma^2 N\Delta t}{p^2}, p\right)$$

$$= \left(\mu - \frac{\sigma^2}{p}\right)T - \Gamma\left(\frac{\sigma^2 T}{p^2}, p\right).$$

The reason why $\ln R_{1,\Delta t} + \cdots + \ln R_{N,\Delta t}$ does not tend to normal as $\Delta t \to 0$ is that $\Gamma(\sigma^2 \Delta t/p^2, p)$ becomes highly skewed for $\Delta t \to 0$ and this increasing degree of non-normality offsets the increasing number of summands in $\ln R_{1,\Delta t} + \cdots + \ln R_{N,\Delta t}$.

In the present setting the central limit theorem is applied under the variance-optimal measure Q. It is easy to verify that if stock returns are IID under P and the interest rate is deterministic, then the stock returns will be IID under Q as well. In turn this implies that log returns are IID under Q.

Moreover, by construction we have $E^Q[R] = R_f$ (see equation (12.42)). We know from the Taylor expansion that as long as the returns are within $\pm 10\%$, we will have $\ln R = R - 1$, and therefore also $E^Q[\ln R] = r$ with very good precision. Finally, for the small values of returns that one observes on daily horizons, it is the case that $\text{Var}^Q(\ln R)$ is very close to $\text{Var}^P(R)$.

The mathematical machinery is provided by convergence in distribution. The central limit theorem implies that

$$X_{N,\Delta t} = \frac{\sum_{i=1}^{N} \ln R_{i,\Delta t} - N E^Q[\ln R_{\Delta t}]}{\sqrt{N \, \text{Var}^Q(\ln R_{\Delta t})}}$$

converges to a standard normal variable X in distribution for Δt fixed as N increases to infinity. This in turn implies that for any bounded continuous function f,

$$\lim_{N \to \infty} E^Q[f(X_{N,\Delta t})] \to E^Q[f(X)].$$

A call option pay-off is not bounded from above but we know that $E^Q[f(X)]$ is finite and therefore the error from truncating f at a very high value can be made arbitrarily small. The result is the Black–Scholes formula with

$$r^{\text{BS}} \triangleq E^Q[\ln R] \approx r \quad \text{and} \quad \sigma^{\text{BS}} \triangleq \sqrt{\text{Var}^Q(\ln R)} \approx \text{Var}^P(R).$$

The practical implication of all this is that one should expect the mean value process to be very close to the conventional Black–Scholes value when the time to maturity is large, even if the log returns over short horizons have high kurtosis.

12.4 Derivation of Optimal Hedging Strategy

We wish to find the optimal control to minimize the expected squared replication error,

$$\min_{x,\theta_0,\dots,\theta_{T-1}} E_0[(V_T^{x,\theta} - H_T)^2], \tag{12.45}$$

where $V_T^{x,\theta}$ is the time T value of a self-financing portfolio generated by initial wealth x and trading strategy $\{\theta_t\}_{t=0,\dots,T-1}$ denoting number of shares.

12.4.1 First Attempt at a Solution

To illustrate this problem let us consider a very simple example with three dates $t = 0, 1, 2$, two basis assets (stock and bond) and one focus asset to be hedged (call it option). We will assume that the stock return is either high $R_u = 1.2$ or low $R_d = 1.0$ and that the risk-free return is $R_f = 1.05$. The initial stock price is $S_0 = 1$ and there are no dividends. At time $t + 1$ the value of the (self-financing) hedging portfolio is

$$V_{t+1} = V_t R_f + \theta_t S_t (R_{t+1} - R_f);$$

thus depending on the realization of the stock return the wealth evolves as follows:

$$V_0 \begin{cases} V_1(u) = V_0 R_f + \theta_0 S_0 (R_u - R_f) \begin{cases} V_2(uu) = V_1(u) R_f + \theta_1(u) S_1(u)(R_u - R_f), \\ V_2(ud) = V_1(u) R_f + \theta_1(u) S_1(u)(R_d - R_f), \end{cases} \\ V_1(d) = V_0 R_f + \theta_0 S_0 (R_d - R_f) \begin{cases} V_2(du) = V_1(d) R_f + \theta_1(d) S_1(d)(R_u - R_f), \\ V_2(dd) = V_1(d) R_f + \theta_1(d) S_1(d)(R_d - R_f). \end{cases} \end{cases}$$

and numerically

$$V_0 \begin{cases} V_1(u) = 1.05 V_0 + 0.15 \theta_0 \begin{cases} V_2(uu) = 1.1025 V_0 + 0.1575 \theta_0 + 0.18 \theta_1(u), \\ V_2(ud) = 1.1025 V_0 + 0.1575 \theta_0 - 0.06 \theta_1(u), \end{cases} \\ V_1(d) = 1.05 V_0 - 0.05 \theta_0 \begin{cases} V_2(du) = 1.1025 V_0 - 0.0525 \theta_0 + 0.15 \theta_1(d), \\ V_2(dd) = 1.1025 V_0 - 0.0525 \theta_0 - 0.05 \theta_1(d). \end{cases} \end{cases}$$

Suppose we are hedging a binary call option with strike $K = 1.1$, such an option will pay

$$H_2(uu) = 1, \qquad H_2(ud) = 1, \qquad H_2(du) = 1, \qquad H_2(dd) = 0.$$

Suppose further that stock returns are independent and that high and low returns are equally likely. Then we have

$$\min_{x,\theta_0,\dots,\theta_{T-1}} E_0[(V_T^{x,\theta} - H_T)^2]$$
$$= \min_{V_0,\theta_0,\theta_1(u),\theta_1(d)} [\tfrac{1}{4}(V_2(uu) - H_2(uu))^2 + \tfrac{1}{4}(V_2(ud) - H_2(ud))^2$$
$$+ \tfrac{1}{4}(V_2(du) - H_2(du))^2 + \tfrac{1}{4}(V_2(dd) - H_2(dd))^2].$$

Closer inspection reveals that this problem has all the features of *one-period* hedging. In matrix notation:

$$V_2 = V_0 \begin{bmatrix} 1.1025 \\ 1.1025 \\ 1.1025 \\ 1.1025 \end{bmatrix} + \theta_0 \begin{bmatrix} 0.1575 \\ 0.1575 \\ -0.0525 \\ -0.0525 \end{bmatrix} + \theta_1(u) \begin{bmatrix} 0.18 \\ -0.06 \\ 0 \\ 0 \end{bmatrix} + \theta_1(d) \begin{bmatrix} 0 \\ 0 \\ 0.15 \\ -0.05 \end{bmatrix},$$

$$H_2 = \begin{bmatrix} 1 \\ 1 \\ 1 \\ 0 \end{bmatrix},$$

$$\varepsilon = V_2 - H_2,$$

$$\min_{V_0, \theta_0, \theta_1(u), \theta_1(d)} \varepsilon^2(uu) + \varepsilon^2(ud) + \varepsilon^2(du) + \varepsilon^2(dd).$$

It is as if we are looking at a one-period hedging with four states: one risk-free and three risky securities. As we discussed in Chapter 2, minimizing the sum of squared replication errors is very similar to a least-squares regression. In this particular case, the regression coefficients, the explanatory variables and the dependent variable are, respectively,

$$\beta = \begin{bmatrix} V_0 \\ \theta_0 \\ \theta_1(u) \\ \theta_1(d) \end{bmatrix}, \quad X = \begin{bmatrix} 1.1025 & 0.1575 & 0.18 & 0 \\ 1.1025 & 0.1575 & -0.06 & 0 \\ 1.1025 & -0.0525 & 0 & 0.15 \\ 1.1025 & -0.0525 & 0 & -0.05 \end{bmatrix}, \quad Y = \begin{bmatrix} 1 \\ 1 \\ 1 \\ 0 \end{bmatrix}.$$

We know that the optimal β is given by the formula

$$\beta = (X^*X)^{-1}X^*Y = \begin{bmatrix} 0.3968 \\ 3.5714 \\ 0 \\ 5.0 \end{bmatrix}. \tag{12.46}$$

Exercise 12.19 asks the reader to verify this solution by constructing a perfect hedge.

The solution derived above is perfectly valid, yet it is hardly a practical one. Imagine a model with 12 periods; such a model would have $2^{12} = 4096$ states and as many regression coefficients. Worse still, consider the model discussed in Section 12.1 with seven values of stock return. This means we have to deal with $7^{12} = 1.38 \times 10^{10}$ states and only slightly fewer regression coefficients. Specifically, the stock portfolio θ_t can now take 7^t different values at time t, thus we have

$$7^0 + 7^1 + \cdots + 7^{11} = \frac{7^{12} - 1}{6} \approx 2.3 \times 10^9$$

portfolio coefficients. Regression with these dimensions is impossible to handle even on the fastest supercomputers.

12.4.2 Importance of Dynamic Programming

To reduce the dimensionality of the problem one has to approach it period by period starting from the terminal date. One first finds the optimal value of θ_{T-1} given V_{T-1}, then the optimal value of θ_{T-2} given V_{T-2} (taking into account the optimal value of θ_{T-1}), etc. Such a recursive approach to solving optimal decision problems is generally called **dynamic programming** and it was pioneered in the 1950s by Richard E. Bellman. In the next section we will show how the principle of dynamic programming is applied to find the optimal dynamic mean–variance hedge.

12.4.3 Bellman's Principle of Optimality

As we have seen above, for large problems it is futile to try to compute all θ coefficients at once. Instead, we will perform this task sequentially, starting with θ_{T-1}. Of course, θ_{T-1} itself can take many different values depending on where we are in the decision tree at $T - 1$, but the beauty of dynamic programming is that we will handle *all* values of θ_{T-1} separately and yet simultaneously. Before we begin in earnest, let us provide a brief overview of what follows in this section.

Overview

First we will extract the one-period problem by using the law of iterated expectations,

$$\min_{x,\theta_0,\ldots,\theta_{T-1}} E_0^P[(V_T^{x,\theta} - H_T)^2] = \min_{x,\theta_0,\ldots,\theta_{T-1}} E_0^P[E_{T-1}^P[(V_T^{x,\theta} - H_T)^2]],$$

that is, by positioning ourselves at an arbitrarily chosen node in the penultimate period. Since we can choose θ_{T-1} separately in each node at $T - 1$ we can isolate the one-period decision further:

$$\min_{x,\theta_0,\ldots,\theta_{T-1}} E_0^P[E_{T-1}^P[(V_T^{x,\theta} - H_T)^2]] = \min_{x,\theta_0,\ldots,\theta_{T-2}} E_0^P[\min_{\theta_{T-1}} E_{T-1}^P[(V_T^{x,\theta} - H_T)^2]].$$

The next step is to evaluate

$$J_{T-1} \triangleq \min_{\theta_{T-1}} E_{T-1}^P[(V_T^{x,\theta} - H_T)^2], \tag{12.47}$$

where J_{T-1} is the smallest possible expected squared replication error. We will obtain one value of J_{T-1} and one value of the optimal hedging strategy θ_{T-1} for each node at $T - 1$. Having computed J_{T-1} our problem is now transformed to solving

$$\min_{x,\theta_0,\ldots,\theta_{T-2}} E_0^P[J_{T-1}].$$

We will repeat the procedure above, positioning ourselves at an arbitrary node at $T - 2$ and by the same reasoning we will obtain

$$\min_{x,\theta_0,\ldots,\theta_{T-2}} E_0^P[J_{T-1}] = \min_{x,\theta_0,\ldots,\theta_{T-3}} E_0^P\left[\min_{\theta_{T-2}} E_{T-2}^P[J_{T-1}]\right].$$

Let us call the optimized value of the corresponding one-period problem J_{T-2}:

$$J_{T-2} \triangleq \min_{\theta_{T-2}} E_{T-2}^P[J_{T-1}]. \tag{12.48}$$

A general pattern begins to emerge. If we denote

$$J_T = (V_T^{x,\theta} - H_T)^2, \tag{12.49}$$

then we have created a recursive structure such that the optimal hedging strategy is obtained from a series of one-period problems,

$$J_t = \min_{\theta_t} E_t^P[J_{t+1}],$$

and at the same time

$$\min_{x,\theta_0,\dots,\theta_{T-1}} E_0^P[(V_T^{x,\theta} - H_T)^2] = \min_x J_0.$$

The above procedure describes the general principle behind dynamic programming. But this procedure is only useful if J_t depends on a relatively small number of state variables for all t. Even if that is the case, it is not at all clear how one will solve the optimization $J_t = \min_{\theta_t} E_t^P[J_{t+1}]$. We will now briefly describe what happens as one solves the one-period optimization problems. Once we perform the optimization in (12.47) we obtain

$$J_{T-1} = k_{T-1}^D(V_{T-1}^D - H_{T-1})^2 + (\varepsilon_{T-1}^D)^2,$$

where k_{T-1}, H_{T-1} and ε_{T-1}^2 depend only on the stock price and the calendar time. At this stage we notice with disappointment that the form of J_{T-1} is *different* from that of J_T in (12.49). With the new functional form of J_{T-1} we now perform the optimization in (12.48). The good news is that

$$J_{T-2} = k_{T-2}^D(V_{T-2}^D - H_{T-2})^2 + (\varepsilon_{T-2}^D)^2,$$

that is, J_{T-2} has exactly the same form as J_{T-1}. Consequently, from now on when computing $J_{T-3}, \theta_{T-3}, J_{T-4}, \theta_{T-4}$, etc., we can recycle the formulae derived for J_{T-2} and θ_{T-2}—no more computations are needed.

12.4.4   One-Period Optimization

Let us now turn our attention to the one-period optimization problem:

$$J_t = \min_{\theta_t} E_t^P[J_{t+1}].$$

To be able to solve this problem we need to know the dependence of J_{t+1} on θ_t. Suppose that

$$J_{t+1} = k_{t+1}^D(V_{t+1}^D - H_{t+1})^2 + (\varepsilon_{T-2}^D)^2, \tag{12.50}$$

with k_{t+1}, H_{t+1} and ε_{t+1} given exogenously. This assumption certainly holds true for $t + 1 = T$ (recall that $k_T = 1$, $\varepsilon_T^2 = 0$, and H_T is the option pay-off). Exactly *how* J_{t+1} is affected by the choice of the delta hedge θ_t is given by the self-financing condition,

$$V_{t+1}^D = R_{f\,t}V_t^D + \theta_t S_t X_{t+1}, \tag{12.51}$$

where $X_{t+1} = R_{t+1} - R_{f\,t}$ is the excess return. To see the dependence of $E_t^P[J_{t+1}]$ on θ_t we need to substitute (12.51) into (12.50) and evaluate the expectation $E_t^P[J_{t+1}]$.

Before we do this, it is useful to introduce the following substitutions to save space:

$$\theta = \theta_t S_t,$$

$$V = R_{ft} V_t^D,$$

$$\begin{aligned}
E_t^P[J_{t+1}] &= E_t^P[k_{t+1}((V - H_{t+1})^2 + 2\theta(V - H_{t+1})X_{t+1} + \theta^2 X_{t+1}^2)]\\
&= E_t^P[k_{t+1}(V - H_{t+1})^2] + 2\theta E_t^P[k_{t+1}(V - H_{t+1})X_{t+1}]\\
&\quad + \theta^2 E_t^P[k_{t+1}X_{t+1}^2].
\end{aligned}$$

Now we look for the θ minimizing $E_t^P[J_{t+1}]$. The first-order condition reads

$$2E_t^P[k_{t+1}^D(V - H_{t+1})X_{t+1}] + 2\theta E_t^P[k_{t+1}^D X_{t+1}^2] = 0$$

and from there

$$\theta^D = \frac{E_t^P[k_{t+1}(H_{t+1} - V)X_{t+1}]}{E_t^P[k_{t+1}X_{t+1}^2]}, \tag{12.52}$$

$$J_t = \min_\theta E_t^P[J_{t+1}] = E_t^P[k_{t+1}(V - H_{t+1})^2] - \frac{(E_t^P[k_{t+1}(H_{t+1} - V)X])^2}{E_t^P[k_{t+1}X^2]}. \tag{12.53}$$

One last manipulation is required, namely we need to transform J_t into the form

$$J_t = k_t^D(V_t^D - H_t)^2 + \varepsilon_t^2.$$

It entails collecting all powers of V in (12.53) and completing the quadratic in V to a square. From (12.53) this is straightforward but tedious; the resulting expressions for k, H and ε^2 are

$$k_t^D = R_{ft}^2\left(E_t^P[k_{t+1}^D] - \frac{(E_t^P[k_{t+1}^D X_{t+1}])^2}{E_t^P[k_{t+1}^D X_{t+1}^2]}\right), \tag{12.54}$$

$$H_t = E_t^P\left[\left(k_{t+1}^D - \frac{E_t^P[k_{t+1}^D X_{t+1}]k_{t+1}^D X_{t+1}}{E_t^P[k_{t+1}^D X_{t+1}^2]}\right)\frac{H_{t+1}}{R_{ft}}\right] \bigg/ \frac{k_t^D}{R_{ft}^2}, \tag{12.55}$$

$$(\varepsilon_t^D)^2 = E_t^P[(\varepsilon_{t+1}^D)^2] + E_t^P[k_{t+1}^D H_{t+1}^2] - k_t^D H_t^2 - \frac{(E_t^P[k_{t+1}^D X_{t+1}H_{t+1}])^2}{E_t^P[k_{t+1}^D X_{t+1}^2]}. \tag{12.56}$$

From (12.52) we obtain the optimal delta hedge:

$$\theta_t^D = \frac{E_t^P[k_{t+1}^D(H_{t+1} - R_{ft}V_t^D)X_{t+1}]}{S_t E_t^P[k_{t+1}^D X_{t+1}^2]}.$$

12.4.5 Variance-Optimal Measure

The reader will have noticed that we have managed to solve the problem without using the variance-optimal probabilities. In fact, equation (12.55) serves as a definition for the variance-optimal change of measure:

$$m_{t+1|t} \triangleq k_{t+1}^D - \frac{E_t^P[k_{t+1}^D X_{t+1}]k_{t+1}^D X_{t+1}}{E_t^P[k_{t+1}^D X_{t+1}^2]} \bigg/ \frac{k_t^D}{R_{ft}^2}.$$

12.4.6   Special Case with IID Returns

The mean–variance hedging formulae will simplify further when the interest rate is deterministic and returns are IID. In such a case the process $\{k_t\}_{t=0,\dots,T}$ becomes deterministic. To begin with, note that $k_T = 1$ is a non-random variable. Now assume that k_{t+1} is non-random and consider formula (12.54). Since k_{t+1} is a constant, we can take it in front of the expectation in (12.54):

$$k_t^{\mathrm{D}} = R_{\mathrm{f}\,t}^2 k_{t+1}^{\mathrm{D}} \left(1 - \frac{(\mathrm{E}_t^P [X_{t+1}])^2}{\mathrm{E}_t^P [X_{t+1}^2]} \right). \qquad (12.57)$$

For IID returns the expression

$$b \triangleq 1 - \frac{(\mathrm{E}_t^P [X_{t+1}])^2}{\mathrm{E}_t^P [X_{t+1}^2]}$$

is the same for all nodes at time t; by assumption, $R_{\mathrm{f}\,t}$ is non-random and k_{t+1} is constant, implying that k_t, too, is constant across all the nodes at time t. So we know that (i) k_{t+1} constant implies k_t constant (for all t), and (ii) k_T is constant. Combining (i) and (ii) we deduce that k_t is indeed constant for all $t = 0, \dots, T$. This line of reasoning is called *mathematical induction*.

Because the process k_t is deterministic, the hedging formulae will simplify too:

$$H_t = \frac{\mathrm{E}_t^P [(1 - aX_{t+1})H_{t+1}/R_{\mathrm{f}\,t}]}{b},$$

$$a \triangleq \frac{\mathrm{E}_t^P [X_{t+1}]}{\mathrm{E}_t^P [X_{t+1}^2]}, \qquad (12.58)$$

$$(\varepsilon_t^{\mathrm{D}})^2 = \mathrm{E}_t^P [(\varepsilon_{t+1}^{\mathrm{D}})^2] + k_{t+1}^{\mathrm{D}} \mathrm{E}_t^P [H_{t+1}^2] - k_t^{\mathrm{D}} H_t^2 - k_{t+1}^{\mathrm{D}} \frac{(\mathrm{E}_t^P [X_{t+1}H_{t+1}])^2}{\mathrm{E}_t^P [X_{t+1}^2]}, \qquad (12.59)$$

$$\theta_t^{\mathrm{D}} = \frac{\mathrm{E}_t^P [(H_{t+1} - R_{\mathrm{f}\,t} V_t^{\mathrm{D}})X_{t+1}]}{S_t \mathrm{E}_t [X_{t+1}^2]}.$$

12.4.7   Interpretation of the Dynamically Optimal Hedging Formula

The dynamic programming solution finds the optimal hedging strategy, which happens to look quite different from the Black–Scholes hedge. To begin with, the dynamically optimal hedge depends on the value of the replicating portfolio V_t^{D}, whereas the Black–Scholes hedge only depends on S_t and t. In the IID case one can show that there is a very close link between the two strategies, which allows us to compare the resulting replication errors.

Recall the one-period optimization:

$$J_t = \min_{\theta_t} \mathrm{E}_t^P [k_{t+1}^{\mathrm{D}} (V_{t+1}^{\mathrm{D}} - H_{t+1})^2 + (\varepsilon_{t+1}^{\mathrm{D}})^2].$$

Because $\varepsilon_{t+1}^{\mathrm{D}}$ is given exogenously (it does not depend on the trading strategy θ_t), we can take it in front of the 'min' sign:

$$J_t = \mathrm{E}_t^P [(\varepsilon_{t+1}^{\mathrm{D}})^2] + \min_{\theta_t} \mathrm{E}_t^P [k_{t+1}^{\mathrm{D}} (V_{t+1}^{\mathrm{D}} - H_{t+1})^2].$$

Furthermore, we know that in the case with IID stock returns, k_{t+1}^D is deterministic *and* exogenous; we can therefore take it in front of the expectation and in front of the 'min' sign:

$$J_t = E_t^P[(\varepsilon_{t+1}^D)^2] + k_{t+1}^D \min_{\theta_t} E_t^P[(V_{t+1}^D - H_{t+1})^2].$$

Writing down the self-financing condition $V_{t+1}^D = R_f V_t^D + \theta_t S_t X_{t+1}$ we obtain

$$J_t = E_t^P[(\varepsilon_{t+1}^D)^2] + k_{t+1}^D \min_{\theta_t} E_t^P[(R_f V_t^D + \theta_t S_t X_{t+1} - H_{t+1})^2].$$

Regression Number 1

The expression

$$\min_{\theta_t} E_t^P[(R_f V_t^D + \theta_t S_t X_{t+1} - H_{t+1})^2]$$

is essentially a least-squares regression with the dependent variable $H_{t+1} - R_f V_t^D$, the explanatory variable X_{t+1} and a slope coefficient $\theta_t S_t$. The conditional probabilities represent weights given to errors in individual states. If we denote

$$\alpha = R_f V_t^D, \qquad \beta = \theta_t S_t, \qquad X = X_{t+1}, \qquad Y = H_{t+1},$$

then

$$\min_{\theta_t} E_t^P[(V_{t+1}^D - H_{t+1})^2] = \min_{\beta} \sum_{i=1}^n p_i (\alpha + \beta X_i - Y_i)^2. \tag{12.61}$$

It becomes obvious that the dynamically optimal hedge β^D is obtained as the slope coefficient in an ordinary least-squares regression of $Y - \alpha$ onto one explanatory variable X (without an intercept!):

$$\beta^D = \frac{\sum_{i=1}^n p_i (Y_i - \alpha) X_i}{\sum_{i=1}^n p_i X_i^2} = \frac{E_t^P[(H_{t+1} - R_f V_t^D) X_{t+1}]}{E_t^P[X_{t+1}^2]}. \tag{12.62}$$

Regression Number 2

It makes sense to ask how the resulting sum of squared errors will change with α. We know that the sum of squared errors will be smallest when α is chosen from the minimization

$$\min_{\alpha, \beta} \sum_{i=1}^n p_i (\alpha + \beta X_i - Y_i)^2, \tag{12.63}$$

that is, when α is the constant term from the regression of Y onto X *and* an intercept. Let us denote the regression coefficients in (12.63) by α^L and β^L:

$$\min_{\alpha, \beta} \sum_{i=1}^n p_i (\alpha + \beta X_i - Y_i)^2 = \sum_{i=1}^n p_i (\alpha^L + \beta^L X_i - Y_i)^2.$$

Using standard regression formulae for α and β we obtain

$$\beta^L = \frac{\sum_{i=1}^{n} p_i (Y_i - \bar{Y})(X_i - \bar{X})}{\sum_{i=1}^{n} p_i (X_i - \bar{X})^2} = \frac{\text{Cov}_t^P (X_{t+1}, H_{t+1})}{\text{Var}_t^P (X_{t+1})}, \tag{12.64}$$

$$\bar{X} = \sum_{i=1}^{n} p_i X_i = E_t^P [X_{t+1}],$$

$$\bar{Y} = \sum_{i=1}^{n} p_i Y_i = E_t^P [H_{t+1}],$$

$$\alpha^L = \bar{Y} - \beta^L \bar{X} = E_t^P [H_{t+1}] - \frac{\text{Cov}_t^P (X_{t+1}, H_{t+1})}{\text{Var}_t^P (X_{t+1})} E_t^P [X_{t+1}]. \tag{12.65}$$

Comparison of Hedging Errors

The optimality of α^L means that the locally optimal hedging error can be written as

$$\sum_{i=1}^{n} p_i (\alpha + \beta^L X_i - Y_i)^2 = (\alpha - \alpha^L)^2 + \sum_{i=1}^{n} p_i (\alpha^L + \beta^L X_i - Y_i)^2. \tag{12.66}$$

This expression is very useful because the second term on the right-hand side is the smallest possible error.

The optimality of β^D implies

$$\sum_{i=1}^{n} p_i (\beta X_i + \alpha - Y_i)^2 = \left(\sum_{i=1}^{n} p_i X_i^2 \right) (\beta^D - \beta)^2 + \sum_{i=1}^{n} p_i (\beta^D X_i + \alpha - Y_i)^2 \tag{12.67}$$

for any β. Choosing $\beta = \beta^L$ in (12.67) we have

$$\sum_{i=1}^{n} p_i (\beta^L X_i + \alpha - Y_i)^2$$

$$= \left(\sum_{i=1}^{n} p_i X_i^2 \right) (\beta^D - \beta^L)^2 + \sum_{i=1}^{7} p_i (\beta^D X_i + \alpha - Y_i)^2. \tag{12.68}$$

Now let us evaluate $(\beta^D - \beta^L)^2$ explicitly. Substituting from (12.62) and (12.64) we find

$$(\beta^D - \beta^L)^2 = (\alpha - \alpha^L)^2 \frac{\left(\sum_{i=1}^{n} p_i X_i \right)^2}{\sum_{i=1}^{n} p_i X_i^2}. \tag{12.69}$$

Finally, in equation (12.68) substitute for $\sum_{i=1}^{n} p_i (\beta^L X_i + \alpha - Y_i)^2$ using equation (12.66) and plug in the value of $(\beta^D - \beta^L)^2$ using (12.69). This gives the desired expression for the dynamically optimal hedging error:

$$\sum_{i=1}^{n} p_i (\alpha + \beta^D X_i - Y_i)^2$$

$$= \left(1 - \frac{\left(\sum_{i=1}^{n} p_i X_i \right)^2}{\sum_{i=1}^{n} p_i X_i^2} \right) (\alpha - \alpha^L)^2 + \sum_{i=1}^{n} p_i (\alpha^L + \beta^L X_i - Y_i)^2. \tag{12.70}$$

IID Hedging Theorem

Equations (12.66) and (12.70) allow us to compare the size of the hedging error in the dynamically optimal ($\beta = \beta^D$) and the locally optimal ($\beta = \beta^L$) cases.

Theorem 12.3 (IID hedging theorem). *For β^D, α^L and β^L defined in equations (12.62), (12.65) and (12.64) we have*

$$\sum_{i=1}^{n} p_i(\alpha + \beta^D X_i - Y_i)^2 = b(\alpha - \alpha^L)^2 + \sum_{i=1}^{n} p_i(\alpha^L + \beta^L X_i - Y_i)^2, \quad (12.71)$$

$$\sum_{i=1}^{n} p_i(\alpha + \beta^L X_i - Y_i)^2 = (\alpha - \alpha^L)^2 + \sum_{i=1}^{n} p_i(\alpha^L + \beta^L X_i - Y_i)^2, \quad (12.72)$$

$$\text{with } b = \left(1 - \frac{(\sum_{i=1}^{n} p_i X_i)^2}{\sum_{i=1}^{n} p_i X_i^2}\right). \quad (12.73)$$

Moreover,

$$\sum_{i=1}^{n} p_i(\alpha^L + \beta^L X_i - Y_i)^2 = \sum_{i=1}^{n} p_i Y_i^2 - b(\alpha^L)^2 - \frac{(\sum_{i=1}^{n} p_i X_i H_i)^2}{\sum_{i=1}^{n} p_i X_i^2} \quad (12.74)$$

by definition of α^L and β^L.

Proof. The proof of (12.71)–(12.73) is between equations (12.61) and (12.70). Equation (12.74) follows from (12.70) by setting $\alpha = 0$. We just need to realize that the optimality of β^D implies

$$\sum_{i=1}^{n} p_i(\alpha + \beta^D X_i - Y_i)^2 = \sum_{i=1}^{n} p_i(Y_i - \alpha)^2 - \sum_{i=1}^{n} p_i(\beta^D X_i)^2.$$

$\square$

It is now enough to realize that $H_t = \alpha^L/R_f$, $\theta_t^D = \beta^D/S_t$, $\theta_t^L = \beta^L/S_t$ and the hedging theorem immediately yields most of the formulae we used in Section 12.1. In particular, equations (12.71) and (12.72) read

$$E_t[(V_{t+1}^D - H_{t+1})^2] = bR_f^2(V_t^D - H_t)^2 + \text{ESRE}_t(H_{t+1}), \quad (12.75)$$

$$E_t[(V_{t+1}^L - H_{t+1})^2] = R_f^2(V_t^L - H_t)^2 + \text{ESRE}_t(H_{t+1}), \quad (12.76)$$

where

$$\text{ESRE}_t(H_{t+1}) = E_t[(R_f H_t + \theta_t^L S_t X_{t+1} - H_{t+1})^2].$$

Define ε_t^2 as the expected squared replication error to maturity conditional on $V_t = H_t$. The recursive application of (12.75), (12.76) gives

$$E_t[(V_T - H_T)^2] = k_t(V_t - H_t)^2 + \varepsilon_t^2,$$

$$\varepsilon_t^2 = E_t[\varepsilon_{t+1}^2] + k_{t+1}\text{ESRE}_t(H_{t+1}),$$

where we take $k = k^D$ for the dynamically optimal strategy and $k = k^L$ for the locally optimal strategy:

$$k_t^D = (bR_f^2)^{T-t}, \qquad k_t^L = (R_f^2)^{T-t}.$$

12.5 Summary

- In practice, option hedging is not riskless; it is therefore important to understand the size of hedging errors associated with a given hedging strategy. There are several ways of measuring the resulting hedging error. In this chapter we have concentrated on the *mean–variance* trade-off. The variance of the hedging error is all one needs to know if options are priced so that the expected hedging error is zero. However, for different strategies mean zero is achieved at different prices; therefore, in general the relevant criterion is the ratio of mean to standard deviation of the hedging error at a given price.

- The mean–variance trade-off of an option hedging strategy can be evaluated in two ways, either by a Monte Carlo simulation or by backward recursion on a state space grid. Both methods have their merits and disadvantages. The former is very easy to implement even with many state variables, but it typically requires many random experiments to arrive at reliable results, particularly with fat-tailed return distributions. The grid method, on the other hand, is faster and guarantees a 'precise' result. On the downside, its implementation requires more sophistication, particularly with many (that is, more than two) state variables.

- Once we have decided on the optimality criterion, in this case the Sharpe ratio of the hedging error, it makes sense to inquire what is the *optimal* hedging strategy. The hedge minimizing the expected squared replication error is called *dynamically optimal* hedge. A closely related suboptimal strategy is the *locally optimal* hedge.

- Suppose one wishes to hedge a derivative security with pay-off H_T by constructing a self-financing portfolio with value $V_t, t = 0, \ldots, T$. The solution evolves around the *mean value process* H_t, which turns out to be the discrete-time analogue of the Black–Scholes value. Both the dynamically optimal portfolio and the locally optimal portfolio are trying to replicate H_t, the difference is in the delta they choose. Both strategies are minimizing $E_{t-1}[(V_t - H_t)^2]$. The locally optimal strategy asks 'if one could choose the value of V_{t-1} to minimize the one-step hedging error $E_{t-1}[(V_t - H_t)^2]$, what would V_{t-1} be?'. The answer is $V_{t-1} = H_{t-1}$ and the corresponding delta would be the locally optimal delta. In other words H_{t-1} is obtained as the intercept from the least-squares regression of H_t onto the excess stock return, and the locally optimal delta is the slope coefficient in that regression. But the locally optimal strategy uses the *same* delta even when $V_{t-1} \neq H_{t-1}$, whereas the dynamically optimal strategy adjusts the delta for the discrepancy $V_{t-1} - H_{t-1}$.

- Thus if $V_{t-1} = H_{t-1}$, the expected squared hedging error in both strategies is the same. If $V_{t-1} \neq H_{t-1}$, then we add an extra term proportional to $(H_{t-1} - V_{t-1})^2$. The constant of proportionality is 1 for the locally optimal strategy and $1 - R^2$ for the dynamically optimal strategy, where R^2 is the non-central 'R^2' from the regression of the risk-free rate onto the excess return. Empirically, this R^2 is very small and from here it follows that the locally optimal strategy is nearly as good as the dynamically optimal strategy in terms of expected squared error.

- The risk of the optimal option hedging strategy is non-trivial, even if we ignore transaction costs. For normally distributed log returns, *Toft's formula* tells us that the squared error is proportional to the expectation of the sum of squared gamma at the rebalancing dates. For returns with higher kurtosis the squared error can be approximated by adjusting Toft's formula multiplied by the factor (kurtosis − 1)/2.

- *Dynamic programming* is a powerful way of rephrasing a single optimization problem with many control variables into a series of simpler mutually related optimization problems each with a small number of control variables. The relationship between individual stages in the resulting recursive procedure is called *Bellman's principle of optimality.* In our example we had to consider three state variables: time to maturity, stock price, and the value of the hedging portfolio. At each point of this three-dimensional grid we had to maximize a quadratic function of future wealth which amounted to computing a least-squares regression of the mean value process onto the excess return and an intercept. The slope coefficient turned out to be the locally optimal delta and the discounted intercept constituted the mean value process for the next stage of optimization.

12.6 Notes

Boyle and Emanuel (1980) were the first to link the one-period squared hedging error to an option's gamma squared, followed by Leland (1985) and Grannan and Swindle (1996). Toft (1996) shows that the expected squared replication error to maturity is proportional to $E_0[\sum_{t=0}^{T} S_t^4 \gamma_t^2]$, where γ_t is the Black–Scholes gamma at time t and S_t is the stock price. This literature does not examine the optimality of the discrete Black–Scholes strategy, merely its performance. An interesting early paper on sequential regressions is Föllmer and Schweizer (1989). There is an exhaustive literature on dynamically optimal mean–variance hedging starting with Duffie and Richardson (1991) through a series of very technical papers (Gourieroux et al. 1998; Laurent and Pham 1999; Rheinländer and Schweizer 1997; Schweizer 1992, 1995), with a dynamic programming solution for discrete Markov chains in Bertsimas et al. (2001) and Černý (1999).

12.7 Appendix: Expected Squared Hedging Error in the Black–Scholes Model

Let $C(t, S_t)$ be the BS price at time t; for us it is an approximation of H_t. H_{t+dt} will be approximated by $C(t + dt, S_{t+dt})$, where $dt = 1$ week. From the Taylor expansion,

$$C(t + dt, S_{t+dt}) = C(t, S_t) + \frac{\partial C(t, S_t)}{\partial t} dt$$
$$+ \frac{\partial C(t, S_t)}{\partial S_t}(S_{t+dt} - S_t) + \frac{1}{2}\frac{\partial^2 C(t, S_t)}{\partial S_t^2}(S_{t+dt} - S_t)^2.$$

Let us now construct a hedging portfolio with initial value $C(t, S_t)$ and θ_t the number of shares. The pay-off of this portfolio will be

$$V_{t+dt} = (1 + r\, dt)C(t, S_t) + \theta_t(S_{t+dt} - (1 + r\, dt)S_t).$$

The hedging error is the difference between V_{t+dt} and $C(t + dt, S_{t+dt})$. Let us evaluate that difference:

$$
\begin{aligned}
V_{t+dt} &- C(t + dt, S_{t+dt}) \\
&= \left(rC(t, S_t) - \frac{\partial C(t, S_t)}{\partial t} - r\theta_t S_t\right) dt + \left(\theta_t - \frac{\partial C(t, S_t)}{\partial S_t}\right)(S_{t+dt} - S_t) \\
&\quad - \frac{1}{2}S_t^2 \frac{\partial^2 C(t, S_t)}{\partial S_t^2}\left(\frac{S_{t+dt} - S_t}{S_t}\right)^2. \quad (12.77)
\end{aligned}
$$

The last expression has non-zero mean. Specifically,

$$
E_t^P\left[\left(\frac{S_{t+dt} - S_t}{S_t}\right)^2\right] = (\mu\, dt)^2 + \sigma^2\, dt \quad (12.78)
$$

is of the order dt. Before proceeding further it is convenient to denote the percentage increase in the stock price Z:

$$Z \triangleq \frac{S_{t+dt} - S_t}{S_t}.$$

The idea now is to collect all the dt terms in equation (12.77), taking into account equation (12.78):

$$
\begin{aligned}
&\left(rC - \frac{\partial C(t, S_t)}{\partial t} - r\theta_t S_t - \frac{1}{2}\sigma^2 S_t^2\frac{\partial^2 C(t, S_t)}{\partial S_t^2}\right) dt + \left(\theta_t - \frac{\partial C(t, S_t)}{\partial S_t}\right)(S_{t+dt} - S_t) \\
&\quad - \frac{1}{2}S_t^2 \frac{\partial^2 C(t, S_t)}{\partial S_t^2}(Z^2 - E_t^P[Z^2] + (\mu\, dt)^2). \quad (12.79)
\end{aligned}
$$

Now if we choose θ_t to be the Black–Scholes delta, that is $\theta_t = \partial C(t, S_t)/\partial S_t$, then the second term in (12.79) vanishes and we obtain

$$
\begin{aligned}
V_{t+dt} &- C(t + dt, S_{t+dt}) \\
&= \left(rC - \frac{\partial C(t, S_t)}{\partial t} - rS_t\frac{\partial C(t, S_t)}{\partial S_t} - \frac{1}{2}\sigma^2 S_t^2\frac{\partial^2 C(t, S_t)}{\partial S_t^2}\right) dt \\
&\quad - \frac{1}{2}S_t^2 \frac{\partial^2 C(t, S_t)}{\partial S_t^2}(Z^2 - E_t^P[Z^2] + (\mu\, dt)^2).
\end{aligned}
$$

In addition,

$$
rC - \frac{\partial C(t, S_t)}{\partial t} - rS_t\frac{\partial C(t, S_t)}{\partial S_t} - \frac{1}{2}\sigma^2 S_t^2\frac{\partial^2 C(t, S_t)}{\partial S_t^2} = 0
$$

by virtue of the Black–Scholes PDE and hence we finally obtain

$$
V_{t+dt} - C(t + dt, S_{t+dt}) = -\frac{1}{2}S_t^2\frac{\partial^2 C(t, S_t)}{\partial S_t^2}(Z^2 - E_t^P[Z^2] + (\mu\, dt)^2). \quad (12.80)
$$

Table 12.8. A sample path of stock returns.

$\ln(S_1/S_0)$	$\ln(S_2/S_1)$	$\ln(S_3/S_2)$	$\ln(S_4/S_3)$	$\ln(S_5/S_4)$	$\ln(S_6/S_5)$
-0.02	0.04	0.00	-0.02	0.00	0.02

Let us denote

$$\gamma = \frac{\partial^2 C(t, S_t)}{\partial S_t^2}.$$

We will now evaluate the mean and variance of the hedging error:

$$\mathrm{E}_t^P[V_{t+dt} - C(t + dt, S_{t+dt})] = -\tfrac{1}{2}\gamma S_t^2 (\mu\, dt)^2,$$

$$\mathrm{Var}_t^P(V_{t+dt} - C(t + dt, S_{t+dt})) = \tfrac{1}{4}\gamma^2 S_t^4 \mathrm{E}_t^P[(Z^2 - \mathrm{E}_t^P[Z^2])^2].$$

The contribution from the variance is more significant. It is shown in Exercise 12.8 that $\mathrm{E}_t^P[(Z^2 - \mathrm{E}_t^P[Z^2])^2]$ can be expressed using mean, variance, skewness and kurtosis of Z as follows:

$$\mathrm{E}_t^P[(Z^2 - \mathrm{E}_t^P[Z^2])^2]$$

$$= (\mathrm{Vol}_t^P(Z))^4 \left(\mathrm{Kurt}(Z) - 1 + 4\frac{\mathrm{E}_t^P[Z]}{\mathrm{Vol}_t^P(Z)} \mathrm{Skew}(Z) + 8\left(\frac{\mathrm{E}_t^P[Z]}{\mathrm{Vol}_t^P(Z)}\right)^2 \right).$$

Recall that the kurtosis of a normal distribution is 3. Kurtosis of returns in our example is 3.28. On the other hand the ratio of mean to standard deviation is 0.11 and the skewness is -0.07, so the second and third terms are -0.03 and 0.09. It is customary to neglect the last two terms, but it may not always be safe to do so, especially if returns have a positive skew. To conclude, the one-period expected squared replication is

$$\mathrm{E}_t^P[(V_{t+dt} - C(t + dt, S_{t+dt}))^2]$$

$$= (\mathrm{E}_t^P[V_{t+dt} - C(t + dt, S_{t+dt})])^2 + \mathrm{Var}_t^P(V_{t+dt} - C(t + dt, S_{t+dt}))$$

$$= \tfrac{1}{4}\gamma_t^2 S_t^4 \tilde{\sigma}^4 \left(\mathrm{Kurt}(Z) - 1 + 4\frac{\tilde{\mu}}{\tilde{\sigma}} \mathrm{Skew}(Z) + 8\left(\frac{\tilde{\mu}}{\tilde{\sigma}}\right)^2 + \left(\frac{\tilde{\mu}}{\tilde{\sigma}}\right)^4 \right),$$

where X is the rate of stock return and $\tilde{\mu}, \tilde{\sigma}$ are its mean and standard deviation. Neglecting the second-order terms we obtain the standard result:

$$\mathrm{ESRE}_t(H_{t+1}) = (\tfrac{1}{2}\gamma_t S_t^2 \mathrm{Var}_t^P(R_{t+1}))^2 (\mathrm{Kurt}_t^P(R_{t+1}) - 1). \tag{12.81}$$

12.8 Exercises

Exercise 12.1 (stock price lattice). Generate the stock price lattice of Figure 12.3 in a spreadsheet.

Exercise 12.2 (mean value process). Extend the spreadsheet of Exercise 12.1 to include the mean value process in a form similar to Figure 12.5. (Hint 1: SUMPRODUCT(A1:A7,B1:B7) will return a scalar product of the two vectors. You can start from spreadsheet *Chapter12Exercise2a.xls*. Hint 2: if you are really stuck, start from *Chapter12Exercise2b.xls*.)

Exercise 12.3 (delta hedge). Building on the previous exercises implement the locally optimal delta hedge θ^L in a spreadsheet and compare it with the continuous-time Black–Scholes delta *à la* Figure 12.6.

Exercise 12.4 (simulation of hedging shortfall). Recompute the shortfall of the dynamically optimal, locally optimal and the Black–Scholes hedging strategy for the sequence of stock returns depicted in Table 12.8.

Exercise 12.5 (one-period expected squared replication error (ESRE)). Building on the spreadsheet developed in Exercises 12.1–12.3 implement the lattice of one-period expected squared hedging errors. For this purpose you may want to use the formula

$$\mathrm{ESRE}_t^P (H_{t+1}) = \mathrm{E}_t^P [H_{t+1}^2] - b R_{\mathrm{f}}^2 H_t^2 - \frac{(a \mathrm{E}_t^P [X_{t+1} H_{t+1}])^2}{1-b},$$

derived in the 'IID hedging theorem' on p. 305, equation (12.74). (Hint: to calculate the last term you may need to use a command similar to SUMPRODUCT(A1:A7,B1:B7,C1:C7).)

Exercise 12.6 (squared error process). Use the recursive formula

$$\varepsilon_t^2 = \mathrm{E}_t^P [\varepsilon_{t+1}^2] + k_{t+1} \mathrm{ESRE}_t^P (H_{t+1}),$$
$$\varepsilon_T = 0,$$

with

$$k_t^{\mathrm{L}} = R_{\mathrm{f}}^{2(T-t)} = 1.0015^{T-t},$$
$$k_t^{\mathrm{D}} = R_{\mathrm{f}}^{2(T-t)} b^{T-t} = 0.9962^{T-t},$$

to generate the dynamically optimal and locally optimal squared hedging errors to maturity in the spreadsheet of Exercise 12.5.

Exercise 12.7 (variance of squared deviations). Denoting $\mu = \mathrm{E}[X]$ and $\sigma^2 = \mathrm{E}[(X-\mu)^2]$ show that

$$\mathrm{Var}((X-\mu)^2) = \sigma^4 (\mathrm{Kurt}(X) - 1).$$

Exercise 12.8. Using the elementary properties of expectation show that

$$\mathrm{Var}(X^2) = \mathrm{E}[(X^2 - \mathrm{E}[X^2])^2] = \sigma^4 \left(\mathrm{Kurt}(X) - 1 + 4\frac{\mu}{\sigma}\mathrm{Skew}(X) + 8\left(\frac{\mu}{\sigma}\right)^2 \right),$$

where $\mu = \mathrm{E}[X]$ and $\sigma^2 = \mathrm{E}[(X-\mu)^2]$.

Exercise 12.9 (Toft's formula). We have seen in equation (12.27) that the expected squared error ε_0^2 of the BS hedging strategy can be expressed as

$$\varepsilon_0^2 = \sum_{t=0}^{T-1} k_{t+1} \mathrm{E}_0^P [\mathrm{ESRE}_t^P (H_{t+1})], \qquad (12.82)$$
$$k_t = R_{\mathrm{f}}^{2(T-t)}.$$

On the other hand, we have shown in equation (12.81) that $\mathrm{ESRE}_t^P(H_{t+1})$ can be approximated using Black–Scholes gamma as follows:

$$\mathrm{ESRE}_t[H_{t+1}] = (\tfrac{1}{2}\gamma_t S_t^2 \,\mathrm{Var}_t^P(R_{t+1}))^2 (\mathrm{Kurt}_t^P(R_{t+1}) - 1). \qquad (12.83)$$

With IID stock returns, $(\mathrm{Var}_t^P(R_{t+1}))^2(\mathrm{Kurt}_t^P(R_{t+1}) - 1)$ is the same in every period and in every node, we shall denote it without time subscript

$$(\mathrm{Var}^P(R))^2(\mathrm{Kurt}^P(R) - 1).$$

Substitution of (12.83) into (12.82) gives Toft's expression for the variance of hedging error in a discretely rebalanced Black–Scholes model without transaction costs:

$$\varepsilon_0^2 = \left(\frac{\mathrm{Kurt}^P(R) - 1}{2}\right) \tfrac{1}{2}(\mathrm{Var}^P(R))^2 \underbrace{\sum_{t=0}^{T-1} k_{t+1}\mathrm{E}_0^P[\gamma_t S_t^2]}_{\substack{\text{Toft's formula for expected squared error} \\ \text{in discretely rebalanced BS model}}}.$$

Toft (1996) shows that with lognormally distributed returns the expression $\mathrm{E}_0^P[\gamma_t S_t^2]$ has the form

$$\mathrm{E}_0^P[(\gamma_t S_t^2)^2] = \frac{S_0^2 e^{2\mu t}}{2\pi\sigma^2\sqrt{T^2 - t^2}}\exp\left(-\frac{(\lambda_t + \tfrac{1}{2}\sigma^2 T)^2 + 2\sigma^2 t\lambda_t}{\sigma^2(T + t)}\right),$$

$$\lambda_t = \ln\frac{S_0}{K} + r(T - t) + \mu t,$$

where r is the risk-free rate per unit of time, μ is the expected rate of return per unit of time, and σ^2 is the variance of log return per unit of time.

For the model of this chapter evaluate $\mathrm{E}_0^P[\gamma_t S_t^2]$ for $t = 0, 1, 2, 3, 4, 5$ weeks and enter the values of

$$\mathrm{E}_0^P[\mathrm{ESRE}_t(H_{t+1})] = (\mathrm{Kurt}^P(R) - 1)(\tfrac{1}{2}\,\mathrm{Var}^P(R))^2\mathrm{E}_0^P[(\gamma_t S_t^2)^2]$$

in a table similar to Table 12.4.

Exercise 12.10 (excess kurtosis in Toft's formula). Suppose that we are hedging a European call option by trading once a day and that the risk-free rate is 0%. Toft's formula for discretely hedged Black–Scholes model gives an expected squared hedging error of 100.00. From the data we find that the kurtosis of daily stock returns is 6.25. What is the (approximate) value of the true squared hedging error?

Exercise 12.11 (hedging errors for the S&P500 Index). Construct a realistic tree to analyse daily rehedging of an S&P500 put option with one year to maturity. Assume that the option is sold at the money. Compute the expected squared hedging error of the dynamically and locally optimal strategies. Assuming that the option is priced in such a way that its implied volatility (annualized) is three percentage points above the historical volatility, compute the Sharpe ratio of the dynamically optimal hedge and contrast it with the Sharpe ratio of the locally optimal hedge.

Exercise 12.12 (equivalence of variance-optimal measure). The file *chapter12-exe12data.gss* contains a histogram of FTSE 100 daily log returns. Assuming that log returns follow the distribution indicated in the file and assuming that the risk-free rate is 0%, find out whether the variance-optimal probabilities in the model with daily rehedging are positive.

Exercise 12.13 (skewness and kurtosis). Evaluate the first four moments (mean, standard deviation, skewness and kurtosis) of the risky return in this chapter both under the objective and under the risk-neutral probability measure.

Exercise 12.14 (skewness and kurtosis in empirical data). Evaluate the first four moments (mean, standard deviation, skewness and kurtosis) in the actual FTSE 100 data under both the objective and the risk-neutral probability measure.

Exercise 12.15 (calibration of returns from empirical data). The code *chapter12-sect3.gss* assumes that weekly returns can have seven different values. Write a code that approximates the historical distribution of weekly FTSE 100 returns with a theoretical distribution with n different values, such that log returns of the theoretical distribution are spaced equidistantly. What value of n is required in order that the theoretical moments faithfully reproduce the population moments? (Try $n = 500$, 100, 50, 10, 5.) Adjust the code so that it can handle other rebalancing frequencies (daily, monthly, etc.).

Exercise 12.16 (compound Poisson jump model). Consider a model where log returns have two Poisson jumps, either -2% or -4%, with equal intensity. Following Section 6.3 calibrate the model to a given volatility σ and mean return μ.

Exercise 12.17 (variance-optimal measure in a jump model). For the calibrated model of the previous exercise compute the variance-optimal probabilities $q(\Delta t)$ (assume $r = 0$) and deduce the risk-neutral intensities of the two jumps. Pick an option with a suitable strike and initial stock value and evaluate the risk-neutral expectation $H_t = \mathrm{E}_t^Q[H_T]$ in this model.

Exercise 12.18 (hedging error in a continuous-time model with two jumps). With H_t in hand from the previous exercise find

$$G_t = \lim_{dt \to 0} \frac{\mathrm{ESRE}_t(H_{t+dt})}{dt}.$$

Decide whether

$$\varepsilon_0^2 = \mathrm{E}_0\left[\int_0^T G_t \, dt\right]$$

is zero or positive.

Exercise 12.19 (optimal hedge in a complete market). Verify that (12.46) is the correct solution by constructing a perfect hedge.

Exercise 12.20 (simple evaluation of locally optimal strategy). For a given but arbitrary hedging strategy θ that only depends on the stock price and calendar time evaluate its expected squared replication error. (Hint: define the mean value process H^θ such that

$$\mathrm{E}_t[R_f H_t^\theta + \theta_t S_t X_{t+1} - H_{t+1}^\theta] = 0$$

and show that

$$\mathrm{E}_t[(V_{t+1} - H_{t+1}^\theta)^2] = R_f^2(V_t - H_t^\theta)^2 + \mathrm{E}_t[(R_f H_t^\theta + \theta_t S_t X_{t+1} - H_{t+1}^\theta)^2].)$$

Appendix A

Calculus

This appendix reviews essential topics in calculus: functions and their derivatives, the Taylor expansion and its application to optimization, and integrals. It is not particularly detailed or rigorous and the reader should consult Binmore and Davies (2001) or a similar textbook for more information.

A.1 Notation

A.1.1 Real Numbers

In calculus we work predominantly with real numbers. The set of real numbers is denoted by $\mathbb{R}$. Occasionally, we need an n-tuple of real numbers (a vector) and the set of all such n-tuples is denoted by $\mathbb{R}^n$. Another way of saying 'x is a real number' is to write $x \in \mathbb{R}$.

A.1.2 Intervals

Intervals are sections of the real line, for example, 'all numbers between 0 and 1'. An interval which includes its endpoints is call **closed** and is denoted with square brackets, for example, $[0; 1]$. An **open** interval does not include its endpoints and is denoted with round brackets, for example, $(0; 1)$. Then we can have mixed intervals like $(0; 1]$ or $[0; 1)$.

To say that

$$0 \leqslant x \leqslant 1$$

we write $x \in [0; 1]$ as the following table suggests:

Normal notation	Interval notation
$a \leqslant x \leqslant b$	$x \in [a; b]$
$a < x \leqslant b$	$x \in (a; b]$
$a \leqslant x < b$	$x \in [a; b)$
$a < x < b$	$x \in (a; b)$
$a \leqslant x$	$x \in [a; +\infty)$
$x < b$	$x \in (-\infty; b)$

A.1.3 Real Function of One Real Variable

These are the most simple functions one encounters in applications. A real function of one real variable takes a real number and assigns to it another real number, for

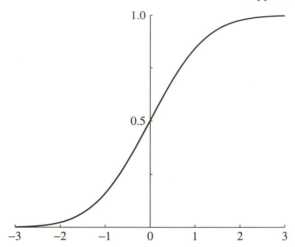

Figure A.1. Cumulative standard normal distribution function $\Phi(x)$.

example,

$$f(0) = 5,$$
$$f(1.5) = 8,$$

and so on. This defines the function f at only two points. More often we give a general recipe, for example,

$$f(x) = 2x + 5.$$

Associated with every function is its **domain of definition**. Very often functions are defined on the whole real line (that is, we can take any real number for x); however, sometimes this is not practical or possible. For example,

$$f(x) = \ln x$$

is only defined for $x > 0$. When performing mechanical manipulation with formulae involving logarithms, one must be aware of this fact.

Sometimes functions are defined *piecewise*, for example,

$$f(x) = x + 2 \quad \text{for } x > 0,$$
$$f(0) = 0,$$
$$f(x) = x^3 - 1 \quad \text{for } x < 0.$$

A.1.4 Examples of Functions

Apart from **elementary functions** like $\ln x$, e^x, x^k, $\sin x$, etc., there are a number of **transcendental functions** that have application in finance. The transcendental functions are usually defined as an integral or a solution to a specific differential equation.

1. Cumulative standard normal distribution (see Figure A.1):

$$\Phi(x) = \frac{1}{\sqrt{2\pi}} \int_{-\infty}^{x} e^{-t^2/2} \, dt.$$

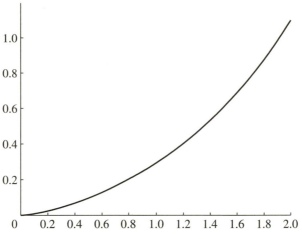

Figure A.2. Graph of $I_{3/2}(x)$.

2. The modified Bessel function $I_q(x)$ satisfies

$$x^2 I_q''(x) + x I_q'(x) - (x^2 + q^2) I_q(x) = 0.$$

This function governs the distribution of future values of the short-term interest rate in the Cox–Ingersoll–Ross model of the term structure (see Figure A.2).

3. Other special functions defined in a similar way include the Beta and Gamma functions, the Exponential integral function, the Logarithmic integral function, the Legendre, Chebyshev, Jacobi, Hermite, Laguerre and Gegenbauer functions, the Hypergeometric function, etc. See, for example, Abramowitz and Stegun (1972).

A.1.5 Properties of Exponential and Logarithmic Functions

One should understand that the logarithmic and the exponential function are inverse to each other, that is,

$$\ln e^x = x,$$
$$e^{\ln x} = x.$$

The properties of the logarithm,

$$\ln xy = \ln x + \ln y,$$
$$\ln x^\alpha = \alpha \ln x,$$

follow from the more obvious properties of the exponential function,

$$e^{(x+y)} = e^x e^y,$$
$$(e^x)^\alpha = e^{\alpha x}.$$

It is advisable to know the above six identities by heart.

A.2   Differentiation

A.2.1   *Functions of One Variable*

By **differentiating** a function we obtain its **derivative**. The derivative measures the rate at which the target function changes with a small change in the variable. Formally, it is a limit of

$$\frac{f(x + \Delta x) - f(x)}{\Delta x}$$

as we let Δx take ever smaller values. The derivative is symbolically denoted

$$\frac{\mathrm{d}f(x)}{\mathrm{d}x} \quad \text{or} \quad f'(x).$$

A.2.2   *Calculation of Derivatives*

It is worth memorizing the derivatives of the most frequently used functions:

Function $f(x)$	Derivative $f'(x)$
x^α	$\alpha x^{\alpha - 1}$
e^x	e^x
$\ln x$	$\dfrac{1}{x}$
$\sin x$	$\cos x$
$\cos x$	$-\sin x$

plus the following five rules:

1. $(\text{const.})' = 0$;
2. $(f(x)g(x))' = f'(x)g(x) + f(x)g'(x)$;
3. $\left(\dfrac{f(x)}{g(x)}\right)' = \dfrac{f'(x)g(x) - f(x)g'(x)}{(g(x))^2}$;
4. $(f(g(x)))' = f'(g(x))g'(x)$.

   A special case of rule 2 when $g(x) = a$ is a constant function gives
5. $(af(x))' = af'(x)$.

Example A.1. Differentiate $\sqrt{x}$.

Solution. We have to think of $\sqrt{x}$ as $x^{1/2}$. After that the result is obtained quickly as

$$(x^{1/2})' = \tfrac{1}{2}x^{1/2-1} = \tfrac{1}{2}x^{-1/2} = \frac{1}{2\sqrt{x}}.$$

Example A.2. Let us differentiate e^x/x.

Solution. We shall take $f(x) = e^x$ and $g(x) = x^{-1}$ and apply rule 2. From the table above

$$f'(x) = e^x,$$
$$g'(x) = -x^{-2},$$

and therefore

$$\left(\frac{e^x}{x}\right)' = e^x x^{-1} - e^x x^{-2} = \frac{e^x}{x}\left(1 - \frac{1}{x}\right).$$

Example A.3. Differentiate $\tan x$.

Solution. We know that $\tan x = \sin x / \cos x$. Hence we set $f(x) = \sin x$ and $g(x) = \cos x$, and apply rule 3. From the table,

$$f'(x) = \cos x,$$
$$g'(x) = -\sin x,$$

and therefore

$$\left(\frac{\sin x}{\cos x}\right)' = \frac{\cos^2 x + \sin^2 x}{\cos^2 x} = \frac{1}{\cos^2 x}.$$

A.2.3 Chain Rule

Rule 4 is called the **chain rule** and is probably the most difficult to understand, because it may not be clear what $f'(g(x))$ means. Calculation of $f'(g(x))$ proceeds in two steps.

1. Replace $g(x)$ with y and calculate the derivative of $f(y)$ with respect to y.
2. In $f'(y)$ replace y with $g(x)$.

Example A.4. Differentiate

$$\frac{1}{1 + \sqrt{x}}.$$

Solution. We have to choose f and g so that

$$f(g(x)) = \frac{1}{1 + \sqrt{x}}.$$

Let us take

$$g(x) = 1 + \sqrt{x}$$

and

$$f(g(x)) = \frac{1}{g(x)}.$$

Now replace $g(x)$ with y and calculate $f'(y)$:

$$f(y) = \frac{1}{y},$$
$$f'(y) = -\frac{1}{y^2}.$$

Now we shall substitute $g(x)$ in place of y:

$$f'(g(x)) = -\frac{1}{(g(x))^2}.$$

To complete the task, let us calculate $g'(x)$:

$$g'(x) = (1 + \sqrt{x})' = 1' + (\sqrt{x})' = 0 + \tfrac{1}{2}x^{-1/2}.$$

Combining all the pieces together we conclude that

$$\left(\frac{1}{1 + \sqrt{x}}\right)' = (f(g(x)))' = f'(g(x))g'(x) = -\frac{\tfrac{1}{2}x^{-1/2}}{(1 + \sqrt{x})^2}.$$

Another example for the chain rule, this time also utilizing properties of the exponential and logarithmic function, is as follows.

Example A.5. Differentiate a^x.

Solution. First we need to rewrite a^x as an exponential function. We know that $a = e^{\ln a}$ and therefore

$$a^x = e^{x \ln a}.$$

Now we use rule 4, taking $f(g(x)) = e^{g(x)}$ and $g(x) = x \ln a$. We have

$$f'(g(x)) = e^{g(x)},$$
$$g'(x) = \ln a,$$

and hence

$$(a^x)' = (e^{x \ln a})' = e^{x \ln a} \ln a = a^x \ln a.$$

A.2.4 Higher-Order Derivatives

Repeating the differentiation process n times, one obtains the nth derivative. The notation for the nth derivative is

$$f^{(n)}(x) \quad \text{or} \quad \frac{d^n f(x)}{dx^n}.$$

The second and third derivatives can be also denoted by f'' and f''', respectively. One computes higher-order derivatives by sequential application of the formula

$$f^{(n)}(x) = \frac{d f^{(n-1)}(x)}{dx}.$$

Example A.6. Calculate the third derivative of $f(x) = e^{-ax}$.

Solution. We have

$$f'(x) = -ae^{-ax},$$
$$f''(x) = (f'(x))' = a^2 e^{-ax},$$
$$f'''(x) = (f''(x))' = -a^3 e^{-ax}.$$

A.3 Real Function of Several Real Variables

We start with an example of a function of two variables:

$$g(x, y) = -xy.$$

The domain of definition is in this case the whole real plane $\mathbb{R}^2$. Some functions, however, require restrictions on the domain of definition. For example,

$$g(x, y) = \ln xy$$

is meaningfully defined only for $xy > 0$.

An example of an n-variable function is

$$g(x_1, x_2, \ldots, x_n) = x_1 + x_2 + \cdots + x_n.$$

A.3.1 Partial Differentiation

A partial derivative is defined as follows:

$$\frac{\partial g(x_1, x_2, \ldots, x_n)}{\partial x_1} \triangleq \lim_{\Delta x \to 0} \frac{g(x_1 + \Delta x, x_2, \ldots, x_n) - g(x_1, x_2, \ldots, x_n)}{\Delta x}.$$

Comparing this definition with the definition of the normal derivative one can see that the *partial derivative is equal to the normal derivative if we regard all remaining variables as constants.*

Example A.7. For $g(x_1, x_2) = x_1 \ln(x_2)$ find

$$\frac{\partial g}{\partial x_1} \quad \text{and} \quad \frac{\partial g}{\partial x_2}.$$

Solution.

$$\frac{\partial x_1 \ln(x_2)}{\partial x 1} = \ln(x_2),$$

$$\frac{\partial x_1 \ln(x_2)}{\partial x 2} = \frac{x_1}{x_2}.$$

A.3.2 Higher-Order Derivatives

We can compose partial derivatives similarly as we can compose normal derivatives. The notation is as follows:

$$\frac{\partial}{\partial x_1} \frac{\partial g}{\partial x_1} = \frac{\partial^2 g}{\partial x_1^2}, \quad \frac{\partial}{\partial x_1} \frac{\partial g}{\partial x_2} = \frac{\partial^2 g}{\partial x_1 \partial x_2}, \quad \frac{\partial}{\partial x_1} \frac{\partial^2 g}{\partial x_1 \partial x_2} = \frac{\partial^3 g}{\partial x_1^2 \partial x_2}, \quad \text{etc.} \quad (A.1)$$

Example A.8. Calculate

$$\frac{\partial^2 (e^{x_1} + e^{x_2})}{\partial x_1 \partial x_2}.$$

Solution. First we will evaluate

$$\frac{\partial (e^{x_1} + e^{x_2})}{\partial x_2} = e^{x_2}.$$

The next step is to calculate

$$\frac{\partial}{\partial x_1}\left[\frac{\partial(e^{x_1}+e^{x_2})}{\partial x_2}\right] = \frac{\partial e^{x_2}}{\partial x_1} = 0.$$

Note. For all well-behaved functions,

$$\frac{\partial^2 g}{\partial x_i \partial x_j} = \frac{\partial^2 g}{\partial x_j \partial x_i}.$$

A.3.3   Partial Derivatives Versus Total Derivatives: the Chain Rule

In certain financial models the formula

$$P = e^{A(t,T)+B(t,T)r}$$

gives the price of a zero coupon discount bond at time t with maturity at time T if the current spot rate is r. When looking at a complicated expression like

$$e^{A(t,T)+B(t,T)r},$$

we need to be explicit about what is treated as a constant and what is treated as a variable. For example, writing

$$P(t) = e^{A(t,T)+B(t,T)r}$$

means that we take r and T as fixed. If we wanted to calculate the change of bond price as a reaction to a small time movement, we would simply use an ordinary derivative

$$\frac{dP(t)}{dt}.$$

On the other hand, if we wished to consider the price as a function of current time and current spot rate

$$P(r,t) = e^{A(t,T)+B(t,T)r},$$

then the price sensitivity with respect to the time movement would be written as

$$\frac{\partial P(r,t)}{\partial t}.$$

Of course, the two expressions $dP(t)/dt$ and $\partial P(r,t)/\partial t$ are the same because both of them treat r effectively as a constant.

Suppose now for a moment that r is not a constant, but it moves deterministically with time, $r(t)$. If we want to find the *total* price change as a result of a small time movement, we have to use the so-called **total derivative**:

$$\frac{dP(r(t),t)}{dt}.$$

By the **chain rule**, the total derivative can be evaluated as follows:

$$\frac{dP(r(t),t)}{dt} = \frac{\partial P(r(t),t)}{\partial r(t)}\frac{dr(t)}{dt} + \frac{\partial P(r,t)}{\partial t}.$$

A.4   Power Series Approximations

Very often one wants to know how the target function, say the price of a security, responds to a small change in underlying variable, say the short-term interest rate. The answer to this question is provided by the **Taylor expansion**:

$$f(x) = f(x^0) + f'(x^0)(x - x^0) + \frac{1}{2!} f''(x^0)(x - x^0)^2 + \cdots$$

$$+ \frac{1}{k!} f^{(k)}(x^0)(x - x^0)^k + o((x - x^0)^k)$$

as long as $f^{(k+1)}(x)$ is continuous around x_0. The symbol $o(\varepsilon)$ denotes *any* quantity much smaller than ε as ε approaches zero, specifically,

$$\lim_{\varepsilon \to 0} \frac{o(\varepsilon)}{\varepsilon} = 0.$$

For example, x^2 is $o(x)$, $10\,000\,000 x^2$ is again $o(x)$, x is $o(\sqrt{x})$, etc. Similarly, the symbol $O(x)$ denotes any quantity not greater in absolute value than a certain multiple of x as x approaches 0. For example,

$$\lim_{x \to 0} \frac{\cos x - 1}{x^2} = -1,$$

which means $\cos x - 1 = O(x^2)$.

We can write the Taylor expansion equivalently as

$$\Delta f(y) = f'(y)\Delta y + \frac{1}{2!} f''(y)(\Delta y)^2 + \cdots + \frac{1}{k!} f^{(k)}(y)(\Delta y)^k + \cdots,$$

where

$$\Delta f(y) \triangleq f(y + \Delta y) - f(y)$$

and the correspondence between y and x variables is $y = x^0$, $\Delta y = x - x^0$.

Example A.9. Find an approximate formula for $\Delta \ln y$.

Solution. Taking the first two elements of the expansion we have

$$\Delta \ln y \approx \frac{1}{y}\Delta y - \frac{1}{2}\frac{1}{y^2}(\Delta y)^2 = \frac{\Delta y}{y} - \frac{1}{2}\left(\frac{\Delta y}{y}\right)^2.$$

Note that $(\Delta y)/y$ can be interpreted as the percentage change in y. For a small change in y (under 5%) it is enough to use just the first term as an approximation:

$$\Delta \ln y \cong \frac{\Delta y}{y}.$$

The exact value of $\Delta \ln y$ and its approximation for $-0.1 \leqslant (\Delta y)/y \leqslant 0.1$ are shown in Table A.1. Note that

$$\Delta \ln y = \ln(y + \Delta y) - \ln y$$

$$= \ln \frac{y + \Delta y}{y}$$

$$= \ln \left(1 + \frac{\Delta y}{y}\right).$$

Example A.10. The price of a pure discount bond with time to maturity T and interest rate r is

$$S = e^{-rT}.$$

Find how the price reacts to a small change in interest rate if the initial interest rate is 10% and time to maturity is five years.

Solution. The Taylor expansion to second order gives

$$\Delta S \approx S'(r)\Delta r + \tfrac{1}{2}S''(r)(\Delta r)^2$$

$$= -Te^{-rT}\Delta r + \tfrac{1}{2}T^2 e^{-rT}(\Delta r)^2$$

$$= S(-T\Delta r + \tfrac{1}{2}(T\Delta r)^2).$$

Substituting $r_0 = 0.1$ and $T = 5$ we have

$$\frac{\Delta S}{S} \approx (-5\Delta r + 12.5(\Delta r)^2).$$

A.4.1 Multivariate Taylor Expansion

In the case where we wish to change several underlying variables independently, we have to use the **multivariate** Taylor expansion

$$g(x_1, x_2, \ldots, x_n)$$

$$= g(x_1^0, x_2^0, \ldots, x_n^0) + \sum_{k=1}^{n}(x_k - x_k^0)\frac{\partial g(x_1^0, x_2^0, \ldots, x_n^0)}{\partial x_k}$$

$$+ \frac{1}{2!}\sum_{k=1}^{n}\sum_{l=1}^{n}(x_k - x_k^0)(x_l - x_l^0)\frac{\partial^2 g(x_1^0, x_2^0, \ldots, x_n^0)}{\partial x_k \partial x_l} + \cdots.$$

With the benefit of matrix notation this formula can be written in a more compact form. Let us introduce the following natural notation:

$$x = \begin{bmatrix} x_1 \\ x_2 \\ \vdots \\ x_n \end{bmatrix},$$

$$\frac{\partial g}{\partial x} = \begin{bmatrix} \frac{\partial g}{\partial x_1} & \frac{\partial g}{\partial x_2} & \cdots & \frac{\partial g}{\partial x_n} \end{bmatrix},$$

Table A.1. Taylor series approximation of $\Delta \ln y$.

Fist-order approximation $\dfrac{\Delta y}{y}$	Exact expression $\Delta \ln y = \ln\left(1 + \dfrac{\Delta y}{y}\right)$	Second-order approximation $\dfrac{\Delta y}{y} - \dfrac{1}{2}\left(\dfrac{\Delta y}{y}\right)^2$
−0.100	−0.105	−0.105
−0.080	−0.083	−0.083
−0.060	−0.062	−0.062
−0.040	−0.041	−0.041
−0.020	−0.020	−0.020
0.000	0.000	0.000
0.020	0.020	0.020
0.040	0.039	0.039
0.060	0.058	0.058
0.080	0.077	0.077
0.100	0.095	0.095

$$\frac{\partial^2 g}{\partial x \partial x^*} = \begin{bmatrix} \dfrac{\partial^2 g}{\partial x_1 \partial x_1} & \dfrac{\partial^2 g}{\partial x_1 \partial x_2} & \cdots & \dfrac{\partial^2 g}{\partial x_1 \partial x_n} \\ \dfrac{\partial^2 g}{\partial x_2 \partial x_1} & \dfrac{\partial^2 g}{\partial x_2 \partial x_2} & \cdots & \dfrac{\partial^2 g}{\partial x_2 \partial x_n} \\ \vdots & \vdots & \ddots & \vdots \\ \dfrac{\partial^2 g}{\partial x_n \partial x_1} & \dfrac{\partial^2 g}{\partial x_n \partial x_2} & \cdots & \dfrac{\partial^2 g}{\partial x_n \partial x_n} \end{bmatrix}.$$

The vector $\partial g / \partial x$ is called the **gradient**. The matrix $\partial^2 g / \partial x \partial x^*$ is called the **Hessian** matrix of the function g. Once can easily verify that the Taylor expansion above can be written as

$$g(x) = g(x^0) + \frac{\partial g(x^0)}{\partial x}(x - x^0) + \frac{1}{2}(x - x^0)^* \frac{\partial^2 g(x^0)}{\partial x \partial x^*}(x - x^0) + \cdots$$

(see also Exercise 1.13 in Chapter 1).

Example A.11. In Example A.10 above find the change in the bond price if both the interest rate r and the time to maturity T change independently by small amounts.

Solution. From the Taylor expansion we have

$$\Delta S \approx \frac{\partial S(r, T)}{\partial r} \Delta r + \frac{\partial S(r, T)}{\partial T} \Delta T$$

$$+ \frac{1}{2}\left[\frac{\partial^2 S(r, T)}{\partial r^2}(\Delta r)^2 + 2 \frac{\partial^2 S(r, T)}{\partial r \partial T} \Delta r \Delta T + \frac{\partial^2 S(r, T)}{\partial T^2}(\Delta T)^2 \right]$$

$$= -T e^{-rT} \Delta r - r e^{-rT} \Delta T$$

$$+ \tfrac{1}{2}[T^2 e^{-rT}(\Delta r)^2 + 2(rT - 1)e^{-rT} \Delta r \Delta T + r^2 e^{-rT}(\Delta T)^2],$$

$$\frac{\Delta S}{S} \approx -T \Delta r - r \Delta T + \tfrac{1}{2}[T^2(\Delta r)^2 + 2(rT - 1)\Delta r \Delta T + r^2(\Delta T)^2].$$

In matrix form,

$$\Delta S \approx \begin{bmatrix} -5 & -0.1 \end{bmatrix} \begin{bmatrix} \Delta r \\ \Delta T \end{bmatrix} + \tfrac{1}{2} \begin{bmatrix} \Delta r & \Delta T \end{bmatrix} \begin{bmatrix} 25 & -0.5 \\ -0.5 & 0.01 \end{bmatrix} \begin{bmatrix} \Delta r \\ \Delta T \end{bmatrix}.$$

A.4.2   Total Differential

For a very small change in the underlying variables we can ignore higher-order terms in the Taylor expansion and write

$$g(x_1, x_2, \ldots, x_n) = g(x_1^0, x_2^0, \ldots, x_n^0) + \sum_{k=1}^{n} (x_k - x_k^0) \frac{\partial g(x_1^0, x_2^0, \ldots, x_n^0)}{\partial x_k}.$$

Since the change in x is small we will write more suggestively

$$(x_k - x_k^0) = dx_k$$

and

$$g(x_1, x_2, \ldots, x_n) - g(x_1^0, x_2^0, \ldots, x_n^0) = dg(x_1^0, x_2^0, \ldots, x_n^0).$$

Then the Taylor expansion becomes

$$dg(x_1^0, x_2^0, \ldots, x_n^0) = \sum_{k=1}^{n} \frac{\partial g(x_1^0, x_2^0, \ldots, x_n^0)}{\partial x_k} dx_k.$$

The expression

$$\frac{\partial g}{\partial x_1} dx_1 + \frac{\partial g}{\partial x_2} dx_2 + \cdots + \frac{\partial g}{\partial x_n} dx_n$$

is called the **total differential** of the function g.

Example A.12. Find the total differential of $S(r, T) = e^{-rT}$.

Solution. We simply take the first part of the approximation that we have calculated in the previous example and replace 'Δ' with 'd':

$$dS = -e^{-rT} T \, dr - r e^{-rT} \, dT,$$

$$\frac{dS}{S} = -T \, dr - r \, dT.$$

A.5   Optimization

The Taylor expansion is instrumental in finding local optima of univariate and multivariate functions. Consider a univariate function $f(x)$ and suppose the point x^0 is its local optimum. From the Taylor expansion

$$f(x) = f(x^0) + f'(x^0)(x - x^0) + o(x - x^0).$$

It follows that $f'(x^0)$ must be equal to 0, otherwise we would be able to increase (decrease) the value of f by moving a small distance to the right or left of x^0. This gives the so-called **first-order condition**:

$$f'(x^0) = 0.$$

This is a necessary, but not a sufficient, condition to find a local optimum. For example, with $f(x) = x^3$ we find $f'(0) = 0$ but $x = 0$ is neither a local minimum nor a local maximum because $f(x)$ is strictly increasing on the whole real line. To see whether one has found a minimum or a maximum it is necessary to look at the *second-order* term in the Taylor expansion:

$$f(x) = f(x^0) + \underbrace{f'(x^0)(x - x^0)}_{0} + f''(x^0)(x - x^0)^2 + o((x - x^0)^2).$$

If

$$f''(x^0) < 0, \qquad\qquad (A.2)$$

then the second-order term is always negative and we have a *local maximum*, whereas if

$$f''(x^0) > 0, \qquad\qquad (A.3)$$

the second-order term is always positive and we have found a *local minimum*. Inequalities (A.2) and (A.3) are called the **second-order conditions**.

A.5.1 *Multivariate optimization*

With multivariate functions the optimization works in exactly the same way. The first-order condition requires the gradient $\partial f / \partial x$ to be zero (in all components), and the second-order condition requires the quadratic form

$$(x - x^0) \frac{\partial^2 f}{\partial x \partial x^*} (x - x^0)^*$$

to be strictly positive for a local minimum, or strictly negative for a local maximum. This is equivalent to requiring the Hessian matrix $\partial^2 f / \partial x \partial x^*$ to be **positive definite** (**negative definite**) to guarantee that x_0 is a local *minimum* (*maximum*).

A.5.2 *Constrained optimization*

Suppose we wish to maximize a multivariate function $f(x)$ subject to a constraint $g(x) = 0$. Assume that x^0 is a local optimum. From the Taylor expansion we have

$$f(x) = f(x^0) + \frac{\partial f(x^0)}{\partial x}(x - x^0) + o(x - x^0),$$

$$g(x) = g(x^0) + \frac{\partial g(x^0)}{\partial x}(x - x^0) + o(x - x^0).$$

The difference from the unconstrained optimization is that

$$\frac{\partial f(x^0)}{\partial x}(x - x^0)$$

does not have to be zero for all values of x but only for those values that satisfy the constraint $g(x) = 0$, which implies

$$\frac{\partial g(x^0)}{\partial x}(x - x^0) = 0.$$

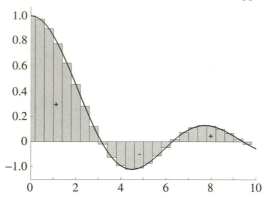

Figure A.3.   Approximation of $\int_0^{10}(\sin x/x)\,\mathrm{d}x$.

Thus for all x such that

$$\frac{\partial g(x^0)}{\partial x}(x - x^0) = 0$$

we must have

$$\frac{\partial f(x^0)}{\partial x}(x - x^0) = 0.$$

This will only be the case if the vector $\partial f(x^0)/\partial x$ is parallel to the vector $\partial g(x^0)/\partial x$, therefore there must be $\lambda \in \mathbb{R}$ such that

$$\frac{\partial f(x^0)}{\partial x} = \lambda \frac{\partial g(x^0)}{\partial x}. \tag{A.4}$$

The coefficient λ is known as the **Lagrange multiplier** and (A.4) is the first-order condition of the constrained optimization.

A.6   Integration

There are two versions of the integral: **definite** and **indefinite**. The definite integral is the area under the curve $f(x)$ between points a and b,

$$\int_a^b f(x)\,\mathrm{d}x,$$

and it should be thought of as the limit of a sum: we approximate the area by a sum of rectangles; a representative rectangle has width Δx. Increase number of rectangles and let all the widths $\Delta x \to 0$; the sum of the areas of the rectangles will tend to the area under the curve. We *define* $\int_a^b f(x)\,\mathrm{d}x$ as the limit of the sum of the areas of the rectangles (see Figure A.3).

Indefinite integration is the opposite process to differentiation, that is, $F(x)$ is the indefinite integral of $f(x)$ if

$$F'(x) = f(x),$$

and we write $F(x) = \int f(x)\,\mathrm{d}x$. The function $F(x)$ is called the **primitive function** $f(x)$.

Note. Unlike in the case of differentiation, for integration we do not have a set of rules that *always* lead to a result.

A.6.1 Elementary Integrals

$$\int e^{ax} \, dx = \frac{e^{ax}}{a} + c,$$

$$\int x^{\alpha} \, dx = \frac{x^{\alpha+1}}{\alpha + 1} + c,$$

$$\int \frac{dx}{x} = \ln(x) + c.$$

A.6.2 Useful Integration Rules

1. $\int (af(x) + bg(x)) \, dx = a \int f(x) \, dx + b \int g(x) \, dx;$

2. $\int f(g(x))g'(x) \, dx = F(g(x))$ (substitution method);

3. $\int f(x)g'(x) \, dx = f(x)g(x) + \int f'(x)g(x) \, dx$ (integration by parts).

Example A.13. Calculate

$$\int (1 + x + e^x) \, dx.$$

Solution. Applying rule 1 and the knowledge of elementary integrals we have

$$\int (1 + x + e^x) \, dx = \int dx + \int x \, dx + \int e^x \, dx$$

$$= x + \tfrac{1}{2}x^2 + e^x + c.$$

Example A.14. Calculate

$$\int e^{-x^2/2} x \, dx.$$

Solution. Here we can apply the substitution method, taking

$$f(y) = e^{-y},$$

$$g(x) = \tfrac{1}{2}x^2.$$

Note that $g'(x) = x$ so that

$$\int e^{-x^2/2} x \, dx$$

is indeed equal to

$$\int f(g(x))g'(x) \, dx.$$

The primitive function to $f(y)$ is

$$F(y) = -e^{-y}$$

as one can quickly verify by differentiating:

$$F'(y) = e^{-y} = f(y).$$

Thus from rule 2 we obtain

$$\int e^{-x^2/2} x \, dx = -e^{-x^2/2} + c.$$

Example A.15. Calculate

$$\int \ln x.$$

Solution. This is an example of integration by parts—rule 3. Take

$$f(x) = \ln x,$$
$$g'(x) = 1,$$

implying $g(x) = x$. Then we have

$$\int \ln x = x \ln x - \int \frac{1}{x} x \, dx = x \ln x - x + c.$$

A.6.3 Evaluation of Definite Integrals

Although the definite integral is defined as a limit of the sum, it is rarely calculated in that way. To evaluate

$$\int_a^b f(x) \, dx$$

we find the primitive function $F(x)$ (the indefinite integral) and then

$$\int_a^b f(x) \, dx = [F(x)]_a^b = F(b) - F(a) \tag{A.5}$$

provided $F(x)$ is continuous between a and b.

Example A.16. Evaluate

$$\int_0^2 e^{-at} \, dt.$$

Solution. First of all, let us find the indefinite integral

$$\int e^{-at} \, dt = -\frac{1}{a} e^{-at}.$$

Now use formula (A.5)

$$\int_0^2 e^{-at} \, dt = \left[-\frac{1}{a} e^{-at} \right]_0^2 = \frac{1 - e^{-2a}}{a}.$$

A.6.4 *Definite Integral as a Function of Its Limit*

Very often we see functions defined as follows:

$$G(t) = \int_0^t g(x)\,dx.$$

For such functions we have

$$G'(t) = g(t),$$

which means that $G(t)$ is a primitive function to $g(t)$. More generally, for

$$G(t) = \int_{a(t)}^{b(t)} g(x, t)\,dx$$

we have

$$G'(t) = b'(t)g(b(t), t) - a'(t)g(a(t), t) + \int_{a(t)}^{b(t)} \frac{\partial g(x, t)}{\partial t}\,dx. \tag{A.6}$$

Example A.17. Find $\Phi'(x)$, where Φ is the cumulative distribution function of the standard normal distribution:

$$\Phi(x) = \int_{-\infty}^x \frac{e^{-t^2/2}}{\sqrt{2\pi}}\,dt.$$

Solution.

$$\Phi'(x) = \frac{e^{-x^2/2}}{\sqrt{2\pi}}.$$

Example A.18. The following problem arises in the calibration of term-structure models. Calculate

$$\frac{\partial A(t, T)}{\partial t},$$

where

$$A(t, T) = \frac{(T - t)^3 \sigma^2}{6} - \int_t^T \theta(t, s)\,ds,$$

$$\theta(t, s) = \int_t^s \mu(u)\,du. \tag{A.7}$$

Solution. By formula (A.6) we have

$$\frac{\partial A(t, T)}{\partial t} = \frac{(T - t)^2 \sigma^2}{2} + \theta(t, t) - \int_t^T \frac{\partial \theta(t, s)}{\partial t}\,ds.$$

From the definition (A.7) it follows that

$$\theta(t, t) = 0,$$

$$\frac{\partial \theta(t, s)}{\partial t} = -\mu(t).$$

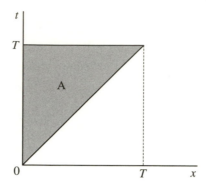

Figure A.4. Area of integration, $0 \leqslant t \leqslant T$, $0 \leqslant x \leqslant t$.

Consequently,

$$\frac{\partial A(t, T)}{\partial t} = -\frac{(T - t)^2 \sigma^2}{2} + \int_t^T \mu(t) \, ds$$

$$= -\frac{(T - t)^2 \sigma^2}{2} + \mu(t)(T - t).$$

A.6.5 Double Integrals

Imagine a situation where the short-term interest rate is given as an integral:

$$r(t) = \int_0^t g(x) \, dx.$$

Now we want to calculate the compounded interest rate from time 0 to time T:

$$f(0, T) = \int_0^T r(t) \, dt.$$

Substituting for r_t we arrive at a *double* integral:

$$f(0, T) = \int_0^T \left(\int_0^t g(x) \, dx \right) dt.$$

The way the integral is written suggests how it should be evaluated: first calculate the inner integral $\int_0^t g(x) \, dx$ and then the outer $\int_0^T r(t) \, dt$. However, the same integral can be written in a completely symmetric way as

$$\int_0^T \left(\int_0^t g(x) \, dx \right) dt = \iint_{\substack{0 \leqslant t \leqslant T \\ 0 \leqslant x \leqslant t}} g(x) \, dx \, dt.$$

The latter integral does not suggest the method of evaluation, it only mentions the function to be integrated, in our case $g(x)$, and the range over which we integrate, in our case the triangle $0 \leqslant t \leqslant T$, $0 \leqslant x \leqslant t$ (see Figure A.4).

An example of the function $g(x)$, considered as a function of two variables x and t, is plotted in Figure A.5.

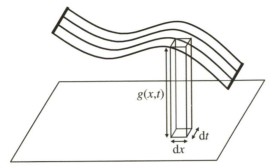

Figure A.5. Two-variable function and its approximation.

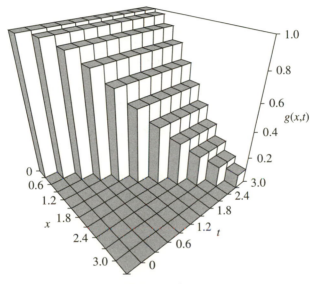

Figure A.6.

Integral in Two Dimensions

In general an integral of a two-variable function over a two-dimensional region will be written as

$$\iint_A g(x, t)\, dx\, dt$$

where A is the area over which we are integrating.

As in the one-dimensional case, the integral can be approximated as a sum of volumes of rectangular objects, but here we have boxes instead of rectangles (see Figure A.5). Figure A.6 shows the approximation of

$$\iint_A g(x, t)\, dx\, dt$$

when A is a triangle $0 \leqslant t \leqslant 3$, $0 \leqslant x \leqslant t$, and $g(x, t) = e^{-x^2/4}$.

It does not matter in which order we add the volume of the boxes in Figure A.6. If we add them first along the x-axis, we will get

$$\int_0^3 \left(\int_0^t g(x, t) \, dx \right) dt.$$

However, we can add them first along the t-axis, and we shall see how it is done in the next paragraph.

Changing the Order of Integration

The integration region in Figure A.4 can be equivalently expressed as

$$x \leqslant t \leqslant T,$$
$$0 \leqslant x \leqslant T.$$

This allows us to integrate along the t-axis first:

$$\iint_{\substack{0 \leqslant x \leqslant T \\ x \leqslant t \leqslant T}} g(x) \, dx \, dt = \int_0^T \left(\int_x^T g(x) \, dt \right) dx.$$

Note that

$$\int_x^T g(x) \, dt = g(x) \int_x^T dt = g(x)(T - x)$$

and therefore the compounded interest can be expressed as a single integral:

$$f(0, T) = \int_0^T g(x)(T - x) \, dx.$$

The 'real' application of changing the order of integration is in Section 11.5.3.

A.7   Exercises

Exercise A.1 (simple differentiation). Differentiate the following with respect to x.

(a) $(3x^2 - 5x + 2)^4$.

(b) $(\ln x + e^x)^4$.

(c) e^{x^2+x}.

(d) $x^2(2x + 1)^3$.

(e) $e^x \ln x$.

(f) $\dfrac{e^x}{(1 + x)^2}$.

Exercise A.2 (partial differentiation and the chain rule). Set

$$f(x, y, z) = x(y^2 + \ln z).$$

(a) Find the partial derivatives of f with respect to x, y, and z.

(b) Define $g(x) = f(x, \ln x, x^2)$. Find $g'(x)$.

(c) Assume, more generally, that $h(x) = f(x, y(x), z(x))$. Find

$$\frac{d}{dx} f(x, y(x), z(x)) \triangleq h'(x)$$

using the chain rule.

(d) Take $y(x) = \ln x$ and $z(x) = x^2$ and substitute this into your result in part (c).

(e) Compare the results in parts (b) and (d).

Exercise A.3 (Taylor expansion). Suppose that production Y is given by the Cobb–Douglas production function,

$$Y(K, L) = K^\alpha L^\beta,$$

where K is the level of capital and L is labour input. Write down the Taylor expansion of Y to first order and decide what is the percentage increase in output, given that both capital and labour increase by 1%. Assume $\alpha = \frac{1}{4}, \beta = \frac{3}{4}$.

Exercise A.4 (differentiating integrals with respect to their limits). Perform the following differentiations.

(a) $\dfrac{d}{dx} \displaystyle\int_{-\infty}^{x} e^{-t^2/2} \, dt$.

(b) $\dfrac{d}{dx} \displaystyle\int_{x}^{+\infty} e^{-t^2/2} \, dt$.

(c) $\dfrac{d}{dx} \displaystyle\int_{0}^{\sqrt{2\ln x}} e^{-t^2/2} \, dt$ for $x > 1$.

(d) $\dfrac{d}{dx} \displaystyle\int_{0}^{x} \left(\int_{0}^{t} f(y, s) \, ds \right) dy$.

Exercise A.5 (definite integrals). Evaluate the following integrals.

(a) $\displaystyle\int_{0}^{t} e^{-1.7s} \, ds$.

(b) $\displaystyle\int_{0}^{t} \sqrt{s} \, ds$.

(c) $\displaystyle\int_{0}^{s} t^{1/2} \, dt$.

(d) $\displaystyle\int_{0}^{+\infty} te^{-t^2} \, dt$.

(e) $\displaystyle\int_{0}^{1} s^{-1} \, ds$.

Exercise A.6 (verifying the solution of a partial differential equation). The *log contract* is a derivative security that pays at maturity the logarithm of the underlying stock price. The Black–Scholes price of the log contract is

$$L(S, r, \sigma, \tau) = e^{-r\tau}[\ln S + (r - \tfrac{1}{2}\sigma^2)\tau],$$

where S is the underlying stock price, r is the (constant) short-term interest rate, σ is the (constant) stock volatility, and τ is the time to maturity.

(a) Verify that L satisfies the boundary condition,

$$L(S, r, \sigma, 0) = \ln S.$$

(b) Verify that L solves the Black–Scholes PDE,

$$-\frac{\partial L(S, r, \sigma, \tau)}{\partial \tau} + rS \frac{\partial L(S, r, \sigma, \tau)}{\partial S} + \tfrac{1}{2}(\sigma S)^2 \frac{\partial^2 L(S, r, \sigma, \tau)}{\partial S^2} - rL(S, r, \sigma, \tau) = 0.$$

Exercise A.7 (call option delta). The Black–Scholes formula for the price of a call option is

$$C(S, K, r, \sigma, \tau) = S\Phi(d_+) - Ke^{-r\tau}\Phi(d_-), \tag{A.8}$$

where

$$d_\pm = \frac{\ln(S/K) + (r \pm \tfrac{1}{2}\sigma^2)}{\sigma\sqrt{\tau}}.$$

Here S is the current price of the underlying stock, K is a fixed strike price, r is the (constant) short interest rate, σ is the (constant) volatility of the stock, and τ is the time to maturity;

$$\Phi(x) = \frac{1}{\sqrt{2\pi}} \int_{-\infty}^{x} e^{-t^2/2}\, dt$$

is the cumulative standard normal distribution function, and we know that

$$\Phi'(x) = \frac{1}{\sqrt{2\pi}}e^{-x^2/2} \triangleq \phi(x).$$

The delta of the option is given as

$$\Delta = \frac{\partial C(S, K, r, \sigma, \tau)}{\partial S},$$

if we take C as a function of S, K, r, σ and τ. It tells us how many shares we should hold in a portfolio which perfectly replicates the option.

(a) Suppose that we take C as a function of S, d_+ and d_- as suggested by equation (A.8):

$$C(S, d_+, d_-) = S\Phi(d_+) - Ke^{-r\tau}\Phi(d_-).$$

Taking into account that d_+ and d_- are functions of S, that is, $d_+(S), d_-(S)$, express Δ using $C(S, d_+, d_-)$, $d_+(S)$ and $d_-(S)$ and the chain rule of Section A.3.3.

Calculate the following.

(b) $\dfrac{\partial C(S, d_+, d_-)}{\partial S}$.

(c) $\dfrac{\partial C(S, d_+, d_-)}{\partial d_+}$.

(d) $\dfrac{\partial C(S, d_+, d_-)}{\partial d_-}$.

(e) $d'_+(S)$.

(f) $d'_-(S)$.

(g) Substitute results (b)–(f) into the chain rule (a) and show that

$$\frac{dC(S, d_+(S), d_-(S))}{dS} = \Phi(d_+) + \frac{\phi(d_+)}{\sigma\sqrt{\tau}} - \frac{Ke^{-r\tau}\phi(d_-)}{S\sigma\sqrt{\tau}}$$

$$= \Phi(d_+) + \frac{\phi(d_+)}{\sigma\sqrt{\tau}}\left[1 - \frac{K}{S}e^{-r\tau}\frac{\phi(d_-)}{\phi(d_+)}\right]$$

$$= \Phi(d_+).$$

Exercise A.8 (call option gamma). The gamma of the call option is defined as

$$\gamma = \frac{\partial^2 C(S, K, r, \sigma, \tau)}{\partial S^2}.$$

Express γ in terms of the option's Δ and evaluate it using the explicit value of Δ obtained in Exercise A.7.

This appendix serves as a refresher course in probability theory. It explains essential concepts such as joint and marginal distribution, cumulative distribution and its density, stochastic independence, conditional probability and expectation, using discrete random variables. We argue that these properties extend to continuous random variables by passing to a limit. We then explain how one describes random variables using the mean, variance and higher moments, the moment-generating function and quantiles. We review the properties of the variance–covariance matrix and of jointly normally distributed variables. If the material included here does not fully satisfy the reader's needs, a more detailed introduction to probability theory can be found in Mood et al. (1974) (see also the notes in Section B.13).

B.1 Probability Space

A **probability space** is the triplet $(\Omega, \mathcal{F}, P)$. It contains information about elementary outcomes in the sample space Ω, all events are collected in the σ-algebra $\mathcal{F}$, and the probability of all events is described by the probability measure P. Each probabilistic model has these three components, even though one does not often mention them explicitly. One example of a probability space in a financial context was given in Section 8.5. Here we give another simple example.

Example B.1. The joint distribution of returns on two car industry stocks, Ford and Honda, is given in Table B.1. Determine the number of elementary outcomes and find the probability of the event $\frac{1}{2}(R_{\text{Honda}} + R_{\text{Ford}}) < 1.0$.

Solution. Each return takes three values and is allowed to move independently of the other return, which means we have nine elementary outcomes. In Table B.2 the probabilities of the elementary outcomes that belong to the event $\frac{1}{2}(R_{\text{Honda}} + R_{\text{Ford}}) < 1.0$ are printed in **bold**. Consequently,

$$P(\tfrac{1}{2}(R_{\text{Honda}} + R_{\text{Ford}}) < 1.0) = 0.4.$$

B.2 Conditional Probability

Let A and B be two events in $\mathcal{F}$ of the given probability space $(\Omega, \mathcal{F}, P)$. The **conditional probability** of event A given that event B occurs, denoted $P(A \mid B)$,

Table B.1.   Joint distribution of R_{Honda} and R_{Ford}.

		R_{Honda}		
		0.9	*1.0*	*1.1*
	0.8	0.1	0.1	0.1
R_{Ford}	*1.0*	0.1	0.1	0.1
	1.2	0.1	0.2	0.1

Table B.2.   Probability of event $\frac{1}{2}(R_{\text{Honda}} + R_{\text{Ford}}) < 1.0$.

		R_{Honda}		
		0.9	*1.0*	*1.1*
	0.8	**0.1**	**0.1**	**0.1**
R_{Ford}	*1.0*	**0.1**	0.1	0.1
	1.2	0.1	0.2	0.1

Table B.3.   Probability of two events.

		R_{Honda}					R_{Honda}		
		0.9	*1.0*	*1.1*			*0.9*	*1.0*	*1.1*
	0.8	0.1	0.1	0.1		*0.8*	0.1	**0.1**	**0.1**
R_{Ford}	*1.0*	0.1	**0.1**	**0.1**		*1.0*	0.1	**0.1**	**0.1**
	1.2	0.1	**0.2**	**0.1**		*1.2*	0.1	**0.2**	**0.1**

$P(R_{\text{Ford}} \geqslant 1.0 \text{ and } R_{\text{Honda}} \geqslant 1.0)$ $P(R_{\text{Honda}} \geqslant 1.0)$

is given by

$$P(A \mid B) = \frac{P(A \cap B)}{P(B)} \quad \text{if } P(B) > 0 \tag{B.1}$$

and is left undefined when $P(B) = 0$. The symbol $A \cap B$ means 'the event A occurs *and* the event B occurs'.

Note.

For B fixed $P(. \mid B)$ is a probability measure on $\mathcal{F}$.

Example B.2. In the set-up of Example B.1, what is the probability that the return on Ford is medium or high ($R_{\text{Ford}} \geqslant 1.0$) given that the return on Honda is medium or high ($R_{\text{Honda}} \geqslant 1.0$)?

Solution. We need to calculate

$$P(R_{\text{Ford}} \geqslant 1.0 \mid R_{\text{Honda}} \geqslant 1.0) = \frac{P(R_{\text{Ford}} \geqslant 1.0 \text{ and } R_{\text{Honda}} \geqslant 1.0)}{P(R_{\text{Honda}} \geqslant 1.0)}.$$

Now referring to Table B.3

$$P(R_{\text{Ford}} \geqslant 1.0 \text{ and } R_{\text{Honda}} \geqslant 1.0) = 0.5,$$
$$P(R_{\text{Honda}} \geqslant 1.0) = 0.7,$$

and consequently $P(R_{\text{Ford}} \geqslant 1 \mid R_{\text{Honda}} \geqslant 1) = 0.5/0.7 = 0.714$.

Theorem B.3 (total probabilities). *If $B_1, B_2, \ldots, B_n$ is a collection of mutually* *disjoint events in* $\mathcal{F}$ *satisfying*

$$\Omega = \bigcup_{j=1}^{n} B_j \quad \text{and} \quad P(B_j) > 0,$$

then for every $A \in \mathcal{F}$

$$P(A) = \sum_{j=1}^{n} P(A \mid B_j) P(B_j).$$

Example B.4. The probability of the pound appreciating significantly within one month is 0.7 if the interest rate goes up during that period, 0.5 if the interest rate remains unchanged and 0.3 if the interest rate goes down. An independent expert believes that in the month to come the Bank of England will either announce a lower interest rate with probability 0.6 or will leave interest rates unchanged with probability 0.4. What is the probability that the pound appreciates significantly within a month?

Solution. Denote the appreciation by A and let I_U, I_C, I_D denote the movements of the interest rate (up, constant, down). Then

$$P(A) = P(A \mid I_U)P(I_U) + P(A \mid I_C)P(I_C) + P(A \mid I_D)P(I_D)$$
$$= 0.7 \times 0 + 0.5 \times 0.4 + 0.3 \times 0.6 = 0.38.$$

Theorem B.5 (multiplication rule). *Let* $A_1, \ldots, A_n$ *be events for which* $P(A_1 \cap A_2 \cap \cdots A_n) > 0$. *Then*

$$P(A_1 \cap A_2 \cap \cdots A_n)$$
$$= P(A_n \mid A_1 \cap A_2 \cap \cdots A_{n-1})P(A_{n-1} \mid A_1 \cap A_2 \cap \cdots A_{n-2})$$
$$\cdots P(A_2 \mid A_1)P(A_1).$$

Example B.6. Researchers were looking at the frequency of market crashes. They found that the probability of a market crash in a given year depends on the number of years during which the market was previously stable. In particular, they deduced that if the market runs for two years without a crash the probability of it surviving another year is 0.8, whereas if the last crash was a year ago the probability of the market surviving another year is 0.9. Immediately after a crash the market survives one year without a crash with probability 0.95. Suppose that this year there was a market crash. What is the probability that the market runs smoothly in the three years to come?

Solution. Let us denote C_n as a crash in year n and N_n as no crash in year n. We are after

$$P(N_3 \cap N_2 \cap N_1 \cap C_0).$$

Using the multiplication rule we obtain

$$P(N_3 \cap N_2 \cap N_1 \cap C_0)$$
$$= P(N_3 \mid N_2 \cap N_1 \cap C_0) \times P(N_2 \mid N_1 \cap C_0) \times P(N_1 \mid C_0) \times P(C_0)$$
$$= 0.8 \times 0.9 \times 0.95 \times 1 = 0.684.$$

B.3   Marginal and Joint Distribution

Definition B.7 (probability density). Let us have two discrete random variables X and Y, taking values x_i, $i = 1, \ldots, m$, and y_j, $j = 1, \ldots, n$, respectively. The function $f_{X,Y}$

$$f_{X,Y}(x, y) = P(X = x, Y = y)$$

is called the joint probability density of the random variables X and Y. The function f_X

$$f_X(x) = \sum_{j=1}^{n} P(X = x, Y = y_j)$$

is called the marginal density of X and similarly f_Y

$$f_Y(y) = \sum_{i=1}^{m} P(X = x_i, Y = y)$$

is the marginal density of Y.

Definition B.8 (cumulative distribution). Take X and Y as above. The function $F_{X,Y}$

$$F_{X,Y}(x, y) = P(X \leqslant x, Y \leqslant y)$$

is called the joint cumulative distribution of X and Y. The function F_X

$$F_X(x) = \sum_{j=1}^{n} P(X \leqslant x, Y = y_j)$$

is called the marginal cumulative distribution of X and similarly

$$F_Y(y) = \sum_{i=1}^{m} P(X = x_i, Y \leqslant y)$$

is the marginal cumulative distribution of Y.

Example B.9. Find the marginal density of R_{Honda} and R_{Ford} in Table B.1.

Solution. To calculate the marginal distribution of R_{Honda}, simply look at Table B.1 and add the probabilities in each column. To obtain the marginal distribution of R_{Ford}, add the probabilities in each row. The result is shown in Table B.4.

Table B.4. Joint and marginal distribution of R_{Honda} and R_{Ford}.

		R_{Honda}			R_{Ford} marginal $\downarrow$
		0.9	*1.0*	*1.1*	
	0.8	0.1	0.1	0.1	0.3
R_{Ford}	*1.0*	0.1	0.1	0.1	0.3
	1.2	0.1	0.2	0.1	0.4
R_{Honda} marginal	$\longrightarrow$	0.3	0.4	0.3	

Table B.5. Two joint distributions with identical marginals.

		R_{Honda}				R_{Honda}		
		0.9	*1.0*	*1.1*		*0.9*	*1.0*	*1.1*
	0.8	0.1	0.1	0.1	*0.8*	0.09	0.12	0.09
R_{Ford}	*1.0*	0.1	0.1	0.1	*1.0*	0.09	0.12	0.09
	1.2	0.1	0.2	0.1	*1.2*	0.12	0.16	0.12

Table B.6. Joint density and joint cumulative distribution.

		R_{Honda}				R_{Honda}		
		0.9	*1.0*	*1.1*		*0.9*	*1.0*	*1.1*
	0.8	0.1	0.1	0.1	*0.8*	0.1	0.2	0.3
R_{Ford}	*1.0*	0.1	0.1	0.1	*1.0*	0.2	0.4	0.6
	1.2	0.1	0.2	0.1	*1.2*	0.3	0.7	1.0
		joint density				joint cumulative distribution		

It is clear that a given joint distribution determines the marginal distributions uniquely. However, the converse is not true; a given marginal distribution can come from many different joint distributions (see Table B.5). The function that links the marginal densities and the joint density is called the **copula**. In practice, one picks the marginal distributions first and then selects an appropriate copula to achieve the right amount of interdependency among the individual random variables (see the notes at the end of the chapter).

Example B.10. Find the joint cumulative distribution of R_{Honda} and R_{Ford} from the density given in Table B.1.

Solution. Proceed from the definition $F(x, y) = P(R_{Ford} \leqslant x, R_{Honda} \leqslant y)$. The resulting F must increase in the left-to-right and top-to-bottom directions (see Table B.6).

B.4 Stochastic Independence

B.4.1 Independence of Events

When $P(A \mid B)$ does not depend on the event B, that is,

$$P(A \mid B) = P(A),$$

then it is natural to say that the events A and B are **stochastically independent** (or simply independent if there can be no confusion with *linear* independence). Equivalently, after writing $P(A \mid B)$ as $P(A \cap B)/P(B)$, we can see that A and B are independent if

$$P(A \cap B) = P(A)P(B).$$

Example B.11. On a given day the market can be bullish or bearish and stable or volatile. The probability of the four outcomes is summarized as follows:

	STABLE	VOLATILE
BULLISH	$\frac{1}{3}$	$\frac{1}{6}$
BEARISH	$\frac{1}{4}$	$\frac{1}{4}$

Are the events BULLISH and VOLATILE independent?

Solution. We have

$$P(\text{VOLATILE}) = \tfrac{1}{6} + \tfrac{1}{4} = \tfrac{5}{12},$$

$$P(\text{BULLISH}) = \tfrac{1}{3} + \tfrac{1}{6} = \tfrac{1}{2},$$

$$P(\text{VOLATILE} \cap \text{BULLISH}) = \tfrac{1}{6},$$

$$\tfrac{1}{6} = P(\text{VOLATILE} \cap \text{BULLISH}) \neq P(\text{VOLATILE})P(\text{BULLISH}) = \tfrac{5}{14},$$

and hence the two events are not independent.

B.4.2 Independence of Random Variables

Definition B.12. Two random variables X and Y are stochastically independent if and only if for any $x, y \in \mathbb{R}$ the two events $X \leqslant x$ and $Y \leqslant y$ are independent, that is, if and only if

$$F_{X,Y}(x, y) = F_X(x)F_Y(y) \quad \text{for all } x, y.$$

Proposition B.13. *When the joint density $f_{X,Y}$ exists, X and Y are stochastically independent if and only if*

$$f_{X,Y}(x, y) = f_X(x)f_Y(y).$$

Proof. For discrete random variables see Exercise B.25 For continuous random variables see Exercise B.9.4.   ☐

The meaning of stochastic independence is best appreciated from the following proposition.

Proposition B.14. *If X_1 and X_2 are independent, then for any functions g_1, g_2 (such that $g_i(X_i)$ are random variables) $g_1(X_1)$ and $g_2(X_2)$ are again independent.*

Proof. Essentially, events of the type $g_i(X_i) \leqslant v_i$ are composed of events of the type $X_i \leqslant v_i$. Since the latter are independent, the former are again independent. A formal proof can be found in Mood et al. (1974).   ☐

B.5 Expectation Operator

Let X be a discrete random variable taking values $x_1, x_2, \ldots x_m$ with density f_X and let g be an arbitrary function. The expected value of a random variable $g(X)$ is defined as follows:

$$\mathrm{E}[g(X)] = \sum_{j=1}^{m} g(x_j) f_X(x_j), \tag{B.2}$$

whereas, for a continuous random variable X,

$$\mathrm{E}[g(X)] = \int_{-\infty}^{\infty} g(x) f_X(x) \, dx. \tag{B.3}$$

- The discrete expectation is calculated as follows. For each value of X evaluate $g(X)$ and multiply it by the probability of the corresponding scenario, then add the contributions of all the scenarios.
- Expression (B.3) can be thought of as a limit of the discrete expectation (B.2); more on this topic in Section B.9.2.
- Definitions (B.2) and (B.3) will also work with several random variables simultaneously; it is enough to think of X as a vector of random variables.

Example B.15. For the distribution of returns in Table B.1 calculate $\mathrm{E}[R_{\text{Ford}}]$ and $\mathrm{E}[R_{\text{Ford}}^2]$.

Solution. This task is best accomplished using the marginal distribution of R_{Ford} given in Table B.4. For each expectation we have to consider the value of R_{Ford} and R_{Ford}^2, respectively, multiply it by the probability of the corresponding state (scenario) and add these values. Specifically,

$$\mathrm{E}[R_{\text{Ford}}] = 0.8 \times 0.3 + 1.0 \times 0.3 + 1.2 \times 0.4 = 1.02,$$

$$\mathrm{E}[R_{\text{Ford}}^2] = 0.8^2 \times 0.3 + 1.0^2 \times 0.3 + 1.2^2 \times 0.4 = 1.068.$$

Example B.16. Calculate $\mathrm{E}[R_{\text{Ford}} R_{\text{Honda}}]$ using the joint distribution in Table B.1.

Solution. Again we have to loop over all scenarios (elementary outcomes) computing the value $R_{\text{Honda}} R_{\text{Ford}}$, multiplying it by the corresponding probability and adding all the contributions. In our particular case,

$$\begin{aligned}
\mathrm{E}[R_{\text{Ford}} R_{\text{Honda}}] = {} & 0.8 \times 0.9 \times 0.1 + 0.8 \times 1.0 \times 0.1 + 0.8 \times 1.1 \times 0.1 \\
& + 1.0 \times 0.9 \times 0.1 + 1.0 \times 1.0 \times 0.1 + 1.0 \times 1.1 \times 0.1 \\
& + 1.2 \times 0.9 \times 0.1 + 1.2 \times 1.0 \times 0.2 + 1.2 \times 1.1 \times 0.1 \\
= {} & 1.02.
\end{aligned}$$

This can be easily written down in matrix form

$$E[R_{\text{Ford}}R_{\text{Honda}}] = \begin{bmatrix} 0.8 & 1.0 & 1.2 \end{bmatrix} \begin{bmatrix} 0.1 & 0.1 & 0.1 \\ 0.1 & 0.1 & 0.1 \\ 0.1 & 0.2 & 0.1 \end{bmatrix} \begin{bmatrix} 0.9 \\ 1.0 \\ 1.1 \end{bmatrix}$$

and computed effortlessly in GAUSS.

B.6 Properties of Expectation

Computing expectations can be time-consuming, especially when dealing with several random variables simultaneously. Knowing the general properties of expectation can help to avoid unnecessary calculations. In turn these properties follow from the properties of summation (or integration as a limit of summation). Let $X_1, \ldots, X_n$ be a collection of random variables and let a be a constant. Then we have the following.

1. Expectation of a constant is that constant:

$$E[a] = a.$$

2. Expectation scales linearly:

$$E[aX] = aE[X].$$

3. Expectation of a sum equals the sum of expectations:

$$E[X_1 + \cdots + X_n] = E[X_1] + \cdots + E[X_n].$$

Proof. Consider two discrete random variables X and Y taking values $\{x_i\}_{i=1}^m$, $\{y_j\}_{j=1}^n$ with joint density $f_{X,Y}$. Then

$$
\begin{aligned}
E[X + Y] &= \sum_{i=1}^m \sum_{j=1}^n (x_i + y_j) f_{X,Y}(x_i, y_j) \\
&= \sum_{i=1}^m \sum_{j=1}^n x_i f_{X,Y}(x_i, y_j) + \sum_{i=1}^m \sum_{j=1}^n y_j f_{X,Y}(x_i, y_j) \\
&= \sum_{i=1}^m x_i \sum_{j=1}^n f_{X,Y}(x_i, y_j) + \sum_{j=1}^n y_j \sum_{i=1}^m f_{X,Y}(x_i, y_j) \\
&= \sum_{i=1}^m x_i f_X(x_i) + \sum_{j=1}^n y_j f_Y(y_j) \\
&= E[X] + E[Y].
\end{aligned}
$$

The same logic applies to three or more variables. $\qquad\square$

4. If $X_1, \ldots, X_n$ are stochastically independent, then

$$E[X_1 \times X_2 \times \cdots \times X_n] = E[X_1] \times E[X_2] \cdots \times E[X_n].$$

Proof. Take X and Y as in the proof of part 2. Independence implies

$$f_{X,Y}(x_i, y_j) = f_X(x_i) f_Y(y_j),$$

hence

$$E[X \times Y] = \sum_{i=1}^{m} \sum_{j=1}^{n} x_i y_j f_{X,Y}(x_i, y_j)$$

$$= \sum_{i=1}^{m} \sum_{j=1}^{n} x_i y_j f_X(x_i) f_Y(y_j)$$

$$= \sum_{i=1}^{m} x_i f_X(x_i) \sum_{j=1}^{n} y_j f_Y(y_j)$$

$$= E[X] \times E[Y].$$

With more than two variables one proceeds in the same way. □

B.7 Mean and Variance

The number $E[X]$, sometimes denoted μ_X, is called the **mean** of the random variable X. The expected squared deviation of the random variable from its mean is called the **variance**, denoted $\text{Var}(X)$ or σ_X^2:

$$\text{Var}(X) \triangleq E[(X - E[X])^2].$$

Example B.17. Use the properties of expectation to simplify the expression for variance.

Solution. Firstly, we will expand the expression $(X - E[X])^2$:

$$(X - E[X])^2 = X^2 - 2XE[X] + (E[X])^2.$$

Now bearing in mind that $E[X]$ is a constant and applying rules 1, 2 and 3 we have

$$E[(X - E[X])^2] = E[X^2 - 2XE[X] + (E[X])^2]$$

$$= E[X^2] - 2E[X]E[X] + (E[X])^2$$

$$= E[X^2] - (E[X])^2.$$

$$\text{Var}(X) = E[(X - \mu_X)^2] = E[X^2] - \mu_X^2.$$

B.7.1 Properties of Variance

1. Variance is independent of the mean in the following sense. If a is a constant, then

$$\text{Var}(X + a) = \text{Var}(X).$$

This is because

$$X + a - E[X + a] = X - E[X].$$

2. Variance increases quadratically with the change in scale:

$$\text{Var}(aX) = a^2 \, \text{Var}(X).$$

This happens because

$$(aX - \text{E}[aX])^2 = a^2(X - \text{E}[X])^2.$$

Example B.18. Calculate the mean and variance of Y if $Y = a + bX$.

Solution. Using the properties of mean and variance we have

$$\mu_Y = \text{E}[Y] = \text{E}[a + bX] = a + b\text{E}[X] = a + b\mu_X,$$
$$\sigma_Y^2 = \text{Var}(Y) = \text{Var}(a + bX) = \text{Var}(bX) = b^2 \, \text{Var}(X) = b^2 \sigma_X^2.$$

B.7.2 Standard Deviation

Standard deviation (also called volatility), denoted $\text{Vol}(X)$ or σ_X, is defined as the positive square root of the variance:

$$\text{Vol}(X) = \sqrt{\text{Var}(X)}.$$

Note that the standard deviation *increases linearly* with the change in scale:

$$\text{Vol}(aX) = |a| \, \text{Vol}(X).$$

B.8 Covariance and Correlation

Covariance is a simple measure of co-movement between two random variables. Formally, it is defined as follows:

$$\text{Cov}(X, Y) \triangleq \text{E}[(X - \mu_X)(Y - \mu_Y)].$$

If the covariance is positive (negative), we expect X_i to be above its mean when X_j is above (below) its mean. In such a case we say that X_i and X_j are **positively (negatively) correlated**.

Example B.19. Use the properties of expectation to simplify the expression for covariance.

Solution. We begin by expanding the expression $(X - \mu_X)(Y - \mu_Y)$:

$$(X - \mu_X)(Y - \mu_Y) = XY - X\mu_Y - \mu_X Y + \mu_X \mu_Y.$$

Consequently,

$$\text{E}[(X - \mu_X)(Y - \mu_Y)] = \text{E}[XY - X\mu_Y - \mu_X Y + \mu_X \mu_Y]$$
$$= \text{E}[XY] - \mu_X \mu_Y - \mu_X \mu_Y + \mu_X \mu_Y$$
$$= \text{E}[XY] - \mu_X \mu_Y.$$

$$\text{Cov}(X, Y) = \text{E}[(X - \mu_X)(Y - \mu_Y)] = \text{E}[XY] - \mu_X\mu_Y,$$
$$\text{Cov}(X, X) = \text{Var}(X).$$

The following two properties are easy to prove from first principles.

1. Shifting the mean does not change the covariance:
$$\text{Cov}(a + X, b + Y) = \text{Cov}(X, Y),$$

2. Covariance scales linearly in both components:
$$\text{Cov}(aX, bY) = ab\,\text{Cov}(X, Y).$$

To find out whether the covariance between two variables is high or low we need a yardstick to compare it against. It turns out the appropriate yardstick is the product of standard deviations $\text{Vol}(X)\,\text{Vol}(Y)$. The scaled value of the covariance is called the **correlation**, and is denoted $\text{corr}(X, Y)$ or $\rho_{X,Y}$:

$$\text{corr}(X, Y) \triangleq \frac{\text{Cov}(X, Y)}{\sqrt{\text{Var}(X)\,\text{Var}(Y)}} = \frac{\sigma_{XY}}{\sigma_X\sigma_Y}.$$

It can be shown (see Mood et al. 1974) that

$$-1 \leqslant \text{corr}(X, Y) \leqslant 1$$

and the equality occurs only if there is a constant a such that $X - \mu_X = a(Y - \mu_Y)$. In such a case we say that X and Y are **perfectly correlated**. Conversely, when $\text{corr}(X, Y) = 0$ we say that X and Y are **uncorrelated**.

B.8.1 Correlation and Independence

- Independent variables are automatically uncorrelated.

  Proof. For independent variables we have $\text{E}[XY] = \text{E}[X]\text{E}[Y]$. Hence $\text{Cov}(X, Y) = \text{E}[XY] - \text{E}[X]\text{E}[Y] = 0$. □

- Uncorrelated variables are *not* necessarily independent. For example, R_{Honda} and R_{Ford} in Table B.1 are uncorrelated but they are not independent.
- If X and Y are jointly normally distributed and uncorrelated, then they are also independent.

B.8.2 Variance–Covariance Matrix

Let

$$X = \begin{bmatrix} X_1 & X_2 & \cdots & X_n \end{bmatrix}^*$$

be a vector of random variables with mean

$$\mu_X^* = \begin{bmatrix} \text{E}[X_1] & \text{E}[X_2] & \cdots & \text{E}[X_n] \end{bmatrix}.$$

We define the **variance–covariance matrix** Σ_X as follows:

$$(\Sigma_X)_{ij} = \text{Cov}(X_i, X_j),$$

meaning that Σ_X is a symmetric matrix with variances on the diagonal and covariances off the diagonal.

In matrix notation Σ can be obtained as

$$\Sigma_X = \text{E}[(X - \mu_X)(X - \mu_X)^*].$$

B.8.3   Portfolio Theorem for Covariances

Apart from storing variances and covariances, the matrix Σ_X is useful for calculating the variance of $Y = \alpha_1 X_1 + \cdots + \alpha_n X_n$. Typically, $X_1, \ldots, X_n$ are returns of different securities and Y is a portfolio return. It is helpful to define

$$\alpha = \begin{bmatrix} \alpha_1 \\ \alpha_2 \\ \vdots \\ \alpha_n \end{bmatrix}$$

and then $Y = \alpha^* X$. We also have

$$\mu_Y = \alpha^* \mu_X.$$

Now we can calculate the portfolio variance

$$\begin{aligned} \text{Var}(Y) &= \text{E}[(Y - \mu_Y)^2] = \text{E}[(Y - \mu_Y)(Y - \mu_Y)^*] \\ &= \text{E}[(\alpha^* X - \alpha^* \mu_X)(\alpha^* X - \alpha^* \mu_X)^*] \\ &= \text{E}[\alpha^* (X - \mu_X)(X - \mu_X)^* \alpha] \\ &= \alpha^* \text{E}[(X - \mu_X)(X - \mu_X)^*] \alpha \\ &= \alpha^* \Sigma_X \alpha. \end{aligned}$$

---

1. **Portfolio theorem.** Let Y be an m-dimensional random variable representing m portfolios generated by portfolio weights $A \in \mathbb{R}^{m \times n}$ from n basis assets X:

$$Y = AX. \tag{B.4}$$

Then the covariance among the new portfolios is given as follows:

$$\Sigma_Y = A \Sigma_X A^*. \tag{B.5}$$

2. As a special case of (B.4) and (B.5) for uncorrelated variables X ($\Sigma_X = I_n$) and $A = \begin{bmatrix} 1 & 1 & \cdots & 1 \end{bmatrix}$ we obtain

$$\text{Var}(X_1 + X_2 + \cdots + X_n) = \text{Var}(X_1) + \text{Var}(X_2) + \cdots + \text{Var}(X_n);$$

the variance of a sum equals the sum of the variances if the summands are uncorrelated.

Example B.20. In econometrics, the ordinary least squares estimator $\hat{\beta}$ is given by the formula,

$$\hat{\beta} = (X^*X)^{-1}X^*Y,$$

where the $n \times k$ matrix X is assumed to be fixed and the n-dimensional vector Y has covariance matrix:

$$\Sigma_Y = \sigma^2 I_n.$$

Find the variance–covariance matrix of the k-dimensional random variable $\hat{\beta}$.

Solution. We have

$$\hat{\beta} = AY,$$
$$\Sigma_{\hat{\beta}} = A\Sigma_Y A^*,$$

where

$$A = (X^*X)^{-1}X^*.$$

Substituting for A and Σ_Y we obtain

$$\Sigma_{\hat{\beta}} = (X^*X)^{-1}X^*\sigma^2 I_n X(X^*X)^{-1}$$
$$= \sigma^2(X^*X)^{-1}(X^*X)(X^*X)^{-1} = \sigma^2(X^*X)^{-1}.$$

B.9   Continuous Random Variables

Recall that for a given random variable X we define the cumulative distribution F_X function as follows:

$$F_X(x) = P(X \leqslant x).$$

The cumulative distribution has the following properties:

1. $F(x)$ is non-decreasing;
2. $F(-\infty) = \lim_{x \to -\infty} F(x) = 0$;
3. $F(\infty) = \lim_{x \to \infty} F(x) = 1$.

Example B.21. Let X be a random excess return between -20% and 30%. Suppose that X is distributed uniformly in $[-0.2, 0.3]$. Intuitively, this means that the probability of X lying in an arbitrary interval $[a, b]$, $-0.2 \leqslant a \leqslant b \leqslant 0.3$, is simply proportional to the length of that interval:

$$P(X \in [a, b]) = \text{const.} \times (b - a) \quad \text{for} -0.2 \leqslant a \leqslant b \leqslant 0.3. \qquad \text{(B.6)}$$

By assumption,

$$P(X \in [-0.2, 0.3]) = 1,$$

and therefore the constant in (B.6) must be 2:

$$P(X \in [a, b]) = 2 \times (b - a) \quad \text{for} -0.2 \leqslant a \leqslant b \leqslant 0.3. \qquad \text{(B.7)}$$

Plot the cumulative distribution $F_X(x)$.

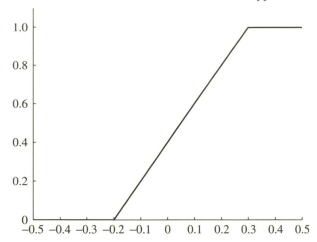

Figure B.1. Cumulative distribution function of a uniform random variable on $[-0.2, 0.3]$.

Solution. We have $F_X(x) = P(X \leqslant x)$. For $x \leqslant -0.2$ this probability is 0, for $x \geqslant 0.3$ it is 1, and for $-0.2 \leqslant x \leqslant 0.3$ it is given by formula (B.7) with $a = -0.2$ and $b = x$:

$$F_X(x) = \begin{cases} 0 & \text{for } x \leqslant -0.2, \\ 2(x + 0.2) & \text{for } -0.2 \leqslant x \leqslant 0.3, \\ 1 & \text{for } 0.3 \leqslant x. \end{cases}$$

This function is plotted in Figure B.1.

B.9.1 Discretization of Continuous Random Variables

The random variable in Example B.21 has one peculiar property: for any $x \in \mathbb{R}$, $P(X = x) = 0$! Thus, seemingly, continuous random variables are quite different from discrete variables. It is, however, a simple matter to approximate a continuous random variable by a discrete random variable.

Example B.22. Divide the interval $[-0.2, 0.3]$ into 10 equal segments. Define a new random variable Y taking 10 values $-0.175, -0.125, \ldots, 0.275$ representing the midpoint of each segment. Assign to each value of Y the probability $f_Y(y)$ equal to the probability that X falls into the given segment. Since the original distribution is uniform and the segments have equal length, the probabilities are equal to $1/10$. Plot the cumulative distribution of Y and compare it with the cumulative distribution of X.

Solution. Since Y is a discrete random variable its CDF will be constant most of the time, jumping by $1/10$ at the points $-0.175, -0.125, \ldots, 0.275$. It has a characteristic zigzag shape shown in Figure B.2. The straight line represents the CDF of the continuous random variable X in Example B.21.

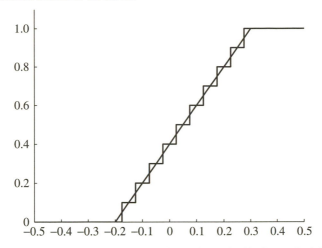

Figure B.2. Discrete approximation of a uniform distribution on $[-0.2, 0.3]$.

B.9.2 Univariate Probability Density

The above discretization can be easily generalized to any continuous random variable taking values on the entire real line. Let us construct segments of length Δx with endpoints $x_i = i \times \Delta x$ for $i = 0, \pm 1, \pm 2, \ldots$. Consider a discrete random variable Y taking values x_i with probability:

$$f_Y(x_i) = P(x_i < X \leqslant x_i + \Delta x).$$

What is the probability that X is between x and $x + \Delta x$? From the additivity of probabilities:

$$P(X \leqslant x) + P(x < X \leqslant x + \Delta x) = P(X \leqslant x + \Delta x),$$

which can be rephrased as

$$P(x < X \leqslant x + \Delta x) = F_X(x + \Delta x) - F_X(x). \tag{B.8}$$

Using the Taylor expansion to first order we have

$$F_X(x + \Delta x) - F_X(x) \approx F_X'(x)\Delta x. \tag{B.9}$$

The function
$$f_X(x) \triangleq F_X'(x)$$
is called the **probability density function** of the continuous random variable X. By virtue of (B.8) and (B.9) the density f_X measures the probability of X falling into a small interval around x *per unit of length*:

$$P(x < X \leqslant x + \Delta x) \approx f_X(x)\Delta x.$$

The expectation of the discretized variable Y is

$$\sum_{i=-\infty}^{+\infty} x_i f_Y(x_i) = \sum_{i=-\infty}^{+\infty} x_i \frac{F_X(x_i + \Delta x) - F_X(x_i)}{\Delta x} \Delta x. \tag{B.10}$$

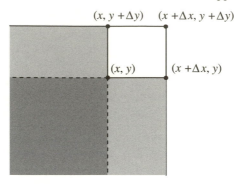

$(x, y +\Delta y)$ $(x +\Delta x, y +\Delta y)$

(x, y) $(x +\Delta x, y)$

Figure B.3.   Discretization of the continuous bivariate distribution.

As $\Delta x \to 0$ the expression $(F_X(x_i + \Delta x) - F_X(x_i))/\Delta x$ becomes $F'_X(x_i)$ and the right-hand side turns into an integral:

$$\lim_{\Delta x \to 0} \sum_{i=-\infty}^{+\infty} x_i f_Y(x_i) = \int_{-\infty}^{+\infty} x F'_X(x)\, \mathrm{d}x = \int_{-\infty}^{+\infty} x f_X(x)\, \mathrm{d}x.$$

For a continuous random variable X with density $f_X = F'_X$, the expectation is defined as the limit of (B.10):

$$\mathrm{E}[X] = \int_{-\infty}^{+\infty} x f_X(x)\, \mathrm{d}x.$$

Example B.23. Suppose that the CDF of the random variable X is

$$F(x) = \frac{e^x}{1 + e^x}.$$

   (a) Find the probability that $0.05 < X \leqslant 0.1$.

   (b) Find the density $f(x)$ and use it to approximate $P(0.05 < X \leqslant 0.1)$.

Solution. (a) From (B.8) we have

$$P(0.05 < X \leqslant 0.1) = F(0.1) - F(0.05)$$

$$= \frac{e^{0.1}}{1 + e^{0.1}} - \frac{e^{0.05}}{1 + e^{0.05}} = 0.0125.$$

(b) First evaluate the density

$$f(x) = F'(x) = \frac{1}{(1 + e^x)^2}.$$

From (B.9) we obtain

$$P(0.05 < X \leqslant 0.1) \approx f_X(0.05)(0.1 - 0.05)$$

$$= \frac{0.05}{(1 + e^{0.05})^2} = 0.0119.$$

B.9.3 Multivariate Probability Density

Now consider a joint distribution with cumulative function $F_{X,Y}(x, y) = P(X \leqslant x, Y \leqslant y)$. To discretize this joint distribution we will divide the plane (x, y) into squares with sides $\Delta x, \Delta y$. Our task now is to find the probability of these little squares:

$$P(x < X \leqslant x + \Delta x, y < Y \leqslant y + \Delta y).$$

Referring to Figure B.3 we can write

$$\begin{aligned} P(x < X &\leqslant x + \Delta x, y < Y \leqslant y + \Delta y) \\ &= P(X \leqslant x + \Delta x, Y \leqslant y + \Delta y) - P(X \leqslant x, Y \leqslant y + \Delta y) \\ &\quad - P(X \leqslant x + \Delta x, Y \leqslant y) + P(X \leqslant x, Y \leqslant y) \\ &= F_{X,Y}(x + \Delta x, y + \Delta y) - F_{X,Y}(x + \Delta x, y) \\ &\quad - F_{X,Y}(x, y + \Delta y) + F_{X,Y}(x, y). \end{aligned} \tag{B.11}$$

The Taylor expansion of (B.11) yields

$$P(x < X \leqslant x + \Delta x, y < Y \leqslant y + \Delta y) \approx \frac{\partial^2 F_{X,Y}(x, y)}{\partial x \partial y} \Delta x \Delta y$$

(see Exercise B.26).

The function
$$f_{X,Y}(x, y) \triangleq \frac{\partial^2 F_{X,Y}(x, y)}{\partial x \partial y}$$

is called the **joint density function** of the continuous random variables X, Y. In general, for n random variables $X_1, \ldots, X_n$, the joint density is

$$f_{X_1,\ldots,X_n}(x_1, \ldots, x_n) = \frac{\partial^n F_{X_1,\ldots,X_n}(x_1, \ldots, x_n)}{\partial x_1 \ldots \partial x_n} \tag{B.12}$$

with the interpretation

$$P\left(\bigcap_{i=1}^{n}(x_i < X_i \leqslant x_i + \Delta x_i)\right) \approx f_X(x_1, \ldots, x_n)\Delta x_1 \times \cdots \times \Delta x_n.$$

B.9.4 Stochastic Independence

Recall that the random variables $X_1, X_2, \ldots, X_n$ are stochastically independent if and only if the events

$$X_i \leqslant x_i$$

are independent for all $x_i \in \mathbb{R}$, that is,

$$P(X_1 \leqslant x_1, \ldots, X_n \leqslant x_n) = P(X_1 \leqslant x_1) \times \cdots \times P(X_n \leqslant x_n)$$

The same equality in terms of a CDF looks as follows:

$$F_{X_1,\ldots,X_n}(x_1, \ldots, x_n) = F_{X_1}(x_1) \times \cdots \times F_{X_n}(x_n). \tag{B.13}$$

Using the expression for joint density (B.12) and the definition of independence (B.13), we find

$$f(x_1, \ldots, x_n) = \frac{\partial^n F(x_1, \ldots, x_n)}{\partial x_1 \ldots \partial x_n} = \frac{\partial^n [F_{X_1}(x_1) \times \cdots \times F_{X_n}(x_n)]}{\partial x_1 \ldots \partial x_n}$$

$$= F'_{X_1}(x_1) \times \cdots \times F'_{X_n}(x_n) = f_{X_1}(x_1) \times \cdots \times f_{X_n}(x_n).$$

For independent continuous random variables the joint density is a product of marginal densities.

B.10   Normal Distribution

The normal distribution is *fully characterized by its mean and variance*. For a random variable X distributed normally with mean μ and variance σ^2 we write

$$X \sim N(\mu, \sigma^2).$$

The PDF for such a random variable is

$$\phi_X(x) = \frac{1}{\sqrt{2\pi}\sigma} \exp\left(-\frac{(x-\mu)^2}{2\sigma^2}\right).$$

$N(0, 1)$ is called the **standard normal** distribution.

Fact. When X has a normal distribution, then $a + X$ and aX are also normally distributed.

Example B.24. If $X \sim N(\mu, \sigma^2)$, what is the distribution of $Y = (X - \mu)/\sigma$?

Solution. Because Y is a linear transform of X we know that the distribution of Y is normal. Thus we only need to find out about the mean and variance of Y. To this end,

$$E[Y] = \frac{E[X - \mu]}{\sigma} = \frac{\mu - \mu}{\sigma} = 0,$$

$$\text{Var}(Y) = \text{Var}\left(\frac{X - \mu}{\sigma}\right) = \frac{1}{\sigma^2} \text{Var}(X - \mu) = \frac{\text{Var}(X)}{\sigma^2} = \frac{\sigma^2}{\sigma^2} = 1.$$

Y has a standard normal distribution.

B.10.1   CDF of a Standard Normal Variable

Let X be a standard normal variable, we will denote its cumulative distribution function by Φ:

$$\Phi(z) \triangleq P(X \leqslant z) = \int_{-\infty}^{z} \frac{1}{\sqrt{2\pi}} \exp(-\tfrac{1}{2}x^2)\, dx.$$

Since the standard normal density is symmetric around zero the area in both tails of the distribution is the same (see Figure B.4), and we have the following symmetry property:

$$1 - \Phi(x) = \Phi(-x).$$

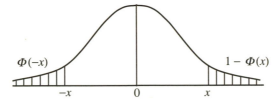

Figure B.4. Density of a symmetric random variable and tail probabilities.

B.10.2 Deriving Black–Scholes Formula

The following example computes the expectation of a truncated lognormal variable, which is needed for the famous Black–Scholes formula.

Example B.25. Evaluate the expectation

$$E[(e^X - e^a)1_{X>a}],$$

where

$$1_{X>a} = 1 \quad \text{for } X > a,$$
$$1_{X>a} = 0 \quad \text{otherwise,}$$

and $X \sim N(\tilde{\mu}, \tilde{\sigma}^2)$.

Solution. One possible solution strategy is to compute the expectation as it stands:

$$E[(e^X - e^a)1_{X>a}] = \int_a^{+\infty} (e^x - e^a) \frac{1}{\sqrt{2\pi}\tilde{\sigma}} \exp\left(-\frac{(x-\tilde{\mu})^2}{2\tilde{\sigma}^2}\right) dx.$$

This works but it is quite messy. A better way is to write X in terms of a standard normal variable Z:

$$X = \tilde{\mu} + \tilde{\sigma}Z,$$

where $Z \sim N(0, 1)$. Then the original expectation becomes

$$\begin{aligned}
E[(e^X - e^a)1_{X>a}] &= E[(e^{\tilde{\mu}+\tilde{\sigma}Z} - e^a)1_{\tilde{\mu}+\tilde{\sigma}Z>a}] \\
&= e^{\tilde{\mu}}E[e^{\tilde{\sigma}Z}1_{Z>(a-\tilde{\mu})/\tilde{\sigma}}] - e^aE[1_{Z>(a-\tilde{\mu})/\tilde{\sigma}}] \\
&= I_1 + I_2.
\end{aligned}$$

This leaves us with two integrals I_1 and I_2. The latter is easy to deal with—it is simply the CDF of a standard normal distribution (see Section B.10.1):

$$I_2 = e^a P\left(Z > \frac{a-\tilde{\mu}}{\tilde{\sigma}}\right) = e^a\left(1 - \Phi\left(\frac{a-\tilde{\mu}}{\tilde{\sigma}}\right)\right) = e^a\Phi\left(\frac{\tilde{\mu}-a}{\tilde{\sigma}}\right).$$

The first expectation can be expressed as

$$\begin{aligned}
I_1 &= e^{\tilde{\mu}} \int_{(a-\tilde{\mu})/\tilde{\sigma}}^{+\infty} e^{\tilde{\sigma}z} \frac{1}{\sqrt{2\pi}} e^{-z^2/2} \, dz \\
&= \frac{1}{\sqrt{2\pi}} e^{\tilde{\mu}} \int_{(a-\tilde{\mu})/\tilde{\sigma}}^{+\infty} e^{-(z^2-2\tilde{\sigma}z)/2} \, dz.
\end{aligned}$$

The important trick is to write the exponent inside the integral as a square; this is accomplished by adding and subtracting $\tilde{\sigma}^2$ inside the bracket in the exponent:

$$\frac{1}{\sqrt{2\pi}}e^{\tilde{\mu}}\int_{(a-\tilde{\mu})/\tilde{\sigma}}^{+\infty}e^{-(z^2-2\tilde{\sigma}z)/2}\,dz = \frac{1}{\sqrt{2\pi}}e^{\tilde{\mu}+\tilde{\sigma}^2/2}\int_{(a-\tilde{\mu})/\tilde{\sigma}}^{+\infty}e^{-(z^2-2\tilde{\sigma}z+\tilde{\sigma}^2)/2}\,dz$$

$$= \frac{1}{\sqrt{2\pi}}e^{\tilde{\mu}+\tilde{\sigma}^2/2}\int_{(a-\tilde{\mu})/\tilde{\sigma}}^{+\infty}e^{-(z-\tilde{\sigma})^2/2}\,dz.$$

The last expression looks like an expectation again, this time

$$e^{\tilde{\mu}+\tilde{\sigma}^2/2}\int_{(a-\tilde{\mu})/\tilde{\sigma}}^{+\infty}\frac{1}{\sqrt{2\pi}}e^{-(y-\tilde{\sigma})^2/2}\,dy = e^{\tilde{\mu}+\tilde{\sigma}^2/2}E[1_{Y>(a-\tilde{\mu})/\tilde{\sigma}}]$$

$$= e^{\tilde{\mu}+\tilde{\sigma}^2/2}P\left(Y > \frac{a-\tilde{\mu}}{\tilde{\sigma}}\right),$$

where $Y \sim N(\tilde{\sigma}, 1)$. Again we can rewrite Y in terms of a standard normal variable Z

$$Y = Z + \tilde{\sigma}$$

and the expectation becomes

$$e^{\tilde{\mu}+\tilde{\sigma}^2/2}P\left(Y > \frac{a-\tilde{\mu}}{\tilde{\sigma}}\right) = e^{\tilde{\mu}+\tilde{\sigma}^2/2}P\left(Z + \tilde{\sigma} > \frac{a-\tilde{\mu}}{\tilde{\sigma}}\right)$$

$$= e^{\tilde{\mu}+\tilde{\sigma}^2/2}P\left(Z > \frac{a-\tilde{\mu}-\tilde{\sigma}^2}{\tilde{\sigma}}\right)$$

$$= e^{\tilde{\mu}+\tilde{\sigma}^2/2}\left[1 - \Phi\left(\frac{a-\tilde{\mu}-\tilde{\sigma}^2}{\tilde{\sigma}}\right)\right]$$

$$= e^{\tilde{\mu}+\tilde{\sigma}^2/2}\Phi\left(\frac{\tilde{\mu}+\tilde{\sigma}^2-a}{\tilde{\sigma}}\right).$$

To conclude, for $X \sim N(\tilde{\mu}, \tilde{\sigma}^2)$ we have

$$E[(e^X - e^a)1_{X>a}] = e^{\tilde{\mu}+\tilde{\sigma}^2/2}\Phi\left(\frac{\tilde{\mu}+\tilde{\sigma}^2-a}{\tilde{\sigma}}\right) - e^a\Phi\left(\frac{\tilde{\mu}-a}{\tilde{\sigma}}\right). \qquad (B.14)$$

B.10.3 Skewness, Kurtosis and the Moment-Generating Function

One can use the higher moments (powers) of a random variable to characterize its distribution. The r**th moment** is defined by the expectation:

$$\mu'_r = E[X^r].$$

More often we make use of the r**th central moment**:

$$\mu_r = E[(X - E[X])^r].$$

Example B.26. For $X \sim N(\mu, \sigma^2)$ we have

$$\mu_r = 0 \quad \text{for } r \text{ odd},$$

$$\mu_r = \frac{r!}{(r/2)!} \frac{\sigma^r}{2^{r/2}}.$$

Thus, for example,

$$\mu_4 = E[(X - E[X])^4] = \frac{4!}{2!} \frac{\sigma^4}{2^2} = 3\sigma^4. \tag{B.15}$$

The normalized third moment

$$\frac{\mu_3}{\sigma^3}$$

is called the **skewness** and is supposed to measure whether the distribution is symmetric around the mean. The normalized fourth moment

$$\frac{\mu_4}{\sigma^4},$$

called the **kurtosis**, is meant to measure how heavy are the tails of the distribution. The normal distribution has a kurtosis of 3 by virtue of (B.15).

The moments of a distribution are concisely captured by the **moment-generating function**,

$$m_X(\lambda) \triangleq E[e^{\lambda X}],$$

since differentiation of m_X with respect to λ gives

$$\frac{d^n m_X(\lambda)}{d\lambda^n} = \frac{d^n E[e^{\lambda X}]}{d\lambda^n} = E\left[\frac{d^n e^{\lambda X}}{d\lambda^n}\right] = E[X^n e^{\lambda X}]$$

and with $\lambda = 0$ the nth derivative of MGF gives the nth non-central moment:

$$m_X^{(n)}(0) = E[X^n].$$

Example B.27. Evaluate the MGF of a normal variable and compute its first derivative.

Solution. For $X \sim N(\mu, \sigma^2)$ we have $\lambda X \sim N(\lambda\mu, \lambda^2\sigma^2)$. It is now enough to apply formula (B.14) with $\tilde{\mu} = \lambda\mu, \tilde{\sigma} = \lambda\sigma, a \to -\infty$ to find

$$m_X(\lambda) = E[e^{\lambda X}] = e^{\mu\lambda + \sigma^2\lambda^2/2}.$$

After differentiation we have

$$m_X'(\lambda) = (\mu + \sigma^2\lambda)e^{\mu\lambda + \sigma^2\lambda^2/2},$$

$$m_X'(0) = \mu,$$

as expected.

B.10.4 Multivariate Normal Distribution

The joint normal distribution is fully characterized by its mean and the variance–covariance matrix. For a $\mathbb{R}^n$-valued random variable X with joint normal distribution with mean $\mu \in \mathbb{R}^n$ and variance–covariance matrix Σ, we write

$$X \sim N(\mu, \Sigma).$$

The PDF for such a random variable is

$$f(x) = \frac{1}{\sqrt{(2\pi)^n |\det \Sigma|}} \exp(-\tfrac{1}{2}(x - \mu)^* \Sigma^{-1}(x - \mu)).$$

Could it happen that Σ is not invertible? If this were the case, then the columns of Σ would be linearly dependent and we could find a linear combination $\alpha \in \mathbb{R}^n$ such that $\Sigma\alpha = 0$. But in that case we also have $\alpha^*\Sigma\alpha = 0$. By virtue of the portfolio theorem (B.4) and (B.5) we have $\alpha^*\Sigma\alpha = \mathrm{Var}(\alpha^*X)$ implying that $\mathrm{Var}(\alpha^*X) = 0$. But the variance can only be zero if $\alpha^*X = \mathrm{const}$. In this case we can express one of the variables as a linear combination of the remaining variables. After we have removed all the redundant random variables, the covariance matrix Σ becomes invertible.

Fact. When X has a joint normal distribution and $A \in \mathbb{R}^{m \times n}$, then the distribution of AX is again jointly normal. In particular, the marginal distribution of each individual variable X_k is normal.

Example B.28. If X_1 and X_2 are joint normal with $\mu_1 = 1$, $\mu_2 = -1$, $\sigma_1 = 2$, $\sigma_2 = 1$ and correlation $\rho = -0.7$, describe the marginal distribution of X_1, X_2, and the joint distribution of $Y_1 = X_1 + X_2$ and $Y_2 = 3X_1 - X_2$. Evaluate the correlation between Y_1 and Y_2.

Solution. We have

$$\mu_X = \begin{bmatrix} 1 \\ -1 \end{bmatrix}, \qquad \Sigma_X = \begin{bmatrix} \sigma_1^2 & \rho\sigma_1\sigma_2 \\ \rho\sigma_1\sigma_2 & \sigma_2^2 \end{bmatrix} = \begin{bmatrix} 4 & -1.4 \\ -1.4 & 1 \end{bmatrix}.$$

It follows immediately that

$$X_1 \sim N(1, 4),$$
$$X_2 \sim N(-1, 1).$$

For the variables Y_1 and Y_2 we have

$$\begin{bmatrix} Y_1 \\ Y_2 \end{bmatrix} = \begin{bmatrix} 1 & 1 \\ 3 & -1 \end{bmatrix} \begin{bmatrix} X_1 \\ X_2 \end{bmatrix},$$
$$Y = AX$$

and $Y \sim N(\mu_Y, \Sigma_Y)$, where

$$\mu_Y = A\mu_X = \begin{bmatrix} 1 & 1 \\ 3 & -1 \end{bmatrix} \begin{bmatrix} 1 \\ -1 \end{bmatrix} = \begin{bmatrix} 0 \\ 4 \end{bmatrix},$$

$$\Sigma_Y = A\Sigma_X A^* = \begin{bmatrix} 1 & 1 \\ 3 & -1 \end{bmatrix} \begin{bmatrix} 4 & -1.4 \\ -1.4 & 1 \end{bmatrix} \begin{bmatrix} 1 & 3 \\ 1 & -1 \end{bmatrix} = \begin{bmatrix} 2.2 & 8.2 \\ 8.2 & 45.4 \end{bmatrix}.$$

The correlation between Y_1 and Y_2 is

$$\rho_{Y_1,Y_2} = \frac{8.2}{\sqrt{2.2 \times 45.4}} = 0.82.$$

B.10.5 Conditional Distribution

For two random variables X, Y the conditional probability density of Y given X is

$$f_{Y|X}(y \mid x) = \frac{f_{X,Y}(x, y)}{f_X(x)};$$

this definition follows naturally from the definition of conditional probability (B.1). For a fixed value of x the function $f_{Y|X}(y \mid x)$ has all the properties of the density function, that is,

$$f_{Y|X}(y \mid x) \geqslant 0,$$

$$\int_{-\infty}^{\infty} f_{Y|X}(y \mid x)\,\mathrm{d}y = 1.$$

Example B.29. Let X and Y be two jointly normal random variables with correlation coefficient ρ. The conditional distribution of Y given X is normal:

$$Y \mid (X = x) \sim N\left(\mu_Y + \rho\frac{\sigma_Y}{\sigma_X}(x - \mu_X), \sigma_Y^2(1 - \rho^2)\right).$$

Conditional distributions are important in filtering, where Y represents an unobserved (latent) variable such as stochastic volatility, and X is an observed variable, such as stock price. The conditional normal distribution is the basis of the so-called Kalman filter.

B.11 Quantiles

The $100 \times q\%$ **quantile** of a random variable X or of its corresponding distribution is denoted ξ_q and is defined as the smallest number ξ such that $P(X \leqslant \xi) \geqslant q$. For continuous random variables we have simply

$$P(X \leqslant \xi_q) = q.$$

Special names for quantiles are the **median** ($q = 0.5$), the **quartile** ($q = 0.25$, 0.5 or 0.75), etc. Quantiles feature prominently in statistical hypothesis testing. In finance, **value at risk** is the size of loss which is exceeded in no more than $100 \times q\%$ of cases, meaning it is calculated as a quantile ξ_{1-q} from the distribution of losses.

Example B.30. A portfolio manager believes that the overnight loss of his portfolio is distributed normally with mean £0 and standard deviation £10 000. Find the 5% one-day value at risk for this portfolio.

Solution. Let us denote the portfolio loss by X, $X \sim N(0, 10\,000^2)$. The value at risk $v_{5\%}$ is by definition a number such that

$$P(X \leqslant v_{5\%}) = 0.95. \tag{B.16}$$

To find $v_{5\%}$ we normalize the random variable on the left-hand side:

$$X \leqslant v_{5\%} \Leftrightarrow$$
$$X - 0 \leqslant v_{5\%} - 0 \Leftrightarrow$$
$$\frac{X - 0}{10\,000} \leqslant \frac{v_{5\%} - 0}{10\,000}.$$

From Example B.24 we know that $Z = (X - 0)/10\,000$ has a standard normal distribution. Equation (B.16) becomes

$$P\left(Z \leqslant \frac{v_{5\%} - 0}{10\,000}\right) = 0.95.$$

If we denote by $z_{95\%}$ the 95% quantile of a standard normal distribution, then

$$\frac{v_{5\%}}{10\,000} = z_{95\%}.$$

We are nearly finished, because $z_{5\%}$ can be found in statistical tables:

$$z_{95\%} = 1.645,$$
$$v_{5\%} = 10\,000 z_{95\%} = 16\,450.$$

The overnight 5% value at risk is £16 450.

B.12   Relationships among Standard Statistical Distributions

Let $X_1, X_2, \ldots, X_n, X_{n+1}, Y_1, \ldots Y_m$ be independent standard normal variables. Note that

$$E[X_i^2] = \text{Var}(X_i) = 1.$$

1. The marginal distribution of $X_1^2 + X_2^2 + \cdots + X_n^2$ is χ^2 with n degrees of freedom. Consequently, the mean of $\chi^2(n)$ is

$$E[X_1^2 + X_2^2 + \cdots + X_n^2] = E[X_1^2] + E[X_2^2] + \cdots + E[X_n^2] = n.$$

   If X_i are independent, then X_i^2 are also independent and therefore also uncorrelated; consequently,

$$\text{Var}(X_1^2 + X_2^2 + \cdots + X_n^2) = n\,\text{Var}(X_i^2) = n(E[X_i^4] - (E[X_i^2])^2) = 2n,$$

   because we know that the kurtosis of a normal distribution is 3, $E[X_i^4] = 3\,\text{Var}(X_i)$, $E[X_i^2] = \text{Var}(X_i)$.

2. The marginal distribution of

$$\frac{X_{n+1}}{\sqrt{(X_1^2 + X_2^2 + \cdots + X_n^2)/n}}$$

   is the **Student** t distribution with n degrees of freedom.

3. The marginal distribution of

$$\frac{Y_1^2 + Y_2^2 + \cdots + Y_m^2}{m} \Bigg/ \frac{X_1^2 + X_2^2 + \cdots + X_n^2}{n}$$

is an F **distribution** with m and n degrees of freedom.

4. If $X \sim N(\mu, \sigma^2)$, then $Y = e^X$ has a **lognormal distribution** with mean

$$\mu_Y = e^{\mu + \sigma^2/2}$$

and variance

$$\sigma_Y^2 = e^{2\mu + 2\sigma^2} - e^{2\mu + \sigma^2}.$$

Conversely, if Y has a lognormal distribution with mean μ_Y and variance σ_Y^2, then $X = \ln Y$ has a normal distribution with mean

$$\mu = \ln(\mu_Y^2 / \sqrt{\mu_Y^2 + \sigma_Y^2})$$

and variance

$$\sigma^2 = \ln(1 + \sigma_Y^2 / \mu_Y^2).$$

B.13 Notes

Mood et al. (1974) is an excellent introduction to probability and statistics; this appendix covers roughly Chapters 1–5. Among the more advanced texts de Finetti is always worth reading for his intuitive ground-up approach. Detailed discussion of probability distributions and their properties is given in Johnson et al. (1993, 1994) and Kotz et al. (2000). Bouyé et al. (2000) is a good starting point to find out about copulas in finance.

B.14 Exercises

Exercise B.1. If two random variables X and Y are uncorrelated, then

(a) $\text{Cov}(X, Y) = 0$;
(b) X and Y are independent;
(c) $E[XY] = 0$;
(d) none of the above.

Exercise B.2. If two random variables X and Y are independent, then

(a) $E[X + Y] = 0$;
(b) $\text{Cov}(X^2, Y^3) = 0$;
(c) $E[X^Y] = (E[X])^{E[Y]}$;
(d) none of the above.

Exercise B.3. Which of the following statements is FALSE, thereby indicating that $F(x) = x^2 e^x / (1 + x^2 e^x)$ is not a CDF?

(a) $F(x) \to 0$ as $x \to -\infty$.
(b) $F(x) \to 1$ as $x \to +\infty$.
(c) $F(x_2) \geqslant F(x_1)$ for all $x_2 \geqslant x_1$.

Exercise B.4. Which of the following statements is FALSE, thereby indicating that $F(x, y) = 2e^{x+y}/(1 + e^x)(1 + e^y)$ is not a CDF?

(a) $F(x, y) \to 0$ as $x, y \to -\infty$.

(b) $F(x, y) \to 1$ as $x, y \to +\infty$.

(c) $F(x_2, y_2) \geqslant F(x_1, y_1)$ for all $x_2 \geqslant x_1$ and $y_2 \geqslant y_1$.

Exercise B.5. Knowledge of the marginal distribution implies the knowledge of the joint distribution.

(a) YES for discrete random variables, YES for continuous random variables.

(b) NO for discrete random variables, YES for continuous random variables.

(c) YES for discrete random variables, NO for continuous random variables.

(d) NO for discrete random variables, NO for continuous random variables.

Exercise B.6. What is the marginal CDF $F_X(x)$ of the joint CDF $F_{X,Y}(x, y) = \exp(x + 2y)/(1 + \exp(x))(1 + \exp(y))^2$?

(a) $\dfrac{\exp(x)}{1 + \exp(x)}$.

(b) $\dfrac{\exp(x)}{4(1 + \exp(x))}$.

(c) $\dfrac{\exp(2x)}{(1 + \exp(x))^2}$.

(d) $\dfrac{\exp(x)}{4(1 + \exp(x))^2}$.

Exercise B.7. You are given a joint PDF

$$f(x, y) = \frac{1}{2\pi \sqrt{(1 - \rho^2)}} \exp\left(-\frac{x^2 + y^2 - 2\rho xy}{2(1 - \rho^2)}\right).$$

Which of the following integrals will give $E[XY]$?

(a) $\displaystyle\int_{-\infty}^{+\infty} \int_{-\infty}^{+\infty} -\frac{\rho xy}{2(1 - \rho^2)} \exp\left(-\frac{x^2 + y^2}{2(1 - \rho^2)}\right) dx\, dy.$

(b) $\dfrac{1}{2\pi \sqrt{(1 - \rho^2)}} \displaystyle\int_{-\infty}^{+\infty} \int_{-\infty}^{+\infty} xy \exp\left(-\frac{x^2 + y^2 - 2\rho xy}{2(1 - \rho^2)}\right) dx\, dy.$

(c) $\dfrac{1}{2\pi \sqrt{(1 - \rho^2)}} \displaystyle\int_{-\infty}^{+\infty} \int_{-\infty}^{+\infty} \exp\left(-\frac{x^2 + y^2}{2(1 - \rho^2)}\right) dx\, dy.$

(d) $\dfrac{1}{2\pi \sqrt{(1 - \rho^2)}} \displaystyle\int_{-\infty}^{+\infty} \int_{-\infty}^{+\infty} xy \exp\left(-\frac{x^2 + y^2}{2(1 - \rho^2)}\right) dx\, dy.$

Exercise B.8. Under what circumstances is it the case that

$$E[f(X)g(Y)] = E[f(X)]E[g(Y)]?$$

(a) Always when X and Y are uncorrelated.

(b) Always when X and Y are perfectly correlated (linearly dependent).

(c) Always when X and Y are stochastically independent.

(d) Always when f and g are measurable functions.

Exercise B.9. Suppose that X_1, X_2 and X_3 are three independent and identically distributed variables, each with two possible values 0.8 or 1.2. How many states are needed to describe the joint distribution of X_1, X_2 and X_3?

(a) 2.

(b) 4.

(c) 6.

(d) 8.

Exercise B.10. The covariance between X and Y is everything below EXCEPT

(a) $E[(X - E[X])(Y - E[Y])]$.

(b) $E[XY - E[X]E[Y]]$.

(c) $E[X - E[X]]E[(Y - E[Y])]$.

(d) $E[XY] - E[X]E[Y]$.

Exercise B.11. If X is a column vector of random variables, how is the variance–covariance matrix obtained in matrix notation?

(a) $E[(X - E[X])^*(X - E[X])]$.

(b) $E[XX^*] - E[X]E[X]^*$.

(c) $X^*X - E[X^*]E[X]$.

(d) None of the above.

Exercise B.12. Match up the PDFs (1)–(4) with the CDFs (a)–(d) (see Figure B.5).

Exercise B.13. You are given two random variables R and S with known means and variances:

$$E[R] = 2,$$
$$\mathrm{Var}(R) = 4,$$
$$E[S] = -1,$$
$$\mathrm{Var}(S) = 2.$$

Find the expected value of $R \times S$ if you know that

(a) R and S are independent:
$$E[RS] =$$

(b) the correlation between R and S is 0.15:
$$E[RS] =$$

Exercise B.14 (joint distribution of returns). Consider two industry sectors: shipping and steel. Suppose that the histogram of historical annual rates of return in these sectors is given in Table B.7.

(a) Are the two returns independent? Justify your answer.

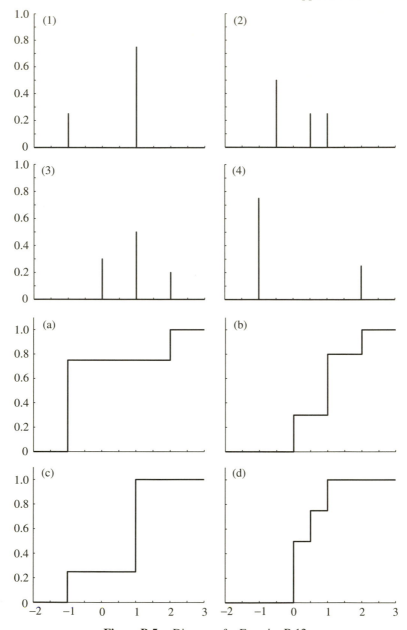

Figure B.5.   Diagrams for Exercise B.12.

(b) Find the expected rate of return in both industries:

$$E[r_{Steel}] =$$
$$E[r_{Shipping}] =$$

Table B.7.   Joint distribution of returns in the shipping and steel industries.

		Shipping				
		−20%	−10%	0%	10%	20%
	−20%	0.02	0.03	0.03	0.04	0.04
	−10%	0.03	0.05	0.05	0.07	0.07
Steel	0%	0.03	0.03	0.03	0.03	0.05
	10%	0.04	0.03	0.03	0.05	0.05
	20%	0.04	0.03	0.03	0.07	0.03

(c) Find the standard deviation of the returns in both industries:

$$\sigma_{\text{Steel}} =$$

$$\sigma_{\text{Shipping}} =$$

(d) Find the covariance between the two returns:

$$\sigma_{\text{Steel,Shipping}} =$$

(e) Prepare a short GAUSS code that performs these operations.

Exercise B.15 (expectation of independent random variables). Assume that X_1 and X_2 are independent random variables with means μ_1, μ_2 and variances σ_1^2, σ_2^2. Find $E[X_1 X_2^2]$.

Exercise B.16 (portfolio rule for covariances). The covariance matrix of two returns, X_1 and X_2, is

$$\Sigma_X = \begin{bmatrix} 0.01 & -0.01 \\ -0.01 & 0.04 \end{bmatrix}.$$

An asset management company created three new portfolios with returns:

$$Y_1 = 0.25X_1 + 0.75X_2,$$
$$Y_2 = 0.5X_1 + 0.5X_2,$$
$$Y_3 = \alpha X_1 + (1 - \alpha)X_2.$$

(a) Find the correlation between Y_1 and Y_2.
(b) Find α such that Y_2 and Y_3 are uncorrelated.
(c) Write down the correlation matrix of the returns Y_1, Y_2 and Y_3 with $\alpha = 0.75$.
(d) Prepare a short GAUSS code that performs these operations.

Exercise B.17 (towards Brownian motion). Consider a time interval $[0, 1]$ and divide it into N equally sized time segments placing ticks at positions

$$t_k = \frac{k}{N}, \quad k = 1, 2, \ldots, N.$$

The distance between two consecutive ticks is then

$$\Delta t = \frac{1}{N}.$$

We associate one random variable ΔX_k with each time tick and assume that

$$\text{Var}(\Delta X_k) = \sigma^2 \Delta t = \frac{\sigma^2}{N}.$$

We assume that $\Delta X_1, \ldots, \Delta X_N$ are uncorrelated. We can think of ΔX_i as a random shock arriving at time t_i.

(a) Find
$$\text{Var}(\Delta X_1 + \Delta X_2 + \cdots + \Delta X_N) =$$

(b) Find
$$\text{Var}(t_1 \Delta X_1 + t_2 \Delta X_2 + \cdots + t_N \Delta X_N) =$$

(Hint: $\sum_{k=1}^{N} k^2 = \frac{1}{6} N(N+1)(2N+1)$.)

(c) What happens to the value of
$$\text{Var}(\Delta X_1 + \Delta X_2 + \cdots + \Delta X_N)$$

as N goes to infinity (the time subdivision gets finer and finer)?

(d) What happens to the value of
$$\text{Var}(t_1 \Delta X_1 + t_2 \Delta X_2 + \cdots + t_N \Delta X_N)$$

as N goes to infinity?

(e) Write the limiting value of $\text{Var}(t_1 \Delta X_1 + t_2 \Delta X_2 + \cdots + t_N \Delta X_N)$ as an *integral*.

(f) Consider two functions of time $a(t)$ and $b(t)$. What is the covariance between $a(t_1)\Delta X_1 + \cdots + a(t_N)\Delta X_N$ and $b(t_1)\Delta X_1 + \cdots + b(t_N)\Delta X_N$ as N approaches infinity?

$$\lim_{N \to \infty} \text{Cov}\left(\sum_{i=1}^{N} a(t_i)\Delta X_i, \sum_{j=1}^{N} b(t_j)\Delta X_j \right) =$$

Exercise B.18 (discretization of a continuous random variable). Suppose that the rate of return X has CDF $F_X(x) = 1/(e^{-10(x-0.05)} + 1)$.

(a) Find the probability that the rate of return is between 0% and 10%:
$$P(0 < X \leqslant 0.1) =$$

(b) Discretize the above distribution into seven brackets:

Return	−20% or less	−20% to − 10%	−10% to 0%	0% to 10%
Probability				

Return	10% to 20%	20% to 30%	30% or more
Probability			

Exercise B.19 (log contract pricing). Calculate the expectation,
$$e^{-rT} E^Q[\ln S_T],$$

if you know that the risk-neutral distribution of $\ln S_T$ is normal with mean $\ln S_0 + (r - \frac{1}{2}\sigma^2)T$ and variance $\sigma^2 T$.

Exercise B.20 (joint distribution of continuous random variables). Suppose that the joint cumulative distribution function of random variables X and Y is given as follows:

$$F_{X,Y}(x, y) = \frac{\exp(2x + 3y)}{(1 + \exp(x))^2(1 + \exp(3y))}.$$

(a) Compute the marginal CDFs $F_X(x)$ and $F_Y(y)$. Are X and Y independent?

(b) Compute the joint density function $f_{X,Y}(x, y)$.

Exercise B.21 (quantiles). Assume that the one-month gain of a mutual fund portfolio is $X = £1000Y - £10\,000$, where Y is distributed as χ^2 with 10 degrees of freedom. Find the performance threshold $\xi_{5\%}$ such that X will underperform $\xi_{5\%}$ only in 5% of cases:

$$\xi_{5\%} =$$

Exercise B.22 (chi-squared and gamma distributions). The $\chi^2(n)$ is a special case of the gamma distribution $\Gamma(\alpha, \beta)$. The density of the gamma distribution is given as

$$f(x) = \frac{\beta^\alpha}{\Gamma(\alpha)} x^{\alpha-1} e^{-\beta x}.$$

What values of α and β must we choose to obtain $\chi^2(n) = \Gamma(\alpha, \beta)$?

Exercise B.23 (power contract pricing). Calculate the expectation

$$e^{-rT} E^Q[S_T^\gamma]$$

for an arbitrary γ if you know that the risk-neutral distribution of $\ln S_T$ is normal with mean $\ln S_0 + (r - \frac{1}{2}\sigma^2)T$ and variance $\sigma^2 T$. (Hint: make use of the moment-generating function of a normal variable.)

Exercise B.24 (generating a desired covariance matrix). A researcher has found that the monthly returns of three investment funds, IF_1, IF_2 and IF_3 have the covariance matrix

$$\Sigma = \begin{bmatrix} 0.01 & -0.01 & -0.02 \\ -0.01 & 0.04 & 0.06 \\ -0.02 & 0.06 & 0.16 \end{bmatrix},$$

and the average returns are 0.05, 0.07 and 0.1, respectively. The returns appear to be independent, identically distributed over time.

In a simulation exercise the researcher would like to generate the future values of the three returns for the next 20 months. For this purpose he uses the random number generator in Excel, creating three uncorrelated series with standard normal distribution, $\varepsilon_1, \varepsilon_2, \varepsilon_3$, given in Table B.8.

The researcher vaguely remembers from his MSc degree that the exercise requires a decomposition of the covariance matrix Σ. He calculates the lower triangular matrix of the Cholesky decomposition of Σ

$$\sigma = \begin{bmatrix} 0.1 & 0 & 0 \\ -0.1 & 0.1732 & 0 \\ -0.2 & 0.2309 & 0.2582 \end{bmatrix},$$

Table B.8.   Random number simulation of three uncorrelated standard normal variables.

	ε_1	ε_2	ε_3
1	−0.300	−1.278	0.244
2	1.276	1.198	1.733
3	−2.184	−0.234	1.095
4	−1.087	−0.690	−1.690
5	−1.847	−0.978	−0.744
6	−2.118	−0.568	−0.404
7	0.135	−0.365	−0.327
8	−0.370	1.343	−0.085
9	−0.186	−0.513	1.972
10	0.866	2.376	−0.655
11	1.661	−1.612	0.539
12	0.902	1.919	−0.085
13	−0.524	0.675	−0.381
14	0.758	−1.444	−0.847
15	−1.522	−0.363	−0.032
16	0.028	−0.323	2.195
17	−1.742	−0.736	−2.578
18	1.448	−1.280	−0.654
19	0.758	0.467	0.875
20	0.596	−1.372	−1.116

but is unsure what to do next. Your task is to generate 20 random values of IF_1, IF_2 and IF_3 using the available information if you know that

$$\Sigma = \sigma\sigma^*.$$

Exercise B.25.   Consider two discrete random variables X and Y. Show that if

$$P(X \leqslant x, Y \leqslant y) = P(X \leqslant x)P(Y \leqslant y),$$

that is, X and Y are independent, then also

$$P(X = x, Y = y) = P(X = x)P(Y = y).$$

Exercise B.26.   Using a Taylor expansion show that

$$P(x_1 < X_1 \leqslant x_1 + \Delta x_1, x_2 < X_2 \leqslant x_2 + \Delta x_2)$$

can be approximated in terms of the cumulative distribution function as

$$\frac{\partial^2 F(x_1, x_2)}{\partial x_1 \partial x_2} \Delta x_1 \Delta x_2.$$

References

Abramowitz, M. and Stegun I. A. (1972). *Handbook of Mathematical Functions* (9th edn). Dover, New York.

Anton, H. (2000). *Elementary Linear Algebra* (8th edn). John Wiley & Sons.

Arrow, K. J. (1971). *Essays in the Theory of Risk-Bearing*. North-Holland.

Ash, R. B. and Doléans-Dade, C. A. (1999). *Probability and Measure Theory* (2nd edn). Academic.

Baxter, M. and Rennie, A. (1996). *Financial Calculus: an Introduction to Derivative Pricing*. Cambridge University Press.

Bertsimas, D., Kogan, L. and Lo, A. W. (2001). Hedging derivative securities and incomplete market: an ϵ-arbitrage approach. *Operations Research* **49**, 372–397.

Binmore, K. and Davies, J. (2001). *Calculus: Concepts and Methods*. Cambridge University Press.

Björk, T. (1998). *Arbitrage Theory in Continuous Time*. Oxford University Press.

Bouyé, E., Durrleman, V., Nikeghbali, A., Riboulet, G. and Roncalli, T. (2000). Copulas for finance: a reading guide and some applications. Groupe de Recherche Opérationelle, Crédit Lyonnais, Working Paper (March).

Boyle, P. P. and Emanuel, D. (1980). Discretely adjusted option hedges. *Journal of Financial Economics* **8**, 259–282.

Carr, P. and Madan, D. B. (1999). Option valuation using the fast Fourier transform. *Journal of Computational Finance* **2**, 61–73.

Černý, A. (1999). Dynamic programming and mean–variance hedging in discrete time. Preprint, The Business School, Imperial College London, October 1999.

Černý, A. (2003). Generalized Sharpe ratios and asset pricing in incomplete markets. *European Finance Review* **7**(2), 191–233.

Cheney, W. and Kincaid, D. (1999). *Numerical Mathematics and Computing* (4th edn). Brooks/Cole.

Cochrane, J. H. (2001). *Asset Pricing*. Princeton University Press.

Cochrane, J. H. and Saá-Requejo, J. (2000). Beyond arbitrage: good-deal asset price bounds in incomplete markets. *Journal of Political Economy* **108**(1), 79–119.

Cooley, J. W. and Tukey, J. W. (1965). An algorithm for the machine computation of the complex Fourier series. *Mathematics of Computation* **19**, 297–301.

Cox, J. C. and Huang, C.-F. (1989). Optimal consumption and portfolio policies when asset prices follow a diffusion process. *Journal of Economic Theory* **49**, 33–83.

Cox, J. C., Ross, S. and Rubinstein, M. (1979). Option pricing: a simplified approach. *Journal of Financial Economics* **7**, 229–263.

de Finetti, B. (1974a). *Theory of Probability*. Wiley Series in Probability and Mathematical Statistics, Vol. 1. John Wiley & Sons.

de Finetti, B. (1974b). *Theory of Probability*. Wiley Series in Probability and Mathematical Statistics, Vol. 2. John Wiley & Sons.

Dowd, K. (1999). A value at risk approach to risk–return analysis. *Journal of Portfolio Management* **25**(4), 60–67.

Duffie, D. (1996). *Dynamic Asset Pricing Theory* (2nd edn). Princeton University Press.

Duffie, D. and Richardson, H. (1991). Mean–variance hedging in continuous time. *Annals of Applied Probability* **1**, 1–15.

Duffie, D., Filipović, D. and Schachermayer, W. (2003). Affine processes and applications in finance. *Annals of Applied Probability* **13**, 984–1053.

Duhamel, P. and Holman, H. (1984). Split radix FFT algorithm. *Electronic Letters* **20**, 14–16.

Duhamel, P. and Vetterli, M. (1990). Fast Fourier transforms: a tutorial review and a state of the art. *Signal Processing* **19**, 259–299.

Eberlein, E. and Keller, U. (1995). Hyperbolic distributions in finance. *Bernoulli* **1**, 281–299.

Föllmer, H. and Schweizer, M. (1989). Hedging by sequential regression: an introduction to the mathematics of option trading. *The ASTIN Bulletin* **18**(2), 147–160.

Frigo, M. and Johnson, S. G. (1998). FFTW: an adaptive software architecture for the FFT. In *Proc. IEEE Int. Conf. on Acoustics, Speech, and Signal Processing, Seattle, WA*, Vol. 3, pp. 1381–1384.

Gourieroux, C., Laurent, J.-P. and Pham, H. (1998). Mean–variance hedging and numéraire. *Mathematical Finance* **8**, 179–200.

Grannan, E. R. and Swindle, G. (1996). Minimizing transaction costs of option hedging strategies. *Mathematical Finance* **6**, 341–364.

Grinold, R. C. (1999). Mean–variance and scenario-based approaches to portfolio selection. *Journal of Portfolio Management* **25**(2), 10–22.

Grossman, S. I. (1994). *Elementary Linear Algebra* (5th edn). Harcourt College Publishers.

Hansen, L. P. and Jagannathan, R. (1991). Implications of security market data for models of dynamic economies. *Journal of Political Economy* **99**(2), 225–262.

Heer, B. and Maußner, A. (2004). *DGE Models: Computational Methods and Applications*. Springer.

Heston, S. (1993). A closed-form solution for options with stochastic volatility with applications to bond and currency options. *Review of Financial Studies* **6**, 327–344.

Hey, A. (1999). FFT demystified. (Available at http://www.eptools.com/tn/T0001/INDEX.HTM.)

Hodges, S. (1998). A generalization of the Sharpe Ratio and its application to valuation bounds and risk measures. FORC Preprint 98/88, April, University of Warwick.

Hull, J. C. (1997). *Options, Futures and Other Derivatives* (3rd edn). London: Prentice-Hall.

Hunt, P. J. and Kennedy, J. E. (2000). *Financial Derivatives in Theory and Practice*. Wiley Series in Probability and Statistics. John Wiley & Sons.

Ingersoll, J. E. (1987). *Theory of Financial Decision Making*. Studies in Financial Economics. Savage: Rowman & Littlefield.

Johnson, N. L., Kotz, S. and Kemp, A. W. (1993). *Discrete Univariate Distributions* (2nd edn). John Wiley & Sons.

Johnson, N. L., Kotz, S. and Balakrishnan, N. (1994). *Continuous Univariate Distributions* (2nd edn). John Wiley & Sons.

Judd, K. L. (1998). *Numerical Methods in Economics*. MIT Press.

Kallberg, J. G. and Ziemba, W. T. (1983). Comparison of alternative utility functions in portfolio selection problems. *Management Science* **29**, 1257–1276.

Karatzas, I., Lehoczky, J. P., Shreve, S. A. and Xu, G.-L. (1991). Martingale and duality methods for utility maximization in an incomplete market. *SIAM Journal of Control and Optimization* **29**, 702–730.

Kolba, D. P. and Parks, T. W. (1977). A prime factor FFT algorithm using high speed convolution. *IEEE Transactions on Acoustics, Speach and Signal Processing*, pp. 281–294.

Kotz, S., Balakrishnan, N. and Johnson, N. L. (2000). *Continuous Multivariate Distributions*. John Wiley & Sons.

Kroll, Y., Levy, H. and Markowitz, H. M. (1984). Mean–variance versus direct utility maximization. *Journal of Finance* **39**, 47–61.

Kushner, H. J. and Dupuis, P. (2001). *Numerical Methods for Stochastic Control Problems in Continuous Time* (2nd edn). Springer.

Laurent, J. P. and Pham, H. (1999). Dynamic programming and mean–variance hedging. *Finance and Stochastics* **3**(1), 83–110.

Leland, H. E. (1985). Option pricing and replication with transactions costs. *The Journal of Finance* **40**(5), 1283–1301.

Luenberger, D. G. (1998). *Investment Science.* Oxford University Press.

McClellan, J. H. and Rader, C. M. (1979). *Number Theory in Digital Signal Processing.* Prentice-Hall.

Madan, D. and Seneta, E. (1990). The variance Gamma model for stock market returns. *Journal of Business* **63**, 511–524.

Markowitz, H. (1952). Portfolio selection. *Journal of Finance* **7**(1), 77–91.

Mood, A. M., Graybill, F. A. and Boes, D. C. (1974). *Introduction to the Theory of Statistics* (3rd edn). McGraw-Hill Series in Probability and Statistics. McGraw-Hill.

Neftci, S. N. (1996). *An Introduction to the Mathematics of Financial Derivatives.* Academic.

Øksendahl, B. (1998). *Stochastic Differential Equations.* Springer.

Oomen, R. C. A. (2002). Modelling realized variance when returns are serially correlated. Warwick Business School.

Page Jr, F. H. and Sanders, A. B. (1986). A general derivation of the jump process option pricing formula. *Journal of Financial and Quantitative Analysis* **21**, 437–446.

Pliska, S. R. (1986). A stochastic calculus model of continuous trading: optimal portfolios. *Mathematics of Operations Research* **11**, 371–382.

Pliska, S. R. (1997). *Introduction to Mathematical Finance: Discrete Time Models.* Blackwell.

Pollard, J. M. (1971). The fast Fourier transform in a finite field. *Mathematics of Computations* **25**(114), 266–273.

Pulley, L. B. (1981). A general mean–variance approximation to expected utility for short holding periods. *Journal of Financial and Quantitative Analysis* **16**, 361–373.

Rader, C. M. (1968). Discrete Fourier transforms when the number of data samples is prime. *Proceedings of the IEEE* **56**, 1107–1108.

Rheinländer, T. and Schweizer, M. (1997). On L^2 projections on a space of stochastic integrals. *Annals of Probability* **25**, 1810–1831.

Ross, S. A. (1978). A simple approach to the valuation of risky streams. *Journal of Business* **51**, 453–475.

Schweizer, M. (1992). Mean–variance hedging for general claims. *Annals of Applied Probability* **2**(1), 171–179.

Schweizer, M. (1995). Variance-optimal hedging in discrete time. *Mathematics of Operations Research* **20**(1), 1–32.

Sharpe, W. F. (1966). Mutual fund performance. *Journal of Business* **39**(1), 119–138.

Sharpe, W. F. (1978). *Investments.* Prentice-Hall International.

Shreve, S. E. (2004). *Stochastic Calculus Models for Finance.* Springer. (Online draft version is currently available via Steven E. Shreve's web page, http://www.math.cmu.edu/people/fac/shreve.html.)

Taqqu, M. S. (2002). Bachelier and his times: a conversation with Bernard Bru. In *Mathematical Finance, Bachelier Congress 2000* (ed. H. Geman, D. Madan, S. R. Pliska and T. Vorst), pp. 1–39. Springer.

Temperton, C. (1992). A generalized prime factor FFT algorithm for any $n = 2^p 3^q 5^s$. *SIAM Journal on Scientific and Statistical Computing* **13**, 676–686.

Toft, K. B. (1996). On the mean–variance tradeoff in option replication with transactions costs. *Journal of Financial and Quantitative Analysis* **31**(2), 233–263.

Von Neumann, J. and Morgenstern, O. (1944). *Theory of Games and Economic Behavior.* Princeton University Press.

Williams, D. (1991). *Probability with Martingales.* Cambridge Mathematical Textbooks. Cambridge University Press.

Wilmott, P. (1998). *Derivatives*. John Wiley & Sons.

Wilmott, P., Howison, S. and Dewynne, J. (1995). *The Mathematics of Financial Derivatives*. Cambridge University Press.

Wippern, R. F. (1971). Utility implications of portfolio selection and performance appraisal models. *Journal of Financial and Quantitative Analysis* **6**, 913–924.

Yavne, R. (1968). An economical method for calculating the discrete Fourier transform. In *Proceedings of the Fall Joint Computer Conference*, pp. 115–125.

Index